KNOW THE
BEGINNING
WELL

An Inside Journey Through
Five Decades of
African Development

KNOW THE BEGINNING WELL

K.Y. Amoako

PWP

AFRICA WORLD PRESS

TRENTON | LONDON | CAPE TOWN | NAIROBI | ADDIS ABABA | ASMARA | IBADAN | NEW DELHI

AFRICA WORLD PRESS
541 West Ingham Avenue | Suite B
Trenton, New Jersey 08638

Copyright© 2020 K.Y. Amoako

Book design: Dawid Kahts
Cover design courtesy of Bladonmore

Cataloging-in-Publication Data can be obtained from the Library of Congress.

ISBNs: 9781569026311 (PB)
　　　　9781569026304 (HB)

For my grandchildren:
Jonah, Kofi, Mena, and Kare.

The future is in your hands.

Contents

PART III – *Around the World*

Part IV – *Toward the Future*

Author's Note

"If you know the beginning well, the end shall not trouble you."

—African proverb

The title of this book is inspired by a favorite proverb, one that I have quoted frequently and used throughout my life to emphasize the importance of knowledge. As an economist, I've always relied on numbers and data to guide me, but even their predictive abilities can't guarantee outcomes. I believe the best way to plan for the future is to know as much as possible about the past. That way, we are more likely to avoid previous mistakes, break unproductive patterns, and benefit from lessons learned. I've written this book to apply that approach to what I know best: African development.

My goal is to contribute something unique to an already rich field, so this book is neither a collection of policy prescriptions nor is it a straight memoir. Rather, it is an inside look at selected aspects of Africa's development journey over the last five decades, told through the eyes of someone who made the same trip. It is a personal account of some of the key policies, people, and institutions that have shaped Africa's post-independence history—and in some cases will continue to shape its future.

My story began at the same time as independent Africa's. I was born in Ghana amid the excitement and optimism of the continent's first independence movement, and I came of age in the immediate postcolonial years. As Africa grew and developed, so did I, right alongside it.

In the 1970s, I joined the World Bank, which effectively held the future of Africa in it hands yet employed very few Africans. Over two decades, I climbed through the ranks, finding myself in the middle of many of the most highly-charged issues, policies, and personalities that defined the Bank during Africa's most turbulent years; from the controversial debate over structural adjustment lending to the eventual shift toward social development, especially gender and education, that defines how the Bank still operates. Along the way, I dealt with despots and charismatic leaders in Africa while navigating colonial attitudes and prejudices inside the Bank— an internal culture the Bank had to change to remain relevant.

In 1995, I joined the United Nations to take over the UN's Economic Commission for Africa (ECA), based in Addis Ababa, as its executive secretary. My arrival at the ECA coincided with the beginning of an exhilarating era of economic and political change in Africa, when optimism rather than pessimism for the future came back in vogue. At the same time, the understanding of what constituted good development policy began to shift as African countries and institutions took on a greater ownership role.

In this, the ECA led the way. We were at the center of dramatic socioeconomic changes in policy and approach at the turn of the century, working with African leaders to define new global partnerships, to push the G8 on debt relief, to come to terms with—and take action on—the HIV/AIDS pandemic, to accelerate the continent's information and communication technology revolution, to elevate gender equality, to take ownership over good governance, and, eventually, to completely redefine the aid dynamic between African countries and donors. Through it all, I worked alongside a new generation of African leaders who were integral in changing the African narrative.

After a decade at the ECA, I realized my journey was not complete. Despite years of unprecedented economic growth, most African countries still relied too heavily on commodities or natural resources to drive their growth—producing short-term benefits but remaining vulnerable to the boom-and-bust cycles of the past. The narrative around Africa had improved, but, in reality, its long-term outlook had not. So I returned home to Ghana and founded the African Center for Economic Transformation (ACET) to help governments and leaders ensure that the momentum of the new millennium was not lost.

When I started ACET, the development practice of economic transformation—structural changes to diversify products, increase exports, invest in technology, attract investments, and modernize processes, all of which enable sustainable growth—had succeeded in Latin America and Southeast Asia but remained largely overlooked in Africa. My goal was to help make transformation synonymous with smart economic policy. As I write this, I'm proud to say ACET has helped play a part in major policy shifts across the continent, so that economic transformation is now seen as the definitive approach to sustainable development and poverty reduction in Africa.

In short, I have lived alongside independent Africa's ups and downs, its successes and its setbacks, and its hopes and dreams. My own hope for the future of Africa is bold but achievable: a continent economically transformed in a generation, led by men and women who are visionary, selfless, and committed to inclusive growth and prosperity. I am blessed to have four grandchildren, and this is the future I envision for them and their generation. I have often called myself an "optimist for Africa," but I am also a realist. That combined outlook informs the actions and ideas contained in these pages.

The book is divided into four parts. **Part I: Inside the Bank** focuses on my early career, which ran parallel to the World Bank's changing attitudes—both internally and externally—toward Africa and social development from the 1970s into the 1990s. **Part II: In Africa** reflects on the value of strong institutions by looking at the different ways the ECA capitalized on a reform agenda to promote economic and social policy advances at the turn of the century, elevating Africa's global voice. **Part III: Around the World** goes behind the scenes of some of the groundbreaking initiatives and global partnerships that accompanied Africa's rise in the new millennium. And **Part IV: Toward the Future** explores the two most critical imperatives for Africa's inclusive and sustainable growth: economic transformation and strong leadership.

Many factors will determine whether Africa continues to make progress and move forward, but the continent's ultimate success or failure is in the hands of those who lead it. I have seen African leadership up close and personal, in all forms, good and bad. So I conclude the book with an exploration of the types of leaders and policies that are needed to secure Africa's future. *Know the Beginning Well,* therefore, is my attempt to share a small part of what I've learned and seen, so that the next generation of Africa's development leaders—be they presidents or policymakers, bureaucrats or technocrats, activists or investors—might have even more knowledge to draw upon.

If they know the beginning well, perhaps the end will not trouble them.

K.Y. Amoako
Accra, Ghana
May 2019

Foreword

By Kofi Annan

One of the highlights of my career came in September 2000, when the United Nations adopted the Millennium Development Goals, a global commitment to lift more than one billion people out of poverty. During the next 15 years significant progress was made but more work remained. Today, the Sustainable Development Goals offer a broad roadmap for continued efforts to end poverty, ensure shared prosperity, and protect the planet through 2030.

Nowhere are these goals more urgent than in Africa, a continent teeming with natural and human resources that has made notable gains but has yet to sustain them. Africa remains a rich continent with too many poor people.

Helping to understand why and charting a better path forward are among the most valuable contributions this book has to offer. K.Y. Amoako approaches Africa's modern development history from a uniquely personal perspective, without losing sight of the big picture. With these insights, he presents a compelling and achievable vision of an Africa transformed under its own direction.

Like K.Y., I too grew up in Africa during a momentous era. I graduated from high school in 1957, the same year the Gold Coast became the independent nation of Ghana. K.Y.'s descriptions of that time and its hopeful promise, which sadly remains unfulfilled, hit close to home. They also ground the lessons contained in these pages in a distinctively African voice. An awareness of history's impact is vital in the search for understanding.

K.Y. traces out the trajectory of development in the past decades, from the optimism at the end of the Cold War to the growing political and economic crises which are destabilizing our current system of relationships and structures. The world continues to be a messy, complex place and K.Y. provides a clear-eyed analysis of how this is affecting modern approaches to development.

Developing countries in Africa now realize that to achieve sustainable growth and escape poverty they must rely on their own resources and abilities. Doing so requires committing to stronger financial mobilization and management, deepening democracy and public integrity, promoting transparency, strengthening their institutions, harnessing abundant labor resources, and working in greater collaboration with the private sector. These are the issues that will drive current and future development strategies and deliver transformation through sustainable growth.

Building these strategies will require many things, especially sound leadership. A litany of selfish, dangerous, or destructive leaders greatly exacerbated the many challenges that independent Africa faced. As this book makes clear, strong, capable states that manage their resources well, provide visionary leadership, and reject authoritarianism and corruption are the ones that are best placed to make lasting gains.

I believe that the drivers of these improvements will be Africa's growing youth population. Throughout my career I have always been struck by the energy, talent, and appetite for knowledge of the continent's youth. They want to create a better, more just world, and I am convinced they have the ambition and the tools, especially through new forms of technology, to do so. As this book underscores, economic transformation, at its core, is about people, so the goal of policies and institutions should be to improve human well-being and ensure that all people have equal opportunities for a better life.

The lessons in this book have the potential to change the way people view Africa and international development. As such, I believe it offers great benefits to anyone with a role to play in Africa's economic transformation and thus to anyone with a hand in realizing Africa's sustainable and more prosperous future.

Kofi A. Annan
May 2018

Abbreviations

ACET	African Center for Economic Transformation
AfCFTA	African Continental Free Trade Area
AfDB	African Development Bank
ADF	African Development Forum
AEC	African Economic Community
AGDI	African Gender Development Index
AGF	African Governance Forum
AISI	Africa's Information Society Initiative
APR	(G8) Africa Personal Representative
APRM	African Peer Review Mechanism
ARIA	Assessing Regional Integration in Africa
ATF	African Transformation Forum
ATR	African Transformation Report
AU	African Union
AUDA	African Union Development Agency
CAA	Cairo Agenda for Action
CAADP	Comprehensive Africa Agriculture Development Programme
CCA	Corporate Council for Africa
CfA	Commission for Africa
CG	Consultative Group
CHGA	(UN) Commission on HIV/AIDS and Governance in Africa

CIDA	Canadian International Development Agency
CPP	Convention People's Party
CSSDCA	Conference on Security, Stability, Development, and Cooperation in Africa
DAC	(OECD) Development Assistance Committee
DATA	Debt, Aids, Trade, Africa
DIFD	(UK) Department for International Development
ECA	(UN) Economic Commission for Africa
EDI	Economic Development Institute
ESPD	(World Bank) Education and Social Policy Department
EU	European Union
FDI	Foreign direct investment
GDP	Gross domestic product
GIIC	Global Information Infrastructure Commission
GNP	Gross national product
HIPC	Heavily Indebted Poor Country (initiative)
HSGIC	(NEPAD) Heads of State and Government Implementation Committee
ICASA	International Conference on AIDS and STDs in Africa
ICT	Information and communication technology
IDA	International Development Association
IMF	International Monetary Fund
IPAA	International Partnership Against AIDS/HIV
LAC	Latin America and Caribbean (region)
MAP	Millennium Africa Recovery Plan
MCC	Millennium Challenge Corporation
MDGs	Millennium Development Goals
NEPAD	New Partnership for Africa's Development
NGOs	Nongovernmental organizations
NICI	National Information and Communication Infrastructure (plans)

OAU	Organization of African Unity
ODA	Official development assistance
OECD	Organisation for Economic Co-operation and Development
OPEC	Organization of the Petroleum Exporting Countries
PCCG	Partner Country Contact Group
PIDA	Programme for Infrastructure Development in Africa
PIE	Project Identification Exercise
PRSPs	Poverty Reduction Strategy Papers
RECs	Regional Economic Communities
SDGs	Sustainable Development Goals
SIA	(UN) Special Initiative on Africa
SPA	Special Program of Assistance for Africa/Strategic Partnership with Africa
TICAD	Tokyo International Conference on African Development
UNAIDS	Joint United Nations Programme on HIV/AIDS
UNICEF	United Nations Children's Fund
UNDP	United Nations Development Programme
UNIP	United National Independence Party
USAID	US Agency for International Development
WDR	World Development Report
WSIS	World Summit on the Information Society
XB	Extra-budgetary (resources)

From left: K.Y., his father Seth, and his brother Kwabena in Ghana in the early 1950s.

Prologue
Sixty Years On

Black Star Square, also known as Independence Square, sits on the edge of the ocean in Accra, the capital city of Ghana. It is one of the largest public squares in Africa, a vast expanse of pavement framed by permanent grandstands on three sides and two towering monuments: Independence Arch, and, across the plaza from it, Black Star Gate, which features the words "Freedom and Justice" inscribed below the four giant stars—black, of course—that sit atop it, each facing outward in a different direction.

The Black Star is seen generally as a symbol of African pride, but it's also closely associated with Ghana, the first country in Africa to gain its freedom. After achieving independence from Great Britain in 1957, Ghana changed its name from Gold Coast and designed a national flag with the Black Star in the center. It was a nod to the Black Star Line, a shipping line founded in 1919 by the Jamaican-born Marcus Garvey to help black Americans return to Africa and the Caribbean. The Black Star Line failed, but Garvey, who died in 1940 and later was awarded Jamaica's Order of National Hero, attracted thousands of supporters by encouraging blacks to be proud of their race and ancestry and return to their homeland, which at the time was under colonial rule. The same spirit of pan-Africanism propelled a young Ghanaian, Kwame Nkrumah, to help lead the push for Ghana's emancipation from the British Empire.

Nkrumah became Ghana's first president and a few years later he commissioned the Black Star Square ahead of a historic visit from the United Kingdom's Queen Elizabeth II in 1961. The square was conceived as a grand display of independence and pride befitting all of Africa, not just Ghana. This reflected Nkrumah's vision for a free but united Africa, so it is appropriate that Nkrumah's legacy hovers all around. In addition to the two large memorials, the square also contains the Eternal Flame of African Liberation, first lit by Nkrumah and still burning. A little farther north stands the Parliament House, designed and built under Nkrumah's direction. A little farther to the west is the Kwame Nkrumah Memorial Park, the centerpiece of which is a museum and the mausoleum that serves as the final resting place for Nkrumah and his wife. At the apex of the mausoleum's sweeping marble exterior sits, appropriately, a single Black Star.

The public square Nkrumah commissioned can accommodate crowds of 30,000 or more, and it is used primarily for special ceremonies and events. It is the memorial heart and soul of Ghana's identity as Africa's first free nation.

While it normally sits empty, the square fills up without fail at least one day every year—March 6, Ghana's Independence Day. The annual celebrations are a sight to behold. The plaza stands packed for what amounts to a national pep rally for a prideful country that has historically held its history in high regard.

So on March 6, 2017, the crowds gathered and filed into Independence Square as usual, but they had a little something extra to celebrate—Ghana's sixtieth anniversary. Normally, a milestone date like that would carry extra weight all alone, but this anniversary felt more compelling for other reasons. It happened to fall just a few months after a bruising, contentious presidential election, which itself fell in the midst of one of the country's worst economic crises.

Celebrated for decades as a pioneer of pan-African leadership and hailed for a quarter-century as a beacon of all that's right with Africa—reliable economic growth, peaceful transfers of power, strong education, and social services—Ghana had fallen on hard times in recent years, its difficulties fueled by major macroeconomic imbalances and development strategies that continued to fall short in planning, execution, or both. In May 2014, political leaders convened an emergency economic summit in Senchi, in the eastern region of Ghana, to try to chart a course for the future that would keep the country solvent and also begin to restore some of the lost luster, both abroad and at home, where citizens had grown increasingly negative over their country's direction and its institutions.

So a few years later, when newly elected President Nana Addo Dankwa Akufo-Addo appointed a 30-member committee to plan the anniversary celebration "Ghana@60," he acknowledged the occasion should be modest and take into account the current economic restraints. After all, he had just a few months prior defeated the incumbent, John Dramani Mahama, by promising to turn around Ghana's faltering economy and be a better steward of state finances. But there would be no question as to whether the celebration would go on.

"Even though the country is going through difficult times, we still have a lot to celebrate as Ghanaians," he said. "We should have good feelings about ourselves."

For many of those raised in Ghana, myself included, the sentiment is familiar.

I was born on September 13, 1944. Still a young boy when my country achieved independence twelve and a half years later, I grew up on the optimism and certainty that Africans were destined for a good life. Such thinking seemed nothing less than inevitable. In my youth, two figures reinforced that perspective, and both towered over me—my father, and Kwame Nkrumah. My father was such a strong believer in Nkrumah's vision of a free and united Africa, dependent only on itself, that it often seemed I was hearing the same voice at home that I heard on the radio. I knew even as a child that when Nkrumah spoke, he was speaking to all of Africa, not just to Ghana, and that when he talked about "raising up the lives of our people," he meant all Africans, not just Ghanaians. Nkrumah spoke for Africa, but he was still Ghana's leader, and there was a good deal of pride in knowing that. I left Ghana in 1969, and over the years lived in America, Ethiopia, and Zambia, traveling to myriad countries along the way. But the pride and optimism of being a Ghanaian—an African—never subsided.

In 2005, the University of Ghana at Legon invited me to deliver an alumni lecture on the country's economic and political history. I used the opportunity to reflect on Ghana's place at the forefront of African independence but also stressed the urgency of keeping Ghana at the forefront of economic and political reform. "In these endeavors," I said, "the Black Star cannot wane."

Almost 10 years later, I spoke at the economic summit in Senchi. It featured plenty of good policy ideas but also plenty of pro-Ghana rhetoric, and my contribution was no exception. "We are not just any nation," I said. "We are the one others looked to for hope, as an example of independence to come. We show the world 'a face of Africa' that is too often overlooked."

In other words, we should have good feelings about ourselves.

As the official Ghana@60 ceremony got underway, the grandstands around Black Star Square were packed with proud Ghanaians who were more than ready to feel good about themselves and their country, including an array of local and foreign dignitaries. On one side of the seats reserved for President Akufo-Addo and his wife Rebecca sat all three of Ghana's living former presidents: Jerry John Rawlings, John Agyekum Kufuor, and John Dramani Mahama, each of whom peacefully transferred power to his successor. On the other side sat Africa's oldest and longest tenured leader, Zimbabwe's Robert Mugabe, in power as prime minister or president since his country gained independence in 1980.

Before taking his seat, President Akufo-Addo, who arrived at the parade grounds in a simple white *batakari*, mounted the ceremonial vehicle to inspect contingents of the Ghanaian armed forces and other public security services, such as the police and fire service units. He moved past the Monument and Tomb of the Unknown Soldier, another of the square's iconic structures, and lit a torch from the eternal flame that burns nearby. He passed the torch to Azumah Nelson, a Ghanaian boxing legend who was going to carry the flame across Ghana's 10 state regions.

Radio and television commentators praised the rich pageantry on display. Dignitaries were dressed in their finest attire, many adorned in Ghana's signature *kente* cloth. A color-coordinated march of the security contingents as well as schoolchildren passed in front of the president before giving way to a feast of traditional dances, dramatic re-enactments and skits from each of the 10 regions. The ceremony reached its climax when a group of master drummers sounded the call for the president to give his maiden Independence Day speech.

The whole scene captured the colorful panoply of Ghana's political and cultural heritage, the kind of national celebration that Nkrumah no doubt envisioned Independence Square hosting long after he was gone. But I doubt he ever envisioned that the words spoken by Ghana's president 60 years later would sound so familiar.

In a speech that lasted about half an hour, Akufo-Addo recognized Ghana's historical roots and founding fathers before warmly paying tribute to "those who fought equally hard for our cultural integrity"—poets, composers, teachers, and others. It was an inspiring, uplifting journey through the past that, in some ways, made the second half of the speech that much harder to take.

Akufo-Addo pointed out that Nkrumah's pan-African vision tied Ghana's future to the rest of the continent, and unfortunately, the difficult times that Ghana went through after independence—one-party rule, military interventions, political instability, economic decline—have indeed been replicated across the continent. And while Ghana stabilized itself with the creation of its fourth (and current) republic in 1992, the economic dividend that was meant to accompany freedom had still not materialized.

"Sixty years after those heady days," he said, "too many of our people continue to wallow in unacceptable poverty. After 60 years, we have run out of excuses. It is time to get our country where it should be."

The challenge before Ghana, he added—though he just as easily could have meant all of Africa—is "to build our economy and generate a prosperous, progressive and dignified life for the mass of our people."

The speech hit the mark, but it was tough to hear. Could this really be the message that the president of Ghana still had to convey, a full 60 years after our country gained its right to self-determination? Of course none of the remarks truly surprised; it had only been a few years since many of those in attendance had shone a light on Ghana's deep structural problems at the Senchi summit. But to hear the president declare that it is "time to get our country where it should be" at a celebration marking *six decades* of our existence, I could not help but stop and think: how much more time do we need? Where was the Ghana that Nkrumah envisioned? Where was the Africa that I had spent my career working toward?

That afternoon, with tens of thousands of Ghanaians gathered to celebrate their country's history and heritage on the grounds designed specifically for such festivities, I wondered what Nkrumah would make of some of the words spoken that day. Of the need for Ghana and the rest of Africa to get its affairs in order. Of the need to stop making excuses for our poverty and underdevelopment.

Nkrumah's final resting place lies just a few hundred meters away from Black Star Square. I imagined he might be turning in his grave.

◆ ◆ ◆ ◆

The message delivered by President Akufo-Addo stood out in part because it all felt so familiar to me, bringing to mind another time in Accra that a high-profile speaker used a high-profile event to lay down some hard truths about Africa's slow progress in the independence era. In July 2009, US President Barack Obama, mere months from taking office after his historic election, visited Accra on a whirlwind tour capped by an address to a special session of Ghana's parliament. The build-up had been enormous and that made the let-down all the more difficult.

Africa had welcomed American presidents before and Ghana in particular had hosted the previous two, Bill Clinton and George W. Bush.[1] But Obama was different. He was the first US president with the "blood of Africa" in him to set foot on the continent. When Ghanaians learned that his first visit to Sub-Saharan Africa would be to their country, they naturally greeted the news with exuberance. Signs went up everywhere: "*Akwaaba* to Ghana," or "Welcome to Ghana." Billboards featuring giant photos of the president and his wife Michelle lined the streets and city walls were painted in their likeness. Street vendors and other traders hawked shirts, scarves, hats, buttons, and mugs—if an image of Obama could be put on it, it could be sold. And it was. The "Hotel Obama" even opened, an actual hotel with rooms named after different periods of the president's life (the "Chicago" or "Harvard" rooms, for instance). The mood in Accra was electric. It was all people talked about.

Interest in Obama's address far exceeded the capacity of the Parliament House, so the event was moved to the much larger Accra International Conference Center, which seats 1,600 and was packed. All the global news channels broadcast the address live and Africans gathered in large groups for viewing parties across the continent. Even the US Department of State got in on the act, taking advantage of the ubiquity of cell phones in Africa to offer speech highlights in English and French via text messaging.

Obama took the lectern to thunderous applause, but, flanked by national flags and seated dignitaries, delivered what could best be described as a "tough love" speech. It was less a celebration of African pride, heritage, and achievement and more about Africa accepting responsibility for the failures of the postcolonial period—for the corruption of its leaders, for the wars that plague the continent, for the diseases that ravage its children, and for the stagnation of economies that has kept Africans poor.

While acknowledging the considerable progress in parts of Africa, Obama pointed out that much of the extraordinary promise that awaited Africa when his father came of age decades before in Kenya had not been fulfilled. And to realize that promise, one must recognize a fundamental truth: development depends on good governance. "That is the ingredient which has been missing in far too many places, for far too long," he said. "And that is a responsibility that can only be met by Africans." The people of the continent must start from the simple premise, he continued, that "Africa's future is up to Africans."

What he was saying, in a sense, is that we Africans had better get our act together: we are here to help, but your development is not for us to decide. At the end of the day, it's about ownership and accountability. Things may be better than before, but you guys have screwed up for too long.

Obama gave a powerful speech, but it wasn't what many Africans expected, or wanted to hear. And I knew that from direct experience.

A few weeks before Obama's arrival in Accra, I had the opportunity to discuss the Obama visit with a delegation of American political, business, and philanthropic leaders, several of whom had served in Bill Clinton's administration and had contacts in the Obama White House. The group, from the ONE Campaign, had come to Ghana to explore developmental issues and learn about what was working, what was not, and what more was needed to empower poor people.[2] I was a member of ONE's policy advisory group, so I hosted a dinner for more than 20 eminent Ghanaians to exchange views with the visitors. During the course of our conversations, I learned that Obama planned to focus his "African message" on the need for improved governance to overcome social and economic problems. He would not be making any major policy pronouncements.

At the time, I sat on the Economic Advisory Council for Ghana's then-president, John Atta Mills. I shared what I had learned with my fellow council members, but they all greeted the news with disbelief. There's no way, they argued, that the first black president of the United States of America, a man of African descent, would make a trip to Ghana just to lecture us on good governance! One member of the council flatly dismissed my details as total hearsay. Surely Obama, a son of Africa, would arrive with a promise to boost aid and a bold new policy initiative, he said—perhaps even a long-awaited Marshall Plan for Africa. He was certain of it.

The call for a Marshall Plan for Africa has been a recurring postcolonial theme. To most, the Marshall Plan means a lot of foreign aid, but it was more sophisticated than that. The plan came about because Europe was at a crossroads. The Soviet Union's political and economic system was a powerful force, endangering the spread of postwar democracy and free markets. The Marshall Plan's grand bargain offered political and economic solidarity, including a strong aid program rooted in national planning, in exchange for which a core of Western European nations agreed to seek trade and monetary union. Those involved realized that the cost of the plan would be high, but that the costs of inaction would be far higher.

At the turn of the century, Africa had experienced only one such compact and that came in the midst of the debt crisis of the 1980s. The United Nations Economic Commission for Africa, or the ECA, proposed a grand bargain of aid to cushion the effects of structural adjustment programs carried out by dozens of African countries at the demands of their major creditors: the World Bank and International Monetary Fund. The Organization of African Unity, the precursor to today's African Union, carried the proposal to a 1986 special session of the United Nations General Assembly, where it was adopted. But the too-frequent result was ineffective adjustment policies supported by inefficient aid. It all added up to a lost period of development from which Africa had just begun to emerge at the dawn of the new millennium.

On November 21, 2000, I addressed the Conference of African Finance Ministers in Addis Ababa. I was midway through a 10-year tenure as the executive secretary of the ECA. My speech took up the call for another grand bargain—a New Global Compact with Africa. African countries would agree to put in place the necessary political and economic reforms to ensure that their economies would take off, while rich countries would agree to support these reforms by committing to invest the necessary resources—through aid, debt relief, and market access. Such a compact would be *with* Africa, not *for* it, and that small preposition conveyed a big meaning: a new sense of partnership.

Subsequent events put the issues raised in that speech at the center of the agenda for change in Africa. But the crux of the Global Compact came from extensive research and planning, and it picked up extra momentum at a groundbreaking meeting of African leaders and donor representatives that I chaired before the conference. We called that meeting the "Big Table" because we brought everyone together as equal participants in an open discussion, and it became a template for improving the dialogue between rich donors of the world and poor countries in Africa. Some of the most influential players in Africa's development scene took part, and while we may not have changed history, we felt we were doing our part to chart a new course.

The principles of the Global Compact became a pillar of the evolving discourse on development, while the idea that African countries and donor countries should hold each other accountable became a key driver in the formation of NEPAD, the New Partnership for Africa's Development, in the early 2000s. NEPAD was the biggest attempt yet by African countries to unite behind a single development framework that aimed to reduce aid dependency, promote debt relief, and rebalance trade while acknowledging the need for political reform through accountability, transparency, and good governance.

None of these events amounted to a Marshall Plan for Africa. But the various development initiatives that emerged in quick succession at the turn of the century altered the traditional North–South conversation in Africa. At the same time, the entire tone of the discussion around African development began to change for the better, because Africa was changing for the better. Economies across the continent surged, from large countries like South Africa and Nigeria to smaller but still stunning turnarounds like

Rwanda. Between 2005 and 2008, Africa enjoyed an average annual GDP growth of 5.5 percent, and by the time Obama came to Ghana in 2009, six of the world's 10 fastest-growing economies over the previous 10 years were in Sub-Saharan Africa.

Taken together, these changes once again renewed hope that African countries *finally* were on the right track toward economic self-sufficiency and fulfilling the promise that Nkrumah had made so long ago, in the first moments of independence—that Africa was ready to fight its own battles and manage its own affairs. It is the same promise that shaped so many African lives, mine included.

Often called the "father of African nationalism" or "father of pan-Africanism," Nkrumah always wanted more than a free Ghana; he wanted "a new Africa in the world." As a result, his influence extended far beyond Ghanaian borders. In 2000, BBC listeners in Africa named Nkrumah the greatest African of the twentieth century. In 2004, in a year-long poll conducted by the New African to choose the greatest African of all-time, Nkrumah placed second to Nelson Mandela—but only by 12 votes.

Nkrumah was born September 21, 1909, in the western region of the Gold Coast. He began his rise to international prominence in 1947 as the secretary-general of the United Gold Coast Convention, a group of African leaders united in their desire to end colonial rule. In 1949, Nkrumah, wanting to move faster and more urgently toward independence, founded his own political party, the Convention People's Party, or CPP, with the motto "Self Government Now." He led boycotts and strikes and served time in prison. But he eventually formed the colony's first African government, paving the way for the independence vote in 1956 and the creation of Ghana as a self-governing state. After the clock struck midnight and March 6, 1957, officially arrived, Nkrumah delivered a brief, rousing address in the earliest hour of Ghana's first day as a free nation. He spoke not only as the leader of a single state but as the voice of a colonized continent. "Our independence is meaningless unless it is linked up with the total liberation of the African continent," he famously said.

Nkrumah was outspoken and unrelenting in his drive for African autonomy, and he inspired multiple generations of young men and women to believe in Africa's potential in the hope that they might realize the potential in themselves. One man who bought fully into Nkrumah's vision was Akwasi Amoako, my father, who passed that same sense of African empowerment along to me. In fact, when I reflect on my upbringing, it is hard to separate Nkrumah and my father as intertwined sources of knowledge and inspiration.

Akwasi, also known as Seth, was not a perfect man by any stretch—he often drank too much, and he could be unnecessarily stern. But he cared deeply about me and my older brother, Kwabena, and he was by far the dominant figure in our lives. My parents divorced when I was two years old and my father took me and Kwabena, while our younger sister Ama, who was six months old at the time of the divorce, went with my mother. As a child, I didn't even know my mother—she and I only formed a relationship many years later, when I went looking for her during my college years. My father remarried (more than once), and when I was young I would stay for short periods with my maternal grandmother Nana Birago, but mostly I grew up without much maternal stability or influence. As I got older, I regretted this missing part of my life, just as anyone might. But through my father's influence, I never felt I was at a loss for support or encouragement.

I knew from an early age that Papa was different from many others. A civil servant who started out as a nurse, he was ethical, educated, and very progressive. He eventually worked his way up to become a health center superintendent, a position few attained in his profession. In areas where they didn't have doctors, he worked in the whole district, often acting like an all-purpose physician. I remember people would come and wake him at three in the morning because someone needed medical attention, or a woman was ready to give birth. And my father would always go. He was a hard-working man but also a "modern" man—he took dance classes to learn how to foxtrot and do the calypso, he loved to have a drink while he smoked his cigarettes, and he read all the time. Much of his reading revolved around Ghana's politics and independence movement. He was very engaged in the process, and by extension, so was I.

Political discussions dominated the talk in local towns and villages. Not everyone backed independence from the beginning, though I am certain my father did. He supported Nkrumah and the CPP, and by the time I was 11 or 12 he would take me along with him to political rallies. I became familiar with the rhetoric about Africa, reading whatever newspaper I could get my hands on, listening to as many radio broadcasts as I could find. My father believed very much in Ghana, in Africa, in the development needed to make us an independent and thriving people. His beliefs greatly influenced my childhood.

At an age when most boys were far more interested in sports and games, I was interested in government and policy. At one point, I won a high-school essay contest arguing in favor of Nkrumah's Volta River development project in the early 1950s, a massive and controversial plan to build a dam and harness hydroelectric power. Papa expected me to be as well informed as he was, and although we also talked about history and literature, politics still seeped into those conversations. His favorite book was George Orwell's *Animal Farm*, and once he had given it to me to read, it became my favorite, too. Papa believed the story, an allegory for political independence, reflected Ghana's own situation at the time. We would recite our favorite passages.

Due to Papa's job, we moved around a lot, but our education always came first. Ghana boasted one of Africa's better school systems and Papa was adamant that we should not waste an opportunity that others less fortunate did not have. Kwabena and I knew that in order to ask our father for favors, we had to be able to show we had earned them. Displays of learning—good grades, stacks of books we had read—became our primary way of doing that. But also, I enjoyed it! I spent hours and hours in libraries, although I probably could have lightened up on my reading list every now and then. Most times, I chose to tear through political biographies that offered riveting examples of leadership: Winston Churchill, John F. Kennedy, and one of my personal favorites, World War II General George S. Patton. (I was such a fan, I must have watched the movie adaptation a dozen times.) I also loved to read great speeches for their messages of hope, empowerment, and optimism. When I was in high school, I became infamous among my friends for always wanting to recite Abraham Lincoln's Gettysburg Address. It may sound simplistic, but I was inspired by men of action, by a display of "can-do" spirit and determination. At home in Ghana, that's how we saw our first generation of independent leaders, too. We admired them. We were inspired by them.

When we were living in Accra, my brother and I would visit the Parliament House, just to stand outside. I was a teenager then, and we would show up in the mornings and watch as the parliamentarians drove up and exited their cars, ready for the day's session. We recognized the prominent politicians, especially those in Nkrumah's cabinet, and we shouted their names. This was the level of political awareness we had, that our father inspired. It is hard now to recall a time when people, much less children, held politicians in such high regard, but such was the pull of independence.

After all, Ghana was a new country. We had our freedom and we had our own destiny. I couldn't possibly have imagined a day when an American president would come to Ghana, much less one of African descent. But if I had, I'm sure it would have seemed magnificent.

The Ghana and Africa that Nkrumah envisioned, stood for, and so passionately promoted, was very different from the reality that Obama described to Ghana's parliament. Nkrumah's goal was to propel Ghana into an industrialized and middle-income country, free of poverty and flush with development, within a few decades. His intent was to transform the economy; the days of over-reliance on smallholder cocoa production and extractive export enclaves bequeathed by the British colonial power, such as minerals and timber, would be over, replaced by an industrialized economy funding robust education, health, and infrastructure sectors. He was an ardent believer in the economic and political integration of Africa, realizing that sustainable development of the African continent would not be possible unless there was a common market or an integrated African economy.

In this way, Nkrumah was ahead of his time. So many of the policies he advocated are core tenets of economic transformation, now accepted as the global blueprint for shaping medium and long-term development strategies. Obama upset many during his first trip to Africa, but his speech in Accra, while arguably too harsh in its tone, nevertheless looked beyond positive growth numbers to emphasize long-term structural changes. And after his eight-year tenure, it became apparent, in retrospect, that he was previewing the new approach toward African development. No, there was no Marshall Plan; but more so than any previous Western leader, Obama promoted African policies that would emphasize the private sector, foreign investments, product diversification, skills development, and technology upgrades, among other things.

These issues matter to African countries. Yet the turnaround that saw so many African economies surge through the first decade of the twenty-first century began, in the second decade, to run up against a harsh reality—the structure of those economies had not changed much since independence. Commodity booms and macroeconomic adjustments had fueled GDP gains that could not be sustained, leaving countries as vulnerable as ever to external shocks. The surface-level growth numbers, paired with soaring interest in African labor and resources from multinational corporations and emerging economies like China, masked the inconvenient truth that Africa still lagged behind the rest of the world in most key economic indicators.

Sure enough, after slowing to 3 percent in 2015, economic growth in Sub-Saharan Africa decelerated in 2016 to its lowest level in years.

The global development community and Africa's leading institutions—the African Union, African Development Bank, and Economic Commission for Africa—all agree that if countries pursue a strategy to transform the structure of their economies, they will build on the growth of the past two decades. The industrialized economies Nkrumah envisioned—those powered by regional cooperation, robust markets, and an influential African middle class—have been slow to come. But they are core components of economic transformation. As such, they remain pillars of Africa's economic future.

Nkrumah inspired a generation of young Africans, including me, with his vision of our future. He told us that after colonial rule, Africa was going to be prosperous, strong, united, and respected. It was not rhetoric. He believed it and he made others believe it. Like my father. Like me. That is how I grew up envisioning Africa's future.

It's how I still do envision it.

◆　◆　◆　◆

So why *is* Africa still poor? The answer is not so clear-cut. The underlying issues that have long plagued Africa are complex, multifaceted, and the subject of countless books that are far more advanced in their arguments than anything I attempt to offer here. Still, I consider four broad explanations worth mentioning for the context they provide, both historically and for the following chapter in this book.

First, history, nature and the world in general have not been kind. Even as countries escaped the shackles of colonialism, African governments were forced to deal with factors they could do little about, such as inherited boundaries that make no sense, hindering regional trade and too often instigating civil strife. Meanwhile, despite Africa's abundance of natural resources, extreme weather wreaks havoc with economies and livelihoods. These are not excuses, just realities for the continent, and factors that must always be taken into account.

Second, Africa's complicated history with development assistance and debt, which reached up to 90 percent of GDP in many African countries, cannot be understated as a chronic impediment to economic progress. For too many years, the debt discussion was never on the table, with aid donors and multilateral institutions trying to reverse Africa's fortunes by simply throwing good money after bad—and often placing unrealistic conditions on Africa in return. It wasn't until the late 1990s that changes in the dialogue around development aid and debt, good governance, and bad policy, all started to coalesce. By the early 2000s, the paradigm for effective African development began a seismic shift in favor of partnerships and greater African autonomy.

Third, inappropriate and short-sighted policies have kept most countries from getting ahead. While external factors have certainly compounded Africa's economic woes over the decades, the root causes usually can be traced back to poor policy choices at home. It is not just that state intervention has been too heavy-handed or market forces too unpredictable or multilateral conditions too unforgiving. It is that most policy structures have ignored the basics—investments in infrastructure, public administration, resource management, and human capital—for short-term, unsustainable gains.

This is one reason that Ghana, seen as one of Africa's most stable and enduring governments, was forced to convene an emergency economic summit. Buoyed by high commodity prices and booming production from oil and gas, Ghana's economy grew from an average of 5.3 percent in the 2000s to 14 percent in 2011—the same year The Economist magazine printed a good-time cover story, "Africa Rising," on the continent's seeming turnaround. Within three years, Ghana was seeking IMF assistance, its currency plunging amid rampant government spending and a current account deficit that exceeded 10 percent of its GDP. Despite the recovery in growth, Ghana's share of manufacturing was in decline, its state capacity had diminished, and its economic focus remained stubbornly stuck on extractives and primary products.

This brings me to my fourth and final explanation: strong, responsible, and visionary leadership has been in short supply, and basic governance has suffered because of it. Bad leadership at both the executive and legislative levels has underpinned so many of Africa's problems, from poor economic management to political instability to opaque institutions, that have too often put narrow interests—or worse still, personal prosperity—ahead of the common good. The independence era has produced a tortured history of dictators, despots, and oppressors who have shamefully exploited Africa's resources and people.

I wish I could say Nkrumah left office on his own terms. But that is not what happened. The early years after independence remained hopeful, but Nkrumah grew increasingly remote and authoritarian. In 1964, Nkrumah declared himself president-for-life and banned opposition political parties. In 1966, after years of political and economic turmoil,

Nkrumah was overthrown in a military coup—a devastating turn of events just seven years after he had proclaimed, "Ghana, your beloved country, is free forever!" Over the next quarter-century, Ghana alternated between military rule and republican government six different times.

When Nkrumah delivered his famous midnight address in 1957, he pointed out the hard work ahead; that the people of Ghana were ready to move beyond past difficulties and take charge of their future. "From now on, we are no more a colonial state but a free and independent people," he said. "We are going to demonstrate to the world, to the other nations, young as we are, that we are prepared to lay our own foundation."

When Akufo-Addo delivered his sixtieth anniversary address in 2017, he pointed out the hard work ahead, that the people of Ghana were ready to move beyond past difficulties and take charge of their future. "We will achieve [our] goals when we move and act as a united people," he said. "Let us mobilize for the happy and prosperous Ghana of tomorrow, in which all of us will have equal opportunities to realize their potential. Then, our independence will be meaningful."

It is easy to consider the strikingly similar message in those two passages and draw a depressing conclusion—that Ghana, like the rest of Africa, has been stuck in place for six decades. But that is not exactly true. Ghana, like the rest of Africa, is not where it *should* be, nor where it *needs* to be, but I refuse to believe that it will never get to where it *can* be—the free, prosperous, and stable homeland for which so many have fought, died, and dreamt.

The decades since independence offer us fascinating lessons in successes, failures, and efforts somewhere in between to tackle Africa's endemic problems. It is our imperative to draw on those lessons as we apply new knowledge to old problems.

The immediate challenge, therefore, is to learn from the past and continue to move forward in a way that will fundamentally transform, not just grow, the African continent. So that in another 60 years, leaders no longer feel the need to tell us it's time to get our act together but instead marvel at what we have accomplished. And so that on the occasion of future celebrations at Black Star Square or anywhere else in Africa, Kwame Nkrumah is no longer turning in his grave, but resting peacefully, content that we have laid our foundation, once and for all.

Notes

1   With Obama's visit, Ghana earned the distinction of being the only Sub-Saharan country to receive three successive American presidents.

2   The ONE Campaign is a global advocacy group formed to ensure that government funds continue to flow to poor countries to fight poverty and preventable disease, especially HIV/AIDS. The dinner I hosted in Ghana also included representatives from (RED), a division of ONE that focuses on raising private sector funds. ONE has played a large role in helping secure almost $100 billion in debt relief for poor countries, many in Africa.

Part I
Inside the Bank

I had to find my footing as a young economist and as an African inside a largely white institution that controlled much of Africa's destiny. It was a tall order, but I crossed paths with some key figures who were moving the Bank, slowly, in the right direction. They helped move me in the right direction, too. The Bank might have been a buttoned-down environment, but I was determined to stand apart.

With Philomena and Zambian President Kenneth Kaunda at a luncheon at the Zambia State House in Lusaka in July 1985.

Chapter 1

Working from the Inside
Experiences from a Changing Era at the World Bank

When I joined the World Bank in 1974, I was quite literally a stranger in a strange land. I had lived for five years in the United States, getting my doctoral degree at the University of California-Berkeley, so I wasn't a stranger to America. But the buttoned-down Bank culture was a far cry from Berkeley's radical and diverse environment, in which I had grown quite comfortable over the years.

I arrived in California in the late summer of 1969, not long after Apollo 11 touched down on the moon. The American astronauts landed in the Sea of Tranquility. I landed in a sea of turmoil. The anti-war movement was in full stride and it often seemed like Berkeley was at or near the center of it all. Just a few months before I came to town, California governor and future US President Ronald Reagan declared Berkeley a state of emergency following violent protests and riots, which broke out when local law enforcement tried to remove student demonstrators camped out on campus property—the "People's Park," as they called it. For two weeks, the US National Guard patrolled the Berkeley campus. It was just one incident in a series of riots over the years with which Berkeley became identified.

I grew up in a politically active environment, but the social unrest in America, fueled by opposition to the Vietnam War and sharp racial tensions, differed from Ghana, which had been a more or less united people. Still, the cries of social justice and equality hit close to home. The activism was infectious, especially being an African man, and I was surrounded by it:

the socialist Black Panther Party, which came to define the "black power" movement in the United States, originated in nearby Oakland, California, and Angela Davis, the outspoken and controversial leftist, joined the University of California faculty in Los Angeles the year I began my studies. I was not an activist by any stretch, but I followed all of this activity closely. I did not march. I did not protest. But my sympathies were with the radical side. Some of their talk might have been over the top, but I could relate to it, especially to the messages of empowerment over oppression. Kwame Nkrumah said many of the same things.

Berkeley boasted a diverse population, and I credit my immersion in that atmosphere for learning how to feel comfortable dealing and negotiating with Africans and non-Africans alike. Despite the inclusive environment on campus, African Americans and Africans generally stayed apart. There was a distance between the two groups and not a lot of social interaction, for reasons mixed up in identity politics. I did not share that perspective, though, and I grew close to a lot of African Americans. Some even had ties to home, like Joe Steward, a former lecturer at the University of Ghana, which is where I first met him. Steward and his wife Andrea had moved to Berkeley from Accra so he could teach in the African American Studies department. He was a friendly face for me, and we became very close. We celebrated in his apartment the night Angela Davis was released.[1] I got drunk that night—the first time in my life—and I may have smoked a little marijuana. But if I did, I did not inhale!

Berkeley was always my first choice. I could have gone to study in Britain, which had closer ties to Ghana, or to other American universities. But I preferred Berkeley because it was a leader in quantitative economics, particularly econometrics: the application of math and statistics to economic analysis. Berkeley had some of the leading thinkers in the field: Thomas Rothenberg, Michael Grossman, and Gerard Debreu, a future Nobel Prize winner. Every graduate student had to specialize in two areas, so I chose econometrics and international economics—the latter because of its relevance to developing countries. The coursework was rigorous, but my first-year advisor, George Akerlof, another future Nobel Prize winner, took a particular interest in me and helped me through the rough patches.

The econometrics class was a small group, mostly of American descent and most with a background in mathematics and statistics. A few hailed from India, some by way of Britain. There were a couple of guys from Brazil, including a very smart man named Pedro Malan, who in 1995 became Brazil's minister of finance. The two Brazilians and I became good friends and we held joint study sessions, because we knew there was strength in numbers. Our major was not an easy one and I worried early on that I might be at a disadvantage. But I held my own against my peers from better-known universities, and that was the first time I truly realized just how valuable my earlier schooling had been.

At Nkrumah's insistence, Ghana invested heavily in education, creating one of the strongest systems in Sub-Saharan Africa, and at my father's insistence, I took full advantage of it. As a teenager I was accepted into the Ghana Secondary Technical School (GSTS), which probably thrilled my father more than me because it was a pretty big deal to get in and because I won a scholarship that included full room and board. GSTS maintained a rigid focus on hard sciences, mathematics, and technology and I was not sure I would be too good at any of that. I grew up as a voracious reader, not a young scientist. But aside from a few bumps in the road, I not only survived GSTS, I performed well. I realized that I had an affinity for numbers after all. In my final year, I was elected senior prefect: following the tradition in British high schools, the role involved assisting the teachers in the administration of the school, representing the school at events, and making public speeches, perhaps an early indication of leadership qualities.

Having made the decision to study economics, I moved on to the University of Ghana. I attended the campus at Legon, a few kilometers outside Accra. It is the oldest and largest tertiary institution in Ghana, and it turned out to be the most important stop I ever made—not for the things I learned, but for the person I met.

In my senior year, one of my friends introduced me to a beautiful woman named Philomena Ansah. Philomena and I went on a first date to a campus concert. Then we went on another date. And then, many more. And before long I knew I had met the love of my life. I graduated in 1968 but stayed on for an extra year as a teaching assistant. Philomena, who was studying the history of religions, graduated in 1969. Although we were leaving Legon at the same time, we had different paths in front of us— me to Berkeley, and Philomena to the University of Cambridge, where she planned to pursue a master's degree. So I made one of my first best decisions: I asked her to marry me. Newly engaged, we went our separate ways, though not for too long.

The following summer, Philomena came to California to visit. I bought a 1965 Ford Mustang, the first car I ever owned, so I could show her around the scenic and romantic San Francisco Bay area.[2] It was a nice time. She visited again the next year, and when she finished her degree in 1972 she returned to Berkeley for good. Two years later, as I was finishing my doctorate, we got married.

The wedding was picturesque, in the beautiful home of a Nigerian friend of ours, overlooking the Bay. And we were surrounded by loved ones, if not in the traditional sense. During the time in California, I grew very close to two separate families, the Banks and the Letiches. They each welcomed me into their homes and lives and I knew how fortunate I was to form such close bonds despite being far away from everyone I knew. The Banks were African American and the Letiches were white, and that's only notable in how little it actually mattered to us.

I met Elijah Banks Jr. at the student union not long after I arrived. He was an undergraduate and much younger than me, but we became fast friends. He invited me over for dinner with his family several times. His father, Elijah Sr., had been a cook in the US Navy, so he knew his way around the kitchen. But he could not hold a candle to his wife, known simply as "Mama Dear." We all called her that because she treated anyone she knew like one of her own, and she took no greater pleasure than in making sure you were well fed. As I got to know the Banks, they wanted to get to know Philomena, too. So whenever she came to town, Mama Dear would cook a big meal for us. Eventually, we joined the Banks and their children for Thanksgiving and Christmas holidays.

My other family began as more of a professional relationship. In those days, Berkeley was not known for being overly interested in African studies or recruiting many African students or scholars. Africa was not ignored, but it was not nearly as common as Latin America or Asia as a field of study or interest. Before long, I met a professor, John Letiche, who taught international economics and had a unique interest in applying his work to Africa. At one time, Letiche had been a consultant for the UN Economic Commission for Africa, which I found out only much later in an interesting coincidence. The point is, our paths crossed, and that proved to be a wonderful opportunity. He took an interest in me because I was one of the few Africans in the department, so he brought me under his wing. He became my thesis supervisor. I also became his teaching assistant, helping him write and research academic papers, and eventually I got to know him very well outside the school walls. He was like a father figure to me and he and his wife Emily always made me feel at home. And he always remained an inspiration, continuing to research and write as a professor emeritus at Berkeley until his death at the age of 98.

These two families made life in America very, very wonderful for me and that took the sting out of being far from home. So at our wedding, Philomena and I brought our American families together. Mr. Banks stood in as the father of the bride and walked Philo down the aisle. And Professor

Letiche gave the toast, as a best man would normally. It was a warm and generous send-off as we prepared for Washington, DC and for raising our own family. When we moved, Philo was already pregnant with our oldest girl, Ama, who was born in November 1974. Two years later, our twin daughters—Nana and Mame—were born.

Philomena and I left Berkeley for good on July 8, 1974, bound for the East Coast. I had lived in the Bay area for five years and left California only once, for a weekend trip to Reno, Nevada on our honeymoon (no luck at the slot machines, unfortunately). Berkeley had been a stimulating environment, culturally and intellectually, and I could not have asked for anything more. But until then, the academic life was the only life I had known and that played into my decision to stay in the United States and join the World Bank. I had an opportunity to work at the world's dominant development institution and the appeal of doing so trumped the desire to return home. The transition proved to be eye-opening.

In the 1970s, American, British, and French nationals dominated the World Bank's upper ranks. In fact, they made up more than half of all Bank staff at that time. These were primarily white men, mostly middle-aged, with very distinct attitudes about the Bank's role, about economic development, and about the world around them. A story from Callisto Madavo, one of the true pioneers at the Bank, best explains the environment.

The Bank employed a small number of Africans when I joined, but almost none when Madavo, a native of Zimbabwe, arrived in 1969. He was a trailblazer; he later became the first Sub-Saharan African vice president in the history of the World Bank. But long before that, in his early days, he accompanied one of these "old-school" Bank officials on a mission to Africa. In the hotel bar of a poor country, the Bank official ordered a glass of white wine. The waiter, an old man of obvious poverty, brought the wine, but it was lukewarm. The Bank official, visibly displeased, called out to the waiter: "Boy, the wine is not chilled enough. Chill it some more." Madavo was incensed at the disrespect—they were in the developing world after all, where wine temperature was not exactly a priority or necessity. Even though the Bank official was of high rank and held influence over Madavo's career, Madavo didn't hold his tongue. He asked his superior to be reasonable and told him that the waiter "was a man, not a boy" and should be treated as such, with respect and not condescension. Madavo shared this story when he retired in 2005, as a way of praising just how much the Bank, in both its policy approach and its institutional diversity, had evolved over the years. Indeed, it's hard to imagine such an encounter taking place today.

That Bank official was a product of his era, an era very much alive when I arrived, though thankfully on its way out. Still, I had to find my footing as a young economist *and* as an African inside a largely white institution that controlled much of Africa's destiny. It was a tall order, but I crossed paths with some key figures who were moving the Bank, slowly, in the right direction. They helped move me in the right direction, too. The Bank might have been a buttoned-down environment, but I was determined to stand apart.

I just didn't think that determination would almost kill me within four years.

♦ ♦ ♦ ♦

So how did I get to the World Bank? I was very focused on Africa's development needs, as I had been even as a young boy. I loved Ghana and took pride in my heritage, but I couldn't escape the reality of living in the developing world. It was just a fact of life. For example, when I was in boarding school at Ghana Secondary Technical School, my father insisted that I come home every academic break, which would not have been so bad if "home" had been closer.

GSTS is in Takoradi, on the Ghana coast, not too far from the country's westernmost point. At the time, my father lived in Tumu, which sits 20 kilometers from Ghana's northern border. The two towns are about as far apart as possible in Ghana, around 900 kilometers depending on the route. And that was the problem; the trip was never easy and the route was never direct. I would leave Takoradi by bus and go north to Kumasi—where I would spend a day or two waiting for another bus to take me to the Bamboi ferry—which would take me up the Black Volta River to the small town of Wa—where I would take another bus the rest of the way to Tumu. The trip took days without any delays, but there were almost always delays.

One year, after having spent the long three-month summer vacation in Tumu, I couldn't wait to get back to school. Just before I was set to leave, a heavy rain rolled in that lasted for days. The dirt roads turned to mud. I waited another week and the roads were still impassable. To make it back to school on time, I had to go farther north, hitch a ride on a cattle truck in what is now Burkina Faso and make my way south again. Ghana had bad roads, unreliable buses, and the most basic transport services. The Bamboi ferry was particularly hazardous since it was not yet fully mechanized; the whole operation depended on a rope.

I tried to make the most of my time in Tumu. I would go on field trips with my father, a health center superintendent, to distribute drugs and other medical supplies to nearby villages—remote places like Wallembelle, Bugubelle, and Gbollu. Through my father's work, I met good people suffering from bad diseases or chronic ailments, often without access to essential services. The poverty in that area was striking, and I was very aware of the problems. Even now, the region remains poorer than southern Ghana, a gap that's yet to be bridged.

I never lost sight of the fact that we had it better than many other African families. We had a good home, we were not poor, we did not go hungry, and we had medicine if we needed it. And I always got to go to good schools. I like to think I never took any of that good fortune for granted as a boy. As an adult, I know I did not; a rare trip to visit my estranged mother ensured as much.

Due to my parents' divorce, I did not meet my mother until I was 12 or 13, and even then it was an accidental encounter at a funeral for a distant relative. My father could not attend, so he sent me to pay our respects. Not long after I arrived—I still can't remember the exact location—three women ran toward me. One of them asked if I knew who she was. "No, I do not," I said.

The woman smiled and hugged me. "I'm your mother."

Imagine my surprise. It was the first time I ever spoke to my mother, Abena Anosowa. It was a strange feeling to meet her so suddenly, so unexpectedly. We talked briefly; I didn't really know what to say. And then it was over.

That chance encounter stayed with me for years. After graduating from Legon, I decided that I would try to find her again on my own. I wanted a chance to know my mother.

When I tracked her down, she was living in the Odumase in the Ashanti region. She had remarried and she had more children with her second husband. She seemed content, but she also lived in true poverty. It was evident all around—in her house, in her belongings, in her clothes. For the first time in my life, at the age of 24, I was able to spend the night under the same roof as my mother, but I felt as much guilt as happiness. I had a good life, so easy by comparison, and soon to be even more enriched by my journey to the United States. So to see my own mother living in such poor conditions had a profound effect on me. When I got to Berkeley, I sent money when I could. Later on, I visited again to help rehabilitate her house. It never seemed like enough. Her life had turned out so much differently from mine, controlled to an extent by opportunity and circumstance. Being aware of that on such a personal level made me want to do more.

When I left Ghana in 1969, I had a clear plan: I would get my PhD, then return home to teach at the University of Ghana. But the realities of raising a family and the deteriorating economic situation in Ghana changed my thinking. Ghana was in economic and political turmoil. The military had overthrown the Nkrumah government in 1966, and a civilian regime under Prime Minister Kofi Abrefa Busia was elected in 1969. That government, in turn, was overthrown in another coup three years later. Meanwhile the country was facing severe economic imbalances with inflation, a severely overvalued exchange rate, and shortages of most essential consumer commodities. Indeed, it was the decision to devalue the Ghana currency that triggered the Busia government's overthrow, a development that influenced the topic of my PhD dissertation. I developed an econometric model of the Ghanaian economy to determine the appropriate exchange rate regime for an economy with Ghana's characteristics.[3]

As the economic situation worsened in the early 1970s, so did the country's governance—a harbinger of things to come for all of Africa. Many Ghanaians who had the opportunity started leaving the country for greener pastures abroad. I began to think that Ghana, at least during that period, might not be the best place to start my own family. At the same time, I had become even more interested in big-picture development economics and I felt a real pull to pursue work with a practical application rather than straight academics. So when I finished at Berkeley, the World Bank seemed like the right place to be, both professionally and personally. Luckily for me, the timing was right from the Bank's side, too.

Even in the 1960s, the Bank attracted criticism from the outside for being old-fashioned or too conservative. Mostly, this concerned its lending practices, which featured little consultation with borrowing countries or other aid agencies and almost no focus on policy or long-term outcomes. Lending for agriculture, for example, was generally confined to hard projects like dams or reservoirs, and most often supported large plantation or commercial agriculture—ventures largely influenced by the experience of former colonial officers who made up a large proportion of the Bank's agricultural staff. As more African countries became independent and joined the Bank, the need for broad-based lending—particularly in agriculture, the main economic engine in many countries in 1960s-era Africa, or in education or other areas of immense need in poor countries—became more apparent. So did the need for Bank staff with fresher perspectives who could better relate to this reality.

In 1963, the Bank established the Young Professional Program, originally the Junior Professional Program, to broaden its outreach and diversify its ranks beyond the usual suspects. Typically, the Bank had recruited mid-career professionals, most of whom came from Western Europe and North America. With this newer program, the Bank began recruiting slightly younger but still experienced professionals, as well as graduates with advanced degrees from leading universities. That's the path I took. During my last year at Berkeley, Bank staff visited campus on a recruiting trip. I applied, traveled to Washington, DC for an interview, and ultimately was accepted.

The program is a sort of one-year probationary job leading to the possibility of full employment at the Bank. Each YP, as recruits are known, is given two six-month assignments in two separate departments, under seasoned managers who evaluate the YP's performance on the job. With a satisfactory performance in both assignments, the YP is confirmed as a regular staff member of the Bank. It's basically pass or fail, and though failures have never been common, the mere possibility has always generated considerable anxiety among recruits.[4]

Introducing YPs into the mix was a big step for the Bank's conservative culture. The program began the same year that George David Woods took over as president, and it was part of his effort to push the Bank toward being a more well-rounded and full-service development institution rather than just a financial institution. The new program was met with a skepticism that lingered in some corners of the Bank for years, but externally it attracted immediate attention. More than 200 people applied the first year. The early cohorts of YPs proved themselves, so the Bank slowly expanded the number of appointments to meet the demand. By 1972, there were 44 applicants for every available slot.

Over time, the YP program became one of the Bank's strongest recruiting tools, and it helped speed up diversification.[5] But it took time. In the very early days, almost all the YPs were men, very few of color. The balance improved over the next decade, though still not to acceptable levels. In a 1978 meeting with the Bank's Arab and African executive directors, Robert McNamara, who succeeded Woods as Bank president in 1968, asked the directors for their support in boosting the number of Arab and African YP applicants, which had tailed off. The issue of race in Bank promotions was becoming more prevalent, and McNamara—a strong supporter of Africans and YPs alike—knew the program was one of the main ways the Bank could broaden its appeal to minorities.

Having been accepted as a Young Professional, I moved to Washington, DC in the middle of July 1974. My first impression of my new home? It was hot, humid, and more unpleasant than I remembered Ghana to be. I had the misfortune of arriving in the middle of summer, but the weather didn't distract from the surroundings. Washington struck me as a lovely, majestic city with its many federal buildings and national monuments, including the White House, barely a few hundred yards from the Bank's headquarters. It was not uncommon to find Bank staff, after lunch at the cafeteria, taking a midday walk around the White House—a tradition I soon indulged in.

My timing for showing up in a new place roiling with political tension continued to be impeccable. Within my first month in DC, the US House of Representatives voted to impeach President Richard Nixon, who resigned a few days later. As I've said, I grew up admiring John F. Kennedy as one of my heroes and I read Theodore H. White's famous book, *The Making of the President, 1960*, many times over. Even as a young adult, I carried an idealized view of democratic politics with me, so I was no fan of Nixon. It was a bit deflating to find myself so close to the White House at its most tarnished moment. Still, I was happy to be in Washington with Philomena, who was five months pregnant when we arrived.

We lived in a sprawling apartment complex in Alexandria, Virginia, a historic town just south of Washington. It cost less money to live a little farther out, but our location, the Hamlet Apartments, had another benefit—many young World Bank staff lived there. For whatever reason, this complex had become a popular "residency" for internationals just starting out at the Bank. Philomena and I lived there one week before my first day on the job, and in short order I found myself carpooling to work with three other YPs, two of them my fellow countrymen. That three Ghanaians would be living in the same place and working the same job—at the same time—wasn't as far-fetched as it might seem.

The original group of Africans in the Bank included a lot of Ghanaians. Among them were Albert Osei and Peter Gyamfi, who paved the way for others. When I started at the Bank, and indeed during most of my two decades there, Ghana had the largest representation among all Africans on its staff. After a while, almost half the Sub-Saharan Africans in the Bank were Ghanaian. So we earned a nickname: "The Ghana Mafia."

The numbers weren't a coincidence. A preponderance of Ghanaians had fanned out across the world during this time, working for international organizations and pursuing advanced degrees at Western universities. Nkrumah's focus on education and human capital development in the early days of independence had a lot to do with that. As Ghana's living conditions worsened in the 1970s, many educated Ghanaians still in the country left for greener pastures abroad. Ghanaians became a huge part of the African diaspora and the Bank naturally became an attractive place to work.

◆　◆　◆　◆

My first assignment was not what I expected. I was to report to a senior economist, Willem Bussink, who would be leading a basic economic mission to Indonesia in a few weeks. A basic economic mission was a big deal in the Bank. Every four or five years, for large and important countries such as India and Korea, the Bank would conduct a comprehensive assessment of the country's economy as a baseline for engagement. The findings determined the Bank's country strategy, including how much money it would lend over a certain period of time and the priority sectors and projects it would support.

The highlight of these assessments was the in-country trip, or "mission," to meet with government officials to share ideas and analysis, collect information, and test recommendations that the Bank team hoped to make. The missions usually spanned several weeks and were comprised of some of the Bank's most experienced economists and sector specialists, augmented by outside consultants to prepare a report in about six months. For an inexperienced YP to be placed on the mission team, let alone given a major responsibility, was highly unusual. Happenstance played a part.

As it turned out, arriving in July had a downside—practically everyone in the Bank would be on vacation in August, just like the rest of Washington, DC. Finding a good assignment was going to be a challenge and it soon became apparent that I might have to wait until early September to begin *anything*—a time frame that would put me at a disadvantage since YPs only had a limited window in which to complete two assignments. The YP program administrator didn't like the sound of that any more than I did and went into overdrive to find me something right away. That's how my CV made its way to Bussink and how I landed such a plum—albeit weighty—assignment.

Bussink, a Dutch national, had already hired one of the best econometricians in the Bank, Sharma Gupta, to create a model of the Indonesian economy in the hope of producing future development scenarios. Gupta and I immediately began work on the econometric model. I focused on data collection and that mostly revolved around Indonesia's booming oil industry. Commercial oil production had begun there as far back as the late 1800s, but the massive price hikes of the early 1970s, pushed by the Organization of the Petroleum Exporting Countries (OPEC), to which Indonesia belonged, brought a sudden windfall. In 1973, Indonesia produced more than a million barrels of oil a day. Oil revenues, which accounted for 70 percent of the state budget, were seen as a bonanza that could transform the economy, sustain economic growth, and greatly reduce poverty.[6] Bussink saw an opportunity for the Bank to make far-reaching and aggressive recommendations to policymakers, and the econometric model would be the primary tool to support those recommendations. As it later became clear, Bussink's enthusiasm and approach, particularly for the modeling work, was not widely shared within the Bank.

Gupta and I got along well. In fact, he became a good friend and an important mentor until he retired. I enjoyed the work and had a good handle on it. But no more than two weeks into the assignment, Bussink called me into his office and shook things up. My role was being changed, he said, and instead of working on the macro model, I would be put in charge of making long-term projections for the investment requirements in key sectors of the Indonesian economy. I had no training or expertise at all in this area. In the Bank, sector specialists—engineers and financial analysts, for example—did this kind of work. Then my surprise turned to panic: I soon learned that the specialist initially slated for this task—a seasoned Bank veteran—chose instead to leave the mission team altogether because he didn't think what he was being asked to do could be finished in the time frame envisioned.

I had three weeks before the mission to Indonesia, so I spent that time reading everything I could about Indonesia's social and infrastructure sectors. I sought out some Bank veterans for their advice, including the man who passed up the assignment in the first place. He was gracious with his time but puzzled by my extra effort. I'm sure he thought I was making too much of it, but he wasn't a YP from Africa. Almost everyone I met or dealt with during my early days at the Bank was kind and hospitable, but too few could relate to the extra pressures and challenges felt by those who came from outside the "typical" Bank culture. Examples weren't always as obvious as the story of cultural disconnect shared by Callisto Madavo;

they could be as subtle as a veteran's bemusement at a rookie's anxiety. That's what made crossing paths with the ones who could relate even more valuable.

Once we left for Djakarta, I didn't feel quite as much stress. That's because the first few days of the mission were almost like a vacation. I boarded a Pan Am 747 flight bound for Hawaii and took my seat in first class, definitely a new experience for me. The Bank sent about 15 staff and consultants on the mission and I traveled in the company of two economists, one from India and the other from Pakistan. Already I was beginning to appreciate the Bank for the diverse nationalities of its staff, even if that wasn't yet the case in upper management. We spent two nights in Maui then flew to Hong Kong for another night, where we stayed at a luxury hotel before the final flight to Djakarta.

Such leisure seems unimaginable now. In those days, the Bank allowed staff on long-haul flights three days' worth of stopovers so they would arrive at their destination fresh, rested, and ready to work. But the privileges of first-class travel and five-star hotels, especially when considered alongside the generous Bank salaries and benefits, had begun to attract intense criticism for being incongruous with a mission to promote development in poor countries. The more the Bank positioned itself as a development institution as well as a lending institution, the more scrutiny its operations got. On that flight to Djakarta, I never imagined that just five years later my job would have me involved in a massive review of the Bank's travel and compensation policies—a review that whittled down those privileges over the ensuing years, including the elimination of first-class travel.

When we got to Djakarta, it was all work: meetings with government officials from morning until early evening, with team members either in pairs or alone. After dinner, we would gather in a hotel conference room and report to the full team our accomplishments for the day, including any key conclusions we were forming. I was always the last to be called upon, and I believe my nerves were apparent. Bussink would usually ask me a couple of questions and make a few suggestions on what I should do the following day, but other members of the team hardly reacted to what I had to say. A few, including my original travel companions, were polite, but it soon became clear that most of them believed my task was a bit quixotic.

The Indonesian officials I dealt with were more encouraging. They were generous with their information and access, and they patiently listened to my queries and requests. I'm sure my nationality had something

31

to do with it. In 1961, Indonesian President Sukarno (one name only) and Kwame Nkrumah joined with three other leaders—India's Jawaharlal Nehru, Yugoslavia's Josip Tito, and Egypt's Gamal Nasser—to form the Non-Aligned Movement, a political alliance among developing countries that sought a middle path between the Western and Eastern blocs fighting the Cold War. It was a powerful statement for developing countries to make. So as a Ghanaian, I was received with warmth and solidarity because of our countries' recent shared history.

We also had larger meetings, where the full Bank team would come together with the most senior Indonesian policymakers. As the new guy on the block, I would sit off to the side or in the back, an inconspicuous onlooker rather than active participant. But I made some valuable observations. First, the Indonesians were on top of their game. They were assertive in their views and confident with their facts, often vigorously disagreeing with the Bank experts. They wanted assistance, not directives, and I quietly sat in awe of their expertise. Second, I noticed how deferential and respectful the Bank staff were toward the government officials. It may not have seemed like a big deal at the time, but very soon in my career I would see a stark contrast in the way my team members treated the Indonesians and the behavior of other Bank staff toward government officials in Africa, which could border on arrogance. It was not uncommon for even the most junior Bank economists to demand meetings with higher-ranking officials than were present. Again, I got lucky because I saw on my very first mission the proper way for Bank staff to carry themselves and I saw how productive respectful interactions could be.

The mission ended after almost six weeks in Indonesia. I decided to forgo the three-day stopover—the same travel policy also applied even on return trips—and head straight home. Philomena was then eight and a half months pregnant, and I spent the final weeks of the mission worrying that she might give birth early in my absence. I made it as far as Chicago before exhaustion got the better of me and I had to spend the night there. I arrived home with little time to spare. My beautiful daughter Ama was born three days later.

A first draft of the assessment, a comprehensive report covering almost every aspect of the Indonesian economy, had to be finished before the end of the year. The team comprised staff from different departments in the Bank, but for efficiency's sake we needed to be in close proximity. It was mid October and we didn't have much time. So we took up temporary residence in a rented space one block from the main Bank complex. I was told it was the first time a team had been sequestered to prepare a report. In other words, we were under extreme pressure. There were no midday strolls around the White House. In my case, Ama refused to cooperate— she wouldn't sleep at night, which meant I didn't either. A newborn and a new job, and no room for error with either one!

It soon became clear that things were not going well. We were missing deadlines and early drafts were not well received. It was a harsh introduction for me to the Bank's culture, where every document is subjected to intense scrutiny in one meeting after another, among different managers, requiring endless rewriting. With an institution that prides itself on analytical rigor, high standards were to be expected. But our report on Indonesia was a different kettle of fish.

As it turned out, many people inside the Bank had expressed serious doubts about the whole scope of the assessment from the very beginning. They didn't think Bussink was being realistic in his determination to craft a blueprint for Indonesia's social and economic transformation—no small endeavor—in so short a time. All of it—Gupta's economic model, the team's analytic findings, my quixotic sectoral projections—was simply more than the allotted time and available resources could accommodate. As we muddled along, the critics were having a field day. Bussink and, by extension, the mission team bit off more than we could chew. As we completely missed the original end-of-year deadline, I came to understand much better why the gentleman originally assigned my task had refused to do it. He wanted to avoid the reputational risk of failure.

In March 1975, almost six months after we returned from Djakarta, the Bank held a review meeting chaired by Bernie Bell, vice president of the East Asia and Pacific region, which included Indonesia. Earlier in his Bank career, Bell had served as a director in Djakarta and was well respected for his knowledge inside the Bank and among Indonesian officials. The conclusion of the review meeting was devastating. Bell and others determined that we should immediately cease work on the assessment; it could not be salvaged through additional work, they said, and it would not be published. It was the first time that the Bank had ever taken such drastic action on a basic economic report. We would have nothing to show for all the effort, which must have cost the Bank a few hundred thousand dollars.

Whether the initial scope of the project was too broad, the goal too aggressive, or our work too hurried, we didn't get the job done and we weren't going to be allowed to finish. There was no way around the sense of failure. I never expected my career at the Bank to begin that way, but

I felt even worse for Bussink. He was a man of integrity and fairness and he genuinely wanted to help Indonesia and its people. He gave me an intimidating assignment, but he believed in me enough to hand me an opportunity rare among YPs and he encouraged me along the way. He pushed me beyond my comfort zone, and he earned my respect because of it.

Still, I worried about how this disaster might reflect on me. Others on the team were established; I was not. Moreover, not more than six pages of the dozens I had produced made it into the document submitted for initial review. That the Bank ultimately rejected the document was beside the point.

One week after the review team's edict, I met with Bussink for my final evaluation, required for all YPs on their assignments. I had given it my all, but I still didn't know what to expect. Based on the meager six pages used in the draft report, my contribution could not be measured as superior. But Bussink was very gracious: he thanked me for my hard work, commented on my fortitude under difficult circumstances, and praised me for being a good team player. Overall, he rated my work as very satisfactory—not outstanding, but I was relieved. And although I'm not sure that I realized it at the time, I had gained valuable insights that would help me navigate my career at the Bank: managing expectations, building team loyalty, treating country leaders with respect, and not being afraid to fail.

Because the Indonesia report had dragged on, I spent almost nine months in that division. As a result, my follow-up assignment was something untraditional: I was sent to the Bank's Economic Development Institute, or EDI, to help prepare teaching materials.

The EDI offered training courses for mid- and high-level officials from developing countries. It was established in 1955 and, based on its initial success, became a permanent part of the Bank two years later. But by the early 1960s, what began as a single, six-month course soon evolved into much more complex contextualized offerings based on the different needs of particular countries or regions. In this way, the institute's transformation to meeting member needs rather than forcing members to conform to standard precepts foreshadowed the broader evolution of Bank approaches to come. The topics covered areas such as macroeconomics, economic planning, and project management, and by the time of my brief assignment in 1975, the institute also boasted a plethora of specialized sectoral courses, such as agro-processing, rural credit, and waste disposal. As the Bank moved to more aggressively transition from a lending institution to a full development institution, the EDI was often at the forefront.

After the high-stress environment I had just come from, my time at the EDI was generally pleasant and passed quickly. There were social functions to keep the visiting officials entertained and occasional field trips away from Washington for hands-on learning, including one that took us to the Appalachian coal country in West Virginia. These activities allowed us to interact in a less informal way with senior foreign policymakers. As a result, I gained more insights into the greater world around me. I learned, for example, how much the officials admired the expertise of Bank staff but disliked the power and influence that the Bank wielded over their countries. One reason it took so long before the Bank addressed this kind of operational disconnect in a meaningful way is because too few of the old guard did not believe that developing countries could direct their own affairs. However, my first experience showed me otherwise— that sometimes, those developing countries might have a much better understanding of their needs than the Bank.

I was confirmed as a regular staff member in August 1975, after which I planned on having a long and productive career at the Bank. It is where I wanted to be and where I believed I could make the biggest impact. But the stress I encountered during that first YP assignment didn't go away with my newfound job security. In fact, it got worse. I landed a good position with one of the Bank's toughest managers, but I soon found myself butting heads with him over important country policy. I also found myself with a larger family to support, after Philomena gave birth to our twin girls in 1976. By the end of the following year, it all caught up with me.

◆　◆　◆　◆

Despite my determination to make a name for myself at the Bank, I was not oblivious to the reality of my surroundings. Among Africans in the Bank, an undercurrent of unease was apparent. No one had any hard evidence at the time, but it seemed that if you were African, promotions were slower to come, plum assignments were tougher to get, and respect was harder to earn. Over the previous decade, the YP program had provided the Bank with an infusion of young, intelligent, and diverse professionals, but moving through the bureaucracy took—and still takes—time. There were only so many avenues for advancement and even fewer for the new generation, since the old generation held most senior positions. For a YP of African descent, finding the right landing spot was not always easy.

The first task for "graduating" YPs is to get one's file in circulation and find a full-time position, and if that position matches up with personal interests then all the better. My preference was to work on Africa and I had a keen interest in one position in particular: country economist for Sudan. The job of a country economist, broadly, is to analyze a nation's data, policies, and key sociopolitical indicators to underpin the Bank's support strategy in that country, which includes lending amounts and priority projects. The YP administrator was responsible for helping place YPs in permanent jobs, and we both agreed that the Sudan position would be a good fit. So he sent my file, which was more or less the equivalent of an application, to the East Africa department, which oversaw Sudan. But he also sent it to the Latin America and Caribbean region for a similar position. It took only a week for me to get an interview with the latter group, and within a few days I had a job offer. I appreciated it, but I really wanted to work on East Africa. The Sudan job was a perfect match for my skills and one reason I opted away from academics was to work on practical development solutions for Africa. Also, the department had earned a great reputation under the leadership of Stanley Please.

A proudly British academic, Please was one of the Bank's early progressive thinkers. He foresaw a different role for the Bank, a much more aggressive and active role, from the moment he arrived in 1963. He believed the Bank's economic strength could be used in poor and developing countries as a force for change, not simply an avenue for aid. Robert McNamara is often credited—and rightly so—for leading the Bank into its more modern era; his famous speech in Nairobi in 1973 in which he stated the need to tackle "absolute poverty" in the developing world is seen as a turning point for the Bank's philosophy and its approach to country policies. But internally, that kind of talk had been going on for years. And Please was among the loudest voices.

In a way, Please is perfectly representative of the worldviews that pushed the Bank in new directions. He expressed particular interest in improving Africa's situation. He saw a region that needed more than borrowed dollars. He believed that states had to have the right policies in place before any long-term development outcomes could be achieved. His beliefs were well known in the Bank and that alone made his department an appealing destination. But he was also known as one of the Bank's strongest supporters of the YP program. A lot of Bank managers were still skeptical, especially since a growing number of YPs were progressive-minded economists inspired by McNamara's anti-poverty message. But Please was an enthusiast. He welcomed YPs and took them under his wing, using his knowledge of the Bank—he had risen steadily from division chief to chief economist to country director—to help guide them. At the same time, he was also known as a punishing manager, a perfectionist who expected nothing but maximum effort.

I had only one problem: Please didn't think I was the right person for the job, and he had no interest in hiring me. He had nothing against me personally. He just didn't think I had what it would take to meet his high standards, mostly because he wasn't a strong believer in the field of econometrics. Young economists didn't bother him; nontraditional backgrounds did. Had I been from Oxbridge, it might have been love at first sight. But I was a YP graduate, and for that reason he agreed to interview me—if I first met with the department's division chief, Anders Ljung, and senior economist, Lyle Hansen, and got their approval. So that's what I did and the meeting couldn't have gone better. We all hit it off and I left the interview even more excited at the prospect of being on their team.

Ljung and Hansen recommended me right away, but then … nothing. Please still didn't want to interview me. I waited a day, then two days, then three days, then four and some more. Meanwhile, I had this other offer from the Latin America and Caribbean region, which needed an answer.

Finally, Please called me for an interview—and that lasted no more than 15 minutes. He was perfectly pleasant but his apprehension was apparent. Sudan was becoming a bigger deal for the Bank; he just didn't see me as enough of a heavyweight.

I left the interview dejected, but once again Ljung and Hansen went to bat for me. They finally wore him down. "If you want the guy you can have him," he told them, "but he'll be your problem."

With that ringing endorsement, I got the job.

The years I spent in that department shaped me, but it was at times a bitter and grueling experience. From the very beginning, I knew I had to prove myself intellectually—and I needed to convince Please that he had made the right decision. But I also had to deal with the diversity issue.

Back then, the Bank divided Africa into two regions, East and West, and Anglo-Saxon staff dominated both. They were almost all British and French nationals who had served in Africa during the colonial days, and the attitude of many toward Africans could easily be called condescending—it didn't matter if the Africans were living on the continent or working down the hall. Needless to say, I was never part of the inner circle. Not long after I was hired, the department staff convened for a meeting to discuss a paper on the Sudanese economy. In my position as country economist, I expected to make the introduction and begin the talk, because that was standard practice. But the gentleman chairing the meeting—not Please—never gave me that chance. He cut me off and instead asked that I take notes, and then he turned to another—non-African—staff member to make the opening remarks. I was terribly offended. But more determined than ever.

When I began my job, three main issues were at the center of the Bank's economic dialogue with Sudan: public enterprise reform, agricultural pricing, and debt management, all interrelated. Private sector development in Sudan was flagging; public enterprises dominated the economy, from agriculture and financial sectors to most large-scale industry. But many of those enterprises were taking losses or simply stagnating. Sudan's irrigated agricultural economy, for example, has always held great potential but rarely lived up to it. The Gezira Scheme, begun by the British in the early twentieth century to distribute water from the Blue Nile through thousands of canals and ditches, was one of the largest irrigation projects in the world. It boosted agriculture in the surrounding region, but it had the capacity to make a much larger impact. The Sudanese government, through poor pricing policy and planning, was not getting as much revenue or production out of Gezira as it could. And that hurt the entire irrigation system. From an economic development standpoint, its water was going to waste.

Gezira offered one example of glaring government inefficiency, but there were others—none bigger than debt management. Once Sudan's long civil war had ended in 1972, the country appeared to be on a path to stability. It had rich resources and plenty of eager investors. Arab countries, in the early years of the OPEC ascendency, recognized Sudan's agricultural potential and began to pour huge capital investments into the state economy to turn Sudan into the "breadbasket of the Arab world." As OPEC money flowed free and easy, other large-scale projects ramped up amid the enthusiasm.[7] There was an expectation that whatever bills Sudan racked up in the present would easily be paid for in the future. But the country lacked basic economic governance. It had no system in place to track all of its borrowing—the amounts, the terms, the purposes. Individual ministers and officials borrowed indiscriminately, and the ministry of finance appeared powerless to exercise any kind of approval authority.

The Bank, meanwhile, was heavily involved. It wanted to be an influential voice and a key player in what everyone perceived to be the ground floor of a Sudanese renaissance. When I joined the East Africa department, the staff members were preparing the Bank's CPP, or country programming paper, for Sudan. A CPP is a confidential document for senior Bank decision-makers, intended to provide guidance on Bank activities. As a result, CPPs need to be rich in detail and confident in their findings. They incorporate a lot of different inputs, including analysis from sectoral specialists, reviews of past economic trends, and projections of future performance. In other words, a CPP is the very definition of analysis in that it relies on as much hard data as possible, but ultimately its recommendations come down to judgment calls.

As the Bank's new country economist for Sudan, I had a major role to play in preparing the CPP, including constant coordination with other Bank staff involved in Sudan, such as the Bank's agricultural experts. We traveled together frequently, meeting with policymakers and other local experts to get a good sense of what was actually going on in the country and to prepare reports or projects for implementation. The IMF was also involved in the major policy issues, and I formed a good relationship with Karim Nashashibi, a brilliant economist who became a counterpart, particularly on the critical issue of agricultural pricing.

I found the work challenging and the pace was relentless. In the first two years, I made multiple trips to Sudan and I logged longer hours in the office than I imagined possible. To Philomena's chagrin, I practically lived at the Bank despite having three infant daughters at home. She's since said that she often felt like a single mother in those days. There's no doubt in retrospect that I pushed too hard, but I had to prove myself. When finished, the CPP would not only go to senior management but all the way to the Bank President McNamara before being implemented. I wasn't doing it all, but the economic projections made the guts of the report and they were my responsibility.

Many in the Bank were bullish on Sudan, especially Stanley Please. He saw the money coming in from other countries and he wanted the Bank to lead, not follow. Among those calling for expansionary lending, he was out front. He was a real optimist, perhaps to a fault. Indeed, he liked to say, "If you're not an optimist on Africa, then you shouldn't be working on Africa!" To his credit, he believed that too many people in the Bank were too negative about Africa's potential and he wasn't afraid to say so. I always admired him for that, but the realist in me refused to get too carried away. Please's position on Sudan made me uncomfortable, because the numbers didn't add up.

One of my duties was to look at the current economic situation and the future projections together, and on that basis provide an assessment of debt versus creditworthiness. Immediately, Sudan's borrowing stood out. And the closer I looked into the weak debt management processes, the more uncomfortable I grew. Saudi Arabia and the other Arab countries were going in with too much money on very short-term lending, creating a potential danger. I didn't see any evidence that Sudan could absorb the influx of financing coming its way without running into major debt problems in the future. So I didn't believe that it could handle an expansionary lending program. I thought the Bank was already contributing to a bad situation and that we would only make things worse if we moved any more aggressively. A debt crisis, I argued, looked unavoidable.

Please disagreed with me—strongly. We already had a tense relationship, because we had rarely seen eye to eye on Sudan and because he never really wanted me in his department in the first place. But the CPP exposed the divide. He wanted to be more aggressive and I wanted to be more cautious. My final analysis included all of the criticisms and concerns I had over Sudan, even though I knew Please didn't share them. As I saw it, my job was to be correct, not a rubber stamp for my boss.

And with that, we embarked on a philosophical tussle. Please told me to change the paper, which I did, but only partially. So he sent it back to me again, and again I held my ground. I wasn't trying to be difficult. In fact, quite a few others on the Sudan team agreed with me, but no one wanted to cross Please. After all, he was our boss. We respected him. Everyone respected him. He was, as I've said, one of the good guys. So even those who agreed with me quietly went along with his wishes. But I couldn't bring myself to do that, even though I was practically committing heresy. Here I was, a young economist barely a few years on the job, butting heads with my universally admired country director on the most fundamental of Bank operations: the size of a country lending program and whether the borrowing country could actually absorb the money. I'm still surprised that I remained as resolute as I did. It must have been the foolishness of youth.

Of course, Please had the final authority, so in the end he got what he wanted—but only for a brief time. The CPP went to the regional vice president, Willi Wapenhans, and others for final review, including the East Africa region's chief economist, Ravi Gulhati. But they had issues with it. Gulhati raised many of the same concerns I had expressed over the proposed lending. Wapenhans asked for the paper to be rewritten right away. So the CPP came back and that's when Please and I finally collaborated. He agreed to ease up, even taking some of my suggestions, and I took the lead in rewriting the full paper, which I somehow pulled off in two weeks. That version made its way to McNamara, who gave it the final approval. I sat in the back of the room during that meeting. When McNamara called the report "extraordinarily good," it was a proud moment. We got the go-ahead to continue the program in Sudan, but at a more restrained pace and with more awareness of the country's mounting debt.

This entire episode had a lasting impact on my career at the Bank. In a short time, I had gained a reputation for being a good analyst and a fast worker. I was willing to go out on a limb and stand by the projections and people took notice. And the "standoff" with Stanley Please certainly attracted attention, because it wasn't every day that a young African economist was willing to push back against an influential British Bank veteran. I had earned respect inside the Bank and that was no small feat.

The following year, in 1978, Please took a different job in the Bank. Before he left our department, he called me into his office and asked me to sit down. He had something to tell me. "I was wrong about you," he said. In the end, that mattered. Not only did he become one of my trusted mentors, we became close associates. A few years later, we again found ourselves working together on the Bank's new lending policy for Africa, and in 1986 we co-authored a paper on ways that big institutions like the World Bank and the Organization of African Unity could find common ground despite philosophical differences—an ironic but fitting topic for the two of us.[8]

In the long run, things worked out. I even gained more self-confidence in my skills: just a few years later, an external debt crisis crippled Sudan and the government eventually collapsed. In the short run, however, the benefits of the job were not so apparent. I had put a lot of pressure on myself to go the extra mile and disprove any doubts about my qualifications to be a country economist. So I worked myself ragged. Essentially, I wore myself down. I soon realized that my early success had come at a great cost to my health.

Hypereosinophilic syndrome is a rare blood disorder caused by an elevated number of white blood cells. Over time, these extra cells can cause discomfort through inflammation but eventually they can cause internal damage to the lungs and heart. Hypereosinophilia can be tough to diagnose because symptoms vary depending on what part of the body is affected, and even then the syndrome is easily masked. Skin inflammation may be as basic as itching and rashes—certainly not symptoms that scream life-threatening blood disorder. Affected lungs can result in shortness of breath. An affected heart may result in extra fatigue. Sometimes, hypereosinophilia can be mistaken for the flu. Other times, for stress.

I had this blood disorder, but I found out only because I encountered an even more apparent health problem—congestive heart failure.

It all started with a bad cold and fever that I couldn't shake in December 1977. The timing was terrible—the holidays were approaching, and we had planned a family trip to Ghana. It was to be my young daughters' first visit to Africa, so we were really looking forward to it. But I wasn't well. After Christmas I began to feel even worse. We had no choice but to postpone the trip. I thought I had the flu, but before long I got admitted to the local hospital in Alexandria, Virginia, with what doctors believed to be a bad case of bronchitis. Soon, fluid began building up in my lungs, and that was when the whole situation got a lot more serious.

Until that point, I had lived a fairly healthy life. I had a bout of malaria as a child, which was sadly common for those living in Africa, but overall I never had reason to worry about my health. I had, however, confronted mortality for the first time only a few months before, when my father passed away in Africa.

He was not an old man, only in his mid sixties, but he had hypertension. I'm not sure that's what killed him, because no one ever really knew. He had retired and moved back to Bompata, a village where we once lived and some of his family resided. He wasn't particularly close to them, but it was home, I suppose. I stayed in touch with him through letters and rare phone calls, but I had not been back to see him since the day I left for Berkeley. When he died, it had been nine years—too long. Even worse, he was dead for two weeks before I knew. Family members sent me a telegram, but Philomena and I had recently moved to a new apartment and so it went to the wrong place.

My father's death hit me hard. I was troubled at the distance that had developed between us, how he never met his granddaughters, and at the thought that he died alone on his farm. He invested so much in me and he gave me so much encouragement, I knew he was proud of where I was. In response, I believe I pushed myself even harder and I was already keeping up a punishing pace between the travel, deadlines, and stress of my stance on Sudan.

Not long after I entered the hospital, the doctors became very worried because they couldn't figure out exactly what was going on. My heart was pumping more weakly than normal and I had a hard time breathing—that was the congestive heart failure—but I didn't fully improve even after they stabilized my heart: that was the undiagnosed hypereosinophilia. The latter was exacerbating the former, though neither triggered the other. I

42

learned later that the hospital had never encountered a patient suffering simultaneously from the two. So they were understandably puzzled.

Things took a turn for the worse when I passed out in my hospital room. I was getting oxygen to help offset the weak blood flow, but I still was bedridden and weak. And I coughed a lot. That's the last thing I remember, heavy coughing, before I blacked out.

Except I don't remember blacking out. I remember seeing my father.

I remember riding in a truck or bus, I'm not sure which, with a group of people I didn't know. We were riding downhill. And then beyond the bus, I saw my father waving, an image as clear and vivid as the last time I saw him face-to-face. And then I was awake.

The nurses revived me, but my heart, they said, had almost stopped. One of the doctors told Philomena just how serious the situation had become. "We're very worried," he said. "We really don't know what's going to happen to him." They were preparing her for the possibility that I might not survive.

With no immediate answers, the hospital transferred me to the National Institute of Health, north of Washington, DC in Bethesda, Maryland. A team of doctors under the leadership of Anthony S. Fauci began looking after me and that was my good fortune. I believe Dr. Fauci saved my life.

At the time, I could tell he was a brilliant physician, but that's selling him short after his amazing career. In 1984, he became the director for Allergy and Infectious Diseases at NIH—a position he held for decades— and he soon moved to the forefront of HIV/AIDS research. He was one of the architects behind the US President's Emergency Plan for AIDS Relief, George W. Bush's $15 billion commitment to fight the HIV/AIDS pandemic. He has long been an expert advisor to world leaders on infectious diseases, including the 2014 Ebola outbreak. Over the years, I've seen him on television dozens of times. And whenever I do, I always smile to myself and say, "There goes my man!"

Dr. Fauci and his team got the heart failure under control; they knew how to treat that. But even after they diagnosed the hypereosinophilia, I didn't improve. My white blood cell count kept going up and they couldn't figure out how to bring it down. The disorder normally produces an elevated cell count for an extended period before dropping once treated. But mine didn't drop. The body can't fight infections in that state, so there was an added urgency to my situation. At one point, NIH rushed one of my blood samples to the Center for Disease Control in Atlanta, Georgia. I really began to wonder if I would recover. But then, after a week or more, the cell count started to fall just as mysteriously as it had first climbed.

With hypereosinophilia, it's not uncommon for an initial cause to never be identified. It is uncommon, however, for the syndrome to seemingly vanish after appearing impervious to antibiotics and other treatment. My case, they said, was a real medical mystery.

After a few weeks of recovery, and with my blood cell count stabilized, NIH released me. I was home for the first time in almost a month and that's where I stayed. The hypereosinophilia might have been a mystery, but the heart issues, fostered by my exhausting pace of the previous four years, were another story. I had to dial it back, the doctors said, for my own good. So I took medical leave from the Bank and didn't go to the office for three months. I recuperated around my wife and young daughters, and I was thankful to be there.

When I was ready to return to work, I tried to ease myself gently back into the routine. At first I worked on a part-time basis, no more than two or three hours a day, and definitely no travel. I planned to gradually increase my time in the office every few weeks or so. But my body wasn't ready to cooperate. Before long, I began to feel worse again. One snowy night, I took my girls to their first NBA basketball game. Afterwards, I relapsed. The emergency team bypassed the local hospital entirely this time and rushed me directly to NIH. My symptoms were the same and the patterns were the same. I was back where I started.

I never got a clear answer because the doctors never had a clear answer. After leaving NIH the second time, I never had another relapse, but I did have to go back for evaluations every six months. Doctors called me a unique case, not only for the dual ailments but for surviving them without any lifelong side effects. In 1985, I began seeing a new physician, Dr. Kevin Nealon, on a regular basis. When he first met me and read my medical history, he was fascinated at what I had survived. He took a lot of interest in my case and I've been fortunate to be under his care ever since.

The ailment has remained as much a mystery to me as what really happened when I "saw" my father the night I blacked out in the hospital. Had it been a fever dream? A near-death experience? My imagination? I'll never know, but that image has stayed with me ever since.

When I returned to the Bank full-time and fully recovered, I had been out for the better part of nine months. My superiors were supportive, but they were also very worried about my durability. I realized the questions about my health were not going away and an answer to the primary one— could I travel overseas?—directly affected my ability to perform my job as a country economist.

The Bank had its own health unit and the woman in charge wanted me to see a specialist recommended by the Bank. I refused to go, because I suspected they were going to come to the conclusion that I was too much of a health risk—and therefore, too much of an insurance liability—to travel on missions. I began to fear my career at the Bank might come to an end. It was ironic; I worked myself to near death to prove my ability, but my ability was now being overshadowed by the poor health that resulted in part from my hard work.

In a way, I had to prove myself all over again.

◆　◆　◆　◆

The issue of racism and discrimination in the World Bank predated my arrival and outlasted my departure. I've mentioned the difficult environment that Africans faced in the 1970s, but the truth is that people of color—whether born in Africa, America, or anywhere else—have always had a tough time reaching the Bank's highest levels. According to data compiled for an internal review in 2003 and reported by the Washington-based Government Accountability Project in 2009, black Bank employees were 36 percent less likely to hold a managerial grade relative to equally qualified, non-black employees. Numbers like these are indicative of a pervasive imbalance, which the Bank has taken increasing steps to address: a racial equality program in 1998, an office of diversity program in 2001, and a code of conduct in 2009 that addressed discrimination and diversity.

Still, the issue persists.

In 2005, the Bank's staff association went on the record to say that "racial discrimination in the Bank is very bad." In 2011, there was not a single black manager in the Bank's highly regarded Development Economics unit, which is at the forefront of the Bank's modern analytical services and poverty reduction strategies. In more recent years, a group of current and past Bank staff formed an organization—Justice for Blacks—to address decades of "systemic racial discrimination." The group has tried to raise awareness through aggressive public information campaigns and open letters to African ministers, policymakers, and Bank leadership.

During my early days, the issue was almost taboo as a talking point in certain circles of the Bank establishment: rarely acknowledged in the open but known to exist. But it was talked about elsewhere, particularly among a small but vocal segment of Africans trying to push the agenda. They formed the Africa Club as an organized outlet inside the Bank to get people talking. This was almost 40 years ago, so while the current awareness is encouraging, the reality that race even remains an issue is disheartening. I have been away from the Bank for too long to speak definitively or with authority on the current challenges, so I'll leave that to the men and women engaged in today's dialogue. What I can speak about, however, is the story behind an earlier turning point, when the issue didn't have nearly as much traction or generate nearly as much attention—but when it coincided with a turning point in my own career.

Not long after I was back from medical leave and once more working full-time, I got a call to meet with the Bank's new vice president in charge of Operations and Personnel Management, Martijn Paijmans. McNamara wanted to improve the Bank's administrative services, so in 1979 he appointed Paijmans—a 17-year Bank veteran known as an "apostle of order, systems, and efficiency"—to take the lead.[9] I'd never met him and I was petrified when I went to see him. The Bank was so worried that I posed a health risk that no one knew what to do with me. My bosses surely didn't want me to travel, so when I got the call from his office, I thought the meeting must have something to do with my health. I feared the new VP would tell me that my capabilities no longer matched my job requirements and that I should leave the Bank. Instead, he told me something else entirely.

Paijmans, who came from the Netherlands, was a smallish man, very intelligent, and very intense. He had a lot of energy and he quickly put my mind at ease because my health turned out to be the least of his concerns.

"The Bank is in trouble," he said. "There are some big problems and big challenges that need to be fixed." He then launched into a long narrative about staff unhappiness regarding salaries, promotional opportunities—or the lack thereof—and the overall condition of administrative service.

The Bank was growing and its mission was changing, he said, but the operational infrastructure was stuck in the past. Morale was getting worse at a time when it should be getting better, since so many young, hungry professionals were joining to carry out McNamara's anti-poverty mission. And it was getting worse because the Bank didn't maximize staff potential. Paijmans had been vocal in the past about what he perceived to be one of the Bank's biggest shortcomings: that it brought in top talent from all over the world and paid them reasonably well but then let them wither because basic functions like personnel management and administration—things he called the Bank's "ignoble side"—weren't up to scratch. The problem as he saw it was a basic mismatch: traditional personnel staff didn't understand the business of the Bank. Since Paijmans came from the operations side—he was an economist who moved up through the ranks like everyone else—McNamara believed he could apply the same rigor from the field to Bank administration.

Paijmans gave me the context and then he told me why I was there.

"You're coming to work for me as my special assistant for personnel and administration."

"Why me?" I asked, more than a little confused that I was being "offered" a job that I hadn't sought nor felt remotely qualified to handle.

"Because I want a good analyst," he said, "a young economist with a critical mind. I looked through several files. I think you're the one."

"Well, what am I coming to do?" I asked, still confused. Then he really won me over.

"I don't know!" he said, as honest an answer as he could give. "But I also don't know what I'm doing. All I know is that we have a big job to do and we can do it together."

There was something about him I found fascinating. His commitment? His enthusiasm? His personality? I figured anyone who would offer a job to a total stranger in such a fashion would be someone I could trust and get along with. The only problem is that I didn't necessarily want to leave my job, and the people in my department didn't want me to leave either. Beyond that, they thought the whole idea was crazy. "Your career is going to be derailed," they said. "This isn't why you came to the Bank." They weren't wrong, at least on the latter point. Paijmans's mandate included every aspect of Bank personnel, from dining services to elevator operations. It was a huge department that extended far beyond my comfort zone of economists, analysts, and policy wonks.

Paijmans gave me two weeks to decide and I did a lot of soul-searching, a process that would become standard for me in just about every future job consideration. But the more I thought about it, the less crazy it seemed. For weeks, I'd feared the Bank was going to show me the door since no one would let me travel and, though I felt fully recovered, I believed a change might do me good after the health woes and Sudan stress. Plus, I simply found Paijmans inspiring. I thought working with him might be a chance worth taking. Not only could I learn from him, but I could learn about the entire institutional structure.

So I took the job. And it was the best decision I could have made.

Why? Because after a few months, the full scope of our mission became clear: we were diving as deep as possible inside the Bank. There were three of us in all: Paijmans, me as a special assistant, and Gautam Kaji, a truly outstanding individual, as senior advisor. My job was to help monitor current practices and create new standards for operating and personnel management units all across the Bank.

We had to set up systems for everything, and for Paijmans those systems started and stopped with accountability, both for individuals and for the institution. He was always asking questions; he was never satisfied with lazy answers. "Because that's how it's always been done" would not suffice. He questioned everything. I picked up more from him about good management practices than I ever imagined needing to know. I also gained a lot from Kaji, who was in the early stages of his own impressive career. Before coming to the Bank, he worked in commercial banking in his home country of India as well as in Hong Kong, the United Kingdom, and the United States. Eventually, he became a vice president. The end result is that I found myself surrounded by brilliant men. I learned what it took to be a manager and I learned what it took to reform an institution. Little did I know how closely both lessons would underpin the rest of my career.

We operated almost like an inspector general's office, taking on decades of entrenched entitlements and poor practices. A lot of hostility came our way. But Paijmans believed the culture needed to change, so from day one he let it be known: we're going to clean up shop.

Two of the biggest targets were travel and compensation.

Remember the generous travel policies for long-haul flights, with leisurely layovers, first-class seats, and five-star accommodations? We conducted a review and found obvious results: that the cost to the Bank—and thus, member countries—was extremely high, both as a financial outlay and as lost productivity. Critics already disliked the policy, seen as an unnecessary extravagance in an organization devoted to development. The Bank's staff union fought hard against any changes, but we won approval for new guidelines that, in the short term, put an end to first-class flights.[10]

Paijmans and Kaji also targeted employee compensation packages. For most Bank staff, the hours were long and the work was taxing. Salaries and benefits, including retirement plans and holiday breaks, were generous—too generous for Bank critics who believed the staff were overpaid. Paijmans was not in favor of rolling back benefits, believing that you needed to pay well to attract top-flight international talent. But he did believe the compensation structure lacked consistency and needed reform. So in early 1980, we brought in an outside group, Hay Associates, to undertake a comparative study. The goal was to establish an objective basis for compensation in relation to other organizations, which the Bank previously did not have. The Hay survey took more than a year, and it led to important revisions in compensation structure.[11]

The bottom line is that Paijmans wasn't afraid to rock the boat. He had McNamara's blessing and both of them wanted to modernize as much of the Bank's internal structure as possible, as quickly and thoroughly as possible. So it came as no surprise that if Paijmans was willing to tackle pensions and salaries, he was willing to tackle an equally delicate issue: diversity.

In 1971, a small group of black employees lodged complaints of racial discrimination inside the Bank. They are believed to have been the first to attempt formal action and, as far as official Bank actions go, nothing much came of their efforts. But more and more, people were talking about race—or grumbling about it, depending on one's vantage point—even if the conversations mostly were behind closed doors.

The dialogue changed dramatically in 1978, when Washington Post reporter William Raspberry wrote two op-ed pieces that focused on the lack of diversity in the Bank's management. "There are zero black division chiefs out of 160," he wrote, adding that division chiefs "represent the lowest managerial rank." Raspberry's op-eds are still considered a bellwether moment in bringing the race issue from the back rooms to the boardroom. The following year, the African members of the Bank's Board of Governors discussed the issue at the annual meetings in Belgrade and called for a more thorough examination.

Since there were no more than a few dozen Africans in an institution of more than 1,000, we were aware of the imbalance inside the Bank. But Raspberry's reporting brought it to public light. McNamara let it be known that he wanted more diversity in the management ranks and emphasized young professional recruitment as a way to get there. An obvious malaise had set in among most of the African staff that needed to be addressed, and it covered everything from rumors about unequal pay to official policy that limited opportunity. African staff, for instance, found it hard to get jobs outside the African region, as the thinking was that the Bank couldn't possibly send an African to advise Brazilians or Koreans or people in other regions. So, Africans were agitating for recognition and opportunity. In October 1978, the Bank's African and Arab directors pressed McNamara on a more specific time frame for recruiting and promoting Africans to senior positions. They also brought to his attention the deep dissatisfaction over the lack of upward mobility and the employment decisions by personnel officers that fueled internal distrust.

It was in this environment that Paijmans, Kaji, and I entered the diversity discussion by launching our internal investigation into hiring and promotion practices. Paijmans was very good in dealing with the different issues that were at play, because it wasn't all about African underrepresentation. Unlike the United Nations and other agencies, the Bank didn't want to use a quota system. So, the ranks were dominated by the British and French and to a lesser extent Americans. One thing that made our study notable was that it expanded the discussion beyond race. The Bank's diversity problem wasn't just a black or white issue—it was a global issue. Germans, for instance, were underrepresented. So were Italians. And Asians. Our study shed light on just how homogeneous the whole institution was.

Still, we had a positive impact on the African situation. We looked at everything: salaries, benefits, recruitment, training, assignments, promotions—all of it. And we found anomalies in individual cases—the African staff member who stayed in his position before promotion much longer than his non-African counterpart. Or the African staff member who received 10 to 20 percent less for doing the same job as his non-African counterpart who had the same education and even came from the same institution; in this case, Harvard University. We couldn't find enough evidence to draw definitive conclusions on discrimination or racism, but we did discover enough cases where the imbalances were glaring. And it did become clear to us that Africans were consistently underpaid and changed jobs less frequently. The good news is that once our study was done, the Bank very quietly began to make changes. Some corrective actions were taken including salary adjustments that fellow Africans told me took them completely by surprise.

We didn't solve the race issue, not by a long shot. But our study was among the first of many, as it turned out, conducted inside the Bank; and it offered much-needed empirical evidence that diversity was an issue that exceeded the frustration among Africans and blacks. After our study, things took on a different dimension inside the Bank.

◆　◆　◆　◆

The downside to being part of a reform movement is the hostility likely to come your way. And that happened with us. We were not the most popular team in the Bank and that made me uncomfortable at first. I was still only a few years into my career, and I didn't yet have the same intestinal fortitude that veterans like Paijmans and Kaji showed. Paijmans could see my unease so one day he called me into his office and gave me a combination pep talk, motivational speech, and tongue-lashing. "Be tough," he said. "And believe in yourself!"

It might sound a little trite to say I took those words to heart, but I did. Others had given me words of encouragement, but his was different and I listened to him. I stopped worrying about my health, my age, or my race as factors in my future. I just focused on the job.

I worked with Paijmans for two years and was a different person because of it. I can trace much of my career to the confidence and assertiveness I gained from this job. I also got a crash course in managerial process.

At the same time, I learned some important lessons about Bank operations. I had seen behind the curtain. I grew more determined to forge my own path and I had a much better understanding of what that would take. From a personal standpoint, I still wanted to work on Africa, and, from a professional standpoint, I wanted a country assignment. In that job, you are the Bank's official representative in a member country and the head of its resident mission. The posts were not easy to get, but working with Paijmans had upped my profile. A country assignment seemed like the right next step. But fate intervened and delayed my plans.

Just as I was looking to leave the personnel and administrative side, I got a call from none other than Stanley Please. Things had gone a little badly for him in the years since we had worked together. He took a post in Indonesia but struggled with his own health problems. He was well respected and admired throughout the Bank, so once he was ready to return to Washington, he was offered a unique assignment: senior advisor to Ernie Stern, the Bank's vice president for all operations and without a doubt the second-most powerful man in the institution behind McNamara.

Ernie Stern was a giant inside the Bank. He also happened to believe a new approach was needed in Africa. So he and Please made a good team. They both decided to form a special task force on Africa that would be responsible for reorienting the Bank's lending policies. When Please called me, he asked that I join the task force. I was the only African asked to be on it and the result of our work, a study widely known as the Berg Report, became a seminal part of the Bank's history. (There's more on the Berg Report in Chapter 3.)

Within the span of two years, I had worked with some of the Bank's most important figures to overhaul internal operations and rethink country programs. Even I was a little surprised at how my path had unfolded and how immersed I had become in the Bank's changing ways.

But counting my time as a YP, I had held four jobs in less than seven years, and I was ready not only to slow that pace down but also to get back to the core of my interests: country programs. I still wanted an overseas assignment, preferably in Africa. But the Bank would not let go of the concerns over my health. I was visiting NIH for regular checkups and was told each time that my heart looked stronger than the time before. Believe it or not, I finally asked for a letter from my doctors to try to prove to the Bank that I was healthy enough to travel for extended periods or to live overseas. The doctors had told me to live my life, to not look back, to get on with my work. They put the same sentiment in the letter. It literally took a note from my doctor for me to continue my career.

Still, the heart episode was a wake-up call. I knew I could no longer push myself to such an extreme. I also knew I wanted to spend more time with Philomena and the girls, who were old enough now to be aware of their surroundings. And for that reason, working in Africa became even more important to me. By 1981, I was finally able to make that happen.

Notes

1   Angela Davis was a controversial figure. She was arrested in relation to a 1970 shooting at a California courthouse despite having no discernible role in the attack. The year before, the University of California-Los Angeles fired her after she admitted membership of the Communist Party. She was an outspoken African American woman and many saw her arrest as being politically and racially motivated. So among the more liberal-minded, she became something of an icon, even for people like me who did not necessarily agree with everything she had to say.

2   That 1965 Mustang has always held a special place in my heart and it's still in the family. I gave it to one of my daughters and her new husband as a wedding present.

3   My dissertation was published in 1980 as part of the "Outstanding Dissertation in Economics" series by Garland Publishing.

4   But an unsatisfactory performance isn't always the end of the road. In some cases, another six-month assignment is given for the YP to prove himself or herself capable.

5   More than 1,500 Bank staff were hired through the YP program across its first 50 years, including future managing directors and vice presidents. The maximum age for acceptance today is 32, with a PhD or master's degree plus relevant work experience required.

6   Indonesia's oil boom did lead to strong economic growth into the 1980s, but it soon ran into the same problems as many African countries that relied too heavily on oil money—political corruption, market distortions, and volatile global demand. Indonesia pulled out of OPEC in 2008 and now imports more oil than it exports, part of a long-term structural transformation of its economy; that's where real sustainable growth lies.

7   The geopolitical enthusiasm included the hunt for oil in Sudan. Two years after the peace agreement that ended the civil war, Sudan granted oil concessions to Chevron, which discovered oil in 1978 but ran into a hotbed of political issues when regional tensions again flared—in part due to the newfound oil reserves and concerns over revenue-sharing between the northern and southern states. In the decades since, the mismanagement of Sudan's resources has been a recurring problem and key contributor to the country's political and economic instability.

8   Equally important, Stanley Please and I became friends. After he retired from the Bank, he and his wife hosted a very small dinner on the night before they left the United States to return to England. The invitees included Mr. and Mrs. Ping-Cheung Loh, a fellow Bank employee and Please's best friend, and Philomena and me—a real honor showing how much our relationship had grown. Three decades later, after Please had passed away, several of his former colleagues, including many he mentored at the Bank, hosted a special event to recognize his contributions. I was delighted to be asked to deliver the keynote address.

9   The description of Martijn Paijmans comes from authors Kapur, Lewis, and Webb in the *The World Bank: Its First Half Century – Volume 1*. Having worked closely with Paijmans, I completely agree.

10   A few years later, the operational travel policies were revisited and in August 1992 new guidelines were put in place that allowed business class and first-class seating but defined when such travel would be allowed rather than it being the standard or default option.

11   The Hay survey compared the salary levels in private and public sector organizations in France, Germany, and the United States. Eventually, the external pressure built up to the point where salaries and benefits were rolled back, though much of that took place after Paijmans retired.

Chapter 2

Up Close and Personal
Valuable Lessons at the Intersection of People, Policy, and Reform

As a young boy in Ghana, I moved around a lot. My family would stay in one place for a year or two, then relocate as my father's work dictated. As I've said, Papa put a premium on education, but he feared our transient lifestyle would be too disruptive to structured learning. So he decided that I should go to boarding school. He found a place he liked in Akropong, in the southeastern part of Ghana, only about 60 kilometers from Accra. This school boasted good "graduation" rates for kids going on to high school, which was important. There weren't too many high schools in Ghana, but the ones we had were very good. Kwame Nkrumah invested heavily in Ghana's education sector, and he had either built new secondary schools or upgraded existing ones across the country. But the best ones were boarding schools with limited capacity, which meant that they also had competitive, nationwide admission processes. My father believed that I would have a better shot at getting into one of these schools if I had a consistent, steady elementary education, preferably at an esteemed school like the one he found in Akropong.

In fact, there were two schools there: a boarding school and a day school, also known as a demonstration school. These were like learning schools for teachers, where trainees would come in and teach. I was sent to the day school, probably because Papa couldn't afford to pay the cost of the boarding school. So I needed a place to live. Normally in that situation, you would move in with local relatives—families were large and it didn't really matter if you knew them or not, as long as there was a relation somewhere down the line. But we had no family in Akropong. So my father got in touch with a local headmaster and arranged for me to live with the headmaster's family. In return, Papa would pay the man a small fee.

But in our culture, payment wasn't enough. A boy in my position also had to earn his own keep. I was expected to be a houseboy, something like a modern-day serf. I wasn't in servitude or in any way demeaned; I was just expected to perform certain chores and duties. But I didn't want to do that and I didn't adapt very well. For someone like me, who had lived a rather sheltered life surrounded by his friends and family and books, these new demands didn't appeal to me at all. I was miserable. I missed my brother. I missed my father. I missed my friends.

I didn't like being away at school and I didn't care that it was for my own academic well-being. I wanted to go back home, so one day I did. I essentially ran away, straight back to my father. And he was not happy about it. In fact, he was furious. He gave me a whipping that I'd never forget. And the next day, he called my bluff.

"You've made your choice," he said. "If you don't want an education, that's fine with me. You won't go back."

He told me that he'd take me to trade school instead, where I could eventually become an apprentice. I'd make an honest living, but I wouldn't be able to read the same books or learn the same things. After a few days, I asked my father to take me back to Akropong. From that point on, I got serious about my education. I graduated and was accepted into the Ghana Secondary Technical School at Takoradi, a quality high school with a focus on mathematics and hard sciences.

That whipping changed my life. There's an old cliché—"knock some sense into you"—and in a way that's what happened. I didn't want to be a quitter. I didn't want to cut and run from a challenge. My father didn't want me to quit either, but he knew that I needed to learn that lesson on my own. I chose to prove myself in an environment that brought with it a fair amount of personal adversity, and I became stronger for it. I got the foundation I needed to continue my education. Without it, I'm not sure how my life would have turned out.

About 25 years later, when I moved my family to Africa to live in Zambia, I found myself in a similar position. I had to prove myself in a tough environment, but what I learned by being there—lessons in national policymaking, local ownership, institutional capacity, development partnerships, and political leadership—gave me great insight into effective development strategies in Africa. And they also gave me an invaluable foundation for the rest of my career.

◆ ◆ ◆ ◆

I wanted to go to Zambia for two reasons. Professionally, I needed field experience; it was time for me to cut my teeth at the country level, preferably in Africa, and I needed to see the programmatic side of the Bank's policies up close. It was the only way to become a complete development economist. Occasional mission trips from headquarters wouldn't be enough. The second reason was more personal: my family needed a break.

We had endured a tough few years. The burden of work and stress that I put on myself had affected my health, but it affected my wife, too. Philomena had been through hell trying to raise three young girls and keep her husband alive at the same time. I wanted Ama, Nana, and Mame, who were now seven and five years old, to get a better sense of their African heritage and I wanted Philomena to get a break. I believed a return to Africa would rejuvenate us. Once the doctors had given me a clean bill of health, the personal and professional timing for a resident mission came together.

At the time, the Bank had two openings in Africa: in Ethiopia and in Zambia. I immediately turned my attention to Ethiopia, which seemed like a perfect fit. It was a challenging environment—the country was in the middle of a 13-year rule by the Derg, an oppressive Communist dictatorship, and its economic and social indicators were dire even by the low standards of early 1980s Africa. But as one of Africa's most populous states, it also commanded attention inside the Bank. It was a high-profile assignment. I lobbied fast and hard for consideration, and my bosses agreed to nominate me for the post.

As the next and final step, Ethiopian officials had to sign off on my nomination. No one expected a problem, since governments automatically endorsed the candidate put forth by the Bank as standard practice. But that didn't happen with me. The Ethiopian government didn't endorse my nomination. In fact, after a few months, the government rejected me, which I believe was the first time such a refusal had ever taken place.

I'm not saying the government was right, but it's true I didn't fit the regular profile. In those days, the Bank tended to fill its resident representative positions with very experienced staff, particularly in the large and important countries like Ethiopia. The incumbent representative was a mid-career, highly respected, urbane, white American man. And he was more or less representative of his peers in similar posts across

Africa. As I've mentioned, the perception inside the Bank was that African governments would not take advice from natives of their own continent—a perception enabled by local leaders who preferred guidance from whites. Ethiopia, where the Derg considered black Africans to be inferior, was a prime example.

Needless to say, I was disappointed, not to mention embarrassed. My nomination for the post went against the grain, but to be rejected, regardless of circumstance or bias, was not an outcome I had ever imagined. Philomena and I wondered if we should just stay put. But the more I thought about it, the more that felt like the easy way out. I thought of my father; I didn't want to cut and run from a challenge. So I turned to the only other option available to me: Zambia.

Zambia's economic outlook was as poor as Ethiopia's, if not worse. But unlike Ethiopia, Zambia was not among Africa's most populous or influential states. The government operated under one-party rule headed by Kenneth Kaunda, a well-respected leader who disliked outside intervention. As a result, the Bank didn't consider Zambia a top priority, so the post carried no prestige. It also offered little in the way of career advancement. A resident posting usually lasted three years, and no ambitious person wanted to spend that long in Lusaka. The assignment was an outpost, not a destination. It had sat unfilled for months.

Although Zambia had a definite downside, it also came with low expectations. If I exceeded them, then perhaps I could boost my career on par with having had a higher profile assignment. So I went back to my bosses and volunteered for the position. My decision surprised them, but after Ethiopia, they understood the motivation. And once again they supported me and put my name forward.

And once again, the local government officials balked.

After the Bank informed the Zambian government that I would be the new resident representative, weeks passed with no response. Through back channels, we finally learned why. Officials knew about the situation in Ethiopia, and they were offended that the Bank would send them not only a young and inexperienced African, but an inexperienced reject! The silence dragged on for months, and I began to wonder what it would mean for me if an African country nixed my nomination a second time. Inside the Bank, appearances mattered.

My immediate boss, Jochen Kraske, the director of the department responsible for Zambia's lending program, had finally had enough. It would be the first of many times that Kraske backed me up in a tough situation. He called Zambian Minister of Finance Kebby Musokotwane to try to work through the impasse directly. The minister expressed his doubts about me and my relative youth, but, thanks to Kraske's lobbying efforts, he eventually offered a proposal: that I go to Lusaka where he and his colleagues could meet me and decide if they found me suitable for the job. It was a highly unusual proposition—one that the Bank declined, not wanting to set a precedent where its appointments were subject to an interview process by member states.

So we had a stalemate, with me caught in the middle, my career in limbo, and my family facing more uncertainty. Unsure what to do next, I turned to my former boss, Martijn Paijmans. I trusted him to give me good advice, and he surely did.

"Don't worry yourself over this," he said. "Just go to Zambia and get them to change their minds." He told me not to stand by while others at the Bank played a game of chicken with my career. He motivated me to get more aggressive. I decided to convince the higher-ups to let me go to Lusaka as the Zambians had requested. I figured it was my best shot to avoid a second rejection.

And after a while, they finally agreed. Now, the pressure would be on me.

A few days before the trip, I received a three-day agenda filled with "meetings," which really were interviews with ministers and government officials, including the governor of the Bank of Zambia. The heads of agencies responsible for Bank-financed projects and programs were also on the list. More people were lined up to interview me in Zambia than had interviewed me for my actual job at the World Bank.

My first appointment was with Musokotwane, the finance minister. I did my homework ahead of time and found an interesting fact: I was a year older than him! Intelligent and well regarded, he was also one of President Kaunda's favorites (and eventually a future prime minister). After we'd exchanged a few general pleasantries, I didn't waste any time playing my trump card.

"What's this talk about me being too young and inexperienced?" I asked, with a half-smile. I wanted him to know I was joking—but not really. "You look younger than me!"

Musokotwane laughed. It broke the ice and it melted the tensions before they could surface. I gave him the full rundown—about my childhood, my education, my ties to Africa, and my experience thus far. I told him that it wasn't easy being an African inside the Bank, but I wasn't intimidated by it either. I also explained the personal value I put on living in Africa while my girls were still young. I could tell I connected with him; he seemed genuinely moved. But when it came to the time for him to talk, I realized the underlying issues went much deeper than me.

In fine detail, he outlined a litany of grievances toward the Bank: the poor attitude of previous resident representatives, the indifference of Bank managers to Zambia's needs, and the general arrogance of the Bank staff as perceived by the Zambians. The problem wasn't that officials found my credentials lacking so much as their belief that the Bank held them in disregard—which my nomination, in which they weren't consulted, seemed to prove.

The timing is important here, because my trip took place in March 1981, just a few months after the Bank had begun its highly controversial structural adjustment lending programs in Africa. The premise behind these programs— covered in more detail in the next chapter—involved conditional lending from the Bank to countries in exchange for policy reforms. The rationale and recommendations for the programs had been laid out in a seminal Bank publication, *Accelerated Development in Sub-Saharan Africa: A Plan for Action*, also known as the Berg Report after its lead author, economist Elliot Berg. I worked on the research team that pulled the report together, so I was very familiar with its details and policy prescriptions. I didn't necessarily agree with all of them, but I did agree with the idea that development investments could have a stronger impact when accompanied by sound structural reforms. The problem that the Bank would run into throughout Africa over the next decade was not just a negative reaction to the perception that the Bank was trying to overreach into African affairs, but that Bank staff didn't bother to seek input and collaboration from local officials.

Once I had heard Musokotwane's concerns directly, the Zambians' request to meet me in person suddenly seemed more than reasonable, whereas the Bank's hardline stance against it seemed much less so. He said most Zambian policymakers, far from being disagreeable or obstinate, welcomed the Bank's help—they just wanted to have a say in how they were helped. That's why it was so important for them to have a resident representative who also believed in that situation. Without meeting me, how would they feel assured? The whole impasse could have been avoided—and months not lost—with simple communication.

After more than two hours, he asked his secretary to cancel the rest of my meetings. Instead, he instructed her to invite all the ministers and officials on my schedule to a cocktail reception the following night.

"Tell them we are welcoming the new resident representative of the World Bank to Zambia," he said.

When I returned to Washington, I had three months to move to Lusaka. I had a lot to learn in a short time, but I also had to get my personal affairs in order. Philomena and I rented our house and put most of our things in storage, including my beloved 1965 Mustang. Leaving it behind almost felt like leaving a member of the family. My daughters were excited for what they saw as a big adventure. When the time came, we flew to Ghana where Philomena and the girls stayed to visit family as I went on to Zambia to get situated. They joined me a few weeks later.

◆　◆　◆　◆

The Republic of Zambia emerged as a new nation in October 1964, when it ceased to be known as Northern Rhodesia and shortly after the Central African Federation—of which it was a part along with Southern Rhodesia (now known as Zimbabwe) and Nyasaland (now known as Malawi)—dissolved. At the time of independence, Zambia's per capita income was among the highest in the region and it was one of the most urbanized countries in Sub-Saharan Africa. The region was rich in copper, which locals had been extracting for hundreds of years—and which attracted the attention of Great Britain during the colonization era.

Under British rule, mining became the prime industry, but no one got rich from it locally. An increasing number of white British workers migrated to the Copperbelt Province, as the whole mineral-rich region was called, and worked alongside Africans. But wages were low and little money stayed in the territory. The British South Africa Company owned the mineral rights and duly exacted royalties.[1] Whatever profits remained were subject to taxation, though the British government retained a large portion and only put small amounts back into circulation. Public investments for roads, schools, and health services were nominal. The first half of the twentieth century brought wildly fluctuating copper prices, which brought periods of labor unrest, particularly among the African workers. By the 1940s, African labor unions had formed to increase bargaining rights while small threads of a civil society—clergy, teachers, mining foremen—began to coalesce. This paved the way for the Northern Rhodesian Congress, which had no real authority but laid the foundation for representative government among the African population.

The Central African Federation was formed in 1953, a move supported by British politicians and seen as a way to consolidate power among the rising numbers of white settlers in Northern and Southern Rhodesia. Despite initial protests over the new federation, an economic boom led to improved labor and living conditions for Africans, at least for a while. But the boom ended toward the end of the 1950s and the jobs dried up. Increasingly, young African nationalists grew more vocal about their economic situation and their dissatisfaction with white majority rule.

In 1958, a splinter group led by a young educator, Kenneth Kaunda, formed the Zambia African National Congress and, soon after, the United National Independence Party. Over the next few years, Kaunda and the UNIP gained clout and support. When the Federation dissolved in 1963, elections were held in early 1964, and the UNIP won a decisive majority. It also won the support of almost a third of white voters. Kaunda became president of the new republic.

Things were good, for a while. The government got the mineral rights held by the British South Africa Company—and the revenues from taxation—so locals finally began to reap the rewards. Kaunda directed long-overdue investments in Zambia's social infrastructure, especially education. Between 1960 and 1971, the number of Africans in Zambia's secondary schools surged from 2,500 to 54,000. But the external shocks that froze most African economies in the early 1970s hit Zambia, and when copper prices began a prolonged tumble, the country fell into steep economic decline. As vulnerable as other commodity-driven economies in Africa were to global markets, Zambia was even more so since copper played such an overwhelming role in its GDP—supplying up to 90 percent of its total foreign exchange earnings.

Ravi Gulhati, then a former chief economist of the World Bank's Eastern and Southern Africa region, published a meticulous account of Zambia's first 35 years and its struggle with political and economic reform. Gulhati noted that Zambia was extremely ill-equipped, politically and administratively, for its independence in 1964. It wasn't just the country's overreliance on a single commodity, but also the crippling legacy of colonialism: Zambia began its independent government with only about 100 university graduates among its population. Zambia's thin reservoir of educated workers and technicians left a debilitating scarcity of skilled economists and administrators to run Zambian institutions.

Beyond that, Kaunda grew increasingly threatened by political opposition. In 1973, he declared one-party rule under the UNIP. Naturally, authoritarian moves followed, such as detaining political opponents and imposing state control over the media. For years, Kaunda had constantly reshuffled colleagues in their government and party roles to reduce the likelihood of a rival ever gaining enough traction to pose a threat. He often made major policy decisions with little or no consultation—and as the hero of Zambia's liberation movement, he rarely faced popular resistance to those policies. It was a poor combination.

As the situation worsened, the Bretton Woods Institutions supplied a steady stream of analyses for policymakers. But beyond a few projects and an IMF standby program, the World Bank and IMF were virtually irrelevant there. The Bank first began promoting economic policy reforms as early as 1972, but political pressure, especially from the trade unions, proved too strong. The Bank tried to press reforms again in 1976, pushing for product diversification and more decentralized controls, but Zambia's response was minimal.

Part of the reason could be traced to the Bank pushing for changes that the government fundamentally opposed. Zambia had undertaken a couple of rounds of notable reforms in the post-independence years—the 1968 Mulungushi and 1970 Matero reforms—that paved the way for most industries coming under state control, including mining. The Bank hoped to reform these "reforms" before full nationalization buried the economy. Unfortunately, that didn't happen.

By the time I took over as the Bank's resident representative in the early 1980s, the per capita GNP in real terms was one-third less than in 1964. The rate of inflation moved from around 15 percent at the end of the 1970s to a peak of almost 50 percent a few years later. Foreign debt had begun to mount, as had arrears in previous loan payments to the Bank and IMF. Zambia's average annual growth rate from 1973 until 1980 in mining—its overwhelmingly dominant economic sector—was *negative* 0.3 percent.

Since gaining independence, Zambia had regressed economically in almost every way.

I wanted the Zambians to see me as a collaborative partner, not as another scold from the World Bank. The biggest knock against me had been my age and experience, so I needed to ensure those criticisms didn't follow me to Lusaka. The best way to do that was to learn everything I could about Zambian affairs. So during the three months before my official start, I dove into research. I also sought out Bank staff with knowledge of the country's current and past economic situation. That process confirmed the impression I got from talking with Musokotwane —that Zambia epitomized many of the structural problems identified in the Berg Report. While exogenous and historical factors were partly to blame for Zambia's difficulties, policy missteps had had a considerable impact; notably a distorted exchange rate, uncontrolled expenditures, and an overreliance on public enterprises at the expense of private investments.

Before I left for Lusaka, I prepared a background paper that applied the Berg Report's analytical framework to Zambia's situation. I even paraphrased the title, calling my paper *Accelerated Development in Zambia: An Agenda for Action*. My goal was to offer policy reform suggestions consistent with the Bank's current lending approach but tailored to Zambia's specific needs. I based it on Bank research, but I added a heavy dose of my own analysis. I also spoke to as many people as I could so that I formed my own opinions about the country's situation. I didn't rely on numbers alone.

The paper consolidated a few key reform ideas around what I saw as Zambia's three most immediate challenges—mining rehabilitation, agricultural pricing, and exchange rate policy—in the hope of nudging policymakers to start to move in a new direction. The common thread that ran through each was also the most critical issue facing the government: its own bureaucracy. It was too big, too ineffective, and too controlling. Nowhere were these constraints more evident than in Zambia's powerful mining sector.

When Zambia gained independence, copper exports buoyed its economy. But Kaunda's government saw the country's Copperbelt as the key to improving the living conditions of the rural poor and increasing employment. So in 1969, the government acquired a controlling stake in Zambia's two main copper-producing companies. That year, the mines produced more than 720,000 tons of copper—a historical peak that wouldn't be matched again. Kaunda's future economic policies depended heavily on proceeds from the nationalized copper industry, but by the mid-1970s the state-run mines were performing poorly. Weak copper prices contributed to the decline, but so did management practices that emphasized mass employment over profitability and state payments over reinvestments in industry infrastructure. In 1982, the government set up a single parastatal organization, Zambia Consolidated Copper Mines, to run the mining operations, but political interference, competing interests, and poor management continually plagued ZCCM.[2] The organization also exemplified Kaunda's government overreach, no matter how well intentioned. In some mining towns, ZCCM provided virtually all the essential services, from water supply to waste removal to health care—a state within a state.

The government's overreach into industry also translated into excessive controls over imports and exports as well as the pricing of basic goods and resources. For instance, the National Agricultural Marketing Board, established in 1969, enjoyed a near monopoly over products like maize and fertilizer but trafficked in all the major agriculture assets—wheat, sorghum, you name it. The board would buy it all up, store it in silos and warehouses and release it as needed, at a single price regardless of basic market factors, such as transport cost and demand. The policy created huge bottlenecks and inefficiencies up and down the line. But Kaunda was a big believer in such "pan-territorial pricing," as it was called. Yet it choked agricultural production; just one of many policy deficiencies.

I had to be careful because I didn't want my paper to be seen as an edict but as a starting point. That's why the essence of the paper boiled down to an argument in favor of the government taking the lead in defining its own policies. This ownership argument was a new one, especially coming from someone representing the World Bank.

Plus, I had another consideration to keep in mind: the internal split among pro- and anti-reformers within Kaunda's leadership team. The more I got to know about Zambia's political economy, the more I realized how deeply it contributed to the country's economic problems. A small group of advisors and policymakers believed that Zambia needed to make deep structural and macroeconomic reforms. But a larger—and more powerful—group had no interest in market-based reforms. These anti-reformers, many of whom were socialist ideologues, dominated the top ranks of the UNIP, and Kaunda was very loyal to the party he had always led.

But that party was steering Zambia over a cliff. The problems that plagued the mining and agricultural sectors were pervasive. In fact, the country's entire sprawling, parastatal sector was ineffective. In his vivid account, *Zambia: The First 50 Years*, author Andrew Sardanis, who moved to Northern Rhodesia in 1950 and participated in Zambia's independence movement and subsequent government under Kaunda, wrote that "competence and expertise were irrelevant" and that senior management in the state-run enterprises and administration was "either political or nepotistic." Companies squandered capital and couldn't manage inventories, leading to severe shortages and spiraling socioeconomic decline. Party leaders, Sardanis wrote, "did not seem to care and did not bother to look for ways out of the vicious cycle."

As a head of state, Kenneth Kaunda—or simply "KK" as he was commonly called—was a complex figure, an emotional and resilient man given to contradictions not common among his peers. He was a calculating, cunning leader who relied extensively on the counsel of those closest to him, yet he would often fire top advisors without warning. He refused to allow multiparty elections and, at least by standard political definition, governed as a dictator. Yet he genuinely wanted to lead as a man of the people. For example, he routinely implemented public policy on a whim, but he remained keenly aware of the opposing forces at play. So if the opposition was loud enough, he might back off a policy as quickly as he enacted it. Conversely, if he truly believed in his heart that a policy improved the well-being of his citizens, he would ignore all evidence or advice to the contrary. As I got to know Kaunda, I understood why he clung to a notion as faulty as pan-territorial pricing—in theory, it was the most equitable way to price goods for every man and woman. To Kaunda, the fact that it made little economic sense hardly outweighed its perceived social worth.

Kaunda followed a political ideology that he named "Zambian humanism," a combination of traditional African values with Western socialism and religious principles, mostly Christian. "I believe that man must be the servant of a vision which is bigger than himself," he wrote in 1966. Kaunda was openly spiritual but not dogmatic and the tenets of humanism, as enumerated by Kaunda himself, reflect that: equal opportunities for all, hard work for oneself and others, a communal approach to national productivity, and a rejection of human exploitation and discrimination. His beliefs drove him to invest heavily in Zambia's educational system as a way to develop, as Andrew Sardanis observed, "plenty of young, enlightened people with good education and open minds."

Philosophy and governance are two separate things, however, and that's where Kaunda ran into trouble.

It was well known among those in Kaunda's orbit that he tried to govern in equal measure with his head and his heart. For a poor, underdeveloped country like Zambia, such an approach often resulted in personal and political conflict. It's one reason he continually rejected policy reforms to open up Zambia. He feared freer markets would naturally favor some more than others, that lifting the state's protective blanket would upend the status quo and cause too much short-term pain to Zambians. Of course, he also feared for his own political survival. Fear of upheaval led to inaction, so as Zambia's state economy cratered, jobs for all those well-educated citizens dried up. For all Kaunda's good intentions, it can't be denied that he brought many of the troubles on himself.

Still, KK was a gracious man who tried to avoid ostentatious displays and his personality endeared him to Zambians and other Africans alike. For instance, he had a habit of serving coffee to guests personally, rather than allowing an aide to do so. He also carried a white handkerchief with him at all times—a symbol of peace, he called it—and it became an iconic image. If you saw KK in public, you often saw a white handkerchief. And if you saw KK cry, which he did with regularity, you saw him pull out a white handkerchief. He was never afraid to let the emotion of a moment overwhelm him.

Like many of his peers, he held on to power for too long and his support eroded amid ever-worsening social conditions. However, unlike many of his peers, he didn't leave office by force but through the ballot box when he finally agreed to multiparty elections. He lost the vote but actually increased his stature by willingly submitting himself for public approval, even in the face of almost certain defeat. That election, held in October 1991, came at the vanguard of Africa's democratic wave—Nelson Mandela's ascension in South Africa was still three years away—and it was credited with galvanizing pro-democracy movements across the continent.

When I crossed paths with Kaunda, that historic vote was a full decade away and he was still at the height of his popularity and influence. He was the first head of state that I got to know on a personal and professional level and it was through him and his diverse group of advisors that I gained my first real insights into the realities of policymaking at the national level of a developing country—and into the dynamics of strong and accountable leadership.

Of course, I didn't roll into Lusaka and immediately start burning the midnight oil with the president. I needed first to create and foster my own local network. I needed to find like-minded allies who recognized the need to get Kaunda to act a lot more with his head and a little less with his heart.

I arrived in Lusaka in July 1981, and I wasted no time in reaching out to ministers and policymakers to introduce myself. I shared copies of the report I had prepared and arranged one-on-one meetings to discuss it. In most cases I didn't need an introduction. I had met many officials at the impromptu reception that Musokotwane organized a few months earlier. And thanks to the controversy surrounding my appointment, I wasn't a complete stranger to the ones I had yet to meet. I also made it a priority to try to build relationships throughout the government—not just the top decision-makers, but the project officers, directors, and analysts. I needed their insights on the big industries, such as mining and agriculture, but I would also need their support in pushing changes. That's how I came to meet some of my closest colleagues, including Mohamed Muhsin.

A Sri Lankan national, Muhsin had moved to Zambia in 1977 to work as an analyst for one of the state mining companies. He caught the eye of Zambian officials, who recruited him to work on a public enterprise commission. Before long, he became the finance director for the mining corporation and a key advisor to Kaunda on state enterprise reform. Luckily for me, he was eager to collaborate.

I learned a lot from Muhsin, including the distance that existed between the Bank and the rank-and-file decision-makers in government. Part of the problem could have been the low priority that Bank headquarters placed on Zambia, which manifested itself at the country level. Regardless of the reasons, I wanted to take a different approach, not because Zambia had suddenly become a higher priority inside the Bank but because I wanted to establish a more productive working relationship. We were still years away from "development partnerships" as a defining trait of donor engagements, but that's how I wanted to come across to policymakers—as a partner. To do that, I had to get to know them.

After a few months on the job, Philomena and I began hosting small social gatherings at our house. Senior Zambian officials as well as members of the diplomatic and donor community were among the guests. Cocktail parties involving Zambians and ambassadors were commonplace long before I arrived, so we weren't breaking new ground. But I saw those parties as an opportunity to build bridges, where officials on both sides could come together in a more casual setting. We had heated policy discussions, but the tone remained civil, as it would be among friends. We also told jokes, played music, danced, and drank good wine. On occasion, my daughters would sneak downstairs after their bedtime. They told me they just wanted to catch a glimpse of the finely dressed diplomats and listen to the music. Before long, the cocktail parties attracted dozens of people.

Contrary to the racial perceptions that prevailed in Washington, the Zambian officials quickly considered me to be one of their own. They welcomed me, my ideas, and, most important, my family. I found the Zambians to be warm and friendly. And most of them—though certainly not all—were as eager as I was to turn things around.

The aggressive manner with which I approached my job attracted attention, particularly among the pro-reformers like Muhsin. Chief among this group was Dominic Mulaisho, who very quickly became another key ally.

When I met Mulaisho, he was Kaunda's top economic advisor, a job he started in 1977 and one that made him a direct conduit to the president. He also was a former teacher, a well-recognized African literary figure, and a veteran of multiple Zambian ministries, including education, land and natural resources, and mines. Prior to advising Kaunda, he had been the chairman of Zambia Consolidated Copper Mines, the state-controlled conglomerate. His years of experience in navigating Zambia's political economy—especially the delicate balance between lawmakers, laborers, union leaders, and private investors—proved invaluable, especially when I found myself entangled in that same complex web. Mulaisho was also a superb writer, so in addition to advising Kaunda on economic affairs, he wrote many of the president's speeches.

The crux of Mulaisho's appeal, besides his obvious intelligence, was his *joie de vivre*. He simply loved life. He had a keen wit and sense of humor, especially about himself. Kaunda, for instance, never missed a chance to lighten the mood of a working lunch by telling a good Mulaisho story. One of his favorites was the tale of the missing shoe. It seems that on one particular trip, Mulaisho lagged far behind the rest of the president's delegation in checking out of his hotel room. So a couple of Kaunda's aides were dispatched to find out what was taking so long. What they found was Mulaisho frantically looking under his bed, holding a shoe in one hand. When they asked what he was doing, Mulaisho said he couldn't leave until he found his other shoe—which he was already wearing. Whenever Kaunda told this story, which he did often, Mulaisho would always laugh along with KK and the audience. He never took himself as seriously as he took Zambia's future.[3]

My relationship with officials like Muhsin and Mulaisho became very important. They had access to all levels of government leaders and they had the respect of their peers who also believed Zambia needed to reform its policies. I have always characterized the three of us as a trio of "co-conspirators." We would meet often, usually at Mulaisho's home, sometimes until the early hours of the morning, strategizing and planning. We needed to outmaneuver the hardliners in the government to ever get Kaunda to back sweeping reforms. Those long nights remain among my fondest memories. We all were doing exactly what we wanted to be doing. We developed a deep friendship that lasted long after I left Zambia, long after Muhsin and Mulaisho left the government, and long after the reforms that we finally helped convince Kaunda to put in place—at his own political peril—came undone.

◆　◆　◆　◆

I met Kaunda for the first time about two months into the job. Mulaisho set it up. He and I had logged countless hours talking about reforms when he said it was time for me to meet with Kaunda directly. He passed along *Accelerated Development in Zambia* for the president to read, and in less than a week KK invited me to his residence.

That first meeting took place in Kaunda's personal study. He and I were alone, with no aides or advisors. Kaunda struck me as gracious, charming—and savvy. For the first 10 minutes at least, he only talked about his love for Ghana and Kwame Nkrumah.

Once the conversation turned to Zambia's economic outlook, I could tell he had read my paper carefully. Kaunda asked detailed questions, and he seemed taken in particular with the emphasis on local ownership. He knew better than anyone that the current system was not working. Zambia's tightly controlled public sector had constrained foreign exchange and led to sharp industrial declines in key areas like manufacturing. Copper, which had long driven the national economy, had turned particularly problematic. The state-owned mining company was suffering substantial losses but did not have the flexibility to respond to global markets or even the natural life cycle of industrial production. The Mine Workers' Union of Zambia stridently opposed wage reductions or layoffs, and so did the Zambia Congress of Trade Unions, the powerful central federation.

We covered a lot of ground, touching on all three of the paper's primary topics—mining, agriculture, and exchange rates—but the conversation kept returning to agriculture and the need for Zambia to move away from one of its signature programs—pan-territorial pricing.

Kaunda's government had always fixed prices, but not until 1971 did it adopt a uniform pricing structure regardless of territory, province, or season. The main objective was to ensure a regular supply of food at low prices for all regions, from the Copperbelt to urban areas. But the policy required huge government subsidies, resulting in soaring budget deficits, fiscal imbalances, and unnatural shifts in crop production. Subsidies for maize and fertilizer were so large that farmers moved away from growing other crops, such as cassava and cotton, that offered strong comparative advantages for certain regions. Over time, the subsidies devoured Zambia's public spending, growing from 1 million Zambian kwacha, the local currency, in 1965 to 205 million in 1980.

The more we talked, the more Kaunda seemed to agonize. I gave him hard evidence that the economics simply were not working, why they were not working, and how they could be reformed.

He had heard variations of these same arguments countless times from his pro-reform policymakers, but now he heard them from a new voice, an impartial observer with no political leanings and no self-interest at stake.

70

We talked for two hours. When we were done, he thanked me for the visit and he commended the research in the report. A few days later, Mulaisho told me that Kaunda had responded well to the meeting. "He said you are a sincere young man we can work with."

A few months later, the outreach efforts paid off. The Zambian government incorporated my paper into a reform framework that officials passed along to the World Bank and IMF for approval. At that point, the issue was no longer whether to reform, but at what pace and volume.

As the saying goes, desperate times call for desperate measures. And desperate times finally compelled Zambia to act. The government had negotiated special debt arrangements with the IMF in 1973, 1976, 1978, and 1981. The latter agreement broke down in 1982. It had also taken World Bank program loans in 1973 and 1976, before relations grew so sour. With Zambia unwilling to make major structural changes, none of these assistance programs had worked. But the country's rising debt and shrinking GDP finally became too much to bear. Kaunda had run out of options.

The first step was to stop the financial bleeding. So beginning in April 1983, Zambia negotiated a new series of stabilization programs with the IMF—and in coordination with the donor countries and other creditors—that restructured debt and devised more controlled aid flows. Against that backdrop, the government then began making significant policy adjustments, starting with its mining sector, then moving on to agriculture and manufacturing. The IMF and the Bank both played a major support role, preparing much of the background work and helping outline the reforms. The Bank also started sending in waves of analysts and technicians to assist the Zambians and work on the reform packages. That alone increased the confidence on both sides of the Bank–Zambia relationship.

Meanwhile, my role deepened. I had gained local trust, so I became the Bank's principal intermediary with the government. But I also acted as the government's chief advocate in its dealings with the Bank and IMF. It was a tricky balance, but it worked.

It all came down to relationships. As I said earlier, I reached out to Zambians beyond the usual ministers or donors and that allowed me to network my way through the decision-makers in the United National Independence Party. As the sole legal political party in Zambia, the UNIP enjoyed unchecked authority and all national policy flowed through its central committee. It was Zambia's nerve center. In fact, the government apparatus was subordinated to the political party, not the other way around. The government included the traditional departments and ministers, but the UNIP—and the central committee—existed separately. Committee members operated like shadow ministers and they held a lot of sway. Eventually, I established a relationship with the head of the party. Even though the UNIP mostly opposed radical reform, the outreach sent a message that everyone should contribute and give input.

It also helped when the Bank's vice president for the region, Edward "Kim" Jaycox, visited Lusaka. His predecessor, Willi Wapenhans, had visited Zambia, but only as a stopover. So when Jaycox made a special trip to meet with local policymakers and politicians, the Bank sent a strong message that it was behind Zambia's efforts. Jaycox cared very deeply about the Bank getting its African programs right. His empathy for Zambia's situation came across even as he spoke about the economic situation with a brutal honesty

Why are these details noteworthy? Because at the time, this kind of approach was extremely important, not to mention unusual, since it took place long before the language of "ownership" had become standard. The Bank's structural adjustment policy fostered a lot of resentment across Africa, so it mattered in local circles if the Bank or IMF seemed genuinely interested in working with governments, not just making demands. The word "conditionality" was toxic, but the motivations behind the approach—to strengthen government institutions, capacities, and policies in order to make aid more effective—were necessary and over time they proved prescient. More than a decade later, those motivations formed the foundation of the ownership agenda that drove global development policy into the new century.

The biggest turning point in the struggle between the pro-reformers and anti-reformers came in October 1983, when Kaunda appointed Luke Mwananshiku as his new finance minister and expanded the ministry's oversight to include the National Commission for Development Planning. From a policy standpoint, this change was seismic.

Mwananshiku saw the need for reform without having to be convinced of the reasons why. He was a good economist, a true technocrat who previously had served as governor of the Bank of Zambia. In that role, he became one of Zambia's most public proponents of reform. But after a dramatic press conference in December 1980 in which he laid bare

Zambia's bleak outlook, he was removed, along with his team of like-minded technocrats. His views directly contradicted those of Leonard Chivuno, a young and brash Soviet-trained engineer who headed the national planning commission. Chivuno was an ideologue who opposed reform and defended the crumbling system. So Kaunda telegraphed a major shift in thinking when he not only brought Mwananshiku back into the government but sidelined Chivuno by placing the planning commission under Mwananshiku's authority.[4]

Around the same, Mulaisho and I urged Kaunda to create a special economic management team to bring together *all* the key policymakers to hash out their decisions—and collectively make recommendations. We hoped such a mechanism would break past patterns, wherein Chivuno or other UNIP hardliners would go directly to Kaunda to try and undermine reform momentum. To our relief, KK endorsed the idea. So we formed the team and named it the "Special Economic Unit"—and it brought policy coordination to the top levels of Zambian government for the first time.

Even though it was a brand-new concept for Zambia, the economic management team proved effective. It encouraged intra-government dialogue and reinforced the idea of local ownership. It also expanded the influence of the pro-reformers, who generally favored consensus and transparency. Through their influence, Kaunda backed an outreach campaign to get public opinion on the side of reforms. The government held week-long meetings around the country to listen to concerns and solicit feedback. Again, this marked a radical shift in approach. The old guard in the central committee had long ignored or disregarded the value of national consensus building.

As the revived relationship between the Bank and the government grew, we were able to try other tactics that proved successful. Two of the biggest were bolstering technical capacity—a necessity when local ownership is the end goal—and re-engaging donors.

The weakness of Zambia's public administration reverberated throughout the government. Kaunda's humanism doctrine, while admirable in design, was more abstract than concrete, and the targets set by Zambia's national development plans reflected as much by favoring idealism over reality.[5] A deeper and more experienced civil service might have been able to counterbalance the poor decisions, but that's not what Zambia had. Instead, it had a few lone voices of reason, like that of Luke Mwananshiku's, that lacked enough support to wage a proper policy fight against the ideologues. To get around this, I pushed the Bank to provide a technical assistance credit so the government could bring in outside experts.

As a result, we were able to recruit some prominent Africans to Lusaka to fill key ministry roles. Between these experts and the increased number of World Bank technicians who had come into Zambia, the government dramatically upped its capacity to make more informed and less ideological decisions.

As for the donors, I knew it was important for the local representatives to feel that their views were being taken into consideration. Without the willingness of the IMF and global creditors to restructure debt and release more funds, Zambia had no room to maneuver and the local donors had a big say in whether that happened. One way we addressed that problem was through the Special Economic Unit, which began to meet periodically with donors to set up coordinating mechanisms. We would often meet in my office, and I would help government officials prepare ahead of time. It was a serious attempt at establishing coordination at the local level.

All these actions were interrelated. For example, policy coordination by the new economic management team enabled serious dialogue with donors around aid coordination because it showed that Zambia was serious about reform. And it gave hope that Kaunda's efforts would not be undercut by his shadow ministers.

The Bank responded to the policy turnaround by raising its commitment levels, and also by convening three high-level donor meetings in Paris between May 1984 and December 1986. Known as consultative group, or CG, meetings, these events have always been very important to borrowing countries. They function like pledging sessions, where donors announce their commitments after studying country data and hearing presentations from policymakers and leaders. The CG meetings, regardless of country or context, are always tense affairs, because the government in question has to sell itself to donors, while the Bank is trying to round up enough donor commitments to meet its suggested targets.

For Zambia, the May 1984 CG meeting was especially dramatic. It was the country's first one in many years and it was the first time Zambia addressed the donor community with a reform agenda.[6] The influx of technical support had helped produce an array of government sector reports outlining a more realistic—and less idealistic—policy framework that donors could back. When the meeting concluded, the Bank had hit its target commitments. A short time later, in 1986, bilateral development assistance to Zambia reached its highest level in six years.

A reform agenda was moving forward, but results were far from assured. Policy reform and financial support needed to go hand in hand, and they still weren't completely aligned. The technical details of the policy overhaul were still being worked out in key areas like copper mining and manufacturing. And the level of engagement by the Bank, IMF and Paris Club had never been more intense—seven different notable agreements on aid and debt restructuring took place over a 20-month period in 1983 and 1984. But there was a reason for the frantic pace of financial activity: none of the efforts were working.

The main thrust of Zambia's whole reform package was to allow the country to regain its macroeconomic balance. Drastic policy changes to curtail government outlays like subsidies were a main part of the equation, but they weren't the only part. Major structural reforms were urgently needed. So even as these agreements were negotiated, they inevitably broke down and the cycle restarted until another agreement was put in place. The breakdowns were due largely to disagreements over exchange rate policy: trying to fix that became of paramount importance.

Without getting into too much detail, Zambia "allocated" foreign exchange through its central bank, a time-consuming and inefficient policy that contributed to wasteful spending and macro distortions. It also severely constrained capital investments. Foremost, the allocation system not only strangled growth, it also promoted favoritism and encouraged corruption—bureaucrats would decide how much money went to mining versus manufacturing versus agriculture, so those who lobbied the best or promised the most would get the biggest allotments. It was all done by fiat. Naturally, the IMF wanted Zambia to change the system as a condition for financial help. But the Fund wanted to completely liberalize it, and Kaunda wouldn't accept that. The allocation system might have been prone to corruption, but in theory, it supported the principles of humanism, which the free market did not. Furthermore, liberalization of foreign exchange would all but wipe out the generous government subsidies that had propped up industries, so from a political standpoint it seemed to be a non-starter.

But by 1984, something had to give. Zambia failed to meet the provisions of its most recent IMF standby that summer and commercial bank credit lines began to dry up. When I previously wrote that Zambia's situation had grown desperate, this was the main reason. The primary stumbling block to reform had been foreign exchange, so even though plans were being put in place for sectoral reforms, foreign exchange policy also had to be revamped. So a group of us came up with a radical plan: an auction.

The final design was complex, but the basic idea was to allocate a certain amount of foreign exchange—for importers, for example—but instead of the government setting the price, other investors would come and bid. It intended to introduce more liberal principles to overhaul Zambia's exchange rate regime without the government having to cede full control of its monetary policy to the free market. Zambia had multiple exchange rates, but each would be determined by the auction. At the time, only a handful of countries worldwide had something similar.[7] But given Zambia's structural characteristics, the auction approach seemed like a good transitional compromise to a more stable, long-term solution.

We had to get the IMF on board first, because Kaunda couldn't announce an auction before having the necessary financial support. We didn't want the IMF to pull the rug out from under our feet, for instance. We needed the Fund to agree to release sufficient foreign exchange to make the auctions viable. Once that deal was in place, we could push Kaunda.

I arranged a meeting with KK to talk about foreign exchange, and it proved to be pivotal. I brought with me a calculation of just how many different decision points—dozens—were involved in the current allocation system. I discussed the perils of having so many bureaucrats making critical financial decisions, and I had the data to back it up. I also pointed out that an auction would be less drastic than what the IMF wanted. He didn't disagree, but his biggest worry was how prices would be affected. He felt he didn't have the political backing from enough stakeholders to take such a step.

He was correct. He didn't.

Kaunda's relationship with the trade unions was severely strained. For example, when he announced a price increase on maize meal, a key agricultural product, as part of the reform package, a huge backlash erupted. The decision infuriated working-class Zambians, and Frederick Chiluba, the head of the Zambia Congress of Trade Unions, called for a strike in retaliation. The ZCTU was a dominant force in driving public opinion, and Chiluba was a popular, influential figure among the rank and file. He also was a frequent foe of the president. In 1981, Kaunda jailed Chiluba and other labor leaders without charges for instigating wildcat strikes. So bad blood existed before Kaunda threatened price increases. Union leaders opposed any kind of reform, which would force major concessions on the mining industry, including job losses and wage restraints. Without widespread support, a foreign exchange auction could be a fatal misstep, and the trade unions held the leverage for fomenting public opinion.

So I made an offer to Kaunda: I could meet with the unions. I would try to sell to them directly the need for reforms and the need to rally around leadership for the sake of national unity. If I went to them as a third-party intermediary, we might help depoliticize the situation, I said. Also, it would send a powerful message if we could get the trade unions on our side. KK agreed rather quickly, although a little reluctantly. Such a move was highly irregular for someone outside the government, much less in the employ of the World Bank. But he trusted me.

The president's office made the arrangements and set up the meeting, and I headed out to the Copperbelt region. I went there because the Mine Workers' Union of Zambia was the strongest and biggest player within the federation. I didn't meet with Chiluba, but I met with other union leaders. I wouldn't call it a hospitable environment, but it wasn't hostile, either. The union reps just wanted to know that all levels of government would share in the pain of economic reform.

"You have to start with the party bureaucracy," one of the men said to me. "The politicians have to show it first. They can't reform on the backs of the citizens."

He made a valid point.

I reported back to Kaunda that the trade unions were willing to meet halfway, but they had to be included in the reform process. They wanted to contribute and be heard. But they needed assurance that the government's bloated party structure, with its inefficiencies and wasted resources, would be reformed in equal measure.

The feedback from the trade unions helped push Kaunda even further toward consensus-building. For too long, the United National Independence Party and its central committee had wielded absolute authority over most policy decisions, so no efforts had ever been made to bring in other voices to be heard. But Kaunda faced different circumstances here. He had already endorsed the week-long public information forums that were held across the country. Those forums had helped increase awareness, but they hadn't necessarily created a groundswell of support for reform.

Kaunda agreed that if subsidies were going to be cut, then so too should government waste, and he wanted to get the word out. He saw the value in building a broad consensus. So Kaunda decided to call a national convention for later that summer.

I was scheduled to leave Lusaka midway through 1984, my three-year assignment having come to an end. But with so much going on, Kaunda asked that I stay on for one more year. I couldn't refuse his request, and I didn't want to.

My final year in Zambia was the most eventful, highlighted by the national convention—only the third one to have been held as of that time. The fact that Kaunda wanted to put the reforms on the table for national debate showed how far he was willing to go to address Zambia's crisis—and how far he had moved from the hardliners that had kept the country closed off. Indeed, for Zambia's growth as a still-young nation, the decision to convene in the name of economic reform was a watershed event.[8]

The convention took place in late July 1984, in the famous Mulungushi Hall, an international conference center that opened in 1970 and soon gained stature as the site of anti-apartheid and pro-independence conferences and negotiations. The convention was a big deal and it attracted everyone: party elites, policymakers, unions, tribal chiefs, you name it. The hall held hundreds and it was full. Kaunda had tasked Mulaisho with writing his address, so Mulaisho pulled Muhsin and me into the process—the three "co-conspirators," at it once more.

As the convention got underway, I found myself caught up in the moment. Kaunda would be delivering more than an opening address—he would be making the public case for a new economic path for Zambia. So much had changed in only three years.

Kaunda spoke to a rapt audience. He described how the economy would be restructured, an "economic crusade" intended to reverse a decade of bureaucratic strangulation. He didn't just gloss over the problems, either. He delved into detail on his country's high prices, product shortages, currency valuation, mining industry woes, and mounting debt. But even in the face of upheaval, he didn't abandon his commitment to his principles. "In the economic, as in the political field," he said, humanism "is our guiding star."

Kaunda made repeated references to Zambia's capacity for reform— as in the need to strengthen it, and sustain it, alongside any set of policy reforms. And those remarks really stood out for me. "We have the capacity to rally round in the agricultural field [and] also in the industrial sector," he said, "but most of this capacity remains grossly underutilized." It can and should be tapped, he argued, with more resources and effort. In other words, ownership without capacity would be meaningless—he had bought in!

Kaunda's speech to the nation—and the political authority behind it—paved the way for the reforms to move forward. In 1985, they arrived in full force. As Ravi Gulhati wrote in his examination of Zambia's reform agenda, "Both the credit and foreign exchange markets were liberalized, radically changing the entire framework of Zambia's macroeconomic policy."

But the government also made important decisions to reform industrial and agricultural policies. In addition, it tried to restructure public expenditure, shifting budgetary resources directly to productive sectors such as agriculture, mines, commerce, industry, and tourism. In 1985, outlays to these sectors rose 28 percent in one year and there was a comparable increase for infrastructure support. Finally, commercial bank interest rates on deposits and loans were decontrolled in September 1985 as a prelude to the establishment of the foreign exchange auction the following month.

Gulhati called the auction a "bold move" that really kicked the reform process into high gear. But the bold move didn't work. The exchange rate policy was central to many of the reform measures, but so were the other sectoral and institutional reforms across the economy.

Unfortunately, there was a limit to Zambia's appetite for overhaul.

We all predicted economic shocks, and Kaunda didn't shy from it. As he made his public case, he was open about the fact that a transition to partial liberalization would be very tough at first. But telling people is one thing and having them experience it is something else entirely. Deregulating industries and foreign exchange opened up new markets, but it caused inflation to rise and prices to soar. As reforms took hold in the mining and agriculture sectors, jobs were lost, wage hikes stalled and subsidies curtailed. All those moves were necessary for economic liberalization, but that didn't mitigate the impact on the people. The high-water optimism of the national convention receded into memory.

By 1986, consumer prices, freed from government controls, had shot up 50 percent. The ineffectiveness of the auction only contributed to the volatility in the consumer and labor markets. Despite their pledges, the Bank and the IMF were not sending money fast enough, and that hurt the foreign exchange rates. Zambia still had to deal with other contributing factors, such as a balance of payments problem and a weak central bank. The combination of all that, along with slow donor disbursements, created very erratic allocations for the weekly auctions. The kwacha appreciated for a brief period, then began a long descent into depreciation.

For Kaunda, the political pressure became too great to bear. Bringing the trade unions to the table was the right thing to do, but it didn't work. Amid the full impact of the reforms, union hostilities with the government actually worsened. Then in 1986, as per capita GDP hit its lowest point since 1963, Kaunda removed many of the key players in the pro-reform movement, including Mulaisho. He reassigned Luke Mwananshiku to the foreign ministry and installed Chivuno as head of the central bank. In February 1987, Zambia suspended the foreign exchange auction, revived it briefly a short time later and then abandoned it for good in May.

Within two years, the entire reform package had unraveled.

Still, it wasn't a complete loss. In the copper industry, for example, the Zambia Consolidated Copper Mines streamlined its management, improved its control systems, opened up its procurement practices, and began long-term corporate planning, though it still suffered losses for years. The exchange auction eliminated the black market, sharply reduced instances of corruption, and demonstrated the value of efficiency in a government apparatus that had all but ignored it. On the agriculture front, the tensions remained so high that very few reforms took hold at the time, but the failed attempts to modernize pricing and distribution at least laid the groundwork for more lasting change the following decade, after Kaunda had been voted out of office and when Zambia was in a stronger position to embark on more macro reforms.

Frederick Chiluba, the influential union leader, succeeded Kaunda in 1991 in a multiparty vote, as the old system finally broke down. On New Year's Eve in 1989, Chiluba had stoked the fires at a labor rally, asking, "If the owners of socialism have withdrawn from the one-party system, who are [we] to continue with it?" Starting in 1999, Zambia's per capita GDP began an upward swing interrupted only by the global recession that hit in 2008 and 2009. In fact, the turnaround in the new century was so strong that respected global economist Steven Radelet named Zambia as one of 17 countries "leading the way" in his 2010 book on emerging economies in Africa.

◆ ◆ ◆ ◆

Zambia attempted a major economic reform that didn't go as planned, but the Bank—and other development observers—learned many valuable lessons. For me, four of those lessons stood out the most.

First, political economy matters. One of the biggest gripes against the Bank and IMF was their propensity to push the same policy prescriptions or set the same loan conditions from country to country, disregarding local context or, even worse, local needs. I realized just how important it was to establish relationships to better understand those needs and, subsequently, get the various special interests and stakeholders together—or at least talking.

Second, partnerships matter. In the early 1980s, the donor community had very little productive dialogue established with Zambian policymakers. But as I saw when I arrived, the government had plenty of eager ministers and technocrats who wanted—and deserved—assurances that they would have substantial input in their country's recovery program.

Third, and along the same line, ownership matters. The Special Economic Unit that we created to encourage intra-government dialogue and counsel Kaunda was a big step forward for empowering local policymakers, who had been shut out by the controlling party bosses. But Zambia proved that even in a one-party state, the ownership principle could take root if given room to grow. I still believe that Kaunda took the time to really consider the suggestions in my economic report because of the emphasis on building capacity. He knew the Zambians, not the Bank, needed to own the reform process. Bringing in outside experts helped but wasn't a long-term solution. Zambia simply didn't have the necessary human or institutional resources to make such drastic changes.

Last, leadership matters. Kaunda wasn't without his faults, but he acted boldly when he needed to and he showed political will. Just as impressive, he genuinely tried to build public support and reach agreement with special interest groups, like the powerful mining union. I would go on to work with many African heads of state over the next two decades, and seeing how Kaunda operated had a big effect on me and how I approached other leaders.

My time in Zambia proved more challenging than I could ever have imagined, while big ideas like the foreign exchange auction proved too aggressive given the country's circumstances. And yet something had to be tried to get the exchange rate under control and to get the IMF back to the table. It didn't work in the moment, but it proved that compromise and collaboration could be reached.

I didn't lose faith in the reforms that were tried. Rather, I gained a better understanding of the environment needed to make them succeed. As much as policy, the Zambia story was one of economic and political governance. Once I had come face-to-face with the realities of national policymaking, I never underestimated those factors again.

◆　◆　◆　◆

Near the end of my stay in Zambia, Kaunda hosted a farewell luncheon for me at the State House, an uncommon gesture since I wasn't a member of the party, a political appointee, or even a diplomat. He invited a small group of government and UNIP dignitaries, including the head of the party as well as many of the people with whom I had worked so closely. Muhsin and Mulaisho were there and so was Kebby Musokotwane, by then the country's prime minister.

As he was known to do at times, KK welcomed Philomena and me by serving us coffee—a moment captured in a photograph that remains a prized possession. After the meal, Kaunda spoke, and, true to form, he made a moving, emotional speech. He said I cared about the Zambian people, and he thanked me for it. He also noted that the World Bank appeared to be changing. He hoped that once I returned to headquarters, I would continue to work for those changes.

When he finished, I rose to give my own remarks. I thanked the people in the room for taking a chance on me and for being collaborative partners. And when I went to thank Kaunda, I saw that he had quietly begun to cry. I stopped talking for a few seconds, long enough for him to pull out his white handkerchief and wipe his eyes. Then I slowly started speaking again.

We left Lusaka in July 1985. I returned to Bank headquarters in Washington, DC and started a new job, one that allowed me to keep working on African policy but apply the lessons from Zambia. While that was a good move for me and the next logical step, leaving Zambia was tough for the family. We had made a nice life there. Philomena tirelessly managed the daily affairs of our household—no insignificant task between three rambunctious girls and the endless stream of job-related luncheons, dinners, and social functions. She excelled at it, of course. We also made lasting friendships. Lusaka boasted a sizable Ghanaian community, many of whom worked for the United Nations. Most prominent among them was Hackman Owusu-Agyemang, the resident representative for the UN's Food and Agriculture Organization. His wife Comfort and their children, who were around the same age as our daughters, became part of our family.

Introducing Ama, Nana, and Mame to the wonders of Africa had been among my primary reasons for wanting a resident assignment in the first place, so we took full advantage. We visited Tanzania's Ngorongoro Crater, one of the Seven Natural Wonders of Africa, and Serengeti National Park, famous for its great migrations. We walked the bridge over Victoria Falls. We traveled to Ethiopia and South Africa and all around Zambia, including the Luangwa River Valley, an extension of the Great Rift Valley that extends along East Africa and boasts a world-famous wildlife sanctuary.

Occasionally, the wonders of Africa could get a little too real. While on a game drive in the Luangwa Valley, we narrowly avoided a herd of elephants in a stampede. Another time, we came face-to-face with a lioness just as she finished feeding her cubs—and when she was in no mood for visitors.

My girls still recall these adventures fondly and I know they enjoyed their time at the Lusaka International School, a virtual melting pot of students from all over Africa and the world. They were also exposed to both sides of Africa's twentieth-century legacy. In the Copperbelt region alone, the remnants of the British colonial period—well-kept bungalows with manicured gardens and exotic flowers—existed alongside impoverished mining camps and villages. We wanted them to understand it all.

Recently, they told me those childhood years remain "an unspoiled dream" that framed their idea of Africa. I feel like I accomplished a lot in Zambia, but nothing else comes close to that.

Notes

1   In 1889, Britain granted a charter to mining magnate Cecil Rhodes's South Africa Company to stake territorial claims. The land became part of Britain's "sphere of influence" in Africa, its strangely cleaved, bean-shaped border the result of negotiation between Britain, other European countries and tribal chiefs—and a lasting reminder of the outsized influence that non-Africans had in carving up the continent's modern-day boundaries.

2   Over almost another two decades, before most operating units were finally privatized again, Zambia Consolidated Copper Mines devolved into "deadweight," as one close associate and renowned Zambia expert put it. ZCCM put practically no capital into operational upgrades or exploration and it failed to safeguard jobs, shedding thousands of workers despite secure employment being one of the primary reasons for nationalizing the industry in the first place.

3   Mulaisho's career was always colorful and always in the service of his country and continent. After leaving the government, he was the founding editor of an economic magazine based in Zimbabwe and created by the Southern African Development Community. Then in 1992, as Zambia began its long overdue transition to a multiparty democracy, he returned home to oversee the Bank of Zambia as its central governor. He passed away in 2013.

4   Kaunda had placed all ministries under the supervision of the UNIP's central committee in an attempt to definitively fuse "party and government" functions. This move gave outsized influence to the political players at the expense of the policymakers and ministries—another reason institutional capacity had grown so weak.

5   For example, at Chivuno's urging, Zambia sharply increased government spending in 1980 to try to prop up its economy despite flat growth. The result was calamitous, as Zambia overshot its budget by 75 percent.

6   It was also a little dramatic behind the scenes. The night before Luke Mwananshiku, the finance minister, was to present Zambia's case to the donors, he realized he had a problem: his speech was terrible. Various government officials had a hand in it, which showed. The tone was way off the mark. It confused ownership with authority and missed the spirit of collaboration almost entirely. He knew the speech was a misfire, so we buckled down and rewrote the entire thing. In the end, the speech hit the mark and was well received, and he delivered it with aplomb—despite a serious lack of sleep.

7   Sierra Leone ran a type of exchange rate auction in 1982 and 1983, and Uganda ran one from 1982 until 1985 before reestablishing an auction in 1992 for a few years. Elsewhere, Bolivia and Jamaica had also established them.

8   The Fifth National Convention, which took place in March 1990, inadvertently turned out to be another watershed moment when Kaunda, dismissing the pro-democracy movement in Eastern Europe, reiterated support for Zambia's one-party state. His declaration inflamed critics, already upset over a series of constitutional amendments he had proposed that would further entrench the UNIP in government. Only a few months later, bowing to public pressure, Kaunda announced a referendum on multiparty elections.

Chapter 3

A Burden to Share
The Complicated, Evolving Relationship Between the Bank and Africa

In 1987, after 13 years at the World Bank, I lost my job. But so did everyone else. Soon after being appointed as the seventh president of the World Bank in 1986, Barber Conable enacted a widespread reorganization to cut costs and improve efficiency in response to mounting criticism from major shareholders. The Bank had become too bloated and sluggish, they said, an overgrown bureaucracy leaning on developing countries to reform when it was in need of reform itself. The result was a drastic and total overhaul of the Bank's structure that eliminated hundreds of jobs, forced remaining staff to reapply for remaining jobs, and tried to reorient operational structure and decentralize decision-making. It was a trying time, emblematic of an extended period of upheaval and uncertainty at the Bank.

I had been back from Lusaka barely two years when this organizational tsunami hit. I was in charge of the Bank's programs for Kenya and Uganda and, while I survived the changes, I suddenly found myself with four more countries in my portfolio: Ethiopia, Mauritius, Somalia, and Sudan. The reorganization came during a period of major change in the Bank's relationship with Africa—a period defined largely by the swelling controversy over structural adjustment lending, a new approach that tied Bank funds to policy reforms at the country level. Along the same lines, governance emerged as a major developmental issue, and capacity development to bolster African ownership took on greater importance. Most countries either weren't yet equipped or lacked the leadership to adequately handle these changes, and the Bank's reputation in Africa nosedived.

The Bank's major shareholders had grown increasingly uncomfortable as the institution's annual budgets continued to rise during a time of global recession and escalating debt crises. As then-US Treasury Secretary James Baker told Conable, a "lot of fat" could be trimmed inside the Bank.

The United States chose the Bank presidents and Baker had recruited Conable, a retired Republican congressman from New York with two decades of experience in US government, for the job. A consummate Washington insider and public servant, Conable offered a distinct contrast to his predecessor, Alden Clausen, who had come from Bank of America— the largest commercial bank in the United States at the time—and possessed good private sector experience that didn't always translate into managing a sprawling bureaucracy. Clausen was hands-off and preferred to delegate, a leadership style that in many ways didn't mix well with the many challenges facing the Bank during his tenure from 1981 to 1985, including a sluggish global economy that slowed growth in developing countries; increased demand for resources to help those countries most affected by the downturn; and offered insufficient replenishments for the Bank's International Development Association (IDA) fund. Meanwhile, the Bank's own operational shifts were causing a lot of internal dissension.

Clausen had the unenviable task of following Robert McNamara, a forceful personality who presided over the Bank from 1968 until 1981 and who had actively transformed the Bank into a more vocal champion of development and the poor. Under McNamara, the Bank had tripled its staff and increased its lending by a factor of 13. He put poverty alleviation at the front and center of Bank operations and had overseen a growing agenda to keep the Bank's expanding operations on track. Clausen didn't want to reshape the Bank as McNamara had done, just maintain a positive status quo. Unfortunately, external events interfered, and as the global economy worsened, pressures on the Bank increased. Around the world, the Bank was trying to get a bigger bang for its buck so to speak, and it had gravitated toward more stringent country lending tied to local economic and political reforms. The approach was controversial from the start, and inside the Bank it caused an ideological rift that only worsened as countries continued to underperform and as administrative costs rose—which, outside the Bank, added fuel to the fire. In fact, Conable received an unexpected surprise soon after coming aboard: the Bank's major shareholders refused to okay the 1986–87 budget, which the outgoing Clausen had submitted.

Criticism of Bank overhead and operating costs had been around for as long as the Bank had existed, particularly from the United States, which is noteworthy since that country held unmatched sway over picking presidents and committing funds. But as Jochen Kraske—one of my former bosses and a Bank historian—wrote in his book *Bankers with a Mission*, "concern about the growth of the Bank's total administrative budget remained muted as long as the Bank's lending and services grew." But by 1986, lending had slowed and opposition to Bank policies continued to fester. Suggestions to pull back activities seemed to go unheeded. There was a growing sense among executive directors and officials in member countries that the Bank, Kraske wrote, "was somehow an organization out of control."

Without the support of shareholders, the Bank would grind to a halt. Conable concluded that something drastic needed to be done to address the external concerns. He decided it was his mandate as president to cut costs and reform operations, a plan he floated by others. A conversation with McNamara convinced him that reorganization would be the way to go.

Many problems were endemic to the Bank's structure, which needed to be reoriented around a country focus. McNamara had actively pushed the Bank toward poverty alleviation, but the Bank as an institution remained stuck in project lending. Building roads and bridges by themselves wouldn't reduce poverty; creating urban and rural employment or helping reform macroeconomic policies, for instance, were essential. But to tackle those kinds of development issues, the Bank needed a better organizational structure to support the shift in operations it had already started to make in the early 1980s.

Conable moved quickly, though his process required several steps. First, he hired an external consulting firm to analyze the Bank's current operations and recommend changes. The consultants found deep displeasure among both veteran and young Bank staff regarding "cumbersome, time-consuming procedures" that didn't do enough to accommodate the "needs and wishes of borrowers"—a common refrain of argument against the Bank from outsiders that was now being repeated from the inside. The consultants suggested that the best way forward would be a complete overhaul of the Bank's operating structure. At that point, Conable appointed an internal Bank task force and a steering committee to implement the changes. Edward "Kim" Jaycox, who had recently been appointed vice president for the Eastern and Southern Africa region, chaired the committee. In the years since my return from Zambia, Jaycox and I had grown close, a relationship that played to my advantage once everything shook out.

The Bank's board approved the reorganization in May 1987 and the overhaul began immediately. The changes were rapid, substantial, and drastic. For starters, the Bank shaped its operations around four regions instead of six: Africa; Asia; Europe, the Middle East, North Africa; and Latin America and the Caribbean. Within the streamlined regional groups, country departments took on increased responsibilities that had previously been divided among other groups. On the personnel side, these changes produced unprecedented upheaval. The Bank eliminated 400 staff positions entirely and everyone else had to reapply for newly merged or created positions.

The selection process for "restaffing" the Bank was the final step and it worked like this: Conable appointed four vice presidents, up from two. The vice presidents selected their directors. The directors selected their division chiefs. And each division chief was allocated a certain number of positions and selected his or her staff to fill them. In essence, Conable rebuilt the Bank not from the ground up, but from the top down.

There were benefits to completely upending the system. For starters, the Bank simply needed a shock to its system. It had become an ever slower-moving bureaucracy, with a personnel management process that was difficult to navigate and too rarely favored diversity in the higher ranks.

The reorganization also rebalanced operational power in the Bank's upper echelon. For years, Ernie Stern, the senior vice president of operations, had wielded unmatched influence inside the Bank, from policy to personnel. After McNamara left, no one had a greater imprint on Bank operations in the early 1980s. The shuffle resulted in a new post for Stern, to the delight of many and to the dismay of others. Stern got things done, but his manner often left a lot to be desired, which I experienced first-hand on more than one occasion.

The reorganization dragged on until October—six months of excruciating stress, tension, and disruption.[1] It proved to be just as painful as could be imagined. It generated ample negative publicity outside the Bank and inside the Bank it adversely affected staff morale—how could it not when all jobs were essentially lost and everyone was forced to compete against colleagues and associates to stick around? Worse, it didn't necessarily achieve its goals.

According to Jaycox, the Bank "gravitated back to the layering and second-guessing and centralization very rapidly," a regression he attributed to the entrenched culture of the Bank.

Still, the reorganization became a touchstone for those on both sides of the growing debate over the Bank's mission and effectiveness. To critics, it was another example of wasted resources, top-heavy demands, and poor execution. To supporters, it represented the World Bank's most substantial effort thus far to try to modernize operations.

And though the reorganization primarily came about as a way to improve efficiency and placate agitated shareholders, it also foreshadowed how the Bank would become more aggressive in shifting its approach in the years ahead. In a report prepared for the executive directors at the end of 1987, Conable recognized the process as "difficult and painful" but added that it had helped reinforce the image of the Bank "as an institution willing and able to confront the need for improvement and change and an institution seeking to be fair and generous to those most affected by the change process."

◆　◆　◆　◆

For better or worse, there was no more dominant player in African development during the 1980s than the World Bank. And in that context, the Conable reorganization had two very positive outcomes for the continent. First, it created a unified Africa region. This might not seem like a big deal, but it was. Prior to 1987, two wholly separate vice presidencies were responsible for Sub-Saharan Africa: the Western Africa region and the Eastern and Southern Africa region. This division made it difficult to apply a coherent strategy to common issues facing the continent. Even worse, the division perpetuated the old colonial division of the continent into Francophone Africa and Anglophone Africa. In fact, for most of the Bank's history, a Frenchman headed the former region and an English-speaking man the latter. The second major development that would shape the future was the appointment of Kim Jaycox as the vice president for the unified Africa region.

Jaycox had been among the earliest young professionals, or YPs, brought into the Bank. American-born and educated, he focused on Africa from the start. In 1965, he traveled to the new country of Malawi, formerly known as Nyasaland under British colonial rule, on a Bank mission. The mission consisted of three members: Jaycox, one of his fellow YPs, and a Bank engineer. They found the project lacked merit, but there was a catch the road, not coincidentally, would have served the private farm of President Hastings Banda, the first president of Malawi. It was up to the mission team to inform the president, but the engineer wanted no part of it. Jaycox and his companion were left to give Banda the bad news. They were taken into the president's chambers, where Banda sat on a raised platform. Jaycox explained that the project didn't make fiscal sense for the Bank presently and was probably a decade away from doing so. Banda didn't like this news. He gripped the arms of his throne, staggered to his feet, and, according to Jaycox, got so worked up that he toppled off the pedestal.

"I thought, 'Oh my God, they're going to take us out and shoot us,'" Jaycox would later recall. The two YPs weren't shot, but they did have to be safely extracted from the room.

Did the whole affair rattle Jaycox? Not at all. Quite the opposite, in fact.

"I found this to be very heady stuff," he said. "And to be working in Africa with these emergent countries in these very difficult situations was really something that I felt I wanted to do."

Jaycox got his wish. His Bank career lasted 32 years, the final dozen of which he spent as the Bank's leading, and often outspoken, voice on Africa. He took over as vice president of Eastern and Southern Africa in 1984 and then assumed the unified Africa vice presidency in 1987 until his retirement in 1996. He had a genuine passion for African development and brought a renewed urgency to the Bank's focus on the continent. When he first became a vice president, the Bank had 14 resident missions in Africa— and only one person in each of those missions. By the early 1990s, the number of missions had more than doubled to 31, with four or five Bank staff in each location.

Among the main forces driving Jaycox beyond his personal interests was the poor state of relations between the Bank and Africa. In country after country, lending programs had stalled or shrunk as African economies cratered and debts ballooned. And in the countries where the Bank operated, the conditional lending tied to policy reforms engendered great hostility among African officials. Jaycox paid special attention to an "African Perceptions" study that the Bank commissioned shortly after structural adjustment lending was introduced in 1980. Completed in 1983, the study was based on interviews with a variety of African stakeholders and the resulting criticisms of the Bank—such as arrogant and insensitive behavior of staff, inadequate knowledge of African affairs, overly harsh demands on African officials, and the low profile and quality of resident missions— alarmed senior management. It also infuriated a fair number of staff who found it unfair and its methodology too one-sided.

A consultant, Dunstan Wai, oversaw the study and spent considerable time in Africa gathering the research. Wai was a native of Sudan, a political scientist with advanced degrees from Oxford and Harvard. He and Jaycox were very close, sharing similar views on what was needed in Africa and what role the Bank should play. Once Jaycox had assumed his first vice presidency in 1984, he hired Wai to be his senior advisor. The African Perceptions study had a profound effect on Jaycox, and both he and Wai were determined to improve on the shortcomings it exposed.

Jaycox's focus and drive eventually earned him a nickname as the Bank's "Mr. Africa." He wasn't universally loved, however, inside or outside the Bank. He was outspoken and stubborn, and he often found himself at odds with African governments and leaders, as well as with other donors, over Bank policies or actions. But he steadfastly supported the Bank's African staff and looked after their career interests. He was an inspiring leader to almost everyone who worked for him, including me.

When Jaycox visited Lusaka toward the end of my stay in Zambia, he had just been appointed VP and his enthusiasm for Africa was infectious. He spoke to me about his plans to make the Bank more responsive to the needs of the countries. He said that he had heard good things about the way I handled a tough situation in Zambia and that he'd like me to be part of his plans. I told him that I would gladly come along, knowing that it would keep me focused on Africa.

A few months later, Jaycox stayed true to his word and submitted my name to the promotions board as division chief for Kenya and Uganda programs in Eastern Africa. Becoming a division chief was a necessary step for anyone to move into senior management. I'm certain that without the strong support of Jaycox, I might not have gotten the same opportunity. And I'm not the only one. It was the Bank's good fortune to have people like Jaycox, who helped push the institution along, sometimes in spite of itself.

The Kenya and Uganda programs division was small, barely a dozen people, with a standard responsibility—to analyze the economic environment of the two countries and, in response, prepare the Bank's assistance strategies. The staff also supported the Bank sector specialists—the agriculturalists, engineers, irrigation experts, and so forth—in designing and implementing the projects that formed the backbone of the Bank's country lending. The division and a few others like it made up the Eastern and Southern Africa programs department, which handled all the Anglophone countries extending from Kenya down to Lesotho and Swaziland.

Things were not going well when I took over, neither in the countries nor back at the office.

Until the mid-1970s, Kenya had been one of the Bank's crown jewels in Africa because it had such good development prospects. Unlike the many countries that had little lasting development to show from colonial rule, Kenya boasted a sound infrastructure, a relatively strong civil service, a viable commercial farming sector, and an industrial base. After gaining independence in 1963, it made tremendous progress for a decade, growing its GDP by 6.6 percent—a period referred to as the "golden years." Its economic foundation seemed solid, so the Bank invested. But Kenya's economy took a sharp nosedive beginning in 1973, hampered by the same oil shocks and economic crises that hurt so many young African economies. Of course, Kenya compounded its external problems with internal shortcomings also consistent across the continent: weak capacity, poor governance, and suspect policymaking. Amid concerns over gross economic mismanagement, the Bank's lending to Kenya plunged more than 96 percent, falling from $600 million in the early 1970s to less than $20 million in 1984.

Though smaller and with fewer expectations, Uganda was even worse off. A case study in the worst excesses of African strongmen and political instability, Uganda in 1985 was emerging from two decades of devastation punctuated by Idi Amin's reign that began in 1971. Amin overthrew the government of Milton Obote, the first leader of independent Uganda, before being forced into exile in 1979. Obote returned to power in 1980, but once again fell victim to a coup in 1985. An interim, though highly unstable, government was put in place. As for the Bank's dialogue and new lending program there, it was practically non-existent.

As poor as the situation was in Uganda, Kenya stood out the most. Its demise as a Bank priority bothered many who felt it was too important a country to just write off. Chief among them was Jaycox. He wanted to send a message that under his leadership attitudes and approaches toward Africa had to change.

Given the current state of Bank operations in Kenya and Uganda—low levels of lending, little engagement with leaders, dormant work programs—the division had very little work to do. Others in the Bank had nicknamed it the "coffee shop" in recognition of the staff's long and frequent breaks. Fully aware of all this, Jaycox viewed the division as an obvious early target for his turnaround.

This is where my background in Zambia came into play. The parallels on the ground were similar, and Jaycox felt my recent experience could help speed up a revamp of the Kenya and Uganda programs. But we both underestimated how hard it would be to close down the coffee shop.

When the Bank announced my appointment, the division staff didn't take it well. Unfortunately, race had a lot to do with it. Many were upset—very upset—that they would now be working under an African. Those who were most offended tried to do something about it. They reached out to Kenyan officials, asking them to oppose my appointment on the grounds that Kenya's economy was more sophisticated than Ghana's economy. Therefore, they argued, it would be an affront to Kenya to have a Ghanaian economist lead the Bank's dialogue.

These were the lengths that some would go to preserve the status quo. Fortunately, those efforts failed. But a tone had definitely been set.

My first day on the job, Jochen Kraske, my immediate boss, set a meeting to introduce me to the staff. Coming into the job, I expected difficulties, but I knew there'd be a silver lining: Kraske. A highly intelligent German national with a wry wit, he had put in a stellar performance in the South Asia region, including serving as director of the large resident mission in Delhi before assuming his East Africa role in 1979. Zambia was under his charge during my four years in Lusaka, and he and I developed a great rapport. He was a very blunt person and made no secret of his admiration for the efficiency of the Indian bureaucracy. He confessed on many occasions that the "lack of competence" often demonstrated by many African officials in comparison simply baffled him. Many mistakenly interpreted his impatience and raw honesty as lacking empathy for the African situation. But I worked closely with him for many years, and I didn't share that view at all. Like Jaycox, he wanted to make the Africa programs a success.

The introductory meeting did not go well. When I walked in the room, no one rose to greet me or showed any interest in being there. Kraske gave me a generous introduction, reviewing my efforts in Zambia and reiterating the confidence that he and Jaycox had in my ability to lead a similar revamp of operations in Uganda and Kenya. The staff members were visibly unmoved, sitting in stony silence until Kraske forced them to speak by asking for their introductions. After going around the table, it was my turn, and I gave my best version of a pep talk, stressing the challenges ahead, the virtue of teamwork, the desperate need in Kenya and Uganda. When Kraske opened the floor to questions, still no one spoke. The meeting lasted less than 30 minutes. It was the start of six months of utter frustration.

By early 1986, I felt I had been handed a double-edged sword. On the one side, I foresaw no immediate prospects for a breakthrough in either Kenya or Uganda, despite a good amount of effort. Or in Uganda's case, as much effort as the dire political situation allowed. On the other, I had to motivate staff that remained resistant to my leadership. And I knew that my performance ultimately would be judged on both metrics.

Soon after taking over, I paid a few visits to Nairobi. I wanted to meet local officials and get their perspective on Kenya's relationship with the Bank. I paid particular attention to the people in the treasury ministry, which served as the focal point for Bank programs. Despite the trouble that my staff tried to whip up over my Ghanaian background, the Kenyans welcomed me warmly and seemed especially pleased to be dealing with a fellow African. I also had a little help from Dunstan Wai, whose wife was Kenyan and had tremendous access to a wide range of officials. He greased the wheels before my first visit, assuring some of the more influential policymakers that I had good intentions and that I would bring a valuable perspective to their situation. They were eager to meet with me—and more eager to unload on the Bank.

I got an earful from them, not unlike what I heard in Zambia. As I mentioned, Kenya had once been a favored country at the Bank, so the money had flowed. Kenya borrowed heavily in the early years of independence and had amassed huge debts, but many of the Bank-sponsored projects and their associated policy and institutional reforms were not carried out, and Kenya still had to service those debts. In addition, relations had soured considerably over the failure of two structural adjustment loans that Kenya received in the early 1980s. The Kenyans felt the Bank had unreasonable expectations, that it had placed too many conditions on the loans and offered too little support to help Kenya meet those conditions. The people I met were quite bitter over the sense that the Bank had set them up to fail, not to mention the unhelpful attitude of some Bank staff. This was especially tough to hear, since I knew some of the Bank staff in question were the recalcitrants in my division.

What I found in Uganda was very different, but even more hopeless. There had been a lot of optimism after the war that ended Idi Amin's rule in April 1979, but the economic and political situation remained bleak. Yoweri Museveni, who had helped to oust Amin and taken a job in the new government, retreated to the bush and launched a new guerrilla war in 1981. After Milton Obote was overthrown a second time and sent into exile in July 1985, the military took over. Six months later, the National

Resistance Army, the military wing of Museveni's National Resistance Movement, seized Kampala and control of the government. Three days later, Museveni was sworn in as president.

Because of the unpredictable security situation and questions of government legitimacy, the Bank had suspended most of its operations during 1985 and only allowed limited travel. Once the NRM had seized power in January 1986, the Bank banned travel completely. I never had a chance to travel to Kampala during my first six months. It seemed an entire half-year had been wasted, though in retrospect that wasn't the case. In October 1985, a small delegation of Ugandan officials traveled to Washington to initiate discussions with the Bank and IMF on a recovery program. It was the only contact I had with any Ugandan official during my first 10 months in the job. As implausible as the prospects of such a program seemed, that meeting laid the groundwork for major reforms which, for a short time at least, would make Uganda a model in Africa.

But that breakthrough was still a few years in the future. In the present, I had to devote most of my attention to managing a fractious staff. One day, I finally reached my breaking point.

I had called a meeting and quite a few people didn't bother to show up on time. They weren't a few minutes late; they were half an hour or more late for a one-hour meeting. I was frustrated, but we proceeded. Among the tardy arrivals was an English gentleman who had become my chief antagonist. He personified the coffee shop mentality, smug and secure in his role. He had been at the Bank for decades, and younger staff in the division took their cues from him. A few minutes after he arrived, I mispronounced a word and, with a condescending snicker and smile, he corrected me using his best Queen's English. Several others burst into laughter, and it wasn't the kind of laughter you go along with. They didn't expect me to laugh with them. They were laughing at me.

My English friend did me a favor, though; he convinced me once and for all that the best course of action in overhauling the division was to gut it.

I went to Kraske the next morning. He knew the challenges we faced at the country level, which included the need to convey that the Bank actually cared about its outcomes. But to convey that, we had to have people who really did care. Kraske had given me ample support since I'd taken the job, so he wasn't surprised when I told him about the previous day's meeting — or that I wanted more committed, sincere employees. It wasn't so much about respecting my authority—though that was important—as respecting the job we were supposed to be doing. Kraske sympathized with me, but he pointed out that the Bank's creaky performance management system did not allow for sweeping change that would adversely affect the careers of veteran staff. Kraske was right, but I had every intention to stand my ground.

"Enough is enough," I said. "I can't stay in this job if I can't improve the staff."

We went to Jaycox and described the extent of the problems. He didn't hesitate to back our request for overhauling the staff, but he offered a simpler solution: "Let's just transfer the troublemakers." And that's what we did, swapping four of the least productive in our division for more motivated performers who actually were eager to do the work. Then we put two of the most veteran staff, including the Englishman antagonist, on a strict performance-monitoring program and encouraged both of them to take early retirement.

This might seem like a hollow victory, or that I simply offloaded my problems on to another manager in another division. But it did more than that. Our division had yet to make much headway on the country work programs, but it gained new respect inside the Bank. And Jaycox got to send the message he wanted to send about a new way of doing business in his region.

Kraske negotiated the transfers and within three months I had four new staff members and two malcontents who had been sidelined. And I didn't have to worry about the others much longer—a few months later, news of the Conable reorganization came down and the whole system was upended.

Despite the stress and uncertainty caused by the reorganization, I didn't worry too much about my future. Jaycox headed the reorganization committee and I knew that in him I had not only a mentor but an advocate. After the dust settled, Jaycox even told me that my division's personnel problems—and the straightforward manner in which I tackled them—underscored the need to face the much larger, but similar, systemic challenges across the entire Bank. Another reason I believed that I'd come out okay had to do with what was going on in Kenya and Uganda. By the middle of 1987, and with some actual staff support, our division had started to make headway.

The reorganization—having unified the Africa region under one vice presidency, held by Jaycox—split Sub-Saharan Africa into six departments. A director was appointed for each department to work under Jaycox and underneath the director was a new position, head of country operations. These six country operations divisions consolidated and replaced the old country programs divisions—such as my Kenya and Uganda division— and brought increased responsibilities: more economic reports, enhanced assistance strategies, and more active engagement in leading policy dialogues. Although the Bank would continue—and still continues—to tweak its organization chart, this overhaul was intended to help address the chronic dissatisfaction among member countries over the Bank's approach.

Callisto Madavo, the Zimbabwe native whose trailblazing career I described in Chapter 1, was appointed the director of the "Africa 2" department that covered six countries: Ethiopia, Kenya, Mauritius, Somalia, Sudan, and Uganda. He and Jaycox then selected me to be head of that department's country operations division. It became known by its acronym—AF2CO.[2]

In other words, I got my job back but I had four more countries added to my Kenya and Uganda portfolio. The result was more work and responsibility but also more authority over the composition of my division. I had to fill 30 positions—20 economists and other high-level staff plus 10 junior staff—in a matter of weeks. For me, it was an opportunity to complete the task I had started in revamping the old division, just on a larger scale.

I had two overriding goals: to compile a team of young, energetic professionals, and to strike a better balance on gender and diversity. Fortunately, I was able to meet both. Once we were fully staffed, the AF2CO division boasted 14 different nationalities. Two-thirds hailed from developing countries and a third were female—a diverse blend of backgrounds and heritage unmatched at the time in any other division across the entire Bank.[3]

With Madavo as my boss, a unique situation in the Bank had suddenly arisen: two Africans now had prime responsibility for directing the Bank's relationship with a group of African countries. It was inspiring—a far cry from a little more than a decade earlier when I was starting my career as the lone African economist in the East African department under Stanley Please.

Over the next few years, we stepped on the gas on all six countries, though Kenya and Uganda continued to command most of my attention. Our work in both places offers good insight into the Bank's shifting approach to Africa during the mid to late 1980s—some of the lowest years in the continent's worst decade. But to grasp the full extent of our work on the ground, it is important to understand how the Bank got to the place it did. Because at that time, the World Bank, and to a lesser extent the IMF, dominated the dialogue around African development. And the overriding issue between the Bank and Africa remained structural adjustment.

◆ ◆ ◆ ◆

The origins of the World Bank's structural adjustment program, or more broadly, policy-based lending, is often traced to *Accelerated Development in Sub-Saharan Africa: An Agenda for Action,* known widely as the Berg Report. Published in 1981, it served as the jumping-off point for a dramatic shift in Bank lending to Africa—a shift that damaged the Bank's standing on the continent but also included a vast increase in resources devoted to Africa. But the roots of the approach that would come to define African development for a decade extend deeper than the Berg Report.

In 1950, the World Bank made its first loan to an African government, Ethiopia, to finance a road rehabilitation project. At the time, Ethiopia and South Africa were the only two Sub-Saharan African countries among the Bank's member states. But as decolonization swept the continent, African membership swelled, leaping from eight to 40 countries between 1962 and 1971. Amid such rapid expansion, the Bank set up a new Africa department, but that only went so far. The Bank's typical engagement process—economic missions, data analysis and research, project proposals and appraisals—was designed to be deliberative, not rapid. Most nascent African countries lacked essential services and the institutional capacity to deliver them quickly on their own. Generally, most new African member countries needed more and different help than that which the Bank was prepared to provide.

During the 1960s, Bank lending to Africa concentrated on transportation and power development, which were standard foreign aid investments of the time. Gradually, more projects began to target agriculture and rural development, reflecting a shift in thinking on the role of aid in development and on poverty reduction. Within 20 years of the first loan to Ethiopia, Bank lending in Africa totaled $2.18 billion. The analytical focus also increased—Bank reports on Africa quadrupled during the 1960s.

Yet even as the Bank paid more attention to Africa, it remained a relatively small and conservative donor. The Bank accounted for no more than 10 to 20 percent of total global aid flows to the region during the 1960s and 1970s and the primary focus remained on one-off projects like roads, dams, and schools. But that approach shifted dramatically by the start of the 1980s—so dramatic that within 15 years there was no region of the world where the Bank was more visible, influential, or invested than in Sub-Saharan Africa. (For the rest of this chapter, the word "Africa" will refer to Sub-Saharan Africa.)

A number of factors contributed to the shift, but, as Carol Lancaster found in *The World Bank: Its First Half Century*, "It was only with the second oil price increase in 1979 and the ensuing balance of payments crisis" that the Bank so rapidly expanded its lending—and "shifted the emphasis in that lending from projects to programs of structural adjustment."

Under these programs, funds were made available to African governments conditional to their adoption of policies designed to help governments adjust their economies to reverse declines and stimulate growth. Among the many goals: to curb inflation, cut budget deficits, improve the balance of payments, tighten monetary policies, liberalize trade, and increase accountability in institutions. The measures employed ranged from lowering import tariffs to devaluing currencies. In addition, the programs favored privatization and deregulation. The stabilization aspects of these programs were generally pursued through the IMF.

The Bank had tested similar types of lending programs meant to influence policy in the past—Latin America, Indonesia, and India, for example, in the 1960s and early 1970s. But their introduction in Africa sparked severe criticism of the Bank. Over time, the critics—both in Africa and abroad—pointed to their negative impact on social and economic conditions in low-income countries. The program was controversial from the start.

Within Africa, government officials, political leaders, and outside observers took umbrage over the extent to which the Bank appeared to want to influence African policymaking. The harshest critics saw structural adjustment as a new form of colonialism that threatened African sovereignty. Of course it didn't help just how few African faces the Bank put forward in the 1980s—which was hard to do, given the low number of Africans working there.

Within the Bank, the program didn't fare much better. Many staff bitterly opposed it on the grounds that it diminished country ownership—which McNamara had actively sought to cultivate—over development policy, de-emphasized poverty reduction, and too openly favored the free market over the state. The resistance was not surprising, since it represented a major move toward policy-based lending at the expense of project lending, which had long dominated Bank operations.

In any event, not everyone thought the Bank's primary focus on projects was in the best long-term interests of its clients, or member countries. Among the most vocal proponents of policy lending was my former boss Stanley Please, who had long wanted the Bank to concentrate more on a country's overall policy environment as the best way to influence development. He believed that Bank projects—which involved a complex array of technicians, economists, analysts, and local leaders—too often took on their own life cycle and didn't allow for enough flexibility to address broader country problems. He also believed that the Bank's heavy project emphasis weakened its ability to use its vast resources to assist countries in crafting macroeconomic policies that could help reverse economic decline or boost growth. And no economies were declining faster at the end of the 1970s than those in Africa.

The first oil crisis in 1973 hit most countries hard, but the shock in 1979 delivered an even more damning blow. It came amid soaring inflation in the West and on top of a collapse in global prices for some of Africa's most important exports, such as commodities, metals, and other raw materials. Meanwhile, even Africa's oil-exporting countries, which benefited temporarily from the price surge, eventually took a hit, since the drop in oil prices a few years later deepened a balance of payments crisis that already existed. Africa's debt began to soar as governments, believing the imbalances to be temporary, borrowed on commercial markets to close the gaps. The global recession of the early 1980s dried up commercial lending, African countries were left with mounting foreign debts they couldn't service, and the continent's "lost decade" was underway.

In response to the mounting crisis, the Bank's executive directors from Africa made a formal request to McNamara at the annual meeting in Belgrade. They asked that the Bank address the "dim prospects for the nations of Sub-Saharan Africa" through a special economic study and, based upon the study's findings, produce a new "program of action" to help Africa. McNamara agreed, and he asked Ernie Stern to oversee the work. Stern knew just where to turn: Stanley Please. Stern shared Please's belief that the Bank should concentrate less on projects and more on a cohesive program of policy reforms to stimulate long-term growth. So he asked Please to become his senior advisor and take charge of the study that had been requested. That's how I got involved.

After working with Stanley Please, I spent two years in Bank operations under Martijn Paijmans as he oversaw valuable but controversial internal reforms. I had hoped for a country assignment as my next move (it would be more than another year before I was sent to Zambia), but Please called and asked that I join the small task force he was putting together to help produce this study. Please had been working in Indonesia and returned at Stern's request, and I felt I couldn't turn him down. I had grown to respect him, I learned a lot from him, and I liked his pitch: that the task force would do its own analysis and come to its own conclusions on recommendations to make for a new Bank approach to Africa. This seemed like a big deal! I was on board. I just had no idea that I was wading into another, even larger controversy.

To the surprise of many, Please and Stern made the decision to go outside the Bank to hire a lead coordinator—Elliot Berg, a well-regarded University of Michigan professor who oversaw the school's Center for Research on Economic Development. Berg, a strong proponent of free markets, had studied and written a lot about African economics.

Our task force consisted of about a half-dozen economists and I had a double distinction—the most junior economist and the only African economist. It was an invigorating experience as we tackled the biggest possible questions.

What factors were most responsible for Africa's situation?

Was it the external factors, such as oil shocks and falling commodity prices?

Was it the internal factors, such as the domestic policies and political instabilities?

How culpable was the state? Or the global lenders?

These were the debates going on in Africa and they were going on inside the Bank as well, including on our task force.

The final version of the Berg Report attributed Africa's stagnation primarily to internal factors, most notably poor governance and state failure. It rejected the industrial policy that many African countries sought, arguing that Africa should return to a focus on export-oriented agriculture. It advocated for less government intervention and unfettered markets to allocate resources. It called for eliminating state subsidies and price controls for wages and imports.

African policymakers reacted sharply. In February 1982, African foreign ministers said the report's "glaring arrogant paternalism" would cost Africans the independence to set their own goals. The next month, the African directors at the World Bank—the same group that had requested the study that led to the Berg Report—denounced it. In April 1982, the Economic Commission for Africa's annual conference of ministers concluded with a declaration that dismissed the Berg Report and reiterated that Africa's official goals and objectives should remain as identified in the

Lagos Plan of Action, which African heads of state had approved in July 1980 as their own response to the continent's crisis.

As an example of pan-African unity and recognition of severe economic problems, the Lagos Plan was admirable. As a viable economic recovery framework for Africa, it fell short.[4] The global development community, including the Bank, didn't embrace it, and that lack of support aggrieved African leaders who felt their own ideas were not being fairly considered. Once the Berg Report came along the following year, it was like throwing a match on a pile of hot tinder.

One of the enduring myths of the Berg Report is that it was a "response" to the Lagos Plan of Action—and an effort by the Bank to subjugate African autonomy. That's simply not true. But that's how many African opinion leaders saw it. Among the most vocal: Adebayo Adedeji, the executive secretary of the Economic Commission for Africa and the driving force behind the Lagos Plan. Adedeji was passionate about Africa, but he was obstinate. When told that the Bank report wasn't meant to undercut the Lagos Plan—and that African governments, via their executive directors to the Bank, had asked for it themselves—Adedeji didn't believe it to be fact. He said it was an insult to be told otherwise. More than three decades later, another generation of African leaders were *still* saying the same thing.[5] Such is the extent of lingering passions over the Berg Report and what it represented to many.

Indeed, the policy recommendations contained within the report were controversial in their own right, but the mere existence of the report created a bitter rift between the Bank and Africa. Once the Bank pushed forward with its adjustment programs despite the opposition, relations frayed even further.

I was in Zambia by this time, so I was well aware of the simmering sentiment. But working at the country level with local policymakers who also wanted a different approach, I could separate the rhetoric from reality. The rhetoric was heated: no African wanted to be seen as a puppet of the World Bank. The reality was that reasonable officials were open to Bank assistance as long as they were not shut out of the decision-making process. In other words, they wanted respect and a shared voice—and rightly so. I didn't forget that lesson once I returned and began working on the programs in Uganda and Kenya.

Few would disagree that history proved the Berg Report's excessive emphasis on free markets and anti-state interventions to be too idealistic—

not to mention wrong. I certainly would not. However, I do still believe, as I believed back then, that lending or financing in the absence of smart, informed policymaking is a waste of resources. This idea, once on the outer edge of development thinking, is now quite commonplace. And although I was on the research team, I did not agree in full with the final report. In fact, I often found myself in respectful disagreement with the principal author. Elliot Berg was a strong academic and an expert on Africa, but he was not an expert *of* Africa. That made a difference. He was committed and passionate, but Western idealism got in the way.[6]

The Bank's *World Development Report 1980*, which came out the same year as the Berg Report, provides an interesting contrast. The *WDR* also dealt with policy adjustments, which McNamara described in the first paragraph of the report's foreword as "a burden that must be shared." The *WDR* was divided into two parts. The first part focused on the need for adjustments in the coming decade as a necessary evil for poverty reduction and human development—the focus of the second part. The *WDR* covered a lot of the same ground as the Berg Report but generally avoided the heavy ideology.

One of the reasons that I accepted the offer from Please was to bring my viewpoints as an African-born economist. I didn't have the credentials of other team members, who had at least 10 or more years of experience over me, but I could tell right away that I held stronger opinions than most of them, save for Berg, of course. My position was junior and I didn't have the clout in 1980 to exert too much influence, but I pushed back whenever I felt it was needed.

For instance, I strongly believed that human capacity—and the lack thereof in most African countries—was a major factor in the poor policies and weak institutions undermining governments. Early drafts completely ignored that fundamental issue. And I never agreed with the outsized role afforded the markets. I argued for more nuance in prescribing how much undeveloped African markets could reasonably accomplish and for more nuance when assessing government capabilities. I grew into a trusted source of feedback for Berg, and over time we settled into a fairly consistent pattern. He would write a few pages and hand them to me. I would look them over and hand them right back.

"No, no, no, Elliot," I would say. "It's not like this because..."

He would listen closely, then always reply, "But I'm writing from the heart."

I'm not trying to disassociate myself from the Berg Report. Indeed, I believe the basic thrust of the recommendations hit the mark, especially the emphasis on getting the fundamentals right, like sound macroeconomic policy and involving the private sector in the production of goods and services and job creation. Most African countries share these objectives today and many are making good progress in attaining them. The key is getting the right balance between the roles of the state and the private sector, which the Berg Report did not do.

◆　◆　◆　◆

Kenya was among the first countries in Africa to go through structural adjustment lending at the Bank, implementing two programs between 1980 and 1983. Both went bust. After the second program collapsed, relations between Kenya and the Bank soured quickly. As would become a typical experience over the next decade, the interpretation of why the programs failed differed between the government and the World Bank and IMF. To the Bretton Woods Institutions, the root causes could be boiled down to weak commitment and poor implementation on the part of the Kenyan officials. But the Kenyans believed the failures were due to harsh lending conditions, unrealistic expectations, and unfair treatment, such as shifting the goalposts and demanding more than the agreed terms.

My job, which started with my initial post as division chief but carried over into the larger AF2CO department after the 1987 reorganization, was to take the lessons learned from the previous misfires and reset relations with Kenya. The most important lesson was one of scope. The earlier programs tried to cover macroeconomic stabilization as well as economy-wide structural policy and institutional reforms. Targeting it all at the same time created too many conditions, caused immense coordination challenges, and stretched implementation capacity too thin. Despite the bad blood, the Kenyan government was open to more Bank assistance, just not under the same terms.

No one wanted to strike out a third time, so we looked for a new way. The end result was an agreement reached with the government to abandon the economy-wide structural loans in favor of a sector-by-sector strategy. These loans became known as sector adjustment loans, or SECALs, and they soon gained widespread popularity across the Bank. We based the approach on a simple premise—that dealing more closely with a concerned sector ministry would engender a greater sense of commitment among the officials in the respective agencies. In the beginning, it was a theoretical assumption. But over time, it proved to be more or less accurate. In Kenya, we embraced SECALs vigorously, and within three years we were preparing loans to support reforms in the agriculture, industrial, and financial sectors.[7]

I visited Kenya every two months, going from ministry to ministry, trying to get to know the local officials and learn how the institutions operated. Kenya's economic decline had undermined its promise as one of Africa's postcolonial success stories, but the country's human capacity remained relatively strong. It boasted educated technicians and sound policymakers who were ready to work with us and were more than capable of carrying on substantive policy discussions. Once we had reestablished good working relations, most of the pieces of the puzzle were in place to try to put the previous failures behind us.

Most, but not all.

The biggest challenge in Kenya was its leadership at the top. Even if we agreed on an economic or sector program, the administration of President Daniel arap Moi would lag on implementation. At best, it was due to political inertia. At worst, it was endemic failings. Corruption had become a major problem and the country's systems lacked transparency and accountability. In fact, a corruption allegation over a major infrastructure project set me on a delicate mission to hand-deliver a letter to Moi. The visit didn't yield much in terms of immediate results, but the aftermath of the controversy influenced the Bank's shift toward recognizing governance as a development issue, not just a political one.

Postcolonial Kenya was in a stronger position to succeed than many of its newly independent African peers. It contained a mix of privately owned and state-run enterprises, and it combined steady growth with decent physical and human infrastructure investments. Between the early 1960s and 1970s, Kenya boasted strong economic growth, reaching as high as 8 percent. The problems began with the 1973 surge in oil costs and were aggravated by a series of factors: drought, trade deficits, unemployment, and deepening poverty.

Following the death of President Jomo Kenyatta in 1978, Moi, who had been vice president since 1967, took over, beginning a 24-year reign as president. He quickly consolidated power, banned opposition parties, and surrounded himself with what the BBC called a "sycophant male court." He continued pro-Western policies started under Kenyatta that ensured large aid flows and Kenya soon reemerged as a relatively "prosperous" African government. But in Kenya, as in many other African countries, corruption was rampant. As political scientist and historian Charles Hornsby wrote, the lack of foreign private investment in Kenya in the 1980s "reflected the high level of bribes demanded as well as the economic environment."

In fact, it was a major infrastructure project in Kenya that finally brought the issue of corruption out of the shadows of global development.

In May 1985, Kenya circulated proposals to several governments and institutions to solicit funding for a new dam and hydroelectric plant to be built in the Turkwel Gorge as part of a major energy initiative. The dam was intended to generate 100–150 megawatts of power and to provide the surrounding communities with irrigation and new income opportunities. The donor community expressed interest, but later in the year, after a few feasibility studies, it was announced that a French consortium, backed by the French government, would be funding the project on commercial terms. A French company, Spie Batignolles, was awarded the job as main contractor, a process that did not go through a competitive tendering process.

The donor community quickly grew suspicious, because the terms of the commercial financing were much more unfavorable to the Kenyan government than what it could have received from other sources, including the World Bank. The Canadian government in particular cried foul. The Kenyan media got in on the act, reporting the lack of competitive bidding and questioning the feasibility studies. Kenya's lack of transparency made project costs very difficult to determine, but rumors and accusations began to fly that the approximate $150 million budgeted cost had soared to more than twice that—implying large kickbacks and internal payoffs.

As this was happening, the Bank was planning its next consultative group meeting in Paris to raise donor support for Kenya's overall development program. A number of donors, led by Canada, strongly objected to holding a donor meeting for Kenya under these circumstances. The Canadians put a lot of pressure on the Bank to investigate the rampant claims of corruption, but the Bank already had its own concerns over the unfavorable financing terms.

The Bank believed the Kenyans needed to reconsider the whole financing structure they had agreed to and was prepared to offer partial funding on its most favorable terms, with lower payments and deferred interest. The decision was made to send a letter directly to Moi, signed by Barber Conable, which made this argument. In order to expedite its delivery, I was asked as head of the division to personally deliver the letter to the Kenyan president. So I set off for Nairobi.

My first stop was the ministry of finance, where I called on Harris Mule, the permanent secretary of the ministry and one of the finest

106

professionals I've ever met. Unlike many in the government, he was known to be incorruptible. He was experienced, educated, and highly respected in Kenya and abroad. I trusted him, but as soon as I mentioned my visit was in connection with Turkwel Gorge he cut me off before I could finish. "Shhhh," he said, refusing to discuss the matter in his office. Later that night, we met for drinks at a hotel. He said he had no details on the project and that it was too sensitive for him to discuss. He agreed to make an appointment for me the following day with his boss, George Saitoti, the finance minister. Saitoti was another Kenyan I easily connected with and we grew closer over the years.[8] But during my visit in 1986, he too refused to discuss Turkwel Gorge, claiming energy projects were outside his area of responsibility.

"But I have this letter and it's urgent," I told him. He said I should meet with Nicholas Biwott, the energy minister and a veteran of Kenyan politics. He was very close to Moi. And very powerful.

I waited around in Nairobi for two more days before I got a call to meet with Biwott. When I arrived at the appointed time, I sat for hours before finally being allowed to see him. It was not a friendly meeting. He had obviously been briefed on the purpose of my visit and it didn't sit well with him. For the first 20 minutes, he only asked questions about my background: how long I had been at the Bank, why I worked there, what my responsibilities were. Then he asked me to explain why I was there, even though I could tell he already knew.

When I told him that I had a letter from Conable to President Moi, he dismissed me with a snide retort: "I see; you are just a delivery boy."

When I told him that the Bank and its donors were urging Kenya to get out of its current questionable financing deal for the Turkwel Gorge dam, he hit the roof. Biwott went on a bitter tirade about the Bank and its condescending attitude toward Africa. If the Bank considered this issue so important, he asked, why hadn't the regional vice president come to see Moi?

"Instead," he said, winding up for a final blow, "they have sent you to do the white man's dirty job for him!"

Biwott was done. He told me I could leave the letter with him to pass along to Moi. If the president wanted to meet me, then I would be contacted. I waited two more days but never got another call. I finally returned to Washington. I don't believe the Bank ever got a response to the letter and I doubt whether President Moi ever actually received it. I had failed miserably as a delivery boy.

Later that year, the Bank went ahead with its consultative group meeting over Kenya. The donors who had complained about Turkwel Gorge were still not happy, but the Bank worked out a compromise of sorts. It promised to put the entire energy sector's investment program on the agenda as a way of getting the Kenyans to also discuss the multimillion dollar dam project. Saitoti, who as finance minister led the Kenyan delegation to the meeting, agreed. He wound up bringing along Biwott and the two of them spoke with bravado and confidence, defending the French financing terms as most favorable to the country. The donors reiterated the importance of ensuring value in public investment programs and, above all, instilling transparency in the process. The meeting was lively and at times tense, but it was not the major confrontation that we all feared. Ultimately, the Bank met its funding targets, and the Kenyans proceeded on Turkwel Gorge with the French contract and their commercial financing.[9]

However, that meeting and the events leading up to it had huge repercussions for how the Bank—and the rest of the world—would come to view the role of governance in development. Within the Bank, it fueled an ongoing debate on whether the institution could keep forbidding its staff from taking political factors into consideration in assessing the viability of an operation. A strict interpretation of the Bank's Articles of Agreement supported the position that the Bank needed only to take into consideration the *economic* justification of a loan; messy political context could be disregarded. Until Turkwel Gorge forced the issue, the Bank didn't want to speak of corruption in the open, much less treat it as an economic factor.

After much soul-searching, Ibrahim Shihata, an Egyptian who at the time was the Bank's general counsel—its chief lawyer—issued a paper justifying the Bank's right to take into consideration corruption and other related political issues. "If the level of corruption is high so as to have an adverse impact on the effectiveness of Bank assistance," Shihata wrote in 1990, "and the government is not taking serious measures to combat it, the Bank can take this as a factor in its lending strategy toward the country."[10]

Around the same time, Kim Jaycox, with the assistance of Dunstan Wai, created the Council of African Advisors, a group of highly-respected men and women of varied backgrounds and professions: policymakers, businessmen, academics, and political figures. Among the members, which numbered about a dozen, were future Liberian President Ellen Johnson Sirleaf and Ali Al'amin Mazrui, a Kenyan academic and literary giant. Jaycox set up the group to provide development advice to the Bank—independent of African governments. The council wound up assisting the production of a major study that examined the evolution of African economies over the first three decades of independence. Published in November 1989, the report was called *Sub-Saharan Africa: From Crisis to Sustainable Growth, a Long-Term Perspective Study.*

In one of the report's major conclusions, many of Africa's development problems over the previous decades could be linked to entrenched leaders and political strongmen who looted public funds and perpetuated a cycle of corruption. Following internal criticism that the view was too political and external criticism that it was too harsh on Africa, the Bank softened its stance but maintained the same core arguments for its future approaches— that in the absence of transparency, accountability, pluralism, rule of law, and respect for human rights, economic growth and development would not take hold. To describe these characteristics, the report coined the term "good governance," now firmly entrenched in development discourse.

In Kenya, the situation continued to deteriorate. In October 1991, the Danish government—historically one of Kenya's biggest donors— announced it would immediately end its 17-year support for rural development after an audit showed that most of the $40 million in that aid program had "disappeared because of corruption." The same year, the British government chose not to give Kenya money to subsidize oil for consumers over fear that politicians would pocket the money. The New York Times quoted US Ambassador Smith Hempstone as saying, "I don't know if Kenya is at the head of the class when it comes to corruption, but they're a contender."

I wouldn't say the World Bank waved a white flag, but we had a hard time gaining any traction in the face of such poor governing conditions. There were good guys, like Harris Mule, but plenty of bad ones, too; enough to thwart our efforts. As other donors were pulling out in 1991, for instance, the Bank decided against a major $100 million program to promote energy production. Meanwhile, the sector adjustment lending that we pioneered in Kenya failed to meet its objectives—though it took off successfully in other countries.

In a November 2000 evaluation, the Bank found little good news when trying to assess the results of almost two decades of program operations. Between 1980 and 1996, Bank commitments in Kenya totaled nearly $3 billion. But, according to the report, "Kenya complied only weakly with Bank conditionality, frequently backtracking on reforms. Disappointing progress occurred under the first two structural adjustment credits (1980–

1983) as well as the subsequent six sector adjustment credits (1986–1992)."
The following year, Kenya's annual growth rate had plummeted to negative
3 percent.

There's an interesting footnote to the Bank's coming to terms with
corruption during this time. Peter Eigen served as the director in the Bank's
Eastern Africa regional office in Nairobi from 1988 until 1991. A good man,
Eigen always had his ear to the ground and never shied from expressing
his frustration—and anger—at the mismanagement of public resources in
Kenya. He and I used to have long talks over dinner at his home, so I always
knew where he stood. Soon after his assignment in Kenya came to an end,
Eigen retired from the Bank. Two years later, he founded Transparency
International to promote accountability in international development.
That organization, based in Berlin, has grown into a global anti-corruption
coalition with chapters in more than 100 countries. Eigen later said that he
had realized something elemental while working in Kenya: the best way to
fight corruption is to let the world know about it.

♦ ♦ ♦ ♦

If Kenya's story in the 1980s exemplified the frustrating nature of an African
state failing to live up to its potential due to poor governance, Uganda's was
the opposite: a story of sound leadership and a commitment to reforms
that set the country on the path to recovery after years of war and economic
collapse.

Let me preface the next few pages by acknowledging the unpredictability
of time. Uganda once put itself in an incredible position to move beyond its
troubled history with reforms that *worked*, only to be held back by the same
leader who had moved it forward. At the time we crossed paths, Yoweri
Museveni took the right steps to turn his country around. But he refused
to leave office. As of this writing, his fifth term will end in 2021, at which
point he will have been in power 35 years—or longer, if he extends it. He's
never laid out a succession plan and Uganda has yet to witness a peaceful
transfer of power since independence from Britain in 1962.

The point of the story here, however, is not how Museveni turned out
but how he began, with Uganda near total collapse. Despite brief attempts
to stabilize and revitalize the economy in the aftermath of the Idi Amin
regime—including donor assistance from the World Bank, IMF, and Paris
Club creditors—recovery remained weak because of lingering structural
problems that had emerged under Amin's rule. For instance, the entire
Ugandan economy turned dangerously inward, with significant protections

given to local industries and the public sector at the expense of outside investments. Amin expelled members of the Asian community, which had dominated the industrial sectors, and expropriated their properties. Efficiency and financial discipline suffered and economic competitiveness disappeared. By 1980, Uganda had become dependent on one crop—coffee, which accounted for 98 percent of its exports. Recovery efforts in the early 1980s stalled, even as GDP weakly grew, because the structural shortcomings were ignored.

By the time Museveni and his National Resistance Movement, or NRM, came to power in 1986, the latest civil war had decimated transport, power, and water facilities, essential commodities were in short supply, prices were escalating rapidly, and the Bank of Uganda had almost run out of reserves. The World Bank wanted to assist, but no dialogue had been established with NRM leaders and a travel ban had been in place since the previous year due to security concerns. We needed an opening to revive the program. In May 1986, we got one.

Uganda's ministry of finance invited a Bank delegation to visit Kampala, the capital and largest city, to discuss the country's rapidly deteriorating economy. The technocrats in the ministry and the central bank believed something had to be done soon, that Uganda didn't have enough time to wait until the dust settled from the latest political coup. We debated the invitation internally for days. Would Uganda's government be capable of taking the necessary actions to tackle its problems? There was considerable skepticism and doubt. We didn't know what to expect from Museveni, who had led a long guerrilla campaign, and we knew the country's human capacity was low.

After much discussion, we made the decision to send not a full team but a single scout to assess the situation and report back to upper Bank management: one staff member would bring fewer security concerns. As head of the division, I volunteered to go.

A pleasant surprise greeted me upon arrival. Museveni had retained many of the deposed government's top officials, including a brilliant young economist named Emmanuel Tumusiime. I had met Tumusiime the previous year, soon after I started the job. He was among a small group of Ugandan officials who had traveled to Washington in the dying days of the previous regime to pitch to the Bank a reform package they hoped to implement. We wanted to help, but we knew it didn't make good sense. With the guerrilla forces of the NRM advancing toward the capital, and Uganda's security situation growing weaker by the day, it was only a matter of time before the government fell. There was nothing the Bank could do.

One of the first things Tumusiime told me after I arrived in Kampala was that he and other holdovers—some of whom had also been part of that Bank visit—remained in favor of major economic reforms. In fact, he said, they had grown so alarmed by the warning signs that they had presented the reforms to Museveni after he assumed power and asked if they could resume talks with the Bank and IMF. Museveni said no. As a lifelong Marxist rebel and a pan-Africanist, he didn't trust the Bank or IMF. He made it clear to Tumusiime and the others that he opposed the policies of both institutions and that he believed neither had anything to offer Uganda.

While I was glad to see Tumusiime, I wasn't encouraged by what he had to say. Government officials had finally reopened the door to the Bank, but they had done it without the backing of their new president, who wanted nothing to do with us. But Tumusiime and his colleagues believed it would be worth the effort for me to pay a courtesy call on the president. I wasn't so sure, but I agreed to go.

Museveni studied economics and political science at the University of Dar es Salaam in Tanzania in the late 1960s, where he became involved with leftist student groups allied with Africa's liberation movement. He returned to Uganda briefly as a political activist, but when Idi Amin came to power in 1971 he went back to Tanzania in exile and established an organization that would help overthrow Amin in 1979. He worked in the transitional government and ran for president in 1980, but lost what he believed to be a rigged election to former President Milton Obote. That's when he helped form the NRM and took charge of the armed wing that waged a five-year guerrilla war. By the time he came to power in 1986, Museveni had spent the better part of 15 years fighting governments and had less than two years working in government. But he wasn't an African warlord who had just come in from the bush. He was educated, intelligent, and so driven to turn his country around that he agreed to meet with a visitor from the World Bank.

Our encounter started pleasantly enough, with the standard protocols on both sides. I explained why I had come to Kampala and that I hoped to gather enough information to restart a Bank assistance program. I recounted the Bank's previous support of Ugandan agriculture, infrastructure, and education projects, all before the situation had deteriorated, so I posed questions and he listened respectfully. When I finished, he laid out the biggest challenges he saw, which centered on the devastation of the country's social and physical infrastructure.

It all felt like a standard affair. But after a few minutes, he took me by surprise.

"I appreciate all that the World Bank has done in the past, helping us build roads and schools," he said, looking at me. He was calm and collected. "But right now we badly need foreign exchange to import fuel and medicine and other critical items. We need $200 million. Will the World Bank help?"

I wasn't sure I heard him correctly. I had no reason to suspect our meeting would take such a sudden turn.

After the fall of Amin, the Bank had tried to help Uganda in the early 1980s with a couple of recovery loans without attaching any major conditions, which would not have been remotely realistic given the condition of the state. The situation was different now, so I wasn't sure what to say. I looked around the room at Tumusiime and the other officials. No one said a word.

I turned back to Museveni and explained that the Bank's business was to promote long-term development through project lending and only on very rare occasions did we provide cash or quick-disbursing funds. If that were to happen, I said, the Ugandan government would have to come up with a policy program we could support.

Museveni grew agitated as I talked. "What do you mean by a *program*?" he asked sharply, the calm instantly gone from his voice. At that point I knew I was in uncharted waters. Once again, I looked at Tumusiime and his colleagues for help. Once again, no one said a word.

I had to think fast. I told the president that it was my understanding that a few weeks prior, he received a proposal of policy reforms from members of his economic team—"ones who are in this very room," I added, just to ensure that if I went down I'd take the silent others with me. "That could be a good starting point."

Museveni exploded. "I knew it!" he said, bolting upright in his chair. "You World Bank people are all the same as the IMF with your conditions." Then he ticked off several measures I knew his economic team had proposed: devaluation of the Ugandan shilling, removal of price controls, public enterprise reforms, liberalizing the coffee market, and more.

He narrowed his eyes and looked back at me.

"What do you find so attractive about them?" he asked, though he didn't let me answer. Before I could speak, he sat back down in his chair and, suddenly calm once more, said, "Let us talk about each one."

That was the beginning of a back and forth that lasted five hours—far from the brief courtesy call I expected.

As the hours rolled by, Museveni really impressed me. He had a deep understanding of the issues and a full awareness of their gravity. He was wrong on many of the technical points, but I grew to admire his determination not to lose an argument. For the first few hours, I pulled my punches. I was deferential and didn't press my arguments too hard.

At midday, he invited the economic team and me to an impromptu lunch, a brief break before we resumed our debate. While I was eating, one of the economic officials walked past me and quickly leaned over to whisper in my ear. This might be a one-time opportunity to make a strong case for reform, he said. I took the hint.

After lunch, I decided to be more aggressive. I got my chance when Museveni again used wrong information to push a couple of technical points. This time I didn't let it pass. "Mr. President, you are incorrect," I told him bluntly. "You're not making any sense."

He stopped speaking and grew silent for a few seconds. Had I crossed the line? Then he stood up.

"Come with me into the garden," he said.

The two of us left Tumusiime and the others in the meeting room and walked outside. We took a seat in chairs placed in the shade underneath a huge, beautiful old tree. No one else was around. He was tired of debating. Instead, he asked me to go back over the issues we had been discussing all morning. In particular, he wanted to know why he should devalue the Ugandan currency. That seemed to be a sticking point. I explained in detail how devaluation would help improve the balance of payments and increase government revenues, among other benefits. He seemed to appreciate that. He didn't argue any other points. He just listened.

After sitting alone in the garden for almost two hours, Museveni called for a few officials to join us. "Keep in touch with Amoako," he said. "Any time he needs to see me, make sure that he does."

That conversation in Kampala kicked off a new era between Museveni's government and the World Bank, a time in which Uganda also made incredible strides in stabilizing its economy and getting on a recovery and growth track. I don't want to imply our half-day debate suddenly flipped a switch in him or somehow saved the day; that certainly wasn't the case. But it did open a door that had been shut. Then it was up to both sides to walk through.

Despite Museveni's willingness to keep an open mind, it still took another year or so to fully embark on a reform program. The process required trust on both sides, and it's a testament to the Ugandan, World Bank, and IMF officials who made it happen and saw it through.[11]

Between 1987 and early 1994, the Bank disbursed about $1.4 billion in loans to Uganda, while economic growth averaged almost 6 percent annually and inflation fell sharply. With the assistance of the Bank as well as the IMF, which disbursed about $446 million over the same period, Museveni and his economic team enacted a series of substantial structural reforms: price liberalization, exchange and payment liberalization, public enterprise reform, financial sector reform, army demobilization, and civil service enhancements. No panacea existed, so even amid the good news major problems persisted: low GDP, weak human capital, and a debt overhang predominantly from non-concessional lending in the early 1980s, before Museveni's government. But Uganda's turnaround is impressive by any standard and even more so when considering the extent of the devastation from which it started. By the mid-1990s, Uganda had gained widespread recognition as one of the most successful turnaround states in Africa—a star performer to be emulated.

Museveni deserves much of the credit. After he got over his initial doubts, he championed the bold changes needed, many times overruling his ministers when he felt they were being too cautious. He displayed a political will for reform that few African leaders had back then. Of course, he needed capable policymakers, and members of his economic team proved strong.

If Museveni drove the political side, Tumusiime drove the technocrats who crafted and implemented. But there were others, like Chris Kassami, a strong advocate for growth-oriented measures who often found himself at odds with the stabilization measures that the IMF pushed. Another critical player was Crispus Kiyonga, Uganda's finance minister who grew impatient with the Bank's slow pace. Often, Kiyonga would call and demand an answer to the same question, over and over: "Where is my money?" I would explain that my division could only do so much. He would keep calling. When I knew I didn't have a good answer, I did what any smart manager would do: avoided him! But in reality, each side knew the other was only a phone call away.

A deep trust developed between our staff in the AF2CO department and the Ugandan policymakers. With two Africans at the top of the department—Callisto Madavo and me—our insistence on local ownership didn't ring hollow or come across as insincere to the Ugandans. They believed we really wanted to help.

Members of our team traveled constantly between Washington and Kampala. And the issues were complex, with difficult political economy implications: fiscal consolidation, including cuts in the defense budget; coffee marketing reforms and agricultural pricing to encourage export diversification; and the return of the Asian properties—the ones seized by Idi Amin—to their owners. A bright young economist, Sanjay Pradhan, who had just come out of the YP program, led our efforts. A future vice president in the Bank, he gained so much respect among the Ugandans that they asked that he come to Kampala for six weeks to work in their ministry of finance. It was an unusual request but we agreed to it.

In May 1994, eight years after the Museveni government reached out, the Bank approved a second adjustment credit of $80 million—a smaller sum reflective of Uganda's gains but also proof that both sides wanted to continue a good story. Tumusiime used to sum up his country's motivations pretty well. He always said Uganda was "not doing any of this" because the World Bank or IMF demanded it but "because it's the right thing to do for the country."

In a 2005 study on economic recovery in low-income countries, researcher Mark Robinson found the design and management of economic and institutional reforms in Uganda "offer important lessons for successful turnaround from a variety of vantage points," including political commitment, the timing and sequencing of reforms, and the role of donors in providing ideas, advice, and financial resources in support of them.

In the years since, Uganda has been ill-served by Museveni's long tenure and lack of policies needed to transform the economy. But a quarter-century ago, when most of Africa was stuck in place or falling behind, Uganda offered hope. And its leaders worked closely—sometimes reluctantly, sometimes angrily, but more times than not productively— with the World Bank and other actors in the development world.

From the Bank's perspective, our relationship was a partnership, where the main goal was to put the Ugandans in the best position possible to achieve their goals—many of which their top policymakers brought to the Bank in the first place, not the other way around.

◆　◆　◆　◆

The story of the Bank's rise in Africa might best be summed up with a familiar saying: be careful what you wish for. According to the Brookings

Institution's World Bank history project, the institution sought—and achieved—increased leadership and influence over an "important and controversial issue: the need for painful, complex, and often politically risky economic reforms." During the 1980s, it achieved that goal but learned that economic reforms, to be successful, often need to be supported by strong institutional and political reforms.

Additionally, the Bank opened itself up to intense scrutiny and controversy over the impact of the strict conditions imposed under adjustment lending, though it did conduct dozens of internal studies to try to better understand the effectiveness of the programs.[12]

By 1990, Bank lending to Sub-Saharan Africa had swelled to almost $4 billion. Of that, approximately 34 percent came in support of some form of adjustment lending, an amount smaller than commonly perceived. At the same time, the Bank increasingly tried to adapt its approach to target country needs, such as increased use of the sector-specific loans we first tried in Kenya.

Still, by the mid-1990s, the chorus of critics had grown sizably. Anti-poverty activists, humanitarian groups, and other nongovernmental organizations (NGOs) roundly criticized the Bretton Woods Institutions—and their donors in the West—for the negative impact structural adjustment had on social development: poverty reduction, health and education services, and so forth.

There's no doubt the heavy debts accrued and public expenditure cuts hindered Africa's ability to invest in human well-being. Though it may not have acted fast enough, the Bank recognized, as it did with governance, that human development mattered for economic development. That's another big operational shift that needed to happen—and one that I was fortunate to be part of.

Notes

1   As Jochen Kraske notes in his book, *Bankers with a Mission*, the change process that Conable began continued for years. In 1989, Conable addressed some of the problems that had arisen in the new structure, while his successor, Lewis Preston, added managing directors in 1991.

2   In addition to the country operations division, three more divisions were under each department with responsibility for sector operations—agriculture, infrastructure, and human development.

3   Looking back now, I know just how fortunate I was to have stumbled across such a dedicated group of men and women, all of them wholly committed to trying to solve the difficult development challenges in their assigned countries. Of the 20 economists

who worked with me during this time, eight would later rise to very senior positions in the Bank, becoming either directors or vice presidents. In baseball, that would be an all-time high batting average.

4   The Lagos Plan of Action broke new ground for what it represented: a blueprint prepared in Africa and endorsed by African countries, from the most Marxist to the most conservative, that attempted to diagnose and fix the continent's economic problems. But in an attempt to champion self-reliance, it was overly nationalistic. It rejected a balanced mix of regional and international investment in favor of a highly introverted and closed-off approach. Multilaterals and big donor countries deemed the plan too unrealistic given Africa's weak skills base and narrow economies and too naive given that international donors would need to pay for most of its proposals.

5   African Union chairwoman Nkosazana Dlamini-Zuma, in a 2013 lecture in Cape Town, South Africa, asked her audience: "Why have we been unable to turn resources, potential, and riches into prosperity?" She then cited external interference as the first answer to her rhetorical question. "When Africans develop their own frameworks, these are immediately followed by other prescripts," she said. "For example, the ink on the Lagos Plan of Action was hardly dry" when the Bank issued the Berg Report and "forced African states into structural adjustment."

6   Elliot Berg wasn't the final voice on the document that came to bear his name. Ernie Stern stepped in, wielded his authority, and actually rewrote significant portions of the report ahead of the final board review, both to inject his opinions and to try to quell internal grumblings.

7   Because Kenya's credit had deteriorated under large debt, funds for all three operations came from the Bank's "soft loan" window, the International Development Association (IDA), and not standard loans from the lending arm. IDA loans have more forgiving interest rates and terms and they remain a major source of assistance for the world's poor countries. This kind of loan was a big sticking point in Kenya. Officials remained angry over the terms of the previous loans, which the Kenyans believed had added to their debt problems.

8   George Saitoti was a key figure in Kenyan politics for decades. He joined Moi's government in 1983 and became vice president in 1988. He also served Moi's successor, Mwai Kibaki, as vice president. We developed a friendship as our careers progressed and he even asked me to write the foreword to his autobiography many years later. He died in a helicopter crash in 2012. At the time, he was serving as Kenya's internal security minister and planning his own presidential run.

9   The Turkwel Dam was completed in 1991 at an allegedly lower cost than originally estimated. According to documents declassified in June 2000, the government conducted multiple feasibility studies and received several competing bids. A Kenyan government investigation cleared high-ranking officials of any wrongdoing.

10   Memorandum of the Vice President and General Counsel, "Issues of 'Governance' in Borrowing Members—The Extent of Their Relevance Under the Bank's Articles of Agreement," Dec. 21, 1990.

11   The Bank's work required enormous collaboration with the IMF—not always an easy task. The mandates of the two institutions require the IMF to take the lead in discussing macroeconomic and stabilization policies with country governments. Without agreement on key issues, such as exchange rate and monetary policies, the Bank cannot

advance far with its operations. But the staff of the two institutions often disagree. During my years at least, Bank staff were often more sympathetic to the position of governments while the Fund took a more "bottom line" approach. We certainly had our share of disagreements in Uganda.

12 The Bank sponsored several post-mortem studies. By mid-1995, 24 reviews on poverty issues and 22 poverty-assessment reports on Sub-Saharan countries had been completed. Most of those reviews reached a similar conclusion: adjustment programs, when implemented consistently, generally helped improve economic performance, but not significantly, and often to the detriment of valuable government services.

Chapter 4

Shifting Perspectives
Behind the Bank's 'Cultural Revolution' for Social Development

To mark their fiftieth anniversary, the World Bank and IMF decided to stage a two-day conference in Madrid, Spain, in late September 1994 as a prelude to their annual meetings a few days later. The stated purpose was not only to celebrate a notable milestone but to use the occasion as "an opportunity for reflection and for reassessing the roles of our institutions as we approach the twenty-first century."[1] They invited notable economists, global finance ministers, and policymakers to speak on a variety of development issues, but those voices weren't the ones that the rest of the world heard. They were drowned out by the roar of party gatecrashers who turned the high-profile event into a made-for-TV debacle.

The Bank president at the time was Lewis Preston, who had succeeded Barber Conable in 1991. As he arrived in Madrid, so many demonstrators had pitched tents along the highway into town that one journalist said the scene resembled a "refugee encampment." These weren't peaceful demonstrators, either.

As delegates collected their credentials, anti-Bank activists staged a "die-in" nearby. Others covered themselves in coarse blankets—in supposed solidarity with indigenous people uprooted by Bank-supported projects—and blocked the conference entrance. About 1,800 journalists were credentialed to cover the conference and Bank–IMF meetings, but some were wolves in sheep's clothing, using their access to promote demonstration marches and disrupt the proceedings from within. A press conference held by Preston came under particular assault. As police searched the bags of journalists entering the room, they seized a pie and a can of shaving cream meant for Preston's face. When the Bank president began to speak, hecklers accredited as journalists stood up and shouted that 50 years of the Bank was enough.

Bank officials anticipated the protests, but the extent and radical nature of the chaos still caught them off guard and it became the defining story of the fiftieth anniversary. A few days after the embarrassing press conference, the ceiling really fell in—figuratively, if not literally. As Preston delivered his keynote speech during the official opening ceremony for the annual meetings, two activists managed to scale the rafters of the conference hall and drop fake dollar bills on the crowd, many with inflammatory inscriptions: "redeemable for ozone destruction" being one example.

Needless to say, this was not exactly the celebration the Bank and IMF had planned.

The disruption in Madrid can be attributed mainly to the "50 Years Is Enough" campaign, a network comprised primarily of environmentalists, anti-poverty activists, and NGOs that formed to protest what they saw as harmful and detrimental policies imposed on poor countries by the Bank and also the IMF. But for the purpose of this chapter I will stick to the Bank. The movement was global and it spread quickly—some 125 groups from more than 50 nations claimed to show up in Madrid. It was a broad coalition of voices that ranged from the militant, such as calling for the Bank's dissolution, to the more measured, such as calling for more aggressive responses to poverty. Among these activists on the political Left, the Bank was seen as too insular, too secretive, too slow, and too beholden to an increasingly globalized financial order.

But the Bank was under fire from critics on the political Right, too. By 1995, net flows of private capital to developing countries neared $250 billion per year—dwarfing the $20 billion or so that the Bank provided. American legislators who remained unhappy with the Bank's operational costs—or simply opposed the Bank outright—began to cite the increased amount of private sector money to argue against the Bank's relevance, or at least in favor of substantial reductions.

The Bank also had to deal with a number of self-inflicted wounds around the same time, the most notable being an internal review known as the Wapenhans Report. In February 1992, only a few months into his term as president, Preston ordered a study of the overall quality of Bank projects. Willi Wapenhans, a well-respected and recently retired Bank vice president, chaired the task force that undertook the review. The group's conclusions were damning: the Bank's procedures and initiatives tended to reward project and program design, including lending, at the expense of implementation and follow-up. As a result, more than one-third of all Bank projects were deemed "unsatisfactory." Any nuance needed to judge the report fairly—such as the many different factors that can affect project performance, or the fact that "unsatisfactory" was a subjective measure— was lost in the ensuing uproar.

But there was more. In 1994, another independent review team that had been commissioned to study a set of dam projects along India's Narmada River criticized the Bank and the government of India for falling short of stated policies and guidelines on resettlement and environmental issues. Meanwhile, the Bank was in the process of building a gigantic new headquarters in downtown Washington, DC—a project beset by delays and cost overruns that easily fed into the emerging narrative of the Bank as bloated and inefficient, unable to manage the construction of its own building, much less projects around the world.

By the time of the annual meetings in Madrid, I had been at the Bank for two decades, and there had *always* been critics calling for more transparency, more accountability, and more reform. But the pressure that had built up by the fiftieth anniversary felt different, more combustible.

The fact is that it had been building for a while, rooted in a growing sense that the structural adjustment policies of the 1980s had so favored austerity measures and free markets that the Bank had lost its soul as a proponent of the poor.

As the first volume of *The World Bank: Its First Half Century* points out, the perception that the Bank had sidelined poverty alleviation seemed to grow year over year, but not without cause. As far back as 1983, an external affairs officer noted that Bank activities had "become markedly less focused on reducing poverty. This is a potential public relations problem." Indeed, that year's annual report had no section devoted to poverty for the first time in many years. Neither did the annual reports in 1984 and 1986, while the 1985 report had a sentence devoted to poverty. An internal evaluation of loan operations for fiscal year 1984 verified the steady decline in lending over the previous five years "for sectors considered to offer the most direct results to the poor," including primary education, population, health, and nutrition, among others.

There were quite a few factors at play, not just adjustment lending demands. Poverty projects were more difficult to implement because of the greater effort required to reach the very poor in most countries. Those projects required more time, staff, and resources, and were much harder to measure. Meanwhile, the G7 finance ministers, whose countries represented the Bank's primary shareholders, were not pushing the Bank on poverty-focused lending, either.

By the second half of the decade, the trend was notable enough to make its way into public dialogue. In May 1987, a symposium in Helsinki, Finland, on economic development in poor countries posed the question: "Has the World Bank abandoned its focus on poverty alleviation?" That same year, the United Nations Children's Fund published a scathing critique of Bank policies under the title *Adjustment with a Human Face.* The book was a collection of case studies intended to demonstrate the "social costs of adjustment," or the decline in the quality of health care, education, and other social needs in countries undergoing structural adjustment lending. Some people inside the Bank questioned the way the book analyzed and presented its data, but on a personal level, it connected with an audience who strongly believed that the Bank need to shift its perspective. In terms of image and perception, the Bank had already lost a war that many probably didn't even know it was fighting.

On December 31, 1991, Lewis Preston issued a directive that reaffirmed the Bank's position on anti-poverty approaches: "Sustainable poverty reduction is the Bank's overarching objective." Going forward, poverty reduction would be the benchmark by which the Bank would measure its performance as a development institution. Preston also said the Bank would take into account a nation's record on social justice and human rights when considering a loan.

The Financial Times, said Preston had "served notice of a cultural revolution" in the Bank's approach. Indeed, both Preston and Conable, who launched multiple poverty-directed initiatives focused on African famine, used their position as Bank president to try to reframe the Bank's position on poverty and social development and push for more action.

For the Bank, the repeated missteps in the early 1990s, on top of the criticism of its adjustment policies, only seemed to reinforce the notion of an institution unmoored from the human side of economic development and unconcerned with the needs and capacities of the countries in which it operated.

"The World Bank is an institution out of time and place," declared the first of three dozen essays published in the 1994 book *50 Years Is Enough: The Case Against the World Bank and the International Monetary Fund.* The book attracted considerable attention when it was released, and while some of the authors seemed more interested in providing shock value than solutions, others offered meaningful arguments. For example, the book's preface is written by Muhammad Yunus, a Bangladeshi economist who in 1983 founded the Grameen Bank, which offers small loans to the poor.

Yunus makes a couple of striking points: that the Bank's conceptual framework was never designed to fight poverty and as a result the fluctuating focus on poverty issues came in the form of "humanitarian add-ons" and social "safety net" programs and thus tackled the symptoms, not the cause; and that the people hired at the Bank were not hired to eradicate poverty from the world but hired for professional qualities that may not, in fact, translate into crafting and carrying out anti-poverty strategies.

In some ways, I believe this thinking was both right and wrong, but I think it also shows the nuance required when criticizing the Bank in broad strokes or at a philosophical level. It's easy to lose sight of the day-to-day contributions of Bank staff who overwhelmingly—at least in my observations—cared more about making a difference in poor countries than anything else. As someone who began working on the social policy side of Bank projects—not just in Africa but globally—during this tumultuous time, I have a slightly different take.

The Bank certainly had its institutional shortcomings in the area of human development. And its rather tortured history of understanding and guarding against environmental impacts, which was one of the main drivers of the anti-Bank movement, has been well documented. But the Bank also began to get more serious about reconciling its rhetoric on poverty reduction with its work on the ground. As always, the process was slow and not nearly as interesting as the images of protesters scaling rafters, so it got far less attention. Yet the shift toward social development is a notable part of the Bank's evolution, and it brought ramifications for Africa as well as my career.

◆　◆　◆　◆

During my first 15 years at the Bank, I worked on Africa more often than not. I had developed a reputation as a young, aggressive manager with a knack for turning around troubled country programs. Being able to focus on African development is what I had hoped to do, so in that regard I was fortunate. But there was a downside. At that time, the Bank had a policy: to be promoted to director, you had to have cross-regional experience. So to take the next step, I knew that I would have to leave the Africa region to work elsewhere, which is how I ended up making a lateral move to the Latin America division. It's not what I ever intended. I wanted to transition to Asia, where the divisions seemed to be a better match for my experience and interests. But I never really had the choice. To understand why is to understand the context of the time—and the insular methods by which Bank staff moved into leadership positions.

The Bank hierarchy was fairly straightforward back then, starting with staff and moving up through division chief, director, and ultimately vice president. There were only so many regions and so many upper management positions—after the Conable reorganization, the whole Africa region only had six directors. So being a division chief was a big deal and a great job to have, one that could sometimes take 20 years or more to get. And since division chiefs outnumbered directors, it was about as high as you could go, on average. Consequently, the relatively few VPs at the top of the command chain wielded enormous power.[2]

At the time, the Bank had what it called "succession planning," wherein the top brass—a few senior managers, vice presidents, and sometimes the Bank president—would meet periodically to discuss open positions and how best to fill them. They would review the division chiefs and make assessments, identifying the ones they believed had the potential to become directors. They would do the same for directors they viewed as possible future VPs.

So division chiefs actually had very little say when moving from one region to another. They would go where the bosses agreed to place them. Sometimes negotiations were involved, sometimes not. If it sounds like I'm describing a small group of men sitting around a backroom table cutting deals and doling out fates, well, that's not too far off.

During one of these meetings in 1990, my name came up. By then, the East Africa division I managed had a top-notch, cohesive staff in place and we were delivering a strong pipeline of projects and studies in partnership with our countries. But I had been there for more than four years: from a career advancement perspective, it was time to move on. The VPs talked nicely about me in the meeting, but that's all it was—talk. The compliments were generous, but they didn't lead anywhere, trailing off with an unspoken word.

"He's done a good job in tough countries (but)…"

"He knows how to put a good team together (but)…"

"He still has growth potential (but)…"

Kim Jaycox was in the room and something didn't sit right with him. Why so much qualified praise without anyone stepping forward to put me in their division? He didn't like the subtext of what he heard. After a short while, he spoke up with a blunt opinion: "Given this guy's track record in Africa, he could get any country job he wanted—if he were not African."

Jaycox might have been the only man in the Bank who could have raised the specter of racism directly to the Bank vice presidents and gotten away with it.

Shahid Husain, the vice president for the Latin America and Caribbean (LAC) region, sat next to Jaycox. Husain had been the VP in East Africa when I began my post-YP career as the country economist for Sudan. I attended a few meetings he chaired, but we never interacted and he certainly did not have a reason to remember me. He was a powerful figure inside the Bank, with an authority and intimidating reputation that preceded him—if you screwed up working under him, you had probably screwed up your career. He joined the Bank in 1963, a Pakistani who came to the Bank, like many others, by way of the London School of Economics and Oxford. He impressed immediately, catching the eye of Robert McNamara and earning his first vice presidency—the first of five throughout his Bank career—in East Africa in 1974. He had been in the upper ranks ever since.

Even after Jaycox made his pitch, the vice presidents still seemed content to pass me over. Except Husain. When no one else spoke up, he turned to Jaycox and said, "I think I have something for him."

Jaycox called me after the meeting and explained what happened. He assured me that my qualifications weren't in doubt, but his assurance didn't make the situation any more pleasant. I appreciated Jaycox going to the mat for me, but once he had told me that he and Husain had agreed to work something out, I told him that I would respectfully pass on LAC. I still wanted to work in Asia and at this point I felt I had built up enough institutional equity to have some input into part of the process. Jaycox seemed disappointed in my lukewarm reaction. He thought I would be excited and he urged me to go talk to Husain.

"Thanks, but no thanks," I said.

A few days later, Husain asked me to his office. I hadn't changed my mind, but I couldn't turn down the request. It was our first meeting, cordial but direct. He wanted me to take over the division responsible for human development projects in the Brazil department. Nancy Birdsall, a well-respected economist who was the current manager, would be taking over the region's environmental division—a clear sign that environmental issues were gaining traction inside the Bank.

Husain had looked over my personnel file closely. He didn't think it made good sense for me to change divisions but do the same job. I needed experience on the project lending side of things, he said, and LAC could offer that.

"You could become a director in two years if you do a good job here," he said.

I expressed my gratitude, but I honestly doubted he had the right person for the job. I didn't speak a word of Portuguese. I had only been to Latin America once and that was for a family vacation. I was a general economist, not an expert on education or health. And I had spent my entire career in the Bank working on macroeconomic and country programs, never project lending. I also had reasons I didn't share with Husain, namely that I worried about being set up to fail in a job that I didn't seek nor possess the qualifications—in my view at least—to hold.

So I told him what I told Jaycox—thanks, but no thanks.

Husain just smiled at me from across his desk. "Mr. Amoako," he said, calmly, "I suggest you take a little more time to make your decision."

I doubt he believed I would ever be so arrogant as to reject the offer. Brazil was an important country for the Bank and it was a big deal for him. It's where he made a name for himself decades before and it's where he was working when McNamara pulled him out and put him on to the path to bigger and better things. But there was even more to it than that.

Husain had gone against the grain in making personnel picks before, including another time he had thrown his weight behind an African, my good friend Callisto Madavo. His situation had been the opposite of mine— he had worked mostly on country projects but needed more experience on the country policy—or "programs"—side. His resumé was sterling, but when he went up for a job as division chief in Pakistan, some people inside the Bank openly questioned whether Pakistanis would accept an African leading the Bank's policy dialogue. When he was a young teenager, Husain had moved to Pakistan following the British partitioning of India into two sovereign countries in 1947. He graduated from the University of Karachi in 1952 and joined the Pakistani civil service in 1956. He was so offended by the racist connotation of the speculation regarding Madavo and the Pakistanis that he firmly intervened to ensure that Madavo got the job. Years later, Madavo would become a vice president in the Africa region.

Husain's patience with me only lasted so long. I took "a little more time" as he suggested not only to think it over but to talk it out. I asked co-workers and colleagues for their advice, openly expressing my hesitations. When word got back to Husain, he wasn't pleased.

So he called me to his office again, with less patience than before. And rightly so. It took me way too long to realize what Jaycox and others had tried to get into my head—I never really had a decision to make in the first place. If the other VPs were so hesitant to hire me now, what would change in another three, four, or six months? Husain had truly made me an offer I couldn't refuse.

And then there was the race issue, which was uncomfortable but couldn't be ignored. Not only did Husain stand up for me, but he sent a clear message to the other VPs in the process. I would be a fool to undercut him.

I sat in his office, this time less cocksure in what I thought I knew, and he smiled at me once again from across his desk. "Mr. Amoako," he said, "have you made your decision now?"

He already knew the answer.

◆　◆　◆　◆

I took over as division chief for the Bank's population and human resources division in Brazil in September 1990 with an eye toward reviving the country's stagnant lending program. It was a scenario I knew well: Brazil had no interest in receiving Bank funds, local policymakers were fed up with what they perceived to be the Bank's strong-armed approach, and the division's operational structure was stretched thin. It was certainly a situation in which I had found myself before, and I soon knew why Husain wanted to put me there.

But the comparison to previous countries on which I had worked, such as Kenya or Uganda, only went so far. In Brazil, the project pipeline was mostly bare and the dialogue with the government was strained, but the division itself had been in great hands under my predecessor, Nancy Birdsall. Knowing I had to follow in her footsteps only added to my initial unease. She has long been one of the world's leading development economists, greatly admired for her impressive career at the Bank and beyond.[3]

Birdsall took over as division chief during the 1987 reorganization, brought in to elevate the quality of the Bank's work on Brazil's social sectors, particularly on education, to try to get the government's attention. The department had published very little analytical work in the past and the ongoing projects were considered traditional and ineffective. In Brazil, key social indicators—such as school enrollment rates, access to education, and infant and maternal mortality—were worse than many countries at lower levels of development or per capita income. It was widely accepted that the poor quality of Brazil's social sectors was holding the country back.[4] The hope was that by providing good recommendations underpinned by solid research, the Bank could reignite the government's interest in a lending program to bolster its social development.

To meet the challenge, Birdsall overhauled the division to bring in a new crop of talented young economists. In a few years, her team turned out some excellent studies that pulled no punches about Brazil's lagging education and health outcomes, attracting the attention of Brazilian economists and a fair amount of publicity in the mainstream media. Nevertheless, the government remained unmoved and the extensive project lending sought by the Bank remained stalled. By the time I came on board in 1990, the pipeline of human development projects in Brazil had plummeted from over $200 million a few years back to less than $30 million, an embarrassingly low level.

Because the program had shrunk so much, only seven people remained in the division when I took it over. One of them, Barbara Bruns, was an articulate protégé of Birdsall's. I had heard great things about her, so before starting the new job I invited her to lunch. She was blunt about the challenges I would face by not knowing the region, its key players, or even its language very well. I opened up to her about my doubts—the same ones I had expressed to Husain. I must have sounded quite dispirited, because Bruns gave me a pep talk that I never forgot. She assured me that the other staff were eager to work with me and ready to move forward. She even cheered me up over the language barrier, saying I could learn Portuguese and she would help push me along.

Getting that reassurance meant a lot, given the broken team that greeted me in East Africa. But she was right. We operated with a skeleton crew for the first six months or so, but everyone bought into the "band of brothers" mentality, though "band of sisters" would be more appropriate—all but one member of our small team was a woman.

In addition to Bruns, Helen Saxenian was another standout, and they both quickly put me through the paces. Saxenian tutored me on health issues and Bruns on education. I wasn't exaggerating when I worried about not knowing the ins and outs of the job—project identification, preparation, appraisal, and supervision; there was much ground for me to cover. They ensured that I learned in a hurry, and everything we subsequently accomplished was largely due to their efforts, not mine. And at their urging, I even took Portuguese lessons.

None of it would have mattered, however, without the strong support and backing of Armeane Choksi, our boss. Choksi and I didn't have a particularly warm relationship at the start and considering the circumstances of my appointment—Husain made the decision to hire me without consulting Choksi—that's hardly surprising. Fortunately, our relationship improved over a short period of time. Choksi admired my leadership style and I grew to admire his manner and intelligence. I also found him fun to be around—an unabashed free-market economist in the true "Chicago school" mold. We didn't share the same philosophies or political leanings, but we shared the same goal: to get results. We became good friends, and his support helped make a tough job easier.

As a developing country, Brazil offered startling contrasts in economic inequality. Sophisticated cities in the southeast region—São Paulo, Rio, Belo Horizonte—had vibrant industries, shopping malls, universities, and world-class hotels. The cultural scene in these cities was dazzling. Dining in São Paulo's top restaurants, you might easily be in London or New York. Even more important, Brazil had a critical mass of scientists, economists, and other academics trained at the world's top institutions but living and working back at home. And yet, in the mostly rural areas in Brazil's northeast, residents lived in extreme poverty, with terrible social services. There, the understaffed and overlooked schools trapped poor children in cycles of repetition before spitting them out, and access to basic health care was extremely limited, a particularly egregious oversight given Brazil's HIV/AIDs crisis and the outsized impact the virus had on the poor and the most vulnerable.

Brazil's open and aggressive media didn't hesitate to criticize the government for its failings. One of the Bank reports produced under Birdsall exposed the inequality of Brazil's public spending on social programs and the country's largest weekly news magazine, Veja, made it the cover story—with an actual picture of the "confidential" World Bank report.

In my first few months on the job, I took several trips to Brasilia, the capital city, to meet with officials in the finance, education, and health ministries. Either Bruns or Saxenian, who both spoke Portuguese fluently and already knew many key government officials, accompanied me on these trips and helped smooth the way. We also met scores of Brazilian experts with compelling diagnoses of Brazil's social problems. But it soon seemed that such efforts might not matter. The government officials we met made it crystal clear that they were not keen at all to borrow from the Bank for the social sectors. And they were adamant against us working toward that end.

They had their reasons, some more noble than others.

In the division, our objective was to revive the lending program in support of three specific outcomes in Brazil: improve the quality of and access to education, improve nutrition and health services, and promote early childhood development. On the "client" side, this involved getting the government to agree to a project's terms and parameters—easier said than done. On the Bank side, the process involved identifying, preparing, and appraising projects for approval by the board of directors, often involving tens of millions of dollars for each project.

Completing a project can take several years—five or more in many cases—so once it's been agreed and approved, there is the follow-through period: supervising the implementation by working closely with the relevant government agency or ministry to ensure that the project stays on track and achieves its particular outcome. On occasion, things do not turn out as intended and a project becomes a "problem project," requiring considerable effort to put it back on track—altering the design, increasing staff, spending more money. Given the Bank's work in low-income and developing countries—many of which are politically or economically unstable, lack sufficient infrastructure, and are deficient in institutional capacity—the margin for error between a "good" project and a problem project is very thin, before factoring in administrative or bureaucratic missteps within the Bank. This is one reason the Wapenhans Report seemed so negative, especially to outside observers—it's a lot harder to get development projects to the finish line than not.

The portfolio I inherited in Brazil was littered with problem projects from the past. For several years, predating Nancy Birdsall's tenure, the country had borrowed hundreds of millions of dollars from the Bank to finance education and health projects, particularly in the poorer northeastern states. Many of the projects had fallen far short of their goals. Moreover, these were standard Bank loans, rather than International Development Association (IDA) "credits," which have longer repayment periods and zero interest. The loans added to Brazil's mounting debt—and the bad blood between local policymakers and the Bank.

Unlike physical infrastructure development that yields quick benefits, such as new roads or irrigation systems, the yield from social sector projects—human capital development—is of a long-term nature, requiring patience and sustained engagement. Brazil's government believed its previous health and education projects, therefore, should have been funded under the more forgiving IDA terms. That argument didn't fly inside the Bank, since Brazil's per capita income was too high to qualify for IDA credits. Believing it had gotten a raw deal and that the Bank was too inflexible, the Brazilian government had little interest in further borrowing for social development.

Still, it wasn't just loan history that hindered the efforts, but Brazil's own macroeconomic and political turmoil. President Fernando Collor de Mello had entered office in 1990 with the promise of getting Brazil's hyperinflation under control but was largely unsuccessful. In the meantime, his administration was caught in a corruption scandal that led to his impeachment in September 1992 and eventual resignation three months later. Finance ministers came and went, as did the ministers in health and other sectors, as several were implicated in the corruption scandal. This situation meant Bank staff had very little stability in terms of government counterparts, at least at the federal level.

When I took over the division, there had only been one new education project in more than six years—and it went to the southeastern state of São Paulo, hardly the place that most needed World Bank support. The real challenge was in the arid, impoverished areas of the northeast, where a handful of family dynasties maintained political power through blatant nepotism and gross misuse of public resources, such as contracting for school supplies that never came.

Background studies on education in the northeast found an average of eight low-level employees on the payroll for every teacher and in-depth audits showed that many of these employees actually worked in other sectors. With no money for teacher salaries, a teacher outside the capital cities in the northeast earned $4 per month—75 percent lower than the national minimum wage. No wonder the caliber of teachers was low and their motivation even lower. Many people I met during my early visits to Brazil—in academia, business, even in government—deplored the situation, but no one seemed to believe it could be disrupted. No one seemed able to imagine, for instance, that education spending could achieve learning results rather than political patronage.

The governors in the region had been expecting a new World Bank project proposal to come their way, structured as usual with a cut for each of the nine states and negotiated politically with the ministry of education. But Bruns had another idea. She wanted to change the incentives and introduce a performance-based approach. After producing evidence that state education payrolls were bloated with tens of thousands of low-level employees and "ghosts," she proposed linking states' share of the project funding to their progress in reducing administrative staff, increasing teaching staff, and raising teacher salaries. Bolstering her innovative idea: the first-ever management audits of the education secretariats in the northeast region, which the Bank initiated and were carried out by McKinsey and Arthur Andersen. The studies provided a detailed and sobering picture of secretariats staffed to do practically everything *but* education.

This preparation work was on my desk the day I arrived, but the dialogue with the government had stalled, partly for the reasons described, partly for its own self-interest. The governors in the northeast clearly perceived the political adjustments this project would trigger and balked. Meanwhile, the federal ministry was no more eager to upset the long-standing and mutually beneficial tradition of education funding for political back-scratching.

Equally problematic in my view was the fact that we had no other project proposals on the horizon. *Zero.* The cupboard, as they say, was bare. This was not a good thing—for the Bank's goals or mine.

The Bank really wanted to reestablish relations with the government for the same reason it had during Nancy Birdsall's tenure: a growing realization among economists that Brazil was on the cusp of turning the corner—which it eventually did, to great acclaim[5]—if it could start to address its inequality and improve its dreadful social indicators. Meanwhile, Shahid Husain's words from our first meeting had stayed with me: "You could become a director in two years if you do a good job here." Though he didn't put an actual deadline on me, I put one on myself. Given how long it takes to go through the project proposal and approval process for projects, I knew that if I wanted to have anything significant to show in just two years, then I needed to find a new way around an old problem.

As I mentioned in Chapter 1, American students made up the majority of my PhD class at the University of California-Berkeley. But there were a few world nationals, including myself and two Brazilians, Pedro Malan and Regis Valdes, with whom I became fast friends. We got along great and even formed our own study and support group, meeting almost every Sunday to go over weekly assignments. After graduation, my two buddies returned to Brazil. Malan later became his country's finance minister, while Valdes went into business and, over the years, made some important government connections. I decided to turn to Valdes to see if he had any advice on how to proceed with the dialogue so that I might make a breakthrough. He agreed to help and arranged a dinner between me and a top official in the education ministry. It was like déjà vu.

For more than two hours, my dinner companion gave me an earful about how frustrated the Bank's approach had made him and his colleagues throughout the government. I learned the old loans weren't the only reason—the Brazilians believed that many of the problematic projects in the northeast were not adequately prepared, were rushed to meet Bank lending targets, and were conceived primarily to advance the career of the staff pushing for them. In other words, a variation on the same argument I had heard since Zambia—that Bank staff weren't collaborating nor taking the needs of the client country into account.

I referred to the studies that Nancy Birdsall's team had prepared, presenting them as the basis for a new pipeline of projects—and proof that the Bank could learn from the past failures. He agreed that we had done some outstanding analytical work but made it clear that Brazil's economists didn't agree with many of the Bank's recommendations. In some areas, he said, they had serious misgivings about the Bank's analysis and conclusions.

So at that point, I proposed something truly innovative—and quite risky—as a way of breaking the logjam: Brazilian officials should determine the areas where they need the most support and make a proposal to the Bank based on those findings. So their proposal, not ours, would form the basis of a new lending program.

"*You* come to *us*," I said.

On top of that, I promised that I and any other Bank staff would stay away from Brazil for at least six months to give the government plenty of time and space to identify priority projects on their own.

My thinking was to create a new template for engagement—with the client country in the lead and the World Bank in the unfamiliar role of listener and support partner. I figured if the Brazilians didn't want to work with the Bank under the traditional terms, why not change the terms?

He agreed to take the idea back to his colleagues, run it up the proper channels, and get back to me with an answer.

We were clear about the technical criteria that potential projects would have to meet, as well as the format and timetable for generating their ideas. As I promised, they would have a six-month window. But beyond that, we were willing to back off and turn what we had over to the Brazilians. We promised to share data and documentation on World Bank projects tackling similar problems in other countries. We offered to pass along the research and studies that Birdsall's team had conducted. We even offered to pay for local Brazilian consultants—identified by the finance and planning ministry—to help out. Essentially, I was willing to turn over the tens of thousands of dollars I had left in my administrative budget to the Brazilians if they were willing to take the lead.

All of this represented a drastic departure from the norm. Typically, the Bank sent its own staff and consultants to the borrowing country to identify a new project in close consultation with local officials. My offer upended decades of that practice.

Within a few short weeks, the Brazilian government agreed to sign on. Armeane Choksi, my boss and the department's, was skeptical at first, but he eventually gave the initiative his full support. And what soon became known in the Bank and Brasilia as the Project Identification Exercise (PIE) was born.

The experiment worked better than I could ever have imagined. The Brazilians took the opportunity to shape their own development agenda and ran with it. In fact, a number of state-level governments formed their own teams of local experts to prepare project proposals. Once the six months were up, Brazil presented us with 24 potential projects. Or, put another way, they generated on average one full project proposal per week.

We didn't want to lose momentum, so we moved quickly. We invited a team of government officials to Washington for a week of intensive technical discussions and also to find common ground. There, we agreed on a priority list of 12 projects for further preparation. Of those 12, eight ultimately were approved by the Bank's board and became a reality. One of these was a pioneering health project for tackling the HIV/AIDS crisis that contributed to Brazil's success in curbing the pandemic.

By the early 1990s, HIV infection rates were soaring, especially in poor and developing regions. Yet Brazil had been among the world's most aggressive countries in trying to slow the spread of the virus. Its first public policy responses, in the form of information awareness campaigns, began in the early 1980s and were incredibly progressive for a time when most world leaders still had their heads in the sand. Still, the virus spread rapidly. Between 1987 and 1989, the total number of diagnosed AIDs cases in Brazil had tripled.

At the same time inside the Bank, and somewhat contrary to popular perception, there were many who knew the institution needed to get more deeply involved in the HIV pandemic. At the time, the Bank could point to only one HIV-related intervention in India, though that project had been considered a success.

Given Brazil's needs and the Bank's motivations, a clear opportunity presented itself. Under the PIE approach, we jointly devised the $160 million AIDS Project I to try to reduce HIV transmissions and also better equip public and private institutions to manage the outbreak. The project became one of the Bank's first full-scale HIV funding interventions and it greatly influenced the design of World Bank lending to fight HIV/AIDS in many other countries.[6]

The credit here goes to Maureen Lewis, a talented health economist and expert who spent more than two decades at the Bank. She was key to the project's success. I had moved on to my next stop before the project ramped up, but I followed it from afar and, knowing its origins, was keen to see it thrive.

Unfortunately, the successful template we pioneered with PIE still couldn't break the logjam over the northeast education project. That required real political leadership at the ministerial level, which was more than we could offer. So it was a stroke of luck that José Goldemberg was named minister of education during my tenure—the first of several visionary ministers who would transform Brazilian education over the next two decades.

One of Brazil's most respected scientists, Goldemberg endorsed our concept of a "competitive model" for the northeast project, with funding allocations based on states' performance. Moreover, he proposed to split the project in two: the first five states to sign on to the new approach would get a larger share of the total funding. But in every case, states would receive their annual allocations *only* after demonstrating they had reached their annual targets recommended by the audits, including hiring more qualified teachers and paying them better.

Eventually, the northeast projects were approved and totaled more than $1 billion, split between the government and the Bank—the largest education loans the World Bank had made at that time. However, the biggest legacy of the projects might have been the relatively small amount allocated to a "national component"—funding for the ministry of education to improve its operations and strengthen its functionality. Foremost among these improvements: the creation of the country's first national learning assessment. Today, Brazil's system of education results measurement is one of the most sophisticated in the world.

The speed and scale of it all was quite astonishing. By mid 1992, the portfolio of projects under preparation in our division alone would represent almost 30 percent of *all* new World Bank projects in the area of human development. Although that figure included projects that we had also developed in Peru and Venezuela—those two countries had been added to my division in 1991   the bulk of the new lending resulted from the Brazil PIE. In just under two years, we went from a barely existent program to a pipeline of social development projects worth approximately $2.5 billion.

The turnaround was a major breakthrough for Bank efforts in Brazil, but I like to think we accomplished much more than that. The steps we took were nontraditional, but they helped show the potential benefits of using a much more collaborative approach and emphasizing local ownership and capacity. We proved it was possible to achieve good results by treating borrowing countries not as faceless clients to whom terms should be dictated but as informed partners who can set their own agendas.

Our efforts were well considered, but they weren't overly complex. We focused on high-value, socially relevant projects. We treated our country counterparts as true partners, talking with them rather than at them. We empowered local leaders to act in their own best interests. And we invested in good, qualified staff.

We were able to do all that because we had support from above. Shahid Husain believed in putting a strong emphasis on human resource development in the Bank's assistance strategies for the three countries I oversaw, the rationale being that Brazil, Peru, and Venezuela had to do more than other countries in this area for their economic development. As such, he allocated considerable resources to the division—pursuant to our success.

Once we had begun to meet the high expectations placed on us, we had the resources to staff up. By the end of the second year, our division had grown from just a few of us to 19. Many would have a big effect on the Bank's future relations with Brazil, including Robin Horn, Alberto Rodriguez, Alexandre Abrantes, and Maureen Lewis. Along with Alcyone Saliba, a Brazilian woman seconded to the Brasilia office, they all developed deep working relationships with their government counterparts once President Fernando Henrique Cardoso came to power in 1995.[7]

And quite a few continued to work on important aspects of the Bank's social development evolution. Barbara Bruns went on to become the lead economist for education in the LAC region and later the first manager of the Bank's Strategic Impact Evaluation Fund, which measures the effectiveness of human development programs to better determine what works and what doesn't. While I was still division chief, Helen Saxenian was selected to work on the *World Development Report 1993: Investing in Health*, which pioneered the concept of DALYs (disability adjusted life years) to measure the state of the health of a population—and the best ways to improve it. Maureen Lewis became the chief economist for the Bank's human development network, which was created in a 1997 reorganization and encompassed a range of sectors including health, nutrition, social protection, and eventually HIV/AIDS.

You might notice a common thread in some of the names I have mentioned. Women made up most of the holdover staff when I started and their numbers swelled as our division grew. At one point, we had 12 total staff and still just one man in addition to me. There were a couple of factors at play here.

The issues at the heart of human development—education, health, population, nutrition, and childcare—seemed naturally to attract more young women economists in the Bank than men. Many men still saw our area of focus as "soft" development and in turn more "appropriate" for women. Regardless, their ignorance was my gain, because the Bank had plenty of brilliant women economists eager for a hard challenge and equal opportunity. Our division had established a reputation for being a very supportive environment for women to flourish and grow their careers. And there were not nearly enough of those in the Bank. After a while, I was gently encouraged to balance out the breakdown a little more. So I did. By the time I left, we were all the way up to four men!

Overall, the experience in LAC had a major impact on me and, I like to think, on the Bank's changing approach to the way it engaged with and responded to a member country's social development needs. My time there wasn't a total success, though; I never did learn to speak Portuguese, despite my best efforts. I even went to Brazil for a three-week immersion program. I picked up enough words and phrases to communicate, but fluency eluded me.

Fortunately, my future didn't hinge on my poor linguistic skills. As I neared the two-year mark in LAC, Shahid Husain asked me to lunch. It turned out that he wasn't so intimidating to work for after all—though I'm sure it helped that I didn't fall flat on my face. As we began to eat, he asked if I remembered when he told me that I had a chance to become a director in two years. I said that I did, and then he just looked at me with a slight smile, just as he had done during our first meeting in his office. I knew then I had hit my mark.

◆　◆　◆　◆

One way to track the timeline of increased awareness of social sector issues inside the Bank is to look at the annual *World Development Report*. First released in 1978, the *WDR* is the Bank's flagship publication, known for its big ideas, its thorough research, and its readability. Generally, its editors subscribe to the notion that a great report isn't worth much if no one wants to read it. Working on the *WDR* is a great assignment in the Bank, but also a temporary one. The lead authors rotate every year, taking leave from their normal jobs. One reason is to keep the report fresh with a constant stream of new voices. Another is to maintain the annual pace; the life cycle of each report is usually two or more years, so different teams work on different reports on a continuous, rolling basis. But the main reason is related to the topical nature of the *WDR*s. Each report is a deep dive into a particular aspect of global development requiring authors with matching areas of expertise.

The annual focus is described in the title, and the very first one reflected the broader pursuits of the Bank during the McNamara era: *Prospects for Growth and Alleviation of Poverty*. Two years later, the topic was *Poverty and Human Development*. After that, however, aside from a 1984 report on population, the *WDR* drifted away from the social sector, focusing on financial systems, agricultural pricing, public finance, trade, and foreign capital, among other topics.

It's not that social issues were ignored entirely for a decade. For example, Ernie Stern, the head of Bank operations, consistently pushed for family planning objectives in loan programs in the 1980s. And population, policy, and health were commonly highlighted in the Bank's country program papers, especially in overcrowded regions like India and Bangladesh. But as the first volume of *The World Bank: Its First Half Century* points out, the Bank generally engaged in social sector projects during this period to serve the larger objective of adjustment lending—to persuade sector officials "to find alternative ways to finance, allocate, and deliver those services" rather than through significant portions of their government budgets.

But then the *WDR* took a dramatic detour. It shifted to human and social development issues in three of the next four editions: poverty in 1990, the environment in 1992 and health in 1993. And even 1991 didn't veer too far from the sudden trend. That year, the *WDR* synthesized key lessons in global development over the previous decades and was organized around four sub-themes, the first of which was "investing in people." The pattern presented a clear shift in tone by the Bank, an attempt to reorient its human resource development initiatives around anti-poverty objectives rather than as components of structural adjustment. It also answered critics who contended that the Bank had pushed poverty and its related issues too far to the side.

The *World Development Report 1990: Poverty* was first out of the gate in this new era, focusing on "the poorest of the world's poor," in its own words. The report defined poverty in broad terms, far beyond the standard economic conception. It argued that a lack of basic human services in the developing world—such as health care, family planning, nutrition, and primary education—were among the most severe consequences of chronic poverty and, as such, required immediate attention and higher spending. It also acknowledged that the development setbacks of the 1980s had fallen "heavily on particular regions," specifically Sub-Saharan Africa and Latin America, making a bad situation worse.

The 1990 *WDR* publicly repositioned the Bank on poverty and social development, but internally the process had been underway for years.

Within months of assuming the Bank presidency in 1986, Barber Conable appointed a task force of senior staff to review the Bank's anti-poverty efforts. He wanted adjustment programs to be better designed so that they reduced the negative impact on income levels and opportunities for the poor. Conable believed strongly in the social dimensions of development and he saw a clear connection between women's health and poverty alleviation. In this way, he believed the Bank had fallen far short and tried to elevate the gender dimension. A new division, Women in Development, accompanied his reorganization in 1987, and two years later he urged the Bank's head of operations, Moeen Qureshi, to ensure that gender stayed central to Bank activities. A short time later, backed by the research and data in the 1990 *WDR*, he declared poverty reduction and women's issues, along with human development in general, to be of "special operational emphasis" for all Bank activities going forward.

At that point it didn't take long for the message to get across—nearly 40 percent of projects approved in 1991 had a special gender component.

Conable retired in August 1991 and was succeeded by Lewis Preston, who reaffirmed in his New Year's Eve directive that alleviating poverty would be the Bank's "overarching objective." Like Conable, Preston wanted to see a bigger commitment to gender in both country programs and Bank operations, calling for more women in management roles. But as the Bank moved to sharpen its focus on poverty and give more attention to contributing factors like health care and education, it became clear that the operational structure needed to change beyond what the Conable reorganization had only recently put in place.[8]

So in 1992 the Bank created a new vice presidency to encompass three reorganized departments. One department focused on internal Bank policy, but the other two covered key social development issues: the Population, Health, and Nutrition department; and the Education and Social Policy department, which became known as ESPD.

Many times in my career I happen to have been in the right place at the right time, and this was definitely one of them. Armeane Choksi was promoted to head the new vice presidency and oversee its three departments. The requirements to get ESPD up and running—building a new team and work program from the ground up—closely mirrored my experience in the Africa and LAC regions. I also happened to be among Choksi's most recent charges, and that mattered; to fill out his leadership team, he looked to people he knew and trusted.[9] He thought I would be a good fit for ESPD, so he asked if I would be the department's first director. I really wanted to return to Africa after my time in LAC, but once again I found myself with an unexpected offer that would be foolish to refuse.

To understand ESPD's significance, it's necessary to know the full circumstances behind its creation—to know *why* it was needed in the first place. The Bank wanted ESPD and its sister department on population, health, and nutrition to address the most glaring gaps in its social sector coverage by trying something new (and long overdue): aligning its robust but mostly isolated research with its actual operations on the ground. Think of the research as taking place in the background, or behind the scenes; then think of the operations, or projects, taking place in the foreground, or out in public. They were two fundamental aspects of the Bank's work, but in terms of the way they functioned, they mostly existed in separate orbits. The criticism that the Bank had historically treated social or human development as "add-ons" to its primary project work stemmed in part from this structure.

As I have said before, the Bank in those days was divided by geographical regions and then by divisions that oversaw the policy programs and project lending in particular countries such as my former Brazil, Peru, and Venezuela division within the Latin America and Caribbean region. At the same time, the Bank had a huge research complex conducting high-level studies and compiling some amazing knowledge on a whole range of issues, especially in the areas of poverty, education, gender, and health care.

The big problem for the Bank was the cultural disconnect. The research staff boasted some top names in their fields of study, but they were so far removed from the operations side as to not have a direct influence. Again, they were doing great work: gathering data, producing studies, traveling to conferences, and making presentations. The operations staff, meanwhile, had their own set of pressures to navigate: working with local policymakers, negotiating loans, designing and implementing projects. Not that they were flying blind or ignoring analytics—this certainly wasn't the case, as my staff from the Brazil division proved. But on a larger scale, the Bank's significant intellectual capital was being used primarily to inform external dialogue, not internal operations.

So even as Conable and Preston "reaffirmed" the Bank's commitment to poverty alleviation over the years, the Bank still needed a way to put that commitment into practice. It was a gradual process that gained momentum after the 1990 *WDR* underscored the need to focus on human and social development issues. The Bank already had a vast reservoir of research on those same issues at its disposal; what it didn't have was a systematic way to ensure that all the different regions and divisions could tap into that knowledge.

ESPD was the answer to the problem. It was created as a hybrid department—a cross between research and operations, pulling in staff from both wings of the Bank, cutting across the regions and consolidating efforts.

For instance, the Bank employed a number of well-respected economists and specialists—people like Elizabeth King, Ralph Harbison, Stephen Heyneman, Marlaine Lockheed, Peter Moock, and Adriaan Verspoor, to name a few. Heyneman, for instance, spent many years in the 1980s in charge of external training in education policy for Bank officials around the world. In 1991, the year before ESPD's founding, Verspoor had published a very insightful study that examined two decades of Bank lending policies for basic education programs.

These men and women were doing great work, but because of the disjointed nature of the Bank's education apparatus—the different regions and departments had their own education groups, in addition to education being a component of the Bank's research complex—their insights didn't always translate to projects.

The Bank wanted ESPD to draw upon existing research and studies, draw lessons from its operations at the country level, and raise the profile of social development so that those issues would eventually become part of the Bank's mainstream—integral components of country operations rather than complementary. Of course, not everyone at the Bank was ready to buy into these new mandates right away, so it would be our job in ESPD to make the case that attacking these issues was tantamount to attacking the root causes of poverty.

Altogether, ESPD comprised four separate issue groups—gender, poverty and social assistance, labor markets and social insurance, and of course education. Getting it off the ground felt like putting together a giant jigsaw puzzle—mixing and matching staff, defining the unit's strategic agenda, and identifying the ways to put that agenda in motion. It's why I was appointed. Choksi wanted someone who understood the fundamental issues at play but could also shape a cohesive unit in short order.

We needed to take people from research and we needed to take people from operations and fuse them together for each of the four areas of focus. Aside from natural or parochial conflicts that you might imagine arising from such an unproven arrangement, I anticipated another problem—a department with too many chiefs and not enough Indians, as the saying goes.

As ESPD got up and running, I realized we didn't have enough staff to create so many small divisions. Besides that, I wanted the flexibility of forming interchangeable teams to collaborate when necessary. The issues on which we had to work—gender, education, jobs—were all interrelated in the context of poverty alleviation anyway. One motivation behind ESPD was to work across the Bank "silos" that had long existed. I was concerned that bringing a disparate group together as one unit then immediately dividing them into four quadrants would undermine that aspiration within our own department!

So I decided to abolish divisions altogether and, with them, division chiefs. Instead, I hired managers for each area of focus. The managers didn't have direct staff working under them; we pooled the personnel so any manager could pull any person into teams to work on specific tasks or reports. I wanted a department that was more flat than vertical, with greater collaboration and less hierarchy. I felt it was the only way to combine seasoned Bank veterans from research and operations into one group successfully.

When I presented the idea to Choksi, he gave me his full support. I could not have attempted such a radical departure from Bank tradition without approval from higher up. Choksi agreed that my plan was risky but he said it was a pioneering move and worth a try.

We pulled together an incredible team. I hired Minh Chau Nguyen, who had worked on numerous country programs, as the head of the gender group. Oey Meesook headed the poverty and social assistance group and Jane Armitage headed labor markets and social insurance. Like Minh Chau, they both came from operations. Peter Moock, one of the Bank's all-stars, headed the education group. He had a deep research background and was also a respected academic. In addition to him, Adriaan Verspoor joined ESPD to bolster our education expertise. I named him as a senior advisor. I also recruited Barbara Bruns from LAC to come over as an advisor.

Not everyone we recruited into the new department was on board with the new structure. Those who came from the research side had the toughest time adjusting. But in fairness, we were asking some veteran Bank staff to forgo a title they had worked years to earn. As I said before, becoming a division chief back then was a big deal and could take a long time. I remember one exchange quite well with a Bank veteran who didn't hide his displeasure.

"I've been a division chief for all these years and now I'll be a manager?" he asked. "A manager for what, a 7-11 convenience store?"

He was incredulous at what he perceived as a professional slight. I tried to explain that he wasn't being valued less, but I understood the frustration.

The staffing model worked out well in the end, and over time it proved prescient. Eventually, the entire Bank moved away from division chiefs and more toward a team approach. The title "manager" came to be used more widely as the first level in managerial positions, while today the Bank uses "task team leaders" to fluctuate easily between projects and departments, going where their expertise and knowledge is put to the best use.

Of course, the whole effort was to try to put this new department in the best possible position to succeed, which at the most basic level meant using the Bank's research to set new, more aggressive policy directions for the Bank and its social development agenda. Given the direction that the Bank's peers were moving, we did feel a sense of urgency so as not to fall behind.

The Organisation for Economic Co-operation and Development, for instance, had elevated social policy in its anti-poverty development strategies, and so too had the United Nations. In 1993, UN Secretary-General Boutros Boutros-Ghali established three new departments to cover more comprehensively the intersection of economic, social, and human development. Amid this growing dialogue, the Bank needed to make its own intellectual contributions and also prove its worth as a thought partner in the social sectors.

A turning point for the Bank and for our new department came in 1994 when the Bank issued a sweeping new operations policy on gender, based primarily on a strategy paper that ESPD produced—the first of its kind published in the Bank. The paper, *Enhancing Women's Participation in Economic Development*, served as a blueprint to bring gender to the foreground of country programs and interventions. More important, it took a strong, unwavering stance—with the data to back it up—that "investing proportionally more in women than in men   in education, health, family planning—is an important part of development strategy, as well as an act of social justice. It directly reduces poverty through substantial economic and social payoffs."

145

Another step forward came the following year. In advance of the Fourth World Conference on Women, held in Beijing in September 1995, ESPD produced a special policy paper, *Gender and Development: Equity and Efficiency,* to serve as the Bank's leading contribution to the conference. But it was more than that; it was the World Bank's first policy paper on gender as a development issue.

Both ESPD's strategy paper and the Bank's institutional policy that flowed from it "gave gender a central place in the Bank's country-level development strategies" for the first time, according to an independent evaluation group study in 2010. "It provided the means to integrate gender considerations into Bank support for the next several years." A few years after the evaluation study, the Bank published the first *World Development Report* on gender equality.

And speaking of the *WDR*, the thematic shift made in the 1990s marked the beginning of a new era. After another poverty study in 2000, the *WDR* explored a variety of social and human development topics, including sustainable development practices, environmental impacts, essential services for the poor, youth skills, inclusive growth, climate change, job creation, human behavioral patterns, and digital societies. And, finally, the *World Development Report 2018* featured education as its own topic for the first time.

The Bank's desire to be more collaborative with its development partners marked a noticeable shift from the "go-it-alone" approach that defined the structural adjustment days. Along those lines, the Bank wanted to play an integral role in the UN's landmark World Summit for Social Development, or "Social Summit" as it came to be known, which took place in Copenhagen in March 1995. The goal of the summit was to reach a consensus for placing poverty reduction and social integration at the core of global development. In other words, to put people first.

As with the gender conference held in Beijing that same year, ESPD was responsible for producing the Bank's contribution. The result, *Advancing Social Development,* offered a strategy to improve economic and social well-being that emphasized the same elements around which ESPD was organized, such as labor-demanding growth and investments in education and health. It also brought in governance since social development gains are so reliant on public resources. *Advancing Social Development* made pronouncements that just a decade earlier might have sounded foreign to the Bank's old guard: "Development must be people-oriented and include efforts to reduce inequality."

The Social Summit attracted more than 100 heads of state and government and delegates from 186 countries. Thousands of NGO representatives also attended. It was the first major UN conference specifically devoted to social development issues. World leaders agreed to the Copenhagen Declaration, a list of 10 commitments that focused on poverty, gender, education, health, and human rights. Many elements of the declaration informed the UN's Millennium Development Goals, which were announced just a few years later.

Planning for the summit took months and months of intense preparation. The UN wanted to see the Bank heavily involved in that process from the start, and the Bank wanted to be involved. At the time, such close communication and collaboration between the two institutions was not very common. As part of this effort, I made regular trips to UN headquarters in New York for meetings, seminars, and working groups. For almost a year leading up to the summit, I represented the Bank with increasing frequency and, to some of those in the UN, became its voice on the connection between poverty and social development.

Around the same time, ESPD had begun to boost its number of specialized policy papers and briefings, many of which were produced in collaboration with UN agencies or other technical groups. Between the external inputs we were seeking for ESPD's research and my participation in the prep meetings for Copenhagen, I began to understand the UN agenda quite well.

Generally speaking, Bank and UN staff hadn't always enjoyed productive relationships, but that's not what I encountered. It was obvious that both sides shared similar views on new development approaches, so on my trips I found eager, collaborative partners. For instance, I got to know Nitin Desai, an Indian economist whom Boutros-Ghali had appointed to head one of the UN's three new social sector departments. Obviously, our areas of interest overlapped, and there was much to discuss. I also met some of the top UN officials, including the undersecretary-generals for agencies such as UNDP, the United Nations Development Programme, and UNICEF, the United Nations Children's Fund. The more time I spent at the UN, the more comfortable I became there, and the more connections I made.

◆　◆　◆　◆

Less than two months after ESPD released its groundbreaking internal report on women and development, the "50 Years Is Enough" campaign disrupted the Bank's annual meeting and anniversary celebration in Madrid. The timing is relevant to point out because the heated rhetoric of vocal critics generally failed to acknowledge the Bank's layers—primarily the many staff who not only helped steer the Bank in a better direction but passionately believed in the value of their work. They were not ones questioning the Bank's legacy, nor were they representative of an institution "slouching" forward, as put forth in the *50 Years Is Enough* book of essays. They were ones who showed up to work every day, trying to find good answers to hard questions to improve people's lives. At least I can say that about the ESPD staff, and the amazing team in the Brazil division, and countless others. They did great work, and I believe their commitment is worth reiterating.

And yet, the ample criticism of the Bank wasn't groundless. It needed to be heard, and it was. As James Wolfensohn wrote in his autobiography, the Bank in 1995 still represented "a unique vehicle for bringing about more equitable economic and social development. The World Bank, in the view of many, had gone woefully out of tune, but it was still the right instrument to play."

Indeed, over the previous 15 years, the Bank had dramatically increased its investments in *people*—from about 5 percent of total lending in the early 1980s to 15 percent in 1994. The composition of those investments also changed, with more emphasis on primary education, girls' education, and health care. By 1994, the Bank was lending more than $2 billion a year for education and $1 billion a year for health. By the time Wolfensohn arrived as president, for instance, the Bank had become the world's largest financier for AIDS prevention programs.

Wolfensohn took over after Lewis Preston, who had been in poor health for years before dying from cancer in May 1995. A native Australian and successful investment banker, Wolfensohn had a self-professed "dream of leading the World Bank" since Robert McNamara retired, when he first hoped to be considered a candidate. Having come to the position of president as someone who actually hoped for and sought the job, Wolfensohn brought a far different energy and attitude to the Bank than his predecessors, and it served him well.

On his first day in the office, he sent the entire staff an open letter brimming with optimism, determination, and big picture goals. He said it was time to transform the Bank into an institution that remained conscious of its financial management and obligations but was driven by ideals—to think of its mission in terms of people first, not numbers. "We care about poverty, the environment, social justice and the other issues that make up the dreams of this institution," he wrote. "These should be our guiding lights."

It was an inspiring, proactive message and it stood in stark contrast to the steady stream of anti-Bank sentiment that seemed to have become the norm. I can't speak for how the memo affected others, but it definitely moved me, so much so that I used the same tactic down the road.

Still, the Bank had to physically navigate its way out of the adjustment era and into the new age of development characterized by anti-poverty objectives, local ownership, and mutual collaboration—essentially the PIE approach in Brazil extrapolated to a full scale.

In 1997 Wolfensohn instituted the Bank's third reorganization in 10 years to strike a better balance between country focus and programmatic objectives, accelerating the Bank's transition from an institution primarily concerned with lending to one that gave equal or more consideration to the needs of the client countries. As part of Wolfensohn's reorganization, the Bank also established "networks" to link staff working on the same issues across the organization and to create a stronger focus on issues that would benefit from additional collaboration with the Bank's partners. The first three networks encompassed poverty reduction, human development, and environmental and social sustainability. They represented a major operational shift for the Bank.

ESPD was abolished and folded into the network structure, which itself was eventually replaced by a new operating model put in place in July 2014. This model emphasized the "client-facing" aspect of traditional regional units and introduced 14 global practices, or thematic areas such as agriculture and education and poverty, to work across all the regions, as well as five cross-cutting areas that include gender and climate change.

According to the Bank, the restructuring was designed to further improve the processes of like-minded collaboration, sharing open knowledge, and making informed decisions "to better serve clients with more integrated programs" in support of economic and social development. The Bank may have a long history of change, but as long as it's willing to evolve around the needs of its members, that's not a bad thing—for the Bank or the countries it was created to help in the first place.

Notes

1   Proceedings of the conference held in Madrid, Spain, "Fifty Years After Bretton Woods: The Future of the IMF and the World Bank," James M. Boughton (editor), September 1994.

2   Vice presidents at the World Bank are still very influential but their numbers have swelled over the years as the Bank has grown and diversified. Today, there are more than two dozen.

3   Nancy Birdsall eventually became the director of the Bank's policy research department. After leaving in 1993, she served as executive vice president of the Inter-American Development Bank and as founding president of the Center for Global Development, a highly respected independent think tank. She is the author, co-author, or editor of more than a dozen books and has produced extensive research on education, health, income inequality, women's economic empowerment, and more. She is a true giant in the field.

4   For example, in 1990, a six-year-old child in the bottom quintile of the income distribution was likely to live in the northeast region and have a mother who had never gone to school. That child would be lucky to complete more than the first few grades of primary school, which in that area of Brazil would be a one- or two-room structure without electricity or water, lacking books and learning materials. The teacher was likely to be hired through political connections with barely more education than her students—60 percent of Brazil's primary school teachers in 1990 had not completed secondary school and 30 percent had not even finished primary school!

5   In 1990, Brazil's GDP was just more than $460 billion. In 2000, it had grown to $644.7 billion. By 2011, it was $2.47 trillion, a growth rate that no doubt exceeded even the most optimistic projections. In that same time frame, Brazil became one of the world's great low-income success stories, rapidly becoming a hub of economic development in the Latin world. The economy finally started to slow in 2014 before taking a more severe downturn, but its rapid turnaround in the 2000s remains a towering achievement.

6   AIDS Project I also produced two follow-ups, AIDS Project II and III, which ran continuously for all but seven months between June 1994 and December 2007.

7   Cardoso helped stabilize the political environment, and, as the first Brazilian president to start a program to address the country's enormous inequalities, he elevated the importance of social development. In the education sector, issues that Bank staff had talked about for years, such as textbooks and assessment, moved to the heart of policy action and lending.

8   The 1987 reorganization actually introduced some rather significant structural problems to the Bank. For example, it severely diminished the personnel and management function and it made the budgeting and top decision-making processes more complex. After a few years, there was much support for further changes.

9   Choksi hired Jim Adams, another of his former division chiefs, to take over the internal policy department when he hired me for ESPD. Jim and I were good friends and longtime colleagues and it would be remiss of me to not mention him or the "twin careers" we enjoyed at the Bank. Jim and I started together as YPs. We worked under Stanley Please at the same time and worked in Africa at the same time. We were promoted to division chief on the same day, so it was only fitting that we made director together, under the same vice presidency!

Chapter 5

Africa Calling
'A Chance to Do Something for What You Believe In'

The first time I saw Kwame Nkrumah in person was November 1961, when Queen Elizabeth II came to Accra on a state visit. The year before, Ghana had officially become a republic and the country was still in a celebratory mood. The Queen spent more than a week in Accra and surrounding areas, and most of the time, Nkrumah was by her side. They came to Takoradi, where I was in school, and it felt like the whole city had lined up to welcome the caravan that brought them to town. I was there too, in the middle of the waving flags and cheering crowds, waiting for a glimpse. I vividly recall seeing their car approach, then pass. The top was open and an umbrella shielded the Queen from the sun, but it was easy to see Nkrumah sitting beside her, waving to admirers like me.

The Queen's visit was quite controversial, in fact, as demonstrations and security fears led many to argue against Elizabeth traveling to Ghana at all. But she did and Nkrumah welcomed her, not as a colonial subject but as a head of state. During the visit, a photo was taken of Queen Elizabeth and Nkrumah dancing together at a ball and it remains a powerful image to this day. There, for the whole world to see, was the Queen of the British Commonwealth, with her crown on her head, in the formal but friendly embrace of an African anti-colonialist, in Africa's first independent country.

Africans are generally proud to a fault, but that week was incredibly special for Ghana. Our new country felt *real*. I can't imagine a more memorable time to have seen Nkrumah in the flesh, with my own eyes. It was an inspirational moment that I've always carried with me.

I never met Nkrumah. I got close to him a few times, such as when I was in the cadet corps at Ghana Secondary Technical School and we were invited to watch as Nkrumah inspected a guard of honor in a nearby military barracks. Nonetheless, I was one of the many made to feel exceptional by his confidence in Africa and its place in the world. His strong pan-African views resonated with my father and, because of that, they resonated even more with me. I devoured his words and ideas, and they molded my belief in African potential, in African greatness, and in the need for Africans to work together, not apart.

Some considered Nkrumah's rhetoric over the top, but he never doubted how difficult the task would be for colonized Africa to raise itself up. So he pulled no punches. When he addressed the UN in 1960, he called for Africa to have a permanent seat on the Security Council, a bold provocation. He chastised Africa's "exploiters and self-appointed controllers" who "strode across our land with incredible inhumanity without mercy, without shame, without honor."

But he also spoke of finding economic stability through peace and a political equilibrium that would benefit African countries as well as the Middle East and Western powers. Thirteen new African nations had taken their seats with the UN that year alone, Nkrumah pointed out, invoking, as he and so many others have done for more than five decades, this "new day" in Africa. "Our tribulations and suffering harden and steel us," he said, "making us a bastion of indomitable courage and fortifying our iron determination to smash our chains."

This was the context for my coming of age, in a country born believing that African self-reliance and determination would lead to prosperity and respect. I grew up absorbing these ideas and passions directly from my father and indirectly from Nkrumah, so the belief that a better Africa was around the corner, and that it was up to Africans and only Africans to lead the way, simply melded into who I became as a person.

◆　◆　◆　◆

By any personal and professional measure, I was in a great place. It was 1994, and I was roughly at the midpoint of my career. I was 50 years old and very happy, with good health and a strong family, and I didn't take either of those treasures for granted. Philomena was doing well and had started her own career at the Bank, and my twin daughters would soon follow their older sister to college. I missed working on Africa, but I had a challenging director's job, an incredible staff, and a growing knowledge of the full scope of economic and social development. In fact, my career was on a bit of a roll.

The Bank's new Education and Social Policy department that I oversaw, ESPD, was not yet two years old and had really taken off. The staffing changes and work program we implemented were lauded inside the Bank, and the department's profile was increasing, thanks to the volume and quality of our work. All the evidence-based analytics we undertook—a progress report on poverty, a study on higher education, the groundbreaking policy paper on gender—were well received among our peers and by the board of directors. In fact, we worked at an almost unprecedented pace within the Bank. By the end of 1994, we were on our way to finishing eight major analytical reports or policy papers in two years. Yes, career technocrats get very excited about these things.

My staff's exceptional work reflected well on me, and I was humbled when my personnel review that year referred to me as a "valuable asset" to the institution and complimented me for having a good sense of strategic priorities. Despite representing the Bank at various UN-sponsored functions and events, I was urged to step up my external efforts even further to become a principal spokesman for the Bank in the social policy field. This encouragement was all very thrilling to me because it helped validate the way I approached my job.

All in all, things were going great. As far as I knew, I had no other place to be.

Then on Thursday, December 8, 1994, at almost 6 p.m., I got a phone call.

I was sitting in my office, buried under a pile of paperwork. I was ready to go home. It was cold outside. I wasn't in the best mood when I picked up the phone. The woman on the other end of the line introduced herself. She was calling from the office of UN Secretary-General Boutros Boutros-Ghali. We exchanged a few general courtesies, but she pretty quickly got to the point.

"Would you be able to come to New York on Tuesday?" she asked. "The secretary-general would like to meet with you."

The call surprised me, but it wasn't totally out of the blue, either. A few months before, in late summer, one of my friends and associates, Ismail Serageldin, asked that I send my CV to Boutros-Ghali. At the time, Serageldin was a vice president at the Bank for Environmentally and Socially Sustainable Development—now just known as Sustainable Development. If I ever start to think of myself as particularly smart or accomplished, I only have to consider Serageldin to put me back in my place. He's been awarded 29 honorary doctorates and he eventually became the director of the historic Library of Alexandria in Egypt. He had a long career at the Bank, but his contributions to development, particularly from a scientific perspective, extend far beyond any one role. He's published more than 60 books and over 200 research papers. He's a brilliant thinker and he's someone I've greatly respected as long as I've known him.

So when he phoned and suggested that I send a CV to Boutros-Ghali's office, I sat up and took notice.

Now, I had never even once considered sending a CV to Boutros-Ghali's office, or any other office for that matter. In fact, I didn't even have a CV to send. I had been at the Bank for 20 years and I had no intention of going anywhere else. At first, I thought Serageldin was joking. He told me he wasn't, but what he wouldn't tell me was why he was making this request in the first place. I asked, but he only chuckled and said, "Well, you'll know when they call you." He told me it was an "important position" and that my name had been mentioned. I don't remember if I felt more honored or confused.

I could put a few pieces of the puzzle together. Since my position as director of ESPD required that I represent the Bank at various UN gatherings, my network of associates inside the United Nations had grown. I was a constant advocate for improved Bank–UN relations while at these events and I know that raised my profile. At the same time, my professional path had begun to cross Serageldin's more frequently, our work dovetailing as the Bank increased its focus on poverty reduction. He also happened to know Boutros-Ghali very well. Both men were Egyptian and each had taught at Cairo University; Serageldin before joining the Bank and Boutros-Ghali before joining the Egyptian government. They had a long association going back decades.

I thanked Serageldin and told him that I'd follow up. But I didn't. I never got around to preparing a CV. I had other things to do, things related to the job I already had that I happened to love. Several more weeks passed and Serageldin called me again. And again he asked that I send a CV to Boutros-Ghali's office. He was adamant that I should at least keep the door open, and since I didn't expect any kind of serious dalliance anyway, I agreed. This time I gave Serageldin my word. I promised to sit down within a few days and cobble something together.

What I saw left me disappointed. The CV just didn't seem very impressive.

As my career had moved progressively forward, I felt each new step I took was bolstering my development credentials. From Sudan to Zambia, from Kenya to Brazil, I had played a real role in facilitating stronger economic and lending policies between the Bank and developing countries. I had met with heads of state in the open and I had met with local policymakers in secret, whatever it took to promote the programs. I had a knack for managing difficult situations, for thinking creatively and not being afraid to share my opinion and for building up divisions through efficient practices and quality staff. And yet, in listing out what I had done, it all seemed so insular. My entire career, all my professional life, I'd only been at the World Bank. From young professional to special assistant to division chief to department director... it was all neatly upward and orderly. But when I looked at my life's direction more objectively, listed matter-of-factly on a few sheets of paper, my contributions as a development professional and as an economist all just seemed... small.

Regardless, I kept my promise to Serageldin and sent off the CV and that seemed to be the end of it. One month passed and I didn't hear anything. Then a second, then a third. Summer turned to fall and fall turned to winter and the growing ESPD workload consumed almost all of my time. I was happy at the Bank and I had no interest in going elsewhere, but I was curious. What had all the urgency been about? So much time had passed, I pressed Serageldin to share some more details. I finally learned that the UN had plans to overhaul its Economic Commission for Africa, which had seen better days and might soon be in need of new leadership. The request for my CV had come in that context. I was glad to solve the mystery but also relieved that nothing had come of it.

Until Thursday, December 8, when I got that phone call.

"The secretary-general would like to meet with you," she said.

I remember it as clear as yesterday. I didn't know what to say. I momentarily froze, but my mind raced.

Should I go? Should I not go?

Should I say yes? How could I say no?

After a few seconds that felt like minutes, I made a decision. I would stall.

I told the woman that I had a scheduling conflict, an important meeting on Tuesday that absolutely could not be skipped. Now, to my credit, I wasn't making this up; Bank board meetings regularly took place on Tuesdays, and as a director I sometimes attended them. But, this being the World Bank, you could throw a dart at a calendar on the wall and hit a day with an "important meeting." I could pick any day of any week and say I had a conflict, though precious few were ever too important to skip. So I wasn't lying. Just exaggerating a bit.

155

I assumed the secretary-general's calendar had precious few openings and that my delay tactic might buy a few extra weeks. Since I knew the likely reason for the call, I could then give serious consideration as to whether I wanted to actually discuss this thing or save everyone some time and gracefully decline.

The woman caller responded kindly to my calendar conflict.

"Of course," she said, not skipping a beat. "I understand. We'll call you back."

It worked! I hung up the phone, thinking I had a few days to figure out the best way to handle this.

She called back in less than five minutes.

"Mr. Amoako, why don't you come on Monday instead?"

◆ ◆ ◆ ◆

The United Nations Economic Commission for Africa, or ECA, is one of five regional economic commissions under the administrative direction of UN headquarters. The commissions are based in diverse geographical locations around the world and operate in response to regional development needs. The ECA, located in Addis Ababa, Ethiopia, functioned as the UN's primary outpost in Africa. I was quite familiar with the ECA.

Founded in 1958 by the UN's Economic and Social Council, the ECA's mandate has stayed mostly consistent over the years: to build up African institutions, articulate plans and strategies, promote cooperation and integration, advocate policies, and provide technical cooperation. Its members, which are also considered its "clients," mirror the membership roster of the United Nations, which is to say, all recognized sovereign African states. Unlike the African Union, the ECA doesn't apply political pressures or suspend membership in the event of political disputes. If a country is a member of the UN, then it's a client of the ECA.

As an institution, the ECA holds a revered place in African history—its inaugural session was the first major gathering of Africans, under the auspices of the United Nations, to talk about African problems on African soil. In a 2009 contribution to the UN Intellectual History Project, Sir Richard Jolly, a notable development economist from the United Kingdom, did a nice job describing the context in which the ECA began operations:

> *The ECA's early years were dominated by political battles against colonialism, racism, and apartheid and preoccupied with the development problems of collective self-reliance, endogenous development, and regional economic integration. Unfortunately ... the rapidity with which African countries became independent*

produced, paradoxically, a negative impact on African solidarity. Independence re-inforced boundaries established by the colonial powers and gave new leaders a vested interest in maintaining them. This was a serious problem for development, which [UN Secretary-General] Dag Hammarskjöld underlined at the ECA's inaugural session when he pleaded that economic integration should be one of the commission's major objectives.

Most African countries were poorly prepared for statehood but leaders envisioned rapid transformation. Independence gave rise to the dramatic expansion of education and training, the localization of the government administration, economic and social planning for economic growth, and development and data collection and the creation of statistical systems. In all of these efforts, the ECA was closely involved.

By the time I got the call from Boutros-Ghali's office, the ECA had been around for more than 35 years, with a strong record of achievement dating back to those early days. In 1962, it helped establish the African Institute for Economic Development and Planning, a pan-African institution created by the UN and located in Dakar, Senegal. African countries were gaining independence at a rapid rate and the African Institute was founded to help these new countries build up their human capital.[1] One year later, in 1963, the ECA led the 23 newly independent African countries in creating the African Development Bank, which officially opened in March 1965, in Abidjan, Côte d'Ivoire. The AfDB grew from its original authorized capital of $250 million to $6.3 billion by 1993. It was another financial resource for Africa's low-income countries and a defining example of the ECA's potential to change the landscape.

Another example of the ECA's work was its role in helping establish a continent-wide network of regional economic communities to promote greater cooperation and trade among African countries. Currently there are eight of these regional communities, which were established throughout the 1970s and 1980s but whose origin can be traced back to 1965. That year, the ECA convened a ministerial meeting of newly independent states at the urging of the Organization of African Unity, itself only recently established, to consider proposals to create sub-regional economic blocs. The communities have had a troubled existence, but they have helped foster regional integration, a signature accomplishment of the ECA through the years.

During this very period, Robert Gardiner served as the ECA's executive secretary, the organization's top position. The executive secretaries of the commissions also carry the title of UN undersecretary-general, so within the UN's hierarchy, the jobs are fairly high up the food chain. Holding the position is no guarantee of influence or effectiveness, but for Gardiner it was. He was an early and vocal proponent of adequate development financing in Africa and he was widely recognized as an eminent economist and thinker whose legacy has only grown over the years. He was a leading force behind the creation of the AfDB, and he later wrote a book recapping the Bank's first 20 years as "an experiment in economic cooperation and development." Within the UN, and certainly during Africa's early postcolonial period, Gardiner was an intellectual force.

Gardiner also was a fellow Ghanaian and ardent pan-Africanist, so my opinion of him may not be objective, but it doesn't have to be. Many others feel the same way. In 1990, a volume of 12 essays by leading African scholars and officials was published under the title *Towards Economic Recovery in Sub-Saharan Africa: Essays in Honor of Dr. Robert Gardiner*. The book analyzed some of Africa's most pressing development issues while simultaneously paying tribute to Gardiner. A former head of the Ghana Civil Service, Gardiner had also been the chief of UN operations in the Congo before he took over at the ECA in 1961. He was a believer in Nkrumah's vision, and he was devoted to using strong institutions as a tool for African progress, starting with the ECA.

During his 14-year tenure, Gardiner worked hard to elevate the organization beyond the slow-moving trappings of many UN bodies. His early years were a whirlwind of activity, as the establishment of the AfDB showed. And, as much as an economist could become a celebrity, he was. As a boy, I remember listening to him talk on the radio. For me, he was another educated Ghanaian who could passionately and intelligently articulate Africa's most pressing needs. In 1965, Gardiner was named as the BBC's prestigious Reith Lecturer, and he delivered a six-part radio series, "A World of Peoples." He was more than the ECA's executive secretary; he was a respected African leader with a global platform.

Because of Gardiner, I became familiar with the ECA's history and stature at an early age. Because of my time at the World Bank, I became familiar with its evolution from the 1970s into the 1990s, a period marked by notable strengths and weaknesses. The ECA's long-time executive secretary during that period, Adebayo Adedeji, strongly disagreed with the Bretton Woods Institutions and had clashed with Bank and IMF officials—a strained relationship of which I was well aware. Adedeji's tenure ended years before Boutros-Ghali reached out to me, but the ECA's overall relations with the Bank and other global organizations had not improved under subsequent leaders.

As I prepared to meet Boutros-Ghali, I wasn't aware just how much of a priority the ECA had become within UN headquarters—or just how far the stock of the institution once led by the great Robert Gardiner had dropped.

◆ ◆ ◆ ◆

When I agreed to go to New York, I expected the meeting to be the beginning of a process. The turnaround between the phone call and the trip was quick—a matter of days—but I had no reason to think urgency would be a factor. Even if Boutros-Ghali had interest in me as a candidate to lead the ECA, he would want to get to know me. And I would want to get to know more about where things stood at the institution. There would be many questions and concerns on both sides, so my flight to New York still felt like the first step of what might be a long and deliberative process.

That thinking would turn out to be very, very wrong.

I arrived at UN headquarters around 9:30 in the morning to find security escorts waiting for me. They checked my identification and then took me straightaway to the secretary-general's office on the famed 38th floor—famed within the vast UN system, at least. Real estate on that floor is so highly regarded that when offices were shuffled as part of an expansion in 1991, the Associated Press even wrote a story about it: "A territorial crisis has erupted at the highest level of world diplomacy…" the article began. With the frequent visits I had made in the preceding years representing the Bank, the UN building now felt like a familiar place. But I had never been to the 38th floor.

As I waited outside the secretary-general's office, I had enough spare time to grow a little nervous. I believe I knew both what to expect and what not to expect at the same time. So my mind wandered back to the stage the UN afforded Nkrumah when he was making the case for Ghana's independence and Africa's freedom. He had used the bully pulpit of the UN General Assembly in 1960 to deliver a memorable and defiant address:

> *I, an African, stand before this august assembly of the United Nations and speak with a voice of peace and freedom, proclaiming to the world the dawn of a new era. … I look upon the United Nations as the only organization that holds out any hope for the future of mankind. Distinguished delegates, cast your eyes across Africa. The colonialist and imperialist are still there. As long as a single foot of African soil remains under foreign domination, the world shall know no peace.*

Nkrumah knew the symbolism that speaking in front of the UN General Assembly carried in 1960. It was powerful. I grew up seeing the UN as a legitimizing force for African independence and I certainly wasn't the only one. The ECA, under Gardiner, was the UN's main outpost in Africa and it helped make things happen, good things, in my eyes, for Africa's development. Whereas anti-UN advocates complained even then about the inefficient or meddlesome institution, the loudest complaints seemed to come from men and women born under self-rule. For those of us from developing countries just coming into our own freedoms, institutions like the UN offered hope, warts and all.

I took a seat in the reception area and prepared for a long wait, often the custom for any high-level meeting at the UN. But an assistant came for me within 10 minutes and ushered me into the secretary-general's office. Things continued to happen faster than I expected.

As I walked into his office, I was surprised to see we were alone. No advisors, no associates. Just the two of us. I had never met or spoken to Boutros-Ghali, who at that time was almost two years into his eventual five-year tenure.

"My brother," he said warmly, taking my hand, "please sit down. There is much to discuss."

A former Egyptian minister and diplomat, Boutros-Ghali became the sixth secretary-general of the United Nations on January 1, 1992. He arrived amid dramatic shifts in the global landscape, as dramatic as any since World War II. These circumstances and his own motivations converged to make him one of the best-known, recognizable, and controversial figures in the world.

One week before he was sworn in, the Soviet Union dissolved. Less than three weeks after that, Serbs in the Bosnia and Herzegovina parliament declared their own republic, escalating the growing tensions that had been building since Yugoslavia began its breakup a year earlier. In the span of a month, Eastern Europe was in disarray, decades-old borders and governments were wiped out and the Soviet superpower collapsed. The same month, Somalia's president was overthrown in a revolution that split the country in violent, opposing camps. Over the next few years, as these regions and others descended into chaos and war, such as Rwanda in 1994, the UN tried to step in.

The concept of UN "peace building" first emerged in the 1970s, but it really gained traction under Boutros-Ghali. In his famous 1992 treatise, "An Agenda for Peace," Boutros-Ghali laid out a much broader mandate for the United Nations, one that incorporated "preventative diplomacy, peacemaking, and peacekeeping." In some ways, it was a direct response to the increasing demands for multinational security forces in the wake of the Cold War's conclusion and the world's quickly shifting borders.

By early 1994, the UN was involved in 18 different peacekeeping operations. But in some parts of the world, particularly in Western countries that supplied the lion's share of UN funds, the changing face of the institution created controversy. The UN's expanding reach under Boutros-Ghali called for a multilateral approach that, at the time, was at odds with the traditionally sovereign nature of foreign policies. Moreover, the loudest critics, such as the US, questioned the UN's capacity to assume this kind of role. The situation grew tense. If Boutros-Ghali wanted to lead the UN into a new era of peace building, then the United States and other donor countries demanded that the UN reform its operations and be more transparent, efficient, and productive with its vast resources.

The successes and failures of the UN missions during this period have been thoroughly documented, and it's not necessary to revisit them here. But the context of the situation is relevant, because the UN under Boutros-Ghali took on unprecedented prominence in world affairs, accumulating ever more critics and watchdogs as a result. There were a lot of eyes on the institution and there was a lot of pressure to ensure its offices and commissions were making maximum contributions in every region of the world. And outside the former Soviet republics, no region was attracting more attention in 1994 than Africa.

Between the well-publicized atrocities in Rwanda, Somalia, and Liberia, where Charles Taylor was leading a destructive civil war, and the much more encouraging changes in Namibia, Ethiopia, and South Africa, where Nelson Mandela ushered out the apartheid era, African countries seemed to be running the full gamut between disaster and opportunity. With its storied history and its mandate to promote economic and social development in Africa, the ECA was well positioned to assist the increasing number of governments in transition.

Boutros-Ghali, under pressure to show that the UN could become more efficient even as its presence on the world stage expanded, believed the ECA needed to play a bigger leadership role in Africa. He also believed the ECA was not currently capable of doing that.

For a few minutes, the secretary-general and I made small talk. He thanked me for making the trip on such short notice. We chatted about family. I marveled at the beauty of his office and its stunning view overlooking New York's East River. Then we started to talk about the UN and the challenges it faced. He spoke of the obvious concerns: shrinking budgets, escalating costs, increasing demands, and the growing chorus of criticism over its recent humanitarian operations. Critics were constantly hammering the UN for its robotic bureaucracy and its perceived—as well as its legitimate—inefficiencies. He explained how he felt it was imperative that all aspects of the UN run effectively, eliminate waste, and produce tangible results. The exchange was short but stimulating, forthright and candid. It was nice. I was engaged but at ease.

Then Boutros-Ghali made a quick pivot in our conversation.

"Mr. Amoako, do you know why I called you up here?" he asked. I told him that I did not. Even though I suspected the reason strongly, I didn't want to sound presumptuous and say so.

He asked if I was familiar with the Economic Commission for Africa.

"Yes, very much so," I told him.

"This organization is very important for Africa," he said, "but right now, it's not in good shape."

And from that, Boutros-Ghali laid out in detail a number of problems he saw at the ECA, problems that primarily concerned its management structure and staff. Workers were not happy, they were not being productive, and morale was poor, he said. He had heard from the commission's member states—its clients—and they were not happy either. They felt the ECA was not offering enough policy support or guidance. And there were personality conflicts with Layashi Yaker, the current executive secretary. Boutros-Ghali had appointed Yaker in 1992 under a short-term contract. That contract was coming to an end in a few months, and Boutros-Ghali told me that he intended to make a change.

Yaker, an Algerian, succeeded Issa Diallo, who served as an acting executive secretary for only about a year. Diallo had the unenviable task of following Adedeji, who had run the ECA for almost 17 years. As much as Robert Gardiner was associated with the ECA in its early days, Adedeji was the man who had put the modern-day ECA on the map.

Adedeji was strident and unapologetic in his views that Africa should not be beholden to excessive Western conditions in exchange for relief and assistance, and this earned him a lot of respect among fellow Africans. Over time, he grew close to heads of state and governments, becoming an influential voice to many. He was vocal and highly visible, and he was the face of the ECA during the creation of the Lagos Plan of Action, an important effort to strengthen African unity and ownership.

Adedeji and Gardiner together ran the organization for 30 years, which was probably too long for only one leadership change. But looking for a third executive secretary in less than five years was no good either. The ECA seemed to be suffering from both malaise and instability at the same time.

Boutros-Ghali made his desire apparent: he wanted to revitalize and renew the commission. He wanted to see its operations reformed. And he wanted to start by changing the way he selected its leader.

Boutros-Ghali said he wanted someone who came from a strong administrative background, without obvious political ties or influences. He wanted a technocrat, someone whose primary interest would be on the substance of the programs and the policy agenda. He wanted someone who understood the complexity of both sides of the aid and lending architecture. And he wanted a proven manager, someone who would be able to right the ship before plotting a new course. Then he said he had "heard a lot" about my career at the Bank and that he wanted me to take over the ECA.

"Is this something you would consider?" he asked.

I don't think my mouth dropped open, but it could have. I had assumed the point of the trip was to talk about the ECA, but I never expected an initial meeting with the secretary-general to end with a job offer. The initial appointment would be a two-year term.

I thanked Boutros-Ghali for his kind words and his confidence in me. I told him that I was very honored by his offer. And I was—honored along with stunned, which I did my best to hide. I agreed that the ECA was an important institution, and I shared with him my memories of Gardiner's radio broadcasts. I told him that I'd need some time, a few weeks, to think about it and that I'd like to consult with some others to gather more information about the organization.

He asked me not to do that.

I needed to keep our conversation quiet, he explained, because no one at the ECA knew he was going to make a change. None of the member countries knew it either. The minute word got out, the suggested nominations and political pressure would roll in immediately. He was willing to withstand any criticisms for appointing a technocrat like me, but only after the fact, when the decision was already announced. He knew different leaders would all have different ideas about whom they wanted and why and it was precisely that kind of political lobbying that he wanted to stop. He wanted to send a message about the urgency of the ECA's mission, and that getting it on track was more important than following past protocols.

He was making a pre-emptive strike to put me in the job, he said, but he had to make a move soon. And he needed a decision fast.

I asked if I could have at least two or three weeks to decide.
He answered quickly. "I can give you one."

Boutros-Ghali was a measured decision-maker and even his critics would have to agree that he didn't act rashly or without reason. His decision to embark on a renewal process for the ECA was not made in haste, nor was it based on personalities or politics. The cold, hard truth was this: in 1994, by all standard objective measures of performance and functionality, the ECA was a broken institution. It lacked relevance, influence, and a clear direction. It possessed an incredible potential to be a force in Africa's emerging voice, but it required a massive makeover. Its recent leadership had shown a remarkable unwillingness or inability—or perhaps both—to make the necessary changes to keep the ECA relevant as the needs of its member countries evolved.

In 1991, after Adedeji retired, the UN commissioned a team of external consultants to conduct a wide-ranging review of the ECA's policy program and its management capacity. The review team closely examined the ECA's structure and its professional outputs, and then they measured those findings against the operational environment for development assistance in 1990s Africa.

Their findings painted a bleak picture.

The ECA's ties with its member countries were weak, with some countries expressing outward frustration at the institution's lack of responsiveness. The ECA's policy program was too broad to be effective, with too many reports being produced by too many organizational divisions with too little follow-up. Many reports had no clear purpose other than to fulfill an output requirement for UN budgeting processes. Meanwhile, the useful analytics that were being produced weren't reaching the right audience because of an inefficient and unorganized communications and public affairs strategy. The review team found that the ECA's approach had become so clouded and aimless that a new mission statement might be warranted so "its staff and constituencies can clearly understand the main *raison d'être* for the ECA."[2]

The problems ran deep and they had become endemic to the institution. Morale was low and division chiefs rarely collaborated. Staff meetings were not common, so internal communication was poor. Results of the work program were not reported consistently and were not reliable. One member of the review team later told me how they were disheartened to see stacks and stacks of undistributed reports sitting on the office floor.

Perhaps most damning, the review called into question the ECA's intellectual rigor and found its advisory and advocacy role compromised by questionable or unsound research: "The [ECA] must ensure that its advice to member states is based on what is known and that reports on its achievements are based on serious evaluation of what has actually been achieved."

The review team tried to consider the strains that the ECA had been placed under—an expanding mandate that stretched the limits of the institution's capacity, and increasing competition from other regional organizations. Competition in this context meant the fight for funding to implement programs and undertake research, as well as the struggle to have its ideas heard and its strategies considered. Some of this competition was coming from within the UN system, from other agencies trying to impose their own agenda.

The task force report recommended that the ECA try to get a grip on its broad mandate by streamlining its mission under a more cohesive and succinct mission statement: "We shall be the voice for Africa's economic and social transformation." It was a straightforward summary of the best option for the ECA going forward, a way for the institution to clear the decks, and focus on reinvigorating the institution's comparative advantages:

> [The] ECA does not face a problem of legitimacy in its mandate; rather it confronts a huge problem of making its impact felt at the operational level. To be relevant and competitive, the ECA needs to do better what it already does best: to provide intellectual leadership in developing ideas and strategies and to reinforce its advocacy role on behalf of Africa—an advocacy backed by technically competent research and analysis. At the same time, the ECA has to cultivate or reinforce excellent relationships with stakeholders in Africa's socioeconomic development.

In a six-page personal memo to executive secretary Issa Diallo, the chair and vice chair of the review team went to great lengths to highlight actions that could be taken to counterbalance some of the report's more negative findings: "You have every right to be discouraged by this long list of problems, but we urge you not to be," they wrote, adding that they were "genuinely impressed with the potential the ECA has as a large collection of professionals, as an institution commanding a significant budget, as a key place for African leaders and the leadership of the ECA's views." Their memo to Diallo offered numerous suggestions for staff restructuring, programmatic reform, and stronger member outreach. "By any means, not everything is broken at the ECA," they added, "but a great deal is running at low speed."

The review team gave its findings to Diallo in November 1991—more than three years before Boutros-Ghali called me to New York. I can't speak to the motivations or constraints that influenced either Diallo or his successor, Yaker, but, whatever the reasons, the ECA had not shown any discernible improvement to UN headquarters during those three years. Nor had it shown any sustained attempt at reform. The detailed set of recommendations from the task force had gone almost completely unheeded.

On the trip back home from New York, I thought I had made a quick decision on what I would do: nothing, other than thank Boutros-Ghali for his offer and move on. I would be lying if I said I didn't feel proud, and while I was more than a little stunned at how the day had unfolded, I was energized by the sheer thrill of it all. I had carried a strong optimism about Africa with me since I was a boy in Ghana, and my talk with Boutros-Ghali had definitely stirred those feelings. I let my mind wander about the possibility of impacting African development on a bigger scale.

Still it felt more like a daydream. I didn't think I could seriously consider the offer. I had too much going on at the Bank. I didn't want to leave my staff, I didn't want to leave my new department, and I didn't want to leave my career. I felt disloyal just thinking about it. Moreover, I couldn't shake the feeling that the job might simply be too much for me.

But my wife disagreed. Naturally I talked to Philomena as soon as I got home, and she rejected my quick resolution. She told me to take a little time and to at least consider the possibilities. She said that I owed it to the secretary-general to take his offer seriously, and, more importantly, that I owed it to myself. Think about the reasons to say yes as well as the reasons to say no, she said.

The next day, I tried to move past the emotions and get serious about the reality. Even before my conversation with Boutros-Ghali, l knew a good bit about the ECA and its internal practices and motivations. For as long as I could remember, the World Bank and the ECA had been fighting and arguing over the best approaches for economic development and poverty reduction in Africa. These fights were more or less rooted in the structural adjustment policies of the 1980s that I described in previous chapters. Over time, the bickering engendered a lot of ill will between the two organizations.

Naturally, I had some concerns that were bigger than my feelings of loyalty to the Bank and my staff. Having spent my entire career at the

Bank, I wondered how eagerly the ECA community would accept me. I was concerned about walking into a potentially hostile environment with a mandate to overhaul it from top to bottom. This would be different from reforming a disappointing division or creating a new department. This would be rebuilding on a whole other scale.

But the biggest issue was the simplest: I didn't really want to leave the Bank. The CV exercise had given me reason to reconsider spending my career in one place, but ultimately I realized that I was quite content. I was on the right path for a potential vice presidency, but even short of that I had reached a level that allowed me to work on some great things. Was I willing to give that up for so much uncertainty? The chance of failure at the ECA seemed at least as high as success, and if I failed I really wasn't sure where that would leave me.

Boutros-Ghali asked me to keep the offer quiet, and I wanted to honor his request. But no one could make such a big decision in isolation, and he was aware of that. He didn't expect me to stay silent; he just wanted me to be discreet. So I decided to discuss the situation with two of the people I trusted the most.

First I went to Kim Jaycox. He was no longer my immediate boss since I had moved on from the African region, but we spoke often and he had become a true mentor. He had always been so encouraging and supportive of all African staff and me, and I never would have become a division chief without him. He knew me, but he also knew Africa; he had lived there. It was a passion for him, so he could relate, even though he wasn't African, to the magnitude of this decision for me—leaving everything I knew for the opportunity to return "home."

We talked in his office, and I listed the pros and cons as I saw them. He listened closely, never interrupting me. When I finished talking, he took a long pause, then told me without hesitation to take the job.

"The ECA needs to be an important institution for Africa, and right now it's not," he said, echoing the words of Boutros-Ghali. He told me he believed I could help get it back on track and if he truly thought otherwise he would say so.

I trusted his opinion not just as a mentor but as an eyewitness. In his position as vice president for Africa, Jaycox had been the point person for the Bank's battles with Adedeji and the ECA in recent years. He had been at the center of the debate over who had the right approach, who had the right strategy, who had the right answers. He knew the ECA inside and out.

We talked a little longer, but his support was unequivocal.

"Go get the experience," he said. "Turn the place around." Then, he offered me the equivalent of career insurance. "If you want to come back to the Bank when it's over," he said, "you can come back."

After talking to Jaycox, I also sought out Shahid Husain. In the few years since I'd worked for him in the Latin America region, he had gone on to become a vice president for personnel and administration—an extremely powerful position. Short of the president and some board members, he was the most influential voice inside the Bank. Husain had all but forced me to take a job under him as a director, even when I doubted my ability. He was right; I was wrong. His opinion mattered to me. And he too advised me to take the job. Like Jaycox, he also told me that I would be welcome to return to the Bank after the two years were up.

The two men most responsible for my career inside the Bank—two men I happened to admire greatly, who had shown their faith in me even when I had none—both told me to take the leap. More importantly, they both assured me that I would have a place to land back if the ECA did not work out.

And yet I could not shake my deep concerns about how I would be received inside the ECA. Not only would I be coming to shake things up, I would be coming from behind enemy lines. How would I handle that?

The more I thought about it, the more I surprised myself. Increasingly, I found my thoughts drifting to what I *could* do, rather than could not—or as Philomena had said, the reasons to say yes, not no. What if my long history and experience at the Bank could actually help reset relations, not just between the ECA and the Bank but between the ECA and African countries? After two decades, I had established some pretty good working relationships in many countries, from political leaders at the top, down through the ranks of policymakers and technocrats. What if I could reposition the institution and apply the same partnership approach that had worked for me at the Bank, but at the ground level of African development?

I began to form my own theories. Getting the institution to function more smoothly would not be enough to make it relevant again; the ECA needed to be connected to the world around it. It needed better relations with the World Bank and other multilaterals. It needed better relations with UN headquarters and other UN agencies. And it needed better relations with the global development community at large. These thoughts encouraged and excited me.

All in all, it took me almost three weeks to come to a decision. When I called Boutros-Ghali, I thanked him for giving me the extra time to make up my mind. I took longer than he preferred, but he never pressured me. I thanked him for that, as well. And then I accepted the job.

◆　◆　◆　◆

Why did I do it? I've reflected on that question a lot over the years, mostly during times of frustration, when the effort didn't seem worth it or when the battle scars seemed particularly painful. In the end, the biggest factor turned out to be the most important one of all—my family.

My kids were at a critical period in their lives. My oldest daughter, Ama, was already in college, but the twins, Nana and Mame, were still in high school. Their education was extremely important to me—just as mine had been to my father—and I didn't want to uproot them. Higher education presents enough challenges without your parents being on another continent. Philomena was also at a crucial point. She had embarked on her own career at the World Bank in information technology. When we moved from California, she quit working until the girls were grown. She had sacrificed years of her career for mine and for our family, and I could not ask to her do that again. For all my indecision about leaving the Bank or being capable enough to do the job, I realized my family was the real reason I couldn't commit. Jaycox and Husain had helped convince me that I was up to the challenge. But taking the job would mean one of two things: living apart from my wife and kids, or utterly disrupting their lives. I was not prepared to do either.

So when Philomena first told me to consider all the possibilities, I did. Or at least I tried. But she could see my uncertainty, and she knew why I was struggling—just as I had seen with Kenneth Kaunda in Zambia, my head and my heart were at odds. So one night she gave me the perspective that, as a husband and father, I simply did not have.

"All your life," Philomena told me, "you've called yourself a pan-Africanist. You've called Nkrumah your hero, for his inspiration and hope. You need to reflect on what this job means for that, not just for us. This is a chance to do something for what you *believe in*. Probably your best chance."

Our conversation was honest, real, and eye-opening. In a few sentences, Philomena clarified a complex situation that I could not. She urged me to take the risk and embrace the opportunity to return to Africa full-time and to dedicate myself to working on the frontlines of African development. And she assured me that she and my daughters would support my decision 100 percent.

I reconsidered how I had spent all my professional life in one place. Then I thought about how well my experience in managing people, planning programs, and building relationships would serve me in this job. I thought about how I would be immersed in the very issues I grew up hearing about from my father, from Gardiner's radio broadcasts, and from Nkrumah's speeches. I decided to study economics with the goal of contributing to Africa's economic dialogue, and what better way, I came to believe, than in this role? I was never a politician and I never intended to be one. If I wanted to contribute directly to Africa's development, this would be, as Philomena said, my best chance.

With my wife and family behind me, and with the option of returning to the Bank if things did not work out, I could listen to both my head and my heart. And each told me the same thing.

It was time to go.

Notes

1   After Ghana gained independence in 1957, the dominoes started to fall. Five African countries gained independence between 1958 and 1959 and 17 others in 1960. After Nelson Mandela's 1994 election in South Africa, 53 countries were independent and all were members of the ECA.

2   "Report of the Task Force on Review and Appraisal of the Policy Orientation, Programs, and Management Capacity of the United Nations Economic Commission for Africa," November 1991.

Part II
In Africa

My goal was to get as many African voices as possible involved so that the ideas we generated were representative, inclusive, and relevant. At the end of the day, it came down to ownership. Ownership over the issues. Ownership over the dialogue. Ownership over the solutions. I wanted to do whatever I could to ensure that the best ideas for Africa were being generated in Africa, by Africans from all walks of life.

With Ethiopian Prime Minister Meles Zenawi at a State House event in Addis Ababa, Ethiopia in 2001.

Chapter 6

Rebuilding the House
Efforts to Reform an Ineffective Institution

The beginning of my tenure at the UN Economic Commission for Africa more or less coincided with the UN's fiftieth anniversary. During the fall of 1995, a series of special events culminated in New York on October 24 with a commemorative session of the General Assembly. "Reform" was the buzzword of the day. Most countries addressed it in their statements, the result being a dizzying array of interpretations of what UN reform should entail. Its thematic popularity ensured that an official call for reform would be included in the joint declaration made by the member states at the end of the ceremony. And it was. "In order to be able to respond effectively to the challenges of the future and the expectations of the United Nations held by peoples around the world, it is essential that the United Nations itself be reformed and modernized"—so stated declaration item no. 14.[1]

The UN has always seemed to be in a perpetual state of reform, an endless cycle of special committees, high-level working groups, and global commissions. A large part of the problem is that the UN, despite its best efforts, has remained resistant to change, a consequence of being a multilateral organization beholden to so many members wielding varying levels of political power and pursuing disparate interests. At the time of the fiftieth anniversary, a paper presented by Sir Brian Urquhart, then a scholar-in-residence at the Ford Foundation, identified five major cycles of UN reform that had taken place—or, a new reform initiative beginning

173

approximately every eight years. Urquhart knew the topic well. He was a personal assistant to the UN's first secretary-general, Trygve Lie, and after retiring he became one of the leading thinkers and authors on UN operational strategy and internal processes. Urquhart was just one among many to use the fiftieth anniversary as a reason to highlight the need for stronger and more lasting reforms amid the wave of ongoing UN publicity.

Indeed, the international spotlight was shining brightly on the organization, and not only to commemorate its half-century. Earlier in the year, The New York Times ran a front-page story—"Mismanagement and Waste Erode UN's Best Intentions"—that called further attention to some of the problems, such as stolen or lost funds, which continued to plague various peacekeeping missions and other efforts under Boutros Boutros-Ghali's expanded mandate. Publicly, the UN was taking a beating. The pressure to show progress, at any or all levels, was enormous, and it seemed as if no part of the organization was immune from judgment, certainly not the regional economic commissions.

For critics both inside and outside the UN looking at cost and efficiency, the regional commissions were an easy target. Hard results were sometimes tough to discern and their mandates and expenditures were constantly being called into question. So it didn't help when an outfit like the ECA was functioning at such a low-impact level.

In June 1995, about five months after I'd accepted the job to run the ECA but a month before I started, UN headquarters sent its own person, Karl Paschke, to Addis Ababa to review the agency. Paschke, a German diplomat, was the UN's first-ever under-secretary-general for internal oversight, appointed the year before in response to the growing criticism around UN practices and inefficiencies. The UN's internal auditing system was not thought to be very strong, nor did the audit division report regularly to intergovernmental bodies. Paschke's appointment was aimed at strengthening the internal oversight at a time when the UN was really on the hot seat and his efforts made headlines. The aforementioned New York Times story focused heavily on Paschke's early findings, for example. Coming amid such heightened awareness of UN operations, Paschke's visit to Addis attracted considerable attention.

Over three days, he held a series of meetings with ECA officials and the heads of UN specialized agencies. Once finished, he gave a statement to the press. And he made it clear that he didn't like what he had seen. Paschke said that the ECA was too theoretical and that its mission needed to be rethought in view of the changing global economy. "In order to expedite the overall change expected in the ECA," the Ethiopian World Herald quoted Paschke as saying, "it needs restructuring, job descriptions need to be rewritten, and individual work plans of units should be revitalized with a thorough introspection on the part of the commission itself."

My term as executive secretary didn't begin until the following month, but Paschke shared his findings with me. And he was quite candid.

Much like the most intractable corners of the UN bureaucracy, he said, the ECA resisted change. He found that little progress had been made in addressing the issues identified by the sweeping 1991 external review, despite many of the same problems—professional isolation, internal control weaknesses, poor skills development—being flagged *again,* in a separate UN analysis, two years later. Twice in four years, key organizational problems had been identified without demonstrable action being taken. Paschke expressed severe concerns over the future of the institution.

"The problems are endemic," he told me, "top to bottom. And they're corrosive."

Around the same time, I learned a very important term that was pivotal to understanding the culture at the ECA: "the House." All the staff—the international staff, the professional staff, the local support staff—rarely referred to the ECA by its name; they all spoke of it as "the House." It was a statement of ownership, of being bonded together under the same roof, like a family. The staff weren't literal shut-ins, but most of them weren't receptive to those they perceived as outsiders. The ECA was their house. It operated under their rules.

Makha Sarr, the ECA's deputy executive secretary who was also the acting head in the months preceding my arrival, didn't agree with Paschke's findings. In a long but polite memo, Sarr argued that Paschke's public remarks did not "do enough justice" to the ECA's current work or past contributions. Paschke responded to Sarr a few days later, with a short and equally polite letter that acknowledged the ECA's past successes while standing firmly behind his gathered opinion: that for the ECA to pursue its work, the institution needed a major reform process.

"I came away with serious doubts about the continuing relevance of the ECA's mandate and its impact on African states," Paschke wrote.

A few days later, on July 10, 1995 I took over, with Paschke's sobering assessment as a baseline and a single tall task in front of me: I had to rebuild the House. Fortunately, I had a head start.

◆ ◆ ◆ ◆

Six months elapsed between the official announcement of my appointment at the ECA and when I actually started work, a delay caused by the need to extricate myself from Bank projects. There was a silver lining, however; I had enough time to do my own research and due diligence. Boutros-Ghali asked me to revitalize the ECA, but he didn't tell me to what end or to what extent, so devising a plan of attack was up to me. I had the external reviews, internal reports, secondhand accounts, and even my own historical knowledge to rely on. But I wanted those inputs to contribute to, not comprise the whole of, my evidence base. In other words, I needed to gather my own data. I already knew my first action at the ECA would be to kick off a major reform process; what I wanted to figure out during this six-month window was how I would go about it.

I called this interim period my "discovery phase" and it consisted of two main thrusts. First, I formed my own small task force to help identify the ECA's most immediate needs, most fixable problems, and most workable solutions. The group consisted of a half-dozen people I trusted completely, either experienced consultants with whom I'd worked in the past or current Bank associates. They helped me comb through a large volume of reports and reviews. Second, I traveled to ECA headquarters in Addis to survey the scene for myself and meet senior staff. I wanted to see the operation on the ground, to know exactly what I had gotten myself into.

Given all this research at my disposal, I rather quickly formed a clear mission statement: for the ECA to regain its relevance at home and abroad, it needed to be at the forefront of strategic policy innovations in Africa. That would be the goal. But at the present time, it was nowhere close, crippled by the problems that Paschke and others had found. I found them too, and they ran much deeper than low morale or weak research. They were structural and financial, and they exemplified how a large development institution could veer off course.

For instance, an unwieldy and ineffective slate of activities constricted the ECA's ability to make an impact in any one area—its efforts were spread too thin across too many fields. At the time of my appointment, it was trying to run almost two dozen separate policy programs. As a result, it too often failed to connect with Africa's most immediate development issues. And it missed opportunities because it didn't have the capacity to act swiftly.

At the time, a number of African governments were undergoing fundamental change, moving from state-dominated to free-market oriented economies, from autocracy to democracy, and in some cases, from conflict to rehabilitation and reconstruction. These countries made up the ECA's membership, and as their needs rapidly evolved, the ECA needed to be in a better position to meet that changing demand and, in certain situations, drive the demand. But based on the evidence collected over the previous few years, the agency did not have the cultural, structural, or organizational strength to carry out its core mandate—providing intellectual leadership and technical support to African countries.

Was this only the result of poor leadership? Hardly. The ECA was not immune to the problems plaguing other UN agencies, such as shrinking resources in the face of rising demands. In fact, one of the big reasons the ECA's work program was stretched so thin was that its guiding body, the conference of ministers, had continually sought more and more assistance over the years. The institution tried to answer the requests, even though it didn't necessarily have the in-house expertise to respond to those requests.

It also didn't have the money to continue operating at its current level.

The UN budgeting system could give even the most astute accountant a headache, but the ECA desperately needed more financial flexibility. When I arrived, the money situation was deteriorating, due mostly to a precipitous drop in resources from outside the standard operating budget, also known as extra-budgetary (or "XB") resources. Regional economic commissions relied heavily on these supplemental funds, which came from donor or other UN agencies, particularly the United Nations Development Programme. But by 1995, the ECA was barely generating any external revenue.[2] Part of the problem was that other UN agencies began to take work (and funds) away from the ECA as its stature diminished, but the ECA also failed to generate enough proposals and lobby for enough funds to cover its costs.

It all added up to a reactive, scattershot strategy in which the ECA wasn't taking the lead on any important issues, not even its own financing. Between shrinking resources, increasing demands, changing needs, and stagnating productivity, the institution was trapped inside itself. My reform plan had to take all of that into account, and that's where the second aspect of my "discovery," the on-site visits, proved extremely useful.

I had two goals for my early trips, which took place in February and May 1995: to gather feedback for my own use, and to introduce myself personally to the staff. I wanted to try to find common ground with those who wanted to make the ECA a better place. Adebayo Adedeji was long gone, but the ECA remained full of loyalists to his policies and procedures—and to his anti-Bank sentiments. I knew many of them would be reluctant to accept me. So in that regard, I wanted to alleviate as many concerns as possible over my background and send an early signal that I valued collaboration.

During my first visit, I gathered the ECA's existing senior management team around a large oval table in the center of the conference room that flanked the executive secretary's office. I let them know that I wanted to hear from them directly and that I valued what they had to say. I hoped to set the tone for a less isolated, insular, and defensive ECA.

Overall, the meeting was productive and honest. Most of them felt frustrated and boxed in by the ECA's direction. They expressed concern over how many reports were being churned out without any regard for impact, or how many conferences were being held without any attempt to build partnerships. They seemed capable if not necessarily enthused. They were supportive of the broad parameters of reform that I described, but I could sense their skepticism.

In retrospect, none of this came as a surprise. I saw for myself a workplace where optimism was hard to come by. Accountability was minimized and merit devalued. Staff reported losing countless hours to useless paperwork, while mundane activities were made unnecessarily difficult, such as cashing money at the in-house bank, which could take up to half a day, or simply riding the elevators, which were achingly slow if they worked at all. Another source of tension came from the support staff—the secretarial pool, the janitorial workers, the maintenance crews, and so on. These folks were almost all locals, Ethiopians who saw the ECA primarily as an employer that helped feed their families. They were vital to the ECA's functional operations but their opinions and ideas were generally disregarded. As a result, this large group felt disenfranchised.[3]

Many of these problems had nothing to do with the institution's intellectual output, but they exemplified everything about its lack of internal dynamism.

It was a wearisome environment for anyone to enter. And just as I had expected, my background stirred up strong feelings. A small but vocal faction were determined to try to block me at every juncture. Some were hardcore, anti-reformists who either didn't support the changes I wanted to make or simply wanted to preserve their own comfortable status quo. Others, best described as the bad apples of the bunch, had more nefarious motivations. They tried to undermine me to assert their own authority, and they exploited my ties to the Bank to stoke fear and paranoia. They simply would not accept that someone from the Bank could have the best interests of the ECA at heart.

Fortunately, the vast majority of staff were not antagonists, and that worked to my advantage. Most people were more than willing to give me a shot, even if many of them, such as the senior managers with whom I first met, seemed skeptical, or if others, like the support staff, were quietly rooting for reforms on the sidelines. The malcontents couldn't change the fact that the ECA staff by and large *wanted* to move in a new direction. They just needed to be convinced that I was serious, capable, and would not impose my will at random.

When I met with the head of the staff union during one of my early visits, he implored me to rely on the people in the House to help turn it around.

"You can come in here and think you are the big cat," he said, "but we are the mice. We will always know this place better than you."

I assured him that I had every intention of using the staff, both professional and support, to build a consensus of support and that I realized I had to win them over. He agreed to give me the benefit of the doubt, and he was among a small handful who stood by me and publicly supported reform from the start—at great risk to his reputation.

Most others had to be brought along. They wanted change; they just needed to see it to believe in it. I couldn't blame them for that.

◆　◆　◆　◆

The key date in the reform process was May 6, 1996, the start of the twenty-second meeting of the African Conference of Ministers of Planning in Addis. The ministers served more or less as the ECA's governing body, so any substantive changes in the ECA's direction and approach had to get their seal of approval. I officially took over the ECA on July 10, 1995, so that gave me a little less than 10 months to finalize reforms before the next ministerial meeting. That might seem like a long time, but it wasn't.

Given the concerns over my Bank background, I knew that whatever I gave the ministers had to be bulletproof. Its arguments needed to be airtight and its details finely tuned. Most of all, it needed buy-in. I didn't expect everyone to go along with me, but I wanted to be able to present a reform agenda as a group effort, rooted in consensus. Internally, I wanted it to unify and inspire innovation. Externally, at least to the ministers, I wanted it to inspire confidence—in the institution and in my leadership. Ten months wasn't a lot of time to pull that off, and I knew that I'd only have one shot to get the ministers on board. I couldn't wait 22 months into my tenure to get the okay to move ahead—my initial appointment was only for two years, after all.

Based on the legwork and research from my "discovery phase," I envisioned a three-pronged strategy for crafting the agenda.

First and foremost, I would engage the staff in the process. I intended to make every effort possible to get them involved from the beginning. I wanted to introduce a stronger brand of accountability in leadership, but I had no intention of imposing edicts.

Second, I would bring in external experts and partners. The steps I envisioned involved unprecedented consultations, reviews, and feedback loops. I wanted a wide variety of voices to comment on what the ECA should be doing, especially those who were looking to the ECA to be a thought leader and authoritative source of information.

And third, I would look for ways to gain flexibility within the rigid UN system, for purposes that were also operational, such as installing my own management and financial teams. The ECA simply had to find new sources of revenue to support its work and to attract the strongest personnel.

Although the primary goal was to devise a work program that would set the ECA on a new course, I didn't want to simply change operational direction; I wanted to remake the place from the inside out.

When I arrived, for example, the institution had an atomized budget spread across almost two dozen areas of focus, and each department wanted to deliver its own "output," regardless of need or demand. These sprawling mini domains rarely interacted with each other, so there was little to no overlap in production or research. My ultimate objective was to tear down that structure and refocus the ECA around a tighter, more cohesive economic agenda driven by collaborative teamwork. So I started with step one of my strategy—engaging the staff.

Given the bloat of the ECA's work program, it was inevitable that internal reforms would lead to collapsed divisions and reduced jobs. Most staff members were intuitive enough to see this coming, so I knew that gaining buy-in would not be easy. And while I had operational roadblocks— primarily the restrictive UN hiring and human resource policies—I also had personal realities to consider. These were people's jobs, their livelihoods. And even though everyone wasn't an all-star, many people wanted the ECA to succeed and wanted to produce meaningful work. The bottom line was that I couldn't change the organization's culture alone, nor did I want to try. That had never been my style. I wanted to enact the changes together, with as many staff as were willing to come along for the ride. It was my job, therefore, to sell them on my vision. For inspiration, I drew on my recent experience.

My 10 years at the ECA almost exactly mirrored James Wolfensohn's tenure at the World Bank. During that decade, he and I developed a strong working relationship at our respective institutions, but we did have a short period at the Bank that overlapped—Wolfensohn arrived on June 1, 1995 and I departed a few weeks later. I'm thankful for that brief overlap, because one of his first actions at the Bank had a big impact on me. New to the job, Wolfensohn sent a short memo to the staff. In it, he introduced himself and described his long-term plans for the Bank. His words were clear and inviting, but also forceful. I had seen a few Bank presidents come and go, but no one before Wolfensohn had begun his tenure with such a direct and transparent approach. It set a tone and gave a direction.

So I did the same thing.

On July 10, I sent an introductory, four-page memo to the full staff, not just the senior managers or executives; I wanted the whole House to see it. The note laid out my proposed blueprint for moving forward. Transparency, I reasoned, would be paramount. I gave the reform agenda a name—"Serving Africa better"—and I boiled it down to three guiding principles: professional excellence, greater cost-effectiveness, and enhanced partnerships. I described the approaches I planned to use in the first six months, including a reliance on staff inputs, and I committed to having a "statement of strategic vision" finalized by the beginning of 1996. In turn, that strategic vision would comprise the core of the formal plan to be presented to the full conference of ministers in May 1996.

Two of the three principles were fairly self-explanatory. On cost-effectiveness, I wanted to make the best possible use of our tight resources through reorganization, better modes of operation, and better use of technology (such as ensuring that the ECA was not left behind at the dawn of the digital revolution). On enhanced partnerships, I envisioned stronger and more fruitful alliances with other organizations, agencies, and member countries. I made one key message clear: the ECA would re-engage with the global community. But to do that effectively, we had to exercise more discretion in what we produced—and be better at producing it.

I sent the memo on my first day in the office. Because as the saying goes, you only get one chance to make a first impression. I knew how many people viewed me with suspicion, and I also knew the environment would only worsen once I launched an aggressive recruitment drive to bring in new blood. So my public introduction needed to accomplish a few different things. I wanted it to be a persuasive argument for change—hopeful and uplifting and forward-looking. But it also had to be transparent and truthful. Once all the changes were in place a few years down the road, many ECA "survivors" told me just how much they appreciated that introductory memo and its honesty and call to action.

It's a lesson I'd pass on to anybody ready to assume a leadership role.

The memo described my intentions, but it was still one-way communication. Reaching out to the staff immediately to seek their inputs seemed like the best way to create a more open work environment and to start narrowing the ECA's focus. I arrived with plenty of knowledge about what had gone wrong and plenty of ideas about where I wanted to go, but I had very few specifics set in stone. I truly wanted the staff to participate and help guide the process.

In the first few weeks, I started with small meetings, either private one-on-one affairs for higher-ranking staff or gatherings of no more than a handful of employees. I asked for their feedback to my ideas and I promised they could speak as freely and openly as possible without fear of recourse. And believe me, some of them didn't hold back. Overall, I found these early exchanges informative and useful. They helped acclimate me to my new surroundings and they gave me a chance to get know the staff as individuals.

My eagerness also led to some early troubles. In those first days, I asked all the professional staff to write a short essay, not more than a few hundred words. I wanted them to share their views of the institution and to evaluate their own skills and performance. My request seemed reasonable enough to me, but asking for self-assessments, which had not been a standard operating procedure in the past, immediately put many people on the defense. I only wanted insights. But from their viewpoint, I was conducting an investigation. The request was not well received.

Honestly, those first few weeks were a little bit like walking on eggshells. But I kept at it. After the small meetings, we moved on to something larger. Historically at the ECA, a gathering of the entire House involved a speech by the executive secretary and little else. It had certainly never been an interactive exchange. So I changed that right away. To follow up on the memo and the small-group meetings, I called a series of town halls—I never referred to them publicly as staff meetings—where I encouraged people to get up and speak. It was heartening to watch people grow more candid and comfortable from one meeting to the next. The town halls added a dose of energy to the place and they set the tone for what came next, which was something even bigger: the "Open Space" forum.

No one quite knew what to make of Open Space, and for good reason. It was unlike anything they had seen. The concept is simple but, in the context of traditional institutional bureaucracy, subversive—the participants control the agenda, from determining topics to setting discussion times to deciding what sessions they will attend and for how long. The principles of Open Space are intentionally egalitarian to foster empowerment and ownership. It may sound a bit utopian, but it's not. I had seen it work before.[4] And it worked at the ECA, too.

My involvement was limited. A week before the on-site retreat, which was held over three days in September 1995, I sent a memo to let staff know what to expect and to pose a few general questions to act as discussion guidelines: How should we deliver our services? How should we partner with other organizations? How do we balance research and assistance? How should we set priorities?

The response was phenomenal.

Over the course of the forum, we convened more than 40 staff-led sessions. Everyone really got into the spirit. The ECA staff had never had an opportunity to speak so freely about the institution in a setting where their thoughts actually mattered. And they took the opportunity and ran with it.

At the end of the retreat, the session leaders met as a group to compile all the recommendations and notes into a single document to carry forward. A few months later, that document evolved into a broader employee report on the state of the ECA—a report that contributed greatly to the eventual reform package. It was an eye-opening account of the ECA's most urgent problems as seen by its staff. It did as much as anything to prove that I wasn't operating alone, that many others wanted the same kind of internal reforms.[5]

In my introductory memo to the staff, I mentioned the concepts of staff empowerment and ownership, but a picture is worth a thousand words and that's what this forum was: a living, breathing snapshot of the ECA's potential to become a more collaborative and dynamic institution. During the closing session, we passed a microphone around the room, encouraging people to share their experiences from the past three days—and their ideas for the future. One after another, by the dozens, people stood up to speak. Some were even openly optimistic about the idea of change.

It was a most encouraging day.

The second step of my three-pronged approach focused on external outreach. Just as the first few months of the reform process were crucial to getting staff on board, they were equally crucial to rebuilding the ECA's brand in the eyes of our member countries and the broader development community at large. I wanted to get intellectual peers and potential partners involved in the reform process, believing it would broaden our appeal and expand our influence more rapidly once we rebuilt our capacity. Also, we needed to increase the resource pool for extra-budgetary funding, which would be very difficult until we earned back some of the lost credibility.

We began by setting up meetings for extensive external guidance from African economic experts, scholars, analysts, and development peers from around the world. We brought groups to Addis for discussions and we commissioned a number of consultant studies.

The two most important studies evaluated employee skill sets against ECA needs and measured the impact and quality of the ECA's prior work. I referred to these dual reviews as efforts to assess our "supply side"—the institution's human resource capacity and skills—and its "demand side"— the technical quality of its previous analytics and report. This process proved to be a great way to bring in outside knowledge while giving us a comprehensive and objective review of the ECA's current operations. Unlike the reviews conducted by Paschke and others, these did not involve the UN in any way and they both boasted a heavy African presence.

We referred to the technical, or demand-side, reviewers as the "Oxford group" because it was led by Paul Collier, the renowned professor of economics at Oxford and director of its Center for the Study of African Economies. The full review team included academics and economists from inside and outside Africa, and their effort was the definition of a "deep dive." They studied dozens and dozens of ECA reports, going as far back as two decades or more and covering most of the institution's primary program divisions: socioeconomic research and planning, trade and development finance, agriculture, natural resources, and public administration, to name a few. Their findings echoed previous assessments: ECA reports were not easy to read, they often lacked a clear focus, and they added little to Africa's development landscape.

Yet the Oxford group did a lot more than reaffirm past findings.

All of those other ECA assessments had lacked a critical component that I found mandatory—a peer-based review of the institution's work. The Oxford group provided one, and it was a shock to the system. One UN associate told me it was "unheard of" to bring in peer reviewers for internal agency products. All the more reason to do it, I replied. Who better than a panel of leading academic and economic experts, many of whom were African, to independently assess the validity and usefulness of the ECA's outputs? They had no vested interests in the results.

Their findings were useful and quite provocative. They argued for the ECA to act as a conduit, a "research user and transmitter," describing the role as "a vital function" for Africa that no other agency currently filled. To an extent, I agreed. I also felt the ECA could do much more to exploit its convening power—and rely less on churning out so many reports. But I didn't believe the ECA should give up on generating its own research. The peer reviewers saw an agency in steep intellectual decline, with limited internal capacity, and their recommendations reflected that. Still, their honesty was needed. And the final report played a big role in shaping our new direction.

The supply-side study, or staff skills assessment, also proved invaluable because it allowed us to put as many people as we could in a position to succeed, while also pointing out the areas in need of extra skills development or administrative attention. For instance, with a good number of staff approaching retirement, the study suggested an aggressive recruitment strategy be balanced with an internal program to develop young professionals for the ECA's long-term benefit. Reorganizing and refining our work program wouldn't get us very far unless we made sure we had the right people doing the right jobs.[6]

The "supply and demand" studies relied on outside expertise to help improve the ECA's day-to-day operations, but they only contributed to the broader goal of external involvement in a narrow way, since the consulting parties had very specific terms of reference.[7] I still wanted higher-profile engagements with the outside world.

In January 1996, we formed an external consultation group tasked with providing views and suggestions on the ECA's comprehensive reform agenda. We brought more than 40 African experts from government, the private sector, academia, NGOs, and civil society to Addis to deconstruct the institution. We laid the past bare and put the future on the table. Part of it was straight public relations and I didn't try to hide it—I wanted the word to spread that the ECA was eager to reach out and incorporate the ideas of others, especially those in Africa, into its new agenda. I also wanted to grease the wheels for the ministerial meeting in May. The ECA's bureau of ministers, which functioned like a working group for the full conference, helped mediate the discussion. Its chairman, Girma Birru, Ethiopia's minister of economic cooperation and development, gave us a full endorsement, saying he was "delighted with the renewal process" and impressed by our obvious initiative. That got the word out that we were shaking things up.

We still had one other key group to involve—our current and future development partners. These were the actors who held the key to the financial resources the ECA so desperately needed, but who in recent years had lost interest in the organization. So in April 1996 we invited almost 30 donor countries and development organizations—including other UN agencies, the World Bank and IMF, and major foundations—to Addis for an ECA partners' forum. For three days, they worked directly with the ECA's senior staff to identify our comparative advantages and best delivery mechanisms. As with the Open Space employee retreat, the forum yielded a very helpful strategy report. Most important, it defined a new "business plan" that promised prominent opportunities for the ECA to contribute to development planning without trying to perform work that other institutions were better equipped to carry out.

In essence, we brought almost all of our potential development partners together and jointly agreed on the most efficient ways for the ECA to reinsert itself in the global dialogue.

By holding a high-level forum just a few weeks before the conference of ministers were to meet, I wanted to send a powerful message—the ECA would no longer stand on the sidelines. And we were confident enough in our reform measures to start re-engaging with the world even before the ministerial conference issued its final approval. In hindsight, it might have been an overly brash measure. But it got the partners excited about our renewal plan and set the ball rolling on external financing. The sooner that happened, the better.

In a short period of time, we had gathered enough information to formulate a clear blueprint to present to the conference of ministers—streamlined divisions built around a set of core programs, higher-quality staff with more technical expertise, the organizational ability to respond in real time, and the initiative and aptitude to create a renewed demand for our work. But unless we gained operational flexibility within the stringent UN bureaucracy, our reform plan would never get off the ground. And that would've been very bad. The only thing worse than doing nothing was creating a big uproar and *then* doing nothing. Tackling the flexibility issue was the third and final part of my three-pronged approach.

When I say "stringent bureaucracy," I'm mainly referring to two administrative issues—hiring and budgeting, areas of any operation that need to run smoothly but were major obstacles at the ECA. Hiring and budgeting roadblocks were endemic to the UN system and I couldn't really control them, yet I knew I would be judged to a large extent by the changes made to remove these roadblocks. Talk about being caught between a rock and a hard place.

After a few months, I went to UN headquarters to make the case that renewing the ECA would require more than sharpening the policy focus. We couldn't produce better reports or provide better services without getting better personnel and better financial support.

I knew there wasn't much to be done about the biennium budgeting process, a big contributor to UN's historic inefficiencies, but I needed to get some room to maneuver on staffing. Getting the current employees more engaged had just been the first step. No amount of enthusiasm could make up for professional deficiencies, and, unfortunately, the ECA had plenty. I could now point to almost a half-dozen studies and assessments that supported the need to go outside the UN system to recruit new hires. But to go outside the system, I had to get the approval of Joseph Connor.

Connor was the "top manager" at the UN, an undersecretary in charge of all personnel, budget, and finance matters. He and I had an interesting connection. He came to the United Nations in 1994, just before I did, and he also had been recruited by Boutros-Ghali to do at a higher level what I was asked to do at the ECA—reform a long history of mismanagement and inefficiency. Our situations ran parallel to each other, so we shared a certain perspective that lent itself to a trusting and productive working relationship. We were fighting in the same bureaucratic foxhole. Because of that, I didn't have to work too hard to convince Connor of the merits of my reform plan. During our first meeting and in subsequent follow-ups, I pitched him on the ideas that I had to upend the ECA's personnel practices and to increase its financial resource flows. I'm not sure how well I could have done my job without him as an ally, because he understood the UN staffing and budget mechanisms were intractable.

For example, everything was managed by a "post" or a specific position. Managers had to allocate a person to the post, so the UN didn't approve financing on a *budget basis* per se, but by approving a certain number of *posts* at certain levels. If this sounds limiting, it was. It didn't help that some parts of the UN, including the ECA, had a habit of parking "temporary" workers to protect a post for a future, permanent hire that might or might not come, at some undetermined time down the road. As a consequence, managers were forced to mix and match workers to fit the predetermined posts and to work around people who might be temporarily posted to a position for which they had no matching skills. I spent one grueling afternoon sitting with a spreadsheet just trying to figure out how many posts the ECA had—because no one could tell me.

In general, the posting system created a suffocating hierarchy of seniority, entitlement, and obstruction. The ECA had a huge internal apparatus reflective of its structure—21 subprograms, which meant 21 people leading them. Some division chiefs also had section chiefs, who weren't necessarily top decision-makers but were still part of an enlarged hierarchy. I intended to streamline that hierarchy right along with the work programs. And then overhaul it.

In almost all cases, promotions had been internal and automatic, and I had no intention of continuing that practice, especially when several of the staff had been hired through political patronage in the first place. I made it known that I would be appointing new people from outside the House to fill most of my senior management jobs. First, I wanted to achieve some semblance of gender and regional balance, which had been blatantly disregarded in the past. Second, I hoped to inject fresh energy and new ideas into the place. I didn't want to cherry-pick through the existing institutional malaise.

Of all the changes I pushed in the first year, hiring "outsiders" directly into top positions caused the biggest stir. It just wasn't common in the UN system. Many of the ECA's old guard took umbrage at my approach, which in their view confirmed some of their worst preconceived notions about me not respecting the House. But I didn't mind raising a few eyebrows. Poor personnel management wasn't the only reason the ECA stagnated as an institution, but it was a big one.

Meanwhile, on the budgeting side, I realized I would have to push a few boundaries there as well. To increase our client responsiveness, we needed to be able to redirect resources as needed, when needed. And the UN's biennium budgeting was anything but responsive. For example, in 1996, we were having to plan for activities through 1998 while fulfilling current obligations originally planned in 1994. A lot can happen in four or five years. The approval system was simply excruciating.

The ECA faced an additional burden due to its severe decline in XB funds. But that's where I saw an opportunity. I wanted to reverse those declines not only to improve the ECA's bottom line but to support new initiatives. More than 90 percent of the regular budget from the UN went to salaries and other administrative costs, leaving little room for anything else, such as special studies and forums—the very things on which the ECA needed to be focusing its energies. So I argued strongly for the authority to seek more resources directly from donors and through partnership agreements. Instead of using XB funds to lightly supplement activities, I wanted to make them an integral part of our operation. Not seeking the most external resources possible was a major budgetary inefficiency.

These ideas were all fairly radical at the time, but Connor was in my corner. The two of us essentially struck a deal. As long as I kept him fully apprised throughout the process, he would let the ECA operate outside the regular UN strictures and function as a "testing ground" for new ideas. Since he was trying to jump-start operational reforms within the larger UN system, he saw the ECA as a possible catalyst. We could bring as much value to UN headquarters as UN headquarters could bring to us—if the reforms worked, of course.

◆ ◆ ◆ ◆

When the ministerial conference convened in May 1996, I presented our full reform agenda, published under the title *Serving Africa Better: Strategic Directions for the Economic Commission for Africa.* "Serving Africa better" is a phrase I used in my introductory memo to the staff and it stuck with me. In three words it captured the motivations behind everything we had done up to that point—and everything we hoped to still do. "The renewal process is the most thorough ongoing reform in the ECA's history," I said in my opening remarks to the ministers. "This is the gateway to the ECA's future."

Ethiopian Prime Minister Meles Zenawi, who at the time was chair of the Organization of African Unity, opened the conference. Most of the ECA's 53 member states sent a delegation, close to four dozen of them—a sign of just how much interest our efforts had generated. These conferences convened regularly but rarely attracted that many attendees. This one was a bigger deal than usual and it showed in the turnout.

In seeking the ministers' support, I wanted to make every effort to convey the same sense of inspiration, optimism, and drive that had motivated me in the first place. So I took the delegates on a detailed trip through the past 10 months—the town hall meetings and Open Space forum with the staff, the extensive consultations with experts and partners, my push for unprecedented operational flexibility, and renewed cooperation with the larger UN apparatus. I revisited the guiding principles of excellence, cost effectiveness, and partnerships, and I laid out my vision of the ECA as a "think tank for Africa, a clearinghouse for best practices, a policy integrator, and a catalyst for people with good ideas."

And then I explained what all that talk meant in practical terms.

Serving Africa Better identified the ECA's comparative strengths, processes, and markets. It included a strategy to ensure the ECA's full participation in Africa's development agenda without duplicating existing efforts. And its details supported my original mission objective: to put the ECA at the forefront of strategic policy innovations in Africa.

To reflect the commission's new goals—and its commitment to focus and efficiency—the final reform plan streamlined the ECA's 21 subprograms into something much more manageable: five overall work programs, each with its own clear goals and objectives.

- **Economic and social policy analysis.** We wanted to refine the ECA's mission to get back to basics—to "put the 'E' back in the ECA," as I would often say. Africa's most pressing social policy issues had substantial economic implications and we intended to extend the ECA's value by deepening our understanding and our contributions in these areas.
- **Food security and sustainable development.** For years, Africa's agricultural production per capita had been in decline as its population increased. We believed the ECA could help find better ways to integrate food, farming, and environmental issues into long-term planning, a necessity to combat poverty.
- **Development management.** We saw the need for African countries to make their public sectors more efficient and their private sectors more robust. We also foresaw a stronger role for civil society. Eventually, this work program proved to be one of the ECA's most effective, underpinning future efforts to strengthen African governance.
- **Harnessing information for development.** Exploiting new technologies would be necessary to participate—and compete—in the expanding global economy. In this area, we had a head start, because the ECA had already been involved in promoting information and communication technologies even before our reform program.
- **Regional cooperation and integration.** Regional integration sat at the heart of the ECA's original mandate and we were adamant that no major initiative stray too far from it. Again, the ECA had some notable successes in this area already, so we didn't have to build a program from scratch; we just planned to be more assertive and efficient.[8]

In addition to these five main work programs, we also identified two thematic areas—gender and capacity building—to incorporate across all of our strategies. Improving gender equality was a matter of justice, but also an economic imperative given the importance of women as a force for sustainable development. Capacity building was an obvious precondition for governments to implement and manage the new policies and ideas we intended to promote.

The entire reform agenda was geared toward putting the ECA in the best position to regain the analytical rigor that had once defined it. Once we could demonstrate credibility, we would have the intellectual authority to complement other research, catalyze action, or take the lead ourselves.

"This," I said, "is the ECA's path to renewal and relevance."

The ministers agreed, unanimously endorsing *Serving Africa Better* and, in the process, giving the institution an unprecedented mandate to overhaul its operations. In their final communiqué from the conference, the ministers lauded the inclusive steps we took to arrive at our framework. The reforms, the ministers concluded, were "long overdue."

In some ways, it seemed like years had passed since I walked into Boutros-Ghali's office one morning and walked out with a job offer. Now, just 18 months later, the ECA had a five-year action plan and an extensive reform package endorsed by Africa's ministers—and backed at the highest levels of the UN.

In a statement presented to the ministerial conference, Boutros-Ghali said the ECA's renewal process "responds precisely to the need to serve member states rather than bureaucratic imperatives." Then he said our work complemented the broader, ongoing efforts to improve UN efficiency and effectiveness. "In many important aspects, the ECA is at the vanguard of renewal and reform in the United Nations."

◆　◆　◆　◆

Enacting major institutional change for the long haul is an ongoing process that doesn't really have a defined end. This is an important point because meaningful reform isn't as easy as flipping a switch on and off. It takes a sustained effort. Cynics may think the constant cycle of UN reforms is proof that the institution can't get its act together, but optimists may see a continuing commitment to improvement. Maybe the reality is somewhere in between, but I've always been an optimist. So while the ECA's reform process began with *Serving Africa Better*, it didn't end there. We kept it going for a decade.

A few years down the road, we undertook a second round of reforms to consolidate our earlier gains. We focused on strengthening the institution rather than overhauling it. And we broadened the participatory process even more. We held a second Open Space retreat and this time included the *entire* ECA staff—the professional staff as well as the hundreds of support staff, from security guards to maintenance personnel. More than 600 people participated, and they emerged with almost 700 recommendations! We identified three dozen priority projects to build on the earlier improvements. For instance, our initial reforms targeted ways to strengthen the empirical data in ECA reports and make them easier to read. The next step was to establish a stronger culture of knowledge management, so that the improved reports we were producing had a maximum impact. These extended reforms constituted our "Institutional Strengthening Program," possible only because of all the effort we invested before it.

Throughout much of this chapter, I've used the plural "we" or "our" as much as, if not more than, the singular "I" or "my." I'll do the same in upcoming chapters. There's a good reason for that: none of the strides by the ECA during these years could have been accomplished without an amazing senior leadership team, a small group of managers and advisors that made up my inner circle. They included Elene Makonnen, Peter da Costa, George Alibaruho, and Ali Todaro. In addition, Bob Berg, an experienced consultant who had worked with previous ECA executive secretaries and knew the UN system well, provided invaluable support. I leaned on these colleagues heavily for strategy, guidance, and advice—a "shadow cabinet" of decision-makers and confidantes that I trusted completely. Their role in shaping the ECA's reemergence cannot be understated. The goals we set for the ECA would never have been reached without their tireless contributions.

In October 1999, Karl Paschke, the UN's inspector-general, returned to the ECA. Four years after he had publicly voiced doubts about the institution's continuing relevance, he arrived in Addis for another round of reviews. His officially stated purpose was to assess "the achievements realized as a result of the program reforms undertaken at the ECA." Also on Paschke's to-do list: analyzing the "complementary measures" we took to increase efficiency, cost-effectiveness, and the quality and timeliness of our services.

At the conclusion of his three-day mission, Paschke recounted his findings in a memo to UN Secretary-General Kofi Annan, who replaced Boutros-Ghali in January 1997. Paschke began by noting that the meetings he held on his previous trip in 1995—with the ECA's then senior management, with permanent representatives, with member states, with donors—had led him to conclude that the institution was not "providing the vision and the leadership necessary for the economic growth of Africa." But, he went on to write, "I am pleased to report that profound reform measures have indeed taken place at the ECA. The commission has renewed its relevance. The ECA [is] functioning well and delivering to its constituents."

Paschke also commended our visible efforts at creating and maintaining partnerships with regional and international organizations, with an emphasis on advocacy and building consensus. And he lauded our commitment to forge stronger strategic alliances. Some partnerships were absolutely necessary, such as with the other continental organizations in Africa, the Organization of African Unity, and the African Development Bank. But others, including those with the World Bank, donor country governments, and civil society, exemplified the scope of our intentions. I wanted the ECA to be a natural partner with Africa's growing intellectual community—its think tanks, its universities, and its NGOs. The ECA needed to shift away from a total reliance on in-house production and toward more aggressive intellectual networking. To some, that was scary new ground we were trying to cover, but it paid off in short order.

"The ECA's relations with donor countries and member states have tremendously improved and they are generally receptive to the commission's renewed vision," Paschke concluded, adding that he was "impressed beyond expectation" with the progress we had made in four years toward transforming the ECA into a viable and relevant organization. Realigning the organizational structure to match our streamlined programs led to stronger outputs that in turn were more effective for member states, he said. "The ECA now occupies a vital place in development efforts in Africa."

Notes

1   Resolution adopted by the UN General Assembly, "Declaration on the Occasion of the Fiftieth Anniversary of the United Nations," October 24, 1995.

2   External resources had long been vital to the institution's bottom line. For example, the ECA's official UN budget for 1990–91 was $61.5 million, but its extra-budgetary resources totaled another $42 million. By the time I arrived four years later, the official budget had increased to $74 million, but the XB resources had plunged to $11 million.

3   The ECA had grown so bloated that by the time I arrived, the support staff numbered almost 400, versus approximately 250 professional staff. The high administrative and overhead costs were bad enough, but the imbalance was made worse by the fact that the support staff didn't have a strong, collective voice. Generally speaking, they wanted to feel as invested in the institution as the professional staff, and rightly so.

4   I first came across the Open Space concept at the World Bank. Giles Hopkins, a great management consultant who also became a great friend, introduced it to me. In a collection of case studies called *Tales from Open Space*, published the same year the ECA held its event, author Harrison Owen traces the origin of the practice to the mid-1980s, though it didn't start to gain real traction until an article about extracting "creativity from chaos" appeared in The Washington Post in 1992.

5   Some highlights of the employee-produced report that came from the Open Space forum included the need to "debureaucratize" the ECA and to remove its "culture of fear"; harmonize work programs both inside the ECA and among other UN agencies; generate more "accurate, relevant, and timely" research data; and only abide staff members who were committed to "competence and confidence, integrity, and loyalty." But the report wasn't just a list of what needed to be fixed; it offered solutions as well. For instance, it included ideas for better human resource management, such as regular consultation meetings and field assignments. It was very insightful.

6   The review, which was for the professional staff only, was administered by an outside group of human resource specialists and it accomplished this most basic objective. It identified more than 50 current staffers with the right qualifications to fill critical jobs in a reorganized ECA. It then identified another three dozen staffers who met the basic requirements for appointment to new posts but would benefit from additional training.

7   The "supply and demand studies" were the most influential consultant efforts to improve ECA performance, but they weren't the only ones. I called in a number of international experts between September 1995 and April 1996 to study almost every major aspect of the ECA's operations, including management and administration, training and human resource development, information technology, and external communications—which the ECA had almost completely disregarded as an integrated component of its work. In spring 1996, we released what I feel was the most comprehensive study of the ECA communication strategies that had ever been done, and it helped redefine the way that the ECA shared its research and promoted its findings to member countries and partners.

8   For instance, the ECA ran smaller sub-regional development centers throughout Africa that were stretched as thin as the ECA, only on a local level. Our reforms decentralized the oversight of those offices to make them more responsive to regional needs, and we made sure the geographic coverage of each location was more equitably distributed.

Chapter 7

A Stronger Voice
Renewing the ECA's Relevance
as an Advocate for Africa

The African finance ministers were not happy. Voicing doubt and frustration over the new debt relief program spearheaded by the World Bank and IMF, the Heavily Indebted Poor Country (HIPC) initiative, the ministers pushed back against terms they found unfavorable. "As many reforming African countries as possible" should have access to the HIPC package, they said in a statement, urging the Bretton Woods Institutions to ease eligibility requirements for countries with a "demonstrated record of strong performance over a long period."

The ministers had gathered in Addis Ababa in early April 1997, for their annual ECA meeting, an event that rarely raised too many eyebrows among the attendees, much less garnered international attention or headlines. But that year's meeting turned out to be different.

For starters, it took place just a few weeks ahead of the Bank's regular spring meetings in Washington, DC when HIPC was a topic on everyone's mind. Launched in October 1996, HIPC was a structured program that aimed to provide relief to countries with a debt burden deemed unsustainable. Through it, the Bank and IMF would reduce and restructure bilateral, multilateral, and commercial debts to enable qualifying countries to service those debts without choking much-needed investments in economic development.

But the initial plan still called for a country to complete six years of a Bank or IMF adjustment program, a condition—and delay—that frustrated African ministers. Specifically, ministers were focused on Uganda, which had a present value of external debt reaching almost $1.9 billion and had been promised debt relief that year, only to learn shortly before the ECA ministerial meeting that creditors had pressured the Bank and IMF to hold off for another few years. This was a big deal for Uganda—Oxfam International calculated the delay would cost Uganda approximately $193 million, or six times its 1997 level of public health spending. Even with the delay, Uganda was first in line for HIPC relief, but confusion over its eligibility generated concern and skepticism among African countries still feeling the effects of structural adjustment policies.

So the timing of the ECA meeting couldn't have been better for policymakers to apply some pressure. According to Uganda Deputy Finance Minister Basoga Nsadhu, who moderated a session on HIPC, his country had intended to bring a message of hope for a breakthrough to its fellow African countries "shackled by debt amidst widespread poverty." Instead, he said, Uganda had to focus on the uncertainties of his new program, such as whether the eligibility requirements were reasonable and if planned "sustainability analyses" for HIPC-targeted countries would be consistent and fair.

Indeed, debt and adjustment issues took center stage at the conference, which also featured discussions on domestic resource mobilization and other important aspects of financing African development. In an opening address, Ethiopian Deputy Prime Minister Kassu Illala, speaking on behalf of Prime Minister Meles Zenawi, expressed doubts about HIPC's conditionality and stringent requirements. Meanwhile, the Bank and IMF sent their own heavy hitters—Callisto Madavo and Jean-Louis Sarbib, the Bank's co-vice presidents for Africa, and A. Basu, the IMF's deputy director for Africa—to counter with more optimistic messages. Presenting this kind of opposing viewpoint during a ministerial conference was an unusual practice, primarily because involving external participants was just as unusual.

The ECA, as the conference host, took on an active role as well. We supplied a background paper, *An Overview of Africa's Debt in the Context of the HIPC Initiative*, which analyzed the causes for the lingering dissatisfaction with the plan to shed an objective light on the disagreement.[1] Our paper warned that the Bank and IMF targets might be too unrealistic for the initiative to succeed. But it also took African governments to task for saying they only accepted the targets because they had no choice.

During my opening session remarks, I sided strongly with the African argument. Without a more flexible application from the Bank and IMF, I said, HIPC could end up "like the mountain that gave birth to a mouse."

It might look good on paper, but the long qualification period would not benefit African countries genuinely burdened by debt, raising concerns that creditors were not genuinely committed to relief. It was a strong position to take. Many African countries were starting to drown in debt and their only real leverage over their creditors was their collective disapproval of poor terms. The way I saw it, one of the best ways for the ECA to serve its members was to help them work in unison.

The conference definitely caused a stir. Later that month, when the Bank and IMF convened their spring meetings, the institutions announced that Uganda would get a $338 million debt reduction through HIPC in April 1998, which was not as early as Uganda—and other African countries watching the process—had hoped, but it was as early as possible given the major creditors' hesitations.

HIPC helped open the door to debt relief as one of the defining issues of African development in the ensuing decade, but the plan also had legitimate issues that African leaders and policymakers were right to question. What made the debate over HIPC at the 1997 ministerial conference unique is not how timely, urgent, and relevant it was—though those aspects shouldn't be discounted—but rather that we had the debate there at all.

Illustrating the ECA's push toward a new way of doing business, the conference format broke with tradition—a tradition in definite need of breaking. Historically, these meetings followed the same, mundane pattern. Ministers would show up, greet each other, and settle in for a parade of addresses. They all wanted their time to speak, either to push an agenda, promote a cause, introduce a resolution, or simply to have their say. There was no follow-up, no real engagement, and no sense of urgency. They would get up, speak for a while—sometimes a long while—and sit back down. After a couple of days, the conference would end. It was a routinely inactive affair.

By 1997, I had been through one cycle of ministerial conferences and seen enough to know that they could be much more meaningful. More contributions out of the attendees would be a start. I also felt the conferences could be a natural way for the ECA to showcase its renewal efforts. The sudden urgency of the HIPC issue gave me an opening to shake up the pro forma feel.

Rather than meandering speeches and empty resolutions, the overhauled 1997 conference featured lively sessions with panel discussions, pointed commentary from ministers and other African attendees, and sharp but respectful exchanges over policy. On the latter, debt relief dominated, but we also covered financial sector reform, capacity building, and capital market development.

In the present day, this format doesn't seem unique at all. But back then the changes were so radical as to cause a minor controversy.

"I have traveled a long way to be here, and I am going to have my say!" one Algerian official barked at me after learning of the format change. I told him that of course he could have his say; if he had brought prepared remarks with him then we would accept them—into the official record, just not on the dais. This was not the answer he wanted.

A few obviously agitated attendees aside, the change in tone and energy was staggering. Being able to focus on a major timely issue like debt relief and the HIPC initiative certainly helped—as did the fact that the conference occurred in the midst of this ongoing debate with the Bank and IMF, a rallying point on which most African officials found common ground. As a result, the conference turned into a major focusing event for African ministers. And it turned into a big moment for the ECA, which provided Africa with a stronger collective voice at an important juncture.

"This new format," I said during my closing remarks, "exemplifies the new ECA: showcasing African talent, promoting substance, and helping Africa find new ways to work together."

It was a way to turn the reforms into something tangible and lasting.

◆　◆　◆　◆

By the mid-1990s, the international focus on Africa's development had become very intense. The challenge of reducing poverty through appropriate domestic policies, and the role of the donors in providing financing for development, took on unprecedented prominence. Underlying the newfound attention was an increasing emphasis on "good governance" and local control, or ownership, over development agendas. With the Cold War in the past and democracy on the move, an emerging generation of African leaders, many who were democratically elected, wanted to take a more proactive approach with the global community.

The need for a credible African institution to engage in this changing landscape was clear and the ECA fit the bill. Unlike the Organization of African Unity, we were not a political entity. And unlike the African Development Bank, we were not tied to lending programs. In my view, the ECA seemed perfectly suited to become a key interlocutor, consensus builder, and stronger advocate for Africa's changing needs.

That's why it was so important to retool the ECA's internal structure—to get the right people working on the right programs. But the institutional reforms were just the first step. The second step was reforming the ways we would go about working on those programs—in other words, *operational* reforms.

The obvious place to start was by sharpening our policy focus to get the most out of our somewhat limited resources. The streamlined work program in *Serving Africa Better* gave us the template, but even within those parameters we had to be judicious about where we chose to focus our energies and to what purpose. And it wasn't always about policy or issues: I believed the ECA needed to put more effort into leveraging its convening power. Only by bringing stakeholders together in more productive and collaborative ways would it become a stronger advocate for Africa. Of course, convening started with the ministers and policymakers that made up its membership, but I wanted to bring in a broader range of contributors to the conversation—the private sector, civil society, even donors. To do that, the ECA needed to strengthen its global partnerships, which were weak and limited. And the best way to increase partner interest was by becoming more relevant and intellectually reliable.

The entire reform framework was interconnected, each big objective tied to another. And the annual ministerial conferences became a proving ground for how this approach could play out successfully.

The ECA hosted a meeting of African finance ministers, such as the one that focused on HIPC, separately from a meeting of the African ministers of planning and development, historically the ECA's governing body. I found the whole setup inefficient and redundant.

Increasingly, the African finance and planning ministers shared key areas of responsibility at the country level. Interaction between the two groups was a matter of necessity. For the ECA, that meant scarce resources being expended for two separate but similar events. So I had a thought: why not combine the two conferences into one ministerial body?

We laid the groundwork at the 1997 meeting of finance ministers by introducing the new format. So many ministers showed up, and the intensity and quality of the discussions were so productive, I grew convinced that combining both conferences into a single annual meeting could yield strong results.

I'm glad to say that's exactly what happened.

Revamped as the Conference of African Ministers of Finance and Planning, the combined event grew more popular every year, eventually becoming a highly influential forum for building consensus and forging new positions on key issues.

By injecting new life into what had long ago become a dull and repetitive affair, the conference meeting no longer plodded amid a sea of forgettable speeches. Instead, it was shaped by intensive preparatory sessions by ECA staff and country technicians to sharpen the focus around timely agenda items. We invited world-class experts to sit on panels that commonly opened session discussions. We began to include the governors of central banks as well as ministers. We reached out to civil society to bring them into the discussion, and we invited special guests from other institutions, including the World Bank.

A hallmark of each joint conference was a succinct, concluding ministerial policy statement, a unified outcome on a single topic of pressing importance, like HIPC. We did away with the dozens of toothless resolutions of the past. This alone added new weight and relevance to the collective voice of African ministers.

Naturally, as the revamped conference grew in relevance, so did the number of participants. In 1996, the meeting of planning ministers drew less than 10 actual ministers. By 2001, the joint conference averaged more than 60 ministers and central bank governors over the next five years.[2]

Combining the ministerial conferences was perhaps the most significant operational move we made to better position the ECA as a stronger advocate for Africa. Of course, it wasn't the only move. Far from it.

We had a lot of irons in the fire, but we still had limited resources. So we knew we had to be smart and selective about where we went "above and beyond" to make the institution a more connected player.

Looking back, some of the most impactful, early efforts to reposition the ECA in the way I envisioned in *Serving Africa Better*—as a key interlocutor, consensus builder, and advocate for Africa— coalesced pretty quickly around two overarching areas: development financing and governance.

Both of these issues cut across all aspects of the new work program and, more importantly, they had rapidly risen to the fore of African development dialogue. In fact, when we convened the new joint Conference of African Ministers of Finance and Planning for the first time, we did so around a major development financing forum that followed up on the HIPC debate and also put African policymakers out in front of even bigger development financing issues.

Before we did all these things, however—before we elevated the ministerial meetings and before we contributed to issues like finance and governance—we had to know the beginning well. In this case, that meant rebuilding the ECA's credibility around its core mission: providing sound advice and analysis as an economic institute. We had to put the "E" back in ECA.

◆　◆　◆　◆

Restoring the ECA's intellectual credibility meant asking ourselves a basic question: how do we best use our resources? The answer was obvious. Quality had to override quantity. In no area did that credo apply more than in published outputs. During 1996–97, the ECA produced 193 publications. More than 80 were recurring publications, which meant valuable human resources were constantly being tied to the production of all these ongoing documents. On top of that, 110 reports were prepared for ministerial and intergovernmental meetings, or by the institution's sub-regional centers throughout the continent. Altogether, the ECA produced a staggering 348 reports, documents, and publications during those two years. The average annual outputs almost outnumbered the professional staff!

Given the lead time for research and production, practically all of these were already being worked on by the time I arrived. I couldn't do anything about those, but I could ensure we ended that nonsense going forward.

Reducing the volume of publications underpinned all our operational reforms. With fewer products to produce, more resources could be devoted to more focused and higher-quality research, improved management systems, and better outreach and dissemination—all enhancements that the ECA needed. It took a few years, but we made huge strides. By the 2002–03 period, the number of recurring publications had been cut by more than half, while non-recurring publications were slashed from 106 all the way down to 35.[3]

Slashing the volume of reports was the easy part, like picking the lowest fruit from a tree. For what remained, we needed first to ensure the work was focused through the proper lens—economic impacts and outcomes— and second to ensure its intellectual integrity. The UN's other regional economic commissions were known for high-quality, intellectually rigorous reports, and I didn't want the ECA to be any different. But something vital was missing: a true flagship report.

After my review, I couldn't point to a single publication that *defined* what the institution stood for or that propelled its research objectives. Moreover, no standing report offered an engaging, relevant, and systematic analysis of Africa's key economic issues. Creating one, I figured, would be the most immediate and obvious way to give the institution a new intellectual identity.

We didn't have to start from scratch. Tucked among the avalanche of outputs was a yearly paper, the *Economic Report on Africa*, intended to provide an analysis of the main socioeconomic trends for the previous year and an outlook for the coming year. But the papers weren't very substantial—only a few dozen pages of text on average—and they tended to offer simple data reviews rather than detailed economic analysis.

For example, here's a truly meaningless sentence from the conclusion of the 1991 report: "The economic prospects for 1991 will evidently depend on both the external and internal factors that have in the recent past significantly influenced the region's economic fortunes." Talk about stating the obvious.

The *Economic Report* was the right kind of product for the ECA, but it fell way short of its potential. The opportunity to make it more impactful was apparent. Africa lacked an empirically sound, year-over-year analysis of its economic development. When our team began producing the *Economic Report on Africa* in 1996, we knew it could become a definitive take on Africa's economic progress. That was the goal; the end result became one of our signature accomplishments.

The timing also worked in our favor. In 1995, Africa had recorded its second-highest growth rate of the decade, the region's GDP had increased for a third straight year, and, in a notable indication of improving economic performance, the continent's 33 least-developed countries grew by 2.4 percent after three years of consecutive decline. So while we didn't overlook the many severe structural problems Africa still faced, we at least had a good message to build on.

The data had to remain front and center but I wanted the reports to become more accessible, more prescriptive, and more urgent than they had been—and especially less dour.

The 1994 report, for instance, projected "uncertain and mixed" prospects for the year ahead, before bleakly adding, "with few real grounds for optimism."

And kudos to anyone who continued reading beyond the third paragraph of the 1991 report, which noted that in spite of the impression that African agriculture "had done reasonably well" for most of the year, "the rains have once again failed and millions of people are threatened with starvation."

We didn't have the capacity to completely overhaul the report right away, but we did improve the tone and expand the scope to be more solution-oriented. Our first report detailed in economic terms a number of urgent social development challenges—such as unsustainable population trends, declining education standards, and containing the HIV/AIDS pandemic—at a time when many African governments had yet to recognize the full economic impact of "soft" social issues. Another big change came in how we treated the future outlook. Rather than a single page or two devoted to macroeconomic forecasts for the year ahead, we outlined a number of medium-term policy challenges that would affect the rest of the decade, particularly the need for new approaches to development financing—"the priority for policy development in the 1990s," as we called it.

Subsequent reports followed the same format: a yearly "state of the economy" report followed by updates on socioeconomic issues and/or major policy challenges for the near and medium term. In the first few years, they covered a wide range of topics that both reflected the current dominant issues—the critical roles of aid, debt, and trade in financing Africa's development, or governance reform and conflict resolution—and forecast future ones—such as structural transformation of African economies as a prerequisite for growth and poverty reduction. We also introduced a systematic peer review into the production process to solicit feedback.

The result of all these enhancements was a broader, more inclusive, and more profound examination of Africa's economic data, with greater relevance to larger audiences.

The real turning point came in 1999, when the *Economic Report on Africa* began to morph into something even more meaningful—a true thought leader.

The 1999 report sharpened its focus to analyze past and future trends from the perspective of a single overarching issue: poverty reduction and sustainability. A thematic approach gave the report a more polished structure and allowed for deeper analysis by the ECA's research staff, which showed up in the report's biggest innovation: three new composite indicators to measure growth and progress. The measurements included rankings of overall economic performance by African countries and two indices—the Sustainability Index and the Policy Stance Index—that related to prospects for reducing poverty.

Other organizations had attempted to construct composite indices, but the ECA's effort represented a departure in scale and ambition. The Sustainability Index aggregated two dozen variables into a single measurement, as opposed to the UNDP Human Development Index, which used only three. The Policy Stance Index improved on previous efforts to measure policy impact (such as the World Bank's *Adjustment in Africa* publication) by clearly separating policy and performance. For example, trade policies were evaluated on the basis of criteria such as tariff levels and customs procedures, rather than on the basis of export performance—making it possible to gain new insights into the extent to which policymakers can influence economic conditions.

The indices took the *Economic Report on Africa 1999* to a new level, but the findings are what caused others to sit up and take notice.

Our report concluded that Africa's macroeconomic performance over the previous four years—with GDP growth averaging 4.5 percent a year— had laid a good foundation for further growth, definitely a welcome contrast to the preceding 15 years of declining per capita income. But we found that economic growth remained far below the level required to make any meaningful dent in poverty. This mattered because cutting poverty in half by the year 2015 had become the world's driving development objective, a goal ratified at the World Summit for Social Development in 1995 and embraced by African governments and their development partners (and soon enshrined as the first target of the Millennium Development Goals the following year).

But the *Economic Report* offered a sobering assessment: for Africa to reduce poverty by half in the targeted time frame, it would need broad-based economic growth, a reduction in gross inequalities, and an average growth rate of at least 7 percent a year—a projection higher and more alarming than most accepted estimates. For instance, only three countries (Botswana, Republic of Congo, and Equatorial Guinea) grew at 7 percent or more in 1998. For Africa to come close to that growth rate, the report concluded, major investment increases would be needed from domestic savings, foreign inflows, and official development assistance (ODA)— "the major challenge of this time for African policymakers and their development partners."

The *Economic Report on Africa 1999* sounded alarm bells throughout the development community. It was the first study to project 7 percent growth as the requirement for sustainable poverty reduction, a figure soon confirmed by the World Bank and others in their own analyses and one that became a defining threshold for anti-poverty initiatives.

The following year, the *Economic Report on Africa 2000* completed the report's transition from an indistinct paper to a true flagship publication. We officially hit the reset button by standardizing the thematic approach (and focusing on a different issue or topic every year forward) and distributing the finished product as a full color booklet enhanced with trend lines, charts, and other graphics. And we expanded the Policy Stance Index to cover almost half of Africa and to incorporate a qualitative element: policy assessment surveys completed in more than 20 countries by public and private respondents, which allowed us to broaden our knowledge base even further. We rebranded it as the first in an annual series.

In their revised form, the reports set a new standard for the ECA, from introducing new tools to measure economic performance of countries to incorporating a peer review to ensure the integrity of the work. Historically, the institution had never held its research up to such scrutiny. They reestablished the ECA's core identity and restored the intellectual credibility that had been lost by stripping away the banal, useless pronouncements in favor of compelling research that actually drove global dialogue. We were clearly on to something; nearly 20 years later, the annual *Economic Report on Africa* was still going strong, closing in on two decades as the ECA's flagship.

◆　◆　◆　◆

While the economic reports helped the ECA regain its footing, it was the issue of development financing that first allowed the new and improved institution to spread its wings and fly. Financial resources were fundamental to meeting poverty goals; as such, development financing permeated practically every aspect of our work program. We believed finance needed to be *the* priority area for African governments, a point emphasized in the *1996 Economic Report on Africa*, the first our new team produced. Without sustainable, varied, and reliable financing for development, anti-poverty measures—and all other transformative development initiatives—were doomed to fail.

That said, financing for development encompassed so many different elements of focus need and concern for African countries—including aid, debt relief, foreign direct investment, domestic resource mobilization, and public–private partnerships—that as a singular issue its scope exceeded our initial capacity. Over time, as the ECA grew stronger as an institution and gained more clout, we became more heavily involved in almost all these aspects of the financing discussion. But as we started out, we had to apply the same standard as to all aspects of our operation: a sharper and more efficient focus.

In *Serving Africa Better*, we identified one critical aspect on which to concentrate—private sector investment:

> *Future growth and development in Africa rests with entrepreneurs and the private sector. The potential for entrepreneurship and private sector development is visible*

everywhere from the trading floors of new African stock exchanges, to the streets in all African countries. But the potential has yet to be fully exploited. It will require active policy support by the state for it to be fully realized.

When talking about development financing in the mid-1990s, the default conversation inevitably turned to aid flows or debt. Private sector financing was recognized as an important piece of the puzzle, but not nearly to the extent that it would be two decades later. Moreover, few African countries had the mechanisms they needed to actively engage the private sector. The ECA targeted three areas: improving regulatory frameworks and market policies to enable successful private investments; strengthening the informal and microenterprise sector, which were key sources of employment; and promoting industrial development. We also anticipated growing opportunities for South–South cooperation, where African countries could attract investments from other developing regions that were more economically advanced.

Meanwhile, an opportunity for something more public presented itself. Prior to my arrival, the ECA had tried on and off for years to hold a conference on private sector investment. But it never got off the ground and had been postponed indefinitely. Much like the *Economic Report on Africa* seemed like a natural showcase for better research, this stalled conference seemed like a great way to announce the ECA's re-emergence as a collaborative partner. Also, it would dovetail nicely with the private sector approach described in *Serving Africa Better*. We got to work and set the date for June 1996.

This would be the first major event I oversaw as head of the ECA, and I wanted to get it right. So I sought assistance from a fellow Ghanaian—President Jerry John Rawlings. I asked him if the Ghana government would host the conference in Accra, with the ECA organizing in conjunction with other partners and co-sponsors. Rawlings had been elected president in 1992 under a new constitution after serving as chairman of a joint military/civilian government for a decade. He was among the growing number of elected leaders anxious to chart a new course for the continent and he saw the value in my proposition. He not only agreed to host the conference, he put the full weight of his government behind it. Ghana rallied support and drummed up attendance, including the participation of numerous heads of state, which turned out to be key.

The event—officially titled the International Conference on Reviving Private Investment in Africa—grew way beyond our initial expectations, with more than 650 attendees. It brought African policymakers together with African business leaders as well as foreign business executives to exchange experiences, open new lines of communication, and jointly articulate a common commitment to reinvigorating private domestic and foreign investments in Africa.

Discussions centered on four major sectors: infrastructure and energy, agribusiness, telecommunications, and financial services—each of which offered enormous potential for investment in growth since they had long been dominated by public sector enterprises in many African countries. Along those lines, one of the key messages to emerge was that in times of severe budgetary constraints and declining aid flows, the public and private sectors needed to work in much closer collaboration if development objectives were going to be reached—a cornerstone of future economic transformation strategies, as well.

By the time it concluded, the conference had accomplished much more than I had ever anticipated, breaking new ground in a number of ways.

First and foremost, it marked the first time that African heads of state had interacted directly with the private sector at an open forum in Africa. The highlight of the whole event turned out to be what we called a "summit roundtable" of heads of state and government in which business executives from Africa, Asia, Europe, and the United States addressed questions to the African leaders: Presidents Alpha Oumar Konaré of Mali, Robert Mugabe of Zimbabwe, Sam Nujoma of Namibia, and of course Jerry Rawlings of Ghana, as well as Côte d'Ivoire Prime Minister Daniel Duncan and South Africa Deputy Prime Minister Thabo Mbeki. Three ministers from Botswana, Senegal, and Burkina Faso representing their heads of state also attended the roundtable, although they didn't participate in the back and forth. I had the honor of moderating.

Aside from Mugabe, the leaders had been politically active in their countries for years but had only recently assumed power through democratic processes. To have them present and engage private sector leaders was a powerful sign of Africa's changing times.

The conference also launched the African Capital Markets Forum, to help build capital markets in Africa by pooling resources and sharing expertise. It offered a way to bring together capital market operators, regulatory and policy agencies, and donor agencies on a consistent basis, which had not been done in Africa before. The forum is no longer around, but it was a valuable, early mechanism for pushing action around capital market development.[4]

Another interesting outcome was accidental but still notable.

To help attract private sector VIPs from the West, I contracted the Washington-based Corporate Council for Africa, at the time a relatively

207

new trade association founded to promote business links between Africa and the United States. The CCA had formed in 1993 through a grant from the US Agency for International Development (USAID) and begun recruiting corporate business members in 1994. Our brief relationship proved mutually beneficial. They did their job by getting powerful companies like Coca-Cola on board for our conference, and we helped supply them with a successful template for their own conferences. One year later, the CCA held its first US–Africa Business Summit outside Washington, DC. It followed the exact same format we used in Accra, heads of state roundtable included. The CCA's biennial summits helped strengthen trade and financial ties between the United States and Africa and they've turned into massive, global affairs.

These type of investment conferences have become commonplace, but the style the ECA pioneered in 1996—global, interactive, African-initiated, and collaborative—was rare at the time. For instance, the World Economic Forum's first meeting on Africa took place in 1990, but it was held in Geneva and focused only on South Africa. It took more than 10 years for that annual meeting to begin its transition to a continent-wide economic summit.

As far as the ECA was concerned, perhaps the biggest outcome of the private investment conference was the demonstration of our convening power. Although the Ghana government played a key role, ECA staff worked hard behind the scenes to line up a diverse roster of partners and co-sponsors: the World Bank, the Global Coalition for Africa, the European Union, and the United Nations Development Programme; the governments of Japan, Korea, the United Kingdom, and Sweden; and a number of private companies such as ABB, a global power and technology company that's operated in Africa since 1926. The wide variety of participants—and the enthusiastic response from them—showed me that the ECA's past reputation might not be too hard to overcome after all.

The year after the investment forum, the African ministers of finance used their ECA conference as a platform to announce their dissatisfaction with the terms and progress of debt relief measures, specifically the HIPC initiative. The one-two punch of both events, in relatively close proximity but covering very different angles of the same issue, seemed to have a positive impact on the new narrative the ECA was crafting as a more unifying, proactive, and pragmatic institution. So it was important for the ECA to carry forward the momentum that had been established.

Before long, we were doing that and more.

By 1999, I was ready to combine the separate ministerial conferences into one joint meeting. It was a big step, so we needed to ensure a big draw. Financing for development seemed obvious. Earlier that year the *Economic Report on Africa 1999* had been published with its thematic focus on the economics of poverty reduction. The 7 percent baseline for per annum growth grabbed the most attention, but the report contained other eye-opening numbers directly related to development financing. For instance, we found that Africa as a whole needed to invest 33 percent of GDP to reach 7 percent annual growth. But with a domestic savings rate of about 15 percent and ODA averaging about 9 percent, Africa faced a significant financing gap to meet the development goals it and its global partners had agreed to. Meanwhile, debt burdens continued to escalate to crisis levels.

We organized the joint conference around a single theme, "The Challenges of Financing Africa's Development," and we used the findings of the 1999 economic report as a jumping-off point. It was a coordinated strategy that underscored how much more efficient—and effective—the institution had become. Only a few years earlier, we could get barely a dozen ministers to show up. By 1999, the multi-stakeholder approach had become the new normal and attendance swelled. Approximately 30 ministers and several governors of African central banks were among the 500 attendees, which also included many private sector officials and what by then had become the usual multilateral and bilateral lineup: the World Bank, IMF, European governments, and other UN agencies.

The joint conference served as a follow-up to the HIPC-focused meeting of finance ministers held two years prior, but it broadened the scope to incorporate the full spectrum of financing obstacles facing Africa at the close of the century: the decline in aid to Africa as donor countries faced budgetary constraints and increased demand from other developing regions; Africa's excessive capital flight, brought on by poor macroeconomic policies as well as illicit transfers; and the continuing burden of external debt weighing down so many African countries.

In fact, in the two years since the finance ministers came together at the ECA to openly debate the merits of HIPC, that initiative remained the only major mechanism for debt reduction on the table. And its slow pace caused immense frustration and anger. By the time our conference convened, only four countries had seen their debt reduced: Uganda, Bolivia, Guyana, and Mozambique.

In an opening statement to the conference, Ethiopian Prime Minister Meles Zenawi acknowledged that HIPC was "a step forward" from previous initiatives launched by creditor nations and institutions but that the steps envisaged by HIPC were "half-hearted and far from adequate"—a fact he believed was recognized even by the authors of HIPC themselves.

The ECA prepared an extensive background paper for the joint conference that drew on data from the *Economic Report on Africa 1999* but delved even further into the structural weaknesses of the current financing architecture. That paper—full of precise projections for necessary levels of debt relief, domestic savings, efficiency of capital, and external resources measured as a proportion of GDP—set the tone for what would become the continent's most frank and inclusive dialogue on financing up to that point. In my opening remarks, I made an effort to lay out several big-picture pathways for reducing poverty but also tried to discuss in honest terms the financial implications they entailed. The donor world seemed eager to slash poverty, but without stronger commitments of support it appeared fragile African countries were being set up to fail.

"Our estimates of the magnitude of external resources required for these poverty reduction targets are so massive," I warned, "that we have concluded they are not likely to be attained."

Hopeful that the donor community would prove more responsive if Africa took a clear, collective stance, I urged the conference to work constructively toward a realistic consensus. We wanted the conference to clarify financing options for countries while also creating a united front for collective action before the situation spun entirely out of Africa's control.

By the conclusion of the three-day conference, the ministers of finance and planning had reached agreement on two significant issues: first, that the existing arrangements to cope with the debt crisis remained inadequate and required substantial revision and augmentation; and second, that the pressures to reduce aid in donor countries should be avoided—and aid flows actually expanded, not contracted—if fundamental development objectives were to be achieved.

The ministerial statement included concrete recommendations not only on debt relief but also on aid flows and capital flight. It called on donors to restructure HIPC "to provide deep, broad, and fast relief" by relaxing eligibility criteria, speeding up the process from eligibility to benefit and investing "substantially greater resources." It took a bold position in defense of Africa's most vulnerable, calling on G7 countries to cancel debts arising from bilateral aid to the poorest countries and seeking "exceptional debt relief"—with the possibility of full cancellation—for post-conflict countries, as well as countries affected by natural disasters and spillover effects from conflict in neighboring countries. Altogether, it was a forceful, sensible declaration that essentially acted as Africa's collective counterproposal to its creditors.

When the financing conference concluded, the ministers requested that the ECA convey the main points of their statement to G7 officials, as well as to the Development Assistance Committee of the Organisation for Economic Co-operation and Development, prior to the G7 June summit in Cologne. We honored the request.

At that point, almost four years into our institutional overhaul, it was clear to me that the ECA's role had irrevocably changed, especially in the way we worked with African policymakers and the development community at large. Of course, we were just one piece of a much larger puzzle, a tremendous worldwide movement to push debt relief to the forefront. But the ECA had been integral to bringing a coherent African voice and position to the debate on debt and finance.

A few weeks later, at the summit in Cologne, leaders of the seven major creditor countries announced major changes to HIPC, saying: "We have decided to give a fresh boost to debt relief." They agreed to lower the threshold for debt to be deemed sustainable, thereby opening the door for more countries to qualify for relief. They also suggested a shorter qualification period and a higher cap for cancellation of bilateral debt, from 80 to 90 percent—the same number suggested by African ministers. The revisions were finalized in September at the annual meetings of the World Bank and IMF, where the program took on a new name: the Enhanced HIPC Initiative. Since then, the Bank and IMF have approved programs under the HIPC initiative for 36 countries, 30 of them in Africa, totaling $99 billion in debt relief.[5]

Meanwhile, the international consensus that led to the HIPC reforms soon resulted in even bigger shifts on debt relief and other financing instruments, many of which mirrored the positions first taken by the African ministers.

In March 2002, the United Nations organized the International Conference on Financing for Development in Monterrey, Mexico. It was the first UN-sponsored summit-level meeting to address financial issues pertaining to global development. It drew more than 250 heads of state and ministers and marked a major turning point in global development cooperation, including pledges to dramatically scale up ODA and to provide sustainable debt financing by matching financing needs and repayment capacities. According to the UN, the conference "succeeded in placing financing for development firmly on the global agenda."

But it was already firmly on Africa's agenda, as it had been for years.

◆ ◆ ◆ ◆

In 1995, the Organization of African Unity, or OAU, adopted the Cairo Agenda for Action to "relaunch Africa's economic and social development"—and to stake an ownership claim. "We reaffirm that Africa's development is first and foremost the responsibility of our governments and peoples," the resolution stated. The Cairo Agenda for Action ostensibly built upon the principles of the Lagos Plan of Action, endorsed by heads of state 15 years prior. But a lot had changed over the time in between, including the composition of the OAU.

The democratic wave that swept over Africa after the fall of the Berlin Wall began a period of rapid political transition. Between 1989 and 1995, Africa saw 35 presidential and parliamentary elections. In the Sub-Saharan region, 29 out of 47 states held their first multiparty elections in more than a generation. The leaders who endorsed the Cairo Agenda for Action were more democratically oriented than their predecessors and eager for Africa to take control over its development agenda. The Cairo resolution reflected those attributes, especially in the section titled: "What we can do for ourselves," which promised the "speedy promotion of good governance" as an objective of sustainable development. By contrast, the word "governance" didn't appear at all in the Lagos plan.

Governance had become a major development issue in a relatively short time. The phrase "good governance" first worked its way into the mainstream in the World Bank's 1989 long-term study on Africa. Within a few years, the development community came to view attributes of good governance—such as accountability, transparency, and the rule of law—as preconditions to sustained economic growth. As a result, the environment in which a state's public institutions operated—the way the state met its basic obligations to citizens—became a huge factor in development strategies. Meanwhile, the Bank and other agencies began to place greater weight on governance indicators when allocating resources.[6] This didn't necessarily sit well with African leaders, especially the newly elected ones who were eager to move beyond the "African big man" narrative and establish closer ties to the West but who recoiled at the perception of externally generated criteria for determining "good governance."

This was the state of the play on governance when we began the process of streamlining and sharpening the ECA's focus. The issue had moved to the top of the global agenda, so we couldn't overlook it. But it remained politically sensitive, and a consensus on best practices had not really emerged. Just as with financing, however, the more we considered governance, the more we realized it cut across just about every aspect of our work program. That's because the ECA approached the issue from a slightly different perspective.

Generally, the donor world occupied itself with *political* governance— those elements relating to free elections, multiparty democracy, press freedom, independence of the judiciary, and so forth. But at the ECA we felt a more comprehensive definition of good governance was appropriate to Africa's economic circumstances, given the continent's history of wars and conflicts, the persistence of poverty, and the poor economic and social indicators generally.

We based our argument around the concept of the capable state, one in which peace and security are guaranteed and sustained. Without peace, there can be no long-term development. And without good governance, there is seldom peace. A capable state creates an enabling political and legal environment for economic progress and equitable growth. It ensures that pro-growth policies also attack poverty and promote education, health, and social safety nets. And it works in tandem with the private sector to generate good jobs and higher incomes. At the core of all this are political stability and the fair and consistent application of the rule of law.

The capable state model had a clear economic component, so it framed the way we considered good governance. That framework would shape our approach for the duration of my decade at the ECA.

Early in 1996, I invited 40 high-level African experts and a number of senior African ambassadors in Addis Ababa to solicit their inputs and feedback for what would become *Serving Africa Better*. In the preceding years, as poverty reduction became the world's overarching development goal, a consensus emerged around three consistent elements to successful anti-poverty strategies: labor-demanding growth, education, and health investments and social safety nets for the poor. The work program we were proposing incorporated those elements, but it acknowledged a fourth: governance. The external experts agreed. In fact, they urged the ECA to focus on promoting governance as a basic pillar for effective development management. It was a worthy goal that we were eager to pursue.

"Governments control a significant share of national resources and shape the environment for the private sector and civil society," the final version of *Serving Africa Better* stated. "Strengthening democratic governance and popular participation in development are vital not only for entrenching democracy, but also for contributing to growth and development."

It was the first step the ECA took to broaden the definition of governance to include socioeconomic factors, and it happened more than five years before a more expansive view of governance became the centerpiece of NEPAD, the New Partnership for Africa's Development, a global African recovery initiative that also included a tool for measuring governance improvements, the African Peer Review Mechanism, or APRM. The ECA played a big role in developing both.

In March 1996, around the same time we were finalizing *Serving Africa Better*, Boutros Boutros-Ghali launched the UN System-wide Special Initiative on Africa, or SIA, as a partial response to the Cairo Agenda for Action. Designed as a 10-year plan, it was the latest in a long line of UN attempts to create a coordinated approach to African development, both across UN agencies and with other partners like the Bank and IMF. Boutros-Ghali set up five interagency working groups on five different issues and he wanted the ECA, along with the United Nations Development Programme, to head up the group on governance. He also asked UNDP Administrator Gus Speth and me to co-chair the full SIA steering committee. So while the initiative covered other areas like water, education, health care, and information technology, our selection as co-chairs placed governance at the forefront.

The SIA didn't move the needle very much on coordination and had very little impact.[7] But it did give the ECA some degree of influence in the direction of governance dialogue, specifically leading to the launch of the African Governance Forum. The AGF was conceived as a platform for bringing together all the stakeholders in the governance arena—public sector, private sector, and civil society—to discuss the issue at the continental level but through the lens of individual, national programs. We hoped that such an open, African-led dialogue would give development partners a green light to make long-term commitments supporting these national programs.

We held the first AGF in Addis Ababa in July 1997. Delegates from 14 African countries attended along with representatives from UN agencies, donor countries, and NGOs. The country delegates described their governance programs, which led to a wide-ranging discussion of local experiences with issues such as decentralization, electoral and parliamentary reforms, human rights, public administration, and more.

The forum—and its frank dialogue built around shared experiences—was a hit. Before adjourning, the attendees agreed that it should be an annual event. We obliged at first, keeping to a yearly schedule through 2002. After that the forums grew more sporadic, primarily because NEPAD adopted most of the underlying principles that drove the AGF discussions. So even though the forums dropped off, their influence persisted.

The AGFs were valuable for helping reshape perceptions of good governance as more than a political issue, but they didn't really provide an objective assessment of country programs and policies. Even at the first forum, I felt the need for something more—a way to treat governance with the same rigor we had started to apply to the rest of the ECA's work program. To do that, we decided to treat a country's governance as we would its economy. We needed to quantify it.

When we introduced comprehensive new performance measurements in the *1999 Economic Report on Africa*, we felt we were on to something good. So that same year we launched a similar effort to monitor and measure progress, at the country level, toward the principles of good governance. To do so, we developed quantitative indicators to measure against agreed-upon codes of governance. It was not easy—it was very complex, in fact—but it was also a big deal.

Other institutions, from multilaterals like the World Bank to global NGOs like Freedom House, a US-based organization founded in 1941, had their own measurement systems and would publish results in the form of world rankings; so did UNDP and the USAID. They all were using their own indicators, but with one common thread—they all came from outside the continent.

As donor countries and investors began to tie aid and development funds to "good governance," it became imperative that Africans controlled what that phrase meant. Creating the first set of truly African-derived governance indicators—and supporting the research to back them up— was a way for the ECA to help give African governments more agency in the dialogue. I also believed our indicators would better reflect where African countries stood.

We created an official name for the project—Measuring and Monitoring Progress Towards Good Governance in Africa—and held the first meeting in September 1999 to begin developing the indicators we would use. After planning that involved numerous expert meetings, methodological workshops, and field-testing suggested indicators in Benin and South Africa, we agreed that the final indicators would reflect dimensions of governance across three broad areas: political representation, institutional effectiveness, and economic and corporate governance. There were 24 indicators in all, seven considered "core."

Our research methodology consisted of three components: a national experts' opinion survey, a national household sample survey, and desk research. We conducted the project in 27 countries over a four-year period (2001 to 2004), sampling opinions from more than 50,000 households and 2,000 experts. We didn't have the capacity to do that much alone, so we partnered with select research groups and local institutions to help. We also organized two national workshops in each country. We wanted to create an accurate portrayal of the state of governance on the continent at the time, with data that could be used as performance benchmarks by governments and citizens alike.

The ECA published the findings as the *African Governance Report 2005*, the first document of its kind produced in Africa. It took longer than planned; we ran into numerous roadblocks, including unacceptable data from a few of the local groups we had contracted. So we delayed the report to strengthen the research, but it was a worthy delay. The final 267-page report returned some encouraging news. It showed that governance was improving in many states and that the overall situation across Africa was markedly better than it was a decade earlier. Almost all African countries were still in need of dramatic improvement but they had improved from the recent past.

The report helped set a baseline for future research that also has come from within, not outside, Africa. The ECA continued to publish governance reports at a four-year interval. *African Governance Report II (2009)* covered 35 countries, a good increase over the 27 countries studied the first time around. *African Governance Report III (2013)*, co-published with Oxford University, dug deeper into the troubled history of African elections and highlighted the central role those elections play in the democratic governance process. The fourth edition, published in 2016, explored the importance of measuring corruption in African governments and institutions and of understanding its international dimensions.

Starting in 2007, the *Ibrahim Index of African Governance* (IIAG), supported by the Mo Ibrahim Foundation, joined the ECA in producing a solely African-driven measurement tool. The IIAG is a more comprehensive collection of quantitative data, consisting of 100 indicators covering every African country and compiled annually as a composite index. As such, it's an incredibly valuable resource.

◆　◆　◆　◆

By the beginning of the new millennium, the ECA's renewal process felt fully realized. With so many changes and new initiatives that either originated with the ECA or involved our input, the reforms had accomplished what I had hoped: one of Africa's oldest institutions had reestablished itself as an influential—and productive—advocate for African affairs.

Not everything worked as planned. The aggressive approach we took was bound to result in a few initiatives falling short. One notable example was the African Center for Civil Society, established in October 1997 to give extra support to NGOs that wanted to build capacity and increase dialogue with governments. The center had been in the works for a while, but we put it on the fast track after the success of the first African Governance Forum a few months prior. That eagerness turned out to be one of our biggest missteps. We didn't have all the pieces in place and we ran into an array of problems from the start. The center struggled to find its footing before shutting down in less than five years.

Still, the sweeping operational overhaul led to significant improvements in every aspect of the organization, from program orientation and priority setting to organizational restructuring and international engagement. We began to insert ourselves into some pretty weighty discussions, but we validated our presence through stronger, more focused research.

Just as important, we proved that when used effectively, the institution's convening power could really move the needle on big issues, as the next two chapters describe. As African countries began to get serious about their underlying problems and Africa's partners began to accept—finally— African input, the ability to connect the two sides mattered. A lot.

Along those lines, the ECA's joint Conference of African Ministers of Finance and Planning really came into its own as a strong, collective voice. The 1999 conference on development financing set the tone, but in the next four years alone the conference provided significant inputs to global outcomes on trade, debt relief, and aid (2000); the creation of NEPAD (2001); governance reform and monitoring (2002); and the emerging aid effectiveness agenda (2003).

In a briefing note to our member states and UN headquarters in late 1997, we recapped the first two years of our administrative and operational reforms. Based on the promise of some of our early successes, we had pledged to continue to strengthen our own research and analytics while operating "as a networker of development expertise in Africa, a clearinghouse for best practices, and a policy integrator for member states."

Within a few short years, we had laid the foundation for a much stronger institution.

Notes

1   For example, this study argued that one major cause of unease among African governments was a potential lack of objectivity on the part of the World Bank and IMF, the HIPC architects but also major creditors—a potential conflict of interest that could have been avoided if an independent commission had been created to guide the initiative's creation and design.

2   Incidentally, our structure for these meetings proved to be such a success that other parts of the UN system began using the "panelists and experts" approach for meetings, including the General Assembly, which adopted the format for roundtable discussions of heads of state.

3   These and other figures relating to the ECA's streamlining efforts were compiled for an internal UN report that measured the progress of our reforms: "Strengthening the Organization: Departmental Self-Assessment," April 2002.

4   We considered it a notable breakthrough just to get the African Capital Markets Forum off the ground. The idea had first gained traction four years earlier, at a 1992 financing conference organized by the Nigerian Securities and Exchange Commission and the African Development Bank. The Capital Markets Authority of Kenya helped organize another conference the following year, which led to the creation of a steering committee. That's when the ECA first got involved as the secretariat of the committee, but after a kick-off meeting in Addis in December 1993, momentum stalled. Our 1996 investment conference finally got it off the ground.

5   Per the World Bank's HIPC 2017 Statistical Update.

6   The World Bank's Country Policy and Institutional Assessment (CPIA) offers a good example. The Bank treats the CPIA as an organic diagnostic tool, periodically revising its measurement criteria to reflect lessons learned and evolutionary thinking. Over time, CPIA criteria have shifted from a largely macroeconomic focus to include a broader range of considerations, such as social and structural factors. In 1997, the Bank officially added governance-related issues to the mix.

7   At that point, there had been three major global UN initiatives aimed at enhancing Africa's development: the UN Program of Action for African Economic Recovery and Development (UN-PAAERD, 1986–90), the UN New Agenda for Development of Africa (UN-NADAF, 1991–2000), and the UN System-wide Special Initiative on Africa (SIA, 1996–2005). Overall, the SIA achieved only modest success at coordinating on the ground. It was widely seen as overly ambitious and imprecise, with too many priorities. The UN Development Assistance Framework and the Poverty Reduction Strategy Papers, introduced a few years later, offered better coordinating frameworks and were widely embraced at the country level.

Chapter 8

The Case for Gender Equality
The Moral and Economic Imperative for Investing in Africa's Women

When my daughters Ama, Nana, and Mame were teenagers, they traveled to Ghana to visit my mother in her village. The girls had a wonderful time, but they also had a big problem—they had to speak through an interpreter, either their mother or me. My daughters, all born in the United States, did not speak a word of Twi, my native language. And my mother, who never set foot in a classroom as a student, didn't speak a word of English. Because of the way my mother's relationship slowly developed with me and my family over time, my daughters didn't know her as well as they knew their maternal grandparents. But from an early age they showed a strong desire to stay connected to their African roots, so they were eager to make the trip, language barrier or not. Still, they were puzzled that their grandmother could not speak basic English.

The fact that my mother, like millions of other African women, never had the opportunity to go to school, much less learn English, didn't occur to my daughters. I'm proud of my heritage, but I wasn't proud to explain the continent's historic inequality between men and women.

In Africa, being a woman has always been a particularly difficult burden. Historically, women have borne the brunt of Africa's underdevelopment, with fewer educational opportunities, greater health risks, and weaker earning potential than men. In addition, women have long been deprived of land and inheritance and forced to contend with deeply ingrained traditions, customs, and belief systems—most following a cultural hierarchy that favors men. I grew up in an Africa that purported to place women and their

219

sacred act of motherhood on a pedestal, yet in reality condemned them to live in patriarchal societies with little or no social mobility.

When I returned to Africa full-time to work at the ECA in the mid-1990s, the disparity was stark. More than half of the women in Sub-Saharan Africa aged 25 or over were illiterate. In Sudan, the ratio of female to male adult literacy was 28 percent. Comparable ratios in Burkina Faso (32 percent) and Sierra Leone (35 percent) were hardly better. Across the continent, many more girls than boys were expected to die before reaching the age of five. In Togo, the difference was 20 percentage points more and in Cameroon 17 points. Once a woman reached childbearing years, the statistics were even more disquieting. One in 20 African women ran the risk of dying from pregnancy-related causes. In the productive sectors, many African women were working 16 or more hours a day between paying jobs and their role as the primary caregiver for their children. In many towns and villages, women were contributing as much as 40-60 percent of the household income, often through physically taxing agricultural jobs or in the low-wage service industry.

There is a Chinese saying that women hold up half the sky. But as I said during my remarks at the Fourth World Conference on Women in Beijing in 1995, "African women hold the heavier half of the sky." That conference gave a huge boost to the cause of gender equality in development and it coincided with my arrival at the ECA.

In the previous chapter, I talked about elevating the ECA as a stronger voice for Africa. Taking a lead on the issue of women in development was another way we did that. There's an obvious moral imperative—the majority of people living in poverty in Africa are women and they already face greater obstacles to escape the poverty trap than men. But from an economic perspective, it is even more urgent, because the empirical evidence for investing in women is overwhelming.

We know for certain that African societies see a greater return on investment in women's education and health than for investment in similar services for men. This is largely due to the strong links between schooling, health, nutrition, and fertility on one hand and skill development on the other. As women's education levels rise, their fertility and child mortality rates fall. The reason: women who read and write are much better able to understand how to better care for themselves and their families. On the work side, similar cause and effect patterns have been proven. Data collected in the early 1990s in Kenya indicated that if all women received just one year of primary schooling, their agricultural productivity would increase by 24 percent.

There's also the issue of peace and stability. We have abundant evidence that most women define human security and power in much more constructive and comprehensive ways than men. Given Africa's long history of instability and civil unrest, and knowing how often widows and single mothers are forced to pick up the pieces in the wake of such conflicts, incorporating women's perspectives into stability strategies just makes sense. That is why the ECA helped establish in 1998 the African Women's Committee on Peace and Development, a high-level advisory group to the OAU. It opened a dialogue with heads of state.

I have always viewed gender equality as an economic development issue and I have worked as much as I can to ensure that others see it the same way. That work has centered primarily around two areas fundamental to gender progress: moving women into positions of power and decision-making, and creating the institutional mechanisms for women's advancement and empowerment. Simply put, women must be in a position to have a say in their future.

Even today, when African women have more opportunities than ever before, they still have the deck stacked against them. That's because they have had a harder time overcoming common development challenges— be they better access to credit or financial assistance, to schools and books, to safe health care, to legal services, or to job markets.

The economic benefits of gender equality are obvious, but trying to ensure sound policy has never been my only motivation. There's always been more to it than that.

I was two when my parents divorced. As a child, I only met my mother once more. We reconnected, but not until I was a young adult. The divorce caused a lot of tension, and my father grew very protective of his sons. I often felt isolated from my mother's side of the family.

In those days, many African men had multiple wives (not uncommon in certain villages and tribes), but my father didn't. He did, however, divorce and remarry frequently, at least four or five times. He stayed with one wife, Vida, longer than the rest. She was kind and caring and the only woman I ever came to think of as a mother. She lived with us into my early teen years, before she and my father split. Naturally, I grew attached to the women coming in and out of my father's life since they also were coming in and out of mine. But as I got older, I realized that my father didn't always treat his wives with respect. It was a different time, and in that way, a much worse time. My father and Vida would fight, she would cry, and I would do my best to offer comfort. It hurt me to see her upset. It's one reason we developed a close bond.

As a result, I developed a heightened sensitivity for treating women with dignity. I grew concerned for their welfare, especially once I realized that an unmarried woman in Africa didn't have a lot to fall back on, and that women lacked the same opportunities as men. After my parents' divorce, my younger sister Ama went with my mother. A few years later she came back to live with us, but in that time, she fell far behind Kwabena and me academically. She had missed out on the good schooling that I got. That never seemed right.

After I tracked down my mother when I was in college, she and I stayed in touch, and we got to know each other as best we could. Her story is not unusual for an African woman. She never went to school. She had several children in all, but not all survived past the age of three. She lost financial security when she and my father divorced, and she lived in poverty. In contrast, my wife Philomena and I were blessed with three daughters who all grew into strong, successful women in their own right. We were privileged to see them excel at school and enter some of the best universities and law schools in North America. We instilled in them a sense of self-confidence and empowerment that my mother never had, nor ever really knew to expect.

My mother and her three granddaughters symbolize the evolution of Africa's women, from a state of illiteracy and repression to expanding opportunity and awareness. Africa has come a long way in a relatively short amount of time, and while the present-day situation remains a work in progress, it's still much improved from where things stood when I began my career.

◆　◆　◆　◆

When I started at the World Bank in 1974, no one was talking about gender, at least not in a substantive way. Very few women filled key positions, whether in the field or in management. That situation changed, but it took a long time. Once I had gained enough clout to start making major personnel decisions in the late 1980s, I tried to do what I could. In fact, moving women into decision-making roles became something of a pattern of mine. As a division chief for Latin America, I hired so many women into my division that I was told to rebalance my staff to include more men. At one point, we had 12 people in our group—but only one man other than me. That poor guy was more often referred to as the "token man" rather than task manager—his actual title. But he took it in his stride.

A few years later, when I was hired as director of the newly created Education and Social Policy department, I built the initial team and once again women dominated the top ranks. Gender was one of ESPD's four main programs, so we quickly became an attractive spot for Bank staff wanting to work on women's issues, which were still not a priority in a general sense. For most country directors, gender was a consideration, not a mandate. It remained a relatively "new" issue.

Officially, the Bank began promoting gender equality in development in 1977, when it hired Gloria Scott to fill a just-created position—advisor on women in development. Scott had spent a decade at the United Nations and before that she worked in Jamaica's ministry of development. Her job was to "focus attention on the subject of women in development and promote an understanding of the key issues and ways to address them in the Bank's operational work."

The following year, the Bank published its first *World Development Report*, which focused on poverty alleviation. In the Foreword, Bank President Robert McNamara explained that the report was a comprehensive analysis of the most "fundamental problems confronting developing countries." Yet in this analysis of fundamental problems, the word "gender" did not appear in the text of a single chapter. "Women" appeared a few times, all in relation to fertility and childbearing. One chapter was devoted solely to Sub-Saharan Africa, making the obvious omission even more depressing. It would take another 35 years, but the Bank devoted the entire *World Development Report 2013* to gender.

Perhaps Gloria Scott's advisory influence helped convince the Bank leadership that overlooking women in the first *World Development Report* was a gross error. In 1979, the Bank highlighted some of the ways its work benefited women with an informative booklet given an unfortunate name: *Recognizing the 'Invisible' Woman in Development*. I know what the title intended to convey, but given the context of the times, it awkwardly reinforced a negative perception of women as quiet, docile, and less than fully realized individuals. At least in the Preface, McNamara recognized the need to make the Bank's activities for women "more effective and useful."

Change came slowly, but it came. In 1984, the Bank added gender to its operations policy and called on staff to regularly consider women's issues for Bank projects. The same year, the Associated Press profiled Gloria Scott and her job, which she vividly described as akin to "pushing the world uphill." That world got a little flatter when Barber Conable soon took over as World Bank president. In Conable, women had a strong advocate for recognizing their role in supporting growth and reducing poverty. In 1987, the Bank created a new division, Women in Development, run by Barbara Herz and tasked with including women's issues in project development—a noticeable step up from Scott's mandate a decade prior to merely "focus attention."

But Conable wanted more. In an eye-opening letter dated April 12, 1989, he wrote to the Bank's vice president for operations to ask for a more urgent, systematic approach to bringing women's issues into Bank activities. Conable said he had been "concerned for some time about the depth and strength" of the Bank's commitment to gender. "Women account for 50 percent of the world's productive human potential," he said. "No country can afford to neglect such a high share of its human resources." In the letter, Conable noted that the upcoming *World Development Report* would deal with poverty and that it would "reflect the fact that many more women than men" live in it.

Despite these efforts and a general acceptance of the need to consider women in development, gender remained on the periphery of the Bank's work, not consistently integrated into most programs and, in some circles of the Bank's old guard, routinely dismissed as inconsequential. The Bank took a step forward in 1993, when ESPD absorbed the Women in Development division to create a broader, but more integrated, approach to gender.

But in 1994, attitudes really began to change—mostly because they had to. That year, the Bank issued its first operations policy on gender, based primarily on a strategy paper that we produced, *Enhancing Women's Participation in Economic Development*. It emphasized ownership at the country level and financial support at the donor level, and it gave the Bank's operations staff a blueprint to follow for incorporating gender components into projects. In the report's Foreword, Bank President Lewis Preston echoed calls to broaden the "women in development" approach into a "gender and development" strategy. The rationale? To recognize that improving the condition of women depended upon the actions and attitudes of *men* as much as women.

The strategy paper became an early, high-profile success for ESPD, shining a spotlight on the people behind it. And most of those people were not men. By the time we published the paper, women occupied three of the four department head posts and made up more than 50 percent of ESPD's staff—ratios unheard of in other Bank departments.

As mentioned in Chapter 4, I actively searched for capable women to bring aboard, but I didn't set any kind of quota. I hired the people I believed to be the best candidates for the jobs. Many of them were Bank superstars in the making. Barbara Bruns was my senior advisor. She went on to become the Bank's lead economist for education in Latin America and the Caribbean. Oey Meesook was the head of the poverty and social assistance group. She became a country director in East Africa before taking over as director of human development for the Africa region. Jane Armitage headed the labor markets and social insurance group. She was hired as an advisor to James Wolfensohn after he became the Bank's ninth president, and she later became a country director. Minh Chau Nguyen was head of the gender group. She worked on numerous country programs at the Bank before joining a global investment firm as a vice president and then continuing her development career with a focus on Asia and her native Vietnam. And there were many others, such as Cecilia Valdivieso, who also worked on the gender program. After she left the Bank, she served as the UNDP's gender coordinator for Asia. The Bank had a deep bench of women economists, especially in the social development field. Their expertise helped push gender into the Bank's mainstream.

ESPD prepared another notable document on gender issues while I was still at the Bank—*Gender and Development: Equity and Efficiency*, the Bank's primary contribution to the Fourth World Conference on Women in September 1995. That conference became a milestone in how the development community viewed gender and, for most multilaterals, it represented their first serious commitments to gender equality on a global scale. I attended the conference as head of the ECA, since it fell just a few months after I left the Bank. But I still took a lot of pride in *Equity and Efficiency*, because we finalized it under my watch and the team I assembled produced it. In addition, and to my unexpected pleasure, the Bank distributed *Enhancing Women's Participation* at Beijing to underscore how serious it was about bringing gender into the mainstream.

◆ ◆ ◆ ◆

The ECA's attention to gender as a development issue goes back to its early years. In response to a groundswell of African women seeking equality, the ECA began its first formal program for women in development in 1971, under Executive Secretary Robert Gardiner. At that time, it was not so obvious that major institutions working for Africa's progress should devote significant energy to gender issues. But Gardiner commissioned a set of studies exploring the implications of women's centrality to development, and in 1975 he oversaw the establishment of the African Training and Research Center for Women. Its small staff was tasked with helping any national, regional, and sub-regional initiatives involved with the advancement of women. Despite that positive beginning, the unit, which shortened its name in 1994 to the African Center for Women, existed for most of its first 20 years on the periphery of the ECA's work. The center's situation was dispiriting, considering that Gardiner's vision predated a much bigger push a few years later by the United Nations to promote women's issues.

Despite the occasional decree, the international community didn't begin to pay close attention to women in development until the mid-1970s when the UN designated 1975 as "International Women's Year" and convened the First World Conference on Women in Mexico City. More and more economic development programs were being implemented in poor countries, so both the year-long observance and the two-week conference were conceived as ways to prevent women from being an afterthought. Both were well received and really got the ball rolling, prompting the UN to declare 1976–85 as the "Decade for Women" and turn its single-year program into a much more aggressive 10-year campaign.

The UN sponsored a Second World Conference on Women at the program's midpoint in 1980 in Copenhagen, and then a third one in 1985 in Nairobi, a landmark achievement for women activists in Africa. By the time of the fourth conference 10 years later in Beijing, awareness had reached new heights. Each conference had attracted twice as many participants as the one before it, with Beijing drawing 17,000 participants and 30,000 more at a related NGO forum. The conference produced the acclaimed Beijing Declaration and Platform for Action, which set a global agenda for gender equality and received endorsement from 189 governments. Even today, that action plan continues to serve as a benchmark for progress.

In the aftermath of the successful Beijing conference, the UN gave each of its five regional economic commissions a mandate to put in place mechanisms to advance the commitments that were made at the international level. For the ECA, this task should have been easy, but it wasn't.

For two decades, the ECA had organized regional conferences on women ahead of the world conferences. These events were intended to energize and mobilize participants ahead of the larger conferences, as well as frame the discussion from the African perspective. For instance, a regional conference held in Dakar, Senegal, in 1994 resulted in an African Platform for Action on gender that was endorsed by the OAU. The lack of movement on it resulted in yet another action plan five years down the road.

Such delayed action was not an uncommon outcome for these regional events, which too often were long on ideas but short on follow-up. Here's another example: along with the OAU and the government of Uganda, the ECA in 1993 co-sponsored a regional conference on women and peace in Kampala to address the growing gender problems posed by Africa's ongoing wars, conflicts, and civil strife.[1] The participants adopted a farsighted framework that called for a standing Women's Committee on Peace and Development. But then, it took five years for that committee to actually form.

The general lack of progress cannot be blamed on the ECA, which has no formal authority to make governments do something they don't want to do. But the ECA's inaction in pushing its member states to honor previous commitments on gender policy left it little moral authority once a higher mandate came down from the UN after Beijing. Since that mandate fell on me as the new executive secretary, the ECA's gender problem was now my problem. And that problem, primarily, was cultural.

"The House" was a male-dominated environment where most senior staff viewed gender equality more as a women's movement than as an economic imperative. Gender did not command the attention of ECA economists as a substantive development issue, so it was not taken seriously. This attitude wasn't unique, though it was certainly outdated. When previewing the First World Conference on Women, The New York Times reported that UN planners were trying to attract more men because "they think governments will take the conference more seriously if it's not an all-women affair." That's because when women meet separately, the Times explained, "it's treated lightly as a ladies' meeting." That article was written in 1974, two decades before I arrived at the ECA to find the same attitude ingrained in the House.

When I took over as executive secretary, a stronger focus on gender was inevitable. First, the international environment after Beijing demanded action from institutions like the ECA. Since it had shown so little urgency for women's issues in recent decades, there was a lot of ground to make up. Second, I left the Bank just as efforts to elevate gender finally began to take off. So it was very much on my mind as I transitioned jobs. Since the ECA needed both administrative and operational reform, I saw an opportunity to continue the "mainstreaming" push, just at a different institution.[2] And I knew the obvious place to start—the African Center for Women, which should have been driving the ECA's gender initiative but instead was stuck in neutral. So I decided to remake it.

The dismissive attitude toward gender undermined the African Center for Women, which was Africa's oldest regional structure for promoting women's issues. Not only was the center severely understaffed, it had few financial resources and a fuzzy, unfocused mission that lacked urgency. It published a useful report the year before I arrived, *Women's Participation in the Economic Sector*, but that was a small victory. I don't mean to diminish the work that went into the report, but the center had little cachet among the member states and next to no influence or sway within the halls of the ECA. It existed, but it barely mattered. Its staff was stretched too thin and its management was too weak.

Historically, the center had a limited function, even when it assisted with large events like the regional conferences it primarily organized, rather than the ones to which it contributed. I wanted it to exist at a higher level. I wanted it to take on aggressive policy work that would bring gender forward and support the post-Beijing mandate given to the regional economic commissions. That meant refining priorities and mobilizing resources to integrate gender into all our activities. Obviously, I needed a strong center to support that plan. And I needed a strong person to run it. Finding its new director became an immediate priority.

I went through a search process for all the management positions that I filled, because I wanted the new leadership team at the ECA to more accurately reflect Africa. So I focused on three criteria: regional balance, gender balance, and an Anglophone-Francophone balance. Depending on the division, some of those criteria were more important than others. With the African Center for Women, obviously, I wanted to look for a woman.

Joséphine Ouédraogo first came to my attention in the mid-1980s when I worked at the Bank. From 1984 to 1987, she was Burkina Faso's minister of family development and national solidarity in Thomas Sankara's government. Sankara was a Marxist revolutionary, often referred to as "Africa's Che Guevara," who seized power as head of state in 1983. On the spectrum of leaders who came to power through a coup, Sankara was better than most. He became the first African leader to denounce AIDS, and he was ahead of his time in promoting women's rights by opposing female circumcision and polygamy and by placing savvy, intelligent women— like Joséphine —in his cabinet. When Sankara was assassinated in 1987, Joséphine co-founded an NGO, but she returned to government in 1995. When I first met her, she had recently taken the position of director-general for international cooperation in Burkina Faso's foreign ministry.

I relied on my top advisors to help me produce short lists of qualified candidates for any of the senior positions I wanted to fill. As we began that process for the African Center for Women, Joséphine's name rose to the top right away. I had never met her, but I remembered her strong reputation as a minister. I had a trip to West Africa coming up, so I reached out to her. She agreed to see me for an interview. We met at the Hotel d'Ivoire in Abidjan, Côte d'Ivoire.

Once we started talking, I knew right away I had the right person. This is the kind of leader the ECA needs, I thought. Her English was not very good and I barely spoke French, but we hit it off anyway. I give Joséphine all the credit. Her knowledge and passion could cut through any language barrier. She had a strong presence and she exuded confidence. I had no doubt she was a natural leader who could turn around the ECA's gender program.

After a long conversation, I asked her if she was prepared to leave Burkina Faso—she had spent her life there—and come to Addis. She said she was. Then I asked her why she wanted to take the job.

"I believe in what the ECA can do," she said. "And I know what women can do. I want to be part of that."

The answer was good enough for me. Joséphine embodied the new image that I wanted for the ECA—vibrant, intelligent, confident, and diverse. She was someone who could take us to the next level. She also inspired me. By the time our meeting ended, I was ready to follow her anywhere. Shortly after, I hired her to take over the center.

Joséphine started in 1997, and over the next few years under her leadership, the African Center for Women made major inroads as a key player in the gender dialogue. In no time, it upped its profile and grew more engaged in regional conferences, training programs, and knowledge-sharing partnerships. It also became more aggressive in its communication and outreach. A few months after Joséphine arrived, the center launched *GenderNet*, a newsletter published under the ECA banner for more than a decade. And it took on bigger studies and produced better research, such as the *African Women's Report 1998*, which examined post-conflict reconstruction from a gender perspective and offered practical strategies to foster gender-balanced development.

With a new reputation as a leading, authoritative voice on women's issues and economic development, the center soon outgrew its name, size, and function. In 1999, the UN agreed to elevate the center in rank and two years later we changed the name to the African Center for Gender and

Development to encompass its broader mandate. We also doubled the staff to a dozen.

Needless to say, our efforts garnered attention, which is what I wanted. Elevating the center gave it a higher internal standing, and that put it on the same level as the economic and social policy division, or the regional integration division, for example. It was an operational move that showed our member states and partners—and the anti-gender holdouts within the ECA—just how seriously we took gender as an economic issue. I had a more practical motivation as well: to open up more funding opportunities for gender-related programs, which was very important for our perpetually cash-strapped operation. It also took a few years to pull off since we first had to reestablish the intellectual bona fides of the center, but in time the UN's Economic and Social Council officially approved the move. And with that, the ECA became the first UN regional economic commission to give gender the status of a division.

We also led the way for other UN agencies to put more women in decision-making roles, though it took a few years to fill out the top ranks exactly as I wanted. My senior management team at the ECA consisted of nine people—eight program heads and a deputy executive secretary—and four of them were women, including my deputy, Lalla Ben Barka, a Malian. All of them, like Joséphine, were brought in from the outside. No other UN economic commission had so many women in senior management.

Once achieved, these two objectives—elevating the African Center for Women and getting more women into leadership positions—represented the culmination of years of effort. It was clear that many of the most skeptical inside the House expected, or at least hoped, that the whole "gender issue" would eventually just go away. Obviously that did not happen!

We laid the groundwork from the start. The first move that caused people to sit up and take notice happened within a few months of my arrival. Along with capacity building, we named gender as one of two overarching issues to cut across all five of the new program areas identified in *Serving Africa Better*, the strategic blueprint presented to ministers in early 1996. We called the decision to prioritize gender "a matter of justice" and explained that the "feminization of poverty and the wider recognition of women as a force for sustainable development" were but two of many compelling reasons to act; an obvious argument, but a necessary one.

After at least two decades of the UN and other big agencies advocating gender equality, real progress in Africa was modest at best. Women remained second-class citizens on much of the continent and in the eyes of most policymakers. Indeed, even as the ministers approved the *Serving Africa Better* blueprint, many remained skeptical over our suddenly progressive approach to gender. But since the issue was folded into the overall reform agenda, it was not seen as an isolated policy push. I believe that's the main reason we didn't encounter too much outside resistance

The first notable turning point for the ECA came in October 1997 at a regional event organized with the World Bank. Held in Addis Ababa, the Conference on Gender and Law: East Africa Speaks brought together ministers, judges, and senior policymakers from six countries as well as representatives from universities and NGOs.[3] It revolved around two main themes: the impact of customary laws and practices on women, and the implementation—or lack thereof—of laws to protect women's rights. Despite legal reform across the continent, women's social and economic status remained too defined by local or ethnic laws deeply rooted in customs.

Our goal with the conference was to strengthen knowledge of legal constraints and open up some new avenues of dialogue both between the countries—to learn from each other—and between the countries and the institutions that supported them, like the ECA. The conference was unique in that the agenda was set and articulated by the countries' practitioners and policymakers; the ECA had hosted regional conferences on gender, but it had not hosted one in which the participating countries took the lead in framing the discussion. In a way, I was applying the same Open Space principle of ownership that had proven so effective with the ECA's institutional reforms.

Organizing the conference was one of Joséphine's first priorities and it presented a nice opportunity for the restructured African Center for Women to show its potential. Now empowered to act on a higher level, the African Center for Women announced its presence as both a leader, by convening the conference with the Bank, and as a facilitator, by seeking inputs from the participating countries, all of which submitted detailed reports of their own gender and law practices and also devised individual action plans.

"We are strengthening our own networks and we need to build partnerships with all the organizations which can support us, but that we can support also," Joséphine said at the conclusion of the two-day conference. "This meeting gave you the opportunity to know the center and to know what the ECA is about."

The conference included just six countries, but it was important for the ECA to show that it meant business in pushing gender equality and in holding countries accountable. It was a small event that generated big enthusiasm. And it showed me that countries were ready for real leadership at a continental level. The OAU at the time was making a little noise on gender, but not much.[4] It had few women in key positions and no real urgency to act. After all, the charter that established the OAU and its mission in 1963 made no mention of women or gender equality, not that many would have expected it to.

I believed the ECA could fill an obvious gap in institutional leadership on the issue, which continued to gain global traction. The year after the world conference in Beijing, the Organisation for Economic Co-operation and Development put women's issues on the same level as all the traditional development challenges. The OECD's International Development Goals included among its six primary objectives the "demonstrated progress toward gender equality and the empowerment of women in education." It was a specific but attainable goal, a starting point for most countries and an important acknowledgement at the highest levels of development policymaking that women's issues must be considered and acted upon.

Africa needed a similar sense of urgency.

As Joséphine and others planned for the gender and law conference, I had begun to consider different ways the ECA could make an even bigger splash. How could we draw attention to gender on a scale that would get even the skeptics interested? By happenstance, the calendar presented an opportunity. The following year would mark the institution's fortieth anniversary, a notable occasion that would dictate an event worthy of high-profile guests. What theme would suffice? In considering the possibilities, I realized the answer to two separate questions was staring me in the face: combine the bigger splash on gender with the notable event for the ECA's anniversary.

I shared the idea with some trusted staff and advisors. Reaction was mixed, though not negative. I acknowledged this would be a bold, potentially divisive move. But once I got it in my head, I knew I wouldn't let it go. I envisioned an opportunity to bring the continent together to consider the contributions of women in development and to discuss the best ways to accelerate women's advancement in the coming century.

Once the Conference on Gender and Law got underway a short time later, I delivered brief opening remarks. I explained that the ECA had organized the event in part to underscore the need for more action in support of the Beijing compact on gender equality. Too little action had been taken in the two years since its agreement, I said. With that in mind, I then announced the ECA would commemorate its fortieth anniversary in 1998 with an expansive forum on African women, their role in development, and their place in society.

"As we strive for gender equality," I said, "let us remember the African saying: 'Paradise is open at the command of mothers'."

A few months later, in December 1997, I had a chance to share the fortieth anniversary plans with my mother. My family and I returned to Ghana for Christmas that year, and we stayed at the official residence of the governor of the Bank of Ghana, a good friend of mine. He and his family lived in another house and used the official residence only for functions, so he insisted that we make use of the large house. We had more space than we needed, so I invited my mother to come up from her village and spend the holidays with us. I didn't get to see her very often, and we never spent holidays together. This was a rare opportunity.

We had set the fortieth anniversary for April 1998, so the compressed time frame meant that I could not unplug from work completely. But I didn't mind because I could talk to my mother about our plans for a major economic conference celebrating African women. I explained to her how gender issues had become a global priority, and how I felt blessed to be in a position to try to make positive changes. My mother did not grasp the full complexities of the economic context, but she understood that any efforts to help women escape poverty and achieve equality was a step in the right direction. She was very supportive.

I spent about two weeks in Ghana before returning to Addis Ababa. The family stayed on for a week more. As I left for the airport, my mother gave me a nice hug and wished me luck with the conference. I promised to give her an update after it was over and I told her to take care of herself. She was a small lady, very petite. I worried about her as any son would. She told me not to worry, as any mother would. It was the last time I saw her.

♦   ♦   ♦   ♦

I could have chosen any issue as the theme for the ECA's fortieth anniversary event. But the more I considered it, the more certain I became to focus on the role of women in development. Although a number of major conferences organized in the 1990s had addressed the gender aspects of other social concerns, such as the environment and human rights, the economic role of women in Africa remained largely unacknowledged. I expected that any conference tied to the ECA's anniversary would attract some real heavyweights, draw a lot of attention, and generate good press coverage. If we announced a standalone forum on gender equality, would I be able to expect the same? Unlikely. So it seemed like a rare opportunity—a chance to convene an African dialogue around an issue that on its own was not yet capable of drawing the same kind of audience.

One way we planned on combating biases or bad attitudes was through emotion. I wanted the fortieth anniversary to be a substantive economic forum focused on gender, but I also wanted it to celebrate African women and all that they are capable of—socially, politically, economically—while still honoring their revered status in Africa as mothers, wives, and daughters. Any real conversation about the role of women in development has to include what they do beyond just raising children, but in Africa the maternal role cannot be ignored, either.

During the planning process, we settled on two proverbs to help frame our theme: "Women hold up half the sky," and "Paradise is open at the command of mothers." I found both inspiring and in recent years had often referenced them when speaking about gender equality. And they seemed appropriate for what we wanted to accomplish. We printed large banners with the proverbs printed on them, so that those sentiments literally hung over the entire proceedings.

Officially titled African Women and Economic Development: Investing in Our Future, the four-day conference exceeded expectations in every possible way, starting with the response. It featured a highly diverse cross-section of Africa, with men and women from government, civil society, NGOs, the private sector, and international agencies. We registered about 1,000 total delegates, but in the end a remarkable *2,600 people* showed up for some portion of the program. It became the largest conference to date the ECA had hosted.

It also became a model for future events. Small breakout discussions flowed naturally from the large plenaries, and they compelled participation, turning them from passive listening experiences into active working groups. As a result, a broader range of experiences and ideas could be incorporated into a final report, as well as the conference dialogue. The working group recommendations, for instance, were presented at the event's conclusion directly to heads of state.

Since kicking off the reform process, the ECA had pulled together meetings with a similar structure, but not on this scale. The revamped ministerial conferences, the 1996 private investment forum, and the

1997 governance forum introduced unique innovations that set them apart—peer level debate, diverse stakeholder participation, direct heads of state engagement—but those elements all came together at the fortieth anniversary conference.

I asked Joséphine to give the welcoming address. She explained that the conference was intended to provide a "space for dialogue and partnerships" to better integrate women's issues into Africa's economic development.[5] To work as envisioned, the conference needed to be seen as an exchange of ideas, not just a series of presentations. She reiterated the desire for engaged debate.

A strong lineup of dignitaries followed Joséphine on the first day. All the speakers offered good ideas and established an uplifting tone, but some turned out to be quite prescient in their remarks.

Gertrude Mongella, the secretary-general of the Beijing conference, suggested that bilateral donors and other partners prioritize social aid packages to target the "miserable condition of women" in areas of education, health, water, and other basic needs. Singling out women as unique beneficiaries of essential services was hardly a priority at the time, but the Millennium Development Goals soon incorporated the idea, and it's now common practice.

Mats Karlsson, the Swedish state secretary in the ministry of foreign affairs, spoke very frankly, saying that global institutions had failed Africa through incoherent policies and inadequate financing. He said African poverty had a "feminine face" and that donors needed to play a larger role in supporting locally driven efforts to fight it, allowing Africans to be the masters of their own destiny.

It was important to me that we get across the message that gender wasn't "just another" topic and that the conference wasn't "just another" meeting. For instance, to show just how strongly we felt about gender being a cross-cutting issue, we invited plenty of officials from ministries *not* primarily responsible for women's issues—such as finance, planning, and agriculture.

"In a very real sense, the advocates for gender progress are advocates for social progress," I said when I addressed the full conference.

The energy of the opening day's plenary gave way to the collaborative working group sessions over the next two days, which gave way to the conference keynote, delivered by UN Secretary General Kofi Annan, on the third day. To my delight, Annan was eager to participate and made the event his first stop on an 11-day tour of African countries. He was a dominant figure over the final two days; in addition to the keynote, he gave closing remarks and participated in what turned out to be the highlight of the entire conference: a heads of state and government forum on the final day.

Like everything else with the conference, the scale of the heads of state forum was big. Seven leaders of African government sat on the stage, including two heads of state—Presidents Festus Mogae of Botswana and Blaise Compaoré of Burkina Faso; two prime ministers—Ahmed Ouyahia of Algeria and Meles Zenawi of Ethiopia; and two vice presidents— Uganda's Specioza Kazibwe and Ghana's John Atta Mills, who became president of Ghana in 2009. Tunisian Secretary of State Sadak Fayala sat in on behalf of President Zine El Abidine Ben Ali. They were joined by two secretary-generals: Kofi Annan and the OAU's Salim Ahmed Salim, who chaired the forum.

On size and star power alone, the forum stood apart from what normally might be expected. The real twist, however, came in the design. We structured it as an open dialogue between the leaders and everyday citizens—not as a standard panel. We selected a group of African women and youth to sit in the front row and ask questions, to which the leaders could respond. This "citizens' panel" represented the collective opinions of the entire conference, culled from smaller panel discussions and the working group sessions. I acted as moderator and I certainly had my hands full—especially with Kazibwe.

Before opening up the forum to the full panel debate, each dignitary had about 10 minutes to make a brief statement, a general overview on the role of women in development, particularly in his or her own country. With so many people onstage, even that short amount of time would add up to 90 minutes or more. So we had to keep things moving. But when it came Kazibwe's turn to speak, she tossed our time guidelines out the window. She went on and on. Her 10 minutes turned into 15 minutes… and then into 20… and then 21, 22, 23, 24… To her credit, she energized the crowd with strong rhetoric and obvious passion. She got a standing ovation when she said Africa should get its "priorities right"— poverty among women and children, for instance—before addressing more controversial concerns like globalization.

"How can we get into the 'global village' when women have no food, shelter or water?" she said. "How can you call yourselves 'men' when there is no food in your homes?"

The crowd loved it. And given what she had accomplished, no one could argue with her knowledge or perspective. In 10 years, she had gone from being a local village leader to an elected representative to a government minister, until, in 1994, she made history by becoming the first female vice president in Africa. She was a leading women's advocate and a trailblazer—but I still couldn't let her talk all day. So as she neared the half-hour mark, I finally wrote a note on a small slip of paper and passed it down the line of dignitaries. "Two more minutes," it said. When the vice president got the note, she briefly glanced at it then stopped talking—long enough to turn her head, stare right through me, and sharply respond, "I'm going to finish what I have to say."

Eventually she wrapped up and the forum proceeded. At the time, the irony of trying to quieten a decorated women's leader at a women's forum was lost on me. So perhaps it worked out for the best that Kazibwe ignored my meek attempt at moderating. We ran long, but no one seemed to care.

This four-hour grand finale gave the conference an unmistakable identity—it removed the invisible barrier between political elites and the audience. Given this opportunity, the African women's panel seated on the front row certainly took full advantage. They asked the leaders about the number of women in government, about the need for equal property rights, and about the lack of educational and training opportunities for young girls. One panelist gave an emotional account of her personal experiences with family members and children displaced by conflict. Had so many people ever seen such a direct back-and-forth between women and heads of state?

One very interesting moment sums up just how unscripted and direct the discussion turned out to be. We were talking about the number of women in parliaments and cabinets and whether countries needed to impose some kind of quota system to ensure stronger female representation.[6] Judging by the tone of the room, most of the audience were in favor. Meles Zenawi disagreed.

"In my experience," he said, speaking directly to the female panelist who had brought up the topic, "if you want something, you have to take it. No one is going to give it to you." He added that when selecting his own ministers or other political appointments, he believed first and foremost "in competence" and looked only for the best people—"not necessarily women."

Kofi Annan turned toward Meles and spoke before anyone else could.

"I'm sure some men in your cabinet turn out to be incompetent," he said. "Why not give women a chance? They have a right to be incompetent too."[7]

That exchange encapsulated so much about the gender debate, and it became one of the event's most talked-about moments. Meles took the gentle rebuke in stride, no doubt relieved that Kofi Annan delivered it rather than Vice President Kazibwe.

By the time it was over, the conference had yielded almost five dozen recommendations, many of which made their way into the national gender policy frameworks at the country level. The ECA played a big role in assisting governments in developing, implementing, and assessing these early frameworks. Kofi Annan, in his closing remarks, urged all African leaders to endorse the conference findings and follow through with implementation.

During the closing session, Bineta Diop of Senegal kindly thanked the ECA for dedicating such a historic event to African women. Years later, Time magazine named her as one of the 100 most influential people in the world. She was among the many notable African women who, like Gertrude Mongella and Specioza Kazibwe, energized the conference by delivering speeches, leading group sessions, and sitting on panels. Some of the others include:

- Ellen Johnson Sirleaf, the former chief of the UNDP Africa Bureau and the future president of Liberia. In 2005, she became the first woman elected as an African head of state;
- Pendukeni Iivula-Ithana, who at the time was Namibia's minister of lands and resettlement. In total she held six different cabinet-level positions, including attorney general, across three decades;
- Winnie Byanyima, a Ugandan parliamentarian, future director of the UNDP's Gender and Development program, and eventual executive director of Oxfam International. During her decade in parliament, she created Uganda's first all-women's caucus;
- Ruth Perry, who made history as modern Africa's first woman head of state when she was appointed chair of Liberia's ruling council in 1996;
- Atsango Chesoni, one of the youth representatives who would later help draft Kenya's revised constitution. In 2011, she became executive director of the Kenya Human Rights Commission.

That partial list now reads like an all-star roster of African trailblazers.

Behind the scenes, women made an equally strong impact. Of the 38 people on the planning committee, 35 were women. They came from the ECA, other UN agencies, and NGOs throughout Africa. (One such woman who deserves special mention is Joyce Mends-Cole, the UNDP gender advisor in Addis Ababa. Not only did she help here, but she consistently used her considerable expertise and extensive network to rally support for our gender program.) For one of the largest and most notable events the ECA had ever hosted up to that point, women almost exclusively ran the show. It succeeded because of their efforts, not mine.

◆ ◆ ◆ ◆

With our intentions firmly established, the ECA embarked on an ambitious women's agenda. Most of that work fell under the purview of the African Center for Women, which remained small but determined—and stretched way too thin. It took years to recruit enough high-caliber staff to reach the level we needed for our capacity to match our ambition. When I reflect on it, I'm still a little surprised by how much we were able to get done. Because we did a lot.

In November 1999, we hosted the Sixth African Regional Conference on Women, the primary objective of which was a five-year review of the commitments made in Beijing and also in Dakar in 1994, at the Fifth African Regional Conference. The major continental bodies—the ECA, OAU, and African Development Bank—prepared evaluations, while 48 member states submitted their own national progress reports. The news was not good. Little progress had been made in most countries due to a lack of coherent strategies, weak financial commitments, systemic discrimination, and so on.

But attendees were ready to move forward. They identified the major impediments to implementing the original Beijing Platform for Action and crafted new strategies for dealing with them. I'm proud to say the recommendations that came out of the ECA's fortieth anniversary event served as the key starting point for the attendees. These new strategies were subsequently adopted by the OAU Council of Ministers as the African Plan of Action.

Despite this positive step, historic indifference remained a worry. It was easy to envision the same governments getting together five or 10 years down the road and conducting the same assessments, identifying the same barriers, and agreeing to the same action plan. Member states had willingly signed on to the newest strategy and agreed to implement national gender policies, but they expressed concern over the lack of tools to gauge results. They made a good point. This kind of technical work was in the ECA's wheelhouse, so we got busy.

In 2002, the ECA finalized a monitoring and evaluation program to accelerate implementation of the African Plan of Action. This way, states could adjust policies and strategies as necessary, based on what was or was not working. The program focused on coordination, accountability, and capacity building, among other things. It defined indicators for consistent measurements and it suggested guidelines for conducting evaluations and analyzing data. The program played a considerable role in helping countries get national gender policies off the ground, which a handful finally did in subsequent years.

As Africa's gender focus sharpened, we worked with governments on economic and legal policies intended to eliminate gender gaps, encourage female entrepreneurship, and put more women in formal sector jobs. With help from donor partners, we established a leadership fund for women, which opened the door for a major new training program. The program's reach was extensive. It trained women in electoral processes and running for office, sponsored trade fairs and study tours, and offered advisory services to civil authorities and management groups on how to incorporate women into areas of responsibility and decision-making. And in an attempt to keep up with the sociopolitical changes going on around us, we developed a plan to bring gender into the Poverty Reduction Strategy Papers that the World Bank and IMF introduced as the basis for concessional lending.

We paid special attention to the role of women in conflict resolution. In 1998, we joined with the OAU to finally establish the African Women's Committee on Peace and Development, first agreed to by policymakers in 1993. This committee received a lot of verbal support over the years; it was included in a continental development plan adopted in Senegal in 1994 and then endorsed by the heads of state in 1995. But that was all talk. Very few leaders cared to act. It took another three years—and the combined efforts of OAU Secretary-General Salim Salim and myself—to get it off the ground. As an all-women's group formed to advise policymakers and decision-makers at a high level, including the OAU and the UN, the committee was a big deal.[8]

One of the biggest contributions to come out of the ECA during this period remains in use today: the African Gender Development Index, an instrument designed to monitor and evaluate the impact of policies introduced to narrow the gap between men and women. The AGDI sprang from the monitoring and evaluation program the ECA created in 2002 to support the OAU's action plan on gender. Just as we had done with governance, we wanted to create a tool that assessed government performance in implementing policies and programs of reform—in this case, policies aimed at ending women's marginalization.

We unveiled the AGDI in September 2004, after two years of intensive studies, including a pilot phase in 12 countries. The next month, the index was endorsed by ministers responsible for gender equality and women's affairs at the Seventh African Regional Conference on Women. The AGDI became the first tool of its kind in Africa, with a focus solely on African realities.[9]

The pilot phase confirmed a strong relation between successful policy implementation and improvements in the situation of women. "Now that a tool exists for demonstrating such progress," I wrote in the initial AGDI synopsis report, "the challenge is for African governments to go beyond commitments to implementation."

The AGDI was a highly technical undertaking that required years of planning and rigorous testing. It took until 2009, much longer than originally planned, before the ECA published the pilot country results. Two years later, the ECA compiled all the data in a full report, the *African Gender and Development Index 2011*. After that, the ECA extended the AGDI to include an additional 24 countries over a second and third phase of studies. In 2016, an AGDI phase four workshop was held in Addis Ababa.

This all happened after my term at the ECA ended and after most of the people who played a key role in the tool's initial development, especially those in the African Center for Gender and Development, were also gone.[10] But the 2011 report acknowledged the AGDI's provenance, that it dated "from eight years of reflection and consultation," and that it was developed under the leadership of Joséphine Ouédraogo. Like me, she had since moved on from the ECA, but she oversaw the AGDI's conception, groundwork, and analytic framework—for which women inside the ECA were almost entirely responsible.

◆ ◆ ◆ ◆

Like so many other development challenges in Africa, gender equality remains a challenging work in progress. Significant gains have been made in recent decades but deep constraints remain. Across Africa, women still struggle to get a proper education, earn a livable wage, and be seen as equals. They struggle to escape their dire circumstance—the World Bank estimates that 1.2 million women in Sub-Saharan Africa go "missing" each year in low- and middle-income countries. And they struggle to escape violence, which remains an everyday reality in Sub-Saharan Africa. As noted in a 2017 study on gender equality from UNESCO, the United Nations Educational, Scientific, and Cultural Organization, the cause of gender-based violence remains, as it's always been, "principally cultural," reflecting societal norms that have long suppressed women's advancements, and endangered lives. As such, making the case for gender equality in Africa is a continuous process that can never be interrupted.

The good news? Basic awareness—recognizing the economic implications of women in development as well as women's rights—has never been higher in Africa, or across the globe. According to the World Bank, 136 countries now have explicit guarantees for the equality of all citizens and non-discrimination between men and women in their constitutions. In Africa, almost all countries have ratified the UN's Convention on the Elimination of All Forms of Discrimination Against Women from 1979; more than half have ratified the African Union's Protocol on the Rights of Women in Africa from 2003. At worst, these actions are symbolic. At best, they catalyze people and institutions to act, and that's where so much of the momentum for change originates.

The World Bank, for instance, had failed to consider women with its first *World Development Report* in 1978 but underwent a cultural sea change over the next three decades. In 1997, two years after I left, the Bank created the Gender and Development Board to harmonize and accelerate gender mainstreaming across the institution. In 2011, it established the Advisory Council on Gender and Development as an external consultative body to also provide guidance and feedback. The following year, *World Development Report 2012: Gender Equality and Development* broke ground as the first *WDR* to focus solely on gender equality, "a core development objective in its own right." And in December 2015, the Bank adopted a broad new gender strategy as a follow-up to the *WDR* recommendations and in support of the UN's Sustainable Development Goals.

The UN also has gotten more serious. In 2010, then-Secretary-General Ban Ki-moon announced "Every Woman, Every Child," a global health initiative targeting the most vulnerable populations with a $40 billion pledge—a level of commitment for women and children's development that once seemed impossible to imagine. That same year, the UN General Assembly created a new agency, UN Women, to lead and coordinate the entire UN system's work on gender equality, with a director at the level of undersecretary-general. In May 2014, UN Women announced a year-long commemoration of the twentieth anniversary of the landmark Beijing conference—one of the many global institutions, NGOs, and civil society groups marking 2015, or Beijing+20, as another hopeful stepping stone.

Also in 2015, the UN adopted the aforementioned Sustainable Development Goals, or SDGs, a set of 17 benchmarks building from the expired Millennium Development Goals, to be reached by 2030. Goal 5 is to "achieve gender equality and empower all women and girls"—a sweeping declaration to end discrimination and harmful practices, eliminate violence, and ensure women's full and effective participation at all levels of political and economic decision-making. The targets are broad, but they are being taken seriously. The Canadian government, for example, in 2017 announced a restructuring of its entire international assistance policy to focus on improving outcomes for women and girls, including a multimillion-dollar program in support of local NGOs working to promote gender equality in developing countries, with a focus on Africa.

The African Union, in its previous incarnation as the OAU, has long acknowledged gender equality as a matter of concern through various charters and protocols but only started to show real commitment in more recent times. The Women and Gender Development Directorate was created in 2000 as a first step toward elevating gender as a development issue. In 2009, the AU adopted its first-ever gender policy "to establish a clear vision and make commitments to guide the process of gender mainstreaming" among its member states. The following year, it launched the 2010-2020 African Women's Decade to great fanfare. With committees at the national level to develop coordinated work plans and budgets and at the regional level to support advocacy campaigns and grassroots action, this was by far the most ambitious gender initiative the AU had ever put forward. The AU established the Fund for African Women in 2011 to support national policymaking and implementation. And in 2015 it enshrined "full gender equality in all spheres of life" as one of the key aspirations for its long-term development blueprint, Agenda 2063. As the women's decade neared its end, the AU in early 2019 consolidated efforts into a new operational strategy for gender equality and women's empowerment in support of Agenda 2063 goals.

I hope the AU's efforts work. As always, follow-through by the leaders will go a long way in determining success or failure. The number of African political leaders genuinely committed to women's rights or who fully grasp the socioeconomic impact of gender still seems few and far between, but increasingly, women are in a position to change that.

Across Africa, more females than ever are involved in the political sphere. According to data from the Inter-Parliamentary Union, the proportion of seats held by women in national parliaments in Sub-Saharan Africa in 1997 was 10.2 percent. In 2019, it was more than 24 percent—meaning that women filled almost one-quarter of all Sub Saharan legislative seats.

Some countries have seen radical gains. Djibouti had zero women in parliament in 2000; by 2019, it had 15, which is not insignificant at all since that number represented 26 percent of parliament seats. Two of the biggest successes have been Rwanda and Senegal, which led the way as early adopters of parity laws that dramatically boosted female representation. As of January 2019, women held 61 percent of seats in the lower house of Rwanda's national legislature, the largest share of any country in the world (and dwarfing the United States, at 23.5 percent).

Representation alone does not equate to the elimination of discrimination, violence, or poverty, but it does strengthen the odds of informed action. According to a World Bank study on gender released in early 2019, only six countries in the world met enough criteria so that men and women could be considered completely equal under the law (covering everything from property ownership to pay to personal safety). But Sub-Saharan Africa, as a region, had the most reforms over the previous 10 years: more than 70 different laws passed that aimed to empower women and girls and ensure their rights.

It's not just the legislative bodies driving change. The UN's NGO Directory for Africa lists more than 650 women's organizations—that's a lot of people working at the grassroots level. The news is equally encouraging in the executive branch at the national level. Since 1980, the proportion of women appointed as cabinet ministers in African countries has increased from 4 percent to more than 20 percent—higher than in Europe. According to the Inter-Parliamentary Union, as of 2019 more women in Africa were in charge of the ministerial portfolios traditionally held by men—defense, finance, and foreign affairs—than ever before. And let's not overlook the very top of the executive branch. At one exhilarating point in 2014, Africa boasted three female heads of state at the same time: Joyce Banda of Malawi, Catherine Samba-Panza of Central African Republic, and Ellen Johnson Sirleaf of Liberia.

In kicking off the Africa Women's Decade, Litha Musyimi-Ogana, the AU's director for gender and development, said, "It's time for action, not just action plans." May her words hold true for the next decade and beyond.

◆ ◆ ◆ ◆

A few months before I left the ECA in 2005, I received a letter. Actually, Kofi Annan received the letter but I got a copy. It was a two-page review of the ECA's work in promoting women's issues over the previous decade, signed by six women representing the ECA's member states and African women's NGOs. The letter is one of the most meaningful I ever received. It read in part:

The ECA has made undisputable strides in institutionalizing a gender program that has gained credibility among African member states. We want to ensure that the gains that have been made are not lost. The executive secretary is appreciated for his consistent advocacy for gender equality and women's empowerment within the ECA. Not a single statement made by Dr. Amoako was without reference to the need for achieving gender equality and women's empowerment as prerequisites for sustainable development. We wish him the best wherever he goes and are confident we have an ardent advocate in him.

The first signature belonged to Gertrude Mongella, who had presided over the Fourth World Conference on Women in Beijing and was also a key participant at the ECA's fortieth anniversary conference. In 2004, she became the first president of the Pan-African Parliament. She and I had a solid working relationship. I can say the same for the other women who signed it.[11]

Their kind words meant everything to me—validation for the decision to bring gender to the fore, inspiration to keep moving forward, and appreciation for a job that I alone could never take full credit. I cannot bestow enough praise on the incredible staff of the African Center for Women, which is now known as the African Center for Gender. They produced rigorous research on women's issues on a level unseen in the ECA's history.

The ECA has continued to build on those gains. In addition to expanding the African Gender Development Index, the ECA has produced more women's reports and studies, embedded gender equality and women's empowerment into long-term strategies, and maintained a focus on gender for workshops and big events, such as the sixth African Development Forum in 2008. I was glad to see this, because I created the ADFs in direct response to the phenomenal success we had in bringing people together at the fortieth anniversary conference, a story the following chapter picks up.

The ECA's women's conference became a touchstone, not just for the way it set a new template for ECA collaboration, but for the manner in which it framed gender as a development issue in Africa—in stark economic terms but without ever losing sight of the cultural and moral considerations of the role of women in African society. The letter from Gertrude Mongella and the other African ladies made special mention of that, commending our effort to celebrate and empower women in all walks of life, whether a career striver or a village mother.

"In order for improved prospects to become reality," I said when I spoke at the conference, "women must envision a different, better future for themselves, with real opportunities and with the odds shifting more in their favor."

My mother was born in a place and of a time where such opportunities for poor African women did not really exist. For her, the odds were too long to ever overcome. I had of course promised to tell her all about the ECA's grand celebration of women, but I never had the chance.

On the eve of the conference, my wife Philomena got a call. My mother had passed away, peacefully, back home in her village. Philomena knew the news would hit me hard, and she was right. So she made the difficult but wise decision to wait until the conference was over to tell me. Had she not, I would have struggled mightily to get through it.

Afterward, I reflected on the proceedings of the previous week in a different light, with an even greater sense of clarity and purpose. And I wondered how many times I must have passed those giant banners hanging in the conference hall—"Paradise is open at the command of mothers"—unaware that the proverb I found so inspiring as a commentary on gender equality had taken on a much more literal, but reassuring, meaning for me.

Notes

1   The recruitment of working-age men into armies and militias often decimated male populations in towns and villages, forcing women into the workforce despite a lack of training or equitable treatment. This had long been a problem in Africa, but it took until the early 1990s before women felt empowered enough to speak out.

2   "Gender mainstreaming" first began to appear in international dialogue after the Third UN World Conference on Women in Nairobi in 1985.

3   The participating countries were Eritrea, Ethiopia, Kenya, Tanzania, Uganda, and Zimbabwe.

4   The Southern African Development Community, one of the seven regional economic bodies created by the OAU, had established a gender unit in 1996 and adopted a policy framework soon after. But that was more a first step than an evolution. It took the OAU until 1992—almost 30 years after its creation—to establish a Gender and Development Directorate, though it was not very effective. The problems were similar to those that undermined the African Center for Women—insufficient staff and funding, and too much bureaucracy, too little passion.

5   The more specific conference sub-themes, which served as jumping-off points for panel discussions and working group sessions, reflected other ECA priorities that were starting to gain more traction, such as information technology, which presented a new window of economic opportunity for women, and good governance, for which women's participation was critical.

6   Rwanda broke new ground in Africa in 2003 when it adopted a new constitution that called for women to fill at least 30 percent of posts in "decision-making organs" across the country. In 2008, the country made history again, by electing 45 women to

parliament out of 80 total seats—the highest share of women MPs for any government in the world. Senegal became the second country to pass a parity law in 2010; in 2012 it elected 65 women to its 150-member National Assembly. By 2015, 16 African countries had gender parity laws. Such laws hardly guaranteed resolute action, but they were a start.

7   Meles, who deserves as much credit for lifting Ethiopia out of the ruins of war as he deserves criticism for his record on human rights, never did warm to the idea of women in government. When I left the ECA in 2005, Meles had been prime minister for a decade but he still had only two female ministers out of almost two dozen. At least he chose wisely. One of them, Aster Mamo, would in 2014 become the first woman granted the rank of deputy prime minister in Ethiopia—under Meles's successor, Hailemariam Desalegn.

8   In 2003, the committee was subsumed into the new African Union Women's Committee and made an advisory body to the AU chair on gender and development.

9   For more on the AGDI's rationale, context, and methodology—as well as acknowledgements of all those who first helped develop the tool—see *The African Gender and Development Index*, September 2004. It is available for download on the ECA's web site.

10   The AGDI is a composite index made up of two parts, the Gender Status Index and the African Women's Progress Scoreboard. The Gender Status Index is classified into three components: social power, which measures human capabilities; economic power, which measures economic opportunities; and political power, which measures political agency. The African Women's Progress Scoreboard focuses on issues such as women's rights that cannot be quantified using conventional statistics. In 2015, the African Development Bank also debuted a measuring tool, the Africa Gender Equality Index, which focuses on similar themes but draws on data to cover 52 African countries.

11   Other signees and their professional roles at the time included: Netumbo Nandi-Ndaitwah, Namibia's minister of women's affairs; Bisi Adeleye-Fayemi, executive director of the African Women's Development Fund; Gladys Mutukwa, chair of the Women in Law and Development in Africa network; Bineta Diop, executive director of Femmes Africa Solidarité; and Lynne Muthoni Wanyeki, executive director of African Women's Development and Communication Network—more commonly known as FEMNET.

Chapter 9

An Agenda for Action
The African Development Forums and a New Urgency for Big Issues

Of the different ideas I tried during my time at the ECA, none took hold faster—or produced a bigger impact—than the African Development Forums. If you have read this far, I know what you're thinking: *Another conference? Another forum?* But it's true. The ADFs, as we called them, were unique and unprecedented in their own way, and they quickly exceeded our most hopeful expectations. The concept filled a vacuum in Africa's public arena and it proved to be an almost perfect embodiment not only of the ECA's mandate and comparative advantages but of the revised priorities we had put in place.

The ECA was in the business of advocacy and policy analysis; it had access to policymakers and opinion leaders; it convened stakeholders and built consensus; it had the capacity to cover a wide range of development issues; and it was charged with enhancing the UN's role in Africa. The forums were tailor-made vehicles for fulfilling all these roles. Despite the large number of procedural conferences and meetings that were a regular part of life in this field, no single venue existed for prominent Africans in both the public and private space to come together on *African* soil and thrash out *African* issues on a regular basis.

The concept of the ADF formed over time, only after I realized that building a larger community around big issues was one of the most effective tools the ECA had at its disposal. It was a mounting realization. The initial success of multi-stakeholder events on private investment and governance had opened my eyes to new possibilities, but the ECA's fortieth anniversary conference on women in development in April 1998 was the true bellwether. Unprecedented in scale and scope for the ECA, it proved that large numbers of busy people, including high-profile leaders in the public and private sectors, would attend a multi-day event in Africa, provided that event was well organized and devoted to a timely topic.

I also found inspiration abroad. I was determined to strengthen ties to many of the foreign governments that controlled the purse strings for development financing. That outreach paid off with an increasingly forthright dialogue with members of the Development Assistance Committee of the Organisation for Economic Co-operation and Development, including invitations to participate in high-level, exclusive retreats and share an African perspective. In those sessions, I found many willing partners eager to help Africa even the playing field with donor countries. One of many topics discussed was having the ECA organize large-scale forums dedicated to singular policy issues that would involve civil society as well as leaders. The success of the women's conference certainly made the idea seem feasible.

But the actual impetus for creating an African-based global forum on development can be linked, ironically enough, to one of the many meetings that Africans regularly attend outside Africa. And to one fortuitous talk with South Africa Deputy President Thabo Mbeki in Tokyo.

In October 1998, the government of Japan convened TICAD II, the second Tokyo International Conference on African Development. It attracted more than a dozen heads of state and prime ministers from participating African and Asian countries. The first TICAD, held in 1993, had been a big success. It was among the earliest large-scale efforts to call for increased South–South cooperation between Africa and Asia's many remarkable economic turnaround stories of the late twentieth century. TICAD II tried to move the process along by establishing joint goals and objectives in specific areas such as social development, agriculture, governance, and private sector development. With representatives from 80 countries and 40 international organizations, it was a huge gathering that brought scores of African ministers, policymakers, and technicians to Tokyo. I was invited and joined the rest of the Africa delegation making the trip.

One evening, the Africa contingent gathered for the shuttle bus ride that would take us to dinner. The bus protocol was well understood. The top African leaders, the heads of state and deputies and so forth, would ride in one bus, while everyone else would take another. As we started to load the shuttles, Mbeki walked past me and took my arm. "Come with me," he said. So I boarded the main bus with him. We took a seat near the back where we began to talk.

Mbeki was widely presumed to be Nelson Mandela's heir apparent. The previous year, he had been elected president of South Africa's ruling political party, the African National Congress. He had spoken for years and at length of his vision for an "African renaissance," a rebirth of African identity and influence in the postcolonial and post-apartheid era. As such, he already was among Africa's most influential leaders. We had only met a couple of times before, at the ECA's private investment conference in 1996, and the following year at a Swedish conference on African development in Stockholm, where he and I served on different panels but had a brief conversation.

I did not see him again until TICAD II. We were there, of course, because the Japanese had invited us to discuss their development agenda for Africa. In Stockholm, the Swedes had invited us to talk about their development agenda for Africa. That point wasn't lost on either of us.

As we settled on the shuttle bus for a short ride, I commented that once again we were meeting thousands of kilometers from home, at the invitation of a donor country eager to talk about Africa. "If we are talking about an African renaissance," I said, "then maybe we should have *them* come to *us*." That way, I said, we Africans would be driving the agenda and our partners would be the observers and participate on our terms, rather than the other way around.

Mbeki laughed but nodded his head. "That sounds like a great idea," he responded, smiling.

I laughed a little too, but I also sensed an opportunity. If Mbeki truly liked that idea, maybe we should act on it. "Perhaps I will take this back to the ECA," I said, "to conceptualize a way to move forward."

Once more, he nodded his head. "I would encourage you to do so."

When I returned to Addis Ababa, my senior staff and I quickly began planning. It didn't take long, because we already had a successful model, the women's conference of just a few months prior, to build from.

A few months later, in May 1999, I shared the idea for the first time with the Joint Conference of African Ministers of Finance and Planning. I introduced it as the African Development Forum, an "innovative activity" that would foster heightened leadership from all segments of society as well as "new partnerships that respond to a vision of development shared by all of Africa's stakeholders." I placed it in the context of the ECA's ongoing renewal and the reputation we had begun to establish as a convening authority. With the ministers' support, the first forum could take place later that year, I suggested. And we had already identified a timely topic: Africa's place in the new information age.

The ministers backed the idea, and the ADFs were born.

During my time at the ECA, we convened four ADFs, each focusing on a single economic and social development issue undergoing a fundamental shift in Africa: technology, HIV/AIDs, regional integration, and governance. As with gender, some of these topics presented a challenge for traditional African policymakers, who had yet to see them as the economic development concerns that they were. But the ADFs provided a powerful way to recalibrate perceptions.

Each ADF produced a consensus statement formed by the diverse cross-section of participants. As a result, the forums opened up new space for civil society, governments, and development partners to work together. They gave average Africans the chance to interact and debate at a high level, which was tremendous and not at all common.

In this chapter, I will revisit the issues at the center of those first four ADFs through the prism of the ECA's approach. The forums played a big role in how we tackled these issues, but they did not represent the full extent of the effort we put forth. They amplified our actions, and they helped focus attention on the economic implications of issues that demanded heightened leadership.

The uniquely collaborative nature of the events gave anyone who participated an ownership stake in the process, which made it easier to build from the consensus and generate actual outcomes. In this way, the ADFs underscored an essential element of the evolution of African development: that solutions to the continent's challenges must start at home.

— ◆ —

ICT

Bringing Africa into the Information Age

Like the agricultural and industrial revolutions that came before it, the global revolution in ICTs—information and communication technologies—is recognized as a major driver of increased wealth and continuously improving standards of living. In rapid fashion, it restructured businesses, altered the demand for skills and employment, and opened up new markets through a faster flow of information and knowledge. More than any free trade agreement, it propelled the shift to a global economy. The end of the

Cold War opened the door to globalization in Africa; the ICT revolution pushed us through.

By the late 1990s, Africa had begun to embrace ICTs, but it still had a long way to go. Relative to the rest of the world, the region got off to a late start in planning for the future, since the future arrived while most of the continent was still stuck in the past. In 1996, for example, 3.6 million people sat on the waiting list for a basic telephone connection, with an average wait of nine years. Telephone operations were run as state monopolies and there were no cellular networks. Importing hardware—computers, modems, fax machines—was a burdensome process bogged down in complex regulation and high tariffs. In terms of modern telecom infrastructure, most of Africa was decades behind.

But the promise of the digital revolution was too great to ignore, and it wasn't just the Internet and World Wide Web. Mobile technology had exploded. Cell phones, with their reliance on satellites and a few well-placed transmission towers rather than miles and miles of high-cost cable, offered an unprecedented opportunity for Africans in even the most remote villages to connect with the world around them. It became more obvious than ever that governments needed to embrace the technology that underpinned the burgeoning information society.

Repeated analyses showed that strengthening telecom infrastructure and services was pivotal in promoting trade and economic growth. In addition, the most stable nations in the aftermath of the industrial revolution proved to be the ones driven by scientific and technological advancements. The most successful among them were the ones that reinvested meaningful percentages of their GDP in research and development to maintain their advantages, increase efficiency, expand knowledge, and, most important, promote innovation. Historically, African countries had not done this, with average investments of about 0.5 percent of GDP compared with 2.5 percent in rich countries. As a result, knowledge gaps were widening even as economies were growing.

I believed in the importance of science and technology-led development for Africa as a basic matter of economic necessity, but the ICT revolution offered an amazing opportunity—a quick way to simultaneously close knowledge gaps and modernize the technology sector by "leapfrogging," or bypassing, older methods entirely. As we began planning for the first African Development Forum, a major goal, therefore, was to help develop, publicize, and support African initiatives that would shape new technology policies and nurture new ways of thinking.

But there was more to it than that. I didn't settle on ICT as the topic of the inaugural ADF by chance. Rather, the advent of the ADF provided a perfectly timed opportunity to consolidate more than three years of intense activity to build an information society in Africa—activity which the ECA had helped lead. While some of that work predated my arrival, I went into the ECA with this issue very much on my mind.

Before I left the World Bank, I had the pleasure of meeting Ernest J. Wilson III. At the time, he was a policy advisor to US Vice President Al Gore and deputy director of the Global Information Infrastructure Commission. Naturally, he was also a highly regarded expert on communications technology. I met him through Bob Berg, a UN consultant and an old hand at ECA affairs. Berg had become a trusted associate, and he was keen that Wilson and I meet. So in my final days in Washington, DC, Wilson dropped by my office for a brief but pointed chat on the economic potential of ICT in Africa. Before departing, Wilson said that he wanted to give me some advice.

"When you get to the ECA," he said, "take this issue seriously."

I promised him that I would.[1]

In that regard, fortune was on my side. When I arrived in Addis, I found passionate ICT advocates already in the House, eager for the ECA to take on a bigger ICT role in Africa but frustrated by years of internal disregard. Technology was not an integral component of the work program, despite the ECA having already been a key player over the past decade. But that was about to change. The ICT revolution had arrived in Africa, and the ECA would soon be helping lead the charge.

◆　◆　◆　◆

The first notable moment for ICT in Africa took place in Europe. In February 1995, a group of G7 ministers and members from the European Commission convened in Brussels for a conference on the emerging information society, and to discuss the need for all countries, including the developing world, to be integrated equally into technology's new world order. The keynote speaker was Thabo Mbeki. He delivered a memorable speech, challenging the rich world to help ensure Africa was not left behind. He illustrated his argument with an example that became an oft-quoted flashpoint, stating that there were "more telephone lines in Manhattan than in all of Sub-Saharan Africa."[2]

Mbeki's address got a lot of attention. It conveyed the message that African leaders were ready to embrace ICT and act. A few months later, they did.

The Regional Symposium on Telematics for Development, an April 1995 gathering organized by the ECA and other partners, including UNESCO and Canada's International Development Research Center, assembled more than 400 telecom officials, systems operators, equipment suppliers, academics, and policymakers to discuss ways for Africa to benefit from the growing tech industry. As an ideas exchange, it was the first of its kind for the industry; it connected Africans from around the continent who had worked in relative isolation and proved that a lot was happening at local levels. Attendees compared and discussed approximately 50 ICT initiatives already underway, and they saw they were not alone. Imagine the experience of a systems administrator from a country with little infrastructure and high-level support being able to talk shop with a counterpart from a country already embracing the industry, like South Africa.

The regional symposium is widely regarded as the first milestone for information technology in Africa. It was there that the importance of building Africa's information infrastructure as a development tool was first stressed; that the concept of leapfrogging was clearly articulated; and that African leaders were publicly challenged to take ICT seriously.

The following month, the ECA ministerial conference responded, adopting a resolution in support of "building Africa's information highway." Some ministers had reservations about investing in new technology while so many countries needed basic services, but enough of them had the foresight to know Africa couldn't let this opportunity pass. The ministers did, however, emphasize the importance of Africa setting its own direction. So they called on the ECA to appoint and oversee a high-level working group that would produce a plan for incorporating ICTs into development policy. It was the first the time the ECA ministerial conference had addressed ICT in Africa.

The working group, which consisted of 11 experts on information technology from across Africa, met in Cairo, Dakar, and Addis Ababa over the course of six months. They formed before I started my job, but I reached out soon after I arrived. It was just one way that I followed Ernie Wilson's advice to take the issue seriously. Another was to make it clear to the handful of staff who had been toiling away to promote ICT that top management was now on their side.

The ECA already had a solid track record in this area—it had helped develop the first email systems in two dozen African countries, beginning as early as 1987.[3] But previous leadership would not commit to investing resources in ICT, despite the warnings from staff that Africa faced being left out of the information age if policymakers didn't become more progressive in their thinking.

No one exemplified that constrained capacity more than Nancy Hafkin, a senior economics officer at the ECA when I arrived in 1995 and now a member of the Internet Hall of Fame. I doubt the regional symposium would have come together without her leadership, and I can't imagine anyone on the continent was ever more focused on getting Africa connected. In a 2012 profile, Wired magazine summed up her impact in one sentence: "Before Nancy Hafkin came along, the Internet in Africa hardly existed."

Nancy arrived at the ECA in the 1980s and she soon took charge of the institution's Pan-African Development Information System, which had been primarily used to store and transmit data between countries—data transmitted by fax or traditional mail. She, however, saw it as a tool to disseminate relevant information to citizens, over a digital communications network. She was among the earliest Internet visionaries, not just in Africa but around the world. Nancy became the face of our work in promoting ICT, but she definitely wasn't alone in driving the issue. Two other women—Karima Bounemra Ben Soltane and Aida Opoku-Mensah—played such an integral role that it would be remiss not to mention their contributions.

By early 1996, the ECA's high-level working group had produced its final product: *Africa's Information Society Initiative (AISI): An Action Framework to Build Africa's Information and Communication Infrastructure*, a seminal document in Africa's ICT history. Meant to be both a vision statement and a road map, it explained how building an information society would stimulate economic growth and provide new opportunities in education, trade, health care, and job creation. And it called for the creation of National Information and Communication Infrastructure (NICI) plans. The ECA conference of ministers endorsed AISI in May 1996, and shortly thereafter, so too did the heads of state during that summer's OAU summit. AISI instantly became Africa's guiding narrative on how to increase the role of technology in development.

A common weakness of ambitious programs developed at the global or regional level is that they are not easily adaptable to the national setting, where implementation really happens. AISI recognized this pitfall by making the NICI plans the key component of its overall strategy, with emphasis on programs and pilot projects that reflected individual country needs. In a way, the national plans decentralized ICT infrastructure development, allowing countries to go at their own pace and within their own capacity while retaining sight of continental goals.

The ECA, meanwhile, assumed a central coordinating, advocacy, and support role for helping countries launch their NICI plans. Multiple agencies and partners had a hand in getting these off ground: UNDP, the World Bank, and others, all of which had different roles to play— capacity building, financing, implementation, and so forth. Some had more resources to invest than others. Our job was to make that collective effort work as efficiently as possible, coordinating among the partners and leading the dialogue at the country level, while also supplying much-needed technical assistance to policymakers and technicians.

For the most part, the system worked. We embarked on NICI plans for seven countries within the first year and more than doubled that total in the second.

Our momentum really picked up after that. In addition to helping set up the NICI plans, we had a bulging to-do list: to encourage the establishment of regional Internet hosts; to guide sector-specific technology applications; to assist governments in creating fair regulatory frameworks that attracted investment; to bolster connectivity; and of course to continue to raise policy awareness.

One significant event with regard to raising awareness took place at the 1997 conference of ministers. We organized a special day-long session with the Global Information Infrastructure Commission (GIIC), a global body of industry leaders established by the G7 and World Bank in the mid-1990s to help bridge the digital divide. It was the first time that the ministers had devoted a full day of their annual meetings to a single, specific theme.[4]

The GIIC session seemed to mark a turning point in both awareness and acceptance among policymakers. We saw a distinct shift in tone at the following year's conference, where ECA technicians spent more time helping ministers plan their country strategies than trying to persuade them of the merits of ICT development. The next year, the tone had shifted yet again, with most ministers eager to talk—or brag— about their countries' accomplishments.

Around the same time, we decided to stage a bigger event to reach a bigger audience: the 1998 Global Connectivity for Africa Conference, which attracted scores of industry types, plus three dozen ministers. In my opening address, I ran through some of the gains made in the three short years since the adoption of the AISA initiative—that 47 African countries had Internet connectivity, compared with a mere four in 1995, and that two dozen countries were in the process of creating or implementing their NICI plans. But I also noted the challenges ahead—that only one African in 10,000 had Internet access, and that abysmal infrastructure was the main culprit. I urged the attendees to devise policy options that would address the underdevelopment and encourage private investment.

The turnout and enthusiasm for the connectivity conference were fantastic, but in some ways we were preaching to the choir. Many attendees, especially from the private sector, were the early adopters. Despite the gains so far and the proliferation of regional conferences like this one (or even larger international events), ICT still had to attract the serious attention of most African decision-makers. Africa needed another catalytic event, like the Telecom Symposium, but one that reached beyond the enthusiasts and usual suspects.

The inaugural African Development Forum turned out to be such an event.

ADF '99, as we called it, drew about 1,000 participants, including for the first time the entire spectrum of high-level ICT stakeholders from government, the private sector, civil society—including academia, the media, and bilateral and multilateral organizations. Though the vast majority of attendees were African, about 20 percent came from other parts of the world.[5] They ranged from community activists and technology experts to ministers and heads of state, including Ethiopia Prime Minister Meles Zenawi and Mali President Alpha Oumar Konaré, both of whom gave inspiring keynotes.

Having Meles and Konaré on board gave the occasion additional gravitas. They were among a small handful of African leaders, along with Rwanda's Paul Kagame and South Africa's Mbeki, who made an early commitment to promoting information technology as a development priority. As the "host country" president, Meles had always been very supportive of ECA events and conferences, and I always welcomed his presence. But in this case, I was particularly proud that Konaré agreed to participate. On the issue of ICT for development, Konaré was already seen as a leader among leaders. Being able to promote his participation lent our new forum instant credibility. Mbeki had agreed to attend, but a scheduling conflict at the last minute forced him to back out. Given that our conversation in Japan had been the catalyst for creating the ADF, I was disappointed that he had to miss it.

We held the forum over four days in October 1999 and gave it an official title: "The Challenge to Africa of Globalization in the Information Age." Admittedly, that title, a little too long with a few too many prepositions, was not our snappiest. But it got the point across. The globalized economy and digital revolution were in many ways intertwined, seismic shifts in the world's socioeconomic order that could flatten or propel Africa. The momentum for ICT had built in recent years, but where would that lead? I wanted it to be a goal-driven forum that yielded something substantial. More than anything, I wanted it to generate momentum for even bigger and better ideas.

In the end we stuck closely to what we knew. ADF '99 followed a similar format to that which had worked so well at the gender conference. We had participants meet in small groups to learn from each other and spur new thinking. We challenged them to devise actionable approaches based on what had already been shown to work in the region. We gave our civil society attendees equal opportunities to speak, just as top policymakers or leaders were given.

The upshot is that the ADF became the first real open forum to demonstrate just how much already was being done in Africa, by Africans, to harness the power of ICTs. Their stories were inspiring, and they occupied center stage. Some of the examples shared included:

- long-distance learning programs to train thousands of teachers and health practitioners in Ethiopia and Senegal;
- wiring the University of Zambia with a campus-wide fiber optic backbone with connections and Internet access to every building and office;
- and the opening of approximately 400 cyber-cafés in Tunisia, which were being managed by young people who had previously been unemployed.

There were many more examples. Such local success stories were not well known at the time, especially within Africa, so we set up an "information marketplace"—an open area where countries, particularly those developing NICI plans, worked in groups to exchange best practices and to explore partnership and funding opportunities with regional organizations and the private sector.

Since this was the first ADF, we wanted to get feedback from the participants. We distributed a survey with a few dozen questions ranging from demographic data to conference orientation. Among those who responded, nearly 90 percent said the conference had helped them identify suitable policy options to pursue for or within their countries. And 97 percent said they would follow up their participation in the conference with activities in support of ICT development. Of course, not that many people charged into the streets and installed local access networks in their towns and villages, but the extraordinarily positive response told us the forum had succeeded at what we wanted it to do: bring people together—policymakers and practitioners—and encourage them to act.

The forum produced an abundance of proposals, which the ECA synthesized into four focus areas: education, e-commerce, health, and policy work. We pursued some very good ideas (such as creating a regional initiative to coordinate the rapidly evolving school networking programs), but, much to my regret, many of them dragged on for months before being quietly dropped. We learned a valuable lesson there because we probably tried to do a little too much.

Still, we found great results with the policy work, centered mostly on further development and enhancements of the NICI plans—one of the main thrusts of recommended follow-up action to come out of the ADF. By the end of the following year, we were working with two dozen countries on formulating their plans. By 2001, we were working with almost 30 countries, 15 of which had completed the process and begun enacting favorable ICT policies.

ICT combined all the major goals I had for the ECA's reform and renewal. We grew into a strong intellectual resource and played a major role in helping African countries develop their first national ICT policies. We were a willing and reliable partner, and we continued to bring people together well after ADF '99.

The ECA had gained enough stature as an ICT leader in Africa to be invited to give the opening presentation at the second Global Knowledge Conference in Malaysia in March 2000. That event also underscored the impact and reach of the ADF, which was regarded as the primary African "feeder event" into the Malaysia conference. Two years later, we organized the launch of the African Stakeholders Network, a clearinghouse for various ICT initiatives across all UN agencies in Africa, which helped reduce duplication and sped up training programs. And when African leaders adopted NEPAD—the New Partnership for African Development—as the continent's guiding development framework in 2002, ICT was one of the main program areas, incorporating elements of the original AISA into it.

◆ ◆ ◆ ◆

When I went to the ECA in 1995, I wanted to make certain that ICT was an institutional priority. So it was heartening to see how quickly the issue gained traction among member countries. For example, Burkina Faso began working on its ICT plan as early as 1996. Its leaders took a pragmatic approach, wanting to apply technology to the country's most immediate challenges, such as poverty, natural resource limitations, and declining social services. Rwanda began its national information and communication strategy in 1998 with a goal of using ICT to modernize government and increase transparency. Nigeria launched its national communications policy in October 1999, the same month as the ADF, with an ambitious plan to quadruple telephone service, end public telecoms monopolies, and integrate national databanks. These countries were among the earliest adopters in Africa.

In 2003 and 2005, the World Summit on the Information Society (WSIS) took place in Geneva and Tunis. It was a summit in two parts, sponsored by the UN and intended to build a consensus on ways to bridge the digital divide between rich and poor states. Delegates from 175 countries spent days debating inclusive growth, regulatory frameworks, innovation, and public–private partnerships. WSIS is seen as one of the key milestones in ICT history because, according to the Internet Society, it "recognized that businesses, civil society, engineers, and everyone—not just governments—should play a role in determining its future."

The AISI initiative preceded WSIS by years. So by the time the global summit convened, the same technology issues under discussion in Geneva and Tunis had already been dissected at the African level, including at the ADF. And in the best cases, like Burkina Faso, Rwanda, and Nigeria, action was well underway.

That's not to say Africa charged ahead to the point where its ICT sector set a new global standard. In the 2017 *Measuring the Information Society Report*, a yearly benchmarking tool published by the International Telecommunications Union, Africa continued to lag behind the rest of the world in ICT performance. Per the report's ICT development index, Africa's average value was 2.64 points, little more than half the global average of 5.11. Only one country, Mauritius, ranked in the upper half of the global index, while 28 of the 38 total African countries that were measured landed in the bottom 25 percent—a reflection of the "generally low level of economic development in the region," the report found.

None of this is surprising, because Africa had to meet the ICT revolution on a vastly uneven playing field from the developed world. There is a long way to go, certainly in relation to the investments in infrastructure and skills training that are needed to close the global gap ahead of next-level technological innovations.

But Africa has had success stories too. It may lag behind, but it's also not been left behind. Look no further than the mobile revolution.

In 2017, mobile technologies and services supported almost 3 million jobs and generated 7.1 percent of GDP in Sub-Saharan Africa, according to research from the GSMA, one of the world's largest mobile associations. That translates into approximately $110 billion in economic value. Projections are for an increase to $150 billion by 2022. The industry's growth has been explosive—from 4 million unique mobile subscribers in 1998 to 259 million a decade later to 444 million, or about 9 percent of total global subscribers, in 2018. For the vast stretches of underdeveloped Africa, mobile technology and related services have been powerful social and economic equalizers. In mobile payments, for example, Africa is leading the world in innovation.

Again, Africa's mobile penetration as a percentage of its population lags behind other regions of the world, but as governments—hopefully—address infrastructure and affordability challenges, and as Africa's youthful population grows to adulthood, the region is expected to see accelerated growth again.

At an AU summit in early 2019, African heads of state directed their ICT ministers to develop a common framework for continent-wide digital priorities and initiatives. A few months later, ministers from across Africa gathered in Geneva, Switzerland, to review proposals in key areas covering infrastructure, private investment, cybersecurity, skills and entrepreneurship, and common digital markets, among other topics. According to a statement released by the International Telecommunications Union, which hosted the event, the ministers departed Geneva committed to "building a new Africa that leverages the tremendous potential of digital technologies to improve lives."

There may be no sector in Africa that offers more opportunity for economic transformation than technology. It touches all industries, all economies, all aspects of citizen life. Making commitments is a necessary step, but lasting progress requires action. Africa has been there before. It can be again.

– ◆ –

HIV/AIDS
Africa's 'Greatest Leadership Challenge'

Standing in front of hundreds of high-powered leaders, I opened the second African Development Forum with a bold challenge: do your jobs better, I said, or risk the annihilation of all of us. "This is a battle for our continent's survival. This is the time to be decisive. This is *our* test. And because Africa is on the front lines of this fight, this is the *world's* test."

I was not being overly dramatic. I was being honest about HIV/AIDS.

In December 2000, when the ECA convened ADF II—we decided to use Roman numerals as a naming convention from that point forward—Africa was in the fourteenth year of the HIV/AIDS pandemic. Calls to arms rang out with increasing frequency. Earlier that year, the International AIDS Conference convened in Durban, the first time the global event had been held in a developing country. The choice of location was pointed—AIDS had become Africa's largest killer, and South Africa had one of the highest HIV prevalence rates in the world. It was found in every country on the continent. It had infected 8.8 percent of our population and was killing 2.4 million people a year, leaving more than 12 million orphans.

African heads of state had passed declarations committing to HIV prevention at OAU summits in 1992, 1994, and 1998. Indeed, national actions had been taken in some countries, but there was a wide disparity in terms of the extent and effectiveness of the responses, not to mention infection rates. At the end of 1999, the estimated number of adults living with HIV/AIDS in Ghana was 3.6 percent. In South Africa, it was 19.9 percent. Mostly, the gap came down to leadership. In many countries, HIV was not fully understood or its impact immediately recognized. But in countries like Uganda or Zambia, where leaders like Yoweri Museveni and Kenneth Kaunda openly supported aggressive counter-measures, the spread of the virus at least was minimized and, in the best cases, reversed.[6]

Preparations for ADF II began as soon as ADF '99 was over, and I mean that quite literally. The ECA and the Joint United Nations Programme on HIV/AIDS, commonly known as UNAIDS, held a planning meeting for the second forum on the last day of the first forum. We moved fast because we had already settled on HIV/AIDS as a topic, for a few different reasons.

I envisioned the ADFs as a mechanism to increase dialogue and action around a timely topic in need of greater policy action, and HIV/AIDS certainly met that requirement. The ECA didn't really deal with health issues because they weren't part of our mandate. But in HIV/AIDS, we had an issue that transcended health impacts. To view it only as a health crisis was to ignore its devastating toll on Africa's working age population and families—and that made it an economic crisis in need of widespread recognition. This realization, plus a confluence of other factors, led to my and the ECA's involvement, which kicked into high gear with ADF II but did not end there.

◆　◆　◆　◆

Unlike gender equality or information technology, HIV/AIDS was never part of my agenda for renewal at the ECA. It wasn't included in *Serving Africa Better* and it remained off our radar in the following years, absent even from a 1997 prospectus on the ECA's upcoming work, *Forging New Partnerships for Africa's Future*. I didn't disregard its importance; I just knew there were other agencies within the United Nations, such as UNICEF, UNDP, and UNAIDS, whose priorities were aligned much more closely to HIV/AIDS interventions than ours. And yet, perhaps more so than with any other major socioeconomic issue, my thinking changed completely. There were two main reasons why.

First, Peter Piot got through to me.

Piot was the executive director of UNAIDS, the joint venture established in 1995 to strengthen the UN's global response to HIV by bringing together the efforts and resources of 11 UN system organizations. He was the founding executive director, a role that made him the UN's chief advocate for worldwide action against AIDS. Piot was a great choice. In 1976, he co-discovered the Ebola virus in Zaire. In the 1980s, he was one of the first scientists to study AIDS in Africa—and to determine that it could be transmitted through heterosexual activity. In the 1990s, he served as president of the International AIDS Society and helped secure expensive antiretroviral drugs to provide to developing countries. The man knew what he was doing and what he was talking about.

Piot arrived at the UN around the same time as I did and we quickly became good friends. We had a lot of conversations those first few years, because he felt like he was struggling to be heard, particularly in Africa. He didn't think leaders were seeing the full implications of the pandemic.

"This is beyond a health crisis," he would say. "It will devastate African economies. Please pay attention to this."

He told me that, over and over. *"Please pay attention."* When someone of his stature tells you to do something, you do it.

I started to look at the situation more closely, reading reports and studying projections but with an economist's eye. The reality was terrifying. Of course HIV wasn't just a health issue—it was crippling Africa's labor force. The virus was having the greatest impact on those in their most productive years. Its rapid spread was decimating workers at the community level, with significant negative consequences for national economies. Damage was calculated as a 0.7 percent annual reduction in GDP, with a projected reduction of 2 percent in the years ahead. All these able-bodied citizens, in the prime of their lives and careers, were dying. Rapidly. The data painted a devastating picture.

As the ECA's annual ministerial conference approached in May 1999, I called Piot with an idea: to put HIV/AIDS on the agenda. This would be the first year of the joint conference, so finance and planning ministers would all be there together. He loved the idea and wanted to participate. Later, he recalled that ministerial meeting as one of the pivotal moments of awareness in Africa.

When we put the data and statistics in front of the ministers, the conference hall fell silent. You could have heard a pin drop. Most of them had never considered HIV/AIDS as part of their domain despite all the economic projections being made—the negative impact on growth rates, on investments, on labor markets, and so on. The research was real and it was relevant. By trying to connect the dots, we helped open their eyes, just as Piot had helped open mine.

The ministers then passed a resolution urging the ECA to work closely with UNAIDS and other institutions to further examine the economic impact of HIV/AIDS in African countries and to "disseminate the data [for] policy development and planning."

Not that I needed more convincing, but the second reason I changed my thinking stemmed from the fallout over a high-profile event a few months later.

In September 1999, the Eleventh International Conference on AIDS and STDs in Africa (ICASA) convened in Zambia with a lot of advance publicity that African leaders were ready to make a bold, collective statement on fighting HIV. The ICASA events were notable for being African-led and grounded in hard science and research, and as the pandemic worsened they had grown in stature. But when the conference opened, only 10 African nations were present, and that wasn't the worst part. Not a single African head of state showed up, not even the host president, Frederick Chiluba, who backed out at the last minute.

The absence of top leaders embarrassed organizers and infuriated the scores of NGO workers, activists, scientists, and researchers who had gathered in Lusaka—almost 5,000 of them in all—under the notion that the five-day conference would be a galvanizing moment for political leadership.

On the first day, the ranking representatives from the participating African countries did agree to unequivocally declare AIDS a national disaster. But the gesture rang hollow, with participants frustrated by a grand statement of political commitment being delivered by vice presidents and ministers. The absence of the Zambian president in particular was a sore point, especially since Chiluba's predecessor, former President Kenneth Kaunda, had become one of Africa's most prominent voices in the fight against AIDS.

I did not attend the conference, but plenty of people I knew called the event a fiasco. Peter Piot was there, as was World Health Organization Director Ebrahim Samba, and they both publicly expressed their disappointment and anger. In the absence of heavyweight political leadership, the conference theme—"Setting Priorities for HIV/AIDS in Africa"—seemed cruelly ironic.

Even though I wasn't there, I was disappointed, too. The fact that it was in Zambia, where I had lived and worked and still felt connected, mattered. But mostly, I had become so much more focused on the urgency of the issue that the whole affair unsettled me. ICASA was a true African-owned event. How could it be so easily overlooked by African leaders when every day seemed to bring more bad news?

At that point, I knew what the focus of the second African Development Forum had to be, even though the first forum had yet to convene. I suppose it's a good thing the first one was not a flop!

The ADF offered the perfect platform to speak about HIV/AIDS in a way that few were doing at the time. I wanted it to build on what we had started with the finance ministers, raising awareness of the economic impacts; but I really wanted to pick up from what took place in Zambia, where thousands of local community and industry leaders from around the world showed up but the president did not. The forum would not only focus on the need for heightened leadership on HIV/AIDS, it would draw on the ECA's convening power to define leadership at *all* levels: within the family, the community, the churches and mosques, the local businesses, and, uppermost, the national political leaders.

After ICASA, the debate over political leadership and HIV had only intensified. The July 2000 International AIDS Conference in Durban had a lot to do with that. The International AIDS Society began staging the conferences in 1985, but the Durban event was considered a breakthrough for putting AIDS treatment on the global agenda—and for conveying the staggering impact of the epidemic in Sub-Saharan Africa to the rest of the world, which had yet to fully grasp the scope of the region's problems.

Holding the conference in a developing country for the first time guaranteed heightened interest, but so did the public pronouncements made by South African President Thabo Mbeki in the weeks prior. Mbeki called into question the reality of HIV infection rates in South Africa and cited poverty, not HIV, as the major cause of AIDS. It was a disheartening example of denialism, made all the worse by the fact that it came from Mbeki, the leader of one of the most HIV-prevalent countries in the world and a man whom so many, myself included, had come to admire as an example of new African leadership.

The controversy led to the unprecedented "Durban Declaration," published on the eve of the conference, in which 5,000 global physicians and scientists reaffirmed HIV as the cause of AIDS. Mbeki still spoke at the beginning of the conference and called for more scientific studies, a speech that Peter Piot, who spoke immediately after Mbeki, said was "very disappointing for many of us."[7] By contrast, Mbeki's predecessor, Nelson Mandela, spoke at the end of the conference and issued a rousing call to arms. "The challenge is to move from rhetoric to action," Mandela said, challenging global leaders, and especially African leaders, to fight HIV/AIDS "at an unprecedented intensity and scale."

The context here is notable because of the increased urgency—and timely relevance—it gave the African Development Forum, scheduled for later that year. All of this unfolded as the ECA was busy planning, and it's one reason I wanted to focus so heavily on leadership. The forum was the first big opportunity for Africa to come together and heed Mandela's call. We took his words seriously and gave the forum a blunt, somewhat provocative theme: "AIDS: The Greatest Challenge to Leadership in Africa."

◆　◆　◆　◆

ADF II opened on December 3, 2000, with Biruk G. Medhin, an Ethiopian community activist, reading a poem he wrote, "The Birds are Singing." It told the story of a father in a hypothetical African village talking to his son about AIDS, and it was meant as a symbolic warning to the citizens of Africa to be safe, help protect their loved ones, and not fear speaking out. It was an emotional, powerful, and uncharacteristically political way to begin a high-level forum, but it set a tone of honesty that remained consistent throughout the four-day event.

"Find the things that will make you a better leader," I urged the audience during my welcome remarks, easily one of the most impassioned, personal speeches I ever gave. "No one is going to save us from the crisis but ourselves."

I spoke of the difference between adequate, good, and great leaders, the latter being the ones who "surpassed even themselves." And I highlighted the obvious link between good HIV/AIDS policy and good socioeconomic development: "Each and every one of the leadership acts necessary to [combat] HIV/AIDS are things we want anyway for a stronger, better developed Africa."

Originally scheduled for October 2000, the ADF had to be pushed back a couple of months due to the complexity of logistics. We had to accommodate an array of partners—the OAU and World Bank, plus UNAIDS, UNDP, UNICEF, among others—but the big challenge was getting enough influential leaders together so that ADF II wouldn't suffer the same fate as ICASA. If we were going to build an AIDS forum around leadership and Nelson Mandela's call to action, we had to have leaders on board. On that level, we succeeded.

There might not have been enough great African leaders who "surpassed even themselves" on the HIV issue at that time, but they did exist. And we got many of them to come to the forum—Rwanda's Paul Kagame, Ethiopia's Meles Zenawi, Botswana's Festus Mogae, and Senegal's Moustapha Niasse, all of whom faced their own AIDS-related crises at home but refused to cower. Botswana at the time had the highest incidence of AIDS in Africa, while Rwanda was trying to overcome a surge of deliberate infections from the recent genocide. And then there were Museveni and Kaunda, two of Africa's most notable and respected voices leading the fight against HIV/AIDS.

Under Museveni, Uganda in 1986 became one of the first countries in Africa to work with the World Health Organization on a national AIDS program. The program operated out of a dozen government ministries, which made Uganda one of the first countries in Africa to attack HIV/AIDS from all policy angles. At the end of the 1980s, Uganda's infection rate ranked among the highest in Africa and the world. But the numbers began to drop around 1993. They continued to decline into the next decade. Tens of thousands still died, so the situation wasn't good, but things would have been much worse without Uganda's extensive awareness and prevention campaign, which included frank dialogue about abstinence, prevention, sexual activities, and voluntary HIV testing. Most leaders weren't willing to have those tough discussions. Museveni was.

Kaunda's case is different—he wasn't a sitting head of state— but also more personal. In 1986, one of his sons died, and the next year Kaunda publicly acknowledged AIDS as the cause. He made a personal plea for the international community to recognize the threat and help fund the fight. I got to know Kaunda very well when I worked alongside him in Zambia so his candor, honesty, and emotion did not surprise me. Once he had left office in 1991, he devoted himself to fighting AIDS with a fierce determination, setting up a foundation for AIDS orphans in Lusaka and aggressively speaking out. More times than not, he found he was the only high-level figure in Zambia—where one in five adults were infected at the end of the twentieth century—willing to break cultural taboos and speak openly about AIDS prevention. He called it "breaking the wall of silence." He also said his mission wasn't just about avenging his son but about fighting a killer disease that threatened to destroy the human race.

Getting both Museveni and Kaunda to attend the ADF was very important to me because I wanted the event to rally leaders by positive example. The trends and indicators were all pointing in the wrong direction, and a leadership crisis was evident, but I didn't want the event to criticize; I wanted it to inspire.

Peter Piot, an obvious choice to deliver a keynote speech, urged attendees to stay positive. "We have the solutions!" he declared, "But we have to apply them on the right scale, the scale of the epidemic itself." Graça Machel, a renowned politician and humanitarian from Mozambique who had married Nelson Mandela in 1998, also brought a message of hope and resilience. Not even HIV/AIDS "can defeat this great continent of ours," she said, hailing the African continent for its "strength, determination, and proven ability to survive." And UN Secretary-General Kofi Annan, who had a big presence at the forum, reminded participants that "we are far from powerless." He said he hoped people in the future "would look back on this forum and say, 'This is where the breakthrough occurred.'" Their words energized the packed conference hall.

Around 1,700 delegates showed up—a more than 50 percent increase over the previous year's forum. There were local community activists and leading members of NGOs, government ministers and policymakers, academics and researchers, and physicians and scientists. There were senior staff and top leaders from fellow UN agencies and other multilateral organizations. And in addition to the heads of state, there were also traditional healers, religious leaders, vice presidents, and ministers, all contributing their time and their ideas.

As with the first ADF, the wide range of participants infused the proceedings with a sense of energy, informality, and discovery. We ensured a major role for youth and women and especially for people living with AIDS. Africans suffering from the disease shared their struggles—standing and speaking to their fellow citizens, to African dignitaries, to heads of state—without fear of being shamed or ostracized. We conducted critical appraisals of current strategies, many of which were not widely known. Museveni, for example, reported how improved sex education in Uganda had not only led to reduced HIV transmissions but had also decreased the number of teen pregnancies. Kaunda reviewed a list of practical policy actions identified by his foundation that could stabilize the recovery of affected families and communities, such as home-based care, fee-free access to drugs and supplies, and income-generating activities for those living with HIV. This was critical knowledge-sharing—quite literally, a matter of life and death.

Even though the subject matter was grim, the mood over those four days tended to be far more hopeful than dour, and it was never dull. At times, it was even uplifting, such as when a group of AIDS orphans staged an interpretive dance that ended with them triumphantly "unmasking" and defeating the virus. At other times, it was defiant, with an undercurrent of controlled anger, particularly among the youth and those living with HIV/AIDS, over how much time and how many lives had been lost.

"We should not have allowed it to get to this stage," said Charlotte Mjele, a young social activist who had no qualms about shaming Africa's weak collective response. She also offered a stirring example of personal leadership, describing how she came to terms with her diagnosis and ignored the social stigma that came with it. "Death was not on my agenda. I was young and I wanted to live," she said, to a standing ovation.

The personal accounts were poignant and effective; they helped humanize a difficult topic and made policy talks more relatable, chipping away at the "wall of silence" Kaunda decried. But the forum was about much more than that. It was also "not just another AIDS meeting," as Peter Piot had said.

To underscore the link between HIV policy and economic outcomes, the ECA and UNAIDS prepared a study that profiled the current state of HIV infections for every country in Africa, plus the government responses. The report, which we presented to the delegates, painted a comprehensive picture of HIV's impact on the continent's social and *economic* fabric. Until then, there had been little systematic analysis of the economic fallout, despite ample anecdotal evidence. Our report compiled the existing evidence from reports, scientific papers, books, surveys, and census data. It filtered that data through selected indicators—impact on macroeconomics, agricultural production, education, etc.— to illustrate how both the demand and supply for sector services and products had been affected by HIV in Africa. It's what the ministerial conference had wanted, and it provided powerful evidence for substantive discussions.

At its core, ADF II was a working meeting. It was preceded by a series of 23 preparatory consultations across Africa at the national level, in which all stakeholders, public and private, jointly set agendas and outlined talking points. In addition, we formed six thematic subgroups (such as youth, people living with AIDS, etc.) that continued to meet through the forum. These subgroups produced their own final statements, which were appended to the forum's major outcome, the Addis Ababa Consensus (formal title: *The African Consensus and Plan of Action: Leadership to Overcome HIV/AIDS*).

The consensus document outlined tasks ahead in key sectors, in both the prevention of HIV/AIDS and the treatment and care of infected people. It also offered specific leadership recommendations for everyone, at all levels—personal, community, national, regional, or international. It was the most expansive blueprint yet devised in Africa for fighting HIV/AIDS from the smallest village to the largest parliament. Within another six months, 29 countries had organized post-forum workshops to see how the consensus could be implemented at the national level.

On the final day of the forum, all the attending heads of state spoke about their country efforts and took questions from the general audience, continuing the innovative format we first used at the fortieth anniversary event. At the time, the ECA was still the only institution supporting forums where civil society could so openly interact with elected leaders.

Most of the political leaders spoke with a disarming sense of humility, not only on the final day but throughout the conference. President Mogae of Botswana plainly admitted that as far as decisive measures go, "we have failed." Museveni talked about his days as a rebel fighter among his fellow soldiers and how he felt the full weight of HIV/AIDS once those soldiers began to die. And Kaunda, in one of the most memorable moments, broke protocol completely when he suddenly started to sing, leading the audience in a verse of the political mobilization song "Forward Ever, Backward Never," which Ghana's Kwame Nkrumah had made famous. Kaunda even modified a few lyrics to reflect the HIV/AIDS challenge.

Kaunda wasn't the only one to get caught up in the moment. Or to break into song. I did it too.

Before the heads of state forum, Kofi Annan announced that a special session of the UN General Assembly, devoted solely to AIDS, would convene the following June. In doing so, he quoted a young girl he had recently met. She told him her country was dying and that it is up to her and her fellow youth "to make sure it stays alive." Facing up to AIDS is a point of honor, Annan said, "not a point of shame." When Annan finished speaking, I took the lectern and led the delegates in singing "Happy Birthday" to Charlotte Mjele, the young woman living with HIV/AIDS who said death wasn't on her agenda. She turned 22 that day, and we had every reason to celebrate her life. Even though she was living with HIV/AIDS, she wasn't a victim. She was a leader.[8]

From the beginning, I viewed ADF II as the start of a process to invest more time and resources, both the ECA's and mine, into HIV/AIDS. The most immediate goal was to generate energy and spread knowledge—about the disease, about new strategies, about development impacts. Beyond the ADF, the short-term goal was to mobilize action on the forum's consensus statement and push the heads of state and government to follow up. In the long term, we wanted to scale up national and international partnerships so that everyone in the world was fully aware of fighting AIDS in Africa. We accomplished all of these goals.

In April 2001, the OAU held a special summit in Abuja on HIV/AIDS and other infectious diseases. That meeting had been set before ADF II, so an open goal at the forum was crafting an action plan that could feed directly into the special summit. In the intervening months, Peter Piot and I stayed in contact with the OAU to make sure that whatever came out of Abuja would build on our and other previous efforts. There was no need to start from scratch, we argued, since the ADF II outcomes addressed specific ways to move forward.

The process played out in a most productive way. With the groundbreaking Abuja Declaration on HIV/AIDS, African governments jointly declared the epidemic as a full-fledged continental emergency and in response they agreed to allocate at least 15 percent of their national budgets over the next 15 years to health programs. Among other commitments, they pledged to remove economic barriers that hindered faster response, support vaccine development, and seek more resources. They also endorsed the ADF II consensus statement, which provided a starting point for much of the Abuja Declaration's broad language, elements of which were still controversial in certain regions—the social stigma of HIV, the vulnerability of migrants and mobile populations, the counter-productiveness of denials, and the essential role of education. And notably, the Abuja Declaration recognized HIV/AIDS as "a devastating economic burden, through the loss of human capital, reduced productivity, and the diversion of human and financial resources to care and treatment."

It was a huge step forward.

A few months later, the UN General Assembly met in its special session on HIV/AIDS, a nine-day event with dozens of side sessions featuring many of the same topics we had touched on in Addis: family and youth, AIDS and poverty, and education and prevention, among others. Many events focused exclusively on Africa, including an African civil society forum and several sessions covering rural challenges, Uganda case studies, international funding, and more. It was the ADF, but on an even bigger scale. Many of the players were the same. Peter Piot played a large role, as did Stephen Lewis, a former Canadian ambassador to the UN and deputy director of UNICEF. He was a passionate advocate for Africa, for its people, and for fighting HIV/AIDS with as much firepower as possible.[9] He had been a visible presence at the ADF, as he was for most events of the kind. I also attended and had the privilege of sitting on a panel with other UN agency heads. Our topic: the socioeconomic impact of the epidemic and how to strengthen national capacities.

In his keynote speech to the General Assembly, Kofi Annan said that he had made the fight against AIDS his "personal priority." I know he was deeply troubled by the toll on human life, but he was also troubled by criticisms that the United Nations was not doing enough. He felt a lot of external pressure and most of it revolved around money. His solution was to establish a global "war chest" to fight infectious diseases, primarily AIDS, tuberculosis, and malaria.

The idea was discussed at the G8 summit in 2000, but it was also a topic of conversation at the ADF, mostly in the margins as Lewis, Piot, and others made a push for more resources. But in his ADF remarks, Annan alluded to the "billions rather than millions" that needed to be spent and how Africa first needed to get mechanisms in place to handle the influx of aid. That's another reason it was so important to start to build consensus among leaders at the ADF. A major financial program was right around the corner, but Africa needed to show it had the fortitude—and a game plan— to put that money to work.

Speaking at the special summit in Abuja, Annan proposed the creation of what became known as the Global Fund, "dedicated to the battle against HIV/AIDS and other infectious diseases." A few weeks later, US President George W. Bush pledged $200 million in seed money. France soon followed with its own early pledge. The fund came into being in January 2002 and shortly thereafter approved its first round of interventions—$565 million for 55 programs in 36 countries. Of that, $308 million, or almost 55 percent, went to Africa.

◆ ◆ ◆ ◆

The tide turned on the approach to HIV/AIDS in Africa, and I think the tipping point came during the short period of time between ADF II and the UN's special session. I believe the ECA forum played a big role— the consensus statement, the recommendations, the public solidarity, the inputs into the Abuja summit, all of it. In the ADF II summary report, which we published about six months after the forum, I noted that after a period of internal discussion and consultation with our partners, including UNAIDS, "we have arrived at a clear sense of ECA's specific role in the follow-up and implementation process." That included integrating HIV/AIDS into most components of our work program—the following year we identified capacity building for HIV prevention as a top policy initiative, for example—monitoring the implementation of the Addis Ababa Consensus, and leveraging our convening power to broker stronger collaboration, primarily through the IPAA, the International Partnership Against HIV/AIDS.

The IPAA had been given significant attention during the ADF, especially from Kofi Annan who had facilitated its establishment by convening five partners—African governments, donors, NGOs, the private sector, and UN agencies—in December 1999 and directing them to develop a mechanism for a coordinated response to the escalating pandemic. The result was the IPAA, a collaborative framework under which ADF II was the first significant step. In fact, the first full meeting of the IPAA representatives took place in Addis Ababa immediately after the end of the forum and yielded a 24-point recommendation plan on next steps.

A year or so later, and in partnership with the World Bank and World Health Organization, the ECA began a treatment acceleration pilot program in three countries—Burkina Faso, Ghana, and Mozambique—to better understand how to scale up the medical response. It was another eye-opening endeavor. We saw that even as more attention and money came Africa's way, implementation lagged far behind. Countries lacked the capacity and tools needed to govern the epidemic at the local level. The policy responses, it seemed, still were not aggressive enough, despite the public proclamations and commitments.

I began to think more seriously about the balance between governing, policymaking, and implementing, and how that interplay would determine the success or failure of Africa's HIV/AIDS interventions. We had witnessed a sea change in recognition and acceptance and an unprecedented influx of financial resources. But what was next? How would we further the discussion so that implementation and capacity commanded the attention of leaders?

A desire to seek answers to these lingering questions led me to create the UN Commission on HIV/AIDS and Governance in Africa, or CHGA. Its purpose was straightforward: to clarify the data on the impact of HIV/AIDS on state structures and economic development, and to accelerate the design and implementation of national policies to govern the epidemic, including the resources coming in.

As I began reaching out to prospective commissioners, I aimed for men and women of high stature— respected leaders in their fields—who would bring credibility. Almost everyone I asked accepted with enthusiasm. Some names are obvious, if only because I've mentioned them so much: Peter Piot and Kenneth Kaunda, for example. We asked Kaunda and Pascoal Mocumbi, who at the time was the prime minister of Mozambique, to serve as the commission's patrons, or its most public faces. All in all, we had 17 commissioners on CHGA, plus Kaunda and Mocumbi. I served as the chair.[10]

We launched CHGA in September 2003 to some fanfare, actually—a by-product of convening the commission in Kofi Annan's name. I only wanted to pursue the idea if the secretary-general agreed to put his weight behind it. His stature as a global leader on HIV/AIDS was unquestioned after the successful launch of the Global Fund, and I knew a commission formed at the behest of the secretary-general would be far more likely to draw attention to the issues I wanted to explore. Fortunately, he liked the idea and urged me to go forward.

Over the next few years, the commission held a series of meetings in Ghana, Morocco, Mozambique, and Washington, DC, among other places. But the heart and soul of the work revolved around sub-regional consultations between CHGA commissioners and a wide range of African citizens. These consultations provided an opportunity to gather shared experiences, discuss successful policy options at the grassroots level, and identify the strongest messages to take forward. The idea was to bring in local citizens, the actual change agents, to testify before the commission. More than 1,000 Africans took part in the consultation process, including policymakers, advocacy groups, NGOs, community-based organizations, people living with HIV/ AIDS, research organizations, and UN agencies. It was the same constituencies we targeted with the ADFs, but this time, instead of bringing them to meet leaders and decision-makers, the leaders and decision-makers went to them.

The information gathered through these local engagements, as well as through original research conducted by the ECA and academic partners on three continents, formed the backbone of a final, 280-page report, *Securing Our Future*. The overall conclusion reinforced the original thesis—that the AIDS epidemic posed a great threat to political stability and social welfare in Africa—but the real value came in the level of detail in the findings. *Securing Our Future* didn't just conclude that HIV/AIDS had reduced the ability of educated and professional Africans to pass on their accumulated knowledge to future generations; it explained how and why, and it offered ways to reverse the trends. I can't pretend to know the full extent of the commission's impact, if such a thing could even be accurately measured. At the very least, CHGA marked a major mobilization effort that kept the conversation going, contributed valuable data to the HIV/AIDS fight, and kept attention focused on the leadership that's required to ensure commitments are carried out.

Through the end of 2018, the Global Fund had disbursed $40 billion worldwide, of which $26.4 billion—more than 65 percent—had gone to Africa. The majority of those funds were directed to more than 300 HIV/AIDS interventions and programs in almost every country on the continent. As a result, 15 million people were on antiretroviral therapy, 75 million AIDS tests had been administered, and more than 19 million pregnant women had been made aware of their HIV status. The Global

Fund counted more than 140 contributing partners to Africa, including governments, multilateral agencies, the private sector, and community groups. This amount of international support was unimaginable not that long ago, when policymakers—and many leaders—still needed to be convinced of the full scope of the pandemic's staggering impact. The positive results are evident.

According to UNAIDS' *Global AIDS Update 2018*, the annual number of global deaths from AIDS-related illness among people living with HIV has declined from a peak of 1.9 million in 2004 to 940,000 in 2017—a decline largely driven by progress in Sub-Saharan Africa, particularly Eastern and Southern Africa, where AIDS-related deaths dropped by 42 percent between 2010 and 2017. Also encouraging, new infections in the region declined by 30 percent. In Western and Central Africa, declines were more modest over the same time—a 24 percent reduction in AIDS-related deaths and an 8 percent reduction in new infections among adults—though still notable.

But challenges remain daunting, especially in Sub-Saharan Africa, which is home to more than two-thirds of all people in the world living with HIV, according to the World Health Organization. Declining death and infection rates are indeed positive, but the raw numbers are still heartbreaking. An estimated 300,000 men and 270,000 women in Sub-Saharan Africa died of AIDS-related illness in 2017, per *Global AIDS Update 2018*. Women continue to account for a disproportionate percentage of new infections among adults at almost 60 percent, while Africa's booming youth population is especially vulnerable. In 2017, more than 90 percent of HIV-related deaths worldwide among adolescents between the ages of 10 and 19 occurred in Sub-Saharan Africa.

Despite the gains, prevalence is still dangerously high and future generations will have to continue to raise awareness, mobilize resources, and keep up the fight not only against infection, but against ignorance and stigma. In the last two decades, at least 30 Sub-Saharan African countries have enacted broad and vague HIV-specific laws that attempt to criminalize HIV in some manner.[11]

Knowledge and action remain powerful tools in the fight, so it's encouraging that the global effort has not waned. The UN General Assembly High-Level Meeting on Ending AIDS, which convened in June 2016, resulted in world leaders adopting a new political declaration to intensify efforts to end the AIDS epidemic by 2030. The following year, a report of UN Secretary-General António Guterres reiterated this commitment, which he called "the highest ambition" within the UN's

2030 Agenda for Sustainable Development. As of this writing, the fast-track targets endorsed by the UN to reach that goal are slightly behind pace, but they are keeping the world focused on moving forward together.

"The greatest achievements of the global AIDS response thus far were forged by open dialogue, broad consensus, shared investment, innovation, and joint action," Guterres wrote in his report. "These are formulas for success that can overcome the biggest barriers."

It was the same formula we tried to employ many years ago at the second ADF. It worked then, and it still can.

$$- \blacklozenge -$$

Regional Integration
In Pursuit of Pan-African Unity

As the African Development Forums grew in size and popularity, so too did the task of planning and organizing them. We had the first meeting for ADF II on the final day of ADF I, but we began preliminary work on the third one almost three months *before* the second one. And even that wasn't enough time to maintain an annual pace. We finally accepted reality—the event had grown to such a scale that we needed more than a year to plan. So we skipped 2001 entirely and instead targeted March 2002 for the third forum, giving us a full 18 months. That turned out to be a fortuitous decision. When planning began, I was motivated by concerns that regional integration policy—always a complex matter—needed to move faster, or Africa risked falling farther behind in a rapidly globalizing world. I did not fully anticipate an alignment of political initiatives that would create tremendous added interest in ADF III.

At their upcoming summit in July 2002, Africa's heads of state were set to officially disband the OAU and regroup as the African Union, bringing along NEPAD as the continent's driving development framework. NEPAD was significant at the time for a lot of reasons, but chief among them were the accountability and cooperation measures which African leaders agreed to in exchange for more equitable and fair development assistance. As the continent's new political body, the African Union would then have the authority— presumably—to enforce and guide such measures. This was the joint agreement African heads of state would enter and it was almost entirely predicated on one general assumption: that after 40 years, African countries were finally ready to work together in meaningful political and economic ways.

Given Africa's poor track record at economic cooperation, the theme for ADF III—"Defining Priorities for Regional Integration"—could not have been more timely; there was no greater overriding issue on the continent in the run-up to the launch of the new African Union. The timing of the third ADF meant we were spotlighting the issue at a point of maximum impact, although regional integration had long been a central part of the institution's identity.

◆　◆　◆　◆

Pan-Africanism was born partly out of the desire for a collective unity of purpose across political, economic, and geographic lines in the early twentieth century, a desire inflamed by the ills of colonialism. It was bad enough that a tiny band of imperialists imposed arbitrary boundaries; what was worse was how poorly they did it, breaking apart ethnic groups, tribes, and families, leaving many areas isolated from valuable land resources. As the independence era progressed, the continent morphed into more than 50 separate nations, many of which made no historical, ethnic, religious, or linguistic sense. Because of all this, a large number of independent nations were economically unviable from the start.

The ECA's original mandate included fostering regional integration for economic growth, and there have been notable efforts. The 1980 Lagos Plan of Action, which the ECA spearheaded, might have had its problems, but at least it tried to unify countries around cohesive economic development. The Lagos Plan helped establish a series of regional economic communities, known as RECs, to strengthen the production and purchasing power of smaller states by creating larger economic blocs. The first one had already formed in 1975 when 15 states in Western Africa banded together. In the wake of Lagos, another five formed.

Unfortunately, the RECs underwhelmed from the start. In 1991, African heads of state recommitted themselves to regional integration, signing a treaty in Abuja that established the African Economic Community as a way to integrate the activities of RECs toward larger goals, such as free trade zones, a central bank, and a common currency.[12]

By the time that I arrived at the ECA, the heads of state had charged a joint secretariat of the OAU, the African Development Bank, and the ECA—the three existing continental institutions—with the responsibility for spearheading implementation of the Abuja Treaty. So by formal mandate, by direction of the OAU, and by my own strong belief in it, regional cooperation and integration immediately became a priority for me

279

at the ECA. It also became one of the five core areas of the ECA's reformed work program.

I spoke on the benefits of greater inter-African cooperation early and often. In my first year on the job, I gave at least a half-dozen addresses on integrating economic activities to ministers, policy experts, and other economists. Arguments in favor of regional integration have largely focused on issues of scale and competition. By overcoming the scale constraints of small markets, regional integration can spur the combination of firms and markets, making them more competitive and leading to greater sustainability and increased productivity. The patchwork quilt of African states has always stood little chance of meeting development challenges unless governments commit to collective action. Excessive tariffs and hostile transport regulations, for example, often prevent African countries from doing business with each other. The RECs were seen as a catalyst for cooperation, but they've never really taken the lead.[13]

The consultation processes that I launched to streamline the ECA predictably concluded that fostering regional integration must be a priority. But we could only do so much. First, we had to work in tandem with the OAU and AfDB as much as possible, per the joint secretariat. It cut down on possible duplications, but it also limited how creative we could be. Second, unlike ICT or HIV/AIDS, regional integration wasn't an issue that required us to raise awareness—everyone knew what needed to be done. Given our comparative advantages, the goal became to advocate, facilitate, and accelerate integration wherever possible.

In *Serving Africa Better*, we described what that meant in real-world terms: to strengthen regional groupings like the RECs, to improve transport and communications systems, and to encourage cooperation in the growing mineral and energy fields. In the following years, new structures were developed, committees chosen, meetings called, partnerships assembled, problems analyzed, and papers produced. A lot of activity, but not a lot of progress.

We tried to push things along in 1998 with the Committee on Regional Cooperation and Integration, a subsidiary organ of the ECA endorsed by the conference of ministers and conceived as the next step for activity coordination. A year later, we combined the committee's first session with a forum on resource mobilization—a serious constraint in pursuing regional ties. True to my determination to forge partnerships wherever possible, the OAU, AfDB, UNDP, World Bank, European Investment Bank, and the African Economic Research Consortium all participated in the session, during which we also assessed the progress made toward meeting the goals of the Abuja Treaty. Of the six stages the Abuja document outlined for establishing the African Economic Community, Africa was still stuck in stage one—strengthening communities—and, considering the ineffectiveness of the RECs, not doing a very good job of that.

Still, we did what we could, which primarily came down to driving the dialogue—and choosing the right battles.

Free trade agreements were proliferating everywhere except inside Africa and a big part of the problem was Africa's inability to integrate its transport sector—planes could not fly in other countries' airspace; ships could not sail along disputed riverways; cars and trucks could not easily cross borders. In general the movement of goods and people was too restricted. In my opinion, discernible economic benefits of regional cooperation would never be seen without tackling transport. It wasn't the only issue of course but, as with resource mobilization, it seemed like a necessary precondition to ever making headway on the African Economic Community's second stage—stabilizing tariff barriers, harmonizing custom duties, and improving inter-African trade prospects in general.[14] Also, donors and African transport ministers had conveyed heightened interest.

The ministers in particular had grown eager to see concrete action taken on an existing agreement: the 1988 Yamoussoukro Declaration, in which 40 African states had promised to "make all the necessary efforts" to integrate their airlines within eight years. The declaration focused primarily on the fundamental need for cooperation. That's because, until the 1990s, most African carriers were owned and operated by the states, which was not a good thing; they were small and inefficient and not responsive to markets, which meant most of them were openly hostile to foreign carriers—and intra-African carriers—to protect their monopolies. As more African governments opened up democratically, the desire to act on Yamoussoukro intensified, but with a major philosophical shift beyond the idea of cooperation toward full liberalization. Transport ministers called for accelerated implementation of the declaration in 1994 and then did so again in 1997. The second time, the ECA listened.

I began making the rounds to drum up external support. I visited Washington, DC to talk to the World Bank, which was very interested in helping build capacity to improve air safety, and I went to Brussels to meet with European Union (EU) officials. During one visit to Washington, I met with US Transportation Secretary Rodney Slater, a very nice man and only the second African American to hold that post. He understood the issues quite well because the US Department of Transportation wanted to get more American airlines into the African market. As I was doing this, the policy experts at the ECA were coming up with an action plan on air transport that we could take to the ministers. I wanted the ECA to offer a framework that put the previous ideas and declarations in more concrete terms.

Once that was ready, we convened the African transport ministers in November 1999—and once again in Yamoussoukro, Côte d'Ivoire—to consider a new set of proposals to liberalize air transport and put Africa on a path to open skies. Those proposals formed the foundation of a new agreement—an updated Yamoussoukro Declaration or, as it's been called to differentiate from what came before, the Yamoussoukro Decision— and were the basis of several supporting studies, such as a look at privatizing ports and railways in select countries.

The new agreement was a real breakthrough. Signed by 44 countries, it endorsed significant changes: removing restrictions on the frequency, capacity, and path of flights; allowing transnational carriers to break into African markets; and increasing regulatory oversight to improve safety. These were big steps.

Granted, what we proposed would essentially dismantle regional monopolies, and that would be harmful to a carrier like Air Afrique and its parent company Air France. For the France-backed Francophone countries, this was bad. But for other countries, like Ethiopia, Kenya, or South Africa, with airlines that would suddenly be able to fly into West Africa, this was quite good. So while there was enough political pressure to get the deal done, I saw first-hand some of the ingrained interests at play that had hindered regional reform in Africa. We were focused on air transport, but it could easily have been any other issue.

From a personal standpoint, one of the biggest disappointments with the role that we played was that we played it alone. Boosting regional integration through air transport had seemed to be a good opportunity for the joint secretariat to work closely together—to lead by example. I made a pitch to Salim Ahmed Salim, who headed the OAU, and Omar Kabbaj, who headed the AfDB, but neither was interested, though both supported the ECA's efforts as we forged ahead.

This was all taking place alongside planning for the first African Development Forum. I still wanted the three organizations to put our collective weight behind something big, and the ADF felt like another opportunity. I envisioned a tripartite event, co-hosted between the ECA, OAU, and AfDB and taking place within the context of the joint secretariat.

Unfortunately, Salim and Kabbaj once again did not share my enthusiasm. They wished me well but passed on co-sponsorship.

A few years later, with regional integration front and center and the ADFs an established brand, we got another chance to lead by example.

When the time came to convene ADF III in March 2002, planning for the African Union was in high gear. I believed the ADF could play a significant role in the process. Economic and political integration was already at the top of everyone's agenda, and I saw ADF III as a singular opportunity for the usual suspects—government officials, policymakers, business leaders, civil society—to debate the primary issue at the heart of the AU: cooperation for shared growth. Indeed, by the time it was over, ADF III turned out to be the highest-profile and most diverse event held to provide substantive, public inputs ahead of the AU's launch.

I saw another opportunity in the forum—a chance to launch a flagship publication dedicated solely to regional integration in Africa. The idea had sprung up inside the ECA not long after the Yamoussoukro conference, the by-product of internal discussions on how to harness and maintain that kind of momentum. We hoped that a regular report might be a direct way to measure progress (or the lack thereof) toward the African Economic Community, and, by extension, move the process along, little by little. Nothing like this existed. It was a void that the ECA was perfectly equipped to fill. We called it *ARIA: The Annual Report on Integration in Africa*, and once the research was underway we realized its publication could coincide with ADF III. It was an aggressive goal, but the potential impact made it worthwhile. After all, there'd be no larger audience to target, given the swelling interest in the ADFs.

The scale of the third forum exceeded any ambitions I might ever have had for the ADFs. What started a few years before as a three-day event had doubled to six days—almost an entire calendar week! Once again attendance topped 1,000, and we followed the same, proven format. We ended with the heads of state forum, as had now become expected, although fewer heads of state attended, a reflection of the forum's timing—just months ahead of the OAU/AU switch—and its more overtly political tone.

Transforming the OAU into a genuine African Union required an enormous amount of work and the complexity of the process can't be understated. It was also a politically sensitive issue; we heard from critics who were skeptical about accelerating regional integration and questioned the usefulness of the AU itself, pointing to the historical ineffectiveness of the OAU. Given that climate, it's not surprising that some top political leaders stayed away.

But in no way was the lower turnout among elected leaders a disappointment, because it was the policymakers, appointees, and operatives—the ones who would really guide policy within the new African Union structure—that we hoped to influence. With that goal in mind, ADF III featured a heavy slate of renowned academics and policy experts, perhaps none more notable than Adebayo Adedeji, the former executive secretary of the ECA. Considered the architect of many African initiatives to promote regional and economic integration, including the Lagos Plan of Action, Adedeji delivered the keynote address, a fascinating historical account of what he described as phases of regional integration in Africa—and the lessons they offered.

Other notable attendees included two Nobel laureates, Robert Mundell and Wole Soyinka, both of whom challenged the forum with provocative thought. Mundell made the persuasive case for an integrated African monetary system, while Soyinka closed the forum as the final speaker with a blistering take on leadership and people's empowerment. Africa should seek a union, he said, "where the fundamental rights of man, woman, and child" always outweigh the interests of borders. "Too much has been sacrificed for a purely service agency—the nation—at the expense of its humanity."

All the ADFs produced consensus statements, but ADF III raised the bar. It ended with agreement on a remarkable 100-point consensus document on the way forward, which recognized that the biggest challenges to integration were not just political but also social; that the AU's future legitimacy depended on its willingness to be transparent and involve civil society; and that true regional cooperation had to occur at every level. That latter point echoed the emphasis we put on HIV/AIDS leadership at the previous forum and it wasn't by accident.

Even though each ADF stood on its own, the issues addressed were so big and all-encompassing that it would have been almost irresponsible to not connect the dots whenever possible. That's one reason that HIV and ICT, as well as gender and other ECA priority issues, were included in the ADF III consensus statement as key components of a cohesive integration strategy. It's why regional integration has always been so prevalent as a development issue—all African-led development, to some extent, comes down to regional cooperation and the need to integrate and harmonize.

Only a few days after ADF III concluded, African foreign ministers convened in the same conference hall and received the consensus statement under the auspices of the OAU. They endorsed it and passed it along to the heads of state to consider at their summit in Pretoria before ushering in the African Union.

The forum had another notable element: collaboration with the OAU and AfDB. Even though they had rejected my initial idea of co-branding, both organizations still supported the first two ADFs; the OAU's Salim had been an active participant in panels and discussions, for example. But that had been the extent of their involvement—up until ADF III, where we turned a corner. When planning first began, we reached out to the others, given the intended focus on regional integration. To my delight, the interest level was high. So we established a steering committee with representatives from the OAU, AfDB, and ECA to provide overall guidance; the committee also included members of the RECs. The OAU's level of involvement was such that for the first time we billed the forum as being "in partnership with the Organization of African Unity."

I chaired the opening session, and after I'd delivered my remarks OAU Secretary-General Amara Essy, who had replaced Salim, spoke. So did AfDB Vice President Cyril Enweze, who filled in at the last minute for Kabbaj. (Salim still attended and participated in a key session on peace and security as an absolute prerequisite for regional integration.) It was a strong display of continental unity. Essy had been elected in 2001 on an interim basis, with the specific task of leading the OAU's transformation into the AU over the course of one year. Some of the comments he made in his opening remarks, therefore, were especially powerful.

"This third ADF constitutes, undoubtedly, a mine of ideas, thoughts, and recommendations for building the African Union," Essy said.

Indeed, that had been the initial goal. And I believe we reached it.

Unfortunately, we didn't quite make the other goal—publishing the *ARIA* report. We had envisioned the launch as one of the main highlights of ADF III. But *ARIA* proved too difficult to finish by then. Our own projections were partly to blame—we were too optimistic about how long it would take to conceive, research, and produce a report of this magnitude— but not completely. As we began work on *ARIA,* the landscape around us shifted more quickly than expected. For decades, regional integration progress had moved at a snail's pace. But the move to the African Union changed all that. Also, in a globalized economy, Africa's economic architecture had to change. Nationally, that meant taking the first steps to open up and transform centralized economies. Regionally and across the continent, it meant putting integration efforts on a fast track.

So the initial objective with *ARIA*—to compile an annual report on the state of integration and cooperation—soon seemed insufficient. We broadened the scope, sought more inputs, and covered every imaginable aspect of regional integration, including macro convergence, communication, energy and infrastructure, knowledge sharing, public goods, movement of people, and of course transport. We published *ARIA* in 2004, and the foreword contained the joint signatures of both me and the AU Commission Chairman Alpha Oumar Konaré. Based on the indicators we'd devised, the initial findings were not very encouraging, identifying "substantial gaps between the goals and achievements of most regional economic communities." But the report also offered policy solutions, conceived by the ECA and endorsed by the AU.

ARIA turned out to be the biggest analysis ever attempted to measure the processes and progress of regional integration in Africa. The ECA wisely abandoned the idea of making it an annual report, though we kept the acronym. We just gave it a better title: *Assessing Regional Integration in Africa*. Eight reports and counting have been produced; perhaps most inspiring, they now carry the joint imprimatur of all three continental bodies: the AfDB, AU, and ECA.

In 2018, *ARIA VIII: Bringing the Continental Free Trade Area About* was published, a fitting and timely topic that focused on Africa's most ambitious effort to date: to realize the long-term benefits of true regional economic integration.

◆ ◆ ◆ ◆

Though approaches and priorities differ, no reasonable debate remains on the imperative of pursuing regional integration in Africa; we know it leads to political stability and sustainable development. It's also the only way to ever maximize the full value of the continent's resources. As The Economist pointed out, if Africa was one country, it would be the world's third most populous and, with a projected $6.4 trillion GDP, would boast the world's fourth largest economy behind China, the United States, and India. Of course, Africa is not a single country, but those numbers underscore the massive potential of a continent working together toward shared goals.

For Africa to ever make significant progress on regional integration, it must confront complex and interrelated challenges: trade facilitation and its costs, trade diversification, maintaining regional infrastructure, border regulations, and the free movement of people throughout the continent, just to name a few. The list is long. So far, lasting gains remain vastly uneven across regional economic communities and countries. And while it's easy to be pessimistic given Africa's history in this area, positive steps have been taken at the leadership level. Most notable among them: the African Continental Free Trade Area, which heads of state and government committed to at a March 2018 summit in Kigali, Rwanda, after years of difficult negotiations to iron out details.

Initially signed by 44 countries, the AfCFTA agreement actually represents something quite remarkable: the largest free trade area agreement since the creation of the World Trade Organization more than two decades prior. Fully established, the AfCFTA would dramatically reshape the continent's economic outlook. It would establish a single market of more than 1 billion people—and twice that or more by 2050—with a GDP of more than $2.6 trillion within the first few years, while also stimulating intra-African trade by up to $35 billion annually. Signing a framework is just the first—and easiest—step to any major accord, but the AfCFTA nonetheless represents the continent's strongest show of unity yet in favor of a potentially powerful Pan-African economy.

Just a few weeks before making the AfCFTA official, African leaders took another big step by endorsing the Protocol on the Free Movement of People, which enshrines the right of African nationals to move freely, reside, work, study, or do business in any of AU's member states—a concept central to the treaty establishing the African Economic Community more than 25 years prior.

There have been other encouraging steps. One of the more notable is PIDA, the Programme for Infrastructure Development in Africa. Adopted in 2012, PIDA is a multibillion dollar initiative set to run through 2040 that focuses on transport, energy, and ICT projects across sub-regions and the continent. A joint venture of the AfDB, AU, and NEPAD, its goal is to remake the physical integration of Africa. Given the historically slow nature of implementing regional infrastructure projects, perhaps PIDA's multi-decade time frame will increase its chances of success.

During his one-year term as chair of the AU in 2018, Rwanda President Paul Kagame spearheaded an aggressive reform agenda to improve the organization's management and finances, strengthen ties to regional bodies, including the RECs, and improve economic integration among member states. Kagame was instrumental in pushing for final adoption of the AfCFTA, for instance. "Reform is not an end in itself," he said to his fellow leaders. "What counts is how we use it to secure a prosperous future for our continent."

As the adage goes, slow and steady wins the race. Let us hope that proves true in this context. Africa's slow and steady march toward regional and economic integration may not have come as fast as hoped, but the AfCFTA, the free movement protocol, and PIDA are all reasons to be optimistic for the future. So is another major milestone that the AU launched in early 2018: the Single African Air Transport Market.

Coming almost 20 years after the Yamoussoukro Decision, on which the publication Quartz Africa said the Single African Air Transport Market is largely based, this ambitious initiative represents the latest—and perhaps final—effort to, in the words of the AU, "create a unified air transport market in Africa as an impetus to the continent's economic integration and growth." According to estimates from the International Air Transport Association, liberalizing even a dozen key routes between African countries could boost economies on the continent with more than 150,000 additional jobs and an extra $1.3 billion in annual GDP. Within the first year, 28 countries had signed on. Thinking back on the ECA's efforts to jump-start integrated air transport in Africa, I can't help but smile and remain hopeful.

– ◆ –

Governance
Bringing It All Together

Shortly after the close of the third African Development Forum, Amara Essy and I held a joint OAU–ECA press conference. I was asked whether I would judge the event a success and, if so, by what criteria? I didn't have to think too long for an answer. I would base the success of ADF III, I explained, on the extent to which the new African Union incorporated the views and suggestions of forum participants. By that standard, it could hardly fail, given the comprehensive nature of the final consensus statement, which many future AU leaders took part in crafting. Whether Kwame Nkrumah's pan-African vision of unity and economic integration ever got any closer raised a different standard entirely, one that the ADF never presumed to meet.

Along the same lines, we tried to measure the success of the first two forums on the basis of their immediate impact, rather than on any long-term success in creating a lucrative information society or defeating the scourge of HIV/AIDS. It's the same way that I looked at the ECA's overall contribution to any socioeconomic issue—pragmatically, methodically, but always realistically. The institution played a role, I played a role, our staff played a role, and the people we convened played a role. Ultimately, that was the point—we all have a role to play, then as now.

That inclusive message of shared responsibility dominated the fourth ADF, the last one under my tenure, because the topic touched every citizen of any African nation: governance. As I wrote in Chapter 7, it didn't take long to realize that the issue of governance would be central for any activity or initiative under the ECA's reformed work program. Governance quickly rose to the top of the global development policy agenda throughout the 1990s and, as this book's subsequent chapters will describe, dominated discussions between Africa and the donor community as both sides worked to craft a more equitable development partnership. The ECA was right in the middle of that, so it seemed fitting to devote an ADF to this all-consuming topic.[15]

Based on the quality and texture of the discussions, I consider ADF IV, "Governance for a Progressing Africa," to be one of the stronger forums organized during my time at the ECA. We took a slightly different approach by scaling back the size to 600 or so people while broadening the parameters of a governance-focused forum. The result was also easily one of the most inclusive dialogues on the full spectrum of governance challenges that Africa had seen.

I asked two of Africa's most powerful women—Gertrude Mongella, chair of the Pan-African Parliament, and Liberia's Ellen Johnson Sirleaf—to deliver back-to-back opening keynotes. Still a few years away from becoming the first African woman elected head of state, Johnson Sirleaf was then the chair of Liberia's Governance Reform Commission. Both women challenged African leaders in candid language to show stronger political will in regard to human well-being. "Respect for dignity and human rights should not be considered new themes," Mongella said, because they are embedded in Africa's rich history and culture.

Along those lines, the forum delved deeply into the history and culture to which Mongella referred by breaking new ground to discuss the *traditional* forms of African governance within the modern debate. Much of the existing research and analysis in Africa had focused on issues concerning the state and its institutions rather than the societal or cultural values and indigenous order to which so many Africans adhered. We wanted to put the issue on the table because no one else had: how do we rise to the challenge of integrating the two systems most effectively to better serve all citizens?

We invited a few traditional leaders to share their views on the relationship between the traditional African systems and the modern elements of governance, and the results were fantastic, expanding the dialogue even further and in distinctly African terms. I was thrilled that a pair of highly respected kings agreed to participate: King Kgosi Lemo Tshekedi Molotlegi of the Royal Bafokeng Kingdom in South Africa, and Otumfuo Osei Tutu II, Asantehene of Ghana.

The Asantehene, the king of the Ashanti people in Ghana, in particular delivered a jolt of energy when he entered the forum in his traditional, royal dress and then proceeded to deliver thoughtful, eloquent, and moving remarks on the need to rely on traditional leaders to bridge cultural and economic gaps in African society. "No chief who commutes from the first world to the second world can fail to appreciate the challenges for integrated national development that is equitable and sustainable," he said.

In general, the amount of ground we covered over a few days was incredible. African judges spoke on the separation of powers and adherence to the rule of law. African parliamentarians spoke on political parties and legislative effectiveness. African civil rights activists spoke on mobilizing citizen participation and protecting democratic space. And the people who attended didn't just sit around passively; they were engaged.

Given such vibrant dialogue, it's no surprise that a number of major recommendations emerged. The ADF IV Agenda for Action focused on 10 priority areas, some of which were obvious actions, such as tackling corruption, but others—leveraging ICT, mainstreaming gender, building partnerships—mirrored the broader, socioeconomic agenda that the ECA had been pursuing. The action plan also urged the inclusion of all Africans in the process, especially those adhering to traditional systems so that their processes would not be ignored when considering broad governance reform. It also reinforced the idea that "good governance" is a development issue as much as a political one—a cornerstone argument of the ECA's approach to governance during my tenure.

ADF IV felt like the culmination of a lot of important work. Not that it was an end point—the effort to get governance right in Africa remains an ongoing and very real challenge—but more like an exclamation point.

For one thing, we presented the early synopsis of a landmark ECA research project that would come out the following year, the *African Governance Report 2005*. The ECA researchers and analysts had worked on that report for years and its findings, shared for the first time at ADF IV, became a centerpiece of the forum. Beyond that, the event offered one of the biggest stages to date for government leaders, the private sector, and civil society to talk in an open environment about two of the most consequential African initiatives of the young century: NEPAD and its core component, the African Peer Review Mechanism, both of which had been crafted, debated, adopted, and launched in the preceding years. ADF IV just seemed to bring together, in a seamless way, all the elements that made these forums special in the first place.

◆ ◆ ◆ ◆

For all they accomplished, the African Development Forums were not without shortcomings. Besides being an enormous amount of work and a logistical nightmare, they were not binding, which frustrated some ECA staff. We could not ensure recommendations and action plans were implemented, nor could we order fellow UN agencies working at the country level to introduce ADF recommendations locally. And in some cases, individual governments either politicized or ignored ideas generated at ADFs. These frustrations were valid, but I never bought into them. Where else before the ADF did the citizen activist or the woman living with AIDS have a chance to directly influence social policy, with a voice no quieter than the minister or parliamentarian who sat a few rows over?

It's true that the ECA has never had the mandate to implement policy, nor the power to compel policymakers to act. But the ECA has always had the mandate to craft bold, innovative ideas and to draw attention to urgent issues. My goal was to get as many African voices as possible involved so that the ideas we generated were representative, inclusive, and relevant.

At the end of the day, it came down to ownership. Ownership over the issues. Ownership over the dialogue. Ownership over the solutions. I wanted to do whatever I could to ensure that the best ideas for Africa were being generated in Africa, by Africans from all walks of life. The ADFs did that.

When he opened the fourth ADF, Meles Zenawi described it as "the leading forum for serious and intellectually rigorous discussion on critical issues relating to Africa's many development challenges"—an incredible accolade and a testament to the extent to which the forums had become a seminal meeting place for anyone and everyone to talk openly, share ideas, and chart the way forward.

As I write this, nine ADFs have been held in all, each on different pressing, modern-day issues. I like the thought of the ADF continuing to evolve along with Africa's needs, involving ever more people in a process proven to work so well.

Notes

1   Ernie Wilson later served as a consultant to an ECA working group on ICT strategies, as well as to the UN Commission on Science and Technology for Development, the World Bank, and the White House National Security Council.

2   In a 1996 world ranking, South Africa (number 35) and Egypt (number 51) were the only African countries "able to absorb new technologies in the information age," according to the World Times Information Imperative Index. Around the same time, The Economist listed South Africa as the only African country "effectively using" information technology.

3   The ECA's early ICT work revolved around two major projects: Computer Networking in Africa, which ran from 1987 to 1991, and then Capacity Building for Electronic Communication, which ran from 1991 to 1995. Both projects were funded by the Canadian government, one of Africa's most committed partners for ICT development.

4   In recognition of the increased prominence that the ECA was giving to ICT issues in Africa, the Global Information Infrastructure Commission eventually asked me to serve a term as a commissioner, which I was honored to do.

5   The diversity of backgrounds at ADF '99 provided a great energy. About 40 percent of attendees were from the public sector, 15 percent from the private sector, 15 percent from NGOs, 15 percent from development agencies, and 15 percent from universities and research institutions. We made a special effort to try to maintain that general balance for subsequent forums.

6   In Kampala, Uganda's main urban area, HIV prevalence among women tested at antenatal clinics surged from 11 percent in 1985 to 31 percent in 1990, before declining to 14 percent in 1998. Throughout the 1990s, Uganda saw a decrease in infection rates among men and women in just about every subgroup.

7   For an insightful, eyewitness account of the discovery and spread of the HIV virus, including its impact in Africa, and the subsequent global response, refer to the 2005 PBS Frontline interview with Peter Piot, "The Age of AIDS." It is available online.

8   Charlotte went on to work as a professional trainer and life coach in South Africa.

9   From June 2001 through 2006, Lewis served as the UN secretary-general's special envoy for HIV/AIDS in Africa. In 2003, he started the Stephen Lewis Foundation to combat AIDS in Africa at the community level. Over the next 15 years, the foundation funded more than 1,100 initiatives, partnering with 300 local NGOs in 15 countries.

10   The full roster of CHGA commissioners, in addition to Kaunda, Mocumbi and myself, included: Seyyid Abdulai, Abdoulaye Bathily, Mary Chinery-Hesse, Awa Coll-Seck, Haile Debas, Richard Feachem, Eveline Herfkens, Omar Kabbaj, Milly Katana, Madeleine Mukamabano, Benjamin Nzimbi, Joy Phumaphi, Peter Piot, Bassary Touré, Paulo Teixeira, and Alan Whiteside. The original commission included three others who were unable to finish the process: Marc Gentilini, Mamphela Ramphele, and Ismail Serageldin.

11   According to data compiled by the HIV Justice Network.

12   The African Economic Community's ultimate goal is ambitious—to eventually merge all the RECs into one African monetary union—which is why it's still a work in progress. In fact, it was a key driver behind the formation of the African Union. Beginning in May

1994, the OAU tried to operate on the basis of its own charter from 1963 as well as in coordination with the principles of the Abuja Treaty. Officially, the organization was referred to as the OAU/AEC. Unable to ratify the necessary amendments to harmonize the two charters, the heads of state in 1999 finally agreed to a single new political body—the African Union—with the ultimate objective of blending the two.

13   The level on which the RECs operate is ideal for boosting intra-state cooperation, making the RECs the theoretical pillars of the African Economic Community envisioned in the Abuja Treaty. But in reality, the RECS have rarely lived up to their promise. The causes are numerous: too few resources, too little clarity, and too much overlap. The ECA established its own sub-regional development centers, but they too proved more problematic than imagined. The sub-regional level holds the key to lasting policy and economic integration, despite the known challenges.

14   The next four stages of integration as outlined in the Abuja Treaty: establishing a free trade zone; establishing a customs union at the continental level through a common external tariff; establishing an African common market after harmonizing all monetary, financial, and fiscal policies; and finally total centralization through a pan-African monetary union, a single African central bank, and a single African currency.

15   For a few years, we had also organized the African Governance Forum. But we could only do so much. As the ADFs grew in stature and prominence, and as some of the key issues discussed at the governance forums were picked up by larger discussions at a global level, we dialed back.

Part III
Around the World

By the late 1990s, a clear consensus had emerged on the need for African ownership over African development. My thoughts on this were clear. I strongly believed that for true African ownership to take root, the relationship had to change. It had to be rebalanced and redefined at the global level, so that African countries were not merely destinations for donor assistance but equal players in development partnerships.

With British Prime Minister Tony Blair at a Commission for Africa meeting hosted by the ECA in Addis Ababa, Ethiopia in 2004.

Chapter 10

A Seat at the Table
Building Partnerships for a New Global Compact on Africa

I returned to the World Bank over two days in November 1997, more than two years after I left. It wasn't my first trip back inside the building; when I was in town I stopped by on occasion, either for friendly visits or informal business talks. But this trip marked the first time I had returned in my official capacity as head of the ECA. I was there for a meeting with the top leadership, including Bank President James Wolfensohn. The official reason for my trip to the Bank was to review ongoing activities between our two institutions. But more so than details on specific projects, I wanted to talk about the big picture. I wanted to talk about meaningful partnerships.

The relationship between the ECA and the Bank had taken a great leap forward since I went to Addis, as had the ECA's reputation as an institution willing to work with others. I still encountered plenty of skepticism in some pockets of the ECA, but I let it be known that stronger relations with the donor world did not mean the ECA would be an underling or have its authority subjugated. In fact, times were changing and the exact opposite was true.

By the late 1990s, a clear consensus had emerged on the need for African ownership over African development. Less certain, however, was what that meant for the traditional relationship between Africa and its bilateral and multilateral donors. My thoughts on this were clear. I strongly believed that for true African ownership to take root, the relationship had

297

to change. It had to be rebalanced and redefined at the global level, so that African countries were not merely destinations for donor assistance but equal players in development partnerships.

Indeed, partnerships had become widely accepted as the key to accelerating Africa's development. In 1996, the Organisation for Economic Co-operation and Development released a seminal strategy document, *Shaping the 21ˢᵗ Century*, in which it outlined a number of goals to improve economic and social well-being in developing countries, including the need for a global "partnership effort" to reach those goals. "We have learned that development assistance will only work where there is a shared commitment of all the partners," the OECD wrote.

In my view, it was important that the ECA be well positioned to champion Africa in this new environment. As the institution grew less insular and international interest in African development began to take off, I felt that we could take advantage of such fortunate timing. To assert an equitable role in any partnership dynamic, Africa needed stronger development capacity and less reliance on expatriate experts and institutions. That's one reason we devoted so much time and energy to improving governance, including institutional development. Meanwhile, I took advantage of the opportunities as they arose to travel globally and push the African agenda, hitting international events from Japan to Europe to North Africa. After a while, one invitation led to another and I began to build a strong network of potential partners.

When we presented *Serving Africa Better* to the African ministers in 1996, we laid out five categories of potential partnerships for the ECA: intergovernmental organizations in Africa (such as the OAU and AfDB), other UN agencies (such as UNDP), donor countries, African universities, and research institutions and civil society. Over the years, we created different levels of partnerships with all of the groups we targeted in that very first document. Fundamentally, we wanted to enable the exchange of knowledge and bring more mutual understanding to the development process.

To underscore our commitment, we convened a large group of external partners to help finalize *Serving Africa Better* before we ever presented it. We hosted representatives from the AfDB, UNDP, the African Economic Research Consortium, 15 Western nations, and the Bretton Woods Institutions, among others. I wanted to send a message that the ECA understood the importance of building partnerships and was ready to help lead the way in a changing world.

By 1997, we were ready to make our presence known, so that summer we issued a glossy publication, *Forging Partnerships for Africa's Future*, in which we laid out a vision for strong alliances between the ECA and the rest of the world. After two years of institutional reform, we stated that we were ready to act as a "vital bridge between African states and their development partners." Because of our mandate and knowledge base, we were in a better position than any other African institution to push that agenda forward. A short time later, we followed up with another publication, *Partnership Africa*, which summarized dozens of partnership projects underway with Canada, the United Kingdom, the Netherlands, Japan, Germany, and more. These joint efforts covered a wide range of social and economic policy initiatives at the center of our work program: gender equality, institution building, governance, ICT, and capital markets, among many others.

We published *Partnership Africa* in 1998. The same year, two major turning points proved we were on the right track.

When I visited Wolfensohn at the World Bank, I had successfully lobbied for the ECA's inclusion in the Partnership for Capacity Building in Africa, a continent-wide skills development program established as a joint collaboration between the Bank, AfDB, and UNDP. It wasn't a monumental initiative, but I wanted the ECA to be assertive and have a role in these kinds of collaborations. That effort paid off because it laid the groundwork for participation in a much more notable partnership, the Bank-led Special Program of Assistance for Africa (SPA).

The SPA was established in 1987 as an informal association of donors to provide quick-disbursing support to debt-ridden Sub-Saharan African countries undergoing structural adjustment programs. After the first 10 years, donors realized that the focus of the program needed to shift, so that funds would be more closely aligned with national development and poverty reduction strategies rather than being tied to structural adjustment. This program was an important initiative for African development, yet it had no sustained African input. We worked with the Bank to identify African policymakers to participate in the deliberations and, in December 1998, we were invited to join the group as a full plenary member. In effect, we became the "African voice" for the SPA.

Around the same time, another move was made to modernize the SPA at the insistence of Jean-Louis Sarbib, one of the Bank's co-vice presidents for Africa along with Callisto Madavo. To reflect the changing tenor of the times, the program needed to rebrand itself. So, out went the "special program for assistance" and in came a new title with the same acronym: Strategic Partnership for Africa. This might seem like an insignificant move, but I was an advocate for it. Semantics mattered and the symbolism of those words carried weight. I believed the effort should be seen in Africa as a mutual commitment, not as an assistance program.

Joining the SPA was notable for the ECA because it enhanced our ability to make sure donors were getting a better understanding of the African perspective. And really, that was the key to effective partnerships, The SPA was seen as a clubby group of donors and we were invited inside, a milestone that punctuated the ECA's rise as a major player in African development. By the end of the decade, the governments of Canada, France, Germany, Japan, the Netherlands, Sweden, and South Korea, as well as the World Bank, IMF, UNDP, and several other UN agencies had all partnered with us directly in some form or the other.

I traveled around the world extensively, selling my optimism, tempered by an honest realism that I know some development ministers and policymakers found refreshing. I became the ECA's indefatigable traveling salesman and I made a point to personally visit our key partners whenever I could: a June 1997 "Partnership Africa" conference in Sweden; the October 1998 Second Tokyo International Conference on Development in Japan; the February 1999 US Ministerial Conference in Washington, DC. The list went on and on.

In fact, my busy schedule almost derailed what ended up as the second major turning point in 1998.

The ECA's increased prominence had attracted the attention of the OECD and its Development Assistance Committee (DAC). I had crossed paths with a few OECD ministers, so that year DAC Chairman Jean-Claude Faure invited me to attend the yearly "Tidewater" meeting, an exclusive, off-the-record retreat for OECD ministers to discuss development issues, including how to best disburse billions of aid dollars, in a frank and mostly unstructured setting. I was honored to be asked, but my schedule ahead of the conference was typically jam-packed, with a week of travel in North America and Europe. To attend Tidewater, which was being held halfway around the world in Nara, Japan, I would have to extend the trip another week. I was reluctant to do that. But one of my top advisors, Elene Makonnen, helped talk me into it. The opportunity was just too important to pass up, she argued. She said there was a chance that I might look back and find Tidewater to be a worthy and memorable trip.

As it turned out, she was right. The Tidewater meeting went great, better than expected and more consequential than I knew at the time. Ultimately, it laid the foundation for one of the most effective innovations to come out of the ECA, the "Big Table" meeting.

300

Without a doubt, the Big Table helped shaped the shifting attitudes on development cooperation between Africa and its donors, and it paved the way for new partnership approaches by doing something no other dialogue ever held on African soil had done—it got the development ministers from rich donor countries and the government ministers from developing African countries in the same room at the same time, sitting face-to-face with no handlers and no entourage. The Big Table opened up a whole new way for these decision-makers to interact—and a whole new world for the ECA.

◆ ◆ ◆ ◆

The first Tidewater event took place in 1968, at the Tidewater Inn in Easton, Maryland. The location changes every year, but the name stuck. The frankness and casual conversation of the Tidewater events instantly set them apart from other OECD meetings—and from any other high-level development conference, too. The idea came about because ministers wanted an opportunity to get away from the formality and the public posturing that is common at official events. They sought a setting where the heads of major bilateral and multilateral donor agencies could join them and talk more openly and freely, without having to speak in only prepared statements or talking points. The meetings were an instant hit with the attendees, and over time, they grew to be very influential affairs because of their intimacy. Tidewater still convenes once a year.

A major difference between the current Tidewater sessions and the earliest days, however, is their makeup. The meetings remain private and intimate, but they are no longer exclusive. In the 1970s, the OECD realized it could probably learn a thing or two from the countries it was attempting to help with a little more diversity in the ranks. So, over the objection of some ministers, occasional meetings began to include leaders from the developing world. The retreats became broader and more inclusive consultations because of it.

By the mid-1990s, the OECD had increasingly turned its focus to Africa. Some countries, like South Africa under Nelson Mandela, offered reasons for optimism, demonstrating that a stable government with sound development policies could yield growth. Most others, suffering from extreme poverty and debt, needed immediate help. Before long, Africa became the number one item on the agenda at Tidewater. But African participants were rarely at those meetings. So it became obvious that including an African voice was a necessity. Because of the ECA's higher profile and improved reputation, as well as my frequent visits to donor capitals, Jean-Claude Faure told me I was an obvious candidate to participate—thus, my invitation to the 1998 meeting in Japan.

I knew almost immediately that the event was worth any additional travel, and I felt silly for coming so close to passing up the opportunity. Conversations centered around harmonizing aid and increasing cooperation for both North–North policies and North–South assistance. The sessions were technical and deliberative and I was impressed with how directly the ministers spoke with each other and how eager most of them were to engage with developing countries early in the aid process. I could tell the ministers were very interested in what I had to say as an African economist. When they invited me back for the following year's conference in Turnberry, Scotland, I jumped at the chance.

That's when the real breakthrough came.

My second trip to Tidewater felt a lot different from the first. For one thing, there was a heightened sense of focus. The official invitation letter, which Faure had sent well ahead of time, set the tone. He asked attendees to reflect on recent Tidewater meetings and find a way to turn all the different ideas and proposals into something actionable. "The concrete conclusions these themes call for—in our countries and among our developing partners—remain to be put into practice," he wrote. Unlike before, everyone arrived with marching orders.

Then there was my own comfort level. I had met most of my fellow attendees the previous year, so I felt less like a guest and more like a full participant. My exchanges with the OECD ministers were more candid, and many of them asked me to speak out as talk turned to Africa's debt overhang, development financing, and trade and globalization policies. I was happy to oblige and share opinions.

I formed a close bond with three development ministers in particular: the UK's Clare Short, the Netherlands' Eveline Herfkens, and Norway's Hilde Johnson. All three women had risen to their roles about the same time—Short and Johnson in 1997, and Herfkens in 1998—and they shared a common interest in wanting to find new ways to reform the aid dynamic with Africa, primarily through better coordination among fellow donor countries and better cooperation with developing countries. Herfkens had been an executive director at the World Bank in the early 1990s, so she and I had a distant association. But I had never met Short or Johnson. Over the years, I became good friends with all of them. But we first bonded at Turnberry, and our interactions there proved to be quite pivotal.

During a coffee break one afternoon, we were all sitting around talking when they commented on how important it was to have an African perspective at Tidewater, especially from someone closely involved with development policy. They said they had learned some new things just listening to me talk. I agreed that it was great to participate, but then I had an urge to state the obvious.

"You all always meet in these reclusive settings and you are always talking about Africa, but I'm the only African here," I said. "It doesn't make sense."

"So why don't you have a meeting in Africa?" one of the ministers (though I cannot recall which) quickly shot back. "Invite all of us and get some other Africans there, too."

We sat silent for a few seconds. It was like the obviousness of it all hit us at the same time. A casual conversation had accidentally sparked a great idea.

"Of course we should do that," I said.

Sixteen months later we did, when the first Big Table meeting convened in Addis Ababa. I can't take credit for the dialogue model itself—that came from Tidewater—but I will take credit for bringing it to Africa and enhancing it, at least as it relates to the equal balance of perspectives on Africa's future.

In subsequent years, I attended two more Tidewater gatherings, in Germany and Portugal. I wasn't the first African ever invited to Tidewater, but I was the only one at the time to attend four straight years. And each time, I was the only non-donor, non-OECD representative present.

By the end of our two days in Turnberry, the OECD ministers and I were in agreement that a special forum in Africa, where Tidewater participants would meet with key African policymakers—at the ministerial level—was the next logical step to foster mutual respect and understanding on both sides. We decided to call it the "Big Table" for two reasons: first, as a literal reflection of the size of the table needed to accommodate more than two dozen people in a roundtable setting, and second, to reflect the "big" role in global development that each participant played for his or her country or agency. We agreed that the meeting should be set up in the same spirit as Tidewater, an informal but topic-driven affair designed to encourage candid dialogue. And we also agreed that balance was critical to success, that there must be an equal number of participants from Africa and from the donor countries and agencies. I offered to host the first meeting the following year at ECA headquarters.

Getting the idea off the ground required some outreach, though. Soon after Tidewater, Eveline Herfkens invited me to address the DAC high-level meeting of OECD ministers in Paris during a special lunch. The purpose was for me to introduce the ECA in a formal setting to the larger group—including those who were at Turnberry—and to explain the objectives of the Big Table. To my relief, the idea was well received. In general, the ministers expressed their support and a number of them assured me they would be happy to participate. I realize the whole idea of an open, equitable exchange of ideas on African soil may seem commonplace now, but in 1999 it was a quantum leap forward for the development ministers to agree to do this.[1]

I wanted the Big Table to be more than a meeting. I wanted it to be a capital "E" *Event*. I knew we needed to be selective with our invitations, not only to ensure a high quality of discussion but to keep the group small enough to retain the same collegial feel that made Tidewater so special. So I took full advantage of a scheduling opportunity.

The ECA was set to convene a meeting of finance ministers to prepare regional positions for two upcoming UN conferences. I expected a large contingent of influential ministers to attend since the UN conferences, which would focus on financing for development and least-developed countries, were highly anticipated. I decided to hold the Big Table on the margins of that ministerial conference, assuming that anyone I would invite to the Big Table would be in Addis already—and therefore would have a harder time saying no!

Once we began preparations, I realized another opportunity was staring me in the face. With the OECD officials already planning to be in town for the Big Table, why not have them stick around for the ministerial conference too? The Big Table already was kind of a radical idea; having the development ministers listen in as observers during an African ministerial conference would be another first—and guaranteed to make the whole affair the *Event* I envisioned.

When I convened the meeting a little after 9 a.m. on November 20, a total of 28 people were sitting around our literal—and metaphorical—big table. Twelve African countries were represented at the level of finance minister or deputy. The attendees weren't chosen at random. We wanted good, smart people, but we also wanted a regional and linguistic balance in the African representation. On the donor country side, we had ministers or heads of agencies from nine countries.[2] This group included Clare Short,

Eveline Herfkens, and Hilde Johnson, who in the time since Turnberry had officially banded together as the "Utstein Group" to promote more action through informal, practical partnerships.[3] Their participation, therefore, was a natural fit. We also had representatives from the AfDB, IMF, World Bank, and OECD, including Richard Carey, the deputy director of DAC, whom I also had met for the first time at Tidewater and found to be a like-minded ally over the years. Additionally, Ellen Johnson Sirleaf, who had been working as a consultant with the ECA over the previous months, joined as the rapporteur. Top to bottom, the table was filled with some of the brightest minds of the day, people ready and willing to try out a new approach.

We laid the ground rules out well in advance. The day was to be an informal discussion, not a legislative meeting. As such, we made a point to avoid the trappings of protocol that could easily get in the way: no background papers, no official statements, no formal requests to speak, and participation was limited to principals only. We allowed one aide to accompany each attendee, but they didn't speak and they didn't sit at the main table.

As the meeting got underway, I definitely felt a little nervous. I had no way of knowing how the day would turn out even though I had a good working relationship or friendship with almost everyone in the room. I was the link between both sides, but that didn't mean I could control the outcome. Would everyone engage with each other and seek common ground, or would the discussion end with little accomplished?

Things didn't get off to an encouraging start. Early comments were stilted and still too formal, even though I insisted we all refer to each other on a first-name basis. In retrospect, I should have anticipated that it would take a little bit of time for everyone to feel each other out. For the African ministers, this was a new experience; it wasn't easy to toss a lifetime of protocol out the window at once.

It took an hour or so, but the ice began to melt. Each time someone spoke, he or she opened up a little more, and before long the day turned into a lively, enthusiastic discussion. The main topics: how the emerging aid architecture built around the International Development Goals (later turned into the Millennium Development Goals) and the World Bank's embryonic Poverty Reduction Strategy Papers, or PRSPs, were working on the ground and whether the necessary financial support was coming into place.

The participants agreed on several points that in the following months and years came to underpin the aid effectiveness agenda (and the Paris

Declaration in 2004): harmonization of donor policies, timely conclusion of bilateral agreements, relaxing aid restrictions, and tackling corruption, which was not only impacting governance but hindering the allocation of aid as budgetary support. This latter issue was a key concern because budgetary support gives countries more flexibility and ownership over uses of financial assistance.

The ownership theme really dominated the day. The African ministers stressed that if they were able to generate genuinely local PRSPs, they would take a big step toward eliminating what one minister called "the imperialism of the Bretton Woods Institutions." The PRSP process was not yet a year old, but the ECA had been heavily focused on how to make the process successful, primarily through the extensive work of Elene Makonnen and Ellen Johnson Sirleaf. The two of them had traveled to a number of African countries to discuss with officials how to ensure African input into the process. Their efforts led to the ECA's proposal for an "African Learning Group," which would promote knowledge sharing among countries. The ministers at the Big Table endorsed it, giving it a stamp of approval that would become even more relevant in the year ahead.

By the time we concluded, we had been talking for nine hours. It was a genuine thrill to watch African ministers and their donor country counterparts engage on an equal footing, without the tensions, doubts, and recriminations that often colored their formal engagements. At the end of the day, as everyone spoke favorably of the meeting's informality, a consensus emerged—the ECA should hold a Big Table every year. And as long as I was at the ECA, we did.

Each Big Table had a notable impact in its own way. We chose themes, which changed yearly, based on one overriding objective—advancing the new partnership between Africa and its development partners. So for that reason, we wanted to rotate locations, between Africa and "donor sites." We held the second Big Table in Amsterdam with a focus on peer review processes and returned to Addis for the third Big Table and a discussion on mutual accountability. Both of these topics, by that time, had moved to the forefront of the partnership agenda. We convened the fourth Big Table as a special session at the World Bank in Washington, DC. The final one was held back in Addis.

The Big Table had a lot in common with the African Development Forums, and both events certainly shared the strand of DNA that emphasized African-led collaboration between top decision-makers. But the difference between the two was stark: the ADFs were large-scale affairs that spanned multiple days and thrived on broad participation, while the Big Table was a small, closed-off session that was not made public or ever intended to be. The two events covered much of the same ground, but in dramatically different fashion.

All of the Big Tables advanced major policy issues of their time, but that first Big Table was truly a major milestone. For the better part of five years I had traveled around five continents, visiting donor countries and their development ministers and diplomats, with the hope that one day the ECA would be able to use its convening power to bring those people closer together with the members we represented. The ECA's outreach program helped set the stage and my participation in Tidewater catalyzed the action, but the Big Table proved that an appetite for new partnerships was getting stronger.

With the first Big Table concluded, I had to pivot immediately to the full ministerial conference the following day. But the Big Table had been like a mental shot of adrenaline! My opening remarks to the ministerial conference had been prepared well in advance of the Big Table, but I was so inspired by the day's discussions that I decided to modify my speech. It already focused on the ways in which the landscape was changing; from the G8 to the UN, African development had surged to the foreground in the new millennium. But I wanted to call even more attention to how much common ground we found in that room. I wanted to articulate my personal vision for an improved partnership approach but also the shared vision of the first Big Table discussion.

I delivered that address, which I titled "A New Global Compact with Africa," on November 21, 2000. It turned out to be one of the most significant speeches I ever made. It helped to reframe the dialogue around African development and it put me squarely in the middle of one of Africa's most dynamic periods of change.

◆　◆　◆　◆

My first few years at the ECA had been all about laying a foundation—institutional reforms, better research and analysis, recruitment and outreach, lobbying and travel. But I could see the hard work paying off. Our growing number of partnerships and joint initiatives proved how much perceptions had changed. My colleagues and I felt we were now in a better position to think big, so we began formulating a vision for addressing Africa's particular needs in an increasingly globalized world. The backbone of that plan started and stopped with partnerships and mutual commitment on both sides. That's where the seeds for the Global Compact were planted. The decision to discuss it at this particular ministerial conference was an easy one, knowing that OECD ministers would be in the audience with African ministers for the very first time.

When the conference convened, hundreds of ministers and officials had filled up the sparkling new UN Conference Center. As I began to speak, I mentioned the "true North–South dialogue" the PRSPs could provide and I mentioned how the OECD's *Shaping the 21ˢᵗ Century* report from a few years back had called for stronger partnerships and policy coherence. I noted that one of the upcoming UN conferences was being referred to as the "new global deal" for least developed countries. "I want to propose that out of this comes a 'New Global Compact with Africa'," I said, before immediately adding for emphasis: "The compact would be *with* Africa, not *for* Africa." Again, semantics matter.

Under the Global Compact as I outlined it, African countries would agree to put in place pro-growth policy reforms while donor countries would agree to support those reforms through such mechanisms as aid, debt relief, and market access—to give African economies the jump-start they needed.

"While we have come a long way toward creating a better understanding and a more conducive environment for Africa's economic recovery," I said, "we are still lacking a bold and comprehensive plan for Africa's irreversible emergence from its current fragile state."

In that context, I highlighted the critical need for increased investment in Africa through better domestic policies, as well as increased and more effective development assistance. I stressed mutual accountability toward development outcomes and long-term commitments. I called for the World Bank to liberalize lending and offer grants to the least developed countries. At the same time, I argued for significant actions on debt, with the goal of finding a lasting exit for indebted countries from their burdens. I also made the case for fair trade rather than free trade, and I urged developed countries to take the lead in removing domestic subsidies and other protectionist measures, while giving African countries the support needed to build domestic industries and trade capacity.

In a nutshell, I was proposing a plan to put the continent on track to sustained economic growth and significant poverty reduction by directly challenging the responsible parties—African leaders and rich donor countries—to do it together, as partners, and to hold each other's feet to the fire. It was a rather progressive—and unusually public—call to action for a UN commission to take. Even though the Big Table had buoyed me, I still wasn't sure what to expect when I was done.

Fortunately, the African ministers reacted with enthusiasm, and Simba Makoni, the minister from Zimbabwe and conference chair, proposed the agenda be revised to take up a formal discussion of the proposal I had just made.

Normally at these ministerial conferences, the opening statements are just formalities. In the past, I had always tried to give substantive remarks, but nothing on the level of the Global Compact. So what was really remarkable about the reaction to the speech was that it compelled the African ministers to want to talk more, among themselves, about what I was saying. So we followed Makoni's proposal and changed the agenda to allow more time to discuss and debate the proposal's implications in finer detail.

I also had to change my own schedule. We had not anticipated the desire to continue talking about it right there and then, so I had to immediately round up senior staff and advisors to give the proposal even more heft.

Over the next 36 hours, the ministers agreed, through an approved resolution, to hold further consultations within Africa on the concepts proposed in the Global Compact and on ways to move it forward. They also advised the ECA to consult with individuals and institutions that "have the potential to best assure that the [Global] Compact moves to implementation," including the UN. Lastly, the finance ministers made a request I didn't see coming; they asked that the ECA present a full version of the proposal—along with a blueprint on how to operationalize it—at the upcoming planning ministers' meeting in Algiers, six months later. Many of the finance ministers said they would make a special trip to attend.

I couldn't have imagined the reaction from the ministers would be so positive and so swift. I remember starting to plan out the next steps in my head the moment we were given our marching orders. What I did not know, however, was that the ECA's plan for a new partnership paradigm was not the only plan in the works. Ours was just the first one out of the gate with a public declaration.

Almost immediately, a number of events that would have a profound impact on our course of action began to unfold in rapid succession, the most notable of which occurred five short days after I proposed the Global Compact.

On November 26, 2000, South African President Thabo Mbeki made a major announcement. By the end of the year, he said, African leaders would present a sweeping new development initiative to rescue Africa from poverty. The Millennium Africa Recovery Plan, or MAP as it became known, was being prepared by the governments of South Africa, Nigeria, and Algeria and, according to Mbeki, it had the support of the United States, Japan, and the European Union. Mbeki unveiled the initiative on behalf of two fellow African presidents: Abdelaziz Bouteflika of Algeria, who was also chair of the Organization of African Unity, and Olusegun Obasanjo of Nigeria. The plan was to be issued in draft form within weeks and launched the following year.

The MAP announcement was seen primarily as a follow-up to that year's G8 summit, held in July in Okinawa, Japan. There, Mbeki, Obasanjo, and Bouteflika discussed a collaborative action plan with the G8 countries to support Africa's development. It was indeed a historic moment—the first time such dialogue had been held between the G8 and developing countries at the highest level. Prime Minister Chuan Leekpai of Thailand also attended. But the roots of the MAP announcement actually go a little farther back.

The September 1999 African heads of state summit in Sirte, Libya is best-known for the declaration that established the African Union in place of the OAU, but it also accelerated movement toward a new relationship between Africa and the donor world—Africa's leaders gave Bouteflika and Mbeki a mandate "to engage African creditors" in the hope of securing total cancellation of Africa's external debt. A few months later, two international coalitions representing smaller and developing countries, the UN's Group of 77 and the Non-Aligned Movement, gathered in Havana, Cuba, where the respective chairmen of the two coalitions, Obasanjo and Mbeki, were urged to be more active on the world stage. Specifically, they were asked to speak up more publicly for the development and debt concerns of the South, especially to the G8 and Bretton Woods Institutions. They got that exact opportunity in Okinawa. A few months later, in October 2000, the three leaders set up a steering committee, appointing two officials each, to begin crafting the outline for a new recovery plan for Africa. Mbeki then made the first public announcement in late November and revealed the MAP to the World Economic Forum in Davos, Switzerland in January 2001. Participation in the MAP, Mbeki said at Davos, "will be open to all African countries prepared to commit to the underlying principles guiding the initiative."

So what was the MAP? It identified several interdependent priority objectives, including the establishment of peaceful and secure societies and a commitment to good governance and fighting corruption. It emphasized infrastructure development, investing in people, and financing mechanisms to meet present challenges, particularly the glaring roadblock presented by Africa's massive debt and the need for debt relief, which Mbeki said was "too slow and miserly." The MAP also called on African leaders to take collective responsibility for these objectives by creating an oversight body comprised of heads of state and government. And like the Global Compact, it encouraged a partnership with developed countries and multilateral institutions in supporting its implementation.

I wasn't aware of the MAP initiative—at all—until I received a phone call from Clare Short after Mbeki made his November 26 announcement. "Have you heard about this?" she asked, seemingly as surprised as I was. I told her that I had not. She said the dynamics of the plan sounded so much like what we had discussed at the Big Table, and even at Turnberry the previous year. It did, but the timing was sheer coincidence.

But then the situation became more convoluted, because while Mbeki, Obasanjo, and Bouteflika were working out the details of the MAP, Senegalese President Abdoulaye Wade was going in another direction altogether.

At the same forum in Davos where Mbeki unveiled the MAP, Wade offered his own African recovery initiative to the world—the OMEGA Plan. According to Wade, *his* plan would be the right blueprint for Africa's future development, and it too would establish a new framework for working with donors. OMEGA placed extra emphasis on investing in Africa's physical infrastructure—roads, rail, public facilities, and the like—as well as its human infrastructure, primarily education. To Wade, inadequate investment in physical and human capital was a precondition as well as an engine of enhanced economic growth.

Regional cooperation among the countries was a central tenet of OMEGA, as was enhanced external resource mobilization (through funding agencies and donors) and a major push to secure untapped sources of domestic financing. Wade envisioned an international authority with a board of directors comprising "debtor and creditor representatives" to oversee implementation. No one could fault him for thinking big, but his timing was less than stellar since he unveiled his plan with no warning and in what appeared to be direct competition to the MAP.

The Omega Plan, the MAP, and the Global Compact had plenty of parallels and overlaps, including the need for stronger regional cooperation and better integration of Africa into the globalized economy. Along those lines, Africa's crippling debt overhang and the need for new relationships had heavily informed all three plans. Each proposal emphasized the need for Africa to determine its own destiny and develop homegrown solutions complemented by productive partnerships with the international community.

But significant differences also existed, not the least of which was the point of origin for each plan. With South Africa's president taking the lead with the MAP and Senegal's president emerging at the last minute with a competing plan, the traditional Francophone-Anglophone divide in Africa suddenly became an issue. Meanwhile, the Global Compact didn't come from a head of state but from an institution serving all African countries—and with strong ministerial backing.

In other words, after years and years of talk, of summits, and conferences and declarations, three similar but uniquely distinct proposals for bold initiatives to address the root causes of Africa's development problem had been unveiled—all within three months.

The African ministers weren't the only audience to give the Global Compact proposal positive feedback. The OECD ministers who attended the Big Table—and who were sitting in on the ministerial conference—liked it too. But Clare Short offered the most enthusiasm. After I finished speaking, she greeted me right away. She complimented the remarks then quickly asked if I could have Kofi Annan send a copy of the speech to Tony Blair. I told her that I would be happy to do so. Blair became UK prime minister in 1997, and he had recently instructed the Department for International Development, which Short oversaw, to take the lead in devising a special UK initiative on African development. As such, she thought Blair would be highly interested in what the Global Compact proposed.

In his time in office, Blair had demonstrated a heightened interest in Africa. His order to DFID came on the heels of remarks he gave at the UN Millennium Summit in September 2000, just a couple of months before the Big Table. That event, held over three days in New York, was thought to be the largest meeting of world leaders in history.[4] Each leader had five minutes to make a statement on whatever global issue they wanted to highlight. Africa was a popular topic, but no leader as prominent as Blair focused so heavily on Africa's plight. Blair devoted almost half of his brief time to Africa, calling out the developed world for a "dismal record of failure" that he said "shocks and shames our civilization." But he also said the time was right to start the process of agreeing on a new way forward.

"Individually, none of us have a decisive impact," Blair said. "We need the political will to broker change that only comes by combining our efforts. We need a new partnership for Africa, in which Africans lead but the rest of the world is committed."

At the time, I had never met Tony Blair, but I took notice of his speech. Africans had heard Western leaders make promises before, but the breadth and specificity of Blair's comments—and the venue he chose to deliver them—raised the possibility that one of the most influential G8 leaders was ready to look at Africa in a different, more equitable, way. From the Big Table and other conversations, I already knew that many key OECD leaders also were ready. Indeed, the latter half of 2000 more or less turned into a tipping point for "global partnerships" as the driving force for African development. The shift was unmistakable, between African leaders being invited to that year's G8 meeting, the strong donor country interest in the Big Table, and the focus on new approaches to Africa at the Millennium Summit. The summit concluded with the adoption of the Millennium Declaration, a commitment to help the world's poorest countries reduce poverty and improve quality of life. The declaration was divided into eight overarching parts, such as "values and principles" and "peace and security," though only one focused on a specific region of the world: "meeting the special needs of Africa." Subsequently, the Millennium Development Goals were agreed to by all 193 members of the UN as a framework for supporting the declaration. The MDGs consisted of eight international goals to achieve by 2015, the final of which was intended to underpin efforts for all the others: "to develop a global partnership for development."

All this movement was happening as I tried to capitalize on the momentum from Tidewater and the ECA tried to expand its partnership network. The Big Table discussions, and the framework for the Global Compact, all flowed from the same line of thinking that informed Blair's Millennium Summit speech and his desire for the United Kingdom to unveil an African plan. We wanted the same thing at the ECA, and the Global Compact was intended to be our contribution. I wrote to Kofi Annan and explained Clare Short's request for a copy of the speech, and he quickly obliged, sending it to the prime minister's office.

As it turned out, that speech was the beginning of a fruitful relationship with Prime Minister Blair. He put his own African recovery initiative on hold when the "homegrown" plans appeared, but he let it be known that the UK would be heavily involved in whatever new framework took shape. Later, he sent Kofi Annan a letter, commending my efforts and saying that he looked forward to working with us as part of this much larger goal.

In December 2001, Blair invited me to London to speak as part of the Millennium Lectures series that he and his wife Cherie had launched. These lectures, which covered a wide variety of topics—the future of education, British identity, science and technology, and international affairs, among others—were delivered at 10 Downing Street, the prime minister's residence, to a hand-picked audience of specialists and opinion-makers. But they also were intended to spark broader debate and dialogue. Naturally, I devoted my address to what I knew best. I called it "Fulfilling Africa's Promise," and I drew on the framework of the Global Compact, highlighting several of the most immediate opportunities that Africans and the international community needed to work together to exploit. Focusing on debt relief, trade policy, aid effectiveness, and good governance, I lauded the new and more open dialogue between Africa and the rest of the world. Three years later, Blair created the Commission for Africa, on which I sat, in the run-up to the UK hosting the 2005 G8 summit in Gleneagles in Scotland.

By the time world leaders—including leaders from Africa—converged in Gleneagles, a lot had changed. Agreements were in place to double aid to Africa, cancel the debts of the world's poorest countries, and support programs to improve governance and strengthen African capacity. Mutual accountability measures were in place, and African ownership had taken a big leap forward. By then, a new global partnership was no longer a distant pipe dream.

◆　◆　◆　◆

At places like Turnberry and the first Big Table, some of the world's leading development policymakers sat beside African officials in ways that had never been done before and each side jointly expressed a desire to radically rethink aid and development processes. At the same time, some African heads of state grew bolder and more vocal over the same processes, while G8 heads of state began speaking out with more frequency and passion, trying to push or pull the rest of the world in the same direction. All in all, the pace of change was dramatic, especially among the rich donor countries.

Implementing a new global partnership was the ultimate goal, but as leaders really began to consider what that meant in practical terms, it became obvious that each side not only had to listen to the other but had to rely on mutual commitments to get anywhere. All the relevant stakeholders were in agreement that more financial resources and support were needed, but both Africans and donors had to accept certain responsibilities together and to respond in kind.

On the donor side, that meant having an ongoing and unprecedented conversation among themselves—and with the African community—over how to boost aid and increase its impact at the same time. On the African side, it meant finally coming together behind a shared vision for the future that, unlike some of the failed action plans of the past, contained real mechanisms to ensure that individual countries adhered to what was expected of them. Supplying that vision was the original motivation behind the Global Compact.

Africa's response was called the New African Initiative, but it eventually became known as NEPAD, the New Partnership for African Development. NEPAD was a significant achievement for the continent, and it came about by reconciling three diverse, African-owned development proposals into one coherent framework.

African finance ministers had given the ECA marching orders to elaborate on the Global Compact and report back in six months with a plan for implementation, but Mbeki's announcement that he, Obasanjo, and Bouteflika had formulated the MAP—and then Wade's release of his OMEGA plan—changed the focus of our initiative. It also altered my role in pushing the partnership agenda. With African heads of state out front, I had to step back, at least publicly.

But behind the scenes, the ECA and I were more involved than ever.

Notes

1   Ministers who regularly attended the Big Table—and with whom I remain in regular contact—still say it was one meeting they never wanted to miss. The quality of discussion was simply on another level compared with standard donor meetings at the World Bank or the UN, where African leaders might be in attendance but not recognized as equal participants.

2   The African countries represented at the first Big Table were Chad, Ethiopia, Guinea, Kenya, Niger, Nigeria, Rwanda, South Africa, Sudan, Uganda, Zambia, and Zimbabwe. The donor countries represented were Canada, France, Germany, the Netherlands, Norway, Sweden, Switzerland, the United Kingdom, and the United States.

3   The Utstein Group also included Germany's Heidemarie Wieczorek-Zeul. The name derived from the location of their original meeting at Utstein Abbey in Norway. The group's forthrightness in calling for a new aid dynamic—the press release announcing their formation directly challenged donors to "get their act together"—made it easier for developing countries, particularly in Africa, to make the same challenges and not be dismissed.

4   The Millennium Summit was a remarkable gathering. According to the UN, more than 150 leaders—heads of state, heads of government, crown princes, vice presidents, and deputy prime ministers included—attended, along with approximately 8,000 delegates from around the world.

Chapter 11

Crafting the New Partnership
A Look Behind the Scenes at Getting NEPAD off the Ground

We were desperately trying to get a deal done—the South Africans in one room, the Senegalese in another, the Nigerians roaming around, and the ECA in the middle of them all. More than once, we were on the verge of a breakthrough, only for me to leave one group, meet with another, and then learn that someone in the first group had changed his mind, sometimes over something as mundane as a single word. A colleague called it "shuttle diplomacy at its most monotonous." Monotonous perhaps, but nonetheless tense, with some big issues at stake.

We were in Algiers, at the Palais des Nations, for the annual joint meeting of African finance and planning ministers. We convened most ministerial conferences at ECA headquarters in Addis Ababa but took this one on the road to Algeria because of its special focus: to finalize the technical details that would merge Africa's competing recovery plans into one framework.

Crafting a singular framework was the overriding goal of the conference. We needed to determine how the OMEGA Plan, backed by Senegal President Abdoulaye Wade, fit in with the Millennium African Recovery Plan, or MAP, that South African President Thabo Mbeki had announced to much fanfare before Wade announced OMEGA. Both initiatives promised new ways to think about Africa's long-term economic development and its relationship with the donor world. In reality, both initiatives were frameworks rather than action plans, though the MAP was a broader development vision than OMEGA. The MAP also had a broader imprimatur, with the joint backing of Nigeria's Olusegun Obasanjo and Algeria's Abdelaziz Bouteflika, and, according to Mbeki, Western development officials. But the MAP lacked technical details and that's where the ECA came in.

It had been almost six months since I proposed the Global Compact at a meeting of finance ministers. At the time, the ministers loved it and directed us to develop a full framework to present for their consideration at our next big event, the upcoming joint conference in Algiers. The ECA got to work straightaway. But once Mbeki and the others came forward with the MAP, we needed to rethink our mission. Since the MAP was more about the big picture rather than processes, it seemed that a detailed version of the Global Compact would dovetail nicely with the MAP—so much so that the two initiatives could actually become one.

UN Secretary-General Kofi Annan believed the same thing. I met with him in New York to follow up on my Global Compact proposal and, in light of the MAP, and he urged the ECA to continue down the path we were on, with the understanding that we would likely need to use our expertise to help fill in the MAP's technical details. I felt good that the secretary-general and I were in agreement and that we both expected the efforts ultimately to merge.[1]

So we decided on a clear course of action—we would draw up a technical plan to operationalize the Global Compact, as the ministers had requested (they served as the ECA's "bosses" after all), but we would do so with the intention of turning that technical plan into the implementation strategy for the MAP. As long as we could successfully mix in elements of Wade's OMEGA Plan, we would have a strong and unified document.

Timing was critical, however. The merger needed to get done during the meeting in Algiers and the calendar offered no respite for delay. The conference began on May 8, 2001. Just a few weeks earlier, at an Organization of African Unity summit in Sirte, Libya, the MAP and OMEGA leaders had presented their plans directly to other heads of state, who recognized the need to bring the two plans together. The heads of state wanted something concrete before their next meeting, scheduled for July in Lusaka, Zambia. That meeting would begin the OAU's transition to the new African Union.

The AU was intended to symbolize a new era of African solidarity and self-reliance, so announcing a thorough recovery plan at the same time made a lot of sense. Plus, it would be a show of good faith to the rest of the world that Africa was serious about taking responsibility for its development future. Momentum for a new partnership between the continent and its donors had never been greater, so African leaders needed an actionable framework to take forward. And they needed it by Lusaka.

For all those reasons, a lot was riding on Algiers, and tensions were evident immediately. The MAP and OMEGA delegations revealed a political divide that was far greater than the actual differences in the two plans. They didn't trust each other and they were not in a compromising mood. Leading up to Algiers, I lobbied African leaders for a good turnout because I knew the stakes were high and, in a way, I got more than I bargained for. Senegal sent a large delegation headed by Finance Minister Makhtar Diop, under orders to ensure the OMEGA Plan stayed intact. I'd met with Wade one-on-one not more than a month before, so I found Senegal's staunch resistance to merging the plans dispiriting. But the bigger concern was getting the key players to come together.

With the conference at a standstill, and the clock ticking toward the closing session, a small group of senior ECA advisors accompanied me as we passed proposals back and forth between the Senegalese, South Africans, and the Nigerians. At this point, I just needed the country delegations to agree in principle on a unified plan; bigger goals had been tossed out the window.

I felt a personal responsibility to ensure that something got done. This was the role I envisioned for the ECA, but what would it say about our newfound credibility—not to mention the viability of a true global compact—if the key African players left Algiers further apart than when they started?

◆　◆　◆　◆

On May 25, 1963, more than 30 independent nations founded the Organization of African Unity in Addis Ababa. It was a momentous occasion, both a triumph of independence and an acknowledgement that the newly freed states needed to work together to improve their economic standing, strengthen their regional ties, and inspire countries still under colonial rule that a united Africa awaited them. More than 30 years later, South Africa shook off apartheid and became the final nation to join the OAU. The group was conceived as an organ of political liberation, and only decades later did it try to become an engine of economic development. But the OAU never really lived up to its potential in either regard and its international credibility grew weak after decades of ineffectiveness and the perception—not necessarily unfounded—that it was run as a "dictators' club."

To start anew, African leaders in July 1999 decided to disband the OAU and replace it with a new African Union, which convened its first assembly of the heads of state on July 9, 2002 in Durban, South Africa. The AU aimed to be a stronger, more inclusive fellowship than the OAU ever was, with a stated resolve to deal with regional conflicts, promote cooperation, and reinforce the emerging voices in African civil society. Its vision statement called for "an integrated, prosperous, and peaceful Africa, driven by its own citizens and representing a dynamic force in the global arena." Mbeki, the AU's first chairman, echoed that vision in his opening address: "Time has come that Africa must take her rightful place in global affairs. Time has come to end the marginalization of Africa. We call on the rest of the world to work with us as partners."

The heads of state backed up the lofty rhetoric. As one of their first major acts at the Durban summit, they ratified the New Partnership for Africa's Development as the continent's cornerstone economy recovery and development program. NEPAD came about as a result of the eventual merger between the MAP and OMEGA plans, a process that began in earnest in Algiers but played out over the better part of two years, and through countless committee meetings, memos, reports, personal visits, and more than a few heated exchanges. To the donor world, NEPAD was Africa's calling card, the continent's entreaty for the new global partnership so widely anticipated. It was a pledge by country leaders to confront the systemic development problems holding their continent back: soaring debt, reduced aid flows, growing economic marginalization, trade imbalances, and especially poor governance. A number of countries had seen democratically elected leaders take office in recent years, but war and poverty persisted. Violent conflict in failing states not only endangered entire populations, it blocked capital investments, prevented regional cooperation, wiped out social services, and bred disease and impoverishment.

The NEPAD program had two overarching objectives: to spur growth and reduce poverty. Its focus had to be in close alignment with the Millennium Development Goals. But its underlying philosophy—a measurable commitment to improve accountability and regional integration at all levels of government—was its strength. That philosophy guided the construction of NEPAD's framework, which was built around a core set of principles all seen as necessary preconditions for Africa's renewal: good governance, peace and security, sound economic policymaking, productive and strategic partnerships, and African-led ownership. The program set lofty goals, with an aim to bridge the infrastructure gap, mobilize reliable financial resources, reverse Africa's brain drain, strengthen production sectors, and open up new markets. And of course, at its center was redefining the ways industrialized countries and multilateral organizations would provide necessary support—the actualization of the new partnership model.

As the plan was being put together, skeptics dismissed it as just another vision statement from African leaders. It was easy to understand why. Failed initiatives, ineffective action plans, and big but ultimately empty declarations litter Africa's development landscape. Like NEPAD, they all were unveiled amid great hope for new beginnings. Unfortunately, none yielded much long-term success.

In the 1980s, the Lagos Plan of Action, Africa's Priority Program for Economic Recovery, and the African Alternative Framework to structural adjustment all tried to boost economic development through pan-African approaches. The Abuja Treaty in 1991 established the African Economic Community and called for a unified continental currency. In 1995, the Cairo Agenda for Action was adopted to "relaunch Africa's economic and social development." These efforts did not meet expectations for a variety of reasons, including a lack of capacity and political will on the part of leaders, too much infighting among African countries, or too much external interference from other organizations. In some cases, the goals were just not practical given the reality on the ground. But at least they tried to offer African solutions to African problems.

With NEPAD, enough critical factors were in place—post-Cold War globalization, the rise of new leadership in Africa, the MDGs, debt and poverty reduction—that the timing finally felt right. Africa needed to produce a better framework than its earlier efforts. But it also needed the right leaders and conditions at home to see it through, and it needed supportive partnerships, not mandates from abroad.

I spoke to the AU Council of Ministers during the July 2002 assembly at Durban, ahead of the final approval by the heads of state. It was the twelfth time I had addressed the council. I even joked to the attendees, "You can be forgiven for thinking: 'Here he is again!'" But it had been an extraordinary year, and I viewed Durban as both an end and a beginning.

"We are coming to the end of a series of international meetings creating added solidarity with Africa," I said, but "we are also entering a new era of internal solidarity."

NEPAD offered the best chance I had ever seen for African countries to work together to advance common goals, with the backing and support of donor countries. Unlike some previous efforts that emphasized vision over realism, NEPAD offered an actual technical strategy to translate vision into reality—and a program of action that flowed directly from that strategy.

Eventually, NEPAD was integrated into the AU's institutional structure, but it originally stood apart as an independent program. Its assimilation into the African Union was probably inevitable, since its evolutionary timeline so closely mirrored that of the AU, and since its creation was as much about politics as policy.

Many words have been written in an effort to deconstruct the program, a wide assortment of books, studies, and analyses brimming with empirical data and arguments. That's not my intention here. Instead, I want to reflect on NEPAD through the prism of my own experiences—the work behind the scenes to build consensus for compromise, the motivations and personalities of the key players, and the biggest issues that emerged on the road to Durban and beyond, including oversight of NEPAD's signature component, the African Peer Review Mechanism. NEPAD brought new energy to African development, but the process of getting it off the ground proved exhausting. In most historical accounts I've read, the process is often glossed over as an inconsequential element of NEPAD's formation. And while I obviously feel a personal attachment to the Global Compact proposal, I can state unequivocally that almost all of its major technical points informed the eventual merger of the MAP and OMEGA plans, which in turn formed the foundation for NEPAD's guiding principles.

I also want to consider NEPAD from a distance. What did it achieve? Did it make Africa better off? Where does it stand now? These are fair and important questions, but they are very difficult to answer, and knowing the context is critical. So before I try, I'll go back to the beginning.

◆ ◆ ◆ ◆

The movement toward mutual partnerships and cooperative development strategies for Africa really began to gain traction with the 1996 publication of the OECD's influential *Shaping the 21st Century*, which called attention to Africa's marginalization and suggested major paradigm shifts in donor relations. The same year, Sweden commissioned a working group within its ministry of foreign affairs to come up with a new policy toward Africa that would reflect the changing attitudes. The working group decided the best way to proceed was to hear from Africans themselves—a novel concept, indeed! The project became known as Partnership Africa, and it was one of the earliest efforts by a single country to bring Africans into direct, high-level dialogue with donors.

"We have felt a need to advance the relationship [toward] a new partnership that transcends the boundaries of traditional development cooperation," Mats Karlsson, the Swedish state secretary for development in the ministry of foreign affairs, wrote in a book of essays published as a follow-up to the project.

In 1997, the Swedish working group organized two Partnership Africa conferences—one in Africa, one in Sweden—in which African invitees were the main participants. The first conference took place in Abidjan, Côte d'Ivoire, in January in cooperation with the African Development Bank and the Nordic Africa Institute, and the second was held six months later in Stockholm. The Swedes invited me to Stockholm, and I eagerly accepted.

Partnership Africa took place before I attended my first Tidewater retreat with the OECD ministers and the Stockholm conference no doubt greased the wheels. But unlike Tidewater, which had a private and clubby atmosphere, the Partnership Africa conferences were broad, open events with more formalized and traditional interactions, like panel discussions. I was invited to participate in one with other African officials that preceded a more notable discussion that featured two future African presidents—Festus Mogae, elected in Botswana in 1998, and Thabo Mbeki, elected in South Africa in 1999.

Mbeki was a very persuasive and passionate speaker and at the time of the event in Sweden he was the deputy president under Nelson Mandela. But he was already a leading voice among a new generation of post-independence, post-apartheid political figures who refused to accept the narrative that Africa was forlorn. Mbeki was born into activism; his father was a leader in the African National Congress and was jailed alongside Mandela. Mbeki spent his early life moving up through the ANC hierarchy and played a key role in the negotiations that ended apartheid. A few years after becoming Mandela's deputy, his profile surged when he delivered his famous "I Am an African" speech in Cape Town on May 8, 1996, a stirring piece of oratory that put African empowerment in urgent, poetic terms without glossing over the past. "Whatever the setbacks of the moment, nothing can stop us now," he said. "However improbable it may sound to the skeptics, Africa will prosper!" It was the kind of speech heard in the early postcolonial days, but not so often during the lost decades.

NEPAD was put in motion because these two factors converged the willingness and urgency of rich countries like Sweden to rethink traditional practices, and the emergence of leaders like Mbeki with enough political will to take the reins of the continent's development agenda. So to grasp how NEPAD gained traction where so many other initiatives fell short, it's important to understand the motivations of the leaders behind it.

Mbeki, Obasanjo, and Bouteflika all took office the same year, 1999, and they were quickly linked by the proximity of their elections and by how vocal they were about fixing Africa's ills. At the top of their list was forcing donors to address the debt crisis, a cause they took directly to the G8. Unlike so many of Africa's autocratic leaders from decades past, they brought legitimacy and they invited collaboration. They also were savvy enough to realize power in numbers, and that a joint plan supported by South Africa, Nigeria, and Algeria—three diverse countries representing three different geographic regions—had a strong chance of gaining international favor. South Africa and Nigeria were considered the two dominant players in Sub-Saharan Africa, while Algeria offered valuable representation from North Africa. After proposing the MAP, they collectively became known as the "troika."

The three men were seen as the new faces of African leadership, although neither Obasanjo nor Bouteflika, like Mbeki, were new to African politics at all.

Obasanjo had actually already served as Nigeria's head of state once before. He took over in 1976 after ruling General Murtala Ramat Mohammed had been assassinated. Mohammed had pledged to turn Nigeria over to civilian rule in 1979 and Obasanjo, a career soldier, followed through on that pledge. He chose not to run for president and instead relinquished military power peacefully, hardly a common occurrence in Africa. Military rule soon returned, and after Nigeria fell into a dictatorship under Sani Abacha in 1993, Obasanjo was imprisoned. When Abacha died five years later, the military promised democratic elections, and in 1999 Obasanjo became Nigeria's first civilian ruler in 15 years.[2]

Bouteflika also was a soldier. He fought against the French for independence in the early 1960s, but a few years later he took part in a coup to overthrow the first government. He spent almost two decades as Algeria's foreign minister before going into self-imposed exile over corruption charges in 1981. He re-entered politics six years later and won election in 1999, though the vote was messy. Algeria spent most of the 1990s in civil war and Bouteflika vowed to restore its reputation and standing in the world.

Bouteflika wasn't as involved as Mbeki and Obasanjo but his presence in the troika was notable and important. Among the North African countries, Algeria has always enjoyed the most solidarity with Sub-Saharan Africa. The relationship goes back to the Algerian Revolution, which began in late 1954 and was one of the continent's earliest colonial rebellions.[3] As a result, Algeria became a close ally of many Sub-Saharan African countries as they gained independence. Bouteflika carried those relations forward. He was a natural ally in the North Africa region for Mbeki and Obasanjo.

Though the MAP carried the imprimatur of all three leaders, Mbeki can fairly be described as the key figure behind it. Mbeki governed as an intellectual, and the MAP fit perfectly into his vision of an "African renaissance," a phrase he referenced so many times and with such conviction that it became synonymous with him. In fact, when Mbeki unveiled the MAP at the World Economic Forum in Davos, he initially called it the "Millennium Africa Renaissance Program," not the Millennium Africa Recovery Plan, its eventual name.

As I've described, I had crossed paths with Mbeki a few times when he was still Mandela's deputy president, and our encounters always seemed productive. It was the conversation I had with him in a shuttle bus in Japan, after all, that spurred me to create the African Development Forums. In 1999, after he had succeeded Mandela, he invited me to speak at the ceremony to mark the launch of the African Renaissance Institute in South Africa. I was more than happy to accept, but that trip came with an added bonus: meeting the great Mandela himself at a dinner Mbeki hosted in his official residence. It was a cozy, informal evening with no more than a dozen guests. Needless to say, spending even a few hours with Mandela was a highlight of my life.

In January 2001, after the Davos summit, I met with Mbeki in a more formal setting: the president's office in Pretoria. I traveled to South Africa to begin the conversation with him and his top advisors on how we would proceed to combine the MAP with the Global Compact. It was an important trip, but it turned out to be just one of many for me in a very hectic few months.

The process of creating what would become NEPAD began in earnest in November 2000, in the immediate aftermath of the conference of ministers at the ECA. That's not an official date, but it's when the momentum that had been building suddenly turned into action. Up until then, the idea of a new partnership plan was still just talk, but the very public introduction of concrete proposals—my Global Compact address and Mbeki's MAP announcement—changed things. It was time to stop talking about what-ifs and get actual details in place.

I can't begin to recall all the working group and committee meetings that followed over the next year and a half—and I'm just referring to the ones that I or an ECA representative attended—and there's really no need, other than to point out that there were *many*. The high-profile events are the ones that really drove the process, so it's worth jumping ahead for a brief moment to put them in chronological order at least once, both as an overall frame of reference and to show just how quickly things moved once the plans were merged:

- In May 2001, the joint conference of ministers in Algiers paved the way for a single plan.
- In July 2001, the OAU summit in Lusaka adopted the framework of that plan, known as the New African Initiative. The G8, EU, and other development partners endorsed the plan the same month.
- In October 2001, the heads of state implementation committee finalized the policy framework of the NAI and renamed it NEPAD.
- In July 2002, heads of state in Durban officially ratified NEPAD and supplemented it with a declaration to establish a peer review mechanism.

So how did we begin? The way I saw it, two things had to happen right away. First, the policy team at the ECA needed to dive into formulating the technical details of the Global Compact; and second, I needed to hit the road for an outreach campaign. In the short run, it seemed inevitable that two separate camps would be working on two separate initiatives; Mbeki needed to present a broad outline of the MAP at Davos in January, and the ECA needed to meet its mandate from the African ministers to have a full Global Compact framework ready for Algiers in May. In the long run, that process seemed inefficient and at cross-purposes. There was no reason, after all, for the two parallel projects to proceed separately. I wanted to keep the lines of communication open, so I scheduled a series of trips to get a better sense of where we were headed.

My first stop was Algeria to meet with Prime Minister Ali Benflis, recently appointed by President Bouteflika, and a small group of policymakers. Since the Algerian government had kindly agreed to host the next joint conference of ministers, and since it was one of the three countries supporting the MAP, Algiers seemed like the right place to start. This was the first conversation I had with anyone directly involved with the MAP, and it was a good one. I realized the MAP initiative was still as much about rationale and vision as about details.

In mid-December, I went to New York to meet with Kofi Annan and other UN officials, where we agreed the ECA should push forward developing the Global Compact, then on to Washington, DC to consult with the World Bank's Africa team, including Callisto Madavo, the regional vice president for Africa. From there, I went to London to meet with UK development officials. Clare Short, the head of DFID, the Department for International Development, was an early supporter of the Global Compact, but she knew the MAP altered the playing field, and not just for the ECA. She told me that Tony Blair would delay his own Africa plan so that the MAP could be unveiled first. Remember, Mbeki had only *announced* a recovery plan; the details were still to be forthcoming in Davos.

Both the World Bank and UK government encouraged the ECA to continue creating a framework for the Global Compact, with the obvious caveat that we should stay in close consultation with South Africa, Nigeria, and Algeria and work together if possible. The meaning was clear—Africa needed one consolidated plan, not multiple ones, to ensure donor backing.

The South Africans heard the same message. Soon after Mbeki announced the MAP, he sent a team of advisors, led by his top economic deputy, Wiseman Nkuhlu, on an outreach mission just like the one I undertook. The delegation visited London, New York, and Washington, DC to explain the objectives of the MAP and to seek support in developing it. At each stop, the officials who met with Nkuhlu—Clare Short, UN Deputy Secretary-General Louise Fréchette, and Callisto Madavo—strongly urged South Africa to collaborate with the ECA.

The message was a practical one, and it also underscored just how far the ECA's credibility had come, which was a particular point of pride for me. But in retrospect, I also understand that message, from the South Africans' perspective, probably did not set the best tone.

Consider the scenario. Here was a high-level delegation, dispatched directly by the president, to consult with some of the West's leading development officials on next steps for a collaborative, African-led recovery plan. And they were told more than once, "Sounds great, go talk to the ECA. Work with the ECA." African pride is a powerful thing, and I should have given a little more consideration to making sure no egos were bruised. I have always believed that Nkuhlu and others developed a misguided notion, at a very early stage, that the ECA—and I in particular—was somehow trying to step on the toes of the elected leaders. That couldn't have been farther from the truth.

The stature the ECA had gained pleased me, and I was eager to move the Global Compact idea forward. Good policy, not public prominence, motivated me. However, not being a politician meant I could move faster. I wasn't beholden to a single state, an electorate, or politics, but rather to the basic principles of the UN mission to improve the African condition. I knew I was acting in the best interests of that mission—and not myself— but my early mistake was presuming that others knew it as well. My focus was solely on developing the best recovery plan possible, and it just wasn't in my nature to take a passive approach.

Shortly before Davos, Nkuhlu invited me to South Africa for an all-day session on the Global Compact and the MAP, the stated goal being a discussion of what the two initiatives had in common. Alec Erwin, the respected minister of trade and industry, joined us for much of the discussion. Before long, it became clear they had another motive: they were "sizing me up." They wanted to get a better sense of my motivations and my ideology. I must have passed their test, because they arranged for me to meet privately with the president in his office.

Since Mbeki and I knew each other, we already had a head start. I offered a few specific proposals intended to solidify the cooperation between the two initiatives: the ECA could participate in all MAP task team meetings, including the drafting sessions; the ECA could serve as the secretariat for the MAP, setting up a neutral and nonpolitical home base; and the ECA could craft an implementation plan within the MAP framework. I also proposed that the upcoming ministerial conference in Algiers be the venue to review and endorse the joint initiative before sending it on to heads of state. We found a lot of common ground quickly. He invited the ECA to join the MAP drafting committee, and I promised that we would attend the committee's next session, which was set for the first week of February (we sent three senior staff members). I then offered to host the committee's final session at the ECA headquarters. He accepted.

Mbeki's motivation was apparent. He didn't want the MAP to be yet another failed attempt at an African-led development plan, so he understood that first and foremost it had to be technically sound. We agreed that the ECA now had the technical capacity to make that happen. We ended the meeting on good terms.

Around the same time that I flew to South Africa, a separate delegation from the ECA traveled to Nigeria for a three-day mission with Nigerian officials in Abuja. The MAP was at the top of their agenda. They shared the same proposals for working together that I'd discussed with Mbeki and got a similarly positive response. In addition, Kofi Annan reached out to the troika directly to reiterate that the ECA's technical apparatus was at their disposal. By then, the key players all agreed—a joint effort was the best way to proceed.

Through the MAP, the three presidents would provide the political rationale and context for the new global partnership and set the agenda of the overarching issues. Through the Global Compact, the ECA would back up that work with policy, program, and implementation details. At the same time, we would continue to work closely with representatives from the three governments so that we could present the framework as a unified plan to the joint conference of ministers at the upcoming spring meeting in Algiers.

But then the OMEGA Plan appeared, and things got complicated.

President Abdoulaye Wade of Senegal had a well-earned reputation as tough, uncompromising, and self-assured; this I knew from personal experience. The first time I met Wade, a very brief encounter in late 1999 before he was elected, we spoke about Africa's challenges and my efforts to reposition the ECA. He immediately suggested that I track down a report that he had written as a consultant for the ECA more than a decade earlier because it "provided the solutions to Africa's problems," he told me. "That's all you'll need."

More than a year later, I spoke with him again, this time when I traveled to Dakar in April 2001 for a formal sit-down to discuss his OMEGA Plan and the need for one joint initiative. I didn't hold out much hope ahead of my trip. Getting Wade, a famously stubborn leader, to agree to compromise would be a task much easier said than done. His obstinacy, in fact, had helped put him in office.

Educated in Senegal and France, Wade practiced law for a number of years before returning home as a professor at the University of Dakar and an outspoken political opposition leader to the ruling Socialist Party. He founded the Senegalese Democratic Party in 1974, won election to the national assembly in 1978, and proceeded to run for president four times over the next 15 years. He served on and off in different presidential administrations. But as a high-profile opposition leader, he was arrested and imprisoned multiple times. Soon, the democratic movement that was spreading across Africa swept through Senegal, and Wade, having refused to give up so many times before, was in the right position to capitalize on it. On his fifth try, in March 2000, he became Senegal's first non-socialist party president since independence and one year later, right around the time of my visit, his political coalition took over the majority of seats in the national assembly. He was a determined leader at the peak of his political power who clearly didn't back down easily.

Wade received me in his private residence at the presidential palace, a striking building perched on the edge of the Atlantic Ocean in Dakar and originally constructed for the governors of French West Africa. He thanked me for coming, and I told him I was glad to be there. I found him to be very attentive as he listened to the main points I wanted to make.

> *"Over the years, many development plans have been proposed for Africa but most have come from the outside," I said, "with few clear priorities and no good way to coordinate them. We have an opportunity to change that. But we have to work together. We should welcome all ideas but still speak with one voice."*

Wade had first presented OMEGA at a Franco-Africa Summit held in Yaounde, Cameroon, in mid-January 2001. A short time later, he took it to the World Economic Forum in Davos. No one could fault him for thinking big or seeing an opportunity to take a leadership role, but the timing of it all raised eyebrows, especially since Mbeki had announced the MAP almost two months before. OMEGA seemed to appear out of the blue. Right away, problems were evident.

First, dueling proposals greatly diminished the chances of *any* proposal succeeding. Africa had a long history of big ideas collapsing under the weight of fractured political agendas. For the kind of partnership agenda being discussed to gain traction, it was imperative that African leaders, especially the ones eager to personify a new era of cooperation and ownership, show they could come together. Uniting behind a single recovery plan was an obvious way to do that.

Second, Wade's proposal, fairly or not, raised the specter of the old divisions between Africa's Francophone and Anglophone countries. The political and cultural split between English-speaking and French-speaking countries had long hindered African unity. English and French colonialists brought different political philosophies with them, and even as countries gained independence, colonial influences remained. Since the Anglophone countries of South Africa and Nigeria were behind the MAP, the OMEGA Plan was seen as more than a competing proposal; it was seen as a Francophone response, upping the political sensitivity of the whole thing. Rumors persisted that the French government was the driving force behind OMEGA. Senegal ministers strongly denied the accusations.

A few weeks before my trip to Senegal, African heads of state convened in Sirte, Libya, to discuss matters relating to the AU's founding. But with two development plans now in play, the leaders also used their summit to try to shepherd the process. The full body heard presentations from both sides, and they endorsed the work by all four presidents—Mbeki, Obasanjo, Bouteflika, and Wade. But then they called for compromise, stating that "every effort should be made to integrate the initiatives being pursued."

As I described in the previous chapter, there were plenty of parallels between the two plans on some big issues like trade and the need for stronger regional cooperation. But OMEGA put a much greater emphasis on infrastructure investments, domestic resource mobilization, and an international authority to oversee implementation. The MAP didn't ignore infrastructure and domestic resources; it just prioritized a broader range of development issues within the context of a more radically altered aid and donor relationship. The OMEGA side generally believed their plan was more homegrown and relied less on the donor countries for direction. So when push came to shove and it was time to talk about blending the plans once and for all, those fundamental differences in philosophy were heightened.

I didn't visit Wade to try to persuade him to abandon the principles in the OMEGA Plan, which would have been a losing proposition from the start, not to mention an insult. In fact, avoiding insult is one of the reasons I went all the way to Dakar. Word had reached Senegal that the ECA would be using the Global Compact to operationalize the MAP; this bothered some of the Senegalese ministers. One of them, on a visit to Addis Ababa, met with me to argue in person for the OMEGA Plan's importance and to express concern that Senegal was not being taken seriously. I hoped my visit with Wade would allay those concerns.

At Wade's residence, I spoke for 15 or 20 minutes, describing the thought processes that had led us to where we were with the MAP. But I explained in great detail the different ways OMEGA could be incorporated into the process. After I finished, Wade began to talk at length about his vision for Africa and how OMEGA fulfilled that vision. But he let it be known—very clearly—that he viewed the MAP as inferior in almost every way. And he seemed offended that the MAP countries, and the troika in particular, did not appear to be taking him seriously. Senegal was ready to talk, he said, as long as the other countries were.

I told Wade that the ECA stood ready to offer his plan the same technical support given to the MAP, but since African leaders had decreed that the two initiatives be merged, it was more imperative for all four leaders to find common ground and agree on a consensus. We were in the final stages of completing the Global Compact as the technical input for the MAP, I told him, and agreeing on the best way to integrate both initiatives needed to be the top priority.

Wade agreed with all of that—as long as the final MAP document helped inform OMEGA, and not the other way around. "The MAP is a manifesto of political will," Wade told me. "The OMEGA is a plan of *action*."

Wade then suggested the MAP be turned into a declaration statement, with OMEGA annexed as the declaration's framework—an alternative that would have rendered the Global Compact and its principles meaningless. He said he would welcome the ECA providing the technical expertise in this scenario, but he would not welcome any attempt to water down the OMEGA by turning it into a general declaration document. That was okay to do to the MAP, but not to the OMEGA.

When our time was up, we were no closer to resolution than when I had arrived. I thanked him for his time and left, my concerns having been confirmed. Wade had no interest in compromise at all.

The ECA by this time had become part of the MAP drafting committee thanks to Mbeki's invitation, and it was immediately clear that working in collaboration was definitely the right approach. We began calling the combined effort by a new name—the Compact for African Recovery— and we hosted drafting sessions at ECA headquarters in Addis. In the meantime, everyone involved continued to drum up support and seek ideas for the final product. The troika leaders began holding bilateral consultations within Africa, while the ECA convened an advisory panel of experts to help us work through the details. In March, we reviewed our work with representatives from various regional organizations, as well as with a few select ministers (the ones who comprised the ECA's conference bureau, which operated more or less like an advisory committee).

But the closer we got to Algiers, the more I began to realize that we were going to run into a serious problem if the situation with Wade and OMEGA wasn't handled carefully. We could come up with the most comprehensive recovery plan possible, but as OECD ministers and others had made clear, our actions had to be louder than our words. We were working toward a final plan for presentation at Algiers, but in the meantime, no one was attending to the obvious elephant in the room—what happened if the Francophone countries all fell in line behind Wade? It could be a disaster.

That's why I went to see Wade in Senegal. It's also why I continued on to Paris immediately after leaving Dakar.

Earlier in the year, Kofi Annan sent a letter to Tony Blair and French President Jacques Chirac to let them know that the UN, through the ECA, would be supporting and working closely with Mbeki, Obasanjo, and Bouteflika to develop their African-owned recovery plan. It was intended to keep two influential world leaders apprised of our progress and also reinforce the notion of unity. But in the meantime, OMEGA had gained momentum and no one was addressing the developing rift.

I went to Élysée Palace and met with Chirac's lead advisor on Africa, Jacques Foccart, commonly referred to in development circles as "Mr. Africa." I talked about the importance of a single initiative, the same kind of presentation I made to Wade. But then I told him there was a common perception "that the French are driving OMEGA." Sticking with it, I said, threatened to divide Africa "at the very moment we need to be working together." Foccart assured me France stood in support of a unified plan and that its support to President Wade was to enhance the OMEGA Plan, not compete with the MAP. He said France was in no way trying to "undermine African solidarity," and that if both programs could be combined, all the better. It sounded, he said, "like more dialogue is needed."

Before I even left Paris, I sent a letter to Wiseman Nkuhlu, Mbeki's point person on the MAP. I attached the minutes of my meeting with Wade so that Nkuhlu, and in turn Mbeki, would get a clear sense of Wade's thinking, including his dissatisfaction with the lack of consultation. But I also had some news to share: despite Wade seemingly digging in his heels, other senior Senegalese officials had assured me before I left Dakar that they were willing to come to Addis Ababa to discuss reconciling the OMEGA Plan with the combined MAP and Global Compact framework. It felt like a small but notable breakthrough.

"I am sure you will agree that it would be important for all of us to meet," I wrote, "to ensure convergence of the MAP and OMEGA Plan before the Algiers meeting in May."

I sent the letter on April 9, just four days after I visited Wade. I suggested that we convene in Addis in 10 days, a date the Senegalese already had agreed to. But I never heard back. Despite the urgency of the letter and the obvious discord conveyed in the minutes, Nkuhlu did not respond. The opportunity was lost.

With only a few weeks to go before Algiers, I began to realize that we would have to devote part of the ministers' conference to basic negotiations. The two sides had not even been in the same room at this point. Our combined framework was essentially done, but the "visions" behind the OMEGA and MAP were not close to being reconciled. We had to get that done before a truly unified plan could be approved to send to the heads of state. In addition, there would be no better time than Algiers to ensure as many other countries as possible had a chance to offer substantive inputs—provided the conference had a strong turnout and the right people showed up. So I quickly turned my attention to that.

In late April, I attended the OAU's special summit on HIV/AIDS and other infectious diseases in Nigeria that produced the landmark Abuja Declaration. I was there on the heels of the second African Development Forum, which had focused on HIV/AIDS and yielded consensus recommendations that were incorporated into the Abuja Declaration. It was, as I described in Chapter 9, a major event. Kofi Annan spoke, as did Obasanjo as president of the host country. Many other heads of state showed up, including Alpha Oumar Konaré, the president of Mali. Konaré was nearing the end of a second five-year term in office and he wielded great influence among his peers. With the Algiers conference now only weeks away, I saw an opportunity to lobby for turnout.

I managed to get Obasanjo, Konaré, and Kofi Annan all in the same place for a few minutes, on the fringes of one of the summit's plenary sessions. I told them that I needed their help to ensure that Algiers was well attended and that the key personnel in the MAP and OMEGA countries would be there. The conference is "probably our best opportunity" to agree on a single initiative ahead of the deadline laid down by the OAU, I said. "Wade is not yet on board."

I briefly recounted my visit to Senegal and France and said that I truly believed if enough ministers came to Algiers ready to work together, "we can get this done and move forward."

The ECA had visited Nigerian officials to discuss the MAP over the previous months, but I had not had an opportunity to speak directly with Obasanjo, as I had with Mbeki. My impromptu pitch was rather unorthodox but may have been the most successful interaction I ever had with him. He and Konaré said they agreed with me and they promised to contact as many heads of state as possible to encourage them to send a ministerial delegation to Algiers.

I've always remembered clearly what Obasanjo said to me as we walked off: "We'll show the world that we are one behind this initiative."

To me, that had been the key all along, which is why it felt so important. But by appealing directly to Obasanjo and Konaré for support, I had left myself no margin for error. Help me get the right people here, I said, and we will be sure to get the deal done. I had essentially put the ECA's reputation on the line, after so many years of building it back up.

◆ ◆ ◆ ◆

The lobbying effort to build interest in the conference paid off. More than 40 countries sent ministerial delegations, about a 75 percent turnout rate. Observers from some of Africa's development partners and other international organizations also showed up. As was customary for these meetings, each country's delegation was headed by a minister of finance or planning. But because we had more at stake in Algiers than normal, some of the leading MAP officials—the point men in their respective countries—also attended, such as Nkuhlu from South Africa, and Ambassador L. Aluko-Olokun, who was Obasanjo's main representative from Nigeria. There were plenty of others, including some who later joined NEPAD's steering committee.

The conference began on May 8, and despite a few other issues on the agenda—following up on the recent HIV/AIDs summit in Abuja, for instance—finalizing a development blueprint was at the top of everyone's list. When the heads of state requested that the competing initiatives be merged into one, they were seeking agreement on a single initiative for moving forward. So that was our first goal for the conference: to get the MAP and OMEGA countries on the same page, clearing the way for all the ministers to endorse the blueprint.

One reason I felt so optimistic is because we had the blueprint ready and laid out in front of them. Now known as the *Compact for African Recovery: Operationalizing the Millennium Partnership for the African Recovery Program*, the joint document simultaneously fulfilled the ministers' request for an elaborated Global Compact document from the ECA and the MAP leaders' vision for an actionable framework. We explicitly stated in the first few paragraphs that the MAP goals "are also the goals of the Global Compact."[4]

Since the framework had already been completed—with the ECA and MAP officials working together, to recall—the expectation was that once all sides came together to endorse it, the conference could then turn its attention to what would come next. Having key players from so many delegations together meant that we could tap into the gathered expertise to shape the plan's policy specifics. We even provided five specific questions in need of immediate consideration to attending delegates before they showed up. These questions were intended to focus and frame the broader "technical discussion" of the *specific* programs that would, eventually, turn the blueprint into action.

So that was our second goal for the conference: to build a consensus on the best way to move the *Compact for African Recovery* forward, the final piece needed to take to the heads of state for endorsement in Lusaka. Following that, the presumption was that a final implementation plan then would be developed through broad stakeholder consultation at the country and regional levels.

All in all, this approach seemed reasonable and imminently doable. The conference was an ECA event and the ministers were the ECA's bosses. They were the policymakers who would be most directly affected by the operational structure of implementing a development plan. They needed to have a prominent role in shaping the architecture. With such strong attendance, the conference afforded a unique opportunity for them to debate the ideas put forward in the *Compact for African Recovery* and refine the proposals as necessary. This approach, I firmly believed, would generate buy-in across the continent at the most fundamental level of government.

But it didn't work. Naturally, I worried that the rift between the MAP and OMEGA countries might overshadow the technical discussion that was needed to give all delegations a chance to contribute to the *Compact for African Recovery*. What I had not anticipated, however, was that rift turning into a gaping divide that would hijack the whole conference—or that the goals of the ECA and the MAP countries were not so similar after all.

We stacked the opening session with a succession of speakers giving strong statements on unity, so that the pressure to come together quickly would feel inevitable. Zimbabwe Minister of Finance Simba Makoni kicked things off by telling the delegates that Africa could not afford three initiatives aimed in the same direction, no matter how noble the origin of each might be. Speaking as the outgoing chair of the conference bureau, he commended the ECA for agreeing to "subsume the Global Compact into the initiative of the sovereigns." Ambassador Lawrence Agubuzu, a Nigerian diplomat who was also assistant secretary-general of the OAU at the time, reminded the audience that the heads of state had already gone on record as supporting a merged MAP and OMEGA plan. Algeria's finance minister, Abdelatif Benachenou, spoke as the host country representative and on behalf of President Bouteflika, who was unable to attend. He also stressed the need for solidarity and for a single vision that could be articulated at global forums, such as the upcoming G8 meeting in Italy.

My opening statement followed and I focused on the virtues of the work we had already done. I stated that the MAP "will give us a better chance of obtaining the changes in development partnership which we seek." I tried to convey a sense of inevitability by explaining how Presidents Mbeki and Obasanjo, as well as Ethiopian Prime Minister Meles Zenawi, as an impartial observer to the competing plans, had all agreed in personal meetings to the combined principles in the joint document that each attendee now held.

As for the OMEGA Plan, I made an effort to commend President Wade's efforts even as I emphasized the similarities between the two proposals. And I tried to be optimistic: "I see very high potential for the merger of the MAP and the OMEGA." Lastly, I implored everyone to embrace the moment to work together.

None of it was enough. Despite everything—the OAU decree for a merged plan, the impassioned words of their peers, the known desires of the donor community—the Senegalese were in no hurry to even discuss, much less endorse, the *Compact for African Recovery*. Just as Wade had given me little reason to think he'd acquiesce to the MAP, his ministerial delegation let it be known they had no intention of deferring the bulk of their plan to the document we had put together. And in spite of my best efforts over the previous months, the MAP team had still failed to engage the Senegalese ahead of Algiers.

The conference agenda collapsed soon after the opening statements were made. Most participants wanted to discuss the details of the *Compact for African Recovery* and move toward a consensus, but the tensions and disagreements among the Senegalese, South Africans, and Nigerians spilled over into the full conference. The plenary sessions, which were intended to address all of the items on the agenda and not just the *Compact for African Recovery*, had to be suspended several times to allow me and the dueling countries to retreat into private rooms. Meanwhile, the other delegations sat stunned and confused, without a clear understanding of what the posturing was really all about. After a few trips to those back rooms, it hadn't taken me long to learn.

Most certainly, I had come into the conference a little too naive. I believed we could find common ground because the plans in principle were not that far apart. An advance group—known as the "technical preparatory committee"—convened a week before the ministers to go over the basics of the *Compact for African Recovery*. While peripheral points remained over specific details, that committee didn't see any major roadblocks. But as I've said, I wasn't a politician, and I didn't think like a politician. The crux of the conflict that erupted in public at Algiers was never about whether the plans should merge but about which side would walk away with the most political clout. The MAP and OMEGA leaders knew Africa's development paradigm was about to shift, and they were vying for influence at home, across the continent, and with the global development community at large.

Within a few hours of opening the conference, rather than helping lead a large-scale technical discussion on the final details of the *Compact for African Recovery* as I had assumed, I suddenly found myself a backroom negotiator, juggling the Senegalese delegation on one side and the MAP countries and their delegations on the other. I wasn't alone in trying to find a middle ground. Representatives from a number of other countries in the conference bureau, including Gabon, Mali, and Tanzania, met several times to try to find a path to compromise, all to no avail.

Political roadblocks were everywhere; both sides had leverage, and neither showed any inclination to give it up. The Senegalese knew the MAP had momentum and widespread support, but they were representing Wade, who didn't want to be left out of the decision-making process and wanted the same influence the MAP leaders had been exerting globally. Meanwhile, the MAP leaders knew Wade did not have broad enough support to derail their plan, even if it didn't all come together at Algiers.

In fact, as the stalemate dragged on, the MAP country delegations seemed to grow increasingly agitated at our insistence on coming out of the conference with a unified plan. This made no sense to me—until it did. As it turned out, the South Africans and Nigerians didn't really want to have a complex technical discussion at Algiers after all. They were still trying to figure out where the MAP "was going to go," as Nkuhlu told me. I can only imagine the look on my face; I was shell-shocked. This whole time, I thought we were operating with the same outcome in mind. We were not.

I viewed the outcome of the conference in a certain way: the ministers would agree on the blueprint we had prepared, and the next stage would be further development of the blueprint toward an implementation plan. That stage would involve the ECA's technical expertise but also widespread consultation at the country level. But the MAP officials had different ideas entirely. They understood the importance of the ministers coming together to endorse a blueprint, but, as Nkuhlu explained, "We don't think this should be the definitive discussion."

In their view, the ECA had a role to play, but only up to a point. We could get the ministers on board, which we did, and we could provide important technical contributions, which we did. But our other ideas— to engage ministers in active debate around the principles laid out in the *Compact for African Recovery* and to take that forward at the country level—

didn't sit well with them. It's not what they wanted or how they saw the final plan coming together at all.

To the South Africans, the creation of the MAP was an extension of Mbeki's articulation of the African renaissance. Mbeki's advisors were determined that the design of the initiative would reflect *his* views and priorities. They viewed it first and foremost as a leadership plan, and they rejected the idea that ministers or other stakeholders should direct its course. The Nigerians felt the same way in relation to Obasanjo. Their ultimate goal at Algiers, which I learned the hard way, was simply to get an endorsement for a single African initiative, the *Compact for African Recovery*, with no concern for the policy details that would underpin it. After Algiers, the MAP senior officials would then take it over, filling in those details under the authority of the heads of state who had appointed them.

Once all this finally became clear to me, at least I knew what I was dealing with. Still, it was hard seeing a good way out. Dozens of ministerial delegations had shown up under the pretense of contributing substantial inputs to the ways in which a unified African recovery initiative would be implemented. But the countries controlling that initiative only wanted a rubber stamp.

And that wasn't the full extent of the trouble, because the troika countries weren't even on the same page, nor had been since the start of the conference.

South Africa and Nigeria believed that by combining their economic and political might, they could generate a bigger impact in their efforts to improve Africa's position in the world economy. To the Nigerians, the MAP also represented a good opportunity to build a stronger bond with the South African government. But Obasanjo's advisors were suspicious of South Africa's motives and jealous of the country's sudden rise as the leading player on the continent. Nigeria saw South Africa, which had not been out from under apartheid rule for very long, as the "new guys on the block." Eventually, this dynamic rose to the surface at Algiers, and added to an already difficult situation. Members of the Nigerian delegation, for example, began privately complaining to me and senior ECA colleagues about the positions the South Africans had taken on the content of the *Compact for African Recovery* document we were trying to agree to.

Then there were the Algerians, who had more or less stayed on the sidelines as the other delegations—Senegal, South Africa, and Nigeria—controlled events. But at one particularly crucial moment in the deliberations, Algerian officials decided to assert themselves, and not in a good way. That's because after two exhausting days, we had finally gotten close to an end point. All of us at the ECA were caught off guard once the full motivations of these delegations came to light, but we had to put our frustration aside and recalibrate expectations. Finding a pathway to agreement on the *Compact for African Recovery* as a single initiative, if not its specifics, became the only goal. It wasn't the technical discussion I had envisioned or promised, but it was enough to prevent the event from being a total failure. And by the end of the second day, we were close.

South Africa, Nigeria, and Senegal had all but signed off on carefully worded language that backed the single initiative, when one member of the Algerian delegation demanded extensive changes. The ECA's senior staff had worked continuously with officials from the country delegations to refine the joint document so that it would be palatable to both the MAP and OMEGA interests—no small feat considering both sides were willing to endorse one initiative—but neither wanted to give up any leverage yet. Unlike the other delegations, Algeria had not been in the middle of the fray. We thought we were done, and it was only at this last minute that Algeria chose to flex its political muscle.

Algeria's sudden curveball brought everything to a halt once again, setting back the progress we made because the Senegalese felt duped, more so as a matter of good-faith negotiations gone awry than anything else. On a substantive level, Algeria's objections were pointless, so inconsequential as to be lost to history. The only motivation was to let everyone else know that the Algerian delegation was just as relevant as the others.

I was furious. I lost what little patience I had remaining, and I blurted out to a packed room of ministers that if they couldn't put the petty politics aside, "Let's just close the meeting and all go home right now."

With the sudden demise of what seemed to be certain agreement, I finally felt like the whole conference could collapse, a disastrous outcome for many reasons. Leaving Algiers with both the MAP and OMEGA still in play and no clear path forward would have ignored the desires of the African heads of state, reinforced old stereotypes among donors and multilaterals, and disillusioned the smaller African countries looking to their larger peers for leadership. Beyond that, a stalemate at such a high-profile event would have been terrible for the ECA, undermining the credibility we had worked so long and hard to reestablish.

With the conference set to conclude the following morning, I decided to make one last-ditch effort and appeal directly to Senegal Finance Minister Makhtar Diop. I knew him to be a reasonable and level-headed man who, like many of us at the conference, realized that Africa simply didn't have the benefit of the doubt in the eyes of the world. Our actions had to speak louder than our words. So I pulled him aside and asked to speak privately. I wanted to ask where he stood and, if necessary, plead my case one final time.

"Something must give here," I said, once we were alone. "This really is just too important."

Wade had put him in a tough position, but he assured me that the bickering between the different delegations would not, in the end, sink the conference, no matter how late the hour.

"My brother," he replied, "do not worry. We know Africa must triumph."

We shook hands and returned to the larger groups.

It took a few more hours still, but in the middle of the night the breakthrough finally happened and the delegations struck a deal. Senegal dropped its opposition to a joint plan and backed the *Compact for African Recovery* with the previously agreed language. The MAP countries agreed to give Senegal an equal voice in the final framework before submitting revisions to the OAU. The Algerians, with some goading, ended their sudden intransigence and made peace with their MAP colleagues, paving the way for the final agreement. And the ECA, as usual, said it would provide the necessary technical support. It wasn't where we had hoped to be, but it was enough to take back to the full conference. And it was far better than where we could have ended up.

The official ministerial statement approved at the end of the conference offered no hint at just how difficult those few days had been. It commended the MAP and OMEGA leaders for their efforts and leadership and the ECA for the quality of the *Compact for African Recovery*. And it affirmed the need to continue working toward the single initiative as an "appropriate framework for Africa's development." In other words, the main task was kicked down the road. But we walked away still moving forward, so I considered it a victory nonetheless.

After the meeting officially closed, I was in my office when a small group led by South African Deputy Minister of Finance Mandisi "Sipho" Mpahlwa walked in. Mpahlwa had participated in the first Big Table meeting six months earlier, and since then he and I had formed a warm relationship. Despite my frustrations at the conference, I tried to never let negotiations get personal. In Mpahlwa's case, he was not the top shot caller, and he could only do so much.

He said that he and some of his colleagues wanted to recognize my efforts over the past few months—and past two days in particular. He called it a "tremendous contribution" to Africa. Mpahlwa then presented me with a set of 10 reprints of paintings by a prominent South African artist. The series depicted the horrors of the apartheid era and the ultimate triumph of the South African people over an inhumane system. He explained that the originals were hanging in a museum in Johannesburg and that on special occasions the South African government would give out a set of reprints to foreign guests or dignitaries. Only 100 reprints were made, so even they were limited, he said.

The paintings were powerful and moving. One showed Nelson Mandela, his face brutalized. Another depicted a pregnant woman behind bars. Another had showed a green and black chain across a map of the continent.

I thanked Mpahlwa and the others for their kindness. Obviously, he had brought the paintings to the conference without knowing just how tough a time we'd have. After all that had happened, the gesture felt even more meaningful. After they left, I sank back in my chair, exhausted and very near tears.

♦ ♦ ♦ ♦

The conference in Algiers might not have produced the intended result, but it made a major impact because it opened the door for actual collaboration between the competing interests. The following month, each side held its own workshop—in Abuja for the MAP and in Dakar for OMEGA—but representatives from Senegal were in Abuja and delegations from South Africa, Nigeria, and Algeria traveled to Dakar. Another workshop was held in Cairo with a joint steering committee, which consisted of the three founding MAP countries plus Senegal and Egypt. Other countries took part in the workshops at different times.

The ministers present at Algiers had "strongly" encouraged the ECA to act as facilitator in future dialogue, per the official conference statement, so we provided technical assistance where we could. After the workshops in June, we hosted a follow-up event that also included African civil society. Unlike the meetings in Abuja and Dakar, these talks were on "neutral ground" and they helped to set the stage for the end game, a final workshop in South Africa in early July. The five steering committee countries gathered in Pretoria, along with representatives from the ECA and OAU, to engage in one last round of debate and negotiation. In the end, a common plan was at long last approved for presentation to the OAU at the Lusaka summit: *The New African Initiative: Merger of the Millennium Partnership for the African Recovery Program and the Omega Plan.*

Following the workshops, Wade led a Senegalese delegation to South Africa, where he and Mbeki discussed the final details of their merged initiatives. According to an interview given a few years later by Senegal Ambassador Balla Sy, the two leaders gave their final endorsements and then together left Pretoria for Lusaka "to demonstrate that they were agreed."

On July 11, African leaders unanimously endorsed the New African Initiative, with the intention to ratify a full operational framework at their summit the following year in Durban, which would be the inaugural meeting of the new African Union. The New African Initiative was a true mixture of all three original proposals. It paid special attention to infrastructure development, acknowledging the OMEGA Plan's primary emphasis, but it incorporated the stronger political rhetoric and vision of the MAP. The core of its operational framework and its implementation methods came from the ECA's Global Compact.

After Lusaka, the pace picked up. Freed from the constraints of dueling initiatives, the leaders were able to shift their focus to building global support for the plan, and they were able to do it with one voice. Mbeki, Obasanjo, and Wade traveled to Genoa, Italy, to present the New African Initiative to the G8, which responded with praise and a commitment to work in partnership with Africa based on the initiative's final framework. Over the next few months, African leaders had a follow-up session with the G8 in England and met with a European Union delegation in Belgium. They also presented it to a United Nations Economic and Social Council summit in Geneva.

Meanwhile, in Africa, they expanded the circle of ownership by forming a 15-member Heads of State and Government Implementation Committee. Obasanjo was named committee chair with Mbeki and Wade as vice chairs. The committee agreed to meet once every four months. Since the implementation committee now included almost one-third of all African countries, the leaders realized they needed a smaller working group to stay on track. So they formed a steering committee, with personal representatives from each of the original founding countries. One of the key functions of the group included close communication and collaboration with the G8 countries to frame the external partnership needed for the plan's implementation. The steering committee included many of the

343

same advisors who had been part of their country delegations in Algiers, including South Africa's Wiseman Nkuhlu, who was picked to chair it.

On October 23, 2001, the full Heads of State and Government Implementation Committee held its inaugural meeting in Abuja.[5] There, leaders finalized the initiative's operating structure, the responsibilities of both the implementation and steering committees, and the full policy framework. They also changed the name one final time to the much more collaborative New Partnership for Africa's Development, or NEPAD.

According to South Africa's historical overview of NEPAD, that meeting in Abuja marked the start of the implementation period. That fact may be technically correct, but it's not altogether accurate. Over the next year, intense diplomatic efforts continued amid a push for debt relief and adequate financing—where the donor side of the "new partnership" came into play—while work intensified on what would become NEPAD's centerpiece, the African Peer Review Mechanism. These were important components that had significant impacts on the program in the long run, including its final ratification the following year. They also were components that kept me in the center of the action for longer than I anticipated.

The road to NEPAD was rocky, and it remained so even after the MAP and OMEGA factions finally came together. In fact, the year between the program's endorsement in Lusaka and its final ratification in Durban was full of challenges. Ensuring accountability and incorporating the African Peer Review Mechanism were two complicated issues, but those efforts played out behind the scenes. Some of NEPAD's biggest troubles played out in public.

African "consensus," at least defined as agreement based on a widespread inclusionary process, was one of the supposed strengths of NEPAD as it was initially promoted. But during the first year or so of discussions, most substantive consultations rarely involved those outside the top levels of a few select governments. The most glaring misstep was the exclusion of civil society, which was almost completely ignored throughout the primary stages of development.

NEPAD's critics had a field day with the fact that Mbeki, Obasanjo, and Bouteflika made multiple trips to the G8 to win support for the program but failed to make any notable outreach efforts to civic groups at home, other than to promote the program, which was not at all the same as actively seeking input. To complicate matters even more, the genesis of the MAP was so closely tied to the G8's desire for an African-owned development plan that the specter of the "Washington Consensus"—a term that became pejorative shorthand for Western-imposed policy prescriptions— reappeared when NEPAD was being shopped for support. I don't believe all of those criticisms were well founded. But the greater point—that the troika failed to effectively involve civil society—is quite valid, and it's a mistake that was repeated throughout the ratification process.

In July 2002, dozens of African trade unions, NGOs, religious groups, and activist organizations emphatically announced their resistance. The African Civil Society Declaration on NEPAD criticized the program for being too focused on raising financial resources and "appealing to and relying on external governments and institutions" at the expense of African input. They called it a "top-down program driven by African elites."

They weren't the first.

A few months earlier, African scholars and activists from academic institutions and civil society groups representing more than 20 countries convened a week-long forum in Ghana. Their ensuing Accra Declaration on Africa's Development Challenges repudiated NEPAD as flawed and issued a damning indictment of the creation process: "In spite of its proclaimed recognition of the central role of the African people to the plan, the African people have not played any part in the conception, design, and formulation of the NEPAD."

Much like the way civil society was boxed out, so too were African ministers. The implementation and steering committees generally avoided their input, leaving many key policymakers in the dark for way too long. I was particularly concerned that the ministers of finance and planning had been sidelined. But each time I raised this concern with the NEPAD steering committee members, I was reminded that NEPAD was "an initiative of African leaders." In other words, once the leaders had finished with it, everyone else would fall in line.

I did not find that response satisfying. So in October 2002—months after the final ratification in Durban—we took it upon ourselves at the ECA to bring the ministers into the loop. We made that month's regular conference meeting all about NEPAD and produced a special report just for the ministerial delegations, *What NEPAD Implies for African Policymakers*. We wanted to give the ministers a better understanding of the program's framework and its main themes. The report was a three-part document and the title of part one—"What is NEPAD?"— underscored just how little information had flowed to their level. The men and women in attendance thanked us repeatedly for putting it together.

Believe it or not, the communication problems actually extended all the way up to other heads of state, the very people whose approval was necessary.[6] For many leaders, it wasn't just an issue of being involved but simply being informed.

On a trip to Dar es Salaam, I asked Tanzania President Benjamin Mkapa what he thought about NEPAD. Mkapa was a highly respected leader, elected in 1995 as the country's third president. I had a good relationship with him, but I had not heard anything regarding NEPAD from his camp. He told me plainly, "I just didn't have a good understanding of it." So I explained everything to him: the objectives, the main areas of focus, the peer review, all of it. It was an eye-opening conversation for him. "Okay, now I get it!" he said.

Other leaders were more suspicious than confused. At the OAU summit in Lusaka, Malawi President Elson Bakili Muluzi aired his concerns openly, unleashing blistering criticisms and invoking the dreaded c-word: conditionality. In the absence of transparent and inclusive dialogue, it was not hard to understand where he or other critics were coming from.

The discussions in Lusaka were actually very difficult and not at all the rubber-stamp of approval that most NEPAD historical accounts make the summit out to be. That's one reason the Heads of State and Government Implementation Committee grew to such an unwieldy number: to include more voices at the highest level. Still, Nigeria and South Africa maintained outsized influence. As chair of the committee, Obasanjo wielded almost absolute authority over the handling of all things procedural. And South Africa continued to dominate the strategic directions. The NEPAD secretariat was placed there after all, and it was funded almost entirely by the South African government. Eventually, a broader array of stakeholders were brought into the process, including more policymakers and civil society organizations, but only in the middle to latter stages.

A more inclusive approach to building consensus from the beginning, rather than when external pressures demanded it, would have produced a smoother launch for NEPAD, though that's easy to say in hindsight—and as someone who didn't have to operate at the political level. But in my view, that's one of the main reasons that the Algiers conference became such an important piece of a larger puzzle. It may not have accomplished what I originally wanted, but it served as a focusing event that eventually brought the key players together and got a fragile process on the right track, before it had the chance to run off the rails for good. Given how difficult the whole process still turned out to be, I do believe that first "unity moment" proved valuable enough to not be lost to history.

That unity moment came at a cost to the ECA though, slowly over the next few years. Leading up to Algiers, during Algiers, and in the aftermath of Algiers, we had nothing but a genuine desire to see the best possible recovery plan put in place, one that would help redefine Africa's relationship with the rest of the world. At the same time, my driving goal for renewing the ECA had been to make it a more useful, relevant, and respected voice for Africa. But some people misinterpreted that enthusiasm and questioned our motives.

In a 2004 academic study that chronicled different African development initiatives, Senegalese diplomats Balla Sy and Bassirou Sene were quoted as saying that the ECA "tried to do a little too much—in the course of which it overstepped its mandate. The perception therefore developed that it was attempting to steal the show from the African leaders."

I do not believe the ECA ever overstepped its mandate, and neither did anyone higher up at the UN—not Kofi Annan, not Louise Fréchette, not any top official who could have ordered us to pull back. Rather, we always had their full support. But the reality of our efforts and the perception of our motivation were two separate things. The mistaken notion that we were trying to hijack a process that political leaders should own certainly affected our working relationships, particularly with the NEPAD steering committee and some of the heads of state on the implementation committee. The tension grew more pronounced over time, but it was less a roadblock and more a nuisance to the good work we were doing behind the scenes, so we pushed ahead.

In fact, for all the effort put into NEPAD ahead of Lusaka, the program was still missing a mechanism that would give practical meaning to the new partnership ideal—a central core around which African countries and donors could coalesce. That meaning came from the ECA in the form of the African Peer Review Mechanism, which I describe in the next chapter.

◆   ◆   ◆   ◆

So was it all worth it? Was NEPAD the game-changing initiative it was seen to be? Things didn't look very good at first. Once in effect, NEPAD's early years mirrored its creation: slow, confusing, and somewhat uncertain. For more than a decade, it was hard to tell where NEPAD was headed or how much it might accomplish. The first big initiative under the NEPAD umbrella, the Comprehensive Africa Agriculture Development Programme, reflected as much.

347

CAADP was a broad set of collective policy reforms designed to boost economic growth in Africa's immense farming industry, improve food security, and make African agriculture more competitive in global markets. AU leaders established CAADP in 2003, just one year after ratifying NEPAD, but it took an inordinate amount of time for anything to happen. It was almost four years before Rwanda signed the first CAADP agreement, then another two years before a second country, Togo, signed. By the end of 2009, six and half years after CAADP launched, only 14 countries had joined.

Part of the problem was what a Brookings review called the "numerous procedural milestones" for participating countries to get up and running, as well as two stiff requirements: first, that countries increase spending on agriculture to at least 10 percent of their national budgets; and second, that countries raise agricultural productivity by an average annual growth rate of 6 percent. More countries signed up in 2010, but a NEPAD report that same year examined CAADP's "biggest disappointments," including the program's failure to resonate at the country level and attract adequate financial resources."

In August 2012, the ECA, the UN's Office of Special Adviser on Africa, and the NEPAD Agency, which had been created to operate the program as a technical body of the AU, jointly published a 60-page report, *Africa's Decade of Change: Reflections on 10 Years of NEPAD*. The report marked the culmination of a year-long series of events and symposiums in Africa and elsewhere—the UN General Assembly even sponsored "NEPAD Week" during its annual meetings in New York—intended to simultaneously celebrate the program and deconstruct it. The *Decade of Change* report was an honest assessment, praising the push for collective ownership but pondering "whether NEPAD represents a step forward, or whether it will [fade] like many other African development initiatives of the 1980s and 1990s."

Ten years in, plagued by insufficient finances and a lack of action, NEPAD was at a crossroads. But then something encouraging happened. NEPAD didn't wither away like all those initiatives. It endured, and more importantly, it evolved.

A multi-donor trust fund was established to finance the development and implementation of the CAADP process at the continental, regional, and national levels. It took a few years to ramp up, but it provided necessary resources to bolster the program and encouraged African governments to step up. By the end of 2018, 47 countries had signed the CAADP agreement, and 39 had formulated a national agriculture plan. While most countries have not reached the CAADP goals, some hit the 10 percent threshold. And in 2015, the UN's Office of Special Adviser on Africa found that average public agricultural expenditures had nearly doubled since the launch of CAADP. "Policy commitment and perseverance at the national and regional levels, as well as global support, helped turn CAADP's difficult beginning into implementation progress," the Brookings review found.

That's a real step forward and it shouldn't be lightly dismissed. In its second decade, other NEPAD programs and projects proliferated, touching on every key sector of African development in four broad areas of focus: regional integration, infrastructure, and trade; industrialization, science, technology, and innovation; national resources, governance, and food security; and human capital development. In early 2019, for example, more than 40 activities were under implementation, and the NEPAD Agency had a footprint in 53 African countries. Although by that point, it was no longer known as the NEPAD Agency.

A confluence of factors revived NEPAD's fortunes, but two stand out. First, African leaders in January 2015 adopted Agenda 2063, a long-term strategy for inclusive growth and sustainable development that aims to consolidate existing continental initiatives around "people-driven" development and the principles of economic transformation. NEPAD was linked as the implementing arm of the Agenda 2063 strategy, with a primary objective of transforming Africa and a new direction as a more results-based program. A few years later, the new direction was further refined as part of a vast slate of institutional reforms instigated by Rwandan President Paul Kagame during his term as AU chair.

Under the reform package, NEPAD was transformed into the African Union Development Agency, or AUDA. According to Ibrahim Mayaki, the long-time head of the NEPAD Agency, the transition was a matter of "expansion and clarity in mandate" to accelerate implementation decisions. As a full-fledged development agency, the AUDA was expected to be able to mobilize more financial resources, develop tools to strengthen local implementing capacity, and act as an institutional conduit between the AU, African governments, and development partners. Perhaps most important, the AUDA, as envisioned by the Kagame reforms, would be more responsive to the rapid transitions on Africa's horizon.

"Demographic transitions, technological transitions, human development transitions, and governance transitions are happening at a very accelerated pace," Mayaki said. "Our responses need to match this."

NEPAD as it was created in 2001 and 2002 no longer exists, and that's not a bad thing. It was a much-needed product of its time to stabilize and equalize the relationship between Africa and donors. Now that Africa's development priorities and needs have evolved, so too has NEPAD. The program had a rough start but eventually found its footing, and those who oversaw it, such as Ibrahim Mayaki, should be commended for learning from early mistakes.

The AUDA is an integral part of Agenda 2063, and it's built on the foundation that NEPAD laid. That in itself is probably enough of a takeaway regarding NEPAD's impact, but I believe the program contributed to Africa's development evolution in a few other very positive ways as well.

First, NEPAD helped codify issues for Africa that are now universally accepted as essential for sustainable political and economic development, such as good governance and sound macroeconomic management. All the other pan-African action plans or initiatives that preceded NEPAD failed in part because they did not give enough weight to these principles.

Second, it revolutionized the concept of African ownership. Since the beginning of the independence era, almost all large-scale development initiatives had been externally driven, or conceived in response to external interventions. NEPAD flipped the script by setting a vision for Africa, conceived by Africans, that the donor world then agreed to support.

Third, it emphasized the importance of long-term investments like infrastructure, particularly the critical importance of regional projects. Senegal's President Wade threw up a roadblock, but NEPAD would have likely devoted much less attention to Africa's sizable infrastructure needs without the influence of Wade's OMEGA Plan.

And fourth, it gave actual structure to the principle of mutual accountability as the defining characteristic of a new development paradigm. This was the real compact between African countries and donor nations—and among the African countries themselves. In a way, mutual accountability was like two sides of the same coin. From the Africa side, it began to take shape once a peer review process was added to NEPAD. From the donor side, it was through stronger aid commitments and debt relief. Today, the dialogue has evolved even further, but mutual accountability was a critical stage in Africa's development history.

So was it all worth it?

It would seem so, but perhaps there's a better, more relevant question to ask: Is Africa better off for it? I believe that's an easy one to answer.

Notes

1   The calculus on this was pretty straightforward. I conceived the Global Compact to tap into the "new partnership" momentum that had been building, both in public (with Mbeki and Obasanjo attending the G8 summit) and behind the scenes—the ECA's first Big Table meeting, for example. I knew many OECD ministers were anxious to try something new and that gave me the courage to try to publicly prod African leaders and donors alike. The MAP was another iteration of this same idea, but with heads of state taking the lead. That's how it needed to be, so I quickly expected the Global Compact would be subsumed, even as the ECA was crafting it.

2   Obasanjo was active on the world stage, moving quickly to strengthen ties with the United States and other Western countries. He said he wanted to build a lasting democracy, and one way to do that was to generate support in the West by rehabilitating Nigeria's image.

3   Algeria fought France for almost a decade, at the same time that Kwame Nkrumah and others were pushing for independence, so Algeria's fight became a rallying point across the continent. Ahmed Ben Bella became Algeria's first president in 1963, and as a pan-Africanist he was one of the founding fathers of the OAU.

4   The final document was a detailed, 53-page blueprint that focused on five areas: strategic "national actions," primarily on governance, peace, and security; joint African and "international actions" fighting HIV/AIDS, improving health, education, technology, and so forth; enhanced partnerships; a transformed aid relationship; and an enhanced role for the private sector.

5   The first meeting included the founding NEPAD countries—Algeria, Egypt, Nigeria, Senegal, and South Africa—plus Ethiopia, Gabon, Ghana, Mali, Mozambique, Rwanda, São Tomé and Principe, Tanzania, Tunisia, and Uganda.

6   I recall one meeting with prominent international development officials that took place before Algiers, when someone expressed concern that the "big guys"—meaning Nigeria and South Africa—were almost exclusively in charge and that other countries were likely to push back if they were not brought into the loop. That proved to be prophetic. The farther along we got, the more grumblings we heard.

Chapter 12

A 'Landmark' Initiative for Governance

The Origin and Impact of the African Peer Review Mechanism

Meeting in Genoa, Italy in July 2001, the G8 devoted much of its attention at that year's summit to poverty reduction in the age of globalization. Leaders discussed some of the most meaningful actions that the world's advanced economies could pursue, including debt relief, trade and investment, better market access, and increased official development assistance. Naturally, Sub-Saharan Africa, where more than 50 percent of the population lived below the international poverty line in 2000, and where such actions were desperately needed, took on increased importance. So did NEPAD, the New Partnership for Africa's Development, which African heads of state would officially endorse just a few weeks later.

The G8 lauded NEPAD for its "principles of responsibility and ownership" and as the basis for new cooperation between Africa and the developed world. For all the measures being discussed to fight poverty, the G8 saw NEPAD as the framework through which African countries would ready themselves—by improving governance, transparency, and the rule of law—to reap the benefits.

So it stood to reason that the G8 countries needed their own framework to further common goals toward Africa and to support African efforts to implement NEPAD. They agreed to the Genoa Plan for Africa, which really was just a brief agreement to develop a concrete action plan to be adopted at their next scheduled summit in Canada's Kananaskis region, near the city of Alberta.

To move forward, G8 leaders agreed to appoint high-level representatives to shape the proposed plan and, in the process, consult closely with African leaders and decision-makers over the following months. The G8 Africa Personal Representatives (APRs) began their discussions in London in October 2001 with a meeting among themselves. But for their next meeting they headed to Addis Ababa, the first of four trips they made to Africa.[1]

The G8 APRs arrived on Thursday, December 6, 2001, for two very busy days. First they met with Ethiopian Prime Minister Meles Zenawi, who was also a member of the NEPAD Heads of State and Government Implementation Committee. On Friday they held discussions with Amara Essy, the interim head of the OAU and then with members of the NEPAD steering committee, including Algeria's M'hamed Achache, South Africa's Wiseman Nkuhlu, Nigeria's Isaac Aluko-Olokun, and Senegal's Chérif Salif Sy. But in between, they spent Thursday afternoon and evening at the ECA. It was a pivotal visit that took place because I had formed a fast bond with Canadian Ambassador Bob Fowler, a well-respected diplomat acting not only as Prime Minister Jean Chrétien's APR but also as chair of the full group of APRs.

Fowler had sent me a letter explaining why the APRs were traveling to Addis: to reach agreement on the elements of NEPAD to which the G8 Africa Action Plan could respond. He wanted to emerge from the Addis meetings, he said, with the parameters of the plan defined, so that in the six months that remained before the G8 summit in Kananaskis, the APRs could focus on the specifics. He said he hoped the ECA could help.

I had only met Fowler two months prior in Washington, DC. We were in town for separate reasons but scheduled a meeting at the behest of others. Fowler said he had been told by many others that the ECA "were the ones to work with" in crafting a sound plan. Conversely, I had been told by UN Secretary-General Kofi Annan to get to know Fowler and stay in close contact with him, given his current responsibility. Fowler began his diplomatic career in the late 1960s, and by the time our paths crossed, he had already served as the foreign policy advisor to multiple prime ministers, as the deputy minister of defense, and as Canada's longest-tenured ambassador to the UN, among other posts. He was a driven public servant, widely recognized as having Africa's best interests at heart—a perception proven completely true in my eyes.[2]

When we first met, however, Fowler had his hands full. In addition to being Chrétien's point person on Africa, he also served as the prime minister's personal representative for the *overall* G8 summit. These men and women are known as sherpas, and they are responsible for negotiating the specifics of whatever big agreements or policies the G8 leaders announce. The host country always takes the lead for ensuring joint outcomes, but the Genoa Plan had upped the stakes. Canadian officials felt extra pressure to deliver on the endorsed action plan, so Chrétien asked Fowler to pull double duty.

When Fowler and I met in Washington, we hit it off instantly. I could tell he wasn't after attention or prestige. He was anxious to learn whatever he didn't already know. For that reason, he took a keen interest in the ECA's work. I told him about all of it—the forums, the economic reports, our supporting role in crafting NEPAD. He listened closely. We promised each other mutual support.

A few weeks later, I invited him to participate in the ECA's second Big Table meeting, which would focus on how to translate the new promises between Africa and donors into something tangible. Big Table II offered the perfect opportunity to talk through ideas with development ministers and African policymakers. Fowler found himself in the middle of that discussion, and it was clear he liked what he heard. He told me he wanted to continue that dialogue, but with the full contingent of APRs. So when the personal reps headed to Africa, Fowler made Addis Ababa and ECA headquarters one of their first stops.

The trip certainly proved necessary. When they arrived, the APRs did not even have an agreed list of priorities, much less a central framework for a plan. There were the political considerations among individual G8 countries that had to be taken into account, and there were the practical considerations of devising a plan that had actual merit—not at all unlike the struggles we had been going through with NEPAD. Fowler conceded to me that he was at a bit of a loss on the best way for the APRs to proceed.

The visit took place in two parts: an afternoon briefing session, and an evening working dinner. During the briefing session, we offered extensive technical details on the parts of our work program that overlapped with the APRs' priority areas of interest: governance, trade and investment, ICT, HIV/AIDs, and food security. A different ECA senior staff member or expert delivered each presentation, a tactic that the APRs commended for demonstrating the depth of our technical expertise, which in turn strengthened the weight of our ideas.

The briefings were good, but the working dinner was even better. In fact, it was dynamic because the G8 reps were so engaged with what we had to say. We made two final presentations that analyzed the challenges of implementing NEPAD across a continent that remained politically and economically disjointed. Then we came to the conclusion—the solution to the challenges as we saw them, which we had been building toward all day: enhanced partnerships, driven primarily by a system of peer review.

"Enhanced partnerships" was an ECA concept, a way to differentiate between African nations that were at different stages of the recovery process: the conflict countries, the struggling countries, and the improving countries—the ones already seeing signs of growth or committed to democratic processes. In these latter countries, the environment for reform was stronger, and the likelihood of development assistance making a lasting impact greater. The aid relationship between these countries and donors would be considered "enhanced," serving as examples for how more aid, less debt, and better trade policies could work in countries committed to pursuing economic and political reforms.

But for enhanced partnerships to be practical, there had to be a way to gauge a country's measure of success toward those commitments. That's where a peer review mechanism, or a process for governments to self-monitor and hold themselves and each other accountable, came into play. The new partnership agenda, by its very nature, entailed a fundamental shift in approach to conditionalities. Self-monitoring would replace externally driven conditions, but there had to be a way for African countries to analyze, measure, and assess whether they were meeting their own goals toward poverty reduction and good governance. Peer review, we argued, would provide the answer.

The G8 reps were excited. I could tell by their body language alone that they liked the idea. From the donor perspective, it was very important that countries had to meet certain standards of accountability. But from the African perspective, we had to ensure that not all countries were seen as the same. The enhanced partnership concept therefore was intended to showcase those countries that had been most successful in meeting certain criteria. In that way, the concept would help tie all of the different aspects of NEPAD together—African accountability, donor responsibility, development assistance, and investment.

At the end of the night, Bob Fowler told me that he had a much clearer focus on how to define G8 support to NEPAD than he had had when the day began. We were sitting next to each other at the same table, and when the final presentation ended, he leaned over and whispered in my ear, "Now I know what my job is."

After their visit to Addis, the G8 APRs prepared four discussion papers intended to frame future meetings. Each paper focused on a different theme: peace and security, knowledge and health, economic growth and private investment, and political and economic governance, including peer review. Over the next six months, as they worked on the donor response to NEPAD, the G8 reps took the concept of enhanced partnerships and peer review and ran with it. For the donors, that idea became the central tenet of their support for NEPAD.

At the same time, similar things were happening on the African side, too.

Just a few weeks before the APRs visited Addis, the NEPAD Heads of State and Government Implementation Committee held its inaugural meeting and agreed to include peer review in the NEPAD framework. It asked the ECA to contribute. We agreed of course, and in a way that felt like a small victory, because we actually had been pushing peer review as a way to reduce donor influence over African affairs throughout the NEPAD process.

I first brought up peer review when I gave my Global Compact speech the previous year, and the ECA continued to make the case for it as we helped merge the Global Compact, MAP, and OMEGA plans into the single initiative that would become NEPAD. We had a very good reason: we wanted peer review to be Africa's ticket to a world beyond traditional conditions. The thinking was clear; if we could monitor ourselves, we could set our own conditions.

But my approach to peer review primarily came from the economic side. That's the prism through which the ECA viewed it. And when the NEPAD heads of state tasked us with crafting a peer review strategy, they commissioned us to work on the *economic and corporate* governance aspect of it; the other aspect to it, *political* governance, was to be handled elsewhere.

The principle of mutual accountability—ensuring each side followed through on its commitments—sat at the heart of NEPAD, and African leaders knew that donors wanted some kind of assurance that their governments would hold up their end of the new partnership. An operational peer review process became the obvious answer. The G8 countries began pushing for it and the heads of state began pushing for it.

Once peer review had become fully enmeshed in the NEPAD process, it took on a different form than I had originally envisioned. Still, the ECA helped open eyes on both the African government and donor sides. And within a year, we had created the framework for what became the African Peer Review Mechanism.

◆　◆　◆　◆

In many assessments, the African Peer Review Mechanism, or APRM, is seen as the most consequential component of NEPAD. Speaking in 2011, Kofi Annan called it a "landmark instrument for good governance currently absent from many other developing regions in the world." But unlike the other unique ideas represented by NEPAD, peer review was not part of the original framework. When the heads of state endorsed the unified recovery plan then known as the New African Initiative at their summit in Lusaka in 2001, peer review was nowhere to be found. And even as African leaders went around the world and sold the idea of NEPAD to the European Union and G8 and other donor partners—and as those partners publicly embraced it—the plan wasn't complete, because the element that would become its "crown jewel" had yet to be added.

Of course, as opinion quickly coalesced around peer review as Africa's response to NEPAD's mutual accountability principle, that omission was addressed. The APRM was presented to the G8 at their 2002 summit in Kananaskis as a major component of NEPAD, and it was roundly praised. Shortly thereafter, African leaders officially endorsed it at their summit in Durban, the same summit that launched the new African Union. After another year or so of structural tinkering, the APRM was considered ready to go.

The APRM is still in use, but it's widely seen as having underachieved its early accolades and recognition. There are numerous reasons why, and I'll explore the most pertinent toward the end of the chapter. But not working out as planned is not the same as being irrelevant, and the APRM will always be relevant for the step forward it represented. Through its acceptance, African leaders demonstrated a newfound willingness to embrace measures of accountability and good governance as integral to the ownership agenda.

So how does it work? A private but high-profile meeting between heads of state to discuss findings gets most of the attention, but it's actually a carefully planned, five-stage process that begins with the collection of background materials, including country self-assessments, and broad public input. This is a great opportunity for civil society to get involved. One of the most thrilling promises of the APRM was the ability for average citizens to offer feedback in ways that could directly influence enhancements in their own government processes. Stage two is a country review mission, which is carried out by a team of experts from academia, business, and other fields. The visiting mission team then prepares and submits a country review report. That's stage three. Throughout these early stages, an appointed "panel of eminent persons" helps guide country assessments and assist the review teams as needed.

Stage four is the actual peer review itself, where the leader of the country under review talks with his or her fellow heads of state about the findings and how to best address those findings. This usually happens on the margins of a summit or other gatherings and it's always done behind closed doors. During the final stage, the report becomes public and its recommendations and follow-up action plan, if there is one, tabled at key institutional meetings, like the Pan-African Parliament. Before any of this begins, though, countries wishing to join the APRM process are required to commit in writing to the codes, standards, and principles of governance that the mechanism outlines.[3]

The APRM was devised as a voluntary process and it still is, but countries were strongly urged to participate upon its adoption because it gave NEPAD the teeth that previous continental recovery initiatives lacked, and it gave donors the assurance that Africa was serious about holding up its end of the partnership bargain. Since NEPAD revolved around Africa's commitment to improving its own political and economic governance, the APRM offered a way to measure which countries were following through on those commitments.

Looking back, it's hard to gauge NEPAD's impact on Africa without taking into full consideration the creation and implementation of the APRM, because neither would have amounted to a whole lot without the other. That may be an overly broad generalization, but the fact of the matter is that NEPAD needed peer review to set it apart from the continental recovery programs of the past. In the context of the new partnership, Africans needed it to win over donors, and donors needed it to justify their relaxed conditionalities.

But the arguments for peer review went much deeper than NEPAD. Through a transparent peer review process, the thinking went, African countries would have a legitimate way to hold each other accountable for weak governance and for policies that failed to support regional growth opportunities. The internal accountability dimension of peer review cannot be overstated—an understood social contract between governments but also between individual states and society. As integral as the idea became to the new partnership, Africa first and foremost needed peer review *for itself*. This line of thinking led the ECA to start focusing on peer review even before it became synonymous with NEPAD.

In 2009, authors Steven Gruzd and Ross Herbert used the experience of the initial five countries to undergo peer review—Ghana, Kenya,

Rwanda, Mauritius, and South Africa—as an opportunity to publish one of the first exhaustive looks at the ins and outs of the review process. They dove deep into the findings from those "pioneer countries" and attempted to bridge the gap between the APRM's theoretical mission and its realistic impact. Their judgment was fair and honest. They called it "unprecedented in its breadth and depth" but acknowledged that the complexity of the system and competing political interests made the APRM challenging for governments to fully leverage the opportunities it presented.

In the years since, as more countries have signed on to peer review, and as more reviews have been completed, the number of publications exploring the APRM's impact—and questioning its value—has proliferated. As with the previous chapter, my intention here is not to tread ground so adequately covered but to review the activities that led to its creation.

◆　◆　◆　◆

For the ECA, the context in which we first seriously considered an African-owned peer review started with the Economic Policy Stance Index, created in 1999 as part of our annual economic report. The index measured economic progress but also encouraged governments to exchange views and monitor each other's performance to better their own. The focus was economic; it's not that we felt political governance lacked importance, it's just that our interest centered on the need for a tool to improve macroeconomic management through peer learning. Naturally, some countries would be able to strengthen their internal processes faster than others, because they were either more committed or more stable. So one of the great appeals of an African-based peer review mechanism would be the ability for the better-performing or worse-performing countries to be measured in relation to each other, by each other—not by donors or multilaterals applying their own standards.

The paths for peer review and NEPAD began to converge in Algiers in May 2001. The document presented at the ministerial conference, *Compact for African Recovery: Operationalizing the Millennium Partnership for the African Recovery Program*, proposed that heads of state, in collaboration with the continental institutions, establish mechanisms for a "peer review of performance on issues of governance and economic management." That document formed the framework for NEPAD (though it was still called the New African Initiative at the time), endorsed by heads of state in July. The next step was taking that framework and putting the meat on the bones, a process that kicked off a few weeks later in August with the first NEPAD steering committee meeting in Dakar.

Presidents Olusegun Obasanjo of Nigeria and Abdoulaye Wade of Senegal addressed the steering committee at a meeting in Dakar. This meeting was more or less the kickoff for the long process of taking the framework that the OAU endorsed in Lusaka and turning it into a detailed plan for ratification the following year. Obasanjo thanked committee members for their work so far then outlined the task: to produce a final product "devoid of repetition, roughness, imprecision, and vagueness." That document would then be presented to the Heads of State and Government Implementation Committee for review in a few months.

Obasanjo then gave the ECA an endorsement by suggesting that the steering committee—which included Algeria, Egypt, Nigeria, Senegal, and South Africa representatives—rely on our expertise. The ECA, he said, could provide the "necessary technical and analytical support" to help guide NEPAD to completion. He called the institution "an intellectual powerhouse." I was quite proud.

Despite the difficult negotiations in Algiers, the ECA had emerged from that conference with a considerable amount of goodwill. For example, a few weeks later, some of our staff attended a meeting in Dakar to discuss next steps for combining the MAP and OMEGA plans. President Wade, Senegalese ministers, and personnel from the OAU and UNDP were also there. According to notes taken, Senegal officials said they held the ECA in high regard as an "honest broker" because it represented all African countries "with no axe to grind."

Obasanjo's endorsement at the steering committee meeting in Dakar seemed to echo that thinking, so we stayed closely involved. As the steering committee got to work, the ECA provided regular feedback and offered suggestions as draft versions flew back and forth. In early September, we hosted the committee for a meeting during which it agreed on the organizational structure that would guide the new initiative, including the parameters of its own role as well as that of the higher-level implementation committee.

Throughout all this, our suggestions were well received—just not for peer review. Politically, it was a delicate matter. And the steering committee consisted mainly of individuals with political backgrounds who put political considerations first. I understood the rationale, but the reluctance to include peer review posed a problem because no other measure being considered gave a *meaningful* definition to the mutual accountability principle. Without it, I felt, NEPAD would not look nearly as unique or firm in its commitment to good governance.

When the Heads of State and Government Implementation Committee, or HSGIC, convened for the first time on October 23, 2001 in Abuja, the framework presented to it did not include any mention of the words "peer review." It did, however, offer a pledge to work "individually and collectively" to promote the principles of good governance. That pledge consisted of two broadly outlined initiatives—one for peace and security and the other for democracy and political governance. The initiatives, according to the NEPAD document, would address obvious needs, such as the need to build capacity to manage conflict; to promote policy measures to address vulnerabilities; and to strengthen political and administrative processes. The lack of specifics, however, posed a problem.

To their credit, HSGIC leaders recognized the shortcoming. They wrote into the plan a vow that within six months they would identify "appropriate diagnostic and assessment tools in support of compliance with the shared goals of good governance." The leaders also promised that African states would support each other in meeting the basic standards of good governance.

Though the official NEPAD document didn't mention peer review, the communiqué issued at the end of the HSGIC meeting did. In it, the committee promised to consider and adopt "an appropriate peer review mechanism and a code of conduct" at its next meeting, expressing hope that Africa's development partners "will complement these efforts." The communiqué was not as high-profile as the approved NEPAD document, but it was still part of the official record. It was a way for committee leaders to be clear about their intentions while buying some time to build wider political support and come up with a viable plan.

A few days later, Wiseman Nkuhlu, chair of the NEPAD steering committee, asked that the ECA take the lead in creating an economic and corporate governance initiative to complement the other two initiatives already promised in NEPAD. "The purpose," Nkuhlu wrote to me in a letter, "is to develop a framework of policies, mechanisms, and instruments" that would demonstrate the continent's commitment to good governance but also to effective enforcement. In addition, the initiative should establish ways "to identify useful information to be shared among countries" as well as the methods for sharing it.

In essence, he had described a peer review mechanism.

We had about four months to put something concrete together before the next HSGIC meeting. The timeline was tight but not necessarily a problem. As the NEPAD process was playing out, the ECA had already moved forward on peer review. In fact, the week before the HSGIC met, we convened the second Big Table, this time in Amsterdam, and peer review was one of the main topics.

After the success of the first Big Table, it was an easy decision to make the consultation between African finance and planning ministers and their OECD counterparts an annual event. And to best embrace the spirit of equal partnership in which the Big Table was conceived, I wanted the location to rotate between Africa and donor countries. Eveline Herfkens, the Dutch development minister, offered to host. Big Table II, as we called it, took place October 14–16 in Amsterdam, and it was bigger in almost every way—more time to meet, more voices to hear, and more topics to discuss. After all, at the first Big Table, talk of a new global compact had been just that—talk. Since then, and in less than a year, that talk had turned into a flurry of activity.

In the months leading up to Big Table II, I traveled a good bit. After the G8's pledge of support for NEPAD at their summit in Genoa, I wanted to reach out to development partners as a follow-up from the ECA's perspective—meaning the technical, not political, side. At the same time, I wanted to drum up momentum for the event in Amsterdam. Many non-G8 donor nations such as Norway, the Netherlands, and Sweden played a big role in African development, so Big Table II gave them a chance to join their G8 partners and African ministers in frank conversation about the new approach. It was during this round of travel that I met Bob Fowler in Washington, DC and invited him to participate.

Altogether, almost three dozen principals attended. Thirteen African countries sent ministerial delegations to sit alongside their counterparts from nine OECD countries. High-level representatives from the African Development Bank, the EU, the World Bank and IMF, UNDP, USAID and, of course, OECD-DAC also attended. Many of the faces were familiar. Donald Kaberuka and Gerald Ssendaula, the finance ministers in Rwanda and Uganda, respectively, and Sipho Mpahlwa, the deputy finance minister of South Africa, were among the returning African policymakers. Among the donor countries and institutions, Clare Short from the UK, Richard Carey from the OECD, and Callisto Madavo from the World Bank were there again.

But with NEPAD moving full steam ahead, I wanted to increase the seats around the table. Some new participants included ministers from Senegal and Algeria and, since both of those countries were NEPAD founding countries, their participation strengthened the lineup. Wiseman Nkuhlu also attended as an observer. From outside Africa, UNDP Administrator Mark Malloch Brown attended, and of course so did Bob Fowler.

Even with a larger group, we maintained the same intimate, collegial, and informal atmosphere. But this time, with the MAP, OMEGA and Global Compact plans all in the rearview mirror, we were no longer focused on hypotheticals but on how to make the new partnership function. The discussions focused on three main topics: governance, aid effectiveness, and peer review. They were tightly connected but carried with them different interpretations, especially governance.

Rwanda's Kaberuka, whose country was still recovering from a devastating period of genocide, made a strong case that peace and security should be the top priorities of a good governance agenda. The table agreed, though others cautioned that good governance, no matter how critical, should not be seen as a litmus test for foreign assistance; governance alone cannot grow economies for the long term. This point underscored a broader issue. As good governance gained traction as the linchpin of NEPAD, some of the G8 countries, especially the United States, preferred to think of the political aspect above all else. For them, it became primarily about promoting democratic systems and leaning on other African countries to pressure dictators and strongmen out of office.

Kaberuka cited Mozambique's successful postwar reconciliation process, and he said it was an example that Rwandan officials hoped to follow as they tried to reestablish their own legitimacy.[4] "Of course good governance is necessary for economic development," Kaberuka said. "And we as Africans are the most interested people in good governance. But ownership of the process is critical."[5] With a very timely example, Kaberuka described how African countries could learn from each other to build better internal systems and, in a way, set the tone for a talk about peer review.

"The new development partnership that Africa is striving for requires a fundamental shift," I said, away from traditional donor conditions and toward mutually agreed outcomes measured through self-monitoring and peer review. "This shift would underpin ownership."

We discussed a broad range of other objectives: to monitor progress toward common goals, to encourage governments to adhere to agreed standards and benchmarks, to encourage mutual learning, to share good practices, and to identify capacity gaps and jointly recommend approaches for addressing those gaps. All these objectives supported good governance, but in a much broader context than political systems. And if viewed through NEPAD, they would address donor country concerns over accountability, as well as give African countries a legitimate ownership claim through self-monitoring their economic and corporate governance.

Muhammad Hassanein of Egypt spoke first, offering a direct endorsement. "Yes, we are ready," he said, adding that concerns over "how it could be done" should not be exaggerated since Africa could rely on professionals already in place in institutions like the AfDB or the ECA to guide the process. Other ministers around the table, including those from Mozambique, Botswana, and Ghana, echoed Hassanein's enthusiasm.

Fowler also spoke in favor of it. If the goal of NEPAD is to produce "a better bang for the buck" in development dollars, he said, then peer review "adds immense value." Gun-Britt Andersson, Sweden's representative to the OECD, said that a learning process was "the best path" for widespread gains in governance, which in turn was necessary for NEPAD to work. Then she added a key point for emphasis: peer review would improve a country's performance as long as it was credible. That wasn't just a donor concern, either.

"Whatever you do," agreed Burkina Faso's minister, "make it credible."

Their thoughts certainly echoed mine. Credibility in the process *had* to be paramount. At the same time, if the process worked, it would bestow its own credibility on the countries agreeing to it. Demonstrated performance—or at the very least, a demonstrated commitment to performance—would give African countries the necessary leverage to make donors live up to their own commitments to boost aid and relieve debt. That line of thinking is what originally led me to the idea of enhanced partnerships, since those countries would be in a better position to benefit from increased development assistance.

"Peer review speaks to ownership," said Sierra Leone minister Kadi Sesay. "There is a need for Africans to review what Africans do."

Kaberuka also weighed in with some very persuasive words. "We talk about lack of ownership and institutional imperialism," he said. "Peer review is an answer to that problem."

As the discussion wrapped up, the sentiment of the ministers was clear: they all stood behind peer review, and they liked the enhanced partnership model as the foundation for it. They also agreed that a governance project already in development at the ECA to establish indicators that would gauge institutional effectiveness and economic management—offered a solid base for generating the necessary data; there would be no need to duplicate that part of the process. And they agreed that existing regional goals should be taken into consideration, as well as the goals of other review processes underway, such as the IMF's Article IV consultations, the World Bank's Country Policy and Institutional Assessment, and the well-regarded OECD-DAC reviews.

The fact that peer review wasn't yet a part of the NEPAD framework didn't dampen the enthusiasm. "Go ahead and do it," said Eveline Herfkens. "Don't wait around for everyone else."

As we soon learned, waiting around would not be an issue. One week later, the Heads of State and Government Implementation Committee held its meeting, stated the desire to incorporate a "diagnostic and assessment tool" into NEPAD, and issued the communiqué that specifically mentioned a peer review process. Six weeks after that, Bob Fowler brought the G8 APRs to Addis, where they decided to make peer review a central element of the action plan they were developing as a complement to NEPAD.

Within the span of two months, support for an African peer review process had coalesced. And from that point forward, peer review became inextricably linked with NEPAD, for better or for worse.

◆ ◆ ◆ ◆

Among the key moments along the timeline of the APRM's development, Big Table II is one of the most meaningful. But because of the event's inherent structure—existing behind the scenes rather than in the spotlight—it is often overlooked, if it's known at all. That's a historical slight. No other occasion afforded so many influential players from inside and outside Africa the opportunity to sit down, in the same room and at the same time, to discuss the merits and conceptual design of peer review in Africa. And it was a thorough, detail-driven discussion. That the head of the NEPAD steering committee and the point man for the G8's action plan simultaneously heard the same feedback is significant. It showed that ministers and heavy hitters on both sides of the new partnership were in general agreement on specific ways to move forward. That knowledge proved valuable as we began work on the economic and corporate governance initiative that the heads of state had requested.

We had two main goals in producing the document: first, to present the HSGIC with a workable blueprint for NEPAD's missing diagnostic tool; and second, to continue to gather as much input and feedback as possible. For example, in January 2002, we hosted an economic and corporate governance workshop put together by Nigeria. That same month, we attended a NEPAD "work-in-progress" meeting that the NEPAD secretariat convened in Pretoria.

When the HSGIC reconvened in Abuja for its second meeting in March 2002, we had the document ready to go—*Codes and Standards for Good Economic and Corporate Governance in Africa: Summary of Key Issues and Declaration of Principles.*[6] In it, we made the technical case, sometimes in excruciating detail, for peer review as the necessary process to hold governments accountable for their commitments.

We argued that good economic governance must rely on harmonious and complementary macroeconomic and trade policies, coherent development strategies and programs, a dynamic domestic private sector, and "monitoring and regulatory authorities" to promote and coordinate economic activity. We tried to stay away from most political governance issues since the committee had a separate initiative on democracy and governance to consider, which was not prepared by the ECA. Nevertheless, we asserted that good *political* governance was an undeniable prerequisite for good *economic* and *corporate* governance and, as such, we recommended that "a single peer review encompassing both the political and economic and corporate aspects of governance for a given country should be conducted where required."

Pleased with what it saw, the HSGIC endorsed both initiatives and officially called for a peer review mechanism to be appended to NEPAD. It was a major turning point. Over the next few months, the two draft initiatives were combined to form the technical backbone for the *NEPAD Declaration on Democracy, Political, Economic, and Corporate Governance*, which was signed by NEPAD leaders ahead of the Durban summit in July 2002. That declaration established the creation of the African Peer Review Mechanism—the on-the-record accountability for good governance principles that had been missing in the original iteration of the NEPAD framework.

But a lot happened in between the time the HSGIC approved the two draft initiatives in March and the time heads of states signed off on creating the APRM four months later. The most high-profile event was the G8 summit in Kananaskis, where leaders unveiled their Africa Action Plan and promised to implement it in coordination with NEPAD. The plan included a strong endorsement of peer review—an "innovative and potentially decisive element" for reaching NEPAD's goals, it said—and a prominent reliance on the ECA's model of enhanced partnerships. But there was a lot going on behind the scenes, too.

The run-up to finalizing the Africa Action Plan occurred alongside the push to harmonize the two governance initiatives into the single NEPAD Declaration, and there was increasing anxiety on both sides to get the mutual agreements right in time for Kananaskis and Durban. No other African organization had the same expertise on the subject matter as the ECA, or had taken on the same kind of leadership role—including close coordination with the HSGIC as well as the G8 APRs. So I expected that we would continue to be involved, both in producing the official APRM framework to be implemented and in guiding the mechanism's eventual stewardship. I was right about the former, but wrong about the latter.

By the time the heads of state had established the APRM in Durban, the ECA's role had been reduced, and the oversight and management of the mechanism had been overtaken by political considerations. I think this hurt the APRM in the long run, even if the outcome probably was inevitable, given the context of peer review's link to NEPAD's formation.

From the beginning, a kind of operational schism existed over NEPAD's most basic aspect—its accessibility. When it was still just the MAP recovery plan, the key figures behind it, South Africa's Thabo Mbeki and Nigeria's Obasanjo, were generally in agreement on what they wanted the initiative to accomplish, but not on its structure. Their viewpoints represented a split in thinking among African leaders that could be broadly categorized in two ways. On one side, there were those who saw the plan as a core program of the new African Union. And since all African countries would be members of the AU, the recovery plan would apply to all countries equally. Obasanjo fell into this group. By contrast, other leaders, including Mbeki, did not originally envision the plan as a "one size fits all" program. Rather than default inclusion via the political body of the African Union, they saw it as a development initiative to exist in conjunction with the AU, one which countries would aspire to join.

Back when the ECA ministers asked us to operationalize the Global Compact, I debated the same issue. Should it be for all of Africa, or should it be for like-minded countries? By like-minded countries, I meant governments that were adhering to the tenets of the capable state as I described in Chapter 7—maintaining peace and security, applying the rule of law, and promoting inclusive and equitable growth, among other characteristics. At the ECA, we debated the ideological and practical consequences of pursuing either path, either for all countries or for like-minded countries.

When I called on Mbeki in January 2001 to discuss what a unified MAP and Global Compact might entail, we had a very thorough discussion on this same topic. His original concept of the MAP was as a plan that would benefit all of Africa—but not a plan that all of Africa would try to enact at the same time. Rather, states that were more stable and farther along economically would lead the way. Then, as more countries met a predetermined set of criteria, they would come along as able. A process for countries to self-monitor their progress would also be needed. This was more in line with the like-minded approach, but with an attainable structure for all countries.

Generally, that's how I came down, too. The fact of the matter was that different countries were at different stages of development, with different capacities and resources, not to mention dramatic disparities in the integrity and quality of leaders. I found myself agreeing with Mbeki a lot during our meeting. It was in the aftermath of that discussion that the ECA developed the enhanced partnerships model and settled on peer review as the engine to propel it.

Ultimately, this was not the path chosen for NEPAD. Rather, the heads of state endorsed the joint initiative, soon to be known as NEPAD, at Lusaka as a blueprint for the whole continent. Even before then, it had become clear that the plan would be an AU initiative, not an independent program. Mbeki and Obasanjo were on the same page, in part because they needed to be.

The process of combining all the elements of the various recovery plans into a single initiative proved arduous, but so did the process of convincing skeptical Africans of the plan's merit. Even though the heads of state backed the plan, tempers flared at Lusaka. There was a lot of concern and disagreement. As I mentioned in the previous chapter, the top-down approach that went into crafting the plan did not sit well with African leaders who felt marginalized or that the program was being imposed on them. Civil society also felt left out—and angry. Buy-in was critical, and that meant no additional conditions to participate.

But with no barrier to entry, a mechanism to ensure countries upheld their commitments to economic and political governance became even more important for keeping the initiative credible. As head of the HSGIC, Obasanjo was aware of this and fully on board with incorporating peer review. But he also had been a proponent of the concept long before NEPAD.

When he was out of elected office, Obasanjo in 1991 organized a special heads of state summit in Kampala that yielded general agreement on the need for democratization, good governance, and improved regional integration in order to boost African development. The meeting resulted in the Kampala Document, which proposed formalizing the agreed principles through the Conference on Security, Stability, Development, and Cooperation in Africa, or CSSDCA. This was one of Africa's earliest attempts to link good governance and development.

Over the next few years, the Kampala Document was presented at OAU summits, but no action was taken. After Obasanjo returned to power in Nigeria's 1998 election, he resurrected the initiative. When African heads of state voted to disband the OAU and create the African Union, they also endorsed the CSSDCA, then being developed as a possible monitoring and evaluation tool for the new AU. This was happening alongside the NEPAD effort, but Obasanjo saw them as linked. In August 2001, a few weeks after the Lusaka summit, Obasanjo said the CSSDCA could be the "anchor point" for both the African Union and NEPAD and that the three initiatives together would form a "tripod support" for Africa's security, stability, and development. It was a few months later, at the first HSGIC meeting in Abuja in October, that he voiced strong support for peer review as a monitoring mechanism to be included in NEPAD.

I can't say that I ever knew or heard much about the CSSDCA; it was never a key point of discussion as we worked on the governance initiative that the HSGIC asked us to produce. There was definite overlap in priorities with NEPAD, and South Africa was one of the stronger supporters. What's notable is that the effort predated NEPAD by a decade, and that Obasanjo helped drive it—and that it was always seen as an OAU/AU initiative to ensure good political and economic governance in conjunction with development cooperation. So it's not surprising that he had favored NEPAD as an AU initiative.

Once the HSGIC had accepted the two governance initiatives presented at its second meeting in Abuja in March 2002 and officially endorsed a peer review process for NEPAD, attention turned to the next logical issue— who was going to run it? The committee members agreed on three points for choosing a secretariat: the secretariat should be "technically competent, credible, and free of political manipulation." These guidelines echoed some of the desires expressed by ministers at the second Big Table. The last point—free of political manipulation—also implied a certain level of independence. Because of how far along we were in our efforts to develop governance indicators, and because we had been peer review's most vocal advocate, the ECA was mentioned as a logical secretariat. After a little more discussion, the heads of state tabled the issue and agreed to pick it back up at their next meeting.

Three months later, the committee gathered for a third time on the sidelines of the June 2002 World Food Summit in Rome. By that point, a decision needed to be made about the APRM's secretariat, because it was one of the last remaining major issues. Also, the Kananaskis summit was right around the corner and Bob Fowler and the G8 APRs were anxious to see the final pieces for NEPAD put into place before unveiling the Africa Action Plan.

I delivered brief remarks before Ethiopian Prime Minister Meles Zenawi officially proposed that the ECA serve as the secretariat. Given the three-point criteria approved in Abuja, Meles said, the ECA seemed to be the obvious solution. No one spoke out against the idea.

This took place a few weeks before the Kananaskis, and the timing was important since the G8 considered peer review the core component of NEPAD. According to Fowler, one issue that greatly concerned the APRs was the technical competence—and political independence—of peer review's eventual secretariat. The ECA had built up substantial credibility in their eyes and would be an agreeable choice.

I never lobbied for the ECA to administer peer review, but, like others, I felt the idea made the most sense. Choosing the ECA would meet the criteria put forth by the HSGIC. It would address the G8's primary concern of competence and credibility. And it would be consistent with what we had heard from the NEPAD leaders; it was only a few months prior that Senegal's President Wade had called the ECA a "fair and honest broker" and Obasanjo had referred to us as "an intellectual powerhouse." In the minds of many, including mine, we left Rome thinking this was a done deal.

But it wasn't, and the ground shifted in a hurry.

After the HSGIC meeting in Rome, Obasanjo and Mbeki led the African delegation to Kananaskis, where the G8 endorsed NEPAD, calling it an "unprecedented opportunity to make progress on common goals." The G8's Africa Action Plan made it clear that donor adherence to the new partnership would hinge on the success of the African ownership agenda. "The prime responsibility for Africa's future lies with Africa itself," the G8 noted in the plan's sixth paragraph. In the seventh paragraph, they endorsed the APRM as a barometer to measure which countries were accepting of that responsibility: "While we will focus particular attention on enhanced partnership countries, we will also work with countries that do not yet meet the standards of NEPAD but which are clearly committed to and working toward its implementation."

The G8 countries were clear in their support for the APRM—and they were content with the ECA's leadership role. The first line item in the Africa Action Plan under the section "Supporting Peer Review" called for continued cooperation between the OECD and the ECA in developing substantive peer review practices. It even urged the ECA to continue participating in the OECD-DAC reviews in Africa, as we had done a few months earlier in Senegal.

For African leaders though, Kananaskis was just a prelude to Durban. All the efforts over the past two years had been in preparation for the launch of the African Union and for the formal launch of NEPAD. With the APRM attached to it, NEPAD got the seal of approval it needed from the donors. That cleared the final hurdle for the heads of state to officially approve NEPAD as Africa's new development framework and the APRM alongside it.

Ahead of the Durban summit, I sent a letter to Obasanjo. It was a little more than two pages. In it, I laid out the ECA's entire thinking on the main issues pertaining to the APRM. Despite the excitement and sudden publicity surrounding it, the APRM still had its share of skeptics, both within and outside Africa. And that was entirely understandable; peer review represented a major change in the way African countries—and donors—would relate to each other. It was imperative for the APRM to start strong, have a good beginning, win over critics, and prove its relevance.

"In the weeks since the Rome meeting," I wrote, "we have been thinking through how to operationalize the APRM so that process meets the criteria set out by the implementation committee." I explained, in fine detail, a five-point plan to get peer reviews up and running, including the establishment of an independent panel of "eminent persons" to oversee reviews and the ways in which that panel and the APRM secretariat would split functions and responsibilities. "The ECA is privileged to be the secretariat for the APRM," I concluded. "We appreciate the continued confidence."

As it turned out, I was being a little too presumptuous.

The committee had scheduled its fourth meeting ahead of the formal summit, and there were no major issues other than giving final approval to the NEPAD and APRM structures, basically a procedural move ahead of endorsement by the full assembly. In fact, one of the most pressing issues was to increase the size of the implementation committee, which had already been done once when it was raised to 15. Now, it would be 20. Discussing the APRM secretariat wasn't even on the preliminary agenda. I attended the meeting expecting to get a final stamp of approval. Instead, I got a dose of political reality.

Obasanjo, the committee chair, ran through the basic agenda— standard comments, decisions, and approvals. It was all very matter of fact, even a little dull. Then he came to the APRM. He said a decision had *not* been made in Rome regarding the secretariat, only a suggestion. And regardless, that suggestion—that the ECA take on the role—needed to be reconsidered. He then launched into a discourse on the reasons why, which boiled down to the fact the ECA acted on behalf of the United Nations, a global body. Citing the history of conditionalities imposed on African countries from outside the continent, specifically the World Bank and IMF, he said there was no need to risk more coming through the UN. Peer review should not be overseen by the ECA, he said, because "the ECA is not an African institution."

The comments cut deeply. *Of course* the ECA was an African institution; it was the oldest African institution! But it was not, however, an institution controlled by the heads of state, as the new AU would be. We had proceeded to plan out a peer review process with the assumption that it would exist alongside NEPAD but independently from the AU's political processes. That's simply not what Obasanjo or some other heads of state on the HSGIC had in mind.

Even though I was in the room, I didn't respond. I wasn't at the main table and it would have been a breach of etiquette and protocol. Meles did reply, since he had been the one to formally recommend the ECA as secretariat. He pointed out that such a move would effectively reverse two decisions—the criteria initially set forth by the HSGIC in Abuja, which called for an independent secretariat; and the agreement made in Rome, to place the secretariat within the ECA.

Obasanjo wasn't swayed. Even if we made the decision, he said, nothing would prevent us from changing it.

On July 8 in Durban, the day of the final session of the OAU and the day before the first session of the new African Union, the full assembly of heads of state and government considered and approved peer review, establishing the APRM. The whole summit was a grand occasion, but moving forward with peer review felt especially momentous, even if for me the past couple of days had taken an unexpected turn.

Shortly thereafter, the HSGIC located the APRM secretariat in Midrand, South Africa, not far from the NEPAD secretariat. Ultimately, the APRM's oversight fell under the direction of the African Union—opening up the possibility for plenty of potential conflicts of interests, the close political affiliation I had wanted to avoid. I always believed the most effective way to introduce peer review to Africa was to keep it as free as possible from the continent's complicated politics. I also worried that the absence of an independent administrator would limit constructive criticism and possibly diminish the role of civil society.

Initially, the decision to sideline the ECA in the APRM process really stung, but I realized in time that it was inevitable. As I've said, compromises had to be made, and placing the secretariat in Midrand sent a reassuring message of unity to African leaders already unsure of whether NEPAD was a "true" African initiative. Once the early idea of a recovery program independent of the AU was abandoned, then it stood to reason that the program's core component would not be overseen by another institution. The decision was in line with Obasanjo's thinking, and it also gave Mbeki a clear political win.

The events in Durban didn't play out as I had expected, but they didn't push the ECA out of the picture entirely, either. In fact, peer review was such a thoroughly conceived mechanism for accountability on Africa's part that attention soon turned to ways to hold the donors' feet to the fire with equal measure. That was the other side of the mutual accountability principle, and it quickly became a priority. At the ECA, we pivoted from peer review to working even more closely with the OECD to bring some donor-side definition to mutual accountability. The HSGIC, including Obasanjo, encouraged and supported our efforts.

◆　◆　◆　◆

In 2018, the African Peer Review Mechanism turned 15 years old. Thirty-seven countries had joined as members, and 21 had undergone the full review process at least once. Of the reviews that had been published, many were well received and generally helpful in their assessments. Naturally, the findings differed from country to country, but some common challenges—in addition to obvious ones such as peace and stability—became evident: job creation and training, capacity constraints, gender inequality, and poor service delivery, to name a few. These issues are all matters of socioeconomic development, so while the process was intended to focus on political, economic, and corporate governance, its scope proved capable of monitoring shortfalls and advancements on a much larger scale. This was encouraging. Unfortunately, the encouraging aspects of the APRM in those first 15 years were few and far between.

Interest and enthusiasm certainly were high in the beginning, though. Almost two dozen countries acceded to peer review shortly after its launch in 2003. A few years later, the *South African Journal of International Affairs* called the APRM "a landmark achievement for Africa" and said it was "potentially the most important reform to ever emerge from the continent." Kojo Busia, a leading expert and author on peer review, wrote in 2010 that the APRM had been a milestone not only for governance reform but also for "institutionalizing domestic accountability practices across the continent."

The enthusiasm proved to be short-lived.

My biggest concern in the aftermath of Durban was not that the ECA had been sidelined, but that the APRM would not be able to make a quick impact with its administrative processes tied so closely to the brand new African Union, which would have to gain its own footing. My concern wasn't too far off the mark. Ghana, the first country to sign up for the APRM, was not reviewed until January 2006—three and a half years after Durban. Those were key years of lost momentum, a frustrating and sluggish start that could have been avoided.

Despite a flurry of activity over the next few years, the entire process soon fell into disarray. Between 2008 and 2016, the APRM secretariat did not have a permanent CEO, reviews ground to a halt, country reports were delayed, and, amid allegations and concerns of financial mismanagement at the secretariat, donor funds and member state dues dried up. Seventeen reviews were carried out within the first decade, but most states failed to implement the national programs that the reviews produced.

Additionally, the review process itself grew problematic, having mushroomed into a much more burdensome procedure than it ever needed to be with multiple layers of bureaucracy and reviews that sometimes dragged on for years.[7] Those lengthy reviews sometimes produced country reports in excess of 450 pages, which were daunting to read and made pertinent information hard to find—an added roadblock when follow-through was already an issue.

One of the best examples is Kenya, which teetered on the edge of civil war following a disputed presidential election in 2007. Kenya's peer review, which was completed in 2006, raised the issue of mounting political and civic tensions, but some country leaders didn't bother to read it, and the leaders who did chose to ignore its warnings. A few years later, Kenya created a new constitution that incorporated a few of the findings from its peer review, but not all.

South Africa offers another example where the review process yielded good and bad results. The draft country report presented to President Mbeki's cabinet in November 2006 highlighted violent crime, fueled by growing income disparities and slow service delivery, as South Africa's number one priority, and listed more than a dozen threats to the country's stability. Xenophobia, the report concluded, was on the verge of undermining South Africa's economic governance capabilities. The good news is that the peer review findings were accurate, as widespread crime and violence surged throughout 2007 and 2008. The bad news, obviously, is that government inaction, based on a disregard for the review's findings, allowed the violence to reach crisis proportions.

There have been successes, especially in the early years when enthusiasm for the APRM was higher. Following its inaugural review, Ghana set about implementing a national action plan with numerous objectives that were directly attributed to the APRM, including new legal protections for whistleblowers and those with disabilities, a reduction in corporate taxes, and revisions to the Supreme Court and president's cabinet. In Nigeria, which was reviewed in 2008, President Umaru Yar'Adua, who succeeded Obasanjo in office, openly agreed with the review findings that poor diversity management had led to intrastate strife and that endemic corruption was a problem, and he underscored his commitment to improving the shortcomings.

One of the more encouraging attributes of the APRM has been the involvement of civil society organizations and the private sector in contributing to national assessments, though the level and extent of their engagement has varied by country. The South Africa assessment, for example, was dogged by controversy from the start because civil society was given less time than government ministries to complete their assessments, and the minister who served as the review's in-country coordinator refused to allow public review of the report before it was finalized. Not to overlook such problems, but non-state actors have at least played a role. In addition to assessment contributions, think tanks have helped conduct research, while civic groups have used review findings to advocate for greater government transparency and accountability.

Still, the APRM remains a mixed bag. Not a single state was reviewed between 2013 and 2016. The process seemed to have run its course. But much like NEPAD, the initiative with which it was inextricably linked, the APRM is evolving to try and live up to its potential.

In June 2015, Kenya President Uhuru Kenyatta was unanimously elected by his peers to serve as the chair of the APR Forum, the name of the committee of heads of state and government from participating APRM countries. Afterward, he delivered a blistering address over what he saw as the APRM's lackluster performance and its "almost rudderless slide into oblivion" in Africa's governance conversations. Among Kenyatta's biggest concerns were the APRM's ongoing financial woes, waning interest from development partners, a general decline in enthusiasm within Africa, and a seeming inability to truly transform leadership across the continent. Kenyatta spoke eagerly of wanting to revitalize the process and make it more effective.

A turning point came in January 2016 with the appointment of a new CEO, South African Professor Eddy Maloka, who quickly embarked on the revitalization strategy Kenyatta had prescribed. Maloka doubled the staff at the secretariat in Midrand, launched the first five-year strategic plan in the APRM's history, pushed for an overhaul of the review process to make it faster and less expensive, increased member state fees, supervised an update to the original 2003 founding document, and began a public campaign to get non-member countries to join up. In 2017, Maloka oversaw the first four new country review missions since 2013 as well as two second-generation reviews in Kenya and Uganda.

As part of the AU reforms introduced by Rwandan President Paul Kagame in 2018, the APRM's official operating structure changed. The mechanism was, at last, fully incorporated into the African Union as a specialized agency and given an expanded mandate that included alignment with the AU's African Governance Architecture and African Peace and Security Architecture platforms. It was also charged with tracking implementation progress of governance-related aspects of the AU's Agenda 2063 and the UN's Sustainable Development Goals—though the specific procedures as to how it would go about doing so were not laid out, making it more of a high-level endorsement for strengthening the APRM and its monitoring capacity than a direct action, at least at the time.

It's encouraging that African leaders are willing to stand behind the APRM, but it will take far more than revitalizing enthusiasm for the process or restructuring its status to give it the "teeth" once envisioned. Foremost, it takes political will and leadership to ensure that all those necessary administrative changes—faster and more efficient reviews, more financial resources, a cohesive vision—actually lead to something tangible in the policy space. If reviews and recommendations are shunted aside or ignored, what good are they?

Consider that even with all the renewed momentum to support the APRM, only 10 heads of state out of the 37 member countries attended the January 2018 APR Forum—and that was considered an impressive turnout compared to previous years. As Steven Gruzd and Yarik Turianskyi of the South African Institute of International Affairs wrote in a policy brief reviewing the APRM's first 15 years: "Without political commitment to the APRM at the heads of state level, it is difficult to imagine the effective functioning of the mechanism, including honest and thorough peer reviews or the implementation of recommendations."

Over time, the APRM has proven to be an extremely effective tool for diagnosing problems, such as the early examples in Kenya and South Africa, and for encouraging political dialogue, at least according to the researchers who have tried to dig into the closed-door meetings of the heads of state. It has involved civil society in encouraging ways and in some cases demonstrably improved governance issues.

On the downside, the lack of an explicit enforcement mechanism and political follow-through remains a fundamental challenge, and the initial operational weaknesses crippled its potential impact in most countries. In a 2009 report that assessed the APRM's first five years, the secretariat was described as being "dogged by politics" and "lacking in clarity"—and that was before it went eight years without a leader. These issues could have been avoided, and, if they had, the APRM's first 15 years—at least—would have been stronger for it.

My outlook on the APRM remains muddled. Its impact on African development in literal terms—such as policy reform—has fallen short, yet I believe Africa remains better off for having it, flaws and all. It pushed leaders further on accountability than anything to have come before, and as a result it helped accelerate Africa's ownership agenda. That result is not insignificant.

A tremendous amount of energy was expended to put the APRM in place, so I hope the revitalization effort pays off. Over time, African development issues have faded from the forefront of the G8's agenda, but the APRM remains a monument to Africa's embrace of ownership and accountability on the one hand, and a nagging reminder of Africa's propensity for unfulfilled potential on the other.

Notes

1   The other African visits were to Pretoria in February 2002, Dakar in April, and Maputo in May.

2   Bob Fowler's drive and commitment to serve almost cost him his life. In 2008, the UN appointed him special envoy to Niger to help broker a ceasefire between the Niger

government and rebels. One night while traveling, local al-Qaeda fighters cut off Fowler's car and kidnapped him and a colleague—the start of a 130-day captivity in the Sahara, which the two men mercifully survived. Fowler described his ordeal in the book *A Season in Hell*, but he also used his kidnapping to discuss important policy and security issues in the age of the ongoing "war on terror."

3   This process is how the APRM generally worked for at least its first 15 years. As of this writing, the African Union is aware of the need to strengthen the process, which could result in changes to the system. But for historical purposes, the process described here is how the APRM operated.

4   After decades of civil war, Mozambique's political leaders reached out to villages, tribes, and elders to set up localized court proceedings as a successful way of rebuilding their civil society and trust in government.

5   Rwanda remains one of Africa's most successful turnaround stories. During the nadir of its civil war in 1994, as many as 1 million people died in 100 days, per reports. Just 15 years later, Fast Company magazine called the country "a new model of economic development." Rwanda was also one of the first countries to sign up for the APRM when it was introduced.

6   The official title was appended a few months after we presented it to the implementation committee, when the NEPAD secretariat published the document in its final form.

7   Once APRM reviews began in earnest, the process evolved into a multilayered organizational structure, starting with the APR Forum of Heads of State and Government, an offshoot of the NEPAD Heads of State and Government Implementation Committee that ranked as the APRM's highest decision-making body. The APR Forum then appointed a Panel of Eminent Persons, consisting of five to seven distinguished Africans, to oversee the selection and assignment of review teams. The APRM secretariat, meanwhile, served as a technical hub and central home of day-to-day operations. Then there were the National Commissions and National Governing Councils to provide strategic direction. With that many cooks in the kitchen, it's no surprise that implementation suffered.

Chapter 13

If We Were Not Poor
Redefining Roles in the Ongoing Effort to Finance Africa's Development

The rest of us sat listening as Donald Kaberuka, Rwanda's minister of finance, carried on a lively conversation with Horst Köhler, managing director of the International Monetary Fund, and James Wolfensohn, president of the World Bank. Kaberuka was trying to make the point that some IMF programs had too many restrictions, were full of too many conditions, and lacked sufficient fiscal space for African countries to grow their economies to meet the Millennium Development Goals, or MDGs. Frustrated by the responses he was hearing, Kaberuka turned to me and said, "You have to protect me for what I'm about to say." Then he looked back at the most powerful men at the IMF and World Bank and told them point-blank that African countries disliked working with their institutions—but had no other choice. "Gentlemen," he added, "if we were not poor, we would not come to you for help."

That acknowledgement, a surprisingly raw statement that no one saw coming, summed up years of frustration for policymakers in developing African countries: without external lending and aid, there can be no long-term development—but at what point will lenders start treating borrowers as partners and not beggars?

Kaberuka's comments came during a special session of the Big Table, hosted by the World Bank on October 28, 2003. The Big Table events had proven to be a very effective way for African leaders and donors to talk to one another openly, and the idea for this "special" event arose at the conclusion of the previous one, held nine months earlier in Addis Ababa.

Whereas the first Big Table addressed the burgeoning global partnership agenda and the second focused on peer review, Big Table III tackled the thorny concept of mutual accountability, or the need for both sides of the new partnership to keep their promises. It convened amid fading optimism. The previous year, African countries had approved NEPAD and the G8 had promised more help and more money. But just six months later, amid delays and uncertainties, each side had begun to question the other's commitment.

A unanimous takeaway from Big Table III was the need for a follow-up, to be held as early as possible, with an exclusive focus on the IMF and World Bank. Why? Because those institutions controlled the purse strings and because they could help keep donor countries accountable—but as long as their own policies undermined effective aid delivery, they would be seen as part of the problem, not the solution. I immediately set out to make the special session happen.

Given the historic tensions that characterized relations between African countries and the Bretton Woods Institutions, I faced two challenges: first, to get the Bank and IMF to agree to participate, and second, to get both Wolfensohn and Köhler to participate personally. Bringing top decision-makers together for candid and informal dialogue had become the Big Table's calling card. If we were to have a special meeting on financing policies, those two gentlemen needed to be there. Wolfensohn and I had a good relationship and I felt certain he would accept the offer, which he did without hesitation. I wasn't as sure about his counterpart at the IMF, though. I had never met Horst Köhler, and the ECA as an institution had very little interaction with the IMF. So it wasn't clear to me that its staff and upper management had an understanding of our role. Unlike the Bank, the IMF had not participated in previous Big Tables, so it was quite a jump to go from nothing to the very top of the organization.

I decided to pay Köhler a personal visit in Washington, DC. Although I had tremendous respect for the IMF staff and for their analytical skills and professionalism, I knew that the institution was more insular than the Bank and far more formal, regardless of the setting. For instance, it was not uncommon to see Bank representatives on an Africa mission dressed in loose pants and shirtsleeves, attire in line with their hosts' wardrobe but also practical for the hot, humid temperatures of Sub-Saharan Africa. But not so for IMF mission reps, who wore full suits and ties all the time. It was the IMF culture and they didn't deviate.

Köhler received me at his office and listened carefully as I gave him the background to the meeting and what we hoped to achieve. He asked a number of fair questions, but he expressed concern that the "special" session would turn into an IMF-bashing session by African ministers who were displeased over his institution's policies. I assured him that in the spirit of the Big Table, where honesty was encouraged but personal attacks were dissuaded, the discussions would be constructive, even if they got heated. Plus, this Big Table was to be held in Washington rather than Addis or in Europe. It would be in the Bank and IMF's backyard. Köhler remained skeptical, but he agreed to participate.

Since a couple of high-profile events in 2002, including a landmark financing conference in Monterrey, Mexico and the Africa-focused G8 summit in Kananaskis, the issue of financing for development had never been more prevalent. For years it had been swept under the rug or seen as an unpleasant afterthought to exciting action plans. No one wanted to talk specifics about money, and when they did, African policymakers, frustrated by decades of conditions and deliveries that didn't match commitments, would listen with a healthy dose of skepticism, and rightly so. After Monterrey and Kananaskis, where big promises were once again made, African ministers were more adamant than ever that donors follow through. For African countries, this was the flip side to the promise of political and economic reform codified in NEPAD.

Altogether, nine African finance ministers and 11 ministers and senior officials from the OECD countries attended, in addition to Köhler and Wolfensohn and other top officers, such as two senior-level Americans, one each from the Treasury Department and USAID. It was an impressive array of dignitaries and experts on both sides, including four of the then "heavyweights" among African finance ministers—Nigeria's Ngozi Okonjo-Iweala, South Africa's Trevor Manuel, Mozambique's Luísa Diogo, and Rwanda's Donald Kaberuka. Among those on the development partner side were Hilary Benn, who had only a few days earlier been appointed as the UK's secretary of state for international development; and Sweden's Ruth Jacoby and the Netherlands' Agnes van Ardenne, both of whom had assumed their posts the year before. Many of the Western ministers from the pre-NEPAD days had moved on and their replacements came on to the scene with the partnership framework established, if not operating smoothly.

Because of the issues at stake and the influence of participants, I considered this to be the "mother" of all the Big Tables, it was a really big deal for the people in that room to be sitting together at the World Bank talking about money. When I joined the Bank almost 20 years earlier, I never imagined being in that seat, sitting at the table, chairing that kind of meeting. I had chaired or organized a lot of meetings over the years. This one carried as much weight as any.

So there we sat, about two dozen of us seated around the large conference table in the boardroom of the World Bank, with me chairing and Kaberuka coming dangerously close to the bashing that I had promised Köhler would not happen. In all honesty, I had been nervous for weeks about how the meeting would go and how to steer the discussion in such a way as to keep it true to the Big Table spirit but away from animosity.

But a funny thing happened after Kaberuka's outburst: the table came alive.

That was a good thing, because the first hour did not go well. The biggest Big Table of all was shaping up to be a big flop. The participants guarded their comments and the discussion lacked the necessary looseness. But along came Kaberuka, who was never one to pull his punches or avoid saying what he really felt. Once he had told Köhler and Wolfensohn that Africans wouldn't bother looking their way "if we were not poor," everything changed. Kaberuka's frankness and his honesty broke the ice by addressing the elephant in the room—that all the grandiose talk of global partnerships wouldn't amount to much if donors didn't change their policies. Understanding what that meant and how to approach it not only defined the Big Table special session in Washington—it came to define global development dialogue in the early part of the new century.

By the time I closed the meeting, we had reached consensus on some pretty significant financing concerns. We agreed that current aid flows to Africa fell far short of what was needed to achieve the MDGs but that achieving the MDGs required more than additional aid dollars; it also required an honest examination of the many domestic and external factors that continued to stunt Africa's growth. On the question of aid effectiveness, we underscored the need for recipient countries to have better policies in place and for donors to provide more coherent assistance in direct support of the MDGs. Finally, Köhler and Wolfensohn promised to push for more flexibility with IMF and Bank practices, reiterating their commitment to local African ownership over the development agenda. Considering the players involved, these agreements really were notable.

Following a rocky start, the well-established spirit of the Big Table prevailed after all. The cooperation and camaraderie thrilled me. And the goodwill continued into the night with a group dinner hosted by Wolfensohn. The mood was relaxed and comfortable as we left most of the work behind and simply enjoyed each other's company. Wolfensohn thanked us for coming and said how valuable he found the day's discussions.

He acknowledged my efforts in bringing everyone together in the first place, and I appreciated the kind words.

In some ways, I viewed the Big Table special session as a follow-up to the 1999 Conference of African Finance Ministers that the ECA had convened to talk about many of the very same issues. That conference, "Challenges for Financing Africa's Development", focused primarily on the amount of official development assistance (ODA) coming into Africa. But we organized it to reinforce the idea that financing for development was about more than ODA flows. Aid certainly needed to be a big part of the overall picture, but aid was dropping for various reasons. Africa still had to move forward, regardless of donor priorities, so we focused on other ways to push Africa's economic and social development in the absence or decline of aid—increasing foreign direct investments, mobilizing domestic resources, addressing the debt crisis, reversing capital flight, and pushing international trade as a driver of development, among other examples. The overarching point: aid couldn't be ignored, but neither could it be the sole foundation for Africa's development financing.

On this topic, the ECA was a little ahead of the curve. The 1999 financing conference got African policymakers talking seriously about their financial options and constraints for meeting ambitious poverty reduction goals ahead of much larger events to come in Monterrey and Kananaskis—and ahead of the G8 agreement in Cologne one month later to speed up the debt reduction process. So in addition to continuing a dialogue that the ECA helped hasten, the Big Table at the World Bank also served as a review of the progress made in the years since and as a benchmark for moving forward with commitments made.

Later that night, after Wolfensohn's dinner, I had trouble sleeping. A couple of thoughts kept running through my head.

The first one had everything to do with me. My time at the ECA would soon be winding down and the day's events had put the circular nature of my journey into perspective. Years before, when I still worked at the Bank, I had occasionally been called to sit at the same table in the same conference room for discussions on Bank policies and lending that had, for better or worse, impacted Africa. The Bank's relations with other institutions were not great. The push for external collaboration was just beginning, although the idea that African ministers might one day descend on the Bank's top leadership en masse would have seemed so far-fetched then as to be foolish. But this day, it had happened, and it didn't seem far-fetched at all. At that moment, all the blood, sweat, and tears seemed worth it.

The second thought that kept me awake was much less personal but much more meaningful: despite the day's productive dialogue and ambitious agreements, what, if anything, might actually come of it? Over the previous year or so, the principle of mutual accountability had proven to be a little too soft to govern the global partnership, and any future progress most certainly would hinge on demonstrable improvements to Africa's aid and financing architecture. Africa was at the apex of its time atop the world's development agenda, but money remained the bottom line. Africa needed more of it and more control over what it got. And though I was deeply involved in different aspects of the aid dialogue, I still had no idea where it was all going, where it would take Africa, or where it would lead me.

◆ ◆ ◆ ◆

Historically, partnerships between donors and aid recipients in Africa had existed in name only. No matter how substantial the ODA flows, strings were always attached and deliveries were often unreliable. Aid had never been cooperative, but it was still better than nothing. But as political forces realigned in the 1990s, the flows began to dry up. Official development assistance to Africa—the continent with the highest rates of poverty and the largest number of least-developed countries—declined from $16 billion in 1996 to $12.7 billion in 2000. In Sub-Saharan Africa, where most of the continent's poor reside, the share of ODA declined from 37 percent to 27 percent during the 1990s. The rich world was putting its money elsewhere.

Why? There were several factors, including a perceived ineffectiveness of aid, an erosion of aid mandates in donor capitals, and budget constraints of donor countries. The United States and other countries experienced an abrupt and harsh recession in the early part of the decade, and by the time economies were humming along again, aid flows had already been cut. Some donors weren't in a hurry to reprioritize aid because in many countries it was tough to make a compelling case for its success.

The Cold War's conclusion also played a role. The thawing of East–West relations had a profound effect on some state budgets that were being propped up by one side or the other. The Soviet Union no longer existed, while the West no longer needed to fund Communist "firewall" governments. This change didn't affect every Sub-Saharan country, but it did affect many of the weakest, such as the Democratic Republic of Congo, then known as Zaire and ruled by Mobutu Sese Seko, a dictator who openly capitalized on Cold War tensions.

But as the world's sociopolitical landscape changed, so did Africa's. Once the post-Cold War wave of democratic governance had moved into the continent—and swept out some of the more unsavory strongmen— arguments for more development assistance aid became a little more palatable to Western powers. At the same time, and for many of those same donors, Africa's debt crisis had become harder to ignore. Soon, creditors came to the sobering conclusion that most of the loans could simply never be repaid.

In 1996, the Bank and the IMF led the charge on the Heavily Indebted Poor Country initiative, which acknowledged that multilateral debts would also need forgiveness. The structured program helped bring debt reduction into mainstream development talks by linking relief to future financing plans, and it also paved the way for the large-scale debt relief to come in the following decade. Africa's soaring debt and crippling poverty, coupled with the rise of a new generation of democratically elected leaders who promised more transparency and better systems, rekindled donor interest because it seemed like joint solutions—actual aid partnerships—might be the best answer. In May 1996, the OECD's Development Assistance Committee, or DAC, adopted its seminal paper, *Shaping the 21st Century: The Role of Development Cooperation*, which emphasized cooperative strategies over straight assistance. It also outlined demand-driven targets that soon formed the foundation for the MDGs. *Shaping the 21st Century* made a partnership approach seem both appealing and urgent.

Indeed, as the new millennium approached, there was no shortage of international initiatives aimed at boosting the ODA and improving cooperation between the rich countries and Africa. Sweden's Partnership Africa Conference, held in 1997, ushered in a sweeping new policy approach in which the Swedish government explicitly advocated for African countries to be treated as autonomous partners, not donor recipient countries. In Japan, the Tokyo International Conference on African Development, first held in 1993, proved so successful that subsequent TICADs followed every five years. Sweden and Japan were far from alone. The United States had the US Growth and Opportunity Act, intended to increase African access to American markets. Canada's "Africa Direct" initiative aimed to establish direct links between Canada and developing African democracies. Germany, emerging from its post-unification period, put Africa squarely on its agenda in 2000 by intensifying its high-level diplomacy, organizing African conferences, and vowing assistance. "Africa shall not become the forgotten continent," the German parliament stated.

Italy also got in on the act, using the occasion of the first European Union-Africa Summit in April 2000 to announce a new national strategy on Africa. That summit, held over two days in Cairo, was a notable milestone; it marked the first time that leaders and ministers from the EU met as a political entity with African countries to talk about the continent's political and economic needs. Sixty-six countries participated, and it produced a declaration that put the most pressing issues—external debt, integration into the world economy, conflict prevention, and global resource mobilization—on the table.

The ECA's 1999 financing conference had covered similar ground the year before, albeit on a continental scale. We'd been hammering on these issues for years, but after the success of the conference we stepped up our research efforts on aid, debt, and trade—the nexus of Africa's financing woes—even more. The increased focus on financing resulted in a higher profile for the ECA, which is how I got involved with the OECD's Tidewater retreats described in Chapter 10. By the time we launched the Big Table meetings, it was clear that Africans and donors alike were ready to put a renewed emphasis on financing for development, which is where NEPAD and the new partnership came in.

◆　◆　◆　◆

When NEPAD arrived, it was a game-changer. It forced donors to deliver on their promises or risk being exposed as less than sincere. Under the agreed framework, development partners were expected to do more than make big pronouncements or keep throwing good money after bad. In other words, in return for African commitments to stronger governance (and the APRM), donors had to pick up their game as well. In general, that boiled down to three improvements African countries needed to see: more aid, effective aid, and coherent aid.

For about the first 30 years of Africa's postcolonial era, when donors talked about aid, they mostly talked about volume. As African policymakers and leaders grew more assertive in seeking ownership over their own development agendas, the flexibility and control over aid became as important as the amount. It was no secret that Africa needed sizable increases in financial assistance to tackle the aggressive targets of the MDGs. But money alone wouldn't suffice. So many of the factors associated with receiving aid—transaction costs, budget support, conditionality, to name a few—needed reforming on the donor side. We talked a lot about "untying" aid, or removing usage restrictions imposed by donors. Along those same lines, African countries needed donors to align their assistance programs to country priorities. Just as important, they needed donors to align their programs with each other. As donor countries proliferated from the 1990s into the 2000s, so did the incoherence of African donor policy. By agreeing to support NEPAD, donors agreed to refocus efforts to fix all these problems.

So as African leaders were busy putting the final touches on NEPAD, the donor countries were looking to combine their separate African initiatives into something uniform. Allow me to step back and recap a bit from the previous chapter. At their 2001 summit in Genoa, G8 leaders agreed to prepare the joint Africa Action Plan to implement commitments made at previous summits and at the United Nations. To drive this effort, each G8 leader selected a personal representative for Africa, or APR. This was the group, chaired by Canadian diplomat Robert Fowler, that had visited the ECA headquarters in December 2001 and locked on to the idea of enhanced partnerships—an ECA model of prioritizing assistance based on the capacity and commitment of countries to put it to the most immediate, effective use. With African leaders planning to present their NEPAD framework at the June 2002 G8 summit in Kananaskis, the G8 wanted to be sure to make a definitive statement of its own.

The action plan was intended to be the collective voice of G8, but some voices were louder than others, specifically those in the United Kingdom and Canada. In the UK, Prime Minister Tony Blair seemed determined to light a fire under the rest of the donor world, while Canada, which had always been a reliable development partner for Africa, wanted to step up even more since it was the host country of the upcoming summit.

Blair had long contemplated a major UK government initiative on Africa. In late 2000 and early 2001, his government started to get more serious about it. But after a few months of preparatory work—which incorporated some of the ideas I first laid out in the "Global Compact" speech to African ministers—the plan was shelved in favor of the larger G8 effort. At the same time, Blair also had his team back off to give African leaders more space to fully develop NEPAD. Blair really did want Africa to take the lead in this process, but he also wanted to rally other countries to the cause. In October 2001, he gave one of the most passionate calls to action on behalf of Africa to ever have come from a leader of the developed world. Using an annual political address to the British Labour Party as his platform, Blair spoke out forcefully in favor of the new partnership approach that NEPAD embodied and he argued that everyone had a "moral duty" to help stabilize the continent. "The state of Africa is a scar on the conscience of the world," he said. The phrase became an immediate rallying cry.

At the same time, Canada was making preparations to take the lead on implementing whatever final plan came out of Kananaskis. In December 2001, the Canadian minister of finance announced the creation of the $500 million Canada Fund for Africa. According to Canadian officials, the fund was established to support the NEPAD proposal and the G8's eventual action plan. During this same time, I formed great relationships with two of my Canadian counterparts: Bob Fowler, and Paul Hunt who was then a vice president and leading figure in CIDA, the Canadian International Development Agency. As CIDA expanded its focus on Africa, Hunt came to rely on the ECA's institutional knowledge. We became strong allies.[1] Canadian Prime Minister Jean Chrétien also put his weight behind our efforts. The idea of enhanced partnerships and peer review as the primary mechanism for measuring which countries rose to that rank really captivated him. The G8 leaders had made it perfectly clear that producing their own plan for Africa depended on Africa developing a peer review. Chrétien was among the most vocal in favor. As the Toronto Sun described it, peer review became his "mantra."

But as Kananaskis drew closer, no one knew what specific commitments, particularly regarding the level of ODA flows, the G8 would be making to support Africa's efforts. By this time, African leaders had put a price tag on NEPAD—approximately $64 billion. It was a hefty sum. So who would pay for it?

All the pro-Africa rhetoric from donors sowed seeds of confusion, even among those who were the most involved. At one point in early 2002, I had an eye-opening conversation with a member of the NEPAD steering committee.

"In terms of this partnership, and since NEPAD is going to cost $64 billion," he began, "will that amount be made available to us immediately?"

I had to shake my head. "No," I said, "It doesn't quite work that way." Whatever form of the eventual financing, I explained, donors were not simply going to give Africa a $64 billion check and wish us well on our way.

Even at the top political levels, African leaders who knew better than to expect multibillion dollar lump sum payments still had legitimate concerns over the details of the G8's plan and whether it would be a bold enough response to NEPAD. I shared the same concerns. So many broken promises in the past were justified on the grounds that African governments had failed to meet various requirements, particularly with governance. The APRM, which donors had championed to give NEPAD its "teeth," was being designed specifically to correct those shortfalls. But what would give the G8's plan a similar bite? How would mutual accountability apply in reality, not just in theory, to donor responsibility?

These were the questions that African heads of state and their top advisors were asking—and they had every reason to. Meanwhile, African civil society, already skeptical of NEPAD due to their lack of involvement in the design, began to grow increasingly restless when figures like $64 billion were tossed around. They wanted to know if leaders were about to sell Africa to the donors.

Sheer volume offered the most immediate way for donor countries to show their commitment. The level of resources pledged by the G8 to support NEPAD and the MDGs needed to be significant, dramatic, and worth the effort being put toward the new partnership. Fortunately, an opportunity had presented itself.

In March 2002, three months before the Kananaskis summit, the International Conference on Financing for Development convened in Monterrey, Mexico. It was the first UN-hosted event to address global financing for developing countries, and it was groundbreaking in scale— more than 800 participants—and in structure: a "quadripartite" dialogue between governments, civil society, the business community, and institutional stakeholders. The outcome was the Monterrey Consensus, in which the rich countries of the world went on record in support of a "fully inclusive and equitable global economic system."

The UN touted the agreement for its official recognition of, first, the need for developing countries to take responsibility for their own poverty reduction and, second, the necessity for rich nations to show their support through open trade and more financial resources. On a global level, the Monterrey Consensus was distinct, but in Africa we'd been talking about those issues for years. When I mentioned earlier that the ECA was ahead of the curve, I meant it: among the six focus areas embraced in the Monterrey Consensus, four were directly parallel to the objectives that emerged from our 1999 financing conference.[2]

At Monterrey, world leaders had promised substantial increases in ODA that were expected to total $12 billion year by year. Increasing aid flows had been an overriding objective, but Monterrey also emphasized that achieving the MDGs demanded "a new partnership between developed and developing countries"—a direct incorporation of the philosophy behind NEPAD. The G8 countries were big players in Monterrey and, with the Kananaskis summit around the corner, the two events were naturally being linked as milestones in development financing and policy. So why not link them even further?

This line of thinking led to a bold idea: that at least half of the proposed $12 billion increase should go to Africa. Fowler understood why African leaders wanted to see a more substantial commitment from donors. But he didn't know if he could get his fellow G8 reps on board in such a short time; they only had a few weeks to finalize the details of the Africa Action Plan. He made a good point, so I suggested he call Kofi Annan to get his endorsement on the record. I knew Annan liked the idea because he and I had talked about it. I wanted to help Bob build the necessary support, so I also reached out to Valerie Amos, the G8 APR from the United Kingdom. She and I had gotten to know and respect each other after her visit to Addis with the rest of the APRs the previous year.[3] She seemed receptive, and I took that as a good sign.

When G8 leaders met on June 27, 2002, to formally unveil the Africa Action Plan, the draft had already been finalized and details agreed upon by their personal representatives. That's how these things go. They are choreographed and ceremonial events to a certain extent, but they have to be. The most powerful men and women in the world don't gather to nitpick fine details of a major plan. But they do debate and consider the broad parameters and that's what happened in Kananaskis. I was honored to be there to witness it.

The G8 invited the four NEPAD founding leaders—Presidents Obasanjo, Wade, Mbeki, and Bouteflika—to the summit for a special consultation on Africa, which also included a lunch and plenty of photo opportunities. Kofi Annan was going, and he asked me to accompany him. A lot of people attended. All the heads of state were in one room and then everyone else—their personal representatives, staff, advisors, and special guests—sat in another. After we finished eating, the special session on Africa began. It was a closed-door meeting, with no more than a few dozen of us in the room. Each G8 leader had a representative or aide and then the four African heads of state. A few dignitaries were there, including Kofi Annan; I attended as one of his guests. I wasn't there to speak, just to listen.

As the host head of state, Canada's Chrétien chaired the meeting. It was a really energetic discussion, with US President George W. Bush, Tony Blair, and others asking the African leaders specific questions on issues of peace, security, and especially governance. Obasanjo, Wade, Mbeki, and Bouteflika were respectful but determined in their exchanges with the world leaders, who were genuinely engaged in the proceedings. After about two hours, it was all over. The meeting ended, everyone shook hands, and the G8 Africa Action Plan was official. All the work over the past few years geared toward getting the donor world to accept a new relationship with Africa—and make new aid commitments to underpin that relationship—came to a head.

In the final plan, the G8 agreed to build a new partnership "based on mutual responsibility and respect." The document praised NEPAD as a "bold and clear-sighted vision" for Africa and referred to itself as a response designed to lay a solid foundation for future cooperation. It also recognized the importance of peer review and incorporated language in direct support of enhanced partnerships, stating that the G8 would work with countries that fell short of NEPAD standards but were committed to showing improvement. And then, in the ninth paragraph, came a crucial reference to the Monterrey Consensus:

> *By 2006, these new commitments will increase ODA by a total of US$12 billion per year. Assuming strong African policy commitments, and given recent assistance trends, we believe that in aggregate half or more of our new development assistance could be directed to African nations that govern justly, invest in their own people, and promote economic freedom.*

The provision had made it into the plan after all, though with a gently phrased "could be directed" rather than a more definitive "will be." I later learned that it had provoked a contentious, last-minute debate among the G8 APRs. But Bob Fowler really liked the idea, so he pushed hard for it. With strong support from Valerie Amos, he got the full group to agree. I congratulated Fowler on helping secure a big win for Africa: an extra $6 billion per year.

Also in the final plan: a special mention of the ECA's efforts on peer review and our relationship with the OECD. A few weeks earlier, the NEPAD Heads of State and Government Implementation Committee (HSGIC) had agreed that the ECA should oversee the African Peer Review Mechanism as an independent body—something that we all knew the G8 APRs wanted, and the implied course of action at the time of Kananaskis. In less than a month, however, the HSGIC reversed its decision and placed the secretariat in South Africa, implicitly tying its operations to the African Union. As I described in the previous chapter, I didn't like the decision because I felt it would undermine the peer review process in the long run. But I also found it surprising to see how quickly African leaders tossed aside an important element of the new partnership agreement before the ink could dry. The location of the APRM secretariat wasn't going to be a deal-breaker, but it had been an understood part of the deal.

And yet, the shift on peer review was a bit of a harbinger of post-Kananaskis tap-dancing as both sides kept a wary eye on the other, their public displays of goodwill tempered by a lifetime of lingering doubts.

◆   ◆   ◆   ◆

It didn't take long for momentum to stall. African leaders adopted NEPAD at the inaugural session of the African Union, held just a few weeks after conclusion of the Kananaskis summit, but implementation roadblocks remained. Chief among them: finalizing the actual processes of a peer review system. That took time, and as the months rolled on, the G8 countries grew impatient at what they perceived to be inadequate progress. Some G8 officials also began to question whether African leaders were really committed to NEPAD's core principles of good governance and peace and security. For them, the true test of African leaders' commitment boiled down to how the new African Union would deal with Zimbabwe, a country in serious political and economic crisis.

Robert Mugabe had kept a tight grip on power since 1980, after a British-brokered peace agreement ended a civil war and led to Zimbabwe's independence. One of Africa's longest-tenured leaders, Mugabe was an unwelcome throwback to the days of African despots. After he was re-elected in 2002 in a vote marred by violence and charges of fraud, the United States imposed economic sanctions against Zimbabwe; the government's relations with the UK were even worse. Zimbabwe had become a political flashpoint. That there were no signs of pressure on Mugabe from the new African Union—and no signs of collective action among African leaders—riled Western donors.

Meanwhile, on the flip side, African leaders grew more and more frustrated that their development partners seemed to be assigning outsized importance to the political governance aspect of NEPAD at the expense of everything else, including the pending peer review process. They bristled at the assumption that they were expected to carry out the foreign policy desires of the West. The frustrations built up, and they only amplified the original doubts that the G8 would give Africa ownership space *and* stand by its commitments.

The warning signs were evident right away, so the ECA began contemplating a next step before tensions accelerated. Our conclusion? That adherence to the mutual accountability principle should be measured in its own right, something that the APRM alone could not do. A mutual monitoring mechanism needed to be put in place that would ensure both sides stayed accountable to the other.

We outlined the basic concept in broad terms. First, tracking any progress under NEPAD required core indicators of country performance and development outcomes, so the broad issues already under consideration for the APRM—political representation, institutional effectiveness, economic and corporate governance—also would be applicable in this context. Second, additional indicators would be needed to measure how closely and consistently donor countries adhered to their promises on ODA flows, policy coherence, debt relief, trade, and support of country-led development strategies.

The idea of a mutual review quickly gained traction. I spoke to Richard Carey, deputy director of the OECD-DAC, and we agreed that our two institutions could work together to build out the concept. African leaders, particularly Obasanjo and the other NEPAD officials, were clamoring for some way to hold donors' feet to the fire, so they embraced the idea. At its November 3, 2002 meeting, the HSGIC underscored the need for a mutual review and made a direct request that the ECA and OECD "urgently conclude work on the institutional framework" for it.

The third Big Table convened a few months later in Addis Ababa to address a singular question: as development partners, how do we keep each other honest? This is the meeting that laid the groundwork for the special session at the World Bank later in the year, but it was eventful in other ways as well. For starters, it gave donor representatives and African leaders their first chance to talk about the post-Kananaskis frustrations directly with one another. Considering that the previous Big Table in Amsterdam had focused extensively on peer review and issues of African accountability, I wanted to put a bigger spotlight on donor responsibility and the emerging dialogue around aid effectiveness, or the idea that aid *quality* mattered as much as aid *quantity*.

Among the 30 or so guests were many Big Table regulars, including Rwanda's Donald Kaberuka, Ethiopia's Sufian Ahmed, Britain's Clare Short, Norway's Hilde Johnson, and Canada's Bob Fowler. But there were plenty of new faces integral to the discussion at hand. Nigeria's Aluko-Olokun represented the NEPAD steering committee. The United States, the largest G8 donor country, sent Andrew Natsios, the administrator of USAID, the US Agency for International Development. And I issued a special invitation to Ethiopian Prime Minister Meles Zenawi, an exceptionally thoughtful and forthright leader.

True to his reputation, Meles deconstructed a litany of problems with the onerous business of donor assistance: the bureaucratic requirements, the contradictory conditions, the lack of clear criteria for compliance, the process of tying aid to the purchase of goods and services from donor countries, and the practice of seeking political influence through assistance. All these issues and more imperiled the effective use of aid, Meles argued, and they needed to be addressed alongside any discussion of ODA flows. His ultimate point was that donor accountability for development financing meant so much more than big commitments. It was the crux of the burgeoning aid effectiveness argument.

Meles' discourse fell on receptive ears. Everyone at the table, including the donor officials, shared the same concerns. That doesn't mean everyone agreed on every issue—Clare Short and Andrew Natsios had a memorably heated exchange over the political sensitivities of donors providing budget support to developing countries, for instance. But where we didn't agree on specifics, we agreed on the need to aggressively tackle the broken functions of development financing, which led to the sit down with the World Bank and IMF. The following month, the principles of aid effectiveness were codified at a major meeting in Rome; an even bigger step would come two years later with the landmark Paris Declaration on Aid Effectiveness.

Shortly before convening the third Big Table, the ECA and OECD-DAC completed work on a concept paper that outlined a plan to put mutual review in place. We proposed a periodic assessment on the performance of African countries and donor partners, followed by a report to be prepared every two years that would cover the major policy areas and commitments made by both sides. It also would cover relevant country programs either underway or in need of development to best meet those commitments.[4] The report would be a joint effort of the ECA and OECD-DAC and presented as a matter of course to all interested parties. And for the sake of transparency, it would also be made available to a wide range of stakeholders outside government, including civil society, academia, and business—basically anyone whose work affected Africa's economic and social agendas and its peace and security.

The concept paper was presented to the Big Table as a topic of discussion but also to get feedback. As much as possible, we wanted to build on existing processes without creating new bureaucratic structures, and the exchange we had around that aspect of mutual review was really helpful in considering the specifics of making such an initiative work.

The concept did not sit well with everyone, though. Andrew Natsios said the US had a problem with the idea of mutual review in the first place, but he really didn't like the process we outlined. He said we were overreaching. "If I take this back to Washington and say that I agreed to it, they'll shoot me," he said.

Nevertheless, the majority of the Big Table agreed with the recommendations in the concept paper, and the ministers who were present urged us to move forward. It then fell to Richard Carey and me to get the necessary approval of the OECD-DAC ministerial council and the NEPAD leaders.

I presented our work to Obasanjo and the rest of the HSGIC on March 9, 2003, just four months after they requested it. To my relief, they expressed strong support; it's what they were looking for, Obasanjo said. But Carey had a tougher time when he took the plan back to Paris, because the full OEC-DAC council was not so receptive. Neither the stated desire of NEPAD leaders nor the general consensus reached by donor ministers at the Big Table mattered much to some countries—especially the US, which proved to be the primary roadblock. Initial consultations between USAID, the Treasury Department, and the White House didn't help, either. The unofficial word coming out of Washington, DC was clear: we're not going to agree for someone else to monitor the United States.

Natsios had been right. But at least he hadn't been shot.

The outlook didn't improve much over the next few months. The African heads of state had made their commitment and were waiting on the donor partners to respond. If the DAC ministers ultimately rejected the plan, Carey and I both knew we'd have a big problem on our hands. Not only would it be an embarrassing setback to both sides, it had the potential to inflame African leaders as a gesture of disregard on the part of the donors. A few days before the DAC's ministerial council meeting, OECD officials invited me to Paris to make the case one final time for mutual review. I promised to do what I could. I described how a mutual review would strengthen NEPAD, how it would work, and why Africans felt it was so necessary. Most important, I argued that the DAC's decision would be seen as a reflection of donor credibility—were donors *really* committed to their promises, and to a productive partnership with Africa, or were they not willing to apply to themselves the same standards asked of us?

After answering a few questions, I was ushered out of the room. It was a short presentation, no more than 20 minutes. A few hours later, the council approved the proposal. I don't know to what extent my visit helped influence the final decision, but it certainly couldn't have hurt.

The ECA and OECD released the first review report in October 2005, a few months after my tenure at the ECA expired. For various reasons, momentum stalled after the inaugural review. But since 2009 the two institutions have produced annual reports titled *The Mutual Review of Development Effectiveness in Africa*. In 2012, Africa's ministers of finance, planning, and economic development reaffirmed the value of the exercise.

◆ ◆ ◆ ◆

The Africa Action Plan allowed the world's richest democracies to speak with one voice, but it didn't compel them to act in unison or equal measure. In fact, it called for each G8 country to determine its own method of support for NEPAD countries, although it still encouraged collective action through international organizations, such as the World Bank and the OECD. The push to define mutual accountability boiled down to a desire to keep those individual and collective efforts on track and in some semblance of synchronicity, at least in relation to long-term goals. So in the immediate aftermath of Monterrey and Kananaskis, the big donors continued to pursue their own path. Three countries—Canada, the United States, and the United Kingdom—took the lead.

The Canadians were first out of the blocks with their $500 million Canada Fund for Africa, which the Canadian finance minister announced six months ahead of Kananaskis. Since Canada was the G8 host country that year, the government wanted to take the lead on implementing the eventual African initiative. So the fund was established explicitly to support the NEPAD proposal and the forthcoming Africa Action Plan through a wide range of programs.[5] In fact, the ECA benefited directly from one such program when the Canadians gave us a generous donation to support our African Trade Policy Center. Though never one of the biggest donors, Canada was consistently among the most pro-African. It's no coincidence that Canada wanted to be out front after Kananaskis.

The United States, by contrast, had been one of the biggest donors but for the most part operated on an independent track in its development assistance strategy, hesitant to align its programs and approaches to that of the other OECD countries. Neither NEPAD nor Kananaskis changed that, much to the frustration of its partners. As played out with the mutual review discussions, the United States simply did not want to be too closely bound to the collective decisions or judgments of others. Yet on two of the most pressing development challenges Africa has ever confronted—debt relief and the fight against AIDS—the White House under George W. Bush boasted a stellar record.

The Bush administration increased US aid for development to Sub-Saharan Africa by more than 640 percent. The year after Kananaskis, Bush announced the President's Emergency Plan for AIDS Relief: a prevention, treatment, and research program that made a huge difference in the fight against HIV/AIDS, raising the number of Sub-Saharan Africans getting anti-retroviral drugs from an estimated 100,000 to 2 million in just five years. In 2005, Bush started a $1.2 billion initiative to fight malaria.

It was clear Bush took Africa seriously even before Kananaskis, especially when he dispatched US Treasury Secretary Paul O'Neill on a 10-day "learning tour" of the continent in May 2002 with Bono, the Irish-born lead singer of the band U2. A passionate human rights activist, Bono was one of the many vocal critics of the war in Iraq who nonetheless embraced Bush's outreach to Africa. Bono's legendary lobbying of the US government to "open America's wallet" certainly raised global awareness, as did the trip with O'Neill. Flying across Africa on the same plane that Bush had chartered for his campaign, the unlikely pair visited South Africa, Uganda, Ethiopia, and Ghana. Time magazine called it Africa's biggest road show "since Stanley met Livingstone." Bono wanted O'Neill to see Africa's poverty up close in an effort to lobby for more assistance. O'Neill, a frequent critic of aid, wanted to ensure that current and future US financial commitments were being put to good use. Their trip—which by most accounts proved to be a high-profile success—eventually brought them to Addis Ababa.

Ahead of their arrival, I received a phone call from Jamie Drummond, who earlier that same year had co-founded the advocacy organization DATA (Debt, AIDS, Trade, Africa) with Bono and others. Drummond wanted to talk about the ECA's work and also get my take on Africa's situation. We had a great conversation, and he invited me to a dinner that Bono and O'Neill would be hosting in Addis for a small group of government officials, diplomats, and development experts. The dinner was a relaxed but highly substantive affair, chock-full of discussion on weighty issues: transparency, corruption, institutional capacity, and leadership. For me, it also marked the beginning of a longer association with Bono and the DATA organization. In 2004, DATA and dozens of other NGOs united to form the ONE Campaign, an umbrella organization dedicated to fighting extreme poverty and disease. After leaving the ECA in 2005, I served on the ONE Campaign's advisory board for a few years.

Of all the US programs initiated post-Kananaskis, the one that resonated with me the most was the Millennium Challenge Corporation. Created in 2004, the MCC and the *Compact for African Recovery*—the eventual operational blueprint for NEPAD that the ECA helped prepare—could have come from the same playbook. The objective of the MCC is to improve US aid to developing countries by linking financial assistance to progress in key areas. Under the MCC, the United States began to sign "compacts" with individual governments to underpin its partnership with them.[6] Through 2018, the MCC had invested more than $13 billion worldwide, with a large portion of those resources supporting programs in almost two dozen African countries.

Canada and the US embraced the momentum out of Kananaskis, and so did the UK, even if it wasn't as immediate. Tony Blair still wanted to make a strong statement on Africa, and he found the perfect opportunity a few years down the road, when the United Kingdom would hold the G8 presidency.

After the Kananaskis summit, Africa had remained on the G8 docket, but to varying degrees of importance. At the 2003 summit in Évian, France, the donors and NEPAD leaders agreed to form the African Partnership Forum as a new, collaborative dialogue. Its format, involving top development ministers and African leaders convening for a frank discussion of priorities and challenges, borrowed heavily from the Big Table's proven template. But Africa garnered less attention when the United States and Russia hosted the G8 in 2004 and 2006.

In the years since Kananaskis, Africa's economic outlook had begun to improve, though the foundation of the new partnership—NEPAD and the African Action Plan—seemed less encouraging. NEPAD got off to a slow start, as detailed in previous chapters, while the G8's plan appeared to be losing a little steam as the financing framework it was intended to be. It seemed obvious that the increased aid promised in 2002 would not be enough to prevent Sub-Saharan African countries from missing most MDG targets. In addition, the United States and other G8 donors continued to pursue their own policies.

With the UK set to host the 2005 G8 summit at the Gleneagles Hotel in Auchterarder, Scotland, Tony Blair decided to refocus the group's agenda on Africa. He and his finance minister, Gordon Brown, whose official title was chancellor of the exchequer, jointly began promoting measures for 100 percent debt relief in poor debtor countries and for accelerated aid spending through a new International Finance Facility. But the centerpiece of Blair's strategy was even more sweeping. On February 26, 2004, Blair announced the formation of the Commission for Africa, or CfA, to "take a fresh look at Africa's past, present, and future." Blair said the world should continue to treat Africa as an "absolute priority" in the coming years and not let the recent momentum wane.

In launching the CfA, Blair aimed to have a comprehensive new study to shape the Gleneagles agenda and give more impetus to the goals originally stated in the African Action Plan. But not everyone was sold. Blair announced the CfA when the war in Iraq was in full swing. Britons pretty solidly opposed their country's involvement in Iraq and Blair's popularity took a hit. Cynics looked at his drive on Africa and saw political calculation—a way to show a more humanitarian side. They dismissed the CfA as Blair's attempt to restore his international reputation by taking on a big African initiative in the midst of an unpopular war. Then there were the skeptics, those who didn't question Blair's motivation but rather his reasoning for wanting to tread the same ground that had seemingly been covered.

I did not share those views, certainly not those of the cynics. Blair had wanted to take the lead on an African initiative for years, when he put his own plans on hold in 2000 once the African-proposed MAP, OMEGA, and Global Compact initiatives all appeared within a few months of each other. Blair's people and I were in close contact during this time, so I know the extent of his desire to recalibrate donor approaches to Africa. In December 2001, Blair invited me to speak at 10 Downing Street as part of his Millennium Lecture Series. I came away from that trip impressed by his sincerity and concern and I believed that when he called Africa's treatment "a scar on the conscience of the world," he truly meant it.

So I was very honored when the British ambassador to Ethiopia, Myles Wickstead, a good friend of mine, conveyed a message: Blair wanted me to serve on his commission. I didn't deliberate too long before accepting, especially once I learned that Meles Zenawi and Benjamin Mkapa, Tanzania's president and another leader I greatly respected, would take part. I knew two other African members of the group: Trevor Manuel, South Africa's finance minister, and Linah Mohohlo, the governor of the Bank of Botswana and another good friend.

In addition to himself, Blair appointed three commissioners from the United Kingdom: Gordon Brown, who eventually succeeded Blair as prime minister in 2007; Hilary Benn, the secretary of state for international development; and Bob Geldof, the famous musician behind 1985's Live Aid concert for famine relief. In total, the CfA consisted of 17 members, all seated after careful consideration of geographical and political balance.

Wickstead left his ambassador's post in Addis Ababa to serve as head of the secretariat.[7]

Despite a highly credible, capable, and experienced roster of commissioners, the CfA caused considerable tension between the UK and the G8 personal representatives for Africa. The APRs had spearheaded the Africa Action Plan and they were the primary conduits between African leaders and their G8 partners. The APRs didn't want Blair's new effort to diminish, overshadow, or potentially nullify their own contributions.

But the uncertainty over Blair's commission was more widespread than that. Once my appointment had been announced, I heard from many people, including ones connected to the African Union, NEPAD, and civil society. They weren't sold. I even heard from associates inside Blair's own government who privately questioned the value of yet another African initiative and report. "We've done this already," someone said to me, "so why does Blair want to do it all again?"

Given the lukewarm reception, it's not surprising that Blair's advisors wanted to try and boost the CfA's popularity with high-profile endorsements. Nor was it surprising that they looked to Bono, easily the world's best-known celebrity activist, as their top choice. What *was* surprising, at least to me, was their request that I personally lobby Bono for his support. I had met him, but we hardly knew each other. So I found the UK's request rather awkward. But I had a trip to Dublin, Bono's home town, to meet with Irish government officials already scheduled, so I agreed to do it.

I reached out to Bono ahead of my trip and, somewhat to my surprise, he quickly accepted my invitation. Once I arrived in Dublin, Bono joined me in my hotel room and we spent a few hours one evening talking about Africa's biggest development challenges, particularly the need for debt relief and HIV/AIDS prevention. When the subject turned to the Commission for Africa, however, I could tell that he wasn't entirely sold on the CfA's merits. I offered him the best reasons I could, such as the need to codify concrete policy recommendations in a more detailed, specific manner than what the Africa Action Plan had done.

But Bono just looked at me and shook his head.

"I still don't get it," he said. "Where is the melody?"

I didn't know what he was talking about. Melody? Did he want me to sing?

A few years later, when serving on the ONE Campaign's advisory board, I learned from Bono's colleagues and staff that he frequently equates "melody" with passion. Just like a song needs a good melody to make it memorable—to drive it—so too does a good cause. That's what he was getting at. Eventually, Bono did back the CfA, and without me having to sing for his support—a good outcome for all involved since I've never been able to carry a tune.

All the CfA commissioners recognized the parameters of our participation and that included the need to explain to key players, particularly in the AU and NEPAD, that we would be producing a serious report based on a serious process. The commission held a series of 10 regional consultations across Africa to involve civil society and larger groups as much as possible. For example, one of the commission meetings in Addis coincided with a meeting of several hundred African women preparing for a major women's conference in Beijing. We used that opportunity to discuss with them the different dimensions of gender equality in the context of the commission's work.

The outreach efforts took off, and by the time our work concluded, the CfA enjoyed fairly broad support. Mkapa and Meles used their influence to convince the NEPAD heads of state that the CfA could help turn up the pressure on the global community to put more financial support behind Africa's improving economic condition. Toward the end of 2004, the NEPAD and CfA secretariats cemented their cooperation through various joint appearances and visits. Outside Africa, the CfA secretariat visited every G8 capital for meetings with top officials, and that helped soften the initial skepticism. The European Commission proved very supportive—a few weeks before Gleneagles, traditional EU member states agreed to a 0.7 percent target for ODA flows within the next decade.

One year after its founding, the Commission for Africa released a sweeping, 450-page report, *Our Common Interest,* in March 2005. It covered the full spectrum of problems facing Africa but gave special attention to financing needs and solutions. The report described how the problems were interlocking and required actions that must be taken together on many fronts—an integrated development package focusing on six broad areas: improving state capacity, avoiding conflict and ensuring peace, investing in social services, promoting growth through entrepreneurship, more trade and fairer trade, and more aid and better aid. It reiterated the need for a successful partnership agenda, it called on donors to support African governments through debt relief and market access in addition to aid, and it embraced the principle of mutual accountability that the ECA had long championed. It also called for an independent body to monitor the commitments on both sides of the partnership, a direct link to the mutual review report that the ECA and the OECD would produce.

In a way, *Our Common Interest* did cover well-worn ground. But it also tried to do more. For instance, it emphasized the need for donors to understand Africa's heritage, traditions, and cultures as a means of establishing a better bond with the continent and its people. Its recommendations were clear and concise, free of the usual technical jargon that limits broad appeal of such a document. And it tried to put a price tag on its recommendations, including $10 billion per year for infrastructure, $10 billion for health care, $8 billion for education. The level of detail in the report helped justify the commission's most notable recommendation: to double aid to Africa in the next three to five years.

Given how controversial Blair's commission seemed at the start, I sometimes wondered if I had made the right decision by taking part. But one of the CfA's objectives was to "help fulfill African aspirations for the future by listening to Africans." The opportunity to be part of that at the highest reaches of global deliberation seemed too valuable to pass up. I also viewed it as an excellent vehicle for promoting the ECA's research. And to an extent, that happened.

Early in the process, the CfA hired renowned economist Nicholas Stern as its director of policy and research.[8] Producing the final report was among his main responsibilities. A few weeks after he started the job, Stern spent a day at the ECA. Our staff made presentations in areas that we knew his team would be addressing in the CfA report, and then we followed up with written submissions covering broader issues that we wanted to push, such as gender, ICT, trade, regional integration, and private sector development. We fully immersed him in years of ECA analysis. At the end of his visit, Stern said he was proud to have been associated "for even one day with the outstanding university" that the ECA had become. Elements of our work permeated *Our Common Interest*.

◆ ◆ ◆ ◆

The G8 leaders convened at Gleneagles in July 2005, three years after they had endorsed the Africa Action Plan and in the midst of unprecedented donor support to Africa. The EU agreement to reach a 0.7 percent target by 2015 was the first big domino to fall, although Canada had promised to double aid to Africa as part of the Monterrey conference in 2002. In April, Japanese Prime Minister Junichiro Koizumi announced Japan's intention to double aid to Africa over the next three years, though he went even further at Gleneagles by committing to a $10 billion increase over five years. Then in June, just a few days before the summit, Bush said that between 2004 and 2010 the US would also double its aid to Africa.

The result of all this activity: a major announcement at Gleneagles that the G8 would double aid to Africa by 2010, an increase of $25 billion per year. That figure blew away previous G8 commitments and it mirrored the amount recommended in the CfA report. In that regard, Blair succeeded in putting Africa at the center of the summit, because the headlines coming out of Gleneagles played up the massive new commitments. It also marked the most direct link from Blair's commission to the outcomes at Gleneagles.

The G8 accepted other major recommendations from the CfA report, most notably on debt relief and trade liberalization, but the promises on trade policy adjustments went nowhere and the debt relief proposals, which the IMF and World Bank did eventually implement, actually predated the commission's work. The commitment on aid was a major advancement, however—and also because the G8 made it clear that African countries should figure out how to best use the resources. Local ownership was one of the key elements of the CfA report. The Africa Action Plan had endorsed the same concept, but in more vague terms.

The Commission for Africa probably fell short of what Blair envisioned because it got little traction after Gleneagles. Even though the African Union eventually gave its support to *Our Common Interest*, the G8 never explicitly endorsed the report. The CfA was intended to bring the G8 closer to a collective approach to Africa, but it couldn't overcome the G8's own lack of cohesion.

As happened with Kananaskis, the glow of Gleneagles began to fade amid the operational realities of donor financing. Nicholas Bayne, an economics professor at the London School of Economics and former British diplomat—he was the UK's G8 personal representative for Gleneagles— wrote that the $25 billion figure eventually became "detached from the calculations that justified it." The G8 repeated its pledge at its next two summits, in Russia in 2006 and in Germany in 2007, but actual aid spending by most G8 members had already started to fall behind the 2010 target. In 2011, the OECD said that, instead of the proposed $25 billion bump, only $11 billion had been delivered. According to the OECD, the failure to meet the $25 billion target had been caused by the "poor performance of several donors," including Germany, France, Italy, and Japan.

Though donors missed most of the lofty commitments they made at Gleneagles, the summit did produce some forward momentum on the principles of mutual accountability, especially in the areas of engagement and transparency. The measures might not have been enough to keep countries beholden to their promises, but they were at least a start.

For example, the G8 agreed to establish a support unit for the African Partnership Forum, which the G8 and NEPAD had created in 2003. The support unit was based at OECD headquarters in Paris and intended to help the forum fulfill its monitoring role. The forum was a direct descendant of the Big Table, whether it was ever explicitly acknowledged or not. During my time at the ECA, we held five Big Table meetings in all, including the special session at the World Bank. But after I left the ECA in 2005, the Big Table stopped. The final one took place in October 2004 and focused on private sector investments. I was never involved with the African Partnership Forum.

The more notable link to mutual accountability from Gleneagles can be found in *Our Common Interest*, which explicitly endorsed a monitoring mechanism to track progress made on both sides of the partnership. At that point, the ECA-OECD mutual review reports had already been established, but the need was obvious and the appetite for a monitoring mechanism remained, even among the donor countries. It was an idea with staying power. The Canadians, for example, had been strong supporters of the mutual review reports. When they hosted both the G20 Summit in Toronto and the G8 Summit in Muskoka in 2010, they drew from the report to introduce mutual accountability processes into the working methods for both summits.

Today, mutual accountability reports on development commitments—and on the wider international cooperation agendas—remain key features of G20 and G7 (no longer G8) operations. At the UN level, mutual accountability is also built into the follow-up processes of the 2030 Agenda for Sustainable Development, and it is a key element of the 2015 Paris Agreement on climate change.

The mutual review process also lived on through the Africa Progress Panel, which Blair formed in 2006 as an offshoot of the Commission for Africa. The idea was to create an eminent global body with enough stature and authority to keep both sides on track with their commitments. Kofi Annan, whose term at the UN was expiring, served as chair. The panel had as much impact as any review effort in its early years, but over time its mandate shifted alongside the decline of traditional donor influence in Africa. That shift was reflected in its mission and annual reports, which focused less on monitoring commitments and more on promoting equitable and sustainable development. It ceased activities in 2017.

◆ ◆ ◆ ◆

Much has been written over the years about an "aid paradox," sometimes referred to as the "micro-macro paradox." In 1987, British economist, researcher, and development expert Paul Mosley gave a good explanation in a book on foreign aid reform. Mosley found no "statistically significant correlation, either positive or negative," between aid flows and GNP growth in developing countries—a macro-level finding that would seem to augment the arguments of those who criticize aid as ineffective. Yet at the same time, Mosley noted that donor agencies like the World Bank consistently reported more success than not on individual projects existing at the local, or micro, level. He cited three potential explanations for the paradox: poor methods of assessment, poor methods of usage, or interference with other forms of development, such as private sector investments, which Mosley called the "backwash" effect. He was attempting to figure out where the disconnect came from—for example, poor policies at the macro level or poor measurements at the micro level?

The answer, as we've learned over the years, was that it came from both. In carefully targeted interventions, aid could yield dramatic results for improved services, such as health and education, but the inability to consistently correlate long-term economic benefits with aid flows rightly called into question ODA's usefulness. That, plus the long history of donor countries failing to meet their commitments or suffocating recipient countries with bureaucracy, offered critics of development assistance plenty of ammunition over the years. After the promised windfall at Gleneagles, they grew even louder.

In 2006, William Easterly published *The White Man's Burden*, a scathing indictment of what he called the West's "utopian agenda" for helping poor countries develop, from a misguided reliance on aid to an overreliance on "planners" who insist on imposing top-down solutions. He pulled no punches in his criticisms, calling out the "alphabet soup of agencies"—USAID, AfDB, etc.—created after WWII, the Bretton Woods Institutions, and even prominent activists like Jeffrey Sachs, Gordon Brown, and my old melody pal Bono. Easterly's first book criticizing Western aid, *The Elusive Quest for Growth*, resulted in the end of his career as a research economist at the World Bank. Also in 2006, Robert Calderisi, another Bank alumnus and former Canadian diplomat, published *The Trouble With Africa: Why Foreign Aid Isn't Working*. Calderisi argued that Africa needed new ideas more than new money and that aid was "slowing political change." In 2009, Dambisa Moyo, a Zambian-born economist educated at Harvard and Oxford, ratcheted up the criticisms further with *Dead Aid*, an argument against "the myth" that aid had helped reduce poverty or increase growth. Of course, there have been many more.

Admittedly, aid has not always worked well and there's plenty of blame to go around. But reducing poverty and growing economies will continue to require more financing than poor African countries can muster. Aid wasn't ever meant to be the final, or only, solution. But to get Africa from point A to point B and on the path to point C—and to save lives at the same time—it's been necessary to fill in gaping budget gaps for the poorest countries or act as a catalytic force for investment in countries that are a little farther along. For example, one commonly cited concern was that by increasing aid, we might be promoting dependency. This is a bit of a straw man argument. Those worried about dependency should be more concerned with whether conditions exist for growth, since the evidence tells us that dependency on aid only results where economies fail to grow.

I suffer no illusions about the historic dysfunction of the aid architecture. We know that promises have been made, broken, and made again. We know that aid volumes have always fluctuated unpredictably, making it impossible for receiving countries to plan effectively for the long term. We know that weak state capacity in poor countries and complex, uncoordinated donor policies have undermined the aid process from the beginning. But eliminating assistance has never been a reasonable solution. I can think of no other professional field, with the possible exception of law, which has been as much maligned as that of development. Yet development aid has helped transform the world and greatly brightened Africa's prospects. And, despite the shortcomings, in the right situation it *can* promote growth. The Commission for Africa report gave detailed examples of direct links between ODA and improved macroeconomic performance, including higher growth and social development. In Mozambique in the 1990s, for instance, aid amounting to 50 percent of GDP drove a 12 percent increase in GDP. A demonstrable relationship between aid and growth could also be found in Ghana, Rwanda, and Uganda, among other countries.

In 2014, the United Nations University World Institute for Development Economics Research concluded a major study on the role and impact of aid in governance, employment, gender equality, the environment and climate change, and other social sectors. The project produced 240 original studies from approximately 300 researchers across 60 countries. This very careful and comprehensive review came to the conclusion that the overall record shows that aid projects and programs do have significant rates of return—a more than 7 percent annual rate over 35 years, according to the aggregate evidence—and that aid does help to foster economic growth over long periods of time.

We now know with certainty, however, that financing development requires a complex suite of solutions, not just a suitcase full of dollars, and that modern-day definitions of what constitutes effective aid have changed dramatically, which the next chapter explores. But most important, we know that financing for Africa's future starts at home, not abroad.

Notes

1   Paul Hunt and I also became good friends—so much so that when I left the ECA in 2005, he presented me with an official jersey of the Canadian national hockey team. For a true-blooded Canadian like him, few gifts could carry more meaning! I framed the jersey, which still hangs in my home.

2   The four parallel objectives between the ECA's 1999 financing conference and the Monterrey Consensus were: mobilizing domestic financial resources, mobilizing foreign direct investment and other private flows, pushing international trade as an engine for development, and tackling external debt. The other two focus areas in the consensus covered increasing technical cooperation and addressing systemic issues such as policy coherence.

3   Also known as Baroness Amos due to her appointment as a British "life peer" in 1997, she went on to become a very active figure in the development world. She served as the interim replacement to Clare Short as the UK's secretary of state for international development, becoming the first black woman to hold a place in the cabinet of the United Kingdom. She eventually became the UN's top official for humanitarian assistance, overseeing UN-led relief efforts around the world.

4   We proposed for the mutual review to cover the following areas: MDG progress and prospects, political and corporate governance, capacity development, aid flows, aid quantity, and policy coherence for African and OECD governments, especially in the areas of agriculture and trade.

5   Canada had a history of this kind of work already, having established in 1986 the highly successful Partnership Africa Canada, a funding mechanism to support collaborations between Canadian and African NGOs. Few Western donors were putting aid dollars in partnership programs in the mid-1980s, so Canada stood out.

6   The Millennium Challenge Corporation compacts are large, five-year grants for countries that meet eligibility requirements, such as capacity for country ownership and good governance, among other criteria. George W. Bush's speech announcing the program, delivered on March 14, 2002 at the Inter-American Development Bank, called for a "new compact for global development, defined by new accountability for both rich and poor nations alike." It certainly sounded familiar!

7   Myles Wickstead documented the Commission for Africa's formation and impact in an essay for the book *Networks of Influence?*. Published in 2009, it is a fantastic resource for anyone seeking a thorough and straightforward analysis of the CfA.

8   Nicholas Stern had been the chief economist and a senior vice president at the World Bank prior to joining the Commission for Africa, but his list of accomplishments before and after are much longer. He was knighted in the United Kingdom for his work in economics in 2004 and a few years later authored a government-commissioned review on climate change that quickly came to be seen as an early seminal study on global temperatures.

Chapter 14

In a New Direction

Making Aid More Effective—and Moving Beyond It

W hen Tony Blair invited me to speak at 10 Downing Street in the months leading up to the G8 Kananaskis summit, I labored for weeks over what I wanted to say. Mine would be the only address in the prime minister's Millennium Lectures Series devoted solely to Africa, and it took place against the backdrop of the final negotiations on the NEPAD and G8 Africa Action Plan frameworks. All around, the world finally was getting serious about issues like African debt and aid. But the more I thought about it, the more I wanted to devote at least part of my lecture to what would come *after* the agreements and promises had been made—to a future where African countries were seen as equals and also where aid could be seen as an additional, not primary, source of development financing. So as I spoke, I highlighted the bold efforts taking place to improve governance, boost economic growth, restore public services, and attract foreign investment. I pointed out that an increasing number of African countries were looking for true development partners, not simply donors, to help finance their future.

I had to keep my remarks grounded in reality, but I also wanted to strike an optimistic tone. I believed big changes loomed on the horizon— "a new paradigm for development cooperation in Africa," I said. On the one hand I was making an obvious reference to NEPAD, but on the other I was calling attention to Africa's improving economic position and, as a result, its future standing among the financiers of global development. I considered this key for African countries to gain the leverage they needed to really make the ownership agenda a reality.

411

Fast forward three years, and I received another British invitation to speak to an influential group in the months leading up to another G8 summit—Gleneagles—that once again would move the needle on Africa's development financing architecture. It was February 2005 and the cross-party Africa Group at the UK parliament, in conjunction with the Royal African Society—a venerable UK organization that promotes African affairs globally—had asked me to make a presentation shortly before the final meeting of the Commission for Africa.

I gladly accepted the invitation, because I saw an opportunity to discuss more than the commission; I wanted to review how dramatically the dialogue around Africa's growth and development—and the financing to support it—had evolved in the few years since I had spoken at 10 Downing Street.

Indeed, the future had started to come at a furious pace.

The continent's overall economic prospects began to brighten considerably in 2003, with growth at nearly 4 percent; that rate increased to 5 percent in 2004. At the start of 2005, the OECD and World Bank estimated even stronger growth in the years ahead. Meanwhile, the climate for security and cooperation had never been better, with the establishment of a Pan-African Parliament and the launch of NEPAD. These encouraging improvements, combined with enthusiasm for tackling the Millennium Development Goals, all played into the unprecedented surge in official development assistance, or ODA, that would soon peak at Gleneagles.

But this surge in donor interest also came with an increased awareness that the handling of ODA, as it moved from the rich world to the developing world, had to improve. For one thing, the number of aid providers and recipients had exploded, from five or six "donors" and a couple of dozen recipients in the late 1950s to more than 200 development agencies sending assistance to more than 150 recipient countries. An obvious result of so many more players was an increasingly chaotic, complex, and disparate architecture for external development financing. Another issue was the growing desire and ability of recipient countries to plan their own development futures, or at least have an equal say. In other words, ownership.

If recognizing that more resources were needed to bolster economies and support development was the first step, then recognizing the need to reform the processes that governed development assistance was the next step. At that point, the environment would be far more conducive for African countries to exert the agency over development resources that they had long sought and, ideally, to plan for a future beyond aid.

In that regard, two notable events took place during this time that helped accelerate the changes to come. The first was in Monterrey, the second in Rome. Both turned out to be breakthroughs in the way developing countries had long been treated and perceived.

At the first International Conference on Financing for Development in Monterrey in 2002, the rich nations of the world not only promised to boost ODA flows to unprecedented levels, they agreed to the need to improve how those resources were distributed and used. The Monterrey Consensus was the most complete development financing framework to date because it went further than simply promising funds and setting conditions. It presupposed successful partnership arrangements, and that was significant for Africa because of how closely it mirrored the core philosophy of NEPAD. The embrace of the partnership agenda is a big reason that donors and recipients were forced to rethink the traditional methods of development financing. So the Monterrey Consensus became one of the first global acknowledgements that aid alone would not guarantee sustainable development outcomes.

The following year, the OECD organized the first High-Level Forum on Aid Effectiveness. Its outcome, the Rome Declaration on Harmonization, clearly defined the steps donors should take to align rules, policies, and procedures so as to lessen the burden of development assistance on recipient countries. More important, it stated that assistance should be delivered foremost in accordance with local country priorities—a practice that may seem reasonably standard now but represented a major leap forward at the time.

Naturally, the Rome Declaration had some gaps, and the OECD only intended it to be a starting point. So a second forum was scheduled in Paris in March 2005, just a few weeks after I traveled to London for my speaking engagement with the UK parliamentarians and the Royal African Society. In addition to reviewing the dramatic changes that had taken place, I took the opportunity to direct attention toward what had become known as the aid effectiveness agenda. I titled my address "Making Aid Work Better for Africa."

But as I had done at 10 Downing Street years before, I also tried to call attention to the need for broader thinking—and changing attitudes—toward financing for development. The OECD-led efforts were great and most welcome, I said, but the end goal for African countries needed to be economic independence from aid and, until that could be achieved, at least the eventual transition to aid as a complementary source of financing. In this way, and with the Paris forum looming on the horizon, I felt I could offer my audience of Western policymakers and influencers a potentially valuable African perspective on a very current topic of discussion.

I described the inextricable link between development assistance and Africa's ability to scale up resources for growth-promoting social investment, infrastructure, and capacity building. Without attention to those issue areas, I argued, Africa had no reasonable hope of attacking the MDGs, much less meeting them—and thus no reasonable hope for sustainable development. Yes, ODA needed to be more efficient and controllable, but African countries also needed support in the form of partnerships, private investments, and policy coherence beyond aid transfers. For example, an ECA study published before my speech showed that if Europe wanted to be coherent in its partnership with Africa, then its Common Agriculture Policy needed to change. With unrestricted market access, I said, African exports would increase by almost $2 billion. My point: boosting aid flows is good, but reforming policies to spur sustainable economic growth is much, much better.

I didn't specifically mention the ultimate goal of transforming economies, but the primary principles I brought up for improving the aid dynamic—ownership, mutual accountability, capacity, and infrastructure investments—would be among the building blocks for transformation. Given that previously aid-reliant countries such as Brazil and South Korea were in the midst of their own transformations, I didn't believe such thinking was a pipe dream. Otherwise, donors would be increasing ODA flows to little long-term effect and missing the bigger picture.

"Aid quantity is insufficient and its quality is not good enough," I said, "but as I predicted three years ago, there has been a shift in the partnership between Africa and rich countries" to improve the outcomes of development assistance. Ultimately, aid effectiveness, at least for Africa, needed to result in African countries having the autonomy to help direct and manage their financial resources in the best way possible to promote growth.

"Evidence tells us that dependency on aid only results where economies fail to grow," I concluded. "With growth, savings are generated and foreign investments attracted, reducing the need for external sources of support."

If global financing for development could evolve in this way, I urged, Africa might finally be in a position to make lasting gains. So it was encouraging when, a few weeks later, the process took another step in a new direction at the OECD's second high-level forum in Paris. It brought together delegates from more than 100 developed and developing countries, international organizations, and other stakeholders to build off the agreements made two years prior. The end result: the Paris Declaration on Aid Effectiveness, which aimed to reorient development efforts around first-hand experience of what worked and what did not work at the country level—a basic concept that historically had remained buried under excessive demands, conditions, and political agendas. The Paris Declaration outlined five fundamental principles for making aid more effective: ownership, alignment, harmonization, results, and mutual accountability.

I attended the Paris forum but played no role. I was pleased, however, that some OECD ministers who had attended past Big Table meetings carried forward many of the recommendations that had cropped up in our discussions.

The Paris Declaration unified many elements for better development practices—such as local ownership, monitoring progress, and mutual accountability—that I and others had been advocating for years. It finally elevated core quality issues from the sidelines to the center of the discussions—a necessary step for countries to get the most out of their financial resources. And while it opened the door for the huge aid commitments from the European Union and G8—commitments that many countries failed to meet, unfortunately—it also recognized, somewhat faintly, the even bigger changes on the horizon: that in recent years, "more development actors—middle-income countries, global funds, the private sector, civil society organizations—have been increasing their contributions and bringing valuable experience to the table."

◆　◆　◆　◆

In December 2003, I returned to Accra for the holidays, for what I expected to be a quiet, mostly uneventful vacation. I wanted to spend time with my family and I needed to do some soul-searching. I was about 18 months away from the end of my tenure at the ECA and had begun to think about the future. I would turn 60 nine months later and, though I might be a little worse for wear, I wasn't ready to put my feet up and call it a day. Africa had finally started to show some real progress and I wanted to stay in the game. But in what way and to what extent?

Over the previous months, I had received a few gentle nudges to consider shifting from one continental institution—the ECA—to another: the African Development Bank. The timing made lot of sense; the current president, Omar Kabbaj, would be stepping down around the same time I would be leaving the ECA. More important, my background made sense—20 years at the World Bank followed by almost a decade at the ECA, a professional mix that closely aligned with the AfDB's role as both a lender and important resource for research and policy advice. As the topic came up more frequently in conversation, such as phone calls with development ministers, I started to consider it more seriously. Still, it wasn't as if I could just wave a magic wand and have the job.

The AfDB presidency is an elected post, not appointed. Given the prestige of the position and the infrequency of its opening—Kabbaj and his predecessor, Babacar Ndiaye, each served 10 years—candidates were already lining up. Winning would require heavy campaigning, and I'd not run for elected office since being voted high school senior prefect when I was 17—hardly the same thing!

Once in Accra, I continued to ponder the possibility of an AfDB campaign in the back of my mind, but I remained undecided. Then one day by happenstance I encountered Ghana's finance minister, Yaw Osafo-Maafo. We knew each other and began talking. Before long, conversation turned to the AfDB election. As finance minister, he was also a governor of the AfDB. He said a few people had reached out to him regarding me as a possible candidate, including some staff at the AfDB. With so much chatter, he wanted to know if I was really interested. If I was, he said, then the government of Ghana would be interested in backing me.

The way these elections work, individual governments nominate a candidate, and then both the government and candidate need to operate in tandem to build support. The fields are often crowded, but generally regional blocs will coalesce around preferred candidates until a few frontrunners emerge. While the individual candidate is the one elected to serve, of course, the actual votes are cast for the nominating country. In my case, voters would choose Ghana, whose nominee I would be. So the elections are a matter of pride not only for the office seeker but for his or her sponsoring country as well.

I told Osafo-Maafo that I had heard similar chatter and had indeed given it careful thought, but I was not yet sure what I would do. He suggested that I meet with Ghana President John Kufuor, sooner rather than later. Osafo-Maafo believed Kufuor would back the idea, and time was of the essence. The election was scheduled for May 2005, less than 16 months away. For this election, that wasn't very long at all since potential candidates—and their sponsor countries—often begin jockeying for support up to two years ahead of time. If I was going to go for it, I had to decide quickly.

I agreed to talk with President Kufuor, and the meeting was set in short order. The two of us plus Osafo-Maafo and Ghana's foreign minister, Nana Addo Dankwa Akufo-Addo, got together to go over the pros and cons of my potential candidacy. We also discussed what a game plan would look like if I chose to run. Akufo-Addo—who would be elected Ghana's president 16 years later—could sense my uncertainty.

"We're behind you if you want to do this," he said, "but do you have the fire in your belly?"

It was a fair question. I really didn't know the answer.

Even though I had begun to think about life after the ECA, I still had a lot going on there. It had to remain my primary focus for the next year and a half. With a potential half-dozen or more competitors, I would have to devote a lot of hours to win the job. And even if I did win, then what? The position would require a daunting commitment. I would be moving instantly from one high-stress job to another, with no time to take a break. Still, I knew I could run a large institution effectively and I had some very strong beliefs about what needed to happen for Africa to build on the economic gains it had started to make. Eventually, I consulted with my family and my own staff, the senior members I trusted the most and whose help I would need to mount a campaign. A few raised real concerns not over my ability to do the job, but on getting elected. They believed I would be a strong candidate, but I couldn't disregard the unique nature of the challenges I faced as an applicant for an elected office.

From the ECA staff to African ministers to heads of state, I had crossed paths with more than a few who either disagreed with my approaches to policy or disliked my background at the World Bank, or both. Similarly, while I knew that my role as a facilitator between donor countries and the NEPAD governments led to many good outcomes, there were others who took a different view—that I was a gadfly, an interloper, a bureaucrat overstepping his bounds. Rounding up enough support would be a tall task, made even more difficult by the rules of the race. Under UN guidelines, I couldn't actually campaign and lobby for myself since I headed a UN agency, so the Ghana government—and supportive surrogates—would need to do a lot more than might normally be expected.

I was aware of the drawbacks, but after the meeting with Kufuor and the others, I warmed to the idea. I decided to go for it.

And I lost.

It wasn't for lack of effort. Once I'd made the decision to run, I went after it at full bore, or at least to the extent my UN limitations allowed. At times, it got a little messy trying to navigate the balance between being the ECA's executive secretary and an AfDB candidate, as a trip to Japan a few months before the election proved. I'll come back to that. First, it's important to understand the process that goes into actually choosing the president.

The AfDB elections are complex affairs, with votes cast by regional and non-regional Bank members. The regional members are African countries; the non-regionals come from outside Africa, mostly traditional donor countries. The president is elected by the AfDB's board of governors, which is made up of representatives of the member states, usually ministers of finance and planning—such as Ghana's Yaw Osafo-Maafo—central bank governors, or duly designated alternates. Voting powers are determined on the basis of payments received, so the larger countries wield the most influence, which is why regional blocs form, either on their own or in support of a larger country's candidate. For instance, as of 2017, Nigeria and South Africa carried the most weight among the 54 regionals. Nigeria had 577,802 total votes, or 8.9 percent of the total voting powers; South Africa had 328,127 total votes and 5 percent of the voting powers. Djibouti, by contrast, had a mere 0.02 percent. Among the non-regionals, the United States' 6.5 percent and Japan's 5.5 percent had the most clout.

In the event of multiple candidates, which the 2005 election produced, a series of votes are held until one country's candidate gets the necessary majority. If that doesn't happen on one ballot, then the country with the lowest total votes is eliminated and a second round of voting takes place. It's all very dramatic and extremely unpredictable, as voters may and do switch allegiances from one round to the next.

Given the structure of the process, it's easy to see why locking up early commitments is vital to staying in the race long enough to winnow the field and make it to the final rounds. The support of a candidate's sponsoring government is crucial and the Ghanaian officials, especially Akufo-Addo, stepped up for me, visiting more than 20 countries on my behalf. As our team canvassed for votes, they got great feedback from both the regional and non-regional countries—so much so that it appeared I was a legitimate frontrunner.

The vote was held in Abuja, on the margins of the AfDB's annual meeting of finance ministers. The ECA senior staff were already there because we were holding our annual conference of ministers meeting the week prior. For years, I had tried to work with the AfDB to schedule our meetings back-to-back, in a single location, to improve efficiency and ideally to increase collaboration between the two institutions. We finally pulled it off in 2005. With many voters gathered so many days before the election, Abuja turned into a hotspot of politicking and lobbying. Unwittingly, the ECA's successful "reform" for making the ministerial meetings more efficient had given my opponents the perfect opportunity to campaign for themselves—and against me, right under my nose!

The day before the election, my team and I remained confident—too confident, as it turned out. We had reason to expect support in the first few rounds would be soft, given how many other candidates had gotten a head start on me and locked up early commitments. But the delegate casting Japan's vote gave me another reason to worry. He asked to have a private, one-on-one conversation, where he delivered an ominous message: "We think you are the best candidate, but my senior vice minister of finance told me not to vote for you."

He didn't have to tell me why. Unfortunately, I already knew.

I entered the AfDB race a few months before I joined the Commission for Africa. My work on the commission paralleled my AfDB candidacy and they even wrapped up about the same time: the CfA published its report in March 2005; the AfDB election was held in May. In the run-up to the report's release, the British wanted some of the commissioners to visit other countries and help drum up support so that the July G8 summit Gleneagles would be a big success. In that context, they asked me to go to Japan. The British government paid for the trip and this was an important point.

Some of my opponents for the AfDB post had been afforded a travel budget by their sponsoring governments—some even used their country's presidential jet—but as a UN employee I faced a different situation. Ghana could back me but the government could not give me funds for travel to help build my candidacy. Nor could I use ECA funds or campaign during ECA trips. It was definitely a tough spot. So I tried to take advantage of the trip to Japan. I met with the senior Japanese finance minister and the British ambassador, but I let the minister's people know ahead of time that, once we had concluded our discussions regarding the Commission for Africa report, it would be nice also to talk about the AfDB. In other words, the basic kind of "meet and greet" that was standard practice for other candidates. There didn't seem to be a problem.

The three of us sat down—the finance minister, the British ambassador, and me—along with the associated staffs of the minister and ambassador. And we had a good discussion. I took the lead in explaining the key messages of the CfA report, why the report was important for Gleneagles, and why Japan needed to support it. It was polite and cordial. Then I made a fatal mistake.

I was in Japan as a formal guest of the British ambassador and therefore the British government. Thus, my briefing to the finance minister was under the authorization of official British business. When we finished discussing the Commission for Africa, I should have ended the official meeting and asked the finance minister for a private word. But I didn't do that. Instead, in front of the British ambassador and his staff, I addressed the Japanese minister: "Your Excellency, I would like to mention that I am a candidate to be president of the African Development Bank and I would appreciate Japan's support and backing."

Immediately, the minister froze. The Japanese are a very formal people and I soon learned through back channels that I offended him deeply by bringing up a Ghana-Japan issue under the guise of a British ambassadorial visit.

After a few awkward seconds that felt like hours, the minister replied.

"Yes, we know," he said. "We have been briefed. And we have received representation from other countries with candidates." His tone was formal and distant, lacking the cordial nature of the earlier conversation. I knew not to say another word on the topic. The meeting ended.

I met scores of dignitaries during my career—too many to count—and this had to be one of my worst gaffes ever. A few months later in Abuja, it came back to haunt me. That year, Japan had 4.5 percent of the votes, the second-biggest non-regional, so losing that country's support hurt. The United States, the largest non-regional, was backing another candidate, while Nigeria, the largest regional, had its own candidate in the race. Still, the night before the election, as my team tallied our supposed commitments, we expected to win. We knew we didn't have the numbers to come out on top in the first round, but we believed the dynamics would shift in our favor for the later rounds.

Instead, we barely survived the first ballot. And in the second round of voting, Ghana was eliminated and my candidacy came to an abrupt end. To say that we were shocked is an understatement. Based on the intelligence gathered, I looked like a finalist at worst. In the end, Rwanda produced the winner: Donald Kaberuka, the country's influential finance minister. A respected policymaker, Kaberuka was an outstanding candidate with broad appeal.[1]

So what went wrong? A lot.

My gaffe in Japan certainly didn't help; it showed my political inexperience as well as the limitations I had as a UN employee. But it was just one contributing factor among many, starting with the time crunch. The government of Ghana was very supportive on my behalf, but it simply didn't have enough time to build a strong coalition among African countries. And there was another complication: President Kufuor was up for re-election at the same time. Although he won, that race didn't wrap up until December 2004, five months ahead of the AfDB vote. Needless to say, some key Ghanaians had bigger priorities than me.

The regional issue also came into play. As I mentioned, winning the AfDB presidency is a source of pride for governments, but there's also a sense that it's a prize to be shared among regions. Kabbaj came from Morocco and his predecessor, Ndiaye, was from Senegal, covering both North and West Africa. Going further back, Wila D. Mung'omba was an East African from Zambia and before him, Kwame Donkor Fordwor came from Ghana, another West African country. West Africans had held the AfDB presidency for 13 of the previous 29 years, including a Ghanaian. Regional "equity" really mattered.

Then there was the Commission for Africa. As I wrote in the previous chapter, the initial response to the commission was lukewarm. Few Europeans or Africans backed it, so my participation wasn't actually a selling point. The UK government also made things harder by sending a letter of support to other European voting members. The move backfired spectacularly. Rather than building support, the letter raised a lot of eyebrows—was I Ghana's candidate, or the UK's?

The CfA backlash played into a more lamentable factor in my loss: quite a few people wanted to take me—and the ECA—down a notch, and the election gave them the perfect opportunity. It was the same issue that dogged us during the APRM process. What I saw as an aggressive effort to strengthen the ECA, others saw as a political and policy land grab. It led to some clear institutional rivalries within Africa and the UN itself. In Abuja, those rivalries played out.[2]

Similarly, the ECA's relationship with the African Union had suffered for the same reason. In 2003, Alpha Oumar Konaré, the former president of Mali, took over as head of the AU. Konaré and I previously had a good relationship—so much so that when he was president he once gave me a goat as a show of friendship! But he believed the ECA, as a UN organization, occupied too much policy space and should defer to the AU. Naturally, relations between our two institutions grew strained. Konaré certainly didn't want to see me take over the AfDB, and he used his influence in the election as he saw fit.

But ultimately, to many voters my background as an economic technician and bureaucrat paled in comparison to someone like Kaberuka, a ministerial-level expert and policymaker. Even with all the other issues at play, that hurdle proved too big to overcome. In retrospect, my chances were not great from the start.

For a while, losing the election felt like the biggest professional misfire of my life. The loss stung, personally and professionally. Despite my initial uncertainty, I had really wanted to win the job. I had grown certain that there was much more I wanted to accomplish, and the AfDB post would enable me to continue that quest. It took months for me to get over the disappointment. But when I did, I saw the silver lining: the election had refocused my energies. I found the "fire in my belly" after all, but it was for something else entirely.

◆　◆　◆　◆

My term at the ECA was set to expire in July 2005, but I stayed on for a few extra months. By the time I officially stepped down in October 2005, I needed an extended break, but I also had a few ECA-related projects to wrap up. I accepted a short-term fellowship at the Woodrow Wilson International Center for Scholars, in Washington, DC, which was a nice landing spot for me to wrap up the outstanding projects and transition into whatever came next. It also allowed me time to reflect on the previous year.

As disappointing as I found the AfDB loss, I began to consider that it might not have been the position itself that I wanted as much as a platform to pursue work that I had come to see as increasingly urgent. The more I had talked about the positive signs of economic growth and the hope for Africa's future, and the more I considered what an "Amoako agenda" at the African Development Bank might have looked like, the more I considered the pressing need for African countries to understand—and embrace—the concept of economic transformation. I had been talking about the need for the structural transformation of African economies for almost as long as I'd been at the ECA. By the time I left, it had become clear that transformation would be required not only to sustain Africa's economic growth but also to make any sizable dent in reducing poverty.

Specifically, African economies needed to undergo the same kind of structural transformation that in recent decades had propelled poor Asian countries to robust and stable economic growth. That meant relying less on commodities, such as oil and minerals, and more on manufacturing, industrialization, exports, and technology. South Korea, for instance, in 2010 completed a remarkable transition from an aid-recipient country to a donor country, the first time since the OECD was established that a non-European country had joined the "advanced nations' assistance club." South Korea had been one of the poorest countries in the world in the aftermath of its 1950s conflict. Donor assistance had been vital to its survival; but once stabilized, South Korea put the right policies in place to reduce its poverty and move beyond aid. Why couldn't an African nation one day accomplish the same? Or two African nations? Or a dozen?

This felt like the inevitable evolution of African development. If I anticipated that transformation would have been at the forefront of my agenda at the AfDB, then why not still focus my energies on it? I surveyed the landscape, and no one was talking much about transformation as a defining characteristic of African development. Between the encouraging growth rates at home and the changing attitudes toward donor relationships abroad, I saw a critical gap to fill.

So after taking a sabbatical to recharge my batteries, I returned home to Ghana in 2007 to establish the African Center for Economic Transformation, or ACET, in Accra. It took a couple of years to get ACET up and running amid all the procedural hassles—staffing, work programs, funding. I can't say I enjoyed going through all those processes yet again, but I embraced the freedom to establish my own African organization with a singular focus on one big idea.

Still, I eased off the gas pedal a little bit, even as I began plotting ACET's future. I wanted to get the organization's foundation right, but I also needed to relax. Almost 30 years after congestive heart failure had put me in the hospital, my heart was going strong but my body needed a break! I didn't disappear entirely. I sat on advisory boards, such as the ONE Campaign, and though I was a little removed from the old circles, I maintained contact with many of the friends, ministers, and policymakers I had known for so long.

I was in Accra when my good friend Richard Carey telephoned in early 2008. He and a few OECD colleagues were in town and they wanted me to meet them for a drink at their hotel bar. Not having seen him in a few years, I was eager to catch up. But when I arrived, he explained that his visit was more than a social call. He and his colleagues had come to Ghana to consult with government officials on preparations for the OECD's Third High-Level Forum on Aid Effectiveness, which Ghana would be hosting in Accra in September 2008.

Carey said the OECD needed to check on the logistical and administrative arrangements for the conference—basically to make sure everything was on track. But the group had a second objective: to convince President John Kufuor that Ghana needed to play a bigger role behind the scenes. The previous two forums were in Italy and France; this one would be the first hosted by a non-donor country. As such, Ghana should be out front, ensuring that all developing countries at the forum were united behind a strong and coherent position from which to negotiate with the donor countries.

"I completely agree," I said, "but how do you do that?"

Carey smiled. "That's why we're here."

The fact of the matter was that things hadn't gone so well since the second high-level forum in Paris. The targets that had been set—and the commitments made—under the Paris Declaration were not being met, while implementation was off track at the country level. The root of the problem could be traced back to the design of the forum itself. Although developing countries took part, the final compromises had been brokered largely among the donor countries. The non-donor countries had not been allowed to contribute when it mattered most. They lacked a full ownership stake in the Paris Declaration, and implementation was adversely affected as a result.

The OECD recognized the problem, Carey explained. Developing countries needed to be involved in the *full range* of decision-making, from beginning to end. And that meant the developing countries speaking with a unified voice. So the OECD wanted to make a proposition to Kufuor: that he appoint someone as a special government envoy to go on a global junket to put the wheels in motion for a common stance among aid-recipient countries for Accra. This way, Carey said, the developing countries would speak from a position of strength. And the biggest misstep from Paris would, in theory, be corrected this time around.

I said that all sounded like a great idea. Then he gave me the kicker: the OECD wanted to suggest Kufuor appoint me as the government envoy.

I told him that I was honored, but it seemed like a lot to take on, for a number of reasons. First, I had begun setting up ACET and I didn't want to divert too much attention from that. Second, after the heavy travel schedule I'd endured at the ECA, I wasn't too keen to embark on a globetrotting tour that would take months to play out. Third and most important, I didn't see how I could—on my own—generate the kind of consensus that the OECD envisioned. We were talking about multiple issues covering diverse country circumstances, interests, and priorities. The suggestion simply seemed beyond the scope of what I, or any one person, could achieve. He asked me to think more about it, and I promised that I would. After a couple of days of reflection, I came up with an alternative.

I proposed that the Ghana government convene a small group of representatives from three regions—Africa, Asia, and Latin America and the Caribbean—to meet a handful of times ahead of the forum and develop a set of common positions. I offered to chair the group and help guide the discussion. The outcome would be along the lines of what Carey and his colleagues wanted, but the process would be more inclusive and collaborative than having a single point person go to countries individually. Ghana's then-finance minister, Kwadwo Baah-Wiredu, liked the idea and agreed to support it.

And so did the OECD.

Working quickly, I identified seven well-respected and influential individuals—government officials, independent experts, researchers, and think tank leaders with extensive experience in aid effectiveness issues—who agreed to join me. The group came to be known as the Partner Country Contact Group, or PCCG, and it represented eight different developing countries: Cambodia, Colombia, Egypt, Liberia, Mauritius, Sri Lanka, and Vietnam. As chair, I represented Ghana.

For more than a year before I got involved, however, the machinery set up by the OECD to plan the Accra forum had been humming. It consisted of two parts.

The first part was the Working Party on Aid Effectiveness, a broad coalition of donor and developing country representatives, plus multilateral agencies. The working party began as a small donor-only grouping ahead of the Rome forum in 2003 and then expanded to include a few developing countries for the second forum in Paris. Leading up to Accra, the working party had grown to a few dozen members and evolved into something that more resembled a partnership.

The second part was the joint secretariat of the World Bank and the OECD's Development Assistance Committee, which also served as the forum's steering committee. It was charged with leading the consultations with the various stakeholders and drafting the recommendations for the upcoming forum's final document—the big takeaway, in other words. So while the working party operated at a big-picture level, guiding the dialogue and setting the tone, the steering committee dictated the contours of the actual outcome. They were the ones with whom our newly formed PCCG would be most involved.

We scheduled two meetings with the steering committee at two key junctures: in May in Paris to provide feedback on the first draft of its working document; and in September, a few days before the start of the forum, to provide final comments on the draft that would be presented to OECD ministers for their approval.

I wanted to get the team together ahead of time, though, so I invited everyone to meet with me in Washington in April. It was a convenient place and time, since most of the PCCG members would be in town for the annual spring meetings of the World Bank and IMF. Our "pre-meeting" proved quite beneficial. Everyone got to know each other and we agreed on the positions that we would present to the steering committee the following month in Paris. I was pleased with the composition of the team. In terms of country-level experience and knowledge, the members were all top-notch. If the OECD ministers wanted more direct input on aid effectiveness from developing countries, they were definitely going to get it.

Jan Cedergren, a Swedish diplomat who had previously been the deputy director general of SIDA, Sweden's international development agency, chaired the meeting in Paris. I took this as a good sign. I knew him from my days at the ECA and found him to be a very reasonable, pragmatic man, well respected inside the development community. If we ran into areas of disagreement, I felt that he, as chair of the steering committee, would be a fair arbiter and take our group's views into account. As it turned out, that's exactly what happened.

A day before our meeting, we were given the first draft of the document that the steering committee had been working on for months, largely in consultation with representatives of the working party. A quick scan of the document, the foundation for what would become the *Accra Agenda for Action*, revealed that we were in agreement with the committee on many of the general issues but were far apart on some of the most fundamental elements of improving development assistance: strengthening country systems, building local capacity, "untying" aid to remove conditions, and measuring mutual accountability. These were core issues for developing countries focused on more authority over immediate resources and better measures to improve the process over the long term.

Keep in mind, however, that the goal of this third high-level forum was not necessarily to break new ground, but to strengthen the implementation of the Paris Declaration. That's why getting developing countries more involved—and taking into account their experiences and frustrations—was so important. But it was definitely alarming to see so many differences between the donor-comprised steering committee's draft of the *Accra Agenda for Action* and the approaches that our country-level partner group had agreed to in Washington. I began to wonder if the whole PCCG effort would be a waste of time.

We gathered for the meeting, and not too long into the morning discussion I noticed two dynamics at play. The first was between our group and the steering committee. On one side, you had people with years of practical experience in aid management within their own countries. On the other, you had representatives of the world's major financing organizations; all of them were stellar economists but most had little or no experience of putting aid to work on the ground. I expected to encounter this dynamic. The other, within the donor group itself, I did not.

Among the dozen or so members of the steering committee, a wide range of opinions existed over their "official" positions on some key issues, including the fundamental ones I had already flagged. The more we discussed the specifics of untying aid or building capacity, for instance, the more I realized that some members of the donor group were aligned much more closely to the PCCG's position than those expressed in the early draft of the *Accra Agenda for Action*. Since the PCCG came into the meeting unified on all the key issues and the steering committee did not, we found ourselves in a surprisingly strong position.

By the end of the first day of the two-day meeting, a remarkable thing had happened: the PCCG was having a profound effect on the steering committee. As we prepared to break, Cedergren proposed that the steering committee alter its operations to allow the PCCG to take on a more active role. Cedergren suggested that four members of the PCCG be absorbed into the steering committee to create a new consensus group with the mandate of developing the final draft of the *Accra Agenda for Action* for adoption at the September forum. The committee approved his proposal unanimously.

This assimilation of developing countries into the highest levels of decision-making had much more to do with the rest of the members of the PCCG than it did with me. I was leading the group, but I didn't have the same on-the-ground experience as my colleagues. So I generally deferred to them, especially to Talaat Abdel-Malek. An Egyptian economist as well as academic, advisor, and consultant, Abdel-Malek stood out for his tenacious and passionate debate on how to improve the North–South dynamic between rich and poor countries so that it actually benefited the poor countries of the global South. In fact, he was so unrelenting in his arguments on the critical role of capacity development that we jokingly referred to him as "Mr. Capacity." His inputs as part of the PCCG, and then the consensus group, earned him a much larger role ahead of the *next* high-level forum: co-chair of the OECD's working party.

In addition to Abdel-Malek, the PCCG members from Sri Lanka and Colombia joined me—along with the initial donor-side steering committee members—in rounding out the consensus group. Between May and September, we met two more times to try to bridge the donor–recipient differences on how to make aid work better for developing countries. We produced a draft of the *Accra Agenda* in July, two months ahead of the forum.

It's not unusual for countries to disagree when it comes to negotiating global agreements, but the differences in opinion among the OECD players over the draft document we produced worsened as the forum approached. By late summer, the lines were firmly drawn. The European Union—the Nordic countries in particular—and the United Kingdom had taken a progressive view on development financing that aligned closely to the views of developing countries. Without getting into too much detail, those views generally allowed for more local control and ownership over the receipt and use of official development assistance. Larger donors, such as the United States and Japan, favored a more conservative agreement that wouldn't appear to shift the balance of power too much toward the developing countries. I worried that these divisions would lead to an acrimonious debate at Accra, potentially preventing a substantive agreement. Such an outcome would be a black eye for Ghana, the host country, and for the new approach that included developing countries.

On September 1, the day before the forum officially opened, the consensus group gathered one last time, but with a few more high-ranking faces in the room. Immediately, it was clear that some of the issues we thought we had settled were now back on the table. We couldn't do much to play peacemaker with the donors, so we stayed focused on core objectives: strengthening capacity for developing countries, lessening conditionalities for more flexibility, and boosting country systems to build healthier institutions. We also argued strongly in favor of giving more space to the private sector and to South–South cooperation: that is, the ability of developing countries to assist one another with both financial resources and technical expertise. The latter point proved especially prescient, given the obvious trends in global financial flows that had already become apparent.

The number of former aid-dependent countries showing signs of an economic turnaround, such as the aforementioned South Korea, had begun to accelerate. In addition to boosting their own GDPs, their growth allowed them to start enacting their own aid policies—either regionally, like Brazil, which quickly emerged as a hub for Latin American financial assistance, or internationally, like China, which used its surging economic might in the new century to invest in development projects around the globe, especially in Africa. By insisting on enhanced South–South cooperation, we were recognizing the arrival of these "new donors" on the scene, signaling another major shift in the prevailing aid architecture long dominated by Western countries and institutions. Pursing this expanded protocol of development cooperation—a broadening of the traditional concept of development assistance—eventually became the center of focus at the subsequent high-level forum in Busan.

The agreement wasn't ironed out as I had hoped before things got underway, but it wasn't tossed aside, either. It took three days of negotiations, but donors finally agreed and endorsed the *Accra Agenda for Action*. It was the product of an unprecedented alliance among developing countries, OECD countries, and more than 3,000 civil society organizations.[3] In retrospect, I believe the act of collaboration itself proved to be as momentous as anything in the document, which notably included the core objectives promoted by the developing countries.

The *Accra Agenda for Action* went further than any previous agreement in recognizing the necessity of true partnerships between donor countries and aid recipient countries. Africa started down that path almost a decade earlier with NEPAD, but the *Accra Agenda* applied those principles on a universal scale.

Equally important, it defined aid and financing for development for a new era. It used evidence gathered by the OECD of what was and was not working at country level to show that simply increasing aid from traditional donor countries was not the answer to sustainable development. Most developing countries, while thankful for the increased commitments of recent years, already knew this.

Events in Accra also enhanced the stature of developing countries as part of the negotiating process. Once planning began for the fourth high-level forum in Busan, the Working Party on Aid Effectiveness had to be reconstituted. But this time it was different. Instead of simply adding more members from developing countries, as it had done previously, the OECD added a co-chair to actually *represent* developing countries: Talaat Abdel-Malck. Developing countries were no longer subsidiary to the decision making process; they were central to it.

The Busan forum convened in November 2011 and its final outcome placed an emphasis on ways for developing countries "to increase independence from aid," including the use of development assistance to catalyze wider domestic and external resource mobilization. It also incorporated a stronger recognition that developing countries deserved ownership over their development agendas and resources. This was an important concession; it acknowledged that progress since Monterrey a decade prior had been uneven and too slow. The same criticism could be applied to Busan. Momentum remains lacking in implementing some of its most celebrated elements, such as removing stipulations at the country level. Cooperation, as always, remains a work in progress.

In general, the agreements produced at these OECD high-level forums have struggled to meet their ambitions, falling short of what the OECD and others had originally envisioned. Part of the problem has been unreliable execution or erratic adherence to the agreed-upon frameworks, but a bigger issue might simply be that time and events passed them by.

I didn't attend the Busan forum. By that time, ACET was going strong and we had our own major event to plan that same year: a three-day, private workshop that convened a few dozen experts to help us set the right course for promoting a full-throttled economic transformation agenda for Africa. I still believed that making aid work better was important, especially in the poorest countries that still need those additional resources the most. But it was evident that dramatic shifts were on the way. Indeed, within a few years, the driving focus of sustainable development in Africa would turn to economic transformation, for which traditional aid and financing would remain relevant but increasingly less so.

◆　◆　◆　◆

In the years between the Rome and Busan forums on aid effectiveness, the external development finance landscape began to change rapidly. In recent years, the change has only accelerated. Traditional ODA to Africa is on a steady decline and is not keeping pace with shifting national priorities. Even though the aid effectiveness agenda helped call attention to the need to improve the delivery and usage of development assistance, many donors have not met their commitments and have remained unreliable in the face of competing demands. Meanwhile, powerful new players in global finance have emerged. China, India, and Brazil, among other nontraditional countries, have invested heavily in Africa; in some cases, so heavily and so aggressively as to spark debate over their motivations. Philanthropies and foundations are providing resources that sometimes bypass government systems entirely. And the private sector has expanded its role, leading to a surge in foreign direct investment (FDI).

This all adds up to a seismic shift in the way African countries are finding funds for development—and in the way that viewpoints on traditional assistance have evolved, for donors and recipient countries alike.

A notable change took place in Doha, Qatar in late 2008, at the second International Conference on Financing for Development, a follow-up to Monterrey. Its outcome, the Doha Declaration, recognized that mobilizing financial resources for development and the effective use of those resources were central to maintaining the global partnership that had emerged over previous years. This marked a big turning point in how development finance was viewed—from "allocating" aid to "mobilizing" resources that included funds from the private sector, finance institutions, guarantees, and philanthropy. This Doha event convened a few months after the *Accra Agenda for Action* was adopted, and it reflected the consensus formed there.

The third International Conference on Financing for Development took place seven years later, in July 2015 in Addis Ababa. It updated the global framework on financing to reflect the new methods and sources of assistance and to ensure priorities were aligned with the recently adopted Sustainable Development Goals. This became known as the *Addis Ababa Action Agenda* and it covered an even broader array of issues. In particular, it highlighted ways in which development assistance can be used not only as primary funds but as a catalyst to generate a larger pool of financial resources—an effort to address obvious financing gaps in an era of declining ODA. As a result, the Addis outcome focused heavily on combating illicit financial flows, improving domestic resource management, addressing trade barriers and debt burdens, and creating more favorable environments for foreign and domestic private sector finance.

Indeed, as we look toward the next era of development financing in Africa, no two components are as crucial as the ability of countries to mobilize their own resources and attract private sector investments. Look no further than the World Bank, Africa's largest source of development financing, as proof.

Every three years, donors meet to replenish the funds for the International Development Association, or IDA, the arm of the Bank that lends money to the world's poorest nations, including fragile and conflict states. The agreement made in December 2016 for the eighteenth replenishment, known as IDA18, included $2.5 billion to mobilize increased private capital and scale up private sector development in IDA countries—a dramatic shift in approach for helping impoverished countries achieve their development goals.

The following April, the World Bank Development Finance Forum convened in Accra, organized around three sectors—infrastructure, with a focus on energy and urbanization; agribusiness; and manufacturing. The forum was the Bank's flagship event in Africa to support its financing for development agenda and it highlighted the sea change in thinking that had taken place. At the meeting, the Bank outlined its "cascade approach," which for the first time emphasized that development organizations should prioritize private finance where possible, then public–private partnerships—and *only then*, if those options are not available, should concessional financing traditionally associated with aid be considered.

What all this means is that the financing architecture that has defined African development since the start of the independence era has been upended. The changes have created an array of choices for countries beyond traditional ODA. But with new opportunities come new questions and concerns. For instance, what methods are countries using to access financing in this new environment? How have new players affected the composition and usages of ODA at the country level? How are country systems—the institutional structures, processes, and coordinating mechanisms—adapting to mobilize and manage financial resources and to ensure their sustainability?

Most countries are already behind the curve. While some have new policies or frameworks in place to reflect the changing landscape, implementation has been poor and institutional reforms have been lacking. It's imperative for governments to adopt progressive policies that leverage the new forms of development financing to their benefit. For example, despite the upward trend, the actual levels of private investment in Africa have been minuscule in relation to overall development spending, and largely focused on a few sectors in a few countries. While investments in sectors such as oil and gas should be welcomed, they are unlikely to spur sustainable economic growth that benefits the broad economy—or lead to true economic transformation, as Chapter 15 details.

African countries face enormous financing gaps, but they also have unprecedented opportunities to control their own fate—an opportunity that didn't exist mere decades ago. As such, they must bear the weight of the ownership they have long sought by addressing long-standing policy challenges, such as enhanced domestic resource mobilization and rule of law, and by making the investment environment attractive, stable, transparent, and mutually beneficial. Developing countries are no longer passive participants but rather active players in a financing environment that looks dramatically different by the day. We've not yet reached a future beyond aid, but we can see it on the distant horizon.

Notes

1   Abuja actually ended in a stalemate. After almost five hours of voting, neither of the final two candidates, Kaberuka and Olabisi Ogunjobi of Nigeria, had the necessary majority. So the election was postponed for two months. The voting members regrouped in Tunisia in July, when Kaberuka won easily. He went on to serve 10 years, and he did a wonderful job.

2   For instance, we got word of senior UN officials actively campaigning against me in the days and hours before the vote. They weren't strangers; they were associates I had worked with over the years. They believed their agencies had been diminished by the ECA's turnaround. A few days after the election, a good friend and associate, Olara Otunnu, a Ugandan who was also a UN undersecretary-general, called me and confirmed the rumors. It was all very disheartening.

3   The role that civil society organizations, or CSOs, played can't be overlooked. Unlike in Paris, where they had a limited impact on the outcome, CSOs were highly involved in the preparatory discussions for the *Accra Agenda for Action*. In fact, a global network of CSOs produced a strong feedback statement in response to an early draft. Their positions closely mirrored those taken by the PCCG members of the consensus group, so we used that opportunity to form an alliance with several CSOs to ensure that we were working together and toward shared objectives.

Part IV
Toward the Future

I am blessed to have four beautiful grandchildren: Jonah, Kofi, Mena, and Kare. Mena lives with her parents in Accra, where she goes to school. She is a child growing up in Ghana, just as I was. When I envision a better future for Africa, I do it through her eyes. When she is grown, what kind of Africa will she see? What kind of opportunities will be available to her? Will her standard of living—her welfare and well-being—be better than it is today?

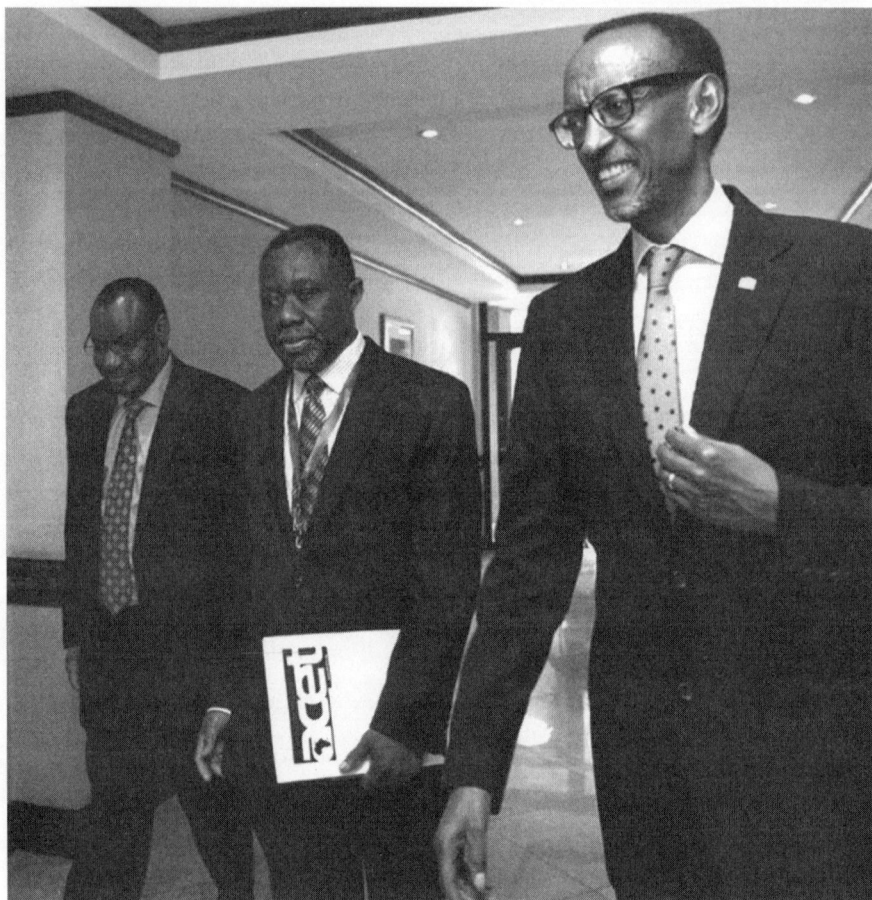

With Rwanda Finance Minister Claver Gatete, left, and President Paul Kagame at the inaugural African Transformation Forum held March 2016 in Kigali.

Chapter 15

Transforming Africa

A Pathway to Inclusive Growth and Sustainable Development

Lake Como, in northern Italy's Lombardy region, lies about 85 kilometers north of Milan, nestled in the foothills of the Alps. It is, quite honestly, one of the most serene and beautiful places I've ever seen. The lake itself is quite large, the third-largest in Italy, ringed by breathtaking mountain vistas. It's shaped liked the letter "Y" turned upside down, with three branches meeting at the picturesque town of Bellagio. The area is known as an upscale resort for the rich and famous, but its beauty and surroundings—the Lombardy region was a center of Renaissance-era art, culture, and thought—also make it an ideal location to seek inspiration. It's where the Rockefeller Foundation established its world-famous Bellagio Center to support "individuals and organizations who are working to improve the lives of poor or vulnerable people." It's also where the African Center for Economic Transformation convened a small but influential group of thought leaders in April 2011 to answer a particularly important question: what does transformation mean for Africa and how do we bring it about?

Structural transformation of an economy entails broadening a country's production structure from one based predominantly on primary commodities, such as oil or fresh fruits, to one based predominantly on industry, such as processing and manufacturing, and knowledge-based services. It means improving infrastructure, from better roads to transport goods to better electrical grids to keep the power on—and industries running. It also means upgrading skills and technological capabilities across all sectors to improve efficiency, respond to new challenges, and be more competitive in global markets—not only with products, but as an attractive destination for doing business.

As might be imagined, such major changes do not come cheaply. The only way for developing countries to tackle such sweeping efforts is through heavy investments from both the public and private sectors. But to attract finance and foreign investment, a country needs to be politically stable, boast strong and capable institutions, and, preferably, be on a growth trajectory to generate the broad array of domestic resources (such as higher private savings and government revenues) that also are needed.

Given the mutually reinforcing nature of economic growth and structural transformation, therefore, it's easy to draw an obvious conclusion: they are inseparable twin objectives that should be the central policy focus of any developing country that is eager not only to grow GDP but to sustain that growth—and improve the lives of its citizens—over the long haul. Taken together, these twin objectives are encapsulated in a single term: economic transformation.

At Bellagio, no one needed a crash course in the nature or benefits of economic transformation. As a development strategy, it had been proven to work time and again, most notably in Asia where it lifted up countries both large and small, from China and its 1.4 billion people to Singapore and its 4 million. What we needed—or in my view, what Africa needed—was a shared understanding for how the continent, with its own unique set of resources and challenges, could apply the same principles and achieve equally successful results.

We met over four days in April, with a group of attendees that included global policymakers, financiers, entrepreneurs, academics, and current and former African ministers. ACET curated the list of participants carefully; we wanted bold thinkers who believed in transformation and understood the vast complexities involved—such as the word transformation itself, an abstraction that means different things to different people. That list included Donald Kaberuka, who had recently won election to a second term as president of the African Development Bank; Tito Mboweni, former governor of the South African Reserve Bank (and future chair of ACET's board of directors); Chukwuma Charles Soludo, former governor of the Central Bank of Nigeria; Rosa Yolanda Munguambe, Mozambique's minister of public service; Kwesi Botchwey, Ghana's former long-serving finance minister; Wonhyuk Lim, a top economist at the Korea Development Institute; Steven C. Radelet, the chief economist for USAID; and Justin Lin, chief economist at the World Bank.

The workshop in Bellagio preceded the Busan High-Level Forum on Aid Effectiveness by almost eight months. The two meetings offer an interesting juxtaposition. Without a doubt, important topics were discussed and agreements made at Busan, but the primary focus remained on refining and improving the relationship between donor and recipient countries, a discussion that had been going on in some form or another for four decades. At Bellagio, we weren't focused on that at all, other than to what extent more equitable approaches by donor countries could lead to more profitable investments for African nations. We were interested in refining—and driving—the dialogue around a development strategy that was beginning to pick up steam.

A handful of African countries had already begun to move along a transformation path, most notably Mauritius, which was doing extremely well after developing one of Africa's most advanced garment industries—a process it began in 1970, just two years after independence. Relying on transformation strategies, Rwanda had instigated one of Africa's great turnaround stories after its mid-1990s civil war. Ethiopia also began to reorient its economy around the same time. By 2010, it had achieved double-digit growth in real terms, averaging 10.6 percent a year over the previous 15 years, outpacing most of its African counterparts and on par with China. Other countries, such as Kenya, which in 2008 launched its transformation-oriented Vision 2030 development program, had more recently taken the important first step of outlining long-term strategies.

Meanwhile, the World Bank and the AfDB had recently adopted new strategies that emphasized regionally integrated infrastructure investments, more diversified production, and rapid growth for manufacturing and services to absorb labor. Global finance paid attention, too. McKinsey & Company, in its 2010 report *Lions on the Move: The Progress and Potential of African Economies*, pointed firmly to transformation as the best way to unlock a $2.6 trillion African market.

This was the big picture context as we met in Bellagio. And for those of us at ACET, the stakes seemed fairly high. We had been up and running for three years and busy from the start. We worked with governments in Liberia, Ghana, Rwanda, and Sierra Leone and we collaborated with more than a dozen African think tanks on transformation-related studies. We worked with the AfDB on a new regional strategy for the Economic Community of West African states and we held numerous advocacy events

439

to raise policy awareness around transformation. As I told the assembled guests in Bellagio, "We hope this is only the beginning."

It was clear which way the winds were blowing and I felt ACET was ready to increase its prominence as a leading policy institution. But to plant that flag, we needed to make a definitive statement on what constitutes transformation for African countries: the pathways to take, the competitive advantages to exploit, the type of goals to set, the measurements to gauge progress. Most important, we needed to be certain that we got such a statement right.

We had a great, diverse group of experts, but we certainly didn't have all the answers. Bellagio was an attempt for opinion leaders to coalesce their thoughts around transformation ideals for Africa, but it also was an opportunity for ACET to deepen its own understanding before the organization took its next step forward. We had begun early preparations for a flagship publication on transformation, but we wanted to be sure that we would have something meaningful to contribute to the dialogue if we followed through with it.

So as I opened the proceedings, I outlined what ACET hoped to attain from the workshop: a shared understanding of economic transformation in Africa, a blueprint for focusing African policymakers on economic transformation, and the best way to position our organization to support those policymakers.

"We would like to benefit from your contributions, as a diverse and richly experienced group, on the prospects and challenges for transformation in Africa," I said, "and receive your guidance on how we can best accelerate Africa's economic transformation."

The ensuing four days were really exhilarating. Our discussions focused on the most fundamental aspects of transformation challenges— financing, infrastructure, harnessing state capacity, and balancing risks and opportunities. We heard from representatives from Brazil, India, South Korea, and Singapore—all countries that had transformed their economies with demonstrable results—and we applied their lessons to Africa's challenges.

At dinner one night, USAID's Steven Radelet made a presentation based on the book he had recently published, *Emerging Africa: How 17 Countries Are Leading the Way*. Radelet's book was among the most notable to focus the world's attention on Africa's unfolding economic promise in the new millennium.[1] Another highlight came courtesy of a good friend of mine, Akbar Noman, an economist specializing in transition economies and senior fellow at the Initiative for Policy Dialogue, an academic think tank headed by Joseph Stiglitz at Columbia University. Noman pointed out that even as new sources of financing emerged in Sub-Saharan Africa, a substantial gap for low-income countries would remain—necessitating more advanced public–private partnerships for investments. It was a key point that's become central to Africa's transformation prospects amid rapid financing shifts.

By the time the workshop concluded, we had found consensus around a number of structural elements in African economies that, when combined with growth, would be the most likely to result in successful transformation and sustainable development. The Bellagio participants encouraged ACET to move forward with a large-scale research project, and we eagerly agreed to incorporate the workshop's deliberations into it. That project, the *African Transformation Report*, would take another three years to finish, but it would also become the kind of definitive statement on economic transformation that Africa lacked.

"The iron of transformation is hot," I told my colleagues before leaving Bellagio. "We must beat it into shape before it cools down!"

◆　◆　◆　◆

I had been talking about transformation for years at the ECA, long before I founded ACET. Even though Africa faced so many pressing challenges, I believed that *any* discussion regarding Africa's long-term development future should not stray too far from the principles of transformation. "Industrialization is crucial to the structural transformation of Africa's economy," I said during a May 1997 address to Africa's ministers of industry. I invoked the idea during my Global Compact speech in November 2000, citing the need to "move faster away from aid dependency" by boosting private investments to finance more sustainable development. In 2000, we made it the featured topic of that year's *Economic Report on Africa*, which was subtitled "Transforming Africa's Economies." From that point, transformation remained a recurring theme in those annual reports, even after I departed.

When I decided to pursue the presidency of the African Development Bank in 2004, I felt I could use the office as a platform to promote economic transformation. Even though I lost the election, I made transformation a central topic of discussion during the time I campaigned. It was clear to anyone who talked with me about the future that I saw transformation as the only viable path for lasting poverty reduction and sustainable development in Africa. So, in a way, I began building support for ACET before I knew that's what I was doing.

Shortly after my term at the ECA expired in 2005, the Kwame Nkrumah University of Science and Technology (KNUST) located in Kumasi, Ghana, awarded me an honorary doctorate. The university also asked if I would come for a short "residency" to deliver a three-part lecture on a topic of my choice. Since I would be addressing Africa's next generation of economists, technocrats, and leaders, the topic seemed obvious: the challenges and opportunities for Africa's economic transformation—a reflection of my growing obsession!

I spent a good bit of time preparing: collecting my thoughts, doing some research, and mapping out the main messages I wanted to convey with my lectures. In doing so, I became more convinced than ever that a broad economic transformation agenda was needed in Africa.

The urgency had never seemed more apparent—if you looked closely.

On the surface, Africa was, at long last, showing hopeful signs. The continent made impressive economic progress in the 1990s; in the second half of the decade, real GDP growth averaged 4 percent a year and several countries enjoyed double-digit growth—a proposition that had seemed outlandish even a few years prior. The investment climate warmed up and capital markets broadened. Export growth nearly doubled. The pace picked up from there.

By 2005, African economies had logged GDP growth of 5.4 percent, topping the 5.2 percent in 2004 and far ahead of the 4.0 percent mark in 2003 and preceding years. According to the ECA's *Economic Report on Africa 2006*, Africa's growth in 2005 was in line with transition economies, higher than Latin America's 4.3 percent. On a disaggregated level, 25 African countries recorded faster growth in 2005 relative to 2004. The strong numbers represented a major turnaround from decades of stagnation.

But the *Economic Report on Africa 2006* also warned that African countries continued to face a perennial shortage of resources to finance public and private investment, constraining their ability to accelerate, or sustain, growth. On the surface, such a claim could seem alarmist. After all, more private capital was coming into Africa than ever before—surging from an average of $6.8 billion in the period between 1998 and 2002 to $17 billion in 2005. But those flows were unequally distributed across the continent, with a marked slant toward oil-rich countries such as Angola, Chad, and Nigeria. And even within those countries, investments were not diverse; in Angola, the oil sector alone accounted for more than 90 percent of FDI in 2005. The oil investments underscored another problem: an overreliance on a booming global commodities market, which is neither predictive nor resilient to shocks—nor particularly strong at creating jobs and adding value to the larger economy.

High global demand for oil and other export commodities wasn't solely responsible for the continent's rising GDP during this time, but even the other key contributing factors had their own warning signs.

For example, macroeconomic management in many countries had improved, resulting in lower inflation and better fiscal accounts. But macroeconomic reforms are like lubricant for an economy. They are a necessary condition for growth but by themselves do not necessarily yield direct, recurring gains over a long period of time; they stabilize rather than propel.

Another example: countries were showing strong performance in the agricultural and service sectors—two areas upon which many African economies historically relied but areas that remain filled with low-wage, non-productive labor. I don't mean non-productive in the sense that workers are lazy, but in the economic sense: jobs that fail to provide additional value to a nation's broader economy or offer little to no upward economic mobility.

The cold hard truth was that the structure of African economies, despite their recent growth, had changed very little since the 1970s. In almost all of them, the primary sectors of either agriculture or minerals still dominated production, but with substandard application of modern technology and few linkages to the rest of the economies. The exports markets, dominated by oil and other commodities, suffered from the same limitations. And aside from South Africa and Mauritius, no Sub-Saharan nation in 2005 had a viable manufacturing sector that was internationally competitive in any product.

The failure in most countries to expand and improve their production and exports, as well as employ more modern and efficient practices, was a primary reason the new growth was not generating enough jobs—and was undermining the long-term viability of any recent GDP gains.

Africa had been down this road before. In the aftermath of independence, many newly formed nations enjoyed booming, commodities-driven growth. Once the external shocks of the early 1970s hit, it all went away, and worse. No one preferred all those years of stagnation to GDP growth, but it was obvious that, without major policy shifts, most African governments were not likely to sustain their gains.

"How many more chances are we going to get?" I asked the audience gathered for my first lecture at KNUST. Without embarking on full-throttled transformation, I said, African countries risked repeating the mistakes of the past—and wasting unprecedented opportunity.

Globalization had rewritten the rules of the game; Africa had never had such potential to expand its markets and compete on a global playing field. And on top of that, at the recent Kananaskis G8 summit, the world's richest nations had just agreed to write off African debts. Coupled with a decade of growth across the continent, I said, this all added up to Africa's best, and perhaps final, opportunity "to break the vicious cycle of underdevelopment, poverty, decline, marginalization, and dependence."

This is what transformation can do for Africa, I added, as it's done elsewhere.

From 1965 to 1990, the 23 economies of East Asia grew faster than all other regions of the world. Most of the growth was attributed to eight economies: Japan; Indonesia, Malaysia, and Thailand, three newly industrializing economies in Southeast Asia; and South Korea, Taiwan, Singapore, and Hong Kong, the four countries that came to be known as the "Asian Tigers." In that time period, real income per capita increased more than four times in the Asian Tigers and Japan and more than doubled in the other three countries. According to the World Bank's 1993 research study, *The East Asian Miracle*, "if growth were randomly distributed, there is roughly one chance in ten thousand that success would have been so regionally concentrated."

The turnaround had staying power, as the Asian Tigers and other countries, especially China, continued to roar over the next 15 years. China had just begun to record its own remarkably high growth rates in the early 1990s, but it would soon grow to become the second-largest economy in the world. The term "miracle" stuck in economic and policy circles, but it wasn't a miracle that elevated the Asian economies from poverty to prosperity: it was transformation. They all embarked on deep, systematic transformation in the decade after World War II, around the same time that Africa's colonial period was nearing its end. It took decades for those processes to play out, but once they did, the results were striking in comparison to Africa.

Economically speaking, much of Africa was at the same level as the Asian Tigers when they started down a transformation path. South Korea, for instance, had the same per capita income as Ghana in 1960, but by 1991 it was more than seven times higher than Ghana's. By 2005, the gap had widened even further, to more than eight times higher. In that same time period, South Korea moved its GDP from $3.9 billion to almost $900 billion. Ghana, by comparison, moved from $1.2 billion to $10.7 billion.

South Korea and the other Tigers didn't all follow the same blueprint, but they did share enough similarities on the path from poverty to prosperity to draw lessons. Their governments focused predominantly on developing industrial capabilities and a strong manufacturing exports base. Their governments invested heavily in the public sector, but often to facilitate even deeper private investments. And their government leaders took active, hands-on approaches to guiding the transformation process, such as creating new institutions designed to plan and carry out strategies. Ultimately, the Asian Tigers succeeded through the combination of creating strong, capable states and unleashing the private sector. Aid was also pivotal; oriented toward growth, it helped eliminate infrastructure bottlenecks and support projects with broad economic impact. Asian countries knew what they wanted, and they crafted clearly defined policies in support.

By 2005, quite a few of the critical preconditions that spurred the Asian turnaround existed across many parts of Africa. Macroeconomic discipline and stability, for instance, were the most consistently present factors across the East Asian economies, and they were finally beginning to show in Africa. Policymaking in many African countries had grown far more pragmatic, another key characteristic of the Asian Tigers that embraced both free markets and state interventions, adopting the best strategies of both, pursuant to circumstance. Additionally, strong leadership and a common vision for progress were vital components in East Asia's drive toward successful development; the countries learned from and relied on each other to accelerate their growth. Through the African Union and NEPAD, African countries had recently committed to following a common framework and implementing a joint vision of development. And of course the changing aid dynamic that favored African ownership mirrored the control East Asia exerted over its external development resources.

Then there was the most basic precondition of all: human capital. The Asian Tigers relied on a growing population to learn skills and fill jobs that aligned with their countries' competitive advantages and transformation goals. Between 1980 and 2005, Africa's population almost doubled, rising from approximately 477 million to 920 million. Projections for the future are even more staggering.

"If asked half a century ago to name the economic success stories for the next decades, only a fool would have picked Hong Kong, Korea, Singapore, or Taiwan," I said to my audience, wrapping up my KNUST lecture. "The reason why such a fool would have turned out to be a visionary is that these countries went to the very core of the meaning of transformation, which literally means going *across, over* or *beyond*, to change the very nature and condition of reality."

After I finished my residency at the university, I knew that I could make a convincing case that Africa needed a continental organization devoted solely to economic transformation. So I published the lectures in a booklet and set out to practice what I now preached.

My premise for founding ACET centered around two questions: How could Africa's recent gains be translated into sustainable growth? And how could the growth be converted into higher living standards for the majority of populations? I envisioned an organization that would work directly with African governments to answer these questions through a transformation lens. But I didn't want ACET to be just another think tank. I wanted it to be action-oriented, undertaking strong research and providing high-quality analysis but also advising governments directly on how to implement policies supported by that same research.

Still, I had my work cut out for me.

At the time, "transformation" in the African context remained primarily a buzzword, not a defining strategy. Most countries and organizations were in the midst of long-term plans built around the Millennium Development Goals and their 2015 target date. Few African countries or development institutions had incorporated transformation strategies into their plans. Naturally, I needed to gauge the potential support of African governments before proceeding.

I consulted several of the leaders with whom I had worked closely during my time at the ECA and shared with them an official proposal for what would eventually become ACET. The group included Ellen Johnson Sirleaf in Liberia, John Kufuor in Ghana, Festus Mogae in Botswana, Bingu Mutharika in Malawi, Jakaya Kikwete in Tanzania, Paul Kagame in Rwanda, and Meles Zenawi in Ethiopia, among a few others. I asked for their feedback and suggestions—and whether they saw a need for what I was proposing in the first place.

The consensus was overwhelmingly positive. I received almost a dozen letters of endorsement in late 2006 and early 2007, many expressing solidarity in the rationale that would ultimately become ACET's core tenet: that economic growth, while welcomed and encouraged, will not be enough by itself to sustain Africa's development. They agreed that transformation must be at the center of national development plans and long-term strategies, with more than one leader making mention of the "timely" nature of my plan. Kagame strongly endorsed a transformation-focused center to "nurture homegrown approaches," as he put it, to tap into the wealth of knowledge and experience in Africa. Somewhat similarly, Mogae lamented that Africa remained "overly dependent on multilateral institutions for policy analysis."

Some of the most encouraging words came from Meles, which was no surprise. During my years at the ECA, he and I had established a very close relationship, warm and friendly as well as professional. But Meles pulled no punches, and if he had hated the idea, he would have said so. Fortunately, he did not. A long-time proponent of transformation-based development strategies, Meles had aggressively promoted industrialization and manufacturing in Ethiopia over the past decade. He offered his full support for the center I proposed, and in doing so he managed to perfectly encapsulate my motivation. He wrote:

> *I fully agree with you that the challenge in African countries, after decades of reform and some encouraging results, is to speed up the pace of economic growth in order to achieve self-sustained development and structural transformation. A center such as the one you plan to establish can provide the independent and country-focused assistance Africa sorely lacks.*

The feedback I got from the heads of state provided high-level validation, but I didn't want to move forward on their support alone. During my decade at the ECA, I saw first-hand the immense value to be gained from a broad and inclusive consultation. I wanted to act quickly with ACET, but I also wanted to be thorough in seeking consensus among the institutions and stakeholders that would be potential partners and collaborators.

Over the course of the next year, I spoke with former colleagues at the World Bank and United Nations. I talked to OECD ministers and representatives from foundations and international think tanks. I sought feedback from African technicians, economists, entrepreneurs, and policymakers. No one discouraged me, or suggested I might be on a quixotic quest. Rather, I heard time and again that African countries serious about sustainable development and inclusive growth would have no choice but to pursue economic transformation on the level of the Asian Tigers. It might take a few years, but as long as respectable growth rates were maintained, it was the only logical next step. If the organization I proposed could help push that process along, then all the better.[2]

It did take a while, but by early 2008 we had enough footing to start ramping up. I had pulled together a solid team of economists and researchers that combined experienced veterans with promising graduates.

I specifically wanted a blend of those who had been on the front lines of development for a few decades and those who would be taking the fight into the future.[3]

Later that year, we held our first notable event: a seminar in which we brought together African research economists from both the diaspora and African think tanks to go through a smaller-scale version of the same process that we would employ a few years later in Bellagio. In a way, we were announcing our presence. The turnout was strong, and we got a helpful publicity boost from one person in attendance: Joseph Stiglitz, a Nobel laureate economist and one of the world's leading thinkers on globalization and development transformation. Stiglitz had been chief economist at the World Bank in the late 1990s, after I had departed. Akbar Noman, one of the colleagues I consulted during my initial ACET "outreach," worked with Stiglitz and he helped set it up.

Stiglitz did more than show up, too; he actually chaired the seminar, then gave a public lecture in Accra, setting the scene for why an organization like ACET was needed. That lecture attracted a lot of attention and represented quite a debut for our new institute; the fact that someone of Stiglitz's stature was already "on board" with ACET helped give us instant legitimacy. It also generated some excitement among our early partners and staff, including me, because I agreed with his research and policy ideas.[4] In his 2006 book *Making Globalization Work*, for example, Stiglitz argued passionately for striking the right balance between the public and private sectors to create inclusive, equitable growth. "Development is about transforming the lives of people," he wrote, "not just transforming economies."

As ACET began working with governments and leaders in Ghana, Liberia, and Rwanda, among other countries, that same philosophy informed our organization's mission statement: to help deliver economic transformation that improves the lives of all Africans.

◆ ◆ ◆ ◆

About three years after the Bellagio workshop, ACET launched its flagship publication, the *African Transformation Report*, in March 2014. It was both a product of the endorsement and guidance we received at Bellagio and the culmination of an exhaustive three-year research program—comprising dozens of country, sector, and thematic studies—that looked systematically at transformation as a broad framework for balanced and sustainable growth.

Our timing could not have been better.

As Africa's economic prospects brightened, so did its defining narrative, shifting from a region wracked by war and poverty to one brimming with opportunity and potential. The growth that propelled Africa in the years preceding the establishment of ACET had only accelerated in the years since, to heights that not long before seemed unimaginable. The size of the African economy had more than doubled since 2000, the beginning of a decade in which six of the world's 10 fastest-growing countries were in Sub-Saharan Africa. By 2014, the continent's global share of FDI had surpassed 5.5 percent—after being as low as 2 percent 15 years prior—and the flow of private capital exceeded foreign aid.

In May 2000, The Economist famously labeled Africa "the hopeless continent" on its cover. In December 2011, it reversed course, calling Africa "the hopeful continent" in a new cover story titled "Africa Rising." The narrative shift was striking. That phrase—Africa rising—quickly became a convenient shorthand for Africa's growth and GDP gains, showing up in books, newspapers, magazines, and as the title of events and seminars. The "rising" narrative exploded the same year that ACET convened its Bellagio workshop, and it was impossible to avoid.

It was a fascinating reversal, but as I watched this narrative take hold from my perch at ACET, I couldn't help but feel uneasy. Those same structural problems that I had been talking about since Africa's modern growth story first began remained, for the most part. Sure, there were countries that had grown in a more sustainable way, such as Mauritius, and countries that had put themselves on a better path, such as Rwanda. But the overwhelming majority of African countries still lagged behind the rest of the world in most economic indicators and poverty rates, and multiple studies showed that even amid Africa's rapid growth, levels of human well-being remained out of whack with GDP per head. As African Development Bank President Donald Kaberuka declared at the Bank's annual meeting in May 2014, "You cannot eat GDP."

From the hopeless to the hopeful continent; it's a good story that gained a lot of traction, but those who were paying close attention knew the economic reality was much more complex. It's not that the "rising" narrative was wrong; it was incomplete. That's where the *African Transformation Report* came in, and why it made such an impact. It filled in the gaps.

For years, those who had been the most vocal about transformation kept saying that African economics needed more than growth to sustain their gains and emulate the success of East Asia and other countries. The *African Transformation Report*, or *ATR*, not only offered empirical evidence to back up that assertion, it laid out a clear vision for African countries to emulate, identified the most immediate paths to transformation, and detailed the various policy and institutional reforms required to get there.

Most notably, the report provided an empirical answer to the question that drove our discussions at Bellagio: what does transformation mean for Africa? The *ATR* boiled it down to five overarching attributes.

It means diversifying production. An essential part of economic transformation is acquiring the capability to produce a widening array of goods and services and then choosing which ones to specialize in based on international relative prices.

It means boosting export competitiveness. Becoming more competitive on international markets opens up the opportunity to expand production, boost employment, reduce unit costs, and increase incomes by better exploiting comparative advantages.

It means increasing productivity, especially on farms and in factories. In most industrialization experiences, the rise in agricultural productivity allowed agriculture to release labor to industry, produce more food to moderate any hikes in urban industrial wages, supply raw materials for processing in industries, increase exports to pay for transformation inputs, and enhance the domestic market for industrial products.

It means upgrading technology throughout the economy. Productivity gains can come from more efficient use of existing resources and technology to produce the same goods and services, but rising productivity can be sustained only through new and improved technologies and increasing ability to master more sophisticated economic activities.

And last but not least, it means improving human well-being. At first glance, this might seem overly vague, but it's not at all. A country cannot develop as long as most of its citizens are trapped in poverty or unable to better their social and financial security. Improving human well-being involves many factors, including incomes, employment, inequality, health and education, as well as peace, justice, security, and the environment. The two most directly related to economic transformation are GDP per capita and employment. If GDP per capita is rising, and job opportunities are expanding, economic transformation will result in shared prosperity and income inequality will be reduced, or at least controlled.

The *African Transformation Report* pulled these five attributes together as part of a simple, three-word phrase to define economic transformation in Africa: growth with depth. Or, more precisely, Growth with DEPTH—an acronym comprising each key attribute: Diversified production. Export competitiveness. Productivity increases. Technology upgrades. Human well-being.

To make the case for growth with depth, we compared Africa's performance with that of eight earlier transformers: Brazil, Chile, Indonesia, Malaysia, Singapore, South Korea, Thailand, and Vietnam. They were plagued 40 years ago by the same weak economic features that characterize many African countries—extreme poverty, low productivity, low technology, and limited exports. Today several of them are upper-middle or even high-income countries.

The *ATR* also introduced the African Transformation Index to translate "growth with depth" into empirical terms. The index offered a comparative baseline to assess the performance and measure the progress of African countries as they move along a transformation path, using the five DEPTH attributes. Nothing remotely close to this had ever been attempted.

Altogether, the *ATR* studied 21 countries in Sub-Saharan Africa. The five highest-ranking on the index—meaning the countries that were most advanced in their transformation approaches—at the time were: Mauritius, South Africa, Côte D'Ivoire, Senegal, and Uganda. The index also measured the attributes all the way back to 2000, which allowed ACET to determine which countries had made up—or lost—the most ground in transforming their economies during Africa's 2000-2010 "boom" decade. The biggest gainers: Uganda, Mozambique, Rwanda, Kenya, and Ethiopia. The biggest decliners: Botswana, Burkina Faso, Cameroon, and, particularly troubling for me, Ghana.

The African Transformation Index was a key selling point of the report but not the only one. In particular, the *ATR* offered recommendations based on the fact that one size does not fit all when it comes to transformation strategy. Our goal was to present ideas, backed by research, that could be tailored to fit the unique challenges and opportunities that each African country faces. The *ATR* identified four overarching pathways to transformation for Sub-Saharan Africa: labor-intensive manufacturing, agro-processing, extractives, and tourism. Most countries enjoy a comparative advantage in one or more of these areas due to Africa's abundant labor and natural resources; they just need to find the right way to exploit their advantages. The *ATR* offered countries the tools to do that.

Moreover, it had something fresh—and important—to say. From the moment we left Bellagio, the full ACET team focused on making sure that the report's research was unimpeachable and its language was clear and compelling. I can't possibly give enough credit to the staff at ACET who oversaw the work, but Yaw Ansu, ACET's chief economist, deserves ample recognition. He was involved in just about every aspect of researching, writing, and producing the final product.[5]

Much to our relief, it was an immediate hit. The African division of the US Chamber of Commerce called the *ATR* "one of the top-notch reports to come out of Africa." The Economist called it "a report grounded in economic reality, unlike many other development blueprints." New African magazine endorsed it as "an agenda to shape new strategies for individual African nations." The Hewlett Foundation deemed it "a major intellectual contribution, not just another report." And Justin Lin, whose term as chief economist at the World Bank had recently ended, called it "a must-read" for governments as well as "anyone concerned about poverty reduction, job generation, and economic development in Africa."

But the best feedback we got in person. Over the next year, we took the *ATR* on a global road show, having been invited to present its findings in several countries, including the Democratic Republic of Congo, Ethiopia, France, Ghana, Italy, Japan, Nigeria, Norway, Rwanda, South Africa, Tanzania, the United Kingdom, and the United States. It was discussed at conferences, meetings, and workshops held in conjunction with the ECA, AfDB, the Center for Global Development, the World Bank, and various national chambers of commerce, and private sector groups. The response blew us away.

One thing working in our favor: the report arrived at precisely the right moment. Economic transformation had rapidly caught on as the global development community began to look beyond 2015 and the expiration of the MDGs. As awareness grew over the need to plan far ahead of the current "African Rising" surge, transformation became the buzzword *du jour*. And the *ATR* offered a groundbreaking exploration of what transformation entails for African countries and the steps to get there.

And yes, it really did break new ground. It was the first report of its kind to define economic transformation for Africa in quantifiable terms.

For ACET, it elevated our profile and put us on the map as a credible source of transformation research as well as implementation strategy—the exact action-oriented think tank I had envisioned. Liberian President Ellen Johnson Sirleaf, one of the heads of state whose counsel and support I initially sought, agreed to contribute a short Foreword to the report. "Years ago, I welcomed ACET's establishment in the expectation that it would give new meaning to African ownership," she wrote. "With this report, ACET has earned that recognition."

By 2015, economic transformation had become the consensus paradigm for Africa's development, a key component of long-term strategies endorsed by Africa's continental institutions and openly integrated into the African objectives of the UN, OECD, World Bank, and numerous think tanks and foundations. ACET and the *African Transformation Report* did not single-handedly turn the tide, but we certainly helped generate some waves. Most of these organizations had either endorsed or were in the process of finalizing strategies centered around transformation by the time we launched the *ATR*. We were mostly moving in tandem, though the early work definitely predated the tipping point to come.

In May 2013, the African Union adopted Agenda 2063, a massive, 50-year development framework built on seven "African aspirations" for the future as well as the numerous past and current AU initiatives it supersedes. The principles of transformation sit at the center of it. The first aspiration, for example, is "a prosperous Africa, based on inclusive growth and sustainable development." The plan is bigger in scope than the AU's past continental initiatives, in part because it aims to integrate regional and national development plans under one umbrella. A five-decade time frame is ambitious, but Agenda 2063 was developed as "a living document" to be adjusted over time, based on the expectation that transformation will produce rapid socioeconomic and cultural change.

Also in 2013, the AfDB launched an updated 10-year strategy with economic transformation as its cornerstone, emphasizing the quality and sustainability of growth and reaffirming the Bank's strategic choices around economic integration, infrastructure, and the private sector. In 2016, Donald Kaberuka's successor as president, Akinwumi Adesina, announced the Bank's "High 5s"— the five priority areas that the Bank will focus on to advance a transformation agenda over the following decade. They are to light up and power Africa, feed Africa, industrialize Africa, integrate Africa, and improve the quality of life for the people of Africa.

In 2014, the UN Secretary-General's High-Level Panel on the Post-2015 Development Agenda—co-chaired by Ellen Johnson Sirleaf—recommended that future global development goals be driven by five big transformative shifts, one being "a profound economic transformation to improve livelihoods by harnessing innovation, technology, and the potential of businesses." Later that year, the UN formally adopted the Sustainable Development Goals, or SDGs, as its primary roadmap through 2030, relying heavily on the recommendations of the panel.

Around the same time, the African heads of state and government united behind a common position as their input to the post-2015 agenda. They identified six pillars to support Africa's long-term development. Economic transformation was the first.

♦ ♦ ♦ ♦

Growth with depth is not mechanical. To pursue it, countries have to develop and implement strategies appropriate to their circumstances. Consider Ethiopia. It achieved double-digit growth rates each year except two between 2005 and 2015, with infrastructure projects and light manufacturing representing the bulk of this growth. In 2012 and 2013, for instance, 37 percent of total public capital expenditure went to road construction alone. You can't attract foreign investors to build industrial parks without roads and infrastructure, and now Ethiopia, the second most-populous nation in Africa, has a half-dozen or more of these parks in different stages of development, with the potential to create millions of jobs in the decades ahead. One of them, Hawassa Industrial Park, opened in 2016 and within a year employed 10,000 people.

Rwanda enjoyed similarly strong growth during the same time period, its GDP per capita growing at an annual rate of 5.2 percent, second only to Ethiopia across Africa. Most developing countries in the world could never dream of this kind of growth, much less achieve it so quickly in the shadow of genocide and mass destruction. Rwanda is one of Africa's most promising transformation stories since it began rebuilding its economy from the ground up with transformation-minded strategies, creating a favorable business environment to attract FDI and trying to ensure job growth through extensive skills training—a necessary step, given the country's depleted postwar human capacity.

A few years ago, I wrote an op-ed with President Paul Kagame, published in newspapers worldwide, that focused on Rwanda's transformative growth. We called it "The African Breadbasket" because of the opportunity available to Africa—with nearly 60 percent of the world's arable, uncultivated land—to create a more resilient global food supply. It described, in part, how Rwanda, an industrial latecomer due to its 1990s collapse, is taking aggressive steps to modernize its agriculture and link it with broader services, such as electricity and education, to accelerate growth across sectors—and to capitalize on the slow pace of agricultural transformation in other countries.

One of those countries, Kenya, hasn't made much progress in agriculture but has been an above-average transformer since 2000 for other reasons. Kenya's strength lies in its technological innovations and sophistication in business, for which it ranked fortieth of 138 countries on the 2016–17 Global Competitiveness Index. That was the second-best score on the continent, behind only South Africa. Kenya's strong growth in the ICT sector (epitomized by the successful M-Pesa mobile telephone financial services platform), its development of the largest techno city in Africa (the Konza Technopolis), and its relatively high levels of education are all assets of a modern economy that can sustain long-term growth—thus, Kenya's ambition to become the "Silicon Savannah."

Other promising transformers have taken their own individual paths as well. The island nation of Mauritius has long been out in front for Sub-Saharan Africa, embarking on its transformation in the 1970s when it first started to move from a mono-crop sugar exporter to a robust, diversified economy built on sugar and textile export processing, tourism, and, more recently, financial services and ICT. In the process, its GDP per capita more than tripled from 1981 to 2010. South Africa, the continent's other leading transformer, is a clear leader when it comes to the level of technology used in production and exports and it trades extensively within the region. Unfortunately, a number of challenges, including persistently high unemployment, corruption scandals, and rising fiscal deficits, have slowed South Africa's strong economy in recent years, putting continued growth at risk.

As these countries show, there is no single formula for economic transformation. Africa is not a single entity but dozens of unique countries, each with its own strengths and weaknesses. Individual approaches are necessary, since what works in one country might not work as well in another. This was, as mentioned, a core concept of the *African Transformation Report*.

And yet, there are standard requirements at the country level to transform national economies—consistent actions that must be taken, regardless of individual considerations or economic circumstance. These are not speculative ideas. They are *concrete actions that countries must take to transform their economies*, drawn from the evidence supplied by those that have successfully gone down this long road. I want to share seven in all.

1. Countries must develop a shared vision and plan.

A national vision and strategy—developed through broad consultations with the private sector, civil society, think tanks, and regional forums—with clear, attainable goals, is imperative to guide economic transformation. Stakeholder buy-in should be earned, not expected.

Ethiopia sought extensive input from outside government before launching its initial five-year Growth and Transformation Plan in 2010, holding countrywide consultations led by senior government officials. The meetings included business leaders, religious leaders, university professors, youth associations, women's groups, and development partners. One of the key issues that arose, civil service reform, became a pillar of the plan.

Actually, it's encouraging how many African countries have put in place long-term strategies centered around transformation and informed by a broad public discourse. Kenya's *Vision 2030* "aims to transform Kenya into a newly industrializing, middle-income country." Like many long-term strategies, it's comprised of a series of medium-term plans. Preparations for the most current of those plans began in August 2012 with country consultations and business, professional, and other stakeholder forums. *Uganda Vision 2040* was launched in April 2013 to transform Ugandan society into a "competitive upper-middle-income country within 30 years with a per capita income of $9,500"—aspirations arrived at following a national consultation process. And in 2016, Botswana launched *Vision 2036*, a "transformative blueprint" led by a presidential task team comprising stakeholders from across the country and including additional outreach from UNDP, UNICEF, and other UN agencies working in the country.

Simply having a well-informed and inclusive development plan is by no means enough to guarantee results. But a transformation strategy cannot get off the ground without one—and it's unlikely to stay on track without a broad sense of collective ownership over its objectives and outcome.

2. Governments must focus on core state functions.

Economic transformation can take place *only* when the economy is managed well, which in turn enables businesses to thrive and transformation to flourish. This may seem obvious, but it's not easy; policy action is required on many fronts. Indeed, the list of state functions that could help provide an environment conducive to business can be very long—too long, given the capacity constraints in most African countries. For that reason, it makes sense for the state to focus on a core set of priority functions that it can perform effectively. Chief among them are sound macroeconomic management that avoids high inflation and excessive public borrowing; a streamlined regulatory environment to encourage innovation and investment; and an exchange rate that keeps exports competitive. The good news for Africa is that decades of reforms have highlighted the importance of these functions, which are now generally well understood and accepted by policymakers in the region—even if actual policies in many countries have yet to catch up.

There are other central functions at which governments must excel in order to transform. They include: planning and managing public investments, particularly infrastructure; improving public procurement to make processes transparent and reduce corruption; administering customs, seaports, and airports honestly and efficiently to facilitate more trade and tourism—and in turn boost government revenues; and building statistical capacity to make more informed decisions.

3. Government agencies must coordinate their actions.

One of the biggest challenges that many Sub-Saharan African countries face in promoting transformation is coordination within government to implement realistic plans. Often, plans are produced by planning agencies using outside experts, resulting in a disconnect when it comes to implementation. That's because if planning and finance operations are separate, as they often are, the planning agency may have little influence in ensuring that expenditures in the plan are actually reflected in the budget.

Since almost any serious transformation initiative cuts across several ministries and agencies, close coordination is imperative. It's the only way to work toward shared goals rather than operating as individual units, a process under which long-term strategies are sure to wither. Ideally, such coordination is carried out by a single agency whose authority is accepted by other ministers and staff. It may be overseen by a powerful minister, or it may be performed by an agency directly under a president, prime minister, or top deputy. Regardless of the coordinating agency's place in the government hierarchy, it must be empowered to convene stakeholders, assign tasks, monitor progress, and lead course corrections when necessary.

It's difficult to find powerful agencies filling that need across most of Africa. But some countries at least are taking steps to improve coordination of economic policy and implementation in government. Botswana has achieved impressive economic growth over the years, moving from one of Africa's poorest countries in the 1960s to an upper-middle-income country, largely on the strength of strong institutions and its flourishing diamond sector. More recently, it has moved to diversify with economic hubs for transportation, agriculture, health, education, innovation, and, of course, diamonds. These efforts have been coordinated by the National Strategy Office, created in 2010 to oversee the performance of all government growth and development entities—and to ensure coherence.

4. The public and private sectors must work together.

There is perhaps no more direct way to say this: successful economic transformation is wholly dependent on a productive working relationship between government and business. Each has a role to play and each is dependent on the other holding up its end of the bargain; otherwise specific and isolated initiatives are unlikely to lead to transformation.

Having an environment in which businesses can thrive is critical because the private sector should spearhead the creation of jobs and be in the best position to upgrade technologies and processes. Governments, meanwhile, must invest in basic infrastructure such as roads and power supplies to boost trade from the local level up and enable firms to expand. And as mentioned previously, they should streamline regulations to encourage entrepreneurship and cut unnecessary red tape. As a matter of standard practice, the public–private relationship must be symbiotic. In relation to Africa's transformation, two areas tower above the rest for public–private partnerships: closing the education and skills gap, and building infrastructure, in particular power and electricity.

By 2050, Sub-Saharan Africa is expected to have a larger and younger workforce than India or China—more than 1.2 billion people. Currently, most countries are grappling with endemic underemployment for a youth population that is already surging. Education is the key to making the labor force an asset. But governments and their development partners must work together to improve education quality and access. Businesses clearly have a role to play here. And to leverage Africa's labor market, it's in their best interests to do so. Technical and vocational education is helpful, but it is expensive—up to six times the cost for general secondary education. The private sector can help offset these costs through practical training programs, fellowships, and curriculum design.

In addition to skills training, infrastructure is the other key area where government and business must work closely to lay the right foundation for any transformation strategy in any country to be successful. Roads, bridges, dams, and facilities are one thing, but Africa cannot transform until it addresses its power problem. Approximately 680 million Africans lack access to reliable power, representing only 56 percent of the population. According to the African Development Bank, per capita consumption of energy in Sub-Saharan Africa (excluding South Africa) is 180 kilowatt hours, compared with 13,000 kwh per capita in the United States. Africa's energy potential, especially for renewables, is enormous but underutilized.

Powering up the continent will cost tens of billions. It simply can't be done by governments alone.

Altogether, even as Africa's millennium boom raised its profile among foreign investors, the reality of doing business there has not yet caught up with its potential as an enviable destination for the private sector. In almost all countries, the regulatory and operational environment is not conducive to starting and running a business, a precondition that must improve to enable transformative public–private partnerships.

5. Governments must integrate African economies.

The need for regional integration—and the lack of progress toward it— is a recurring theme in Africa's development history. The importance of governments working together is only heightened when talking about economic transformation.

For instance, many Sub-Saharan economies are small and have to import most inputs to manufacture. They also lack a large domestic market, which hampers growth and limits employment. These challenges to the manufacturing industry ultimately can be overcome by becoming competitive in global export markets. But in the early stages of industrial development, they make it very difficult for any one country to gain traction in production efficiency, export competitiveness, or any of the growth with DEPTH attributes.

In general, Africa's regional and demographic profile would seem to compel leaders to integrate the continent economically. Kwame Nkrumah certainly called for it, when Ghana was still the continent's only independent country. The limitations of going it alone have always been evident. Among Africa's 54 countries, 37 have GDPs less than $25 billion, and 16 are landlocked. Most have low population densities, poor physical infrastructure, and thick borders. Intraregional trade is a mere 15 percent, higher only than South Asia among developing regions. According to an AfDB report, these constraints make it difficult for African firms to reach competitive economic scales to move up regional—and global—value chains.

I see three key areas of focus for Africa to seize the opportunities that regional integration offers for economic transformation.

The first is financing and building regional infrastructure, including roads and other transport networks, power and energy solutions, and information technology. The second is trade facilitation, including customs and other cross-border regulations. Encouragingly, heads of state in 2018 committed to the African Continental Free Trade Area, which will establish a single market of more than 1 billion people (and is discussed in Chapter 9). The third is an unwavering political commitment to agreed-upon regional projects. For example, the Programme for Infrastructure Development in Africa is a continental initiative that aims to bring some momentum and order to numerous regional projects. It is a long-term plan through 2040 with an ultimate intention to "realize the building of the African Economic Community," first outlined in the 1991 Abuja Treaty.

6. Countries must mobilize and manage their own resources.

For African countries to transform their economies, they will need massive financial help. For example, the AfDB estimates that through 2025 its High 5s agenda will require annual investments of about $300 billion, while the UN's SDGs will require more than $600 billion, roughly 12 times the annual financing deployed for development in Africa over the past decade.

Where will those resources come from? The numbers for infrastructure investment alone illustrate the challenge. The AfDB estimates a $100 billion annual need over the next decade, but continent-wide, investment in infrastructure has averaged only half that over the previous decade. More telling, over 30 percent of those investments have been sourced from the ODA; the private sector, meanwhile, has contributed just 9 percent. For Africa to secure the resources it needs to see its countries transform, such a split is untenable.

It's not that ODA is no longer necessary. Aid is still vital to Africa, in particular for fragile states and the poorest countries and to address strategic priorities in middle-income countries. But as I described in the last chapter, circumstances are very different than they were for the better part of my career. Issues of debt relief, budget support, and mutual accountability are not at the center of Africa's development financing story going forward. Rather, it's the need for countries to be more effective at mobilizing and managing their own resources.

In July 2015, world leaders gathered for the third International Financing for Development Conference and endorsed the *Addis Ababa Action Agenda* as a foundation for financing implementation of the SDGs. That document's main focus was on improving domestic resource mobilization, including the need to widen revenue bases, end illicit financial flows, boost private investments, and integrate financing frameworks with long-term development plans.

In 2016, AfDB President Akinwumi Adesina asked me to serve on a special panel chaired by Kofi Annan and Horst Köhler. Our mission: to advise the Bank on how best to implement its agenda and help finance Africa's transformation. Our view: that the basic long-term solution lies in a very sharp increase in domestic resource mobilization by raising national savings rates well above historic levels in most countries. The panel report noted that Africa's domestic savings rates currently average about 17 percent of GDP, compared with about 40 percent in East Asia. "If Africa were to increase its average savings rate to even 30 percent," the report said, "it would have an additional $280 billion annually in resources—involving no debt obligations."

ACET's research shows that many countries are increasingly focused on ways to strengthen domestic resource mobilization, including leveraging traditional official development assistance to meet new challenges and generate new resources. For instance, countries such as Rwanda and Ghana are among those receiving support from and collaborating with development partners in recent years to increase their capacity to collect domestic revenue, which is a complex process but can be as straightforward as reforming tax policies and administration and curtailing tax evasion.

The AfDB special panel pointed out that stronger domestic resource mobilization should be complemented by initiatives to improve the business climate to spur even more private sector activity and foreign direct investment. The continent's global share of FDI increased from 3.2 percent in 2007 to 11.4 percent in 2016, making Africa the second-fastest-growing FDI destination by capital. Of particular note, investments in areas related to infrastructure—including power, construction, and ICT—made up 44 percent of all FDI into the region in 2015. Per the Financial Times' *Africa Investment Report 2016*, this "clearly demonstrates that foreign investors are thinking long term about Africa's prospects" and are responding to what regional authorities say they need.

Still, projected shortfalls are daunting. The 2017 *Financing for Development: Progress and Prospects* report tracked early progress on the *Addis Ababa Action Agenda*. It was produced by an interagency task force—including the UN system, the Bretton Woods Institutions, the World Trade Organization, and others—and was the first joint assessment of financing for development conducted since adoption of the SDGs in 2015. According to one of its key findings, under current trends, least-developed countries are likely to fall short by large margins. It also pointed to the challenges in financing long-term and high-quality investments—particularly in infrastructure, and especially in the poorest countries.

7. Political leadership must drive the process.

Successful transformation will span 20 or 30 years or more—a period that is often at odds with transfers of power. A transformation vision, however, must be long term, so support for it must be consistent over time. Political will is paramount. It's worth noting that many of the long-term plans that countries have adopted in recent years are actually comprised of a series of short-or medium-term action plans in the range of four to 10 years. This is a wise approach, as it allows for priorities to adjust as political leaders and policymakers come and go and as new or varied needs arise. The experience of the successful countries, however, shows that long-term transformation goals must be maintained once put in place, even if the incremental processes implemented to attain them are adjusted to reflect prevailing political winds.

Earlier in this book, I wrote about my experience working with Brazil in the early 1990s as that country was struggling to turn itself around. At the time, Brazil suffered from crippling stagnation and hyperinflation. As the former head of Brazil's Central Bank put it, "Imagine that the cost of your food and clothing went up by 40 percent every month." It seemed outlandish to imagine Brazil was anywhere near economic stability, much less growth. In 1995, Fernando Henrique Cardoso was elected president and his government, an alliance of his own moderate party and two right-wing parties, embarked on a decade of structural reforms and austerity measures. These moves put Brazil on a new path. By the mid-2000s, the country had grown into an emerging economic power. Brazil fell into recession in 2015 and encountered significant political upheaval shortly thereafter. But it's interrupted growth doesn't diminish the fact that it became one of the new century's great economic turnaround stories—a turnaround that shows how long-term, political commitment to transformation can benefit a country economically if it's supported across party lines.

It's an important lesson for Africa, where most countries are still struggling to find the right mix of strong state leadership and strong democratic processes. One of the biggest questions for African countries going forward is how to navigate that delicate balance.

Mauritius is generally considered the best-run country in Africa, ranking first on the Ibrahim Index in 2016 for overall governance, and not for the first time. It has spent a decade consistently ranked at the top. Not coincidentally, Mauritius has been Africa's top transformer. Granted it is a small nation with a population of just under 1.3 million, but it has held a series of peaceful elections and smooth handovers of power since gaining independence from Britain in 1968. Its democratic stability has defined it, and its leaders have remained committed to the consistent pursuit of transformation strategies. Conversely, Ghana, also a leader in African democracy for the last quarter-century, has experienced dramatic economic peaks and valleys because its frequent shifts in power have not been accompanied by adherence to a consistent long-term plan.

In contrast to both countries, Ethiopia's economy accelerated under the uninterrupted rule of Meles Zenawi, who was president or prime minister for 21 years and played an active role in shaping strategy, including the five-year Ethiopia Growth and Transformation Plan that his government adopted in 2010. It was the first part of a long-term strategy (the second part went into effect in 2015) that focused on deepening infrastructure and social sector investments, modernizing and commercializing agriculture, and fostering industrial growth. In support of the plan, Meles traveled to Beijing in 2011 to make a personal sales pitch to Chinese investors to bring factories back to Ethiopia. He explained that industrial development was a central plank in the country's new economic strategy and asked the investors to consider how a partnership could provide jobs and boost exports for Ethiopia and lower costs for China, which had begun to aggressively target Africa for investment.[6] Within six months of Meles's trip to Beijing, the Huajian Group, a large-scale shoe manufacturer, opened a factory near Addis Ababa; within a few years, the factory employed more than 4,000 workers, more than 90 percent of whom were local Ethiopians, and had become one of the country's largest exporters, helping fuel an industrial revolution.

Time and again, we have seen evidence that nothing can drive a country's pursuit of transformation quite like direct engagement from the very top of the political hierarchy. The structure of that hierarchy, or the exact type of political system that's in place, may vary—an ongoing debate that I pick up in the final chapter—but the engagement must be there, regardless of the system. Without committed political leadership at the top and without the political will to stay the course, transformation will not take root.

As I said, growth with depth is not mechanical, and that includes the DEPTH framework itself. The seven actions described above are necessary regardless of country circumstance, and that will not change; but the global context for economic transformation *will* change, as it's doing right now, all around us. The way that ACET defined transformation was necessary and appropriate when the first *African Transformation Report* was published in

2014, but, in a few short years, the landscape for transformation has become much more complex. As with any approach or framework, adapting to new factors is necessary.

For example, innovation is rapidly changing the way people live and work. The DEPTH framework rightfully emphasized the importance of technology, but the pace of change has exceeded expectations. Digital currencies, social media, robotics, and automation are just a few of the innovative elements that are having an outsized impact on economies and their key inputs, such as information and communications, business development, labor markets, especially vocation and skills training. Likewise, the importance of data security and privacy have become central policy issues shaping transformation strategies.

Africa's access to capital markets and other debt is also changing the nature of transformation because of the way it's changing economies. Given their low domestic savings rates, African governments have rapidly accumulated debt from international markets, particularly China, which has dramatically altered Africa's economic landscape since the turn of the century. Between 2001 and 2016, the Chinese lent Africa approximately $130 billion. According to the BBC, the newly signed value of Chinese contracted projects in Africa totaled $76.5 billion in 2017 alone. By 2018, China had become the single largest bilateral financier of infrastructure in Africa, surpassing the AfDB, European Union, European Investment Bank, International Finance Corporation, World Bank, and G8 countries combined. The rapid influx of financing has produced sizable debts, but it's also created jobs, enhanced infrastructure, and boosted industries.

The Growth with DEPTH model is in some ways premised on a traditional transformation process that draws from the success of the East Asian economies, but is also deeply steeped in Western economic models. In an age of increasingly technological-fueled globalization, those models are changing faster now than at any point since the Industrial Revolution. For example, more and more research is pointing to diminished returns from manufacturing, making it critical for developing countries to raise productivity in other areas, such as services. But this brings additional transformation challenges, since high-productivity service segments cannot absorb as much labor as traditional manufacturing, while low-productivity services do not generally foster growth.

In a 2017 study, Margaret McMillan, Dani Rodrik, and Claudia Sepulveda outlined two challenges in this regard: the "structural transformation" challenge, which is how to ensure that resources flow to the modern economic activities that operate at higher levels of economic productivity; and the "fundamentals" challenge, which is how to accumulate the skills and broad institutional capabilities needed to generate sustained productivity growth. Regardless of the frameworks in which we tackle transformation, African policymakers will need to address both of these challenges in a rapidly changing world.

◆　◆　◆　◆

In addition to the seven concrete actions discussed, there is one more aspect to transforming Africa that should be considered universal, though it's not a specific policy or political action—the need to support and learn from one another. Nkrumah's vision of a consolidated Africa never came to pass, but Africa has been able to pull together to some degree, starting with the African Union on down to smaller alliances such as the regional economic communities. Neither the AU nor the RECs are without their shortcomings, but African countries can accomplish more together than they can apart. With economic transformation, that ethos is as important as ever. So it's important to keep trying.

My biggest disappointment with the *African Transformation Report* didn't lie with the report itself but in the follow-up. ACET did a great job at getting the word out. We garnered a good bit of press and took the report around the world. We were proud that "growth with depth" set a standard for countries to pursue and even more proud when many of the countries we already worked with asked for further engagement. But overall, action on the report's recommendations lagged behind the pace we had hoped for. The blueprint had been laid out and the research had been roundly endorsed. But the most important step—getting more countries to act—seemed to be falling through the cracks.

As ACET began preparations for the second *African Transformation Report*, we took stock of everything that had gone into compiling the first one, including follow-up on the findings.[7] Now that we knew what transformation meant for Africa and how African countries should go about transforming, we realized that we faced a two-pronged issue. First, how could we get countries more engaged to learn from each other in the same way that the *ATR* offered, but on a continual basis rather than every few years? And second, how could we keep the *ATR*'s recommendations relevant as we encouraged countries to pursue them?

Perhaps the one thing that has defined my career, regardless of where I worked, is the belief that bringing people together to jointly find approaches to existing problems is always the best, most beneficial path forward. So it was in that context that, more than 40 years into my career, I created the African Transformation Forum, or ATF, which I hope will maintain the momentum to transform economies well into the future.

ACET convened the inaugural ATF in March 2016 in Kigali. After making overtures to President Kagame, Rwanda quickly agreed to host the forum and work in collaboration with ACET to put it together. Given the country's success in its early stages of transformation, holding this first forum in Kigali seemed like a no-brainer. It drew almost 300 participants, a broad mix of public and private sector officials representing almost three dozen countries across Africa, Asia, Europe, and North America. Participants hailed from every major transformation stakeholder group: government leaders, national policymakers, business executives, entrepreneurs, and civil society, as well as international development organizations, global foundations, and leading African institutions.

In addition to top government officials and ministers from Rwanda and other countries, the forum featured a diverse array of Africans leaders from key organizations, including Carlos Lopes, who held my old job as executive secretary of the ECA; Makhtar Diop, vice president for Africa at the World Bank; Antoinette Sayeh, director of the IMF Africa department; and Ibrahim Mayaki, CEO of NEPAD. It was highly encouraging to have the participation of these organizations and their high-ranking officials at the time.

Claver Gatete, Rwanda's minister of finance and development planning, joined me in opening the forum along with Carlos Lopes. I had done this so many times before over the previous decades—welcoming participants, setting the stage, trying to outline what we hoped to achieve. But the ATF felt more personal. I'm sure part of the reason was that this one, unlike all the other forums and events, came from an organization that I built from the ground up.

In my remarks, I described the "remarkable consensus," both within and outside Africa, around economic transformation as the key to sustained growth and prosperity. After many ups and downs, I said, transformation "has united us, endorsed by the African Union, African Development Bank, the ECA, and African heads of state and government as the continent's leading development paradigm. We are in agreement. Now we must take it forward."

The two-day forum covered the full range of concerns and challenges that countries face as they try to create and implement a transformation agenda: improving the quality of basic education to upgrade skills, generating long-term employment and meeting future labor demands, increasing access to finance, improving trade to take full advantage of Africa's regional markets, raising agricultural productivity, boosting innovation and industry, attracting the private sector, and mobilizing enough resources to carry out sustainable strategies.

It was a robust, substantive two days that underscored the need for coordinated, collaborative, and committed action at the country level and across borders to address the most urgent transformation issues. So the forum ended with the launch of a new platform to try to meet those needs: the Pan-African Coalition for Transformation—a broad network of policymakers and experts working across sectors to drive transformation policy and institutional reforms.

ACET had developed the parameters ahead of time, hoping for endorsement of just such a collaborative mechanism. African economies may find it difficult to replicate the pace of change experienced by the fast transformers in East Asia or even Latin America because it's more difficult now for developing countries to reach the level of competitiveness required to participate effectively in global value chains. The global economy is more crowded than ever, so transformation for Africa may take longer. But a platform for mutual support can help prop up a process that could easily go awry given the length of time involved.

Near the end of the forum, Kagame offered his full support. "No institution or individual has all the resources or answers," he said. "The right strategy is to use our limited means to send clear signals to the market and to partners about how best to allocate and utilize these resources. Working together, with an understanding of the strategic environment, we can speed up progress."

That's the hope at least: to get individuals working together, to combine knowledge and know-how to help transform their countries more rapidly. I have no idea at this point if the African Transformation Forum, which ACET envisions as a biennial event, will take root and become part of the continent's development fabric. But ACET convened a second forum in June 2018 that not only drew more participants than the first one but concluded with an exceptionally frank dialogue between African heads of state, including Kagame and Ghana President Nana Akufo-Addo, and private sector leaders, including Aliko Dangote, Africa's most successful businessman, on the types of policies, investments, and leadership that transformation requires. All that really matters is that some avenue exists to help maintain momentum and keep the transformation agenda moving forward. I've spent an entire career trying to bring people together to jointly tackle the biggest challenges facing Africa. With economic transformation, that's still my goal. And, as always, I remain ever hopeful.

Notes

1   Radelet highlighted five changes that helped spur the turnaround in African countries: better governance, smarter economic policies, debt relief and improved donor relations, improved use of technology, and a new generation of policymakers and business leaders. The changes he identified have all remained central to successful transformation policies.

2   It takes a long time to establish a non-profit policy institute, primarily because enough funding has to be lined up to ensure solvency. And that, in turn, takes a lot of faith on the part of partners holding the purse strings. ACET was very fortunate to have strong, early support from the World Bank, the government of the Netherlands, and the Hewlett and Rockefeller Foundations.

3   The first group of people who came on board included Yaw Ansu, ACET's chief economist, and Edward Brown, ACET's head of Policy Advisory Services. They had both spent more than 25 years at the World Bank and boasted expertise in regional economic and sustainable development. Like me, they both were born in Ghana. Another Ghanaian, Marianna Ofosu, was very young but incredibly smart; she functioned more or less as a chief of staff. With the other staff, I made it a point to look outside Ghana and recruit from other countries, including two bright young women, Buddy Buruku and Eugenia Maina, from Uganda and Burkina Faso, respectively. Another young hire, Francis Mulangu, was from the Democratic Republic of Congo, while the more seasoned Julius Gatune came from Kenya.

4   A true giant in his field, Stiglitz is one of the most influential economists of the century. As a long-time critic of the "Washington Consensus," he wasn't a great fit at the World Bank, which he has faulted, along with the IMF, for promoting policies that favor the financial community over the developing world and that overemphasize free markets at the expense of sound regulatory structures. He joined the faculty of Columbia University in 2001 and has written numerous books deconstructing global economics and its impacts, especially on the developing world. I've always been grateful for what he contributed to help get ACET off the ground.

5   Additional credit goes to a friend and associate I've known for most of my career, Bruce Ross-Larson, who served as the *African Transformation Report*'s primary editor. He and his team in Washington, DC helped shape the *ATR* so that it was as enjoyable to read as it was informative.

6   China increased its financing commitments in Africa dramatically from around $5 billion in 2006 to $10 billion in 2009 to $20 billion in 2011. While that number represented only about 3.2 percent of total FDI in Africa at the time, it was a much larger share of China's overall investments.

7   While the first *African Transformation Report* in 2014 focused broadly on the state of transformation in Africa up to that point, subsequent reports focused on more specific sectors or policy areas that directly impact transformation, such as agriculture, technology, and demographic shifts.

Chapter 16

Leadership for the Africa We Want
The Key to the Continent's Future Lies with Those Who Shape It

The African Union headquarters, which opened to great acclaim in January 2012, is a sprawling complex dominated by a glittering glass and concrete office building that soars more than 100 meters high on the edge of downtown Addis Ababa, Ethiopia. It is one of the city's tallest and most recognizable structures. Funded entirely by the Chinese, the project wasn't without controversy. But once the headquarters opened, its financing seemed less important than what it represented—a physical symbol of strong African leadership. So in that sense it's entirely fitting—and not at all surprising—that a slightly larger than life-sized statue of Kwame Nkrumah stands nearby, atop a marble pedestal etched with words Nkrumah spoke in May 1963 at the founding of the OAU, the predecessor organization for which he so strongly advocated: "Africa must unite."

The AU's Nkrumah statue is cast in bronze but shines a brilliant gold in the sun. It depicts Nkrumah in ceremonial clothes, the northern Ghanaian smock or *fugu* he wore to declare independence in March 1957, with his right hand raised high in a show of strength and his left foot slightly in front of his right as if he, like Africa, is on the move. His head tilts upward, looking toward the sky. It perfectly encapsulates Nkrumah the visionary leader who inspired a generation to believe in their heritage and their endless possibilities.

Approximately 4,300 kilometers away, a visually similar but quite different statue stands in Kwame Nkrumah Memorial Park in Accra, Ghana.

The park has a compounded history; it's where the British colonialists who once ruled the region played polo, which is why Nkrumah—embracing the symbolism—chose that spot to declare "Ghana is free forever" on the eve of independence. So it seemed a fitting location for a memorial park in his honor. There are actually two statues of Nkrumah in the park: one in front of the mausoleum that contains his remains, and one behind it. The one out front is tall and imposing. The other one is not, and it's this one that invokes comparison to the figure at the African Union.

This statue too sits on a marble pedestal, though much smaller. It too is cast in bronze, but it's aged and dull and no longer shines in the sun. It too depicts Nkrumah in the northern *fugu* with his right hand raised in a show of strength and his left foot slightly in front of his right, as if he, like Ghana, was once on the move. But his head does not tilt upward. In fact, there is no head at all. Rather, the head is mounted on its own pedestal beside the body. This statue once stood in front of Ghana's old Parliament House, the same place I would visit as a child, inspired by Nkrumah. But amid the 1966 coup d'état that ended Nkrumah's rule, it was toppled and decapitated. Some years ago, it was reinstalled in the park. At one point, it, like the statue in Addis Ababa, perfectly encapsulated Nkrumah the visionary leader.

These two statues, on opposite sides of the continent, represent the best and worst of African leadership in the most literal sense—a golden vision versus a broken dream.

Africa has long struggled with the issue of political leadership, starting with the first class of leaders who, through tremendous commitment and personal bravery, fought for the continent's freedom from colonial rule: icons including Nkrumah, Julius Nyerere of Tanzania, Kenneth Kaunda of Zambia, Ben Bella of Algeria, and Sékou Touré of Guinea. Not all lived up to their potential, but they are revered as visionaries and inspirational leaders nonetheless. Also revered is a group of young, courageous, or charismatic leaders who died or were assassinated before some could prove their worth: Patrice Lumumba of Congo, Thomas Sankara of Burkina Faso, Amílcar Cabral of Guinea Bissau, and Samora Machel of Mozambique, for example. They offered hope that was taken away. And of course Nelson Mandela belongs in his own class. The end of apartheid in South Africa arrived a generation later than freedom in other African countries, but Mandela inspired like few others—before, during, and after his presidency.

At the other extreme are numerous African leaders who could be counted among the very worst tyrants and despots in modern history. The real worst of the worst—Idi Amin in Uganda, Mobutu Sese Seko of the

Democratic Republic of Congo, Charles Taylor in Liberia, Jean-Bédel Bokassa in the Central African Republic—committed severe atrocities and human rights abuses, bringing untold misery and deprivation to millions of their own people. Amin is believed to be responsible for as many as 300,000 killings. Bokassa answered criticisms by simply declaring himself emperor. They embodied the face of Africa's "big man" rule and, consequently, failed states.

Indeed, poor leadership has undermined African ambitions from the start, exacerbating the incredible hurdles that most newly independent states already faced—weak institutional capacity, poor policy and planning choices, and ethnic strife, to name a few—and commonly resulting in tragedy. Between 1965 and 1995, Sub-Saharan Africa registered almost 30 cases of armed conflict or civil war (an average of about one per year), with more than 10 million estimated casualties in about the same time frame. Nearly that many were severely injured or disabled for life. For many Africans, basic survival under oppressive conditions was all that mattered.

Decades of fragmented and disappointing leadership is one of the main reasons that African countries continue to be concerned about development this long after independence. It's a big reason why Africa has not united, at least not in the sense that Nkrumah and other early pan-Africanists envisioned. The OAU was so ineffective that it was easier to dissolve and reconstitute as a new body than reform. The AU has given more reason to be optimistic than its predecessor, especially after the signing of the African Continental Free Trade Area agreement. But in the years ahead, can the AU live up to its pan-African aspirations? To the same lofty heights that its new building symbolizes?

The answer will depend on the ability of Africa's current and future leaders to succeed where so many of their predecessors failed: promoting sound policies and providing stable leadership. Given what we now know, the policies must be rooted in transformation, and the leadership must be consistent, committed, and engaged. Leadership from the top is essential—perhaps the most essential precondition for successful transformation that exists. Everything else flows from it. National strategies. Core institutional competence. Stable investment environments. Productive public–private partnerships. Without the right executive political leadership, everything else falls apart.

For that reason, the last words I have concern the intersection of leadership and transformation, which I believe is the key to Africa finally fulfilling its promise. The most obvious and relevant place for me to start is, naturally, at the beginning, which just so happens to be the place that's most personal to me—where I came from, where I returned, and where I hope my grandchildren, and their children, one day see the future long imagined.

◆ ◆ ◆ ◆

Ghana offers an interesting, if disappointing, case study in the context of economic transformation and leadership. Known as the Gold Coast as a British colony because of its rich and plentiful natural resources, independent Ghana turned from a beacon of freedom for other countries to follow into a cautionary tale to avoid, all in less than a decade and largely due to the leadership of the man most responsible for its freedom in the first place, Kwame Nkrumah. Not only did Ghana have the foundation to implement a transformation agenda at the same time as East Asia, it had a visionary leader who embraced many of the core concepts and necessary policies. Had Nkrumah become a truly transformational leader, Ghana's history would have been markedly different.

Nkrumah wasn't one of Africa's notorious bad men of absent character, even though his righteous passion to free Africa eventually distorted his judgment, as ideological motivations sometimes do. He was, however, ill prepared to govern in the sense that he couldn't effectively transition from the political leader of a movement into the pragmatic leader of a state. He was so determined to showcase Ghana as a proving ground that he simply tried to move too far, too fast, with too little recognition of the complexities of reasoned political and economic management.

The warning signs were evident in the pro-independence slogan he made famous: "Seek ye first the political kingdom and all else shall be added unto you." If only it were that simple. Nkrumah founded the Convention People's Party, or CPP, in 1949 as a pro-independence movement. While the CPP was well suited for the struggle for sovereignty, it was not the right apparatus for the rigors of policymaking. But Nkrumah envisioned Ghana at the forefront of a new economic order, with an economy propelled by intense and rapid state investment to generate power, build infrastructure, and create jobs, particularly in manufacturing. Colonial powers had displayed little regard for investing in the social and human capital of the populations they ruled, leaving behind in most countries weak technical capacity and a lingering distrust of private enterprise and markets. "Capitalism is too complicated a system for a newly independent nation," Nkrumah had said.

A trip to the Soviet Union in 1961 left him so impressed by Soviet industrialization efforts that he returned to Ghana and announced his Seven-Year Plan to rapidly establish factories and industrialize. But Ghana's government was already a debacle. It had poured too much money too quickly into state-owned companies that were plagued by mismanagement, graft, and patronage. At the same time, its policies undermined historically successful markets, such as cocoa, by overtaxing and taking revenues to cover ballooning costs elsewhere. Ghana was the world's leading producer of cocoa, for example, but government policy choked a vibrant and potentially lucrative industry. Ultimately, the CPP had neither the awareness among its rank and file nor the commitment among its top leadership to enact the complicated economic agenda Nkrumah sought.

The early years between 1957 and 1960 were not so bad. The Nkrumah government maintained sound fiscal management, and the country was seen as politically stable, free of restrictive controls, and attractive to foreign investment. It had also accumulated some $500 million in foreign exchange reserves on the strength of its exports: mainly cocoa, gold, and other raw minerals. Prospects seemed bright, but the groundwork for future problems was already being laid.

One of Nkrumah's biggest missteps as a governmental leader was an unwillingness to bend or compromise his vision, particularly when it came to economic planning. The distinction is important, as Nkrumah was definitely a believer in development planning. But he paid little heed to sound economic principles, despite some excellent thinkers around him.

Independent Ghana proved to be an attractive destination for technicians and intellectuals abroad who were energized by the opportunity for an African country to prove its autonomy. Ghanaians and non-Ghanaians alike wanted to contribute, including Arthur Lewis, widely considered a founding father of development economics. Born in St. Lucia, Lewis was one of the twentieth century's foremost economists and a true intellectual pioneer—the first black professor in a British university and also at Princeton University, and the first person of African descent to win the Nobel Memorial Prize in Economics, which he did in 1979. But before that, he spent time in the Gold Coast as a principal economic advisor to Nkrumah from 1957 to 1958, then returned to Ghana briefly in 1963. It did not go well.

Lewis grew interested in the Gold Coast during the late 1940s and early 1950s as he worked as a consultant with the nationalist movement Nkrumah led. To Lewis, decolonization appeared inevitable, and the region seemed ripe for devising successful growth formulas. As Robert

473

Tignor wrote in his biography on Lewis: "Not only did the country have a sound infrastructure and a relatively high standard of living, but its charismatic leader, whom Lewis knew and admired and of whose leadership he expected great things, seemed to embody just the right mix of idealism, talent, and savvy to lead his people to political and economic successes." In 1953, Lewis drafted a blueprint for industrialization in the Gold Coast. A few years later, he left the University of Manchester to work alongside Nkrumah and guide Ghana's economic program. Lewis's arrival in October 1957 gave Nkrumah increased optimism over Ghana's future, Tignor wrote.

Though the two men spoke a similar language, Lewis soon found that he and Nkrumah disagreed on some fundamental tenets of policy, primarily where to direct resources and how aggressively Ghana should try to industrialize. Lewis argued that Ghana should move slowly and did not have the financial or human resources to invest too heavily or too quickly in manufacturing at the expense of less flashy but attainable goals, such as improving product diversification and efficiency. Nkrumah disagreed. At the time, Lewis was working on a draft of a five-year development plan for 1959 through 1964. He initially projected a £70 or £80 million investment in economic development for this period. Lewis advised ministers to show restraint when drawing up their budget proposals, but Nkrumah wanted something else entirely. He wanted big and bold, and nothing exemplified his thinking more than the proposal closest to his heart: the Volta River project, a massive hydroelectric initiative that he had championed for years.

Nkrumah saw Volta as the centerpiece of his strategy to transform Ghana's economy, arguing that it would give the energy and industrial sectors enough of a boost to jump-start rapid industrialization across the country. The project was an enormous undertaking with two major components: a hydroelectric dam and an aluminum smelter. Given the project's scale and projected costs, economists like Lewis, as well as those in the World Bank, urged a slow approach. But Nkrumah insisted that sizable resources for Volta be included in Lewis's five-year plan.

By the time Nkrumah presented the plan to the National Assembly in mid-1959, the price tag for development investments had ballooned to £343 million—a breathtaking increase over Lewis's initial £70-80 million projection. The final numbers concerned Lewis, but only from afar; he had left Ghana in December 1958 after being marginalized to a point where he no longer felt effective.

The point here is not that Lewis was right and Nkrumah wrong. Lewis's tenure in Ghana was very brief in the grand scheme of things. But it's a very telling example of how deeply politics and economics are intertwined in developing countries, and how the chief players—in this case, political leaders like Nkrumah and economists or technicians like Lewis—need to work together, rather than at cross-purposes. Of course, the onus for ensuring such relationships always rests with political leadership, and it's one of the differentiating qualities between those leaders who succeed in truly improving the lives of their people and those who do not, even if their motivations, as was mostly the case with Nkrumah, are genuine.

By 1960, Ghana had begun its turn. Between 1961 and 1965, government revenue increased by 42 percent while expenditure increased 63 percent. More telling, development expenditure rose by 79 percent, almost twice incoming revenues. It was in the middle of this period that Nkrumah devised his Seven-Year Plan in an effort to speed up his industrialization goals even further. The plan attracted a lot of criticism because its dramatic spending proposals seemed detached from Ghana's economic reality. By 1963, the country was on the brink of bankruptcy. By 1965, its foreign exchange reserves were depleted and its foreign debt totaled almost $800 million. Unable to borrow from governments or foreign banks, Ghana racked up hundreds of millions of additional debt to suppliers and contractors. And its parastatal strategy had flopped. The government had invested in more than 30 state enterprises, but only two showed a profit, and most were largely devoid of linkages to the rest of the economy.

As his political support waned and Ghana's outlook worsened, Nkrumah declared Ghana a one-party state in early 1964, stamping out political dissent and declaring himself president for life. It had been less than a year since he joined the other founding fathers of the OAU in signing a charter that affirmed "freedom, justice, and dignity" of the African people.

On January 22, 1966, Nkrumah inaugurated the Volta River project's massive Akosombo Dam, calling it one of his "greatest dreams" and affirming that his "faith in it never faltered, in spite of the disappointments and frustrations." One month later, Nkrumah was deposed in a military coup.

Kwesi Botchwey—a well-respected Ghanaian statesman and former long-serving finance minister—noted in a series of lectures in 2010 that Nkrumah was undone by his own mistakes as well as the circumstances of his time. For instance, Nkrumah was far from being alone in the belief that some form of African socialism was the answer for new states that had long been exploited by colonial settlers and foreign companies. It was the prevalent thinking of the day, and it was shared by other highly influential and charismatic figures—such as Julius Nyerere in Tanzania, Jomo Kenyatta in Kenya, and Kenneth Kaunda in Zambia—as well as many development economists. This historical context helps add texture to understanding Nkrumah's approach, because he was both wrong and right. It helps that, with the luxury of hindsight, we can see Nkrumah wanted the right thing for Ghana—to structurally transform the country and its economy—but went about it the wrong way.

The almost wholly state-controlled economic model he advocated has been proven inadequate for development, yet we know that for a country to transform, the state must play a strong role in mobilizing resources, coordinating activities, fostering appropriate incentives, and investing in infrastructure, both human and physical. Nkrumah built a network of schools and universities in Ghana that became the envy of developing Africa. And his crowning achievement, the Volta River project, has generally been a qualified success. It didn't spearhead the rapid growth Nkrumah imagined, but the dam remains the principal supplier of hydroelectric power in Ghana.

In his lectures, Botchwey pointed out that Nkrumah's imprint remains everywhere—"in the macroeconomic and real sectors of Ghana's national economy, in the banking and insurance industries, in the country's basic infrastructure." He credited Nkrumah's "genius" at recognizing and harnessing the power of political organization, as he did with the Convention People's Party. And he said Nkrumah, though rightly criticized for his political evolution into an authoritarian, nonetheless epitomized a leader of visionary influence.

I don't disagree. I've said it before in this book and I'll say it one final time: despite the shortcomings, Nkrumah was a man ahead of his time. Yet his legacy is indeed a complex matter, one that Ghanaians have long struggled to reconcile. His political and economic records are mixed, but the inspiration he engendered and the vision he set forth were unmatched in African history.

I was one of the many young people Nkrumah inspired to action, so there's a question I ask myself all the time: had he turned out to be the right kind of leader for Ghana, would Africa's poor record on leadership— and in turn, development—have been better? Nkrumah struggled with the role of the state versus the private sector. He struggled to find the right balance between being a strong leader and an authoritarian one. He also failed to lay a solid foundation; Ghana alternated between civilian and military rule during the 1970s and 1980s, with a half-dozen leadership changes in 15 years. None of that turmoil can be blamed on Nkrumah, but the opportunity his government had to build strong institutions and set a transformative course in Ghana's earliest days was not realized.

In the end, Nkrumah got many things wrong, in both policy formulation and implementation. And those things that went wrong in Ghana went wrong in so many of the countries that followed Ghana into independence. In that sense, Ghana became a poor role model, rather than an inspiration, for the rest of Africa. Had he pursued a different, more positive path, one can't help but wonder: what if?

♦ ♦ ♦ ♦

One afternoon in May 2014, five prominent African figures gathered in front of a packed conference room at the Serena Hotel in Kigali: President Paul Kagame of Rwanda; Olusegun Obasanjo, the former president of Nigeria; William Ruto, the deputy president of Kenya; Nkosazana Zuma, chairwoman of the African Union Commission; and Mo Ibrahim, the founder and chairman of the Mo Ibrahim Foundation, a leading authority on governance in Africa. Two other eminent Africans joined the discussion, not on stage with the others but from the floor: Thabo Mbeki and Benjamin Mkapa, the former presidents of South Africa and Tanzania, respectively. The group had come together to discuss the most fundamental of questions: where do we find—and how do we nurture—the visionary leadership that is essential for Africa's future?

Without a doubt, these leaders were among the most influential in Africa over the previous two decades. I knew some better than others. I had worked closely with Mbeki and Obasanjo, of course, during the creation of NEPAD and the African Peer Review Mechanism (APRM), while ACET had formed a good working relationship with Kagame and his government due to Rwanda's reliance on economic transformation strategies. But they all had the kind of history and reputation that imbued them with authority on the topic at hand. More than 500 people came to the Serena Hotel to hear what they had to say, including me.

Their discussion was a highlight of that year's annual meeting of the African Development Bank, a special event that celebrated the AfDB's first 50 years and looked ahead toward the next 50. The event's theme—"The Africa We Want"—simultaneously reinforced Africa's renewed agency over its development agenda and the fact that we're still looking for answers after a half-century.

The seven leaders quickly came to the conclusion that Africa needs a critical mass of leaders across all areas of society to transform the continent—not just in the public sector but in businesses, among civic and religious communities, within families, and so forth. Such individuals often exist outside the standard political structure of the state, yet they too should be visionaries and people of action. The leaders also agreed that Africa needed more women in prominent leadership positions, and more opportunities for the youth.

As a spectator, I eagerly waited for the panelists to describe learning from their own experiences and to dive deeply into the question of *political* leadership—especially the glaring leadership deficits responsible for much of Africa's poor outcomes: the wars, conflicts, corruption, brutality, and poverty. To my disappointment, that never really happened.

I don't disagree that leadership at all levels of society is fundamental to transforming Africa. It does take a collective commitment to improve the quality of life, whether it's the entrepreneur training local workers or the religious leader wading into the political process on behalf of the disenfranchised. But the research, literature, and recorded experiences of transformed countries is clear: success in developing countries begins and ends with transformational political leaders. So how do we define such leaders, especially in the context of the economic transformation process itself?

Robert I. Rotberg, one of the foremost scholars on this subject, offers a straightforward evaluation that sets a reasonable standard: successful leaders possess an array of skills that allow them to transform political visions into economic growth, inclusive prosperity, and human well-being within their countries. In other words, the vision is just the start—"what leaders are *meant* to provide," as Rotberg writes in his book *Transformative Political Leadership*.

Consider what we know to be true: economic transformation holds the key to Africa's future, and the right political leadership is the key to successful transformation. Therefore, a true transformational leader must accomplish more than unleashing a movement, cultivating a cult of personality, or simply enduring in office. He or she must govern effectively and, ideally, as selflessly as possible. In this context, political will requires more than fortitude. It requires the discipline to set and maintain a strategy, and learn and adapt, if needed, to deliver the goods: to ensure steady growth and material uplift in the service of the citizenry—not of the vision itself. It requires pragmatism over ideology.

For years, scholars have examined the importance of political leadership to the fortunes of nations. They have concluded what may seem obvious but is nevertheless vital to stability and prosperity: good leadership separates endeavors that succeed from those that fail. Nowhere is this idea more relevant than in the developing world. That's because developed countries often boast value systems that are fully rooted, political institutions such as legislatures and judiciaries that are independent and strong, and economic practices that are open and inclusive. For those reasons, Rotberg argues, the added value of enlightened leadership "is much greater in those regions where political cultures and political institutions are still embryonic." It is precisely in those places, he says, that sound leadership qualities are most essential—and, consequently, a distinguishing factor in successful transformation.

In short, in the developing world, the quality of political leadership matters far more than it does elsewhere. So for Africa to transform, it must fully commit to holding its leaders to a higher standard. Historically, it has not done that. "African leaders—not a lack of capital, access to world markets, or technical expertise—are to blame for the continent's underdevelopment," South African author and policy analyst Greg Mills wrote in 2010's *Why Africa Is Poor*.

Nigerian political scientist Claude Ake, who died in 1996 and was one of Africa's foremost authorities on political economies, argued that development would only succeed when decisions were made by the people and taken out of the hands of corrupt leaders. "Development strategies in Africa, with minor exceptions," he said, "have tended to be strategies by which the few use the many for their own purposes." At the ECA's third African Development Forum in 2002, Wole Soyinka, a Nobel laureate in literature and political activist, delivered a rousing closing address that echoed Ake's belief that the people should be empowered because African leaders had historically proven unworthy of their roles. He bemoaned the "roll call of dictators" throughout post-independence history and said prospects for change had too often been quashed when the call for a new leader had regularly "turned up yet another monstrosity."

Such pessimism by distinguished Africans is not at all unfounded. And the reason this still matters so much is because Africa's political leadership situation remains a matter of grave concern. In his 2011 book *The Fate of Africa: A History of the Continent Since Independence*, historian Martin Meredith chronicles Africa's half-century quest for economic and social development by focusing on key events and figures, in particular the rise and fall of a litany of African leaders. And the fact that so many of those leaders "fell" is a big part of the problem. By the end of the 1980s, not a single African head of state in three decades had allowed himself to be voted out of office, leaving most African states incapable of serving the public good and hollowed out by decades of political mismanagement, fear, and corruption.

Angola's José Eduardo dos Santos and Zimbabwe's Robert Mugabe ruled their countries with near-total autonomy for almost four decades—38 and 37 years, respectively. Though Mugabe did not go willingly, both men left office within a few months of each other in 2017. There have been many more like them. By 2019, a full dozen political rulers in Africa's post-colonial era had retained power for 30 years or more, including four who were still in office and others nearing that mark.[1]

At the AfDB's "Africa We Want" event, Mbeki came closest to addressing the chronic leadership deficit most directly by calling for a "real, critical, truthful self-assessment" of the performance of African leaders—a tacit acknowledgement that the APRM, which had been put in place more than a decade earlier, had not accomplished as much as it needed to accomplish.

"We are afraid to speak frankly to one another about the wrong things that we are doing," Mbeki said, warning that leaders will be meeting in another century to discuss the same question if nothing changes. "I think critical self-assessment of the continent… would be an important step in terms of producing the kind of leadership that Africa wants."

It's worth reiterating that Mbeki was not actually serving on the AfDB's panel but participating from the floor. The invited panelists shared some interesting observations, but the event ended without any of them specifically addressing the lack of transformative political leadership as a root cause for many of the continent's problems. To me, this seemed like a missed opportunity, because Africans in general do not give high marks to their political leaders.

On countless occasions over the years, I've been engaged in discussions on African development with friends or colleagues with a vested interest in the social and economic progress of African countries—activists, policymakers, public servants, business executives, and so forth—when talk inevitably turns to political leadership. With alarming regularity, I've watched with equal bemusement and sorrow as colleagues struggle to come up with a meaningful list of current or recent African leaders worthy of admiration. In fact, the exercise usually ends in frustration when they are unable to name more than five or six leaders at a time. I admit that this is a very unscientific way of identifying good leaders, but at least there is a much better one.

In 2007, the Mo Ibrahim Foundation launched the Ibrahim Prize, an award celebrating excellence in African leadership. Given to former executive heads of state or government by an independent committee, the

Ibrahim Prize recognizes African leaders who developed their countries, lifted people out of poverty, and paved the way for sustainable and equitable prosperity. In the process, it aims to inspire future leaders by highlighting exceptional role models for the continent.[2] Unfortunately, the Ibrahim Prize has also called attention to Africa's dearth of quality leadership—in its first 10 years, it was only awarded four times: to Joaquim Chissano of Mozambique in 2007, Festus Mogae of Botswana (2008), Pedro Pires of Cabo Verde (2011), and Hifikepunye Pohamba of Namibia (2014).

The Ibrahim Foundation acknowledges that the standards are high and that it doesn't expect to name a recipient every year, but the prize is *intended* to be an annual honor. So it's hard to overlook the negative message sent by the infrequency of the awards, intended or not. Being elected fairly, leaving office peacefully, and improving the lives of citizens should not be an impossible bar to clear on a continent comprised of 54 countries. Once it seemed that awarding the prize was the exception rather than the rule, media coverage reflected as much. "The shame ends," is how the South African newspaper Mail & Guardian referenced Pohamba's award in 2014. A few years later, Newsweek magazine called it the "hardest prize to win in Africa."

The informal poll that I often see my colleagues and friends conduct in identifying the contemporary African leaders they admire may be unscientific, but the results are not that far-fetched after all, it seems.

Throughout my career, I've had the opportunity to meet and work with many top political leaders in Africa, holding extensive discussions on issues that were affecting either their countries' development or the larger pan-African agenda: peace and security, regional integration, agriculture, governance, financing, debt, aid, trade, and more. I've spoken with many about delicate but demanding socioeconomic challenges, such as gender equality and HIV/AIDS treatment and prevention. And during the 10 years I spent as executive secretary of the ECA, I had the privilege of participating in almost all the discussions at the OAU/AU heads of states and government summits, including closed and confidential sessions. From these vantage points, I came to know and admire a number of these leaders. A few of them I even came to know as friends.

At the same time, I gained my own education in leadership traits, practices, and policies that, at least from an economic technocrat's point of view, seemed to work better than others. In short, I've encountered plenty of bad leaders but also plenty of good ones who stand out as exceptional, in one way or another, amid Africa's parade of disappointments. While the continent certainly has had its leadership challenges, I think it's important not to overlook some of the success stories. It's from their experiences that we can draw lessons for the future.

For instance, I was delighted when the first Ibrahim Prize was awarded to Joaquim Chissano, "the antithesis of the African big man," as the London Independent accurately described him. After winning elections in 1994 and 1999, Chissano stepped aside rather than seek a third term in 2004, something he had the political support and constitutional authority to do. He also helped turn Mozambique around after more than 15 years of civil war. I had a number of encounters with him during his tenure as president and came to admire him as a thoughtful, sincere, and soft-spoken visionary. He quickly grasped the importance of the information society, for example, a subject he and I often discussed. He helped make Mozambique an African leader in the ICT revolution.

I also developed a strong personal relationship with—and great respect for—another Ibrahim Prize winner, Botswana's Festus Mogae. He was one of two heads of state to sit on the panel that closed the ECA's fortieth anniversary event on gender in 1998. Later, he participated in the ECA's African Development Forum on HIV/AIDS at a time when Botswana was being crippled by the pandemic. After winning the Ibrahim Prize in 2008, Time magazine called him "Africa's good leader" and praised Botswana's remarkable growth and progressive HIV/AIDS policies, drawing a direct contrast with more infamous leaders such as Robert Mugabe. But Mogae also stands out as much for what he did *not* do as for what he did: he didn't undermine the gains that had been made before him.

Unlike most African countries, Botswana has actually had a few outstanding political leaders, including Sir Seretse Khama, the country's first president, and Quett Masire, who followed Khama after his death. Khama created a paradigm for African leadership that stood apart from peers and proved formative for Botswana's early development: a devotion to rule of law, wise investment in infrastructure, an absence of internal strife, and a refusal to condone corruption. His leadership laid a foundation for future growth that Masire built on. By the time Mogae became president in 1999, Botswana's political stability had been solidly established and its economic health was strong, thanks to sensible management of its diamond wealth. Mogae could have undermined the legacy he inherited by exploiting Botswana's standing for personal gain, a pattern that has played out in other African states. Rather, he pushed policies that managed to further improve the lives of his constituents, exemplifying the best traits of political leadership.

I met Mogae shortly before he became president, at a Swedish forum on African development. At that event in Stockholm, Mogae served on a panel with another future president who deserves mention here, Thabo Mbeki. I had a lot of dealings with Mbeki, ground I've already covered extensively throughout this book. But if I'm going to recount my experiences with strong, effective political leaders, I must again mention Mbeki, who was in office from 1999 to 2008.

Mbeki had the unenviable task of following the great Mandela, but he became the face and voice of the African renaissance he championed. At home and abroad, his passionate, articulate vision of pan-African achievement earned him recognition as the continent's de facto leader as Africa began to assert itself with more assurance and authority on the global stage. He was the driving force behind NEPAD, without which the APRM likely would not have been adopted, and he was instrumental in establishing the African Union to be a more effective pan-African body than the OAU had been. Appropriately, in my opinion, he was selected as the AU's inaugural chairman.

And yet, while no leader is without fault, Mbeki unfortunately undermined much of the goodwill he had earned in the eyes of the world with the manner in which he handled the HIV/AIDS crisis, as described in Chapter 9. Some 20 years after Mbeki entered office, South Africa still had more people living with HIV/AIDS than any other country in the world. And that's not the only big issue affecting South Africa, which in the 2010s faced the dual challenge of serious structural constraints, which stunted growth and deepened unemployment and inequality, and poor political leadership, which mired the country in corruption and scandal. Much of the latter can be laid at the feet of Mbeki's successor, Jacob Zuma, but the structural issues date back to Mbeki's time in office. Still, South Africa has strong institutions compared to most in the region, and a solid foundation for transformation, ranking second on ACET's African Transformation Index in both 2000 and 2010.

In 2005, Foreign Affairs magazine profiled Mbeki's South Africa as "a tale of two countries"—one a dramatic success story of economic growth and a stable political system, the other a cautionary tale of government leaders not doing enough to improve the lives of its citizens. In this way, Mbeki shows transformational leadership is not always easily classified.

Two other leaders I got to know and respect were Benjamin Mkapa and John Kufuor. Mkapa was the third president of Tanzania, and his two terms in office between 1995 and 2005 overlapped precisely with my time at the ECA. Mkapa came to power with strong support from former president and pan-Africanist icon Julius Nyerere, and he helped jump-start Tanzania's growth by liberalizing the economy and pursuing more private sector investments and partnerships. Kufuor succeeded Jerry John Rawlings as president of Ghana in 2001, and it marked the first time in Ghana's post-independence history that one civilian government peacefully transferred power to another. Rawlings ruled for 20 years and did a lot to stabilize Ghana, but Kufuor demonstrated immense leadership by opening up the country—to donors, foreign investors, the private sector, and even its own citizens. Kufuor spearheaded the repeal of criminal libel laws, stronger rules to fight corruption, and safety and judicial reform. Kufuor projected a very positive image for Ghana, and he was determined to strengthen country systems and services. Under Kufuor, Ghana became the first country to undergo the APRM.

The last leader I want to mention in this group is Ellen Johnson Sirleaf, a Nobel Peace Prize winner and the first woman elected as an African head of state. She spent a short time as a consultant and advisor to me and the ECA before she returned to Liberia and won the presidency in 2005, and I was always awed by her determination. She had made a good life for herself without going back to Liberia, but she was a vociferous critic of President Charles Taylor and driven to start rebuilding her country in the aftermath of his rule. When she took power, Liberia was in complete chaos with broken infrastructure, dysfunctional institutions, and a population decimated by death or displacement brought on by 14 years of civil war. Her policies helped rejuvenate stagnant sectors like iron ore mining and rubber production, reduce public debt, and boost primary-school enrollments. In her first four years, Liberia's GDP per capita doubled; it remained painfully low, but at least it moved upward. Perhaps her greatest challenge arrived in her second term, dealing with the Ebola crisis in 2014 and 2015. It killed thousands across West Africa but Liberia moved fast to contain it.

She stopped Liberia's freefall, but she had to navigate a corrosive political economy based on coercion and bribery. Liberia's patronage system is deeply rooted, and its lack of reform has proved to be a hindrance to deeper economic and political progress—the biggest criticism against Johnson Sirleaf's time in office. Yet she inherited a shell of a country and her top priority, unapologetically, was to stabilize and rebuild institutions—a messy practice that required tough choices. In that difficult environment, I think she did a remarkable job.[3]

Johnson Sirleaf served two six-year terms. She left office in December 2017, replaced by former football star George Weah in Liberia's first democratic transfer of power in more than 70 years. A few months later, she became the fifth winner of the Ibrahim Prize—the first woman, of course, to receive the award.

A shared trait among the aforementioned leaders—Chissano, Mogae, Mbeki, Mkapa, Kufuor, and Johnson Sirleaf—was their willingness to step aside peacefully, after a certain number of years in office. Relinquishing power as mandated by a country's constitution is another low bar to clear for excellence, but given Africa's difficult history, those who do should be commended.

There are other leaders I worked with and came to know equally well, however, who fall into a different subset. I call this second group the "marathon runners," men who held on to power for 20 years or more. Such longevity is usually frowned upon by advocates of good governance, and for sure not all these leaders—or their country governments—were well served from the length of their stay. Some have been called dictators, and at a certain level that's not wrong. But they have all exhibited leadership traits that were unique in their own way and, within the context of this discussion—and my personal interactions—deserve mention. There are five in all.

The first one I want to mention is the most problematic when viewed through a historical lens: Yoweri Museveni. Once he came to power in Uganda in 1986, Museveni displayed a leadership trait that often sets apart the great ones: a willingness to change his mind and go against his own ideology for the greater good. Uganda's situation was dire, and though Museveni was highly skeptical and distrustful of World Bank and IMF assistance, he agreed to it. For the most part, Museveni's early efforts to stabilize and grow the economy worked. By the new century, Uganda was widely regarded as one of the most successful turnaround states in Sub-Saharan Africa. According to a 2005 World Bank analysis, the Museveni government had succeeded "with sustained improvement in rates of economic growth and poverty reduction, and in bringing peace to many parts of the country after years of political instability and civil strife."

I wrote about my early dealings with Museveni in Chapter 3, and what I said about him then—that I saw a political will for reform that few African leaders had at the time—remains true. It was strong leadership in action, as was his bold and progressive guidance on measures to combat the

HIV/AIDS crisis in Uganda in subsequent years. But what I said about his later days also remains true—that his steadfast refusal to step aside, after more than three decades, as well as his drift toward repressive policies and authoritarianism, is not the type of leadership that Africa needs. Despite Uganda's strong growth, with GDP averaging 5.8 percent in the 1990s and 6.7 percent in the 2000s, and despite new opportunities from oil, the structure of the economy has barely shifted in two decades, stagnating rather than expanding. In other words, Museveni's lengthy rule hasn't been about bettering his country in a long time.

Kenneth Kaunda of Zambia is another leader of lengthy tenure that I got to know well during my time at the World Bank in the 1980s, as I described in Chapter 2. And while the economic reforms he ultimately implemented in Zambia didn't take—some of which he rolled back due to political pressure before they could succeed—he charged into them against enormous political headwinds because he knew it was the right thing to do. Unlike Museveni, he showed a pragmatic streak throughout his time in power, including accepting when it was time to go even if he didn't necessarily want to.

Kaunda ruled for almost 30 years, and Zambia went through a lot of ups and downs during his time. But it's hard for me to imagine any leader caring more personally for the well-being of his fellow citizens than Kaunda. He didn't always make the right policy choices, but he acted boldly when needed and tried to build consensus around a shared vision. I truly believe he always had the best interests of Zambia—and Africa—at heart, even when out of office. Like Museveni, he became a vocal leader in the fight against HIV/AIDS and a key partner in the ECA's efforts to elevate the issue as an economic crisis.

I've always considered my four years in Zambia crucial for the lessons I learned about policymaking and development, and much of the credit goes to Kaunda. Through him, I saw directly how much strong, informed leadership at the top matters. More than a decade later, I saw the same thing with Meles Zenawi.

Meles, who served as Ethiopia's president or prime minister from 1991 until his death in 2012, is someone else I've mentioned frequently throughout this book. That's because I worked more closely with him than with any other African leader. We simply saw eye-to-eye on numerous economic positions and long-term solutions to Africa's development challenges. When I founded ACET, Meles supported our mission because he believed, unequivocally, in the need for economic transformation to elevate African countries from the ranks of the world's poor. Meles and

I would talk about transformation challenges and solutions for hours at a time. I got to know him on a personal level, and I respected his determination to transform Ethiopia.

And yet I realize that his final legacy may not be known for years to come. For one reason, ethnic tensions gradually grew more pronounced during his rule, due in large part to a system of political representation that he helped devise.[4] Those tensions escalated into serious disturbances after the May 2005 general election, the first multiparty vote held in Ethiopia, in which the opposition made large gains. Government-backed security forces clamped down, resulting in the deaths of dozens of protestors. Tensions have worsened in the time since, often erupting into violence and threatening Ethiopia's security and stability.

There's also the issue of Ethiopia's promising but unfinished transformation journey. Deputy Prime Minister Hailemariam Desalegn succeeded Meles and in many respects maintained the policies of his predecessor. He ensured that Ethiopia completed its first Growth and Transformation Plan and continued to oversee significant investments in industry and infrastructure, including the large-scale privatization of state-owned enterprises. Hailemariam stepped down in 2018, however, amid increasing civil unrest. He was succeeded by Abiy Ahmed, a relatively unknown politician and former intelligence officer who quickly launched a whirlwind of even more dramatic changes. Abiy released thousands of political prisoners, invited back exiles, and initiated peace talks with Eritrea after decades of hostilities. He lifted bans on press freedoms and made women's empowerment a priority. Abiy also championed privatizing industry and liberalizing key economic sectors long considered off-limits to non-state intervention. In other words, he dramatically opened up the political landscape that Meles had kept tightly controlled. However, Abiy, like Hailemariam and Meles before him, faced the simmering ethnic tensions that are never too far below the surface in Ethiopia. In 2019, an attempted regional coup was thwarted, but multiple high-ranking government officials were killed.

Ethiopia's economic outlook remains positive, but the initial uncertainty and unrest in the years after Meles's death dampened enthusiasm. As the country's social and political context continue to change, I hope the development gains are not lost but will instead lead to the political reconciliation the country needs to sustain its economic progress. Perhaps only then will we be able to know the full extent of Meles's legacy—and the outcome of the transformation vision he championed well before most other African leaders.

Meles offers an interesting comparison to the next leader in this group, Paul Kagame of Rwanda. Both men were able to put their countries on a steady path to transformation due in part to their lengthy stay in power. Meles ran Ethiopia for 21 years before his death; Kagame, still in power as of early 2019, has run Rwanda even longer. After helping defeat Hutu forces to end Rwanda's genocide in 1994, Kagame became the country's de facto leader. He was elected to his first seven-year term as president in 2003 upon ratification of a new constitution. After winning re-election in 2010, Kagame created quite a controversy by seeking, and winning, a third seven-year term—after saying he would leave office and after a 2015 referendum was passed to change the constitution to allow him to run again. In announcing his decision in a televised address, Kagame said, "I can only accept" the request, via the referendum, to remain in office, but added: "I don't think what we need is an eternal leader."

What he says is true, but at the same time, Kagame expressed reservations about stepping aside because he feared state institutions weren't strong enough to exist outside the oversight of his authority—a common rationale among African strongmen. And he certainly has critics and opponents who have admonished his decision to stay in power as well as Rwanda's crackdown on dissent or political opposition. Yet Kagame does not fit alongside the many despots and dictators who clung to office at all costs, because rather than pillaging or looting his country, Kagame, like Meles, instead oversaw an incredible turnaround.

Africa has rarely seen a head of state on the continent as development-oriented, as well as resourceful and pragmatic, as Kagame. Under his leadership, an utterly devastated and broken country grew its GDP from approximately $1.7 billion in 2000 to $8.4 billion in 2016. After that, growth leveled off. But it remains upward, and the key to sustaining it, as the World Bank's 2017 economic update on Rwanda made clear, is to continue the transformation-focused strategy Kagame has championed: namely, more private sector investment, greater agricultural productivity, and further regional trade.

At the AfDB's "Africa We Want" symposium, a participant asked Kagame, who served as a panelist, point-blank to share his thoughts on succession. Kagame's candid response said volumes about his leadership philosophy: the issue isn't how long you stay, Kagame responded, "but what you leave behind."

This brings me to the last person to mention here, Jerry John Rawlings, who ushered in Ghana's modern era of multiparty democracy. Like Kagame, Rawlings led his country before winning his first official election. In fact,

Rawlings led a coup to overthrow the government not once, but twice. The first time, in 1979, he handed power back to a civilian government. The second time, on December 31, 1981, he assumed power and ruled as a dictator for a decade. Under public pressure, he stood for election in 1992, won, and was re-elected in 1996. In 2000, Rawlings agreed to step aside and the man who had lost to him four years earlier, John Kufuor, was elected. Kufuor was from a different political party, and the peaceful transfer of power was notable as the first in the country's history.

Like other marathon runners I've discussed, Rawlings should be commended for his ability to change course, which he did more than once. As a military leader, Rawlings brought some political stability to Ghana, but it came at a pretty high cost. Ghana had a notoriously poor human rights record in the 1980s under his regime, a major stain on his legacy. Rawlings's early socialist leanings also led to a worsening economic situation, which was bad to start with. But Rawlings was able to put ideology aside when it was clear his policies weren't working. Eventually, he dropped subsidies and price controls to curb inflation, privatized state-owned companies to attract external investment, devalued the currency to boost exports, and engaged the Bretton Woods Institutions to help prop up and stabilize the economy. By the early 1990s, Ghana had one of the highest growth rates in Africa. By then, opposition to his military regime had grown, and he agreed to democratic elections.

Although I got to know Rawlings well over occasional interactions, I probably worked less directly with him than with any other marathon runner. But he was a big help in my efforts to revitalize the ECA. For instance, he put the weight of his government behind the first major conference I oversaw, a 1996 forum on private finance. We held the forum in Accra, and Rawlings's support ensured a big turnout, which played a significant role in the new tone we were trying to set.

To reiterate, these two groups are not intended to represent a list of Africa's best political leaders over the past few decades. Rather, they are among those who demonstrated some of the traits that we know are required of political leaders—especially in the context of promoting an economic transformation agenda. I also want to be clear that it's not my intention to make direct comparisons—the challenges faced by Ellen Johnson Sirleaf or Paul Kagame were far different than the environment into which Festus Mogae or Thabo Mbeki arrived. A leader like Kenneth Kaunda had to establish a newly independent country, while Meles Zenawi had to restore order to an existing but broken country.

And yet, if we consider these leaders and what they did or did not achieve when drawing lessons on economic transformation, we run directly into an issue that must be thoughtfully considered: what system of political governance is most beneficial for producing the type of leadership that will foster economic transformation?

For instance, we can see that both Meles and Kagame have had considerable success in taking their countries down a transformation path, but that success was met with ample criticisms over an apparent disregard for—or at the very least a lack of attention to—the principles that have come to define good governance in the modern day. As African countries and the development community have turned their attention to transformation as the defining paradigm for sustainable development, they have also turned their attention to trying to balance this issue. The question posed is not easy to answer, but it merits consideration because it has implications for Africa's transformation agenda.

◆　◆　◆　◆

In the late 1950s, the economies of Hong Kong, South Korea, Singapore, and Taiwan all had features that characterize many African countries today—widespread poverty, low productivity, low technology, and limited exports. But as detailed in the previous chapter, they ignited one of the most sustained booms in history through economic transformation. In 1981, East Asia had more poor people than any other region in the world; nearly 80 percent of its population lived in absolute poverty. By 2005, that percentage had plunged to 18 percent, a figure all the more striking when compared with Sub-Saharan Africa, where the percentage of people living in extreme poverty—approximately 50 percent—remained almost unchanged over the same period.

Such a rapid and systematic gain in multiple countries at the same time is almost impossible to comprehend. There are many explanations, but there's only one overarching, common factor: leadership. According to historian Michael Schuman, East Asia benefited from leaders in government and business who faced remarkably similar sociopolitical headwinds but all shared mutual goals: to reduce poverty, build thriving economies in postwar landscapes, and elevate Asia's standing in the world. And they realized that the surest way to achieve their economic goals—and to sustain them—was through transformative policies.

It's important to note that not all Asia's transformative leaders were saints. Far from it, in fact. Some of them systematically suppressed democracy and human rights, using torture or worse to maintain power. Some were guilty of patronage or peddling political influence, occasionally on a large scale. Others turned a blind eye to business tycoons as they created monopolies or manipulated markets in the name of jobs and growth. While it's impossible to justify any of these actions, Schuman concludes, it is equally impossible to deny the results.

Indeed, it is not uncommon to find economists, intellectuals, and development experts who compare the divergence in growth and transformation between Africa and the East Asian countries and identify the leadership factor as the key variable. And that creates a moral and ethical quandary when looking to Asia as an example for Africa. In which cases do the ends justify the means?

In a 2017 profile of Kagame's Rwanda, for example, The Economist noted that the country was "more prosperous than ever before. It is also a more repressed one." The article touched on the confounding dichotomy of a country transformed under an economically progressive leader that nonetheless bans independent media, actively discourages political opposition, and detains citizens without charge or due process. And yet, donor countries love Rwanda's efficient management of aid and development financing, while foreign investors love Rwanda's hospitable business climate that discourages patronage and bribes. Kagame's supporters and admirers, according to the profile, take the view "that a strongman with a long-term plan can be better for development than lots of squabbling factions. Too often in Africa, multiparty politics has degenerated into tribal feuding. Rwanda, of all places, cannot take that risk."

As much as the lessons from East Asia are noteworthy, they are not all directly applicable to Africa. The continent today is very different from the Asia of yesterday, as are the processes and strategies that will drive transformation, not to mention the social and cultural histories. But what about the type of political system and the leadership it produced?

Generally speaking, most African countries have moved toward multiparty democracy, often with messy but nonetheless hopeful results. The East Asian experience, however, was decidedly non-democratic. And that brings up the complex debate at the heart of the discussion around political leadership for Africa's economic transformation: can an African country with a multiparty system of government—which promotes regular transfers of power among competing political interests—"deliver the goods" to the same degree as a developmental state—one characterized by the presence of a strong development-oriented leader, centralized power, and a lower degree of political competition?

Allow me to reiterate why this issue is so fundamental to the discussion of African political leadership. It's a point I made in the previous chapter but it can't be overstated: economic transformation is a long-term process that requires discipline and the implementation of a consistent vision by policymakers committed to achieving that vision. The gains are not linear, and the political will must be strong enough to weather the ups and downs. In Africa's true multiparty democracies, meaning those with legitimate political competition, such discipline has proven elusive; Ghana, with its inability to gain traction on transformation, is a great example. By contrast, Rwanda, began its turnaround with a strong leader who has stayed in power long enough to keep the long-term vision on track—and to start to see the contours of that vision turned into reality.

Previously, I described Kagame, among others, as a "marathon runner," reflecting a description of development leadership that Kagame himself once gave. Development, he said, "is working toward an idea of what one wants now. But the reality of the situation, as well as what is actually required to achieve what one wants, comes into play. These two things must be balanced. So development is a marathon, because the reality is that development takes time."

There is a broad consensus among respected economists that developing countries are best served by a strong, capable state that provides visionary leadership, manages resources, and directs development. However, a *capable* state doesn't necessarily have to be a *developmental* state of the type that has a highly centralized system of power and single-party or autocratic rule. A multiparty democracy can be a capable state—provided the leaders and the democratic processes don't undermine the traits I just outlined. So far in Africa, that's been the big challenge.

To illustrate the point, we can return to Ghana.

When Jerry Rawlings's military regime took over in 1981, it had been 15 years since Nkrumah was overthrown. In the interim, Ghana had endured a destructive cycle of political coups and economic mismanagement. The hope that was prevalent in the post-independence years was long gone. But Rawlings stabilized the government and, before long, the economy started to grow. That stability and growth came with a cost. The policy changes Rawlings pursued to improve the economy were working, but Ghanaians wanted a return to civilian rule and pushed back against the authoritarianism and human rights abuses of the military regime. This coincided with the end of the Cold War and the wave of multiparty elections around the world, so donors got involved, too.

Rawlings relented and agreed to hold democratic elections in 1992, ushering in Ghana's Fourth Republic, even though he felt Ghana was not ready for it—something he was quite vocal about. He feared the gains made on economic growth and stabilization would be sacrificed, but at the time he had little choice. Rawlings won in 1992, and then he won again four years later before agreeing to step aside. His decision to leave after two terms, peacefully transferring power to an elected leader of an opposing party, once again elevated Ghana as "a model for Africa in terms of its democratic practices," as US President Barack Obama said during his 2009 visit to Accra.

But cracks appeared in the foundation almost immediately.

The move to a multiparty system split Ghana's policymakers into two political parties, generally rooted in past regional divisions evident since independence. These parties, the left-leaning National Democratic Congress (NDC) and the right-leaning National Progress Party (NPP), flow from historic pro-Nkrumah and anti-Nkrumah sentiment, respectively, and they have seldom worked together constructively. They have also traded off the presidency with regularity: Rawlings and the NDC ran Ghana for eight years, then gave way to Kufuor and the NPP for eight years. In 2009, the NDC regained power for the next eight years—first under John Atta Mills, who died in office during his first term, then under John Mahama, who succeeded Mills before winning his own four-year term. In 2016, the NPP once again returned to power under Nana Addo Dankwa Akufo-Addo.

On the plus side, these handovers have all been peaceful and the elections themselves have gone relatively smoothly. On the down side, the constant turnover has produced repeated interruptions in economic planning, since policy directions have ping-ponged back and forth based on the political philosophy of the governing party and its leader.

This is not uncommon in democracies; elections have consequences and to the victor go the spoils. But in a developing country, democracy alone is not enough to unleash development and foster sustainable economic growth, despite the romantic notion that it can be. The institutional apparatus must be in place so that long-term goals are not compromised by political swings to the left or right. Most importantly, the leaders across the political spectrum must be working toward the same destination, even if the paths they take to get there vary.

This is where Ghana's democratic process has stumbled.

During the new century boom years, Ghana flourished, thanks to an economy that grew from its average of 5.3 percent in the 2000s to an astonishing 14 percent in 2011—a peak year during which the World Bank moved Ghana from low-income to lower-middle-income status. Its economy was the fastest-growing in Sub-Saharan Africa. But then Ghana's GDP began an annual decline, the result of years of poor macroeconomic management and falling commodity prices that had driven the boom. Ghana's economic structure was not advanced nor diversified enough to withstand the shocks, and it lacked a foundational plan on which to fall back as a "fail-safe." Flush with revenues after the 2007 discovery of oil, Ghana had multiple strong-performing sectors from which it could have aggressively expanded its local processing, manufacturing, and industrialization policies to boost value chains. But that didn't happen.

Consider the pattern that I've seen play out repeatedly in Ghana. New leaders are elected and promise to act on campaign priorities—smarter spending and better macroeconomic management are usually at the top of the list. But after two or three years, and with the next election on the horizon, the government starts to overspend or enact short-sighted policies to win favor with voters and retain power. Fiscal discipline breaks down, deficits swell, inflation rises—prompting the need for smarter spending and better macroeconomic management. Another four-year cycle begins, and the process starts anew.

The bottom line is that Ghana's modern political system has not been oriented around long-term development planning or ensuring economic sustainability, such as transformation. It has been oriented around the political process itself—seeking votes and trading favors to secure power, then manipulating macroeconomic policies to retain power in the short term rather than to benefit the country's development in the long term.

The consequences have accumulated, from well-documented cases of corruption in the legislative and judicial branches of government, to weak procurement and contracting processes riddled with loopholes, to poor oversight of public resources and investment. In June 2014, with the country facing severe economic difficulties, the Mahama government called an emergency national forum in Senchi. The goal: for public and private sector stakeholders to try to reach a common understanding over the complex challenges Ghana faced and agree on the way forward. It was a bold acknowledgement that the country had veered too far off track. A few months later, and with obvious dissatisfaction, Mahama agreed to open discussions with the IMF on a recovery program to prop up the Ghanaian economy.

Not long before the Senchi forum, ACET, in conjunction with the Ghana Center for Democratic Development, conducted a study on Ghana's state capacity to drive economic transformation—and, in turn, generate inclusive growth and economic prosperity for its citizens. What did we find?

- That Ghana's administrative capacity was hampered by a lack of adequate financing and human resources.
- That the technical capacity of the civil service was generally weak and not configured to help drive growth and transformation.
- And that the regulatory capacity was only moderately able to enforce the nation's laws.

It's impossible to look at Ghana's story since Rawlings ushered in the Fourth Republic in 1992 on the one hand, and Rwanda's story since Kagame embarked on the postwar rebuild in 1994 on the other, and not compare them. Two very different systems of political leadership produced two very different results.

According to the USAID Human and Institutional Capacity Development Project for Rwanda, which was conducted over five years ending in 2017, Rwanda has made considerable strides toward achieving middle-income status and becoming a knowledge-based economy. To bridge the gaps needed to achieve its ambitious development plans, the government prioritized capacity development and established a new institution responsible for managing public and private sector capacity building. Likewise, the Legatum Prosperity Index 2018 found that among Sub-Saharan countries Rwanda had most improved its business environment over the previous decade by implementing comprehensive reforms, such as reducing the time to start a business, increasing access to credit, and strengthening investor protections. By comparison, Ghana's rankings for business environment had declined each year since 2015. Barely a quarter-century removed from genocide, Rwanda had enjoyed annual growth rates that exceeded 8 percent for a decade, foreign investment that had tripled, and improvement across most human well-being indicators, such as a 50 percent reduction in infant mortality and expansive health care. Per the World Bank, Rwanda is one of the few countries anywhere in the world that has managed fast economic growth, robust reductions in poverty, and a narrowing of inequality.

There's no doubt Kagame's unchallenged leadership at the top, in conjunction with a rigid political and policy apparatus, has underpinned

Rwanda's rapid development. Conversely, Ghana's rotating leadership at the top, combined with fluctuating policy priorities and uneven macroeconomic management, has perpetuated the country's inability to turn its growth cycles into lasting gains.

Based on these examples, the answer to the question I posed—can a multiparty system be as effective as a developmental state in producing sustainable development—would seem to be clear. But it's not at all.

I've thought a lot about where I come down in this debate, because I think it's one of the most important questions developing countries in Africa will face as they navigate the demands of economic transformation. Much of the evidence at our disposal supports the idea that developing countries tend to excel at making transformative gains under the developmental state approach versus the more unpredictable nature of multiparty democracies. That said, as impressive as the developmental states led by Meles and Kagame have been, the ways of Rwanda and Ethiopia are unique to Rwanda and Ethiopia. Their methods are not how every country in Africa can go, nor should go.

As has been emphasized so many times before, Africa is not a single entity; one size does not fit all. A country's circumstances dictate the way forward. Rwanda, ravaged by civil war and depleted human capacity, took its only viable path to return from ruin. Ghana, on the other hand, helped pioneer a type of democracy in Africa that, while not necessarily conducive to promoting uninterrupted transformation or consistent development, stayed consistent to the vision of personal freedoms on which Kwame Nkrumah first rallied the country.

Somewhere in the middle is Botswana, which underscores the point that each country must find its own way. Botswana is regarded as the continent's longest continuous multiparty democracy. No other mainland African nation enjoys what Botswana embodies: a flourishing democracy, prosperity, good roads, solid rule of law, and effective government at several levels. But the same Botswana Democratic Party has governed the country since independence in 1966, winning most elections in a landslide. So while it's a multiparty system with term-limited leaders, the governing political philosophy has not dramatically shifted as one leader goes out and another comes in. This does make a difference.

I have focused a lot on Ghana and Rwanda because of the stark contrasts they offer in this discussion on leadership, growth, and transformation—not because they are representative of the whole continent. They both offer truly instructive lessons from which transforming countries must learn. The type of substantive development planning necessary to pursue economic transformation requires a cohesive vision and implementation commitment that supersedes political ideology or party. That's not a problem in a developmental state like Rwanda. In a true multiparty democracy like Ghana, it is, so leaders must take that consideration into account.

But I believe Ghana can offer something more. I believe it has yet another chance to be a model for the rest of Africa—provided that it builds a better foundation for the future. In my view, there are four immediate ways to do so: through the constitution, political parties, public sector, and leadership.

First, on the constitution, it is critical that the separation of powers and the system of checks and balances become more distinct and firm. Likewise, constitutional reforms focused at local levels could decentralize decision-making and allow chief executives and assembly members to be chosen in open, multiparty elections. Second, political parties must turn policy platforms into medium-term policy programs, and they must have their activities and financing better regulated. Third, in the public sector, Ghana must ensure the integrity, independence, and capability of its institutions through merit-based selection, promotion, and compensation—which will help safeguard against the surrounding political climate. Fourth, leadership needs to be strengthened at all levels, including among traditional chiefs, religious leaders, the private sector, civil society, and academia. This includes improving the gender balance among elected officials and appointees, where Ghana falls well behind many of its peers.[5]

Ghana blazed a trail to independence but poor policy choices led it astray. It pursued true multiparty democracy ahead of most African nations but let political processes get in the way. The question is whether it has learned enough from its past to strengthen its democratic institutions while charting a successful transformation course. We already know the developmental state model can work in that way. If it can get its house in order, Ghana will be able to show Africa how the multiparty democracy model can work, too—and that a democracy can also be developmental.

◆　◆　◆　◆

I began this book—and this chapter—by reflecting on Ghana's past. To end it, I want to consider Ghana's future. Or, its potential future, given the right leadership and decision-making. Ghana is not the only African country with lessons to teach us or golden opportunities to grasp under a transformation strategy. But it is the most personal one for me. After all, it's where I was born and raised. It's where I returned after more than 30 years away. It's where my mother and father lived and died and where my brother and sisters have spent most of their lives. It's where I met my wife Philomena and where one of our daughters, Nana, lives with her husband Sam and daughter Mena.

Ghana is home. It always will be. So its future matters to me.

The real long-term challenge for Ghana, as with most resource-rich African nations that have experienced growth of an unequal or unstable nature, is to figure out what's necessary to maximize the value of its resources, stabilize and diversify its growth, and ensure sustainable development. This is economic transformation in a nutshell, and, as I've described, Ghana is a prime candidate to benefit from it.

After winning the 2016 presidential election, Nana Akufo-Addo promised to focus on accelerating growth by diversifying and expanding the economy. A medium-term program of economic and social development policies, which Akufo-Addo presented to parliament in late 2017, identified a number of diverse industrial initiatives as "anchor pillars of growth" for economic transformation, including petrochemicals, iron and steel, pharmaceuticals, automotives, and garments and textiles.

The government also pledged to combat a "mindset of dependency" in both the public and private sectors. Indeed, a country will only excel through transformation if government leaders and citizens alike are committed to hard work, ethical behavior, and the fair and just treatment of all people. This is, of course, a broad-stroke characterization; no country is ever free of corruption or societal ills. But it is not naive to recognize the historical importance of collective will in transforming societies. It requires more than pledges, though. And in a developing country, it requires the people in positions of authority—the government and business—to empower and support civil society, traditional communities, and families, particularly women and youth.

If Ghana stays the course, and if its present and future political leaders continue to equate political power with improving the lives of the citizens, it can realize a transformative level of change. Its future could be every bit as bright as the one Nkrumah promised so long ago.

I have always believed in that vision, and I still do.

I am blessed to have four beautiful grandchildren: Jonah, Kofi, Mena, and Kare. As I just mentioned, Mena lives with her parents in Accra, where she goes to school. She is a child growing up in Ghana, just as I was. When I envision a better future for Africa, I do it through her eyes. When she is grown, what kind of Africa will she see? What kind of opportunities will be available to her? Will her standard of living—her welfare and well-being—be better than it is today?

In early 2017, I addressed a group of officials at a public–private symposium in Berlin on this very topic. They were interested in hearing my take on Ghana's potential for economic transformation. And so I shared not just what I *hoped* the future would look like for Mena but what the data tells us *is possible*. Looking ahead to 2040, I said, Mena will be 30 years old. If Ghana's political leaders stick with a transformation strategy between now and then, Mena will see a vision turned into reality amid phenomenal changes...

... An economy that is diversified, stable, and providing its citizens with higher and steadily rising levels of real income. Its GDP could be four to five times larger than it is today, with an average GDP growth rate of around 7 percent. As a result, its population would be significantly better off than now, with per capita GDP three times higher.

... An economy that is generating more productive jobs and a workforce that is better equipped to excel. Eighty percent of all secondary and tertiary school graduates who enter the labor market could get formal sector jobs within two years of graduation after getting an education of reasonably good quality. Between 2010 and 2013, for example, fewer than 8 percent of those graduates were able to find formal sector jobs.

... An economy that is no longer based on traditional agriculture, raw materials extraction, and low-value services but an economy based on modernized agriculture and manufacturing, value addition in extractives, and high-value services, such as those in the professional and technology industries. Its share of manufacturing in GDP would be 25 percent—as opposed to its current 5 percent. Its level of medium and high technology products in manufacturing could be about 30 percent, as opposed to where it stands now—just 15 percent in medium technology and nothing in high technology.

... An economy that is far more diversified and better able to compete on the global export markets, as well as more resilient to outside shocks, including those stemming from climate change. In 2016, just five goods accounted for more than 85 percent of Ghana's total exports. By 2040, the total export share of those same five goods could drop down to as low as 40 percent as industrial and manufacturing advancements unleash new industries.

... An economy supported by higher—and more efficient—levels of national investment. By 2040, if Ghana grows with depth, it will have higher domestic savings and increased external resources flowing in, allowing the government to ramp up investment as a percentage of GDP to levels associated with the explosive growth of countries in East Asia.

... An economy featuring dramatic advances in energy and transport infrastructure to power and propel future economic growth. Renewable and alternative energy could account for more than 20 percent of Ghana's total power generation, and the first nuclear power station could be operational. A national rail network could connect all regional capitals and other strategic areas, such as food-growing and mining communities.

If Mena saw all these things, then she would see a country that is becoming more sustainable and a society becoming more inclusive. She would see a country building a solid foundation on which to deploy policies, such as social protection programs, that would better reach the poor and vulnerable—increasing life spans, closing income gaps, and reducing poverty. Because at its core, economic transformation is about people: their jobs, their prosperity, their livelihood, their mutual contributions to Ghana's—and Africa's—future.

There's a short story, a parable, I have told often about some mischievous young boys who set out to embarrass the village wise man. The boys wanted to prove that the old man was no smarter than anyone else. They went to him with a bird, and asked him if it was dead or alive. If he said it was dead, they would let the bird fly; if he said it was alive, they would wring its neck and kill it. One way or another, the wise man had to lose. "Old man," they said, "is the bird dead or alive?" The wise man looked at the boys, paused for a minute, and replied thoughtfully, "Young men, the answer is in your hands."

There's no way to predict the future with any level of certainty, but the answer to the challenges and problems that we face will remain, as it always has, in our collective hands. The journey must begin with worthy and capable political leaders, but we all must see it through. Collectively, African societies must commit, just as political leaders are expected to commit. We have more than enough data to make an educated guess on the pathways to transform Africa. That's what I've tried to do here, at the end of this book—make an educated guess for one country at the beginning of an arduous journey, and also demonstrate the power of that journey to remake the African narrative.

I do not know if Mena will see the Ghana I just described, or the future of the country I have envisioned my whole life, but I hope she does. And I believe she will. My journey is nearing its conclusion. Her journey—and a better one for Africa—is just beginning.

Notes

1 The four leaders were Teodoro Obiang Nguema of Equatorial Guinea, Paul Biya of Cameroon, Yoweri Museveni of Uganda, and Omar al-Bashir of Sudan, ousted soon thereafter in April 2019.

2 Another goal of the Ibrahim Prize is to ensure that Africa continues to benefit from the experience and expertise of good leaders even after they leave office by enabling them to continue work in public service. With a $5 million initial payment plus $200,000 a year for life, the prize is believed to be the world's largest, exceeding the $1.3 million Nobel Peace Prize.

3 This is more than a personal opinion. Since its founding, ACET has worked extensively with the government of Liberia—perhaps more so than with any other country—on institutional and policy reforms, infrastructure development, and the restructuring of key finance and planning functions.

4 After the prolonged civil war in Ethiopia that culminated in the overthrow of the Derg regime, Meles helped impose a new system that subdivided the government into numerous regions that, in theory, were given independent autonomy. In reality, however, at the federal level, the ruling Ethiopian People's Revolutionary Democratic Front, a coalition of four ethnic–based parties, is dominated by Meles's ethnic Tigrayans. Despite making up fewer than 10 percent of the country's population, Tigrayans tend to control the country's economy, military, and its security sectors.

5 In a 2017 lecture that I was invited to deliver at the University of Ghana at Legon, I went into great detail on Ghana's political history and the different ways the country could become a true leader in multiparty democracy in Africa. Titled "Positive Politics for Ghana: A Stronger Democracy for a Stronger Economy and a Stronger Future," I consider the speech one of my most substantive because of the importance of a healthy, vibrant, and transparent democracy to Ghana's development.

The full lecture is available on ACET's web site: http://www.acetforafrica.org.

K.Y. and Philomena's four grandchildren in Accra in 2015. From left: Mena, Kare, Jonah, and Kofi.

Acknowledgements

I can trace the roots of this book to a late evening conversation in 1995 with my wife, Philomena, my partner in all things. I described that conversation in Chapter 5, when Philomena told me to disregard my doubts about leaving the World Bank to return to Africa. I would not have taken that leap without her encouragement, nor would I have had the opportunity to be involved in so many amazing aspects of African development. I am eternally grateful for her support and guidance.

On various legs on my journey, I have been fortunate to have had many companions who inspired me, supported me, or worked with me on the policies, initiatives and endeavors described in these pages. Several of them are mentioned in the book, and I thank all of them for what they taught me and helped me accomplish. Two people who had an outsized influence on my life and career and who encouraged me to write the book recently passed away: John M. Letiche, my professor at the University of California, Berkeley, and Callisto Madavo, my friend and colleague at the World Bank. I live every day with affectionate memories of our personal and professional relationships.

With similar regard, I also want to acknowledge the contributions of the late Kofi Annan—first and foremost to African and global development, but also to my career. Kofi's achievements are inspiring no matter one's nationality, but to be able to work alongside him at the United Nations as a fellow Ghanaian was especially uplifting. I am forever grateful that he contributed the Foreword to this book, just a few months before his passing in August 2018.

There are quite a few people who, at one point or another, played an important role in helping get this book over the finish line. If you have been a sounding board or a guest reader, thank you. And if you have offered feedback and suggestions, thank you. I deeply appreciate those contributions and friendships. I would like to recognize and thank David Ladds and associates at Bladonmore in the United Kingdom for their generous assistance and direction in producing the cover. I also want to recognize Bruce Ross-Larson. For almost three decades, Bruce and his colleagues at Communications Development Inc. in Washington, DC have provided excellent editorial services for many of the publications I have been associated with. Throughout the conception, writing, and editing of this book, I sought Bruce's guidance and counsel, and for that I am forever grateful.

And finally, I would like to thank Jason Craig Thompson for his help in writing. For several years, Jason was at my side researching all parts of my career from the time I started at the World Bank through my work at the ECA and on my current efforts with the African Center for Economic Transformation. Jason's intelligence, hard work, and meticulous attention to detail as we drafted—and redrafted—the various chapters were truly remarkable. Without the contributions of this talented researcher and journalist, the book would have been less complete, less accurate, and far less compelling. He has my everlasting gratitude and bond of friendship.

Index

Convention People's Party (CPP) xvi, 9–10, 38–39, 40, 472–73

Copenhagen 146–47, 226

Corporate Council for Africa (CCA) xv, 208

Côte d'Ivoire 157, 207, 229, 282, 323

D

da Costa, Peter 192

Dakar 157, 226, 239, 255, 329–33, 342, 361, 378

Dangote, Aliko 467

Dar es Salaam 112, 346

DATA (Debt, AIDS, Trade, Africa) 399

Davis, Angela 20, 52

Davos 310–11, 325–28, 330

debt x, 7, 8, 13–14, 16, 38–41, 63, 71, 74–75, 78, 86, 100, 115, 118, 132, 195–98, 203, 205–06, 208–11, 217, 299, 301–02, 308, 310–12, 314, 320–21, 324, 344, 350, 353, 356, 365, 385, 387–88, 395, 398, 400, 402–05, 409, 411, 431, 460–61, 464, 468, 475, 481, 484

debt relief x, 8, 16, 195–98, 205, 208, 210–11, 217, 308, 311, 314, 344, 350, 353, 387, 395, 398, 400, 402–03, 405, 460, 468

democracy, multiparty 83, 213, 488, 491–92, 496–97, 501

Democratic Republic of Congo 386, 452, 468, 471

Department for International Development, UK (DFID) 312, 327

Derg, The 57–58, 501

Desai, Nitin 147

Desalegn, Hailemariam 247, 487

developmental state 491–92, 496–97

Development Assistance Committee (DAC). *See* Organisation for Economic Co-operation and Development–Development Assistance Committee (OECD-DAC)

development financing 158, 200, 203, 205–06, 209, 217, 250, 302, 385, 392, 396, 411–13, 428, 431–32, 460, 491

Diallo, Issa 162, 165–66

Diogo, Luisa 383

Diop, Bineta 238, 247

Diop, Makhtar 319, 340, 466

Djakarta 31, 33

Djibouti 243, 418

Dlamini-Zuma, Nkosazana 118

Doha 431

Doha Declaration 431

Donkor Fordwor, Kwame 421

dos Santos, Jose Eduardo 480

Drummond, Jamie 399

Duncan, Daniel 207

Durban 263, 267, 320–22, 326, 343, 344–45, 358, 367–68, 372–75

E

East Asia 33, 444–45, 449, 461, 467, 472, 490–91, 500

East Asian Miracle, The 444

Easterly, William 407

Ebola 43, 264, 484

510

M-Pesa 455

Mugabe, Robert 4, 207, 394, 480, 482

Muhsin, Mohamed 67–69, 78, 82

Mulaisho, Dominic 68–69, 71, 73, 78, 80, 82–83

Mulangu, Francis 468

Mule, Harris 106, 109

Muluzi, Elson Bakili 346

Mung'omba, Wila D. 421

Munguambe, Rosa Yolanda 438

Museveni, Yoweri 94–95, 110–16, 263, 268–70, 272, 485–86, 501

Muskoka 406

Musokotwane, Kebby 58–60, 63, 67, 82

Musyimi-Ogana, Litha 244

Mutharika, Bingu 446

mutual accountability 306, 308, 350, 357–58, 361, 374, 382, 386, 391, 394, 398, 403, 405–06, 414–15, 426, 460

Mutual Review of Development Effectiveness in Africa, The 398

Mwananshiku, Luke 72–73, 80, 84

N

Nairobi 36, 94, 106–07, 110, 226, 246

Namibia 161, 207, 238, 247, 481

Narmada River 123

Nasser, Gamal 32

National Information and Communication Infrastructure (NICI) plans xvi, 256–60

National Institute of Health (NIH) 43–44, 52

Natsios, Andrew 395–97

Ndiaye, Babacar 416, 421

Nealon, Kevin 44

Nehru, Jawaraharial 32

New Partnership for Africa's Development (NEPAD) iv, xvi, 8, 214, 217, 260, 278, 287, 290, 315, 317, 320–26, 335, 344–76, 379, 382–83, 388–95, 397–98, 400, 402–03, 406, 411–13, 417, 429, 445, 466, 477, 483
Declaration on Democracy, Political, Economic, and Corporate Governance 367–68
Heads of State and Government Implementation Committee (HSGIC)xvi, 343–44, 346, 354, 357, 361–63, 366–67, 368, 369, 370–71, 373–74, 379, 393, 395, 397
secretariat 346, 367, 373, 379
steering committee 345, 347, 354, 361, 362, 366, 390, 395

Netherlands, the 46, 299–300, 302, 315, 363, 383, 468

New African Initiative (NAI) 326

New York 86, 109, 131, 147, 153, 159, 161, 166, 173, 174, 227, 312, 318, 327, 348

Nguema, Teodoro Obiang 501

Nguyen, Minh Chau 144, 225

Niasse, Moustapha 268

Niger 315, 378

Nigeria 8, 261, 310, 315, 318, 324, 327–28, 330, 334–35, 339–40, 342, 346, 351, 354, 361, 366, 368, 370, 376, 383, 395, 418, 420, 433, 438, 442, 452, 477

Sukarno 32

sustainability 149, 196, 203, 280, 432, 453, 494

Sustainable Development Goals (SDGs) xvii, 242, 453, 460–61

Swaziland 91

Sweden 208, 300, 315, 322–23, 363, 365, 383, 387, 426

Swedish International Development Cooperation Agency (Sida) 426

Switzerland 262, 310, 315

Sy, Balla 343, 347

Sy, Chérif Salif 354

T

Taiwan 444–45, 490

Takoradi 24, 56, 151

Tanzania 82, 112, 246, 338, 346, 351, 401, 446, 452, 470, 476–77, 483–84

Taylor, Charles 161, 471, 484

Teixeira, Paulo 292

Thailand 310, 444, 451

think tanks 193, 376, 439, 447–48, 453, 455

Thompson, Jason 504

Tidewater meetings 300–05, 307, 313, 323, 388

Tito, Josip 32

Todaro, Ali 192

Tokyo International Conference on African Development (TICAD) xvii, 250 51

Touré, Sékou 292, 470

trade xv, xvi, 70, 76, 286–87, 398–99, 460–61, 471

transformation. *See* economic transformation

Transparency International 110

Tumu 24–25

Tumusiime, Emmanuel 111–16

Turianskyi, Yarik 378

Turkwel Gorge 106–08

Turnberry 302–05, 311, 314

U

Uganda 84–85, 91–97, 102, 110–16, 119, 129, 195–97, 209, 227, 236, 238, 246, 263, 268–70, 273, 292, 315, 351, 363, 377, 399, 408, 451, 456, 468, 470, 485–86, 501
economic stabilization 114
National Resistance Movement (NRM) 95, 111–12

Uganda Vision 2040 456

UK Parliament Africa Group 412

United Gold Coast Convention 9

United Kingdom 1, 48, 156, 208, 299, 313, 315, 389, 392, 398, 400–01, 409, 410, 428, 452

United Nations (UN) iv, x, xv, xvi, xvii, 22, 82, 145–47, 152–62, 164–66, 168, 173–75, 177, 180, 184, 186–94, 201, 209, 211, 214, 217–18, 226–27, 229–30, 235, 238, 240, 242, 244, 246, 249, 254, 260–61, 264, 269, 270–78, 291–92, 298, 300, 304, 307–13, 315, 318, 327–28, 333, 347–49, 354, 373, 377–78, 391, 406, 409, 417, 419–21, 433, 453, 456, 460–61
2030 Agenda for Sustainable Development 278, 406
Convention on the Elimination of All Forms of Discrimination